NETWORK SECURITY

PRIVATE Communication in a PUBLIC World

NETWORK SECURITY

PRIVATE Communication in a PUBLIC World

CHARLIE KAUFMAN • RADIA PERLMAN • MIKE SPECINER

Prentice-Hall of India Private Limited
New Delhi - 110 001
2005

This Indian Reprint—Rs. 325.00
(Original U.S. Edition—Rs. 2218.00)

NETWORK SECURITY—Private Communication in a Public World, 2nd Ed.
by Charlie Kaufman, Radia Perlman and Mike Speciner

ISBN-81-203-2213-4

Published by Asoke K. Ghosh, Prentice-Hall of India Private Limited, M-97, Connaught Circus, New Delhi-110001 and Printed by Jay Print Pack Private Limited, New Delhi-110015.

Si spy net work, big fedjaw iog link kyxogy

CONTENTS

ACKNOWLEDGMENTS

Despite the controversies that crop up around security issues, it has been our experience that people in the security community are generally generous with their wisdom and time. It's always a little scary thanking specific people, for fear we'll leave someone out, but leaving everyone out seems wrong. It's not even the fair thing to do, since some people would be more egregiously wronged by being left out than others.

Eric Rescorla and Hilarie Orman have been particularly helpful with answering questions and reviewing chapters for this edition. Other reviewers, and people who have been helpful answering questions, include Tom Wu, Kevin Fu, Marshall Rose, Joe Tardo, Joe Pato, Seth Proctor, Timothy Spiller, Tom Rice, Kristen McIntyre, Gary Winiger, Dan Harkins, Peter Memishian, Jeff Schiller, Burt Kaliski, Tony Lauck, Phil Karn, Ron Rivest, Steve Crocker, Steve Kent, John Linn, Steve Hanna, Jim Bidzos, Dave Jablon, Ted Ts'o, Matthew Barnes, Keith McCloughrie, Jeffrey Case, Kathrin Winkler, Philippe Auphelle, Sig Handelman, Phillip Hallam-Baker, Uri Blumenthal, Serge Vaudenay, and Boyd Roberts.

We could not have done Chapter 24 *More Security Systems* without help from the various companies involved, since for the most part the security systems were previously undocumented. We'd like to thank Al Eldridge from Iris (Lotus Notes), Amir Herzberg and Mark Davis from IBM (KryptoKnight), Walt Tuveli from OSF, and Cliff Van Dyke from Microsoft (LAN Manager and Windows NT security) for explaining their systems to us, doing timely reviews of what we wrote, and being enthusiastic and supportive of the project. Although nearly 67% of us work for companies that have products in this area, the opinions we offer are ours alone, and not those of our companies.

Mary Franz, our editor at Prentice Hall, has been enthusiastic and optimistic and patient with us throughout. She's shown good judgment about when to be helpful, when to keep out of the way, when to nag, and when to just look soulful so we feel guilty enough to meet a deadline.

Despite the fact that this book has kept both of his parents busy for a significant part of his life, Ray Perlner has kept us inspired with his wholehearted and unselfish enthusiasm for the project. He's shown genuine interest in the subject matter, offered useful advice during interauthor arguments, helped search for quotes, reviewed part of the book, and particularly liked the subscripted pronouns. If we overdo those, it's just because it's fun to see him giggle. Dawn Perlner has also been a great supporter of the project, and manages to convince a surprising number of her friends, as well as complete strangers, to buy the book.

And of course we thank you, our reader. We welcome your comments and suggestions. Compliments are always welcome. We hope to update the book periodically, so if there are topics you wish we'd covered or errors you'd like us to correct, let us know. Errata can be found at http://www.phptr.com/networksecurity.

Our current email addresses are ckaufman@us.ibm.com, radia@alum.mit.edu, and ms@alum.mit.edu. But we've found that email is not always reliable and email addresses change. If all else fails, you can contact the publisher, Prentice Hall, particularly our editor Mary Franz (mfranz@prenhall.com), and find out our current addresses.

We wish to thank the following for their permission to use their quotes in this book:

- Quote on page 10 from *The Hollywood Book of Quotes*, Omnibus Press.
- Quotes on page 17 and page 25 Copyright © 1994 Newsweek, Inc. All rights reserved. Reprinted by permission.
- Quote on page 43 reprinted by permission of Singer Media Corporation.
- Quote on page 19 reprinted by permission of Turner Entertainment.
- Quote on page 117 courtesy of Donald Knuth.
- Quote on page 253 reprinted by permission of *The Wall Street Journal*, Copyright © 1992 Dow Jones & Company, Inc.

1 *INTRODUCTION*

It was a dark and stormy night. Somewhere in the distance a dog howled. A shiny object caught Alice's eye. A diamond cufflink! Only one person in the household could afford diamond cufflinks! So it was the butler, after all! Alice had to warn Bob. But how could she get a message to him without alerting the butler? If she phoned Bob, the butler might listen on an extension. If she sent a carrier pigeon out the window with the message taped to its foot, how would Bob know it was Alice that was sending the message and not Trudy attempting to frame the butler because he spurned her advances?

That's what this book is about. Not much character development for Alice and Bob, we're afraid; nor do we really get to know the butler. But we do discuss how to communicate securely over an insecure medium.

What do we mean by communicating securely? Alice should be able to send a message to Bob that only Bob can understand, even though Alice can't avoid having others see what she sends. When Bob receives a message, he should be able to know for certain that it was Alice who sent the message, and that nobody tampered with the contents of the message in the time between when Alice launched the message and Bob received it.

What do we mean by an insecure medium? Well, in some dictionary or another, under the definition of "insecure medium" should be a picture of the Internet. The world is evolving towards interconnecting every computer, and people talk about connecting household appliances as well, all into some wonderful global internetwork. How wonderful! You'd be able to send electronic mail to anyone in the world. You'd also be able to control your nuclear power plant with simple commands sent across the network while you were vacationing in Fiji. Or sunny Libya. Or historic Iraq. Inside the network the world is scary. There are links that eavesdroppers can listen in on. Information needs to be forwarded through packet switches, and these switches can be reprogrammed to listen to or modify data in transit.

The situation might seem hopeless, but we may yet be saved by the magic of mathematics, and in particular cryptography, which can take a message and transform it into a bunch of numbers known as ciphertext. The ciphertext is unintelligible gibberish except to someone who knows the secret to reversing the transformation. Cryptography allows us to disguise our data so that eavesdroppers gain no information from listening to the information as transmitted. Cryptography also allows us to create an unforgeable message and detect if it has been modified in transit. One method of accomplishing this is with a **digital signature**, a number associated with a message and its sender that can be verified as authentic by others, but can only be generated by the sender. This should seem astonishing. How can there be a number which you can verify but not generate? A person's handwritten signature can (more or less) only be generated by that person, though it can be verified by others. But it would seem as if a number shouldn't be hard to generate, especially if it can be verified. Theoretically, you could generate someone's signature by trying lots of numbers and testing each one until one passed the verification test. But with the size of the numbers used, it would take too much compute time (for instance, several universe lifetimes) to generate the signature that way. So a digital signature has the same property as a handwritten signature, in that it can only be generated by one person. But a digital signature does more than a handwritten signature. Since the digital signature depends on the contents of the message, if someone alters the message the signature will no longer be correct and the tampering will be detected. This will all become clear if you read Chapter 2 *Introduction to Cryptography*.

Cryptography is a major theme in this book, not because cryptography is intrinsically interesting (which it is), but because many of the security features people want in a computer network can best be provided through cryptography.

1.1 ROADMAP TO THE BOOK

After this introductory chapter, there are five main sections in the book:

- **Part 1 CRYPTOGRAPHY** Chapter 2 *Introduction to Cryptography* is the only part of the cryptography section of the book essential for understanding the rest of the book, since it explains the generic properties of secret key, message digest, and public key algorithms, and how each is used. We've tried our best to make the descriptions of the actual cryptographic algorithms nonthreatening yet thorough, and to give intuition into why they work. It's intended to be readable by anyone, not just graduate students in mathematics. Never once do we use the term *lemma*. We do hope you read Chapter 3 *Secret Key Cryptography*, Chapter 4 *Modes of Operation*, Chapter 5 *Hashes and Message Digests*, and Chapter 6 *Public Key Algorithms* which give the details of the popular standards, but it's also OK to skip them and save them for later, or just for reference. Chapter 7 *Number Theory* and Chapter 8 *Math with AES and Elliptic Curves* gives a deeper treatment of the mathematics behind the cryptography. Reading them is not necessary for understanding the rest of the book.
- **Part 2 AUTHENTICATION** Chapter 9 *Overview of Authentication Systems* introduces the general issues involved in proving your identity across a network. Chapter 10 *Authentication of People* deals with the special circumstances when the device proving its identity is a

human being. Chapter 11 *Security Handshake Pitfalls* deals with the details of authentication handshakes. There are many security flaws that keep getting designed into protocols. This chapter attempts to describe variations of authentication handshakes and their relative security and performance strengths. We end the chapter with a checklist of security attacks so that someone designing a protocol can specifically check their protocol for these flaws.

- **Part 3 STANDARDS** This portion of the book describes the standards: Kerberos versions 4 and 5, certificate and PKI standards, IPsec, and SSL. We hope that our descriptions will be much more readable than the standards themselves. And aside from just describing the standards, we give intuition behind the various choices, and criticisms where they are overly complex or have flaws. We hope that our commentary will make the descriptions more interesting and provide a deeper understanding of the design decisions. Our descriptions are not meant to, and cannot, replace reading the standards themselves, since the standards are subject to change. But we hope that after reading our description, it will be much easier to understand the standards.
- **Part 4 ELECTRONIC MAIL** Chapter 20 *Electronic Mail Security* describes the various types of security features one might want, and how they might be provided. Chapter 21 *PEM & S/MIME* and Chapter 22 *PGP (Pretty Good Privacy)* describe the specifics of PEM, S/MIME, and PGP.
- **Part 5 LEFTOVERS** Chapter 23 *Firewalls* talks about what firewalls are, what problems they solve, and what problems they do not solve. Chapter 24 *More Security Systems*, describes a variety of security systems, including Novell NetWare (Versions 3 and 4), Lotus Notes, DCE, KryptoKnight/NetSP, Clipper, SNMP, DASS/SPX, Microsoft (LAN Manager and Windows NT), and sabotage-proof routing protocols. Chapter 25 *Web Issues* talks about the protocols involved in web surfing: URLs, HTTP, HTML, cookies, etc., and the security issues these raise. We close with Chapter 26 *Folklore*, which describes the reasoning behind some of the advice you will hear from cryptographers.

1.2 WHAT TYPE OF BOOK IS THIS?

We believe the reason most computer science is hard to understand is because of jargon and irrelevant details. When people work with something long enough they invent their own language, come up with some meta-architectural framework or other, and forget that the rest of the world doesn't talk or think that way. We intend this book to be reader-friendly. We try to extract the concepts and ignore the meta-architectural framework, since whatever a meta-architectural framework is, it's irrelevant to what something does and how it works.

We believe someone who is a relative novice to the field ought to be able to read this book. But readability doesn't mean lack of technical depth. We try to go beyond the information one might find in specifications. The goal is not just to describe exactly how the various standards and de facto standards work, but to explain why they are the way they are, why some protocols designed for similar purposes are different, and the implications of the design decisions. Sometimes engineering tradeoffs were made. Sometimes the designers could have made better choices (they are human after all), in which case we explain how the protocol could have been better. This analysis should make it easier to understand the current protocols, and aid in design of future protocols.

The primary audience for this book is engineers, especially those who might need to evaluate the security of, or add security features to, a distributed system; but the book is also intended to be usable as a textbook, either on the advanced undergraduate or graduate level. Most of the chapters have homework problems at the end.

Not all the chapters will be of interest to all readers. In some cases we describe and critique a standard in great detail. These chapters might not be of interest to students or people trying to get a conceptual understanding of the field. But in many cases the standards are written fairly unintelligibly. People who need to understand the standard, perhaps to implement it, or maybe even to use it, need to have a place where it is described in a readable way (and we strive for readability), but also a place in which mistakes in the standard are pointed out as such. It's very difficult to understand why, for instance, two fields are included which both give the same information. Sometimes it is because the designers of the protocol made a mistake. Once something like that is pointed out as a simple mistake, it's much easier to understand the specification. We hope that reading the descriptions in the book will make the specifications more intelligible.

1.3 TERMINOLOGY

Computer science is filled with ill-defined terminology used by different authors in conflicting ways, often by the same author in conflicting ways. We apologize in advance for probably being guilty sometimes ourselves. Some people take terminology very seriously, and once they start to use a certain word in a certain way, are extremely offended if the rest of the world does not follow.

> *When I use a word, it means just what I choose it to mean—neither more nor less.*
>
> —Humpty Dumpty (in *Through the Looking Glass*)

Some terminology we feel fairly strongly about. We do *not* use the term *hacker* to describe the vandals that break into computer systems. These criminals call themselves hackers, and that is how they got the name. But they do not deserve the name. True hackers are master programmers, incorruptibly honest, unmotivated by money, and careful not to harm anyone. The criminals termed "hackers" are not brilliant and accomplished. It is really too bad that they not only steal money, people's time, and worse, but they've also stolen a beautiful word that had been used to describe some remarkable and wonderful people. We instead use words like *intruder, bad guy,* and *impostor.* When we need a name for a bad guy, we usually choose *Trudy* (since it sounds like *intruder*).

We grappled with the terms *secret key* and *public key* cryptography. Often in the security literature the terms *symmetric* and *asymmetric* are used instead of *secret* and *public*. We found the terms *symmetric* and *asymmetric* intimidating and sometimes confusing, so opted instead for *secret key* and *public key.* We occasionally regretted our decision to avoid the words *symmetric* and *asymmetric* when we found ourselves writing things like *secret key based interchange keys* rather than *symmetric interchange keys*.

We use the term *privacy* when referring to the desire to keep communication from being seen by anyone other than the intended recipients. Some people in the security community avoid the term *privacy* because they feel its meaning has been corrupted to mean *the right to know,* because in some countries there are laws known as *privacy laws* which state that citizens have the right to see records kept about themselves. *Privacy* also tends to be used when referring to keeping personal information about people from being collected and misused. The security community also avoids the use of the word *secrecy,* because *secret* has special meaning within the military context, and they feel it would be confusing to talk about the secrecy of a message that was not actually labeled top secret or secret. The term most commonly used in the security community for keeping communication from being seen is *confidentiality.* We find that strange because *confidential*, like *secret*, is a security label, and the security community should have scorned use of *confidential*, too. In the first edition, we chose not to use *confidentiality* because we felt it had too many syllables, and saw no reason not to use *privacy.* For the second edition we reconsidered this decision, and were about to change all use of *privacy* to *confidentiality* until one of us pointed out we'd have to change the title of the book to something like *Network Security: Confidential Communication in a Non-Confidential World*, at which point we decided to stick with *privacy.*

> Speaker: *Isn't it terrifying that on the Internet we have no privacy?*
> Heckler_1: *You mean* confidentiality. *Get your terms straight.*
> Heckler_2: *Why do security types insist on inventing their own language?*
> Heckler_3: *It's a denial-of-service attack.*
>
> —Overheard at recent gathering of security types

We often refer to things involved in a conversation by name, for instance, *Alice* and *Bob*, whether the things are people or computers. This is a convenient way of making things unambiguous with relatively few words, since the pronoun *she* can be used for Alice and *he* can be used for Bob. It also avoids lengthy inter- (and even intra-) author arguments about whether to use the politically incorrect *he*, a confusing *she*, an awkward *he/she* or *(s)he*, an ungrammatical *they*, an impersonal *it*, or an incredibly awkward rewriting to avoid the problem. We remain slightly worried that people will assume when we've named things with human names that we are referring to people. Assume Alice, Bob, and the rest of the gang may be computers unless we specifically say something like *the user Alice*, in which case we're talking about a human.

> *With a name like yours, you might be any shape, almost.*
> —Humpty Dumpty to Alice (in *Through the Looking Glass)*

Occasionally, one of the three of us authors will want to make a personal comment. In that case we use *I* or *me* with a subscript. When it's a comment that we all agree with, or that we managed to slip past me_3 (the rest of us are wimpier), we use the term *we*.

1.4 NOTATION

We use the symbol ⊕ (pronounced *ex-or*) for the bitwise-exclusive-or operation. We use the symbol | for concatenation. We denote secret key encryption with curly brackets preceded by the key with which something was encrypted, as in $K\{message\}$, which means *message* is secret key encrypted with *K*. Public key encryption we denote with curly braces, and the name of the owner of the public key subscripting the close brace, as in $\{message\}_{\text{Bob}}$. Signing (which means using the private key), we denote with square brackets, with the name of the owner of the key subscripting the close bracket, as in $[message]_{\text{Bob}}$.

Table of Notation

⊕	bitwise exclusive or (pronounced *ex-or*)
|	concatenation (pronounced *concatenated with*)
$K\{message\}$	*message* encrypted with secret key *K*
$\{message\}_{\text{Bob}}$	*message* encrypted with Bob's public key
$[message]_{\text{Bob}}$	*message* signed with Bob's private key

1.5 PRIMER ON NETWORKING

You have to know something about computer networks to understand computer network security, so we're including this primer. For a more detailed understanding, we recommend PERL99, TANE96, COME00, STEV94, KURO00.

Networks today need to be very easy to use and configure. Networks are no longer an expensive educational toy for researchers, but instead are being used by real people. Most sites with networks will not be able to hire a full-time person with networking expertise to start and keep the network running.

1.5.1 OSI Reference Model

Somehow, a book about computer networks would seem incomplete without a picture of the OSI (Open Systems Interconnection) Reference Model, so here it is.

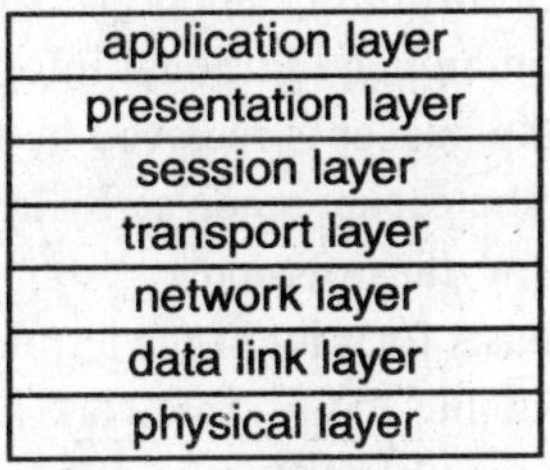

Figure 1-1. OSI Reference Model

The OSI Reference Model is useful because it gives some commonly used terminology, though it might mislead you into thinking that there is only one way to construct a network. The reference model was designed by an organization known as the International Standards Organization (ISO). The ISO decided it would be a good idea to standardize computer networking. Since that was too big a task for a single committee, they decided to subdivide the problem among several committees. They somewhat arbitrarily chose seven, each responsible for one layer. The basic idea is that each layer uses the services of the layer below, adds functionality, and provides a service to the layer above. When you start looking at real networks, they seldom neatly fit into the seven-layer model, but for basic understanding of networking, the OSI Reference Model is a good place to start.

1. **physical layer**. This layer delivers an unstructured stream of bits across a link of some sort.
2. **data link layer**. This layer delivers a piece of information across a single link. It organizes the physical layer's bits into packets and controls who on a shared link gets each packet.

3. **network layer**. This layer computes paths across an interconnected mesh of links and packet switches, and forwards packets over multiple links from source to destination.

4. **transport layer**. This layer establishes a reliable communication stream between a pair of systems across a network by putting sequence numbers in packets, holding packets at the destination until they can be delivered in order, and retransmitting lost packets.

5. **session layer**. The OSI session layer adds extra functions to the reliable pair-wise communication provided by the transport layer. Most network architectures do not have or need the functionality in this layer, and it is not of concern to security, so for the purposes of this book we can ignore it.

6. **presentation layer**. This layer encodes application data into a canonical (system-independent) format and decodes it into a system-dependent format at the receiving end.

7. **application layer**. This is where the applications that use the network, such as web surfing, file transfer, and electronic mail, reside.

A layer communicates with the equivalent layer in a different node. In order to get data to a peer layer, though, the layer at the transmitting node gives the data to the layer below it (on the same node), which adds a header containing additional information if necessary, and that layer in turn gives it to the layer below. As the packet is received by the destination node, each layer reads and strips off its own header, so that the packet received by layer n looks to that layer just like it did when it was sent down to layer $n-1$ for transmission.

This seven-layer model is the basis for a lot of the terminology in networking, and a good first step towards understanding networks, but today's network protocols do not neatly fit this model. Throughout the book we sometimes use the OSI terminology by discussing things such as encryption at layer 2 vs. layer 3 vs. layer 4, or use the terms *data link layer*, or *transport layer*.

1.5.2 IP, UDP, and TCP

Today the most common protocols are the ones standardized by the IETF (Internet Engineering Task Force). All the IETF documents are on-line and freely available from the web site www.ietf.org. The protocols are specified in documents known as RFCs. (RFC is an abbreviation for "Request for Comments", but the time to comment is when the documents are in the more preliminary "internet draft" stage. Nobody wants to hear your comments on RFCs.)

The IETF's protocol suite is usually referred to as the "TCP/IP suite", after the most common layer 3 (IP) and layer 4 (TCP) protocols at the time the suite was being nicknamed. IP (Internet Protocol), the layer 3 protocol, is defined in RFC 791. Its job is to deliver data across a network. To get a letter mailed with the postal service, you put it in an envelope that specifies the source and destination address. Similarly, the IP layer adds an envelope (a header) to the data that specifies the source and destination addresses.

But the IP address only specifies the destination machine. There might be multiple processes at the destination machine all communicating across the network, so it's necessary to also specify which process should receive the data. This is similar to putting an apartment number on the envelope in addition to the street address. IP doesn't identify the processes, but instead has a 1-octet field that specifies which protocol should receive the packet, and the rest of the information necessary to identify the destination process is contained in the layer 4 header, in the PORT fields.

The two most important layer 4 protocols in the IETF suite are TCP (Transmission Control Protocol, defined in RFC 793) and UDP (User Datagram Protocol, defined in RFC 768). TCP sends an unlimited size stream of data, reliably (either all data is delivered to the other end without loss, duplication, or misordering, or the connection is terminated). UDP sends limited-sized individual chunks, with best-effort service. Both TCP and UDP have fields for SOURCE PORT and DESTINATION PORT, which specify the process to whom the data belongs. TCP additionally has sequence numbers and acknowledgments to ensure the data arrives reliably.

Some port numbers are "well-known", i.e., permanently assigned to a particular service, whereas others are dynamically assigned. Being able to contact someone at a well-known port makes it easy to establish communication. In contrast, if Alice and Bob were going to attempt to communicate by going to public telephones wherever they happened to be, they'd never be able to communicate, since neither one would know what number to call. But if one of them were listening at a well-known telephone number, then the other could call from anywhere. This is very similar to the use of well-known ports.

To communicate with a particular service, say the telnet service, at some machine at IP address x, you'd know that telnet uses TCP, and is always assigned to port 23. So in the IP header, you'd specify x as the destination address, and 6 (which means TCP) as the protocol type. In the TCP header, you'd specify port 23 as the destination port. Your process would be at a dynamically assigned port, but the recipient process at node x would know which port to reply to by copying the port from the source port in the received TCP header.

This will all become much more relevant when we discuss firewalls in Chapter 23 *Firewalls*, and how they can distinguish telnet packets (which firewall administrators would usually like to block) from, say, email packets (which firewall administrators would usually like to allow).

1.5.3 Directory Service

Having a telephone line into your house means you can access any phone in the world, if you know the telephone number. The same thing is true, more or less, in computer networks. If you know the network layer address of a node on the network, you should be able to communicate with that node. (This isn't always true because of security gateways, which we'll discuss in Chapter 23 *Firewalls*.)

But how do you find out another node's network layer address? Network layer addresses are not the kind of things that people will be able to remember, or type. People instead will want to access something using a name such as File-Server-3.

This is a similar problem to finding someone's telephone number. Typically you start out by knowing the name of the person or service you want to talk to, and then look the name up in a telephone book. In a computer network there is a service which stores information about a name, including its network layer address. Anything that needs to be found is listed in the service. Anything that needs to find something searches the service.

We call such a service a **directory**, though some people like to reserve the term "directory" for something in which you search based on an attribute (e.g., "find all the people who live on Main Street") rather than look up something based on knowing its name. Those people would call a simple service in which you look up information (rather than do complex searches) a **naming** service. We see no reason to make that distinction. It might be nice to search for all items that match a certain attribute, but usually the name will be known, and the attributes of that name will be fetched.

Rather than keeping all names in one directory, the directory service is typically structured as a tree of directories. Usually a name is hierarchical, so that the directory in which the name can be found is obvious from the name. For example, an Internet name looks like radia@east.sun.com. The top level consists of pointers to the directories com for commercial enterprises, edu for educational institutions, gov for U.S. government, and various country names. Under com, there are various company names.

Having multiple directories rather than keeping all names in one directory serves two purposes. One is to prevent the directory from getting unreasonably large. The other reason is to reduce name collisions (more than one object with the same name). For instance, when you're looking up a telephone number for your friend John Smith, it's bad enough trying to figure out which John Smith is the one you want if you know which town he lives in and the telephone company has separate directories for each town, but imagine if the telephone company didn't have separate books for each town and simply had a list of names and telephone numbers!

Ideally, with a hierarchy of directories, name collisions could be prevented. Once a company hired one Radia Perlman, they just wouldn't hire another. I_2 think that's reasonable, but someone with a name like John Smith might start having problems finding a company that could hire him.

> *Now why did you name your baby* John*? Every Tom, Dick, and Harry is named* John.
>
> —Sam Goldwyn

For electronic mail addresses, conflicts must be prevented. Typically, companies let the first John Smith use the name John@companyname for his email address, and then perhaps the next one will be Smith@companyname, and the next one JSmith@companyname, and the next one has to start using middle initials. But for directories of names, there is usually no way to avoid name collisions within a directory. In other words, both John Smiths will use the same name within the company. Then, just like with a telephone book and multiple John Smiths, you have to do the best you can to figure out which one you want based on various attributes (such as in the telephone directory, using the street address). And just like in "real life," there will be lots of confusion where one John Smith gets messages intended for a different John Smith.

The directory service is very important to security. It is assumed to be widely available and convenient to access—otherwise large-scale networking really is too inconvenient to be practical. The directory service is a convenient place to put information, such as a user's public cryptographic key. But the directory service, although convenient, is not likely to be very secure. An intruder might tamper with the information. The magic of cryptography will help us detect such tampering so that it will not be necessary to physically secure all locations that store directory service information. If the information is tampered with, good guys will detect this. It might prevent good guys from accessing the network, since they won't be able to find information they can trust, but it will not allow bad guys unauthorized access.

1.5.4 Replicated Services

Sometimes it is convenient to have two or more computers performing the same function. One reason is performance. A single server might become overloaded, or might not be sufficiently close to all users on a large network. Another reason is availability. If the service is replicated, it does not matter if some of the replicas are down or unavailable. When someone wants to access the service provided, it doesn't matter which of the computers they reach. Often the user can't even tell whether there's a single copy of the service or there are replicas.

What are the security issues with a replicated service? You'd want the user to have the same authentication information regardless of which replica was authenticating the user. If authentication information is stored at each replica, then coordinating the databases, for example after a change password command, can be tricky. And if the identical exchange will work with any of the replicas, then having an eavesdropper repeat the authentication handshake with a different replica might be a security problem.

1.5.5 Packet Switching

A really naive assumption would be that if people wanted computer A to talk to computer B, they'd string a wire between A and B. This doesn't work if networks get large, either in number of nodes (n^2 wires) or physical distance (it takes a lot of wire to connect each of 10000 nodes in North America with each of 10000 nodes in Asia). So in a network, messages do not go directly from sender to recipient, but rather have to be forwarded by various computers along the way. These message forwarders are referred to as packet switches, routers, gateways, bridges, and probably lots of other names as well.

A message is generally broken into smaller chunks as it is sent through the network. There are various reasons for this.

- Messages from various sources can be interleaved on the same link. You wouldn't want your message to have to wait until someone else finished sending a huge message, so messages are sent a small chunk at a time. If the link is in the process of sending the huge message when your little single-chunk message arrives, your message only has to wait until the link finishes sending a chunk of the large message.
- Error recovery is done on the chunk. If you find out that one little chunk got mangled in transmission, only that chunk needs to be retransmitted.
- Buffer management in the routers is simpler if the size of packets has a reasonable upper limit.

1.5.6 Network Components

The network is a collection of packet switches (usually called routers) and links. A link can either be a wire between two computers or a multi-access link such as a LAN (local area network). A multi-access link has interesting security implications. Whatever is transmitted on the link can be seen by all the other nodes on that link. Multi-access links with this property include Ethernet (also known as CSMA/CD), token rings, and packet radio networks.

Connected to the backbone of the network are various types of nodes. A common categorization of the nodes is into *clients*, which are workstations that allow humans to access the resources on the network, and *servers*, which are typically dedicated machines that provide services such as file storage and printing. It should be possible to deploy a new service and have users be able to conveniently find the service. Users should be able to access the network from various locations, such as a public workstation a company makes available for visitors. If a person has a dedicated workstation located in one location, such as an office, it should be possible with a minimum of configuration for the user to plug the workstation into the network.

Historically, another method for users to access a network is through a *dumb terminal*. A dumb terminal is not a general-purpose computer and does not have the compute power to do cryptographic operations. Usually a dumb terminal hooks directly into a host machine, or into a *terminal server* which relays the terminal's keystrokes via a network protocol across the network to the host machine (the machine the user logs into). Very few dumb terminals remain today, but their legacy lives on in the form of software-based terminal emulators implemented in most PCs and workstations. Even though these devices are capable of complex calculations, for backward compatibility, they don't do them.

1.5.7 Destinations: Ultimate and Next-Hop

A network is something to which multiple systems can attach. We draw it as a cloud since, from the point of view of the systems connected to it, exactly what goes on inside is not relevant. If two systems are on the same cloud, one can send a message to the other by attaching a header that contains a source address and a destination address, much like putting a letter into an envelope for delivery by the postal service.

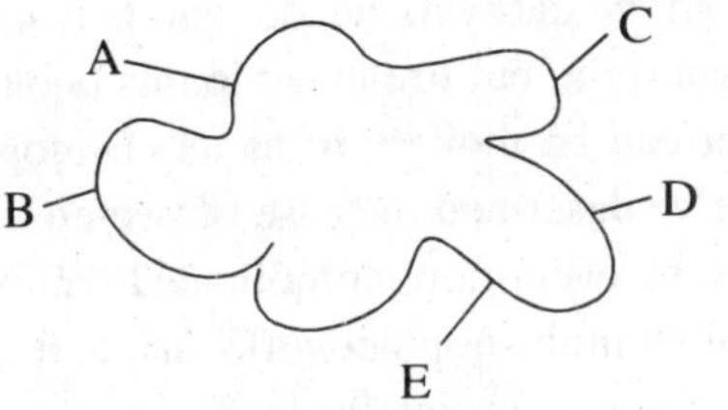

Figure 1-2. A Network

But how do you connect to the network? With a point-to-point link to a packet switch inside the network, things are reasonably simple. If A wants to send a message to B, A will put A as source address and B as destination address and send the message on the point-to-point link. But what if A is connected on a LAN? In that case, in order to transmit the packet through the network, A has to specify which of its neighbors should receive the message. For example:

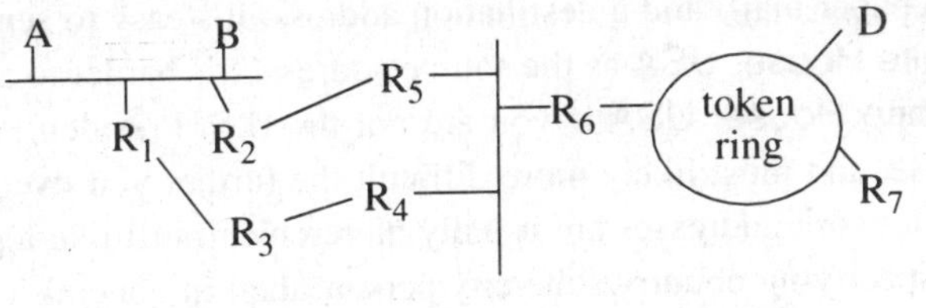

Figure 1-3. Network Connections

If A wants to send a message to D it has to know (somehow—if you care how, you can read my_2 book [PERL99]) that the appropriate neighbor for forwarding the packet is R_2. So when A transmits the message there are two destinations: R_2 as the next recipient and D as the ultimate recipient. A reasonably simple way of thinking about this is that the data link layer worries about transmission across a single link. The data link header has a source address and a destination address which indicate the transmitter on that link and the receiver on that link. The network layer worries about transmission across a multi-hop network. It has a header that carries the original source and ultimate destination. The data link header is removed each time a message is received, and a new data link header is tacked onto the message when it is forwarded to the next hop.

When A transmits the packet, the network header has source A, destination D. The data link header has source A, destination R_2. R_2 forwards the packet to R_5. Since R_2 is connected to R_5 with a point-to-point link, the data link header will not have addresses. But when R_5 forwards the packet to R_6 across the LAN, the network layer header will (still) be source A, destination D. The data link header will be source R_5, destination R_6. When R_6 forwards it (across the token ring LAN) the network header is still the same, and the data link header has source R_6, destination D.

Most likely A's data link address will look different from its network layer address, so it's a bit sloppy to say source A in both the data link header and network header. But this is all irrelevant to security. Fascinating in its own right, but irrelevant to this book.

The network layer header can be thought of as an envelope for the message. The data link header is an outer envelope. We've described the case of two envelopes—a network header inside a data link header. The world can be even more complicated than this. In fact, the "data link layer" might be a multi-hop network with multi-hop networks inside it as well. So a message might wind up with several envelopes. Again this is fascinating stuff but irrelevant to this book.

1.5.8 Address Structure

What do addresses look like? In terms of security, the main issue is how difficult it is to forge a source address, and how easy it is to arrange for the network to deliver packets to you when they are addressed to someone other than you. For instance, think of a letter as having a source address (the return address, it's called in paper mail) and a destination address. It's easy to send a letter to anyone and put President, White House, USA as the source address. It's harder to arrange to receive mail sent to President, White House, USA if you are not the U.S. President, especially if you don't live in the White House, and most likely more difficult the further you live from the address you'd like to impersonate. Network addresses are usually hierarchical, just like a postal address. If we think of the address as specifying country/state/city/person, then in general it will be easier to arrange to receive someone else's messages if you reside in the same city (for instance by bribing a postal employee), and most difficult if they're in a different country.

Forging source addresses is easy in most network layers today. Routers can be built more defensively and do a sanity check on the source address, based on where they receive the packet from. After some highly publicized denial of service attacks, where vandals overwhelmed victim sites with nuisance traffic, many routers are now deployed with this feature of checking source addresses and discarding traffic received from an unexpected direction. It's not a perfect solution, though. As typically implemented, it requires extra configuration (so the routers will know what source addresses to expect from which directions), somewhat violates my_2 philosophy (as a layer 3 specialist) that routers should be self-configuring and adapt to topological changes, and slows down the router because it has to make an extra check when forwarding a packet.

1.6 ACTIVE VS. PASSIVE ATTACKS

A passive attack is one in which the intruder eavesdrops but does not modify the message stream in any way. An active attack is one in which the intruder may transmit messages, replay old messages, modify messages in transit, or delete selected messages from the wire. A typical active attack is one in which an intruder impersonates one end of the conversation, or acts as a man-in-the-middle (see §6.4.1 *The Bucket Brigade/Man-in-the-Middle Attack*).

1.7 LAYERS AND CRYPTOGRAPHY

Encryption and integrity protection are sometimes done on the original message or on each chunk of the message, and if on each chunk, it might be done end-to-end or hop-by-hop. There are interesting tradeoffs and implications of these choices. If done on the original message, it can be protected while being stored, and the infrastructure does not need to even know whether the data it is moving is cryptographically protected. This means that the location where the cryptographically protected message is kept, and the infrastructure for transmitting the message, need not be trusted.

Encryption hop-by-hop can foil traffic analysis, i.e., it hides from eavesdroppers the information about which parties are communicating. Thus it is useful even if encryption is being done at other layers. If done hop-by-hop, the packet switches must be trusted, because by definition of hop-by-hop, the packet switches will see the plaintext.

If done end-to-end as the data is being transmitted, if individual chunks are separately encrypted and integrity protected, then the data that arrives intact can be used, whereas if there's only a single integrity check for the entire message, then any corruption or loss will require retransmitting the entire thing, since (by definition of cryptographically protecting the data as a whole instead of individual chunks) there will be no way to know where the loss/corruption occurred.

1.8 AUTHORIZATION

Network security basically attempts to answer two questions: "who are you?" and "should you be doing that?" **Authentication** proves who you are. **Authorization** defines what you're allowed to do. Typically the way a server decides whether someone should have access to a resource is by first authenticating the user, and then consulting a database associated with the resource that indicates who is allowed to do what with that resource. For instance, the database associated with a file might say that Alice can read it and Bob and Carol can both read and write it. This database is often referred to as an **ACL (access control list)**.

Another model of authorization is known as the **capability model**. Instead of listing, with each resource, the set of authorized users and their rights (e.g., read, write, execute), you would have a database that listed, for each user, everything she was allowed to do.

If there were only a single resource, then the ACL model and the capability model would be basically the same, since in both cases there would be a database that lists all the authorized users and what rights each has to that resource. But in a world in which there are many resources, not all under control of one organization, it would be difficult to have a central database listing what each user was allowed to do (for instance, all the files that user is allowed to read), and it would have scaling problems if there were many resources each user was allowed to access.

Some people worry that ACLs don't scale well if there are many users allowed access to each resource. But the concept of a **group** answers that concern. A very basic form of group implemented in some systems is that each user is a member of one group, and someone with special privileges assigns users to groups. There is a special group known as "world", which includes everyone. Alice would be allowed to read a file if her name was listed on the ACL with read access, or if her group was listed on the ACL with read access, or if "world" was given read access.

Extensions to the idea of groups that might be useful:

- allow a user to be in multiple groups (researchers, security experts, U.S. citizens)
- allow anyone (not just someone with special privileges) to create a group. Allow anyone to name that group on an ACL they are authorized to administer.
- allow a group for which the user explicitly invokes his membership. This type of group is known as a **role**. The main difference between what people think of as a role and what people think of as a group is that the user always has all the rights of all the groups he is a member of, but only has the rights of the role he has explicitly invoked. Some people would claim that if the user is allowed to assert multiple roles, he can have only one of them active at any time.

We discuss ways of implementing very flexible notions of groups in §15.8.3 *Groups*.

1.9 TEMPEST

One security concern is having intruders tap into a wire, giving them the ability to eavesdrop and possibly modify or inject messages. Another security concern is electronic emanation, whereby through the magic of physics, the movement of electrons can be measured from a surprising distance away. This means that intruders can sometimes eavesdrop without even needing to physically access the link. The U.S. military Tempest program measures how far away an intruder must be before eavesdropping is impossible. That distance is known as the device's **control zone**. The control zone is the region that must be physically guarded to keep out intruders that might be attempting to eavesdrop. A well-shielded device will have a smaller control zone. I_1 remember being told in 1979 of a tape drive that had a control zone over two miles. Unfortunately, most control zone information is classified, and I_2 couldn't get me_1 to be very specific about them, other than that they're usually expressed in metric. Since it is necessary to keep intruders away from the control zone, it's certainly better to have something with a control zone on the order of a few inches rather than a few miles (oh yeah, kilometers).

> *CIA eavesdroppers could not intercept the radio transmissions used by Somali warlord Mohammed Farah Aidid; his radios, intelligence officials explained, were too "low tech."*
>
> —Douglas Waller & Evan Thomas, *Newsweek*, October 10, 1994, page 32

1.10 KEY ESCROW FOR LAW ENFORCEMENT

Law enforcement would like to preserve its ability to wiretap otherwise secure communication. (Also, sometimes companies want to be able to read all data of their employees, either to enforce company policies, or to ensure data is not lost when an employee forgets a password or leaves the company.)

In order for the government to ensure it can always wiretap, it must prevent use of encryption, break the codes used for encryption (as it did in a military context during World War II), or somehow learn everyone's cryptographic keys. The Clipper proposal was proposed in the mid-90's and attempted the third option. It allows the government to reconstruct your key (only upon court order and with legitimate cause of course). This is made possible through the use of a device known as the Clipper chip. A lot about Clipper was classified by the government as secret (and classified by a lot of other people as evil). We describe the basic technical design of Clipper in §24.9 *Clipper*. Although the Clipper proposal appears to have been a failure, and the government appears to have for the moment at least given up on attempting to control cryptography, the Clipper design was fascinating, and is worth learning about. The simple concept is that encryption is done with a special chip (the Clipper chip). Each chip manufactured has a unique key, and the government keeps a record of the serial number/encryption key correspondence of every chip manufactured. Because not all people have complete trust in the government, rather than keeping the key in one place, each key is broken into two quantities which must be ⊕'d in order to obtain the actual key. Each piece is completely useless without the other. Since each piece is kept with a separate government agency, it would require two U.S. government agencies to cooperate in order to cheat and obtain the key for your Clipper chip without a valid court order. The government assures us, and evidence of past experience supports its claim, that cooperation between U.S. government agencies is unlikely.

The Clipper proposal was always controversial, starting with its name (which violated someone's trademark on something unrelated). Why would anyone use Clipper when alternative methods should be cheaper and more secure? The reason alternatives would be cheaper is that enforcing the ability of the U.S. government to wiretap adds a lot of complexity over a design that simply encrypts the data. Proponents of Clipper gave several answers to this question:

- The government would buy a lot of Clipper chips, bringing the cost down because of volume production, so Clipper would wind up being the most cost-effective solution.
- Encryption technology is only useful if both parties have compatible equipment. Since the U.S. government would use Clipper, to talk securely to the U.S. government, you would have to use Clipper. So any other mechanism would have to be implemented *in addition* to Clipper.
- Again, since encryption technology is only useful if both parties have compatible equipment, if Clipper took over enough market share, it would essentially own the market (just like VHS, a technically inferior standard supposedly, beat out Beta in the VCR marketplace). Since Clipper would be one of the earliest standards, it might take over the marketplace before any other standards have an opportunity to become entrenched. The argument was that most people wouldn't care that Clipper enables wiretapping, because they'll assume they have nothing to fear from the U.S. government wiretapping them.
- The government claimed that the cryptographic algorithm in Clipper was stronger than you could get from a commercial source.

Civil libertarians feared Clipper was a first step towards outlawing untappable cryptography. Clipper proponents say it was not. It's true that outlawing alternatives was not part of the Clipper proposal. However, there have been independent efforts to outlaw cryptography. Those efforts have been thwarted in part with the argument that industry needs security. But if Clipper were deployed, that argument would have gone away.

Clipper was designed for telephones, fax, and other low-speed applications, and in some sense is not relevant to computer networking. Many people regard it, however, as a first step and a model for taking the same approach for computer networks.

The Clipper proposal was a commercial failure, and export controls are currently relaxed. However, the technical aspects of such designs are fascinating, laws can change at any time, and export controls have created other fascinating and arcane designs that we will describe throughout the book, for instance, §19.13 *Exportability*.

1.11 KEY ESCROW FOR CARELESS USERS

It is prudent to keep your key in a safe place so that when you misplace your own key you can retrieve a copy of the key rather than conceding that all your encrypted files are irretrievably lost. It would be a security risk to have all users' keys stored unencrypted somewhere. The database of keys could be stored encrypted with a key known to the server that was storing the database, but this would mean that someone who had access to that machine could access all the user keys. Another possibility is to encrypt the key in a way that can only be reconstructed with the cooperation of several independent machines. This is feasible, and we'll discuss it more in §24.9.1 *Key Escrow*.

Some applications don't require recoverable keys. An example of such an application is login. If a user loses the key required for login, the user can be issued a new key. A user may therefore want different keys for different uses, where only some of the keys are escrowed. For applications that do require recoverable keys, protection from compromise can be traded off against protection from loss.

1.12 VIRUSES, WORMS, TROJAN HORSES

Lions and tigers and bears, oh my!
—Dorothy (in the movie *The Wizard of Oz*)

People like to categorize different types of malicious software and assign them cute biological terms (if one is inclined to think of worms as cute). We don't think it's terribly important to distinguish between these things, but will define some of the terms that seem to be infecting the literature.

- **Trojan horse**—instructions hidden inside an otherwise useful program that do bad things. Usually the term Trojan horse is used when the malicious instructions are installed at the time the program is written (and the term *virus* is used if the instructions get added to the program later).
- **virus**—a set of instructions that, when executed, inserts copies of itself into other programs. More recently, the term has been applied to instructions in email messages that, when executed, cause the malicious code to be sent in email to other users.
- **worm**—a program that replicates itself by installing copies of itself on other machines across a network.

- **trapdoor**—an undocumented entry point intentionally written into a program, often for debugging purposes, which can be exploited as a security flaw.
- **logic bomb**—malicious instructions that trigger on some event in the future, such as a particular time occurring.
- **zombie**—malicious instructions installed on a system that can be remotely triggered to carry out some attack with less traceability because the attack comes from another victim. Often the attacker installs large numbers of zombies in order to be able to generate large bursts of network traffic.

We do not think it's useful to take these categories seriously. As with most categorizations (e.g., plants vs. animals, intelligence vs. instinct), there are things that don't fit neatly within these categories. So we'll refer to all kinds of malicious software generically as **digital pests**.

1.12.1 Where Do They Come From?

Where do these nasties come from? Except for trapdoors, which may be intentionally installed to facilitate troubleshooting, they are written by bad guys with nothing better to do with their lives than annoy people.

How could an implementer get away with writing a digital pest into a program? Wouldn't someone notice by looking at the program? One of the most famous results in computer science is that it is provably impossible to be able to tell what an arbi rary program will do by looking at it*, so certainly it would be impossible to tell, in general, whether the program had any unpleasant side effects besides its intended purpose. But that's not the real problem. The real problem is that nobody looks. Often when you buy a program you do not have access to the source code, and even if you did, you probably wouldn't bother reading it all, or reading it very carefully. Many programs that run have never been reviewed by anybody. A major advantage offered by the "open source" movement (where all software is made available in source code format) is that even if you don't review it carefully, there is a better chance that someone else will.

What does a virus look like? A virus can be installed in just about any program by doing the following:

- replace any instruction, say the instruction at location *x*, by a jump to some free place in memory, say location *y*; then
- write the virus program starting at location *y*; then

* This is known in the literature as *the halting problem*, which states that it is impossible in general to tell whether a given program will halt or not. In fact it is impossible in general to discern any nontrivial property of a program.

- place the instruction that was originally at location *x* at the end of the virus program, followed by a jump to *x*+1.

Besides doing whatever damage the virus program does, it might replicate itself by looking for any executable files in any directory and infecting them. Once an infected program is run, the virus is executed again, to do more damage and to replicate itself to more programs. Most viruses spread silently until some triggering event causes them to wake up and do their dastardly deeds. If they did their dastardly deeds all the time, they wouldn't spread as far.

How does a digital pest originally appear on your computer? All it takes is running a single infected program. A program posted on a bulletin board might certainly be infected. But even a program bought legitimately might conceivably have a digital pest. It might have been planted by a disgruntled employee or a saboteur who had broken into the computers of the company and installed the pest into the software before it was shipped. There have been cases where commercial programs were infected because some employee ran a program gotten from a friend or a bulletin board.

Often at holiday times people send email messages with attached programs and instructions to run them. While this used to require extracting the email message to a file and possibly processing it first, modern email systems make it very convenient to run such things... often just by clicking on an icon in the message. Often the result is some sort of cute holiday-specific thing, like displaying a picture of a turkey or playing a Christmas carol. It could certainly also contain a virus. Few people will scan the program before running it, especially if the message arrives from a friend. And if you were to run such a program and it did something cute, you might very well forward it to a friend, not realizing that in addition to doing the cute thing it might very well have installed a virus that will start destroying your directory a week after the virus is first run. A good example of a Christmas card email message is a program written by Ian Phillipps, which was a winner of the 1988 International Obfuscated C Code Contest. It is delightful as a Christmas card. It does nothing other than its intended purpose (I_1 have analyzed the thing carefully and I_2 have complete faith in me_1), but we doubt many people would take the time to understand this program before running it (see Figure 1-4).

Sometimes you don't realize you're running a program. PostScript is a complete programming language. It is possible to embed a Trojan horse into a PostScript file that infects files with viruses and does other damage. Someone could send you a file and tell you to display it. You wouldn't realize you were running a program by merely displaying the file. And if there was any hope of scanning a C program to find suspicious instructions, there are very few people who could scan a PostScript file and look for suspicious PostScript commands. PostScript is, for all practical purposes, a write-only language.

As mail systems get more clever in their attempt to make things more convenient for users, the risk becomes greater. If you receive a PostScript file and you are running a non-clever mail program, you will see delightful crud like Figure 1-5

```
/* Have yourself an obfuscated Christmas! */
#include <stdio.h>
main(t,_,a)
char *a;
{
return!0<t?t<3?main(-79,-13,a+main(-87,1-_,main(-86,0,a+1)+a)):
1,t<_?main(t+1,_,a):3,main(-94,-27+t,a)&&t==2?_<13?
main(2,_+1,"%s %d %d\n"):9:16:t<0?t<-72?main(_,t,
"@n'+,#'/*{}w+/w#cdnr/+,{}r/*de}+,/*{*+,/w{%+,/w#q#n+,/#{l,+,/n{n+,/+#n+,/#\
;#q#n+,/+k#;*+,/'r :'d*'3,}{w+K w'K:'+}e#';dq#'l \
q#'+d'K#!/+k#;q#'r}eKK#}w'r}eKK{nl]'/#;#q#n'){)#}w'){){nl]'/+#n';d}rw' i;# \
){nl]!/n{n#'; r{#w'r nc{nl]'/#{l,+'K {rw' iK{;[{nl]'/w#q#n'wk nw' \
iwk{KK{nl]!/w{%'l##w#' i; :{nl]'/*{q#'ld;r'}{nlwb!/*de}'c \
;;{nl'-{}rw]'/+,}##'*}#nc,',#nw]'/+kd'+e}+;#'rdq#w! nr'/ ') }+}{rl#'{n' ')# \
}'+}##(!!/")
:t<-50?_==*a?putchar(31[a]):main(-65,_,a+1):main((*a=='/')+t,_,a+1)
:0<t?main(2,2,"%s"):*a=='/'||main(0,main(-61,*a,
"!ek;dc i@bK'(q)-[w]*%n+r3#1,{}:\nuwloca-O;m .vpbks,fxntdCeghiry"),a+1);
}
```

Figure 1-4. Christmas Card?

```
%!PS-Adobe-3.0
%%Creator: Windows PSCRIPT
%%Title: c:\book\spcaut.doc
%%BoundingBox: 18 9 593 784
%%DocumentNeededResources: (atend)
%%DocumentSuppliedResources: (atend)
%%Pages: (atend)
%%BeginResource: procset Win35Dict 3 1
/Win35Dict 290 dict def Win35Dict begin/bd{bind def}bind def/in{72
mul}bd/ed{exch def}bd/ld{load def}bd/tr/translate ld/gs/gsave ld/gr
/grestore ld/M/moveto ld/L/lineto ld/rmt/rmoveto ld/rlt/rlineto ld
/rct/rcurveto ld/st/stroke ld/n/newpath ld/sm/setmatrix ld/cm/currentmatrix
ld/cp/closepath ld/ARC/arcn ld/TR{65536 div}bd/lj/setlinejoin ld/lc
/setlinecap ld/ml/setmiterlimit ld/sl/setlinewidth ld/scignore false
def/sc{scignore{pop pop pop}{0 index 2 index eq 2 index 4 index eq
and{pop pop 255 div setgray}{3{255 div 3 1 roll}repeat setrgbcolor}ifelse}ifelse}bd
```

Figure 1-5. Typical PostScript Code

If you wanted to display the file, you'd have to extract the mail message and send it to the printer, or input it into a special program that displays PostScript on your screen. However, a clever mail program might look at the message, recognize that it was PostScript, and automatically run the PostScript code to display the message. Although this is convenient, it is dangerous.

There are various other clever features being added to mail programs. Some mail programs allow the sender to send a program along with the mail message. Usually the mail message will arrive and display some sort of icon. If the receiver clicks on the icon, the transmitted program is executed. Someone, to illustrate this point, sent such a mail message. It displayed only as a button that said *push me*. When the person who received the message clicked on the box, it came up with a message that said, *I could have just reformatted your hard drive*.

In the first edition of this book, we said "Before the technology for clever mail goes much further, we ought to consider how we can reap the benefits of such cleverness while minimizing the security risks". We can now confidently say that it has gone much further, no one has worried at all about security, and as anyone who has been stung by the email virus of the week can attest, the situation is a disaster.

There remain dangers associated with booting from floppy disks. If the hard drive of a computer were completely wiped clean, there has to be some way to come up again, so machines provide the feature that if there is a floppy in the drive when the machine is powered on, the machine boots off the floppy. This can be disabled, but it rarely is. Even if system software becomes sophisticated about security, it won't be able to protect against Trojan horses on the boot device. When you turn on many machines with a floppy disk inserted into the drive (intentionally or accidentally), they execute the code on the floppy in a privileged mode. If there is a virus in that code, it can infect the system.

Most PCs are configured to detect a CD-ROM placed in the drive and will execute a startup program automatically when a new one is inserted. This may have been a relatively safe thing to do when writable CD-Rs were a rarity and most CD-ROMs were commercially manufactured, but today it is likely viruses will spread this way. With CD-RWs becoming common, viruses can spread across your CDs the way they once did across floppies.

1.12.2 Spreading Pests from Machine to Machine

How might a virus or worm spread from machine to machine? An infected program might be copied to a floppy or other medium and moved to another machine. Or, as we said, a mail message might carry the infection. But it is also possible for the pest to explore the network and send itself to other machines, once it is running in one machine on a network. Such a pest is called a worm.

One method a worm can employ to transmit itself to another machine is to actually log into the other machine. It can do this by guessing passwords. Sometimes things are set up to make it really easy; for instance, account name/password pairs might be stored in script files so that a naive user can access remote resources automatically. If the worm manages to find that information, it can easily log into other machines and install itself. Sometimes machines have trapdoor debugging features, such as the ability to run a command remotely. Sometimes it isn't even necessary to log in to run such a command. And if intruders can execute commands, they can do anything.

> ***The only reason all the computers in the world haven't crashed at the same time is that they're not all connected together yet.***
>
> —Dave Cheriton

In the first widely publicized example, a Christmas-card-type email message displayed a pretty animated tree on the screen, but also scanned the user's directory for all possible correspondents, including distribution lists, and mailed itself to them. Each time a recipient read a copy of the message, it sprang into life and mailed itself off to all the mailboxes it could locate from that node. This was written by someone who was not trying to attack systems—he was just trying to be "cute" but didn't consider the likely consequences of his action. Although this program did not destroy data, like a classic worm it completely overloaded and disabled the corporation's electronic mail.

Email borne viruses have become the most common kind in the last few years, taking advantage both of bugs in email systems and naive users. The "ILoveYou" virus was particularly virulent because users were willing to take a chance and run the attachment when the message had a seductive subject line.

Worms have also become more effective at spreading as more machines are continuously connected to the Internet via cable modems and DSL, but not carefully configured for security. In several cases, insecure default configurations or bugs in services that were enabled by default provided fertile ground for worms to spread.

1.12.3 Virus Checkers

How can a program check for viruses? There's rather a race between the brave and gallant people who analyze the viruses and write clever programs to detect and eliminate them, and the foul-smelling scum who devise new types of viruses that will escape detection by all the current virus checkers.

The most common form of virus checker knows the instruction sequence for lots of types of viruses, checks all the files on disk and instructions in memory for those patterns of commands, and raises a warning if it finds a match hidden somewhere inside some file. Once you own such a virus checker, you need to periodically get updates of the patterns file that includes the newest viruses. To evade detection of their viruses, virus creators have devised what is known as a **polymorphic virus** which changes the order of its instructions, or changes to functionally similar instructions, each time it copies itself. Such a virus may still be detectable, but it takes more work and typically requires a coding change and not just a new pattern file. Modern virus checkers don't just periodically scan the disk. They actually hook into the operating system and inspect files before they are written to disk.

Another type of virus checker takes a snapshot of disk storage by recording the information in the directories, such as file lengths. It might even take message digests of the files. It is designed to run, store the information, and then run again at a future time. It will warn you if there are suspicious changes. One virus, wary of changing the length of a file by adding itself to the program, compressed the program so that the infected program would wind up being the same length as the original. When the program was executed, the uncompressed portion containing the virus decompressed the rest of the program, so (other than the virus portion) the program could run normally.

It would be natural for viruses to attack the virus checkers rather than just trying to elude them. One could even imagine a virus spread by the mechanism a virus checker uses to keep its pattern files up to date. Such a virus has not been seen at the time of this writing, but it is something to look forward to.

1.12.4 What Can We Do Today?

The world was a scary place before computer viruses came along, and will most likely continue to be scary. How can you know whether you can trust a program not to do bad things when you run it? Wouldn't it be nice to have the equivalent of a lie-detector test for programs?

> *Ames slipped by a lie-detector test because no one had told the polygrapher he was under suspicion.*
>
> —Douglas Waller & Evan Thomas
>
> *Newsweek* article on CIA and traitor Aldrich Ames, October 10, 1994

Given that there is no infallible method to test a program for hidden bad side effects, we can't be completely safe, but there are some precautions that are worth taking:

- Don't run software from suspicious sources, like bulletin boards or people who aren't as careful as you are.
- Frequently run virus checkers. Have the industry employ people whose job it is to keep up with virus technology and come up with vaccines.
- Try to run programs in the most limited possible environments. For instance, if you have a PC in order to get real work done, and you also want to play games, sometimes using shareware or games copied from bulletin boards, have two machines. If you run a game with a virus, you'll only wipe out your games. A somewhat more practical way to accomplish this is to have a machine with multiple disks and a physical switch that connects only one of them at a time.
- When your system puts up a warning saying that something is dangerous, don't do it!
- Do frequent backups, and save old backups for a long time.
- Don't boot off floppies, except in an extreme circumstance, such as the first time you unpack your machine and turn it on. In those circumstances, be extremely careful about what floppy you boot from.

But mostly, the situation is pretty bleak, given the design of the operating systems for PCs. Maybe in the future, some of our suggestions in the next section might be implemented.

1.12.5 Wish List for the Future

I_2 always assumed computers were designed in such a way that no program that ran on the machine could possibly injure the machine. Likewise, it should not be possible to send a piece of information to a machine that might damage the machine. People are designed properly that way, aren't they?

Sticks and stones may break my bones but words will never hurt me.
(chant designed to encourage bullies to get physical)

But one of my_2 first programs consisted of something that just sat around and waited for interrupts, and processed the interrupts. The program itself, not counting the instructions for processing the interrupts, was `HERE: JUMP HERE` (that's not the exact instruction, because I_2 don't want to divulge the brand of computer). I_2 discovered (the hard way) that you weren't supposed to do that, because it burned out core at the instruction that kept getting executed over and over. Gerry Sussman, while a high school student, wrote a program that broke magnetic tapes. The guru who guarded and ran the mainframe didn't believe Gerry when he boasted that he could write a program to break tapes, so Gerry wrote his program to go down the entire row of tape drives, breaking the tape in each one. Another example was a machine designed with a small amount of nonvolatile memory, but the type that wore out after a finite number of writes, say 10000. That kind of memory is fine for something like saving terminal settings, since a human has to type the key sequence to cause a write, and a human won't do it very often. But if the same kind of memory is used for storing parameter settings received by a network management message, then it is possible to break the machine within seconds by sending it parameter settings over and over.

In an ideal world, it should be possible to load a floppy and examine the contents without fear. You should be able to receive any email message without fear. If it is a multimedia message, it should be possible to play the audio, display the video, print the text, or waft the odors without damage to either the machine or files stored on the machine. A file is just a bunch of bits. If the file claims to be audio, it should be possible, without risk of any type of harm, to play the file. Likewise, if the file claims to be something worthy of printing, it should not cause any harm to print the file.

Programs are a bit trickier. It should be possible to run a program and have confidence that it will not affect the files stored on your machine or the basic integrity of the operating system.

We know none of these "shoulds" are true today. The files on your machine can be virus-infected through email, by displaying a PostScript file, or simply by inserting a floppy disk or CD-ROM (on some machines). How could systems be designed more defensively?

One simple feature would be a write-protect switch on your hard disk. Sometimes you run programs that you know should not be writing to your hard disk. A game program shouldn't be writing to your hard disk. Perhaps it wants to record highest score, but consumers might be willing to do without that frill if it means that they can run any game they want without fear of wiping out their life's work. Legitimate game manufacturers could design their games to work with write-protected hard disks. There is still the risk that the social misfits who design games that spread viruses could design their games to work with write-protected hard disks, but have their program check to see if some user has forgotten to write-protect the disk, and then launch the virus.

Timesharing systems used to be much more defensive. You could not run a program that would write into some other user's memory, or modify any portion of the disk that you were not authorized to write into. But PCs make the assumption that there is only one human on the machine at a time, and that human ought to be able to do anything it wants. To make matters worse, to enable snazzy maximally flexible features, there are all sorts of surprising places where someone can insert a program that will be executed.

The operating system ought to be built more defensively. PCs should have accounts just like timesharing systems so that you can set up a game account that can't affect the rest of the system. Likewise, your normal account shouldn't be able to alter system software. You should be able to easily run a program with the right to access only a single directory (its own). The world is moving in this direction, but progress is slow.

1.13 THE MULTI-LEVEL MODEL OF SECURITY

Computer security has become sufficiently important that it was inevitable that governments would decide they needed to "do something about it". And when governments want to know something about security, they turn to the experts: the military. And they develop standards and measurement tools by which security can be measured that are unbiased so as not to favor any one organization. And they mandate that anyone they can influence buy products meeting those standards.

The problem is that *secure* is not as simple to define as, say, *flame-retardant*. The security threats in different environments are very different, as are the best ways to counter them. The military has traditionally focussed on keeping their data secret (and learning the secrets of the other side). They are less concerned (though probably shouldn't be) about data getting corrupted or forged. In a paper world, forgeries are so difficult and so likely to expose the spies placing them that this threat takes a back seat. In the computerized environment, modification or corruption of data is a more likely threat.

1.13.1 Mandatory (Nondiscretionary) Access Controls

O negligence! ... what cross devil made me put this main secret in the packet I sent the king? Is there no way to cure this? No new device to beat this from his brains?

—Shakespeare's *King Henry VIII*, act 3, scene 2

Discretionary means that someone who owns a resource can make a decision as to who is allowed to use (access) it. **Nondiscretionary access controls** enforce a policy where users might be allowed to use information themselves but might not be allowed to make a copy of it available to someone else. Strict rules are automatically enforced about who is allowed access to certain resources based on the attributes of the resource, and even the owners of the resources cannot change those attributes. The analogy in the paper world is that you might be given a book full of confidential information, but you are not allowed to take the book out of the building. In the military, information often has a security classification, and just because you have access to secret information does not mean you can forward it as you see fit. Only someone with the proper clearance can see it, and clearance levels are decided by a separate organization based on background investigations—not based on whether someone seems like a nice guy at lunch.

The basic philosophy behind discretionary controls is that the users and the programs they run are good guys, and it is up to the operating system to trust them and protect each user from outsiders and other users. The basic philosophy behind nondiscretionary controls is that users are careless and the programs they run can't be presumed to be carrying out their wishes. The system must be ever vigilant to prevent the users from accidentally or intentionally giving information to someone who shouldn't have it. Careless users might accidentally type the wrong file name when including a file in a mail message, or might leave a message world-readable. The concept is to confine information within a **security perimeter**, and thus not allow any information to move from a more secure environment to a less secure environment. A secure system would have both discretionary and nondiscretionary access controls, with the latter serving as a backup mechanism with less granularity.

Now of course, if you allow the users out of the building, there is an avenue for information to leak out of a secure environment, since a user can remember the information and tell someone once the user gets out of the security perimeter. There really is no way for a computer system to prevent that. But the designers wanted to ensure that no Trojan horse in software could transmit any information out of the perimeter, that nothing a user did inadvertently could leak information, and that users couldn't spirit out larger amounts of information than they could memorize.

1.13.2 Levels of Security

What does it mean for something to be "more sensitive" than something else? We will use a somewhat simplified description of the U.S. Department of Defense (DoD) definitions of levels of security as an example. It is a reasonably general model and similar to what is done in other contexts. It is sufficient to understand the security mechanisms we'll describe.

The security label of something consists of two components:

- A **security level** (also known as classification), which might be an integer in some range, but in the U.S. DoD consists of one of the four ratings unclassified, confidential, secret, and top secret, where unclassified < confidential < secret < top secret.
- A set of zero or more **categories** (also known as **compartments**), which describe kinds of information. For instance, the name CRYPTO might mean information about cryptographic algorithms, INTEL might mean information about military intelligence, COMSEC might mean information about communications security, or NUCLEAR might mean information about types of families.

Documents (or computer files) are marked with a security label saying how sensitive the information is, and people are issued security clearances according to how trustworthy they are perceived to be and what information they have demonstrated a "need to know."

A clearance might therefore be (SECRET;{COMSEC,CRYPTO}), which would indicate someone who was allowed to know information classified unclassified, confidential, or secret (but not top secret) dealing with cryptographic algorithms or communications security.

Given two security labels, (X,S_1) and (Y,S_2), (X,S_1) is defined as being "at least as sensitive as" (Y,S_2) iff $X \geq Y$ and $S_2 \subseteq S_1$. For example,

(TOP SECRET, {CRYPTO,COMSEC}) > (SECRET, {CRYPTO})

where ">" means "more sensitive than".

It is possible for two labels to be incomparable in the sense that neither is more sensitive than the other. For example, neither of the following are comparable to each other:

(TOP SECRET, {CRYPTO,COMSEC})

(SECRET, {NUCLEAR,CRYPTO})

1.13.3 Mandatory Access Control Rules

Every person, process, and piece of information has a security label. A person cannot run a process with a label higher than the person's label, but may run one with a lower label. Information is only allowed to be read by a process that has at least as high a rating as the information. The terminology used for having a process read something with a higher rating than the process is **read-up**. Read-up is illegal and must be prevented. A process cannot write a piece of information with a rating lower than the process's rating. The terminology used for a process writing something with a lower rating than the process is **write-down**. Write-down is illegal and must be prevented.

The rules are:

- A human can only run a process that has a security label below or equal to that of the human's label.
- A process can only read information marked with a security label below or equal to that of the process.
- A process can only write information marked with a security label above or equal to that of the process. Note that if a process writes information marked with a security label above that of the process, the process can't subsequently read that information.

The prevention of read-up and write-down is the central idea behind mandatory access controls. The concepts of confinement within a security perimeter and a generalized hierarchy of security classes were given a mathematical basis by Bell and La Padula in 1973 [BELL74]. There is significant complexity associated with the details of actually making them work. There has been significant subsequent research on more complex models that capture both the trustworthiness and the confidentiality of data and programs.

1.13.4 Covert Channels

A **covert channel** is a method for a Trojan horse to circumvent the automatic confinement of information within a security perimeter. Let's assume an operating system has enforced the rules in the previous section. Let's assume also that a bad guy has successfully tricked someone with a TOP SECRET clearance into running a program with a Trojan horse. The program has access to some sensitive data, and wants to pass the data to the bad guy. We're assuming the operating system prevents the process from doing this straightforwardly, but there are diabolical methods that theoretically could be employed to get information out.

The Trojan horse program cannot directly pass data, but all it needs is for there to be anything it can do that can be detected by something outside the security perimeter. As long as information can be passed one bit at a time, anything can be transmitted, given enough time.

One kind of covert channel is a **timing channel**. The Trojan horse program alternately loops and waits, in cycles of, say, one minute per bit. When the next bit is a 1, the program loops for one minute. When the next bit is a 0, the program waits for a minute. The bad guy's program running on the same computer but without access to the sensitive data constantly tests the loading of the system. If the system is sluggish, its conspirator inside the perimeter is looping, and therefore transmitting a 1. Otherwise, the conspirator is waiting, and therefore transmitting a 0.

This assumes those two processes are the only ones running on the machine. What happens if there are other processes running and stopping at seemingly random times (from the point of view of the program trying to read the covert channel)? That introduces noise into the channel. But communications people can deal with a noisy channel; it just lowers the potential bandwidth, depending on the signal to noise ratio.

Another kind of covert channel called a **storage channel** involves the use of shared resources other than processor cycles. For instance, suppose there were a queue of finite size, say the print queue. The Trojan horse program could fill the queue to transmit a 1, and delete some jobs to transmit a 0. The covert channel reader would attempt to print something and note whether the request was accepted. Other possible shared resources that might be exploited for passing information include physical memory, disk space, network ports, and I/O buffers.

Yet another example depends on how clever the operating system is about not divulging information in error messages. For instance, suppose the operating system says file does not exist when a file really does not exist, but says insufficient privilege for requested operation when the file does exist, but inside a security perimeter off limits to the process requesting to read the file. Then the Trojan horse can alternately create and delete a file of some name known to the other process. The conspirator process periodically attempts to read the file and uses the information about which error message it gets to determine the setting of the next bit of information.

There is no general way to prevent all covert channels. Instead, people imagine all the different ways they can think of, and specifically attempt to plug those holes. For instance, the timing channel can be eliminated by giving each security level a fixed percentage of the processor cycles. This is wasteful and impractical in general, because there can be an immense number of distinct classifications (in our model of (*one of four levels*, {*categories*}), the number of possible security perimeters is $4 \cdot 2^n$, where n is the number of categories).

Most covert channels have very low bandwidth. In many cases, instead of attempting to eliminate a covert channel, it is more practical to introduce enough noise into the system so that the bandwidth becomes too low to be useful to an enemy. It's also possible to look for jobs that appear to be attempting to exploit covert channels (a job that alternately submitted enough print jobs to fill the queue and then deleted them would be suspicious indeed if someone knew to watch). If the bandwidth is low *and* the secret data is large, and knowing only a small subset of the secret data is not of much use to an enemy, the threat is minimized.

How much secret data must be leaked before serious damage is done can vary considerably. For example, assume there is a file with 100 megabytes of secret data. The file has been transmitted, encrypted, on an insecure network. The enemy therefore has the ciphertext, but the cryptographic algorithm used makes it impossible for the enemy to decrypt the data without knowing the key. A Trojan horse with access to the file and a covert channel with a bandwidth of 1 bit every 10 seconds would require 250 years to leak the data (by which time it's hard to believe the divulging of the information could be damaging to anyone). However, if the Trojan horse had access to the 56-bit key, it could leak that information across the covert channel in less than 10 minutes. That information would allow the enemy to decrypt the 100-megabyte file. For this reason, many secure systems go to great pains to keep cryptographic keys out of the hands of the programs that use them.

1.13.5 The Orange Book

The National Computer Security Center (NCSC), an agency of the U.S. government, has published an official standard called "Trusted Computer System Evaluation Criteria", universally known as "the Orange Book" (guess what color the cover is). The Orange Book defines a series of ratings a computer system can have based on its security features and the care that went into its design, documentation, and testing. This rating system is intended to give government agencies and commercial enterprises an objective assessment of a system's security and to goad computer manufacturers into placing more emphasis on security.

The official categories are D, C1, C2, B1, B2, B3, and A1, which range from least secure to most secure. In reality, of course, there is no way to place all the possible properties in a linear scale. Different threats are more or less important in different environments. The authors of the Orange Book made an attempt to linearize these concerns given their priorities. But the results can be misleading. An otherwise A1 system that is missing some single feature might have a D rating. Systems not designed with the Orange Book in mind are likely to get low ratings even if they are in fact very secure.

The other problem with the Orange Book rating scheme is that the designers focused on the security priorities of military security people—keeping data secret. A rating of B1 or better requires implementation of multi-level security and mandatory access controls. In the commercial world, data integrity is at least as important as data confidentiality. Mandatory access controls, even if available, are not suitable for most commercial environments because they make some of the most common operations, such as having a highly privileged user send mail to an unprivileged user, very cumbersome.

Mandatory access controls do not by themselves protect the system from infection by viruses. Mandatory access controls allow write-up, so if some unprivileged account became infected by having someone carelessly run, say, a game program loaded from a bulletin board, the virus could spread to more secure areas. Ironically, if it was a very secure area that first got infected, the mandatory access control features would prevent the infection from spreading to the less secure environments.

The following is a summary of what properties a system must have to qualify for each rating.

D – Minimal Protection. This simply means the system did not qualify for any of the higher ratings; it might actually be very secure. No system is ever going to brag about the fact that it was awarded a D rating.

C1 – Discretionary Security Protection. The requirements at this level correspond roughly to what one might expect from a classic timesharing system. It requires

- The operating system must prevent unprivileged user programs from overwriting critical portions of its memory. (Note that many PC operating systems do not satisfy this condition.)
- Resources must be protected with access controls. Those access controls need not be sophisticated; classic owner/group/world controls would be sufficient.
- The system must authenticate users by a password or some similar mechanism, and the password database must be protected so that it cannot be accessed by unauthorized users.

There are additional requirements around testing and documentation, which become more detailed at each successive rating.

C2 – Controlled Access Protection. This level corresponds roughly to a timesharing system where security is an important concern but users are responsible for their own fates; an example might be a commercial timesharing system. The additional requirements (over those required for C1) for a C2 rating are

- access control at a per user granularity—It must be possible to permit access to any selected subset of the user community, probably via ACLs. An **ACL** is a data structure attached to a resource that specifies the resource's authorized users. C2 does not explicitly require ACLs, but they are the most convenient way to provide the granularity of protection that C2 requires.
- clearing of allocated memory—The operating system must ensure that freshly allocated disk space and memory does not contain "left-over" data deleted by some previous user. It can do that by writing to the space or by requiring processes to write to the space before they can read it.
- auditing—The operating system must be capable of recording security-relevant events, including authentication and object access. The audit log must be protected from tampering and must record date, time, user, object, and event. Auditing must be selective based on user and object.

It is reasonable to expect that C2-rateable systems will become ubiquitous, since they contain features that are commonly desired and do not represent an unacceptable overhead. It is somewhat surprising that such systems are not the norm.

B1 – Labeled Security Protection. Additional requirements at this level are essentially those required to implement Mandatory Access Controls for secrecy (not integrity) except that little attention is given to covert channels. Requirements for B1 above those for C2 include

- Security Labels: Sensitivity labels must be maintained for all users, processes, and files, and read-up and write-down must be prevented by the operating system.
- Attached devices must either themselves be labeled as accepting only a single level of information, or they must accept and know how to process security labels.
- Attached printers must have a mechanism for ensuring that there is a human-readable sensitivity label printed on the top and bottom of each page corresponding to the sensitivity label of the information being printed. The operating system must enforce this correspondence.

B2 – Structured Protection. Beyond B1, there are few new features introduced; rather, the operating system must be structured to greater levels of assurance that it behaves correctly (i.e., has no bugs). Additional requirements for B2 include

- trusted path to user—There must be some mechanism to allow a user at a terminal to reliably distinguish between talking to the legitimate operating system and talking to a Trojan horse password-capturing program.
- security level changes—A terminal user must be notified when any process started by that user changes its security level.
- security kernel—The operating system must be structured so that only a minimal portion of it is security-sensitive, i.e., that bugs in the bulk of the O/S cannot cause sensitive data to leak. This is typically done by running the bulk of the O/S in the processor's user mode and having a secure-kernel mini-O/S which enforces the mandatory access controls.
- Covert channels must be identified and their bandwidth estimated, but there is no requirement that they be eliminated.
- Strict procedures must be used in the maintenance of the security-sensitive portion of the operating system. For instance, anyone modifying any portion must document what they changed, when they changed it, and why, and some set of other people should compare the updated section with the previous version.

B3 – Security Domains. Additional requirements for B3 mostly involve greater assurance that the operating system will not have bugs that might allow something to circumvent mandatory access controls. Additional requirements include

- ACLs must be able to explicitly deny access to named individuals even if they are members of groups that are otherwise allowed access. It is only at this level that ACLs must be able to separately enforce modes of access (i.e., read vs. write) to a file.
- active audit—There must be mechanisms to detect selected audited events or thresholds of audited events and immediately trigger notification of a security administrator.
- secure crashing—The system must ensure that the crashing and restarting of the system introduces no security policy violations.

A1 – Verified Design. There are no additional features in an A1 system over a B3 system. Rather, there are formal procedures for the analysis of the design of the system and more rigorous controls on its implementation.

1.13.6 Successors to the Orange Book

Gee, I wish we had one of them Doomsday machines

—Turgidson, in *Dr. Strangelove*

Governments are rarely willing to adopt one another's ideas, especially if they didn't contribute. They would rather develop their own. The publication of the Orange Book in 1983 set off a series of efforts in various countries to come up with their own standards and classifications. These efforts eventually merged in 1990 into a single non-U.S. standard called ITSEC, followed by a reconciliation with the U.S. and the development of a single worldwide standard called the Common Criteria in 1994. Version 2.1 of the Common Criteria became an international standard in 1999.

The details of the various rating systems are all different, so passing the bureaucratic hurdles to qualify for a rating under one system would not be much of a head start toward getting an equivalent rating in another (much as different countries don't recognize each other's credentials for practicing medicine). The following table is an oversimplification that we hope won't be too offensive to the advocates of these rating systems, but it does allow the novice to judge what is being claimed about a system. In a partial acknowledgment of the multifaceted nature of security, many of the systems gave two ratings: one for the features provided and one for the degree of assurance that the system implements those features correctly. In practice, like the artistic and technical merit scores at the Olympics, the two scores tend to be closely correlated.

TCSEC (Orange Book)	German (Green Book)	British CLEF	ITSEC	Common Criteria
D	Q0		E0	EAL 0
				EAL 1
C1	Q1/F1	L1	C1/E1	EAL 2
C2	Q2/F2	L2	C2/E2	CAPP/EAL 3
B1	Q3/F3	L3	B1/E3	CSPP/EAL 4
B2	Q4/F4	L4	B2/E4	EAL 5
B3	Q5/F5	L5	B3/E5	EAL 6
A1	Q6/F5	L6	B3/E6	EAL 7

1.14 Legal Issues

The legal aspects of cryptography are fascinating, but the picture changes quickly, and we are certainly not experts in law. Although it pains us to say it, if you're going to do anything involving cryptography, talk to a lawyer.

1.14.1 Patents

One legal issue that affects the choice of security mechanisms is patents. Most cryptographic techniques are covered by patents and historically this has slowed their deployment. One of the important criteria for selection of the AES algorithm (see §3.5 *Advanced Encryption Standard (AES)*) was that it be royalty free.

The most popular public key algorithm is RSA (see §6.3 *RSA*). RSA was developed at MIT, and under the terms of MIT's funding at the time there are no license fees for U.S. government use. It was only patented in the U.S., and licensing was controlled by one company which claimed that the Hellman-Merkle patent also covered RSA, and that patent is international. Interpretation of patent rights varies by country, so the legal issues were complex. At any rate, the last patent on RSA ran out on September 20, 2000. There were many parties on that day.

To avoid large licensing fees, many standards attempted to use DSS (see §6.5 *Digital Signature Standard (DSS)*) instead of RSA. Although in most respects DSS is technically inferior to RSA, when first announced it was advertised that DSS would be freely licensable, i.e., it would not be necessary to reach agreement with the RSA licensing company. But the company claimed Hellman-Merkle covered all public key cryptography, and strengthened its position by acquiring rights to a patent by Schnorr that was closely related to DSS. Until the patents expired, the situation was murky.

> *"I don't know what you mean by* your way,*" said the Queen: "all the ways about here belong to me..."*
>
> —*Through the Looking Glass*

Some of the relevant patents, luckily all expired, are:

- Diffie-Hellman: Patent #4,200,770, issued 1980. This covers the Diffie-Hellman key exchange described in §6.4 *Diffie-Hellman*.
- Hellman-Merkle: Patent #4,218,582, issued 1980. This is claimed to cover all public key systems. There is some controversy over whether this patent should be valid. The specific public key mechanisms described in the patent (*knapsack* systems) were subsequently broken.
- Rivest-Shamir-Adleman: Patent #4,405,829, issued 1983. This covers the RSA algorithm described in §6.3 *RSA*.
- Hellman-Pohlig: Patent #4,424,414, issued 1984. This is related to the Diffie-Hellman key exchange.

1.14.2 Export Controls

> *Mary had a little key*
> *(It's all she could export)*
> *And all the email that she sent*
> *Was opened at the Fort.*
>
> —Ron Rivest

The U.S. government used to impose severe restrictions on export of encryption. This caused much bitterness in the computer industry and led to some fascinating technical designs so that domestic products, which were legally allowed to use strong encryption, could use strong encryption where possible, and yet interoperate with exportable products that were not allowed to use strong encryption. We describe such designs in this book (see §19.13 *Exportability*). Luckily, export controls seem to be pretty much lifted. For historical reasons, and in case they become relevant again (we sure hope not), we couldn't bear to delete the following section. It was written for the first edition of this book, and was timely in 1995 when that edition was published:

The U.S. government considers encryption to be a dangerous technology, like germ warfare and nuclear weapons. If a U.S. corporation would like to sell to other countries (and the proceeds are not going to be funding the Contras), it needs export approval. The export control laws around encryption are not clear, and their interpretation changes over time. The general principle is that the U.S. government does not want you to give out technology that would make it more difficult for them to spy. Sometimes companies get so discouraged that they leave encryption out of their products altogether. Sometimes they generate products that, when sold overseas, have the encryption mechanisms removed. It is usually possible to get export approval for encryption if the key lengths are short enough for the government to brute-force check all possible keys to decrypt a message. So sometimes companies just use short keys, or sometimes they have the capability of varying the key length, and they fix the key length to be shorter when a system is sold outside the U.S.

Even if you aren't in the business of selling software abroad, you can run afoul of export controls. If you install encryption software on your laptop and take it along with you on an international trip, you may be breaking the law. If you distribute encryption software within the U.S. without adequate warnings, you are doing your customers a disservice. And the legality of posting encryption software on a public network is questionable.

PART 1

CRYPTOGRAPHY

2 INTRODUCTION TO CRYPTOGRAPHY

2.1 WHAT IS CRYPTOGRAPHY?

The word *cryptography* comes from the Greek words κρυπτο (*hidden* or *secret*) and γραφη (*writing*). So, cryptography is the art of secret writing. More generally, people think of cryptography as the art of mangling information into apparent unintelligibility in a manner allowing a secret method of unmangling. The basic service provided by cryptography is the ability to send information between participants in a way that prevents others from reading it. In this book we will concentrate on the kind of cryptography that is based on representing information as numbers and mathematically manipulating those numbers. This kind of cryptography can provide other services, such as

- integrity checking—reassuring the recipient of a message that the message has not been altered since it was generated by a legitimate source
- authentication—verifying someone's (or something's) identity

But back to the traditional use of cryptography. A message in its original form is known as **plaintext** or **cleartext**. The mangled information is known as **ciphertext**. The process for producing ciphertext from plaintext is known as **encryption**. The reverse of encryption is called **decryption**.

plaintext —encryption→ ciphertext —decryption→ plaintext

While cryptographers invent clever secret codes, cryptanalysts attempt to break these codes. These two disciplines constantly try to keep ahead of each other. Ultimately, the success of the cryptographers rests on the

Fundamental Tenet of Cryptography

If lots of smart people have failed to solve a problem,
then it probably won't be solved (soon).

Cryptographic systems tend to involve both an algorithm and a secret value. The secret value is known as the **key**. The reason for having a key in addition to an algorithm is that it is difficult to keep devising new algorithms that will allow reversible scrambling of information, and it is difficult to quickly explain a newly devised algorithm to the person with whom you'd like to start communicating securely. With a good cryptographic scheme it is perfectly OK to have everyone, including the bad guys (and the cryptanalysts) know the algorithm because knowledge of the algorithm without the key does not help unmangle the information.

The concept of a key is analogous to the combination for a combination lock. Although the concept of a combination lock is well known (you dial in the secret numbers in the correct sequence and the lock opens), you can't open a combination lock easily without knowing the combination.

2.1.1 Computational Difficulty

It is important for cryptographic algorithms to be reasonably efficient for the good guys to compute. The good guys are the ones with knowledge of the keys.* Cryptographic algorithms are not impossible to break without the key. A bad guy can simply try all possible keys until one works. The security of a cryptographic scheme depends on how much work it is for the bad guy to break it. If the best possible scheme will take 10 million years to break using all of the computers in the world, then it can be considered reasonably secure.

Going back to the combination lock example, a typical combination might consist of three numbers, each a number between 1 and 40. Let's say it takes 10 seconds to dial in a combination. That's reasonably convenient for the good guy. How much work is it for the bad guy? There are 40^3 possible combinations, which is 64000. At 10 seconds per try, it would take a week to try all combinations, though on average it would only take half that long (even though the right number is always the last one you try!).

Often a scheme can be made more secure by making the key longer. In the combination lock analogy, making the key longer would consist of requiring four numbers to be dialed in. This would make a little more work for the good guy. It might now take 13 seconds to dial in the combination. But the bad guy has 40 times as many combinations to try, at 13 seconds each, so it would take a year to try all combinations. (And if it took that long, he might want to stop to eat or sleep).

With cryptography, computers can be used to exhaustively try keys. Computers are a lot faster than people, and they don't get tired, so thousands or millions of keys can be tried per second. Also, lots of keys can be tried in parallel if you have multiple computers, so time can be saved by spending money on more computers.

Sometimes a cryptographic algorithm has a variable-length key. It can be made more secure by increasing the length of the key. Increasing the length of the key by one bit makes the good guy's

*We're using the terms *good guys* for the cryptographers, and *bad guys* for the cryptanalysts. This is a convenient shorthand and not a moral judgment—in any given situation, which side you consider *good* or *bad* depends on your point of view.

job just a little bit harder, but makes the bad guy's job up to twice as hard (because the number of possible keys doubles). Some cryptographic algorithms have a fixed-length key, but a similar algorithm with a longer key can be devised if necessary. If computers get 1000 times faster, so that the bad guy's job becomes reasonably practical, making the key 10 bits longer will make the bad guy's job as hard as it was before the advance in computer speed. However, it will be much easier for the good guys (because their computer speed increase far outweighs the increment in key length). So the faster computers get, the better life gets for the good guys.

Keep in mind that breaking the cryptographic scheme is often only one way of getting what you want. For instance, a bolt cutter works no matter how many digits are in the combination.

> *You can get further with a kind word and a gun than you can with a kind word alone.*
>
> —Willy Sutton, bank robber

2.1.2 To Publish or Not to Publish

Some people believe that keeping a cryptographic algorithm as secret as possible will enhance its security. Others argue that publishing the algorithm, so that it is widely known, will enhance its security. On the one hand, it would seem that keeping the algorithm secret must be more secure—it makes for more work for the cryptanalyst to try to figure out what the algorithm is.

The argument for publishing the algorithm is that the bad guys will probably find out about it eventually anyway, so it's better to tell a lot of nonmalicious people about the algorithm so that in case there are weaknesses, a good guy will discover them rather than a bad guy. A good guy who discovers a weakness will warn people that the system has a weakness. Publication provides an enormous amount of free consulting from the academic community as cryptanalysts look for weaknesses so they can publish papers about them. A bad guy who discovers a weakness will exploit it for doing bad-guy things like embezzling money or stealing trade secrets.

It is difficult to keep the algorithm secret because if an algorithm is to be widely used, it is highly likely that determined attackers will manage to learn the algorithm by reverse engineering whatever implementation is distributed, or just because the more people who know something the more likely it is for the information to leak to the wrong places. In the past, "good" cryptosystems were not economically feasible, so keeping the algorithms secret was needed extra protection. We believe (we hope?) today's algorithms are sufficiently secure that this is not necessary.

Common practice today is for most commercial cryptosystems to be published and for military cryptosystems to be kept secret. If a commercial algorithm is unpublished today, it's probably for trade secret reasons or because this makes it easier to get export approval rather than to enhance its security. We suspect the military ciphers are unpublished mainly to keep good cryptographic methods out of the hands of the enemy rather than to keep them from cryptanalyzing our codes.

2.1.3 Secret Codes

We use the terms *secret code* and *cipher* interchangeably to mean any method of encrypting data. Some people draw a subtle distinction between these terms that we don't find useful.

The earliest documented cipher is attributed to Julius Caesar. The way the **Caesar cipher** would work if the message were in English is as follows. Substitute for each letter of the message, the letter which is 3 letters later in the alphabet (and wrap around to A from Z). Thus an A would become a D, and so forth. For instance, DOZEN would become GRCHQ. Once you figure out what's going on, it is very easy to read messages encrypted this way (unless, of course, the original message was in Greek).

A slight enhancement to the Caesar cipher was distributed as a premium with Ovaltine in the 1940s as *Captain Midnight Secret Decoder rings*. (There were times when this might have been a violation of export controls for distributing cryptographic hardware!) The variant is to pick a secret number n between 1 and 25, instead of always using 3. Substitute for each letter of the message, the letter which is n higher (and wrap around to A from Z of course). Thus if the secret number was 1, an A would become a B, and so forth. For instance HAL would become IBM. If the secret number was 25, then IBM would become HAL. Regardless of the value of n, since there are only 26 possible ns to try, it is still very easy to break this cipher if you know it's being used and you can recognize a message once it's decrypted.

The next type of cryptographic system developed is known as a **monoalphabetic cipher**, which consists of an arbitrary mapping of one letter to another letter. There are 26! possible pairings of letters, which is approximately 4×10^{26}. [Remember, $n!$, which reads "n factorial", means $n(n-1)(n-2)\cdots1$.] This might seem secure, because to try all possibilities, if it took 1 microsecond to try each one, would take about 10 trillion years. However, by statistical analysis of language (knowing that certain letters and letter combinations are more common than others), it turns out to be fairly easy to break. For instance, many daily newspapers have a daily cryptogram, which is a monoalphabetic cipher, and can be broken by people who enjoy that sort of thing during their subway ride to work. An example is

Cf lqr'xs xsnyctm n eqxxqgsy iqul qf wdcp eqqh, erl lqrx qgt iqul!

Computers have made much more complex cryptographic schemes both necessary and possible. Necessary because computers can try keys at a rate that would exhaust an army of clerks; and possible because computers can execute the complex algorithms quickly and without errors.

2.2 BREAKING AN ENCRYPTION SCHEME

What do we mean when we speak of a bad guy Fred *breaking* an encryption scheme? The three basic attacks are known as **ciphertext only, known plaintext**, and **chosen plaintext**.

2.2.1 Ciphertext Only

In a ciphertext only attack, Fred has seen (and presumably stored) some ciphertext that he can analyze at leisure. Typically it is not difficult for a bad guy to obtain ciphertext. (If a bad guy can't access the encrypted data, then there would have been no need to encrypt the data in the first place!)

How can Fred figure out the plaintext if all he can see is the ciphertext? One possible strategy is to search through all the keys. Fred tries the decrypt operation with each key in turn. It is essential for this attack that Fred be able to recognize when he has succeeded. For instance, if the message was English text, then it is highly unlikely that a decryption operation with an incorrect key could produce something that looked like intelligible text. Because it is important for Fred to be able to differentiate plaintext from gibberish, this attack is sometimes known as a **recognizable plaintext** attack.

It is also essential that Fred have enough ciphertext. For instance, using the example of a monoalphabetic cipher, if the only ciphertext available to Fred were XYZ, then there is not enough information. There are many possible letter substitutions that would lead to a legal three-letter English word. There is no way for Fred to know whether the plaintext corresponding to XYZ is THE or CAT or HAT. As a matter of fact, in the following sentence, any of the words could be the plaintext for XYZ:

The hot cat was sad but you may now sit and use her big red pen.

[Don't worry—we've found a lovely sanatorium for the coauthor who wrote that.

—*the other coauthors*]

Often it isn't necessary to search through a lot of keys. For instance, the authentication scheme Kerberos (see §13.4 *Logging Into the Network*) assigns to user Alice a DES key derived from Alice's password according to a straightforward, published algorithm. If Alice chooses her password unwisely (say a word in the dictionary), then Fred does not need to search through all 2^{56} possible DES keys—instead he only needs to try the derived keys of the 10000 or so common English words.

A cryptographic algorithm has to be secure against a ciphertext only attack because of the accessibility of the ciphertext to cryptanalysts. But in many cases cryptanalysts can obtain additional information, so it is important to design cryptographic systems to withstand the next two attacks as well.

2.2.2 Known Plaintext

Sometimes life is easier for the attacker. Suppose Fred has somehow obtained some ⟨plaintext, ciphertext⟩ pairs. How might he have obtained these? One possibility is that secret data might not remain secret forever. For instance, the data might consist of specifying the next city to be attacked. Once the attack occurs, the plaintext to the previous day's ciphertext is now known.

With a monoalphabetic cipher, a small amount of known plaintext would be a bonanza. From it, the attacker would learn the mappings of a substantial fraction of the most common letters (every letter that was used in the plaintext Fred obtained). Some cryptographic schemes might be good enough to be secure against ciphertext only attacks but not good enough against known plaintext attacks. In these cases, it becomes important to design the systems that use such a cryptographic algorithm to minimize the possibility that a bad guy will ever be able to obtain ⟨*plaintext*, *ciphertext*⟩ pairs.

2.2.3 Chosen Plaintext

On rare occasions, life may be easier still for the attacker. In a chosen plaintext attack, Fred can choose any plaintext he wants, and get the system to tell him what the corresponding ciphertext is. How could such a thing be possible?

Suppose the telegraph company offered a service in which they encrypt and transmit messages for you. Suppose Fred had eavesdropped on Alice's encrypted message. Now he'd like to break the telegraph company's encryption scheme so that he can decrypt Alice's message.

He can obtain the corresponding ciphertext to any message he chooses by paying the telegraph company to send the message for him, encrypted. For instance, if Fred knew they were using a monoalphabetic cipher, he might send the message

The quick brown fox jumps over the lazy dog.

knowing that he would thereby get all the letters of the alphabet encrypted and then be able to decrypt with certainty any encrypted message.

It is possible that a cryptosystem secure against ciphertext only and known plaintext attacks might still be susceptible to chosen plaintext attacks. For instance, if Fred knows that Alice's message is either Surrender or Fight on, then no matter how wonderful an encryption scheme the telegraph company is using, all he has to do is send the two messages and see which one looks like the encrypted data he saw when Alice's message was transmitted.

A cryptosystem should resist all three sorts of attacks. That way its users don't need to worry about whether there are any opportunities for attackers to know or choose plaintext. Like wearing both a belt and suspenders, many systems that use cryptographic algorithms will also go out of their way to prevent any chance of chosen plaintext attacks.

2.3 TYPES OF CRYPTOGRAPHIC FUNCTIONS

There are three kinds of cryptographic functions: hash functions, secret key functions, and public key functions. We will describe what each kind is, and what it is useful for. Public key cryptography involves the use of two keys. Secret key cryptography involves the use of one key. Hash functions involve the use of zero keys! Try to imagine what that could possibly mean, and what use it could possibly have—an algorithm everyone knows with no secret key, and yet it has uses in security.

Since secret key cryptography is probably the most intuitive, we'll describe that first.

2.4 SECRET KEY CRYPTOGRAPHY

Secret key cryptography involves the use of a single key. Given a message (called plaintext) and the key, encryption produces unintelligible data (called an IRS Publication—no! no! that was just a finger slip, we meant to say "ciphertext"), which is about the same length as the plaintext was. Decryption is the reverse of encryption, and uses the same key as encryption.

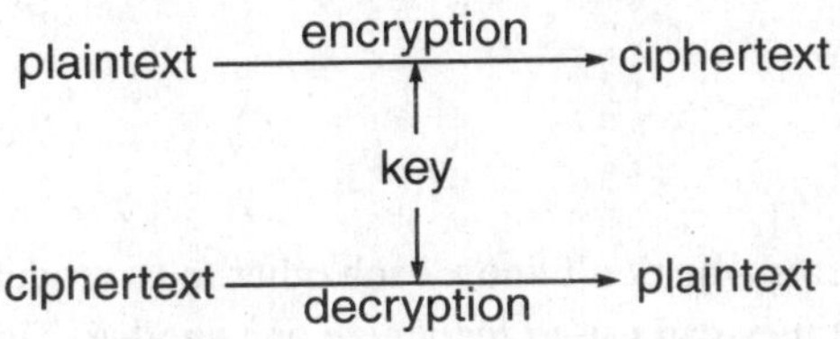

Secret key cryptography is sometimes referred to as **conventional cryptography** or **symmetric cryptography**. The Captain Midnight code and the monoalphabetic cipher are both examples of secret key algorithms, though both are easy to break. In this chapter we describe the functionality of cryptographic algorithms, but not the details of particular algorithms. In Chapter 3 *Secret Key Cryptography* we describe the details of some popular secret key cryptographic algorithms.

2.4.1 Security Uses of Secret Key Cryptography

The next few sections describe the types of things one might do with secret key cryptography.

2.4.2 Transmitting Over an Insecure Channel

It is often impossible to prevent eavesdropping when transmitting information. For instance, a telephone conversation can be tapped, a letter can be intercepted, and a message transmitted on a LAN can be received by unauthorized stations.

If you and I agree on a shared secret (a key), then by using secret key cryptography we can send messages to one another on a medium that can be tapped, without worrying about eavesdroppers. All we need to do is have the sender encrypt the messages and the receiver decrypt them using the shared secret. An eavesdropper will only see unintelligible data.

This is the classic use of cryptography.

2.4.3 Secure Storage on Insecure Media

If I have information I want to preserve but which I want to ensure no one else can look at, I have to be able to store the media where I am sure no one can get it. Between clever thieves and court orders, there are very few places that are truly secure, and none of these is convenient. If I invent a key and encrypt the information using the key, I can store it anywhere and it is safe so long as I can remember the key. Of course, forgetting the key makes the data irrevocably lost, so this must be used with great care.

2.4.4 Authentication

In spy movies, when two agents who don't know each other must rendezvous, they are each given a password or pass phrase that they can use to recognize one another. This has the problem that anyone overhearing their conversation or initiating one falsely can gain information useful for replaying later and impersonating the person to whom they are talking.

The term **strong authentication** means that someone can prove knowledge of a secret without revealing it. Strong authentication is possible with cryptography. Strong authentication is particularly useful when two computers are trying to communicate over an insecure network (since few people can execute cryptographic algorithms in their heads). Suppose Alice and Bob share a key K_{AB} and they want to verify they are speaking to each other. They each pick a random number, which is known as a **challenge**. Alice picks r_A. Bob picks r_B. The value x encrypted with the key K_{AB} is known as the **response** to the challenge x. How Alice and Bob use challenges and responses to authenticate each other is shown in Figure 2-1.

If someone, say Fred, were impersonating Alice, he could get Bob to encrypt a value for him (though Fred wouldn't be able to tell if the person he was talking to was *really* Bob), but this information would not be useful later in impersonating Bob to the real Alice because the real Alice

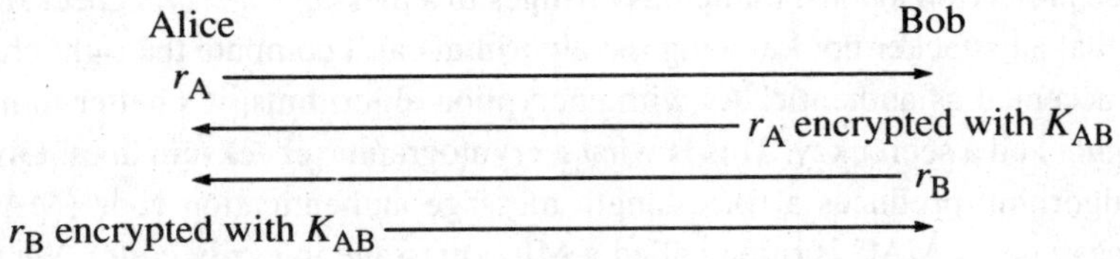

Figure 2-1. Challenge–response authentication with shared secret

would pick a different challenge. If Alice and Bob complete this exchange, they have each proven to the other that they know K_{AB} without revealing it to an impostor or an eavesdropper. Note that in this particular protocol, there is the opportunity for Fred to obtain some ⟨chosen plaintext, ciphertext⟩ pairs, since he can claim to be Bob and ask Alice to encrypt a challenge for him. For this reason, it is essential that challenges be chosen from a large enough space, say 2^{64} values, so that there is no significant chance of using the same one twice.

That is the general idea of a cryptographic authentication algorithm, though this particular algorithm has a subtle problem that would prevent it from being useful in most computer-to-computer cases. (We would have preferred not bringing that up, but felt we needed to say that so as not to alarm people who already know this stuff and who would realize the protocol was not secure. Protocol flaws such as this, and methods of fixing them, are discussed in Chapter 11 *Security Handshake Pitfalls*.)

2.4.5 Integrity Check

A secret key scheme can be used to generate a fixed-length cryptographic checksum associated with a message. This is a rather nonintuitive use of secret key technology.

What is a checksum? An ordinary (noncryptographic) checksum protects against accidental corruption of a message. The original derivation of the term *checksum* comes from the operation of breaking a message into fixed-length blocks (for instance, 32-bit words) and adding them up. The sum is sent along with the message. The receiver similarly breaks up the message, repeats the addition, and *checks the sum*. If the message had been garbled en route, the sum will not match the sum sent and the message is rejected, unless, of course, there were two or more errors in the transmission that canceled one another. It turns out this is not terribly unlikely, given that if flaky hardware turns a bit off somewhere, it is likely to turn a corresponding bit on somewhere else. To protect against such "regular" flaws in hardware, more complex checksums called CRCs were devised. But these still only protect against faulty hardware and not an intelligent attacker. Since CRC algorithms are published, an attacker who wanted to change a message could do so, compute the CRC on the new message, and send that along.

To provide protection against malicious changes to a message, a *secret* checksum algorithm is required, such that an attacker not knowing the algorithm can't compute the right checksum for the message to be accepted as authentic. As with encryption algorithms, it's better to have a common (known) algorithm and a secret key. This is what a cryptographic checksum does. Given a key and a message, the algorithm produces a fixed-length message authentication code (MAC) that can be sent with the message. A MAC is often called a MIC (message integrity code). We prefer the term MIC, and MIC is used in standards such as PEM (see Chapter 21 *PEM & S/MIME*), but the term MAC seems to have become more popular.

If anyone were to modify the message, and they didn't know the key, they would have to guess a MAC and the chance of getting it right depends on the length. A typical MAC is at least 48 bits long, so the chance of getting away with a forged message is only one in 280 trillion (or about the chance of going to Las Vegas with a dime and letting it ride on red at the roulette table until you have enough to pay off the U.S. national debt).

Such message integrity codes have been in use to protect the integrity of large interbank electronic funds transfers for quite some time. The messages are not kept secret from an eavesdropper, but their integrity is ensured.

2.5 PUBLIC KEY CRYPTOGRAPHY

Public key cryptography is sometimes also referred to as **asymmetric cryptography**. Public key cryptography is a relatively new field, invented in 1975 [DIFF76b] (at least that's the first published record—it is rumored that NSA or similar organizations may have discovered this technology earlier). Unlike secret key cryptography, keys are not shared. Instead, each individual has two keys: a private key that need not be revealed to anyone, and a public key that is preferably known to the entire world.

Note that we call the private key a *private key* and not a *secret key.* This convention is an attempt to make it clear in any context whether public key cryptography or secret key cryptography is being used. Some people use the term *secret key* for the private key in public key cryptography, or use the term *private key* for the secret key in secret key technology. We hope to convince people to use the term *secret key* only as the single secret number used in secret key cryptography. The term *private key* should refer to the key in public key cryptography that must not be made public.

Unfortunately, both words *public* and *private* begin with *p*. We will sometimes want a single letter to refer to one of the keys. The letter *p* won't do. We will use the letter *e* to refer to the public key, since the public key is used when encrypting a message. We'll use the letter *d* to refer to the private key, because the private key is used to decrypt a message. Encryption and decryption are two mathematical functions that are inverses of each other.

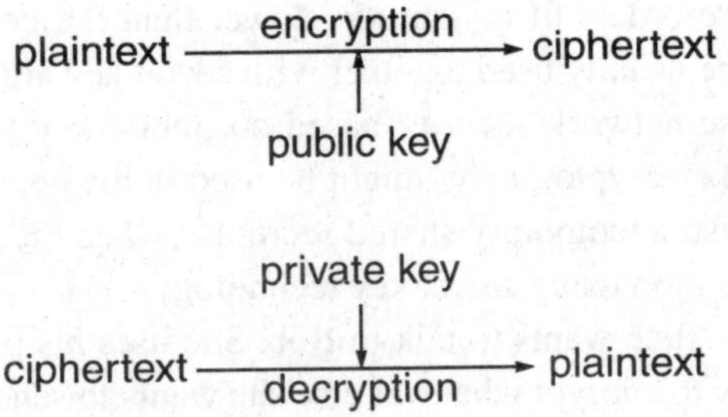

There is an additional thing one can do with public key technology, which is to generate a **digital signature** on a message. A digital signature is a number associated with a message, like a

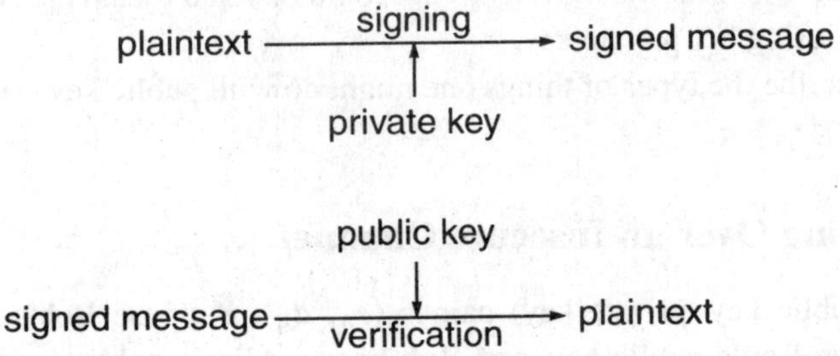

checksum or the MAC described in §2.4.5 *Integrity Check*. However, unlike a checksum, which can be generated by anyone, a digital signature can only be generated by someone knowing the private key. A public key signature differs from a secret key MAC because verification of a MAC requires knowledge of the same secret as was used to create it. Therefore anyone who can verify a MAC can also generate one, and so be able to substitute a different message and corresponding MAC. In contrast, verification of the signature only requires knowledge of the public key. So Alice can sign a message by generating a signature only she can generate, and other people can verify that it is Alice's signature, but cannot forge her signature. This is called a signature because it shares with handwritten signatures the property that it is possible to recognize a signature as authentic without being able to forge it.

2.5.1 Security Uses of Public Key Cryptography

Public key cryptography can do anything secret key cryptography can do, but the known public key cryptographic algorithms are orders of magnitude slower than the best known secret key cryptographic algorithms and so are usually used together with secret key algorithms. Public key cryptography is very useful because network security based on public key technology tends to be more easily configurable. Public key cryptography might be used in the beginning of communication for authentication and to establish a temporary shared secret key, then the secret key is used to encrypt the remainder of the conversation using secret key technology.

For instance, suppose Alice wants to talk to Bob. She uses his public key to encrypt a secret key, then uses that secret key to encrypt whatever else she wants to send him. Since the secret key is much smaller than the message, using the slow public key cryptography to encrypt the secret key is not that much of a performance hit. Only Bob can decrypt the secret key. He can then communicate using that secret key with whoever sent that message. Notice that given this protocol, Bob does not know that it was Alice who sent the message. This could be fixed by having Alice digitally sign the encrypted secret key using her private key.

Now we'll describe the types of things one might do with public key cryptography.

2.5.2 Transmitting Over an Insecure Channel

Suppose Alice's ⟨public key, private key⟩ pair is $\langle e_A, d_A \rangle$. Suppose Bob's key pair is $\langle e_B, d_B \rangle$. Assume Alice knows Bob's public key, and Bob knows Alice's public key. Actually, accurately learning other people's public keys is one of the biggest challenges in using public key cryptography and will be discussed in detail in Chapter 15 *PKI (Public Key Infrastructure)*. But for now, don't worry about it.

Alice		Bob
encrypt m_A using e_B	$\longrightarrow$	decrypt to m_A using d_B
decrypt to m_B using d_A	$\longleftarrow$	encrypt m_B using e_A

2.5.3 Secure Storage on Insecure Media

This is really the same as what one would do with secret key cryptography. You'd encrypt the data with your public key. Then nobody can decrypt it except you, since decryption will require the use of the private key. For performance reasons, you probably wouldn't encrypt the data directly with the public key, but rather randomly generate a secret key, encrypt the data with that secret key, and encrypt that secret key with the public key. As with secret key technology, if you lose your private key, the data is irretrievably lost. If you are worried about that, you can encrypt an additional copy of the data encryption key under the public key of someone you trust, like your lawyer. Or you can store copies of your private key with someone you trust (see §24.9.1 *Key Escrow*).

Public key technology has an important advantage over secret key technology for this application. Alice can encrypt a message for Bob without knowing his decryption key.

2.5.4 Authentication

With secret key cryptography, if Alice and Bob want to communicate, they have to share a secret. If Bob wants to be able to prove his identity to lots of entities, then with secret key technology he will need to remember lots of secret keys, one for each entity to which he would like to prove his identity. Possibly he could use the same shared secret with Alice as with Carol, but that has the disadvantage that then Carol and Alice could impersonate Bob to each other.

Public key technology is much more convenient. Bob only needs to remember a single secret, his own private key. It is true that if Bob wants to be able to verify the identity of thousands of entities, then he will need to know (or be able to obtain when necessary) thousands of public keys. In Chapter 15 *PKI (Public Key Infrastructure)* we discuss how this might be done.

Here's an example of how Alice can use public key cryptography for verifying Bob's identity assuming Alice knows Bob's public key. Alice chooses a random number r, encrypts it using Bob's public key e_B, and sends the result to Bob. Bob proves he knows d_B by decrypting the message and sending r back to Alice.

Alice		Bob
encrypt r using e_B	⟶	decrypt to r using d_B
	⟵ r	

Another advantage of public key authentication is that Alice does not need to keep any secret information in order to verify Bob. For instance, Alice might be a computer system in which backup tapes are unencrypted and easily stolen. With secret key based authentication, if Carol stole a backup tape and read the key that Alice shares with Bob, she could then trick Bob into thinking she was Alice (or trick Alice into thinking she was Bob). In contrast, with public key based authentication, the only information on Alice's backup tapes is public key information, and that cannot be used to impersonate Bob.

2.5.5 Digital Signatures

Forged in USA

engraved on a screwdriver claiming to be of brand *Craftsman*

It is often useful to prove that a message was generated by a particular individual. This is easy with public key technology. Bob's signature for a message m can only be generated by someone with knowledge of Bob's private key. And the signature depends on the contents of m. If m is modified in any way, the signature no longer matches. So digital signatures provide two important functions. They prove who generated the information, and they prove that the information has not been modified in any way by anyone since the message and matching signature were generated.

Digital signatures offer an important advantage over secret key based cryptographic MACs—**non-repudiation**. Suppose Bob sells widgets and Alice routinely buys them. Alice and Bob might agree that rather than placing orders through the mail with signed purchase orders, Alice will send electronic mail messages to order widgets. To protect against someone forging orders and causing Bob to manufacture more widgets than Alice actually needs, Alice will include a message integrity code on her messages. This could be either a secret key based MAC or a public key based signature. But suppose sometime after Alice places a big order, she changes her mind (the bottom fell out of the widget market). Since there's a big penalty for canceling an order, she doesn't fess up that she's canceling, but instead denies that she ever placed the order. Bob sues. If Alice authenticated the message by computing a MAC based on a key she shares with Bob, Bob knows Alice really placed the order because nobody other than Bob and Alice know that key. If Bob knows he didn't create the message he knows it must have been Alice. But he can't prove it to anyone! Since he knows the same secret key that Alice used to sign the order, he could have forged the signature on the message himself and he can't prove to the judge that he didn't! If it was a public key signature, he can show the signed message to the judge and the judge can verify that it was signed with Alice's key. Alice can still claim of course that someone must have stolen and misused her key (it might even be true!), but the contract between Alice and Bob could reasonably hold her responsible for damages caused by her inadequately protecting her key. Unlike secret key cryptography, where the keys are shared, you can always tell who's responsible for a signature generated with a private key.

2.6 HASH ALGORITHMS

Hash algorithms are also known as **message digests** or **one-way transformations**.

A cryptographic hash function is a mathematical transformation that takes a message of arbitrary length (transformed into a string of bits) and computes from it a fixed-length (short) number.

We'll call the hash of a message *m*, *h*(*m*). It has the following properties:

- For any message *m*, it is relatively easy to compute *h*(*m*). This just means that in order to be practical it can't take a lot of processing time to compute the hash.
- Given *h*(*m*), there is no way to find an *m* that hashes to *h*(*m*) in a way that is substantially easier than going through all possible values of *m* and computing *h*(*m*) for each one.
- Even though it's obvious that many different values of *m* will be transformed to the same value *h*(*m*) (because there are many more possible values of *m*), it is *computationally infeasible* to find two values that hash to the same thing.

An example of the sort of function that might work is taking the message *m*, treating it as a number, adding some large constant, squaring it, and taking the middle *n* digits as the hash. You can see that while this would not be difficult to compute, it's not obvious how you could find a message that would produce a particular hash, or how one might find two messages with the same hash. It turns out this is not a particularly good message digest function—we'll give examples of secure message digest functions in Chapter 5 *Hashes and Message Digests*. But the basic idea of a message digest function is that the input is mangled so badly the process cannot be reversed.

2.6.1 Password Hashing

When a user types a password, the system has to be able to determine whether the user got it right. If the system stores the passwords unencrypted, then anyone with access to the system storage or backup tapes can steal the passwords. Luckily, it is not necessary for the system to know a password in order to verify its correctness. (A proper password is like pornography. You can't tell what it is, but you know it when you see it.)

Instead of storing the password, the system can store a hash of the password. When a password is supplied, it computes the password's hash and compares it with the stored value. If they match, the password is deemed correct. If the hashed password file is obtained by an attacker, it is not immediately useful because the passwords can't be derived from the hashes. Historically, some systems made the password file publicly readable, an expression of confidence in the security of the hash. Even if there are no cryptographic flaws in the hash, it is possible to guess passwords and hash them to see if they match. If a user is careless and chooses a password that is guessable (say, a word that would appear in a 50000-word dictionary or book of common names), an exhaustive search would "crack" the password even if the encryption were sound. For this reason, many systems hide the hashed password list (and those that don't should).

2.6.2 Message Integrity

Cryptographic hash functions can be used to generate a MAC to protect the integrity of messages transmitted over insecure media in much the same way as secret key cryptography.

If we merely sent the message and used the hash of the message as a MAC, this would not be secure, since the hash function is well-known. The bad guy can modify the message and compute a new hash for the new message, and transmit that.

However, if Alice and Bob have agreed on a secret, Alice can use a hash to generate a MAC for a message to Bob by taking the message, concatenating the secret, and computing the hash of *message|secret*. This is called a **keyed hash**. Alice then sends the hash and the message (without the secret) to Bob. Bob concatenates the secret to the received message and computes the hash of the result. If that matches the received hash, Bob can have confidence the message was sent by someone knowing the secret. [Note: there are some cryptographic subtleties to making this actually secure; see §5.2.2 *Computing a MAC with a Hash*].

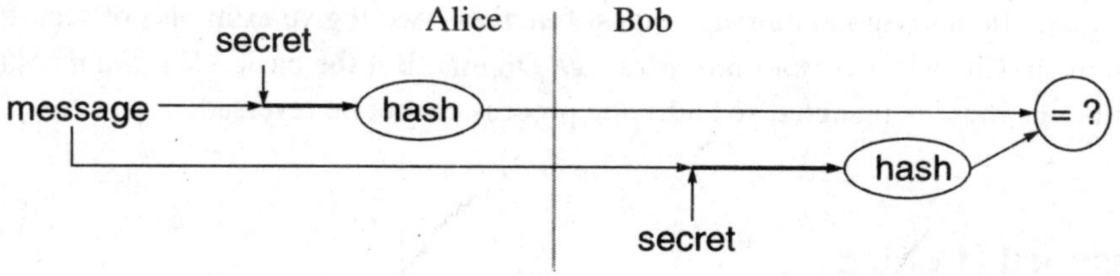

2.6.3 Message Fingerprint

If you want to know whether some large data structure (e.g. a program) has been modified from one day to the next, you could keep a copy of the data on some tamper-proof backing store and periodically compare it to the active version. With a hash function, you can save storage: you simply save the message digest of the data on the tamper-proof backing store (which because the hash is small could be a piece of paper in a filing cabinet). If the message digest hasn't changed, you can be confident none of the data has.

A note to would-be users—if it hasn't already occurred to you, it has occurred to the bad guys—the program that computes the hash must also be independently protected for this to be secure. Otherwise the bad guys can change the file but also change the hashing program to report the checksum as though the file were unchanged!

2.6.4 Downline Load Security

It is common practice to have special-purpose devices connected to a network, like routers or printers, that do not have the nonvolatile memory to store the programs they normally run. Instead, they keep a bootstrap program smart enough to get a program from the network and run it. This scheme is called **downline load**.

Suppose you want to downline load a program and make sure it hasn't been corrupted (whether intentionally or not). If you know the proper hash of the program, you can compute the hash of the loaded program and make sure it has the proper value before running the program.

2.6.5 Digital Signature Efficiency

The best-known public key algorithms are sufficiently processor-intensive that it is desirable to compute a message digest of the message and sign that, rather than to sign the message directly. The message digest algorithms are much less processor-intensive, and the message digest is much shorter than the message.

2.7 HOMEWORK

1. What is the dedication to this book?
2. Random J. Protocol-Designer has been told to design a scheme to prevent messages from being modified by an intruder. Random J. decides to append to each message a hash of that message. Why doesn't this solve the problem? (We know of a protocol that uses this technique in an attempt to gain security.)
3. Suppose Alice, Bob, and Carol want to use secret key technology to authenticate each other. If they all used the same secret key K, then Bob could impersonate Carol to Alice (actually any of the three can impersonate the other to the third). Suppose instead that each had their own secret key, so Alice uses K_A, Bob uses K_B, and Carol uses K_C. This means that each one, to prove his or her identity, responds to a challenge with a function of his or her secret key and the challenge. Is this more secure than having them all use the same secret key K? (Hint: what does Alice need to know in order to verify Carol's answer to Alice's challenge?)
4. As described in §2.6.4 *Downline Load Security*, it is common, for performance reasons, to sign a message digest of a message rather than the message itself. Why is it so important that it be difficult to find two messages with the same message digest?

5. What's wrong with the protocol in §2.4.4 *Authentication*? (Hint: assume Alice can open two connections to Bob.)
6. Assume a cryptographic algorithm in which the performance for the good guys (the ones that know the key) grows linearly with the length of the key, and for which the only way to break it is a brute-force attack of trying all possible keys. Suppose the performance for the good guys is adequate (e.g., it can encrypt and decrypt as fast as the bits can be transmitted over the wire) at a certain size key. Then suppose advances in computer technology make computers twice as fast. Given that both the good guys and the bad guys get faster computers, does this advance in computer speed work to the advantage of the good guys, the bad guys, or does it not make any difference?

3 SECRET KEY CRYPTOGRAPHY

3.1 INTRODUCTION

This chapter describes how secret key cryptographic algorithms work. It describes in detail the DES and IDEA algorithms. These algorithms take a fixed-length block of message (64 bits in the case of both DES and IDEA), a fixed-length key (56 bits for DES and 128 bits for IDEA) and generate a block of output (the same length as the input). In general, a message won't happen to be 64 bits long. In §4.2 *Encrypting a Large Message* we'll discuss how to convert the basic fixed-length block encryption algorithm into a general message encryption algorithm.

3.2 GENERIC BLOCK ENCRYPTION

A cryptographic algorithm converts a plaintext block into an encrypted block. It's fairly obvious that if the key length is too short (for instance, 4 bits), the cryptographic scheme would not be secure because it would be too easy to search through all possible keys. There's a similar issue with the length of the block of plaintext to be encrypted. If the block length is too short (say one octet, as in a monoalphabetic cipher), then if you ever had some paired ⟨plaintext, ciphertext⟩, you could construct a table to be used for decryption. It might be possible to obtain such pairs because messages might only remain secret for a short time, perhaps because the message says where the army will attack the next day.

Having a block length too long is merely inconvenient—unnecessarily complex and possibly having performance penalties. 64 bits is a reasonable length, in that you are unlikely to get that many blocks of ⟨plaintext,ciphertext⟩ pairs, and even if you did, it would take too much space to store the table (2^{64} entries of 64 bits each) or too much time to sort it for efficient searching.

The most general way of encrypting a 64-bit block is to take each of the 2^{64} input values and map it to a unique one of the 2^{64} output values. (It is necessary that the mapping be **one-to-one**, i.e.

only one input value maps to any given output value, since otherwise decryption would not be possible.)

Suppose Alice and Bob (who happen to speak a language in which all sentences are 64 bits long) want to decide upon a mapping that they can use for encrypting their conversations. How would they specify one? To specify a monoalphabetic cipher with English letters takes 26 specifications of 26 possible values, approximately. For instance,

a→q b→d c→w d→x e→a f→f g→z h→b etc.

How would you specify a mapping of all possible 64-bit input values? Well, let's start:

0000000000000000→8ad1482703f217ce
0000000000000001→b33dc8710928d701
0000000000000002→29e856b28013fa4c

Hmm, we probably don't want to write this all out. There are 2^{64} possible input values and for each one we have to specify a 64-bit output value. This would take 2^{70} bits. (Actually, nitpickers might note that there aren't quite 2^{70} bits of information since the mapping has to be a **permutation**, i.e., each output value is used exactly once, so for instance the final output value does not need to be explicitly specified—it's the one that's left over. However, there are $2^{64}!$ different possible permutations of 2^{64} values, which would take more than 2^{69} bits to represent.) [Remember $n!$ (read "n factorial") is $n \cdot (n-1) \cdot (n-2) \cdot (n-3) \cdots 3 \cdot 2 \cdot 1$. It can be approximated by Stirling's formula: $n! \approx n^n e^{-n} \sqrt{2\pi n}$]

So let's say it would take 2^{69} bits to specify the mapping. That 2^{69} bit number would act like a secret key that Alice and Bob would share. But it is doubtful that they could remember a key that large, or even be able to say it to each other within a lifetime, or store it on anything. So this is not particularly practical.

Secret key cryptographic systems are designed to take a reasonable-length key (i.e., more like 64 bits than 2^{64} bits) and generate a one-to-one mapping that looks, to someone who does not know the key, completely random. **Random** means that it should look, to someone who doesn't know the key, as if the mapping from an input value to an output value were generated by using a random number generator. (To get the mapping from input i to output o, flip a 2^{64}-sided coin to choose the value of o—or if such a coin is not readily available, a single coin could be flipped 64 times. Since the mapping must be one-to-one, you'll have to start over again choosing o if the value selected by the coin has been previously used.) If the mapping were truly random, any single bit change to the input will result in a totally independently chosen random number output. The two different output numbers should have no correlation, meaning that about half the bits should be the same and about half the bits should be different. For instance, it can't be the case that the 3rd bit of output always changes if the 12th bit of input changes. So the cryptographic algorithms are designed to *spread bits* *around*, in the sense that a single input bit should have influence on all the bits of the output, and be able to change any one of them with a probability of about 50% (depending on the values of the other 63 bits of input).

There are two kinds of simple transformations one might imagine on a block of data, and they are named in the literature as *substitutions* and *permutations* (which is the only reason we are using those names—we would have chosen different words, perhaps the term *bit shuffle* instead of *permutation*). Let's assume we are encrypting k-bit blocks:

A substitution specifies, for each of the 2^k possible values of the input, the k-bit output. As noted above, this would be impractical to build for 64-bit blocks, but would be possible with blocks of length, say, 8 bits. To specify a completely randomly chosen substitution for k-bit blocks would take about $k \cdot 2^k$ bits.

A **permutation** specifies, for each of the k input bits, the output position to which it goes. For instance, the 1st bit might become the 13th bit of output, the 2nd bit would become the 61st bit of output, and so on. To specify a completely randomly chosen permutation of k bits would take about $k \log_2 k$ bits (for each of the k bits, one has to specify which bit position it will be in the output, and it only takes $\log_2 k$ bits to specify k values).

A permutation is a special case of a substitution in which each bit of the output gets its value from exactly one of the bits of the input. The number of permutations is sufficiently small that it is possible to specify and build an arbitrary 64-bit permuter.

One possible way to build a secret key algorithm is to break the input into manageable-sized chunks (say 8 bits), do a substitution on each small chunk, and then take the outputs of all the substitutions and run them through a permuter that is as big as the input, which shuffles the bits around. Then the process is repeated, so that each bit winds up as input to each of the substitutions. (See Figure 3-1.)

Each time through is known as a **round**. If we do only a single round, then a bit of input can only affect 8 bits of output, since each input bit goes into only one of the substitutions. On the second round, the 8 bits affected by a particular input bit get spread around due to the permutation, and assuming each of those 8 bits goes into a different substitution, then the single input bit will affect all the output bits. Just as when shuffling a deck of cards, there is an optimal number of rounds (shuffles). Once the cards are sufficiently randomized, extra shuffles just waste time. Part of the design of an algorithm is determining the best number of rounds (for optimal security, at least enough rounds to randomize as much as possible; for efficiency reasons no more rounds than necessary).

Another important feature of an encryption mechanism is it must be efficient to reverse, given the key. An algorithm like the one above would take the same effort to decrypt as to encrypt, since each of the steps can be run as efficiently backwards as forwards.

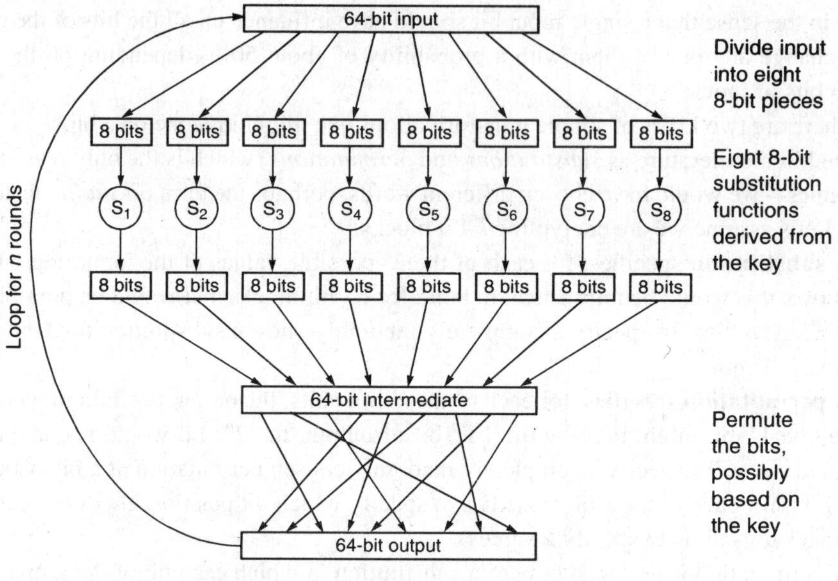

Figure 3-1. Example of Block Encryption

3.3 DATA ENCRYPTION STANDARD (DES)

DES was published in 1977 by the National Bureau of Standards (since renamed to the National Institute of Standards and Technology) for use in commercial and unclassified (hmm...) U.S. Government applications. It was designed by IBM based on their own *Lucifer cipher* and input from NSA. DES uses a 56-bit key, and maps a 64-bit input block into a 64-bit output block. The key actually looks like a 64-bit quantity, but one bit in each of the 8 octets is used for odd parity on each octet. Therefore, only 7 of the bits in each octet are actually meaningful as a key.

DES is efficient to implement in hardware but relatively slow if implemented in software. Although making software implementations difficult was not a documented goal of DES, people have asserted that DES was specifically designed with this in mind, perhaps because this would limit its use to organizations that could afford hardware-based solutions, or perhaps because it made it easier to control access to the technology. At any rate, advances in CPUs have made it feasible to do DES in software. For instance, a 500-MIP CPU can encrypt at about 30 Koctets per second (and perhaps more depending on the details of the CPU design and the cleverness of the implementation). This is adequate for many applications.

Why 56 bits?

Use of a 56-bit key is one of the most controversial aspects of DES. Even before DES was adopted, people outside of the intelligence community complained that 56 bits provided inadequate security [DENN82, DIFF76a, DIFF77, HELL79]. So why were only 56 of the 64 bits of a DES key used in the algorithm? The disadvantage of using 8 bits of the key for parity checking is that it makes DES considerably less secure (256 times less secure against exhaustive search).

OK, so what is the advantage of using 8 bits of the key for parity? Well, uh, let's say you receive a key electronically, and you want to sanity-check it to see if it could actually be a key. If you check the parity of the quantity, and it winds up not having the correct parity, then you'll know something went wrong.

There are two problems with this reasoning. One is that there is a 1 in 256 chance (given the parity scheme) that even if you were to get 64 bits of garbage, that the result will happen to have the correct parity and therefore look like a key. That is way too large a possibility of error for it to afford any useful protection to any application. The other problem with the reasoning is that there is nothing terribly bad about getting a bad key. You'll discover the key is bad when you try to use it for encrypting or decrypting.

The key, at 56 bits, is pretty much universally acknowledged to be too small to be secure. Perhaps one might argue that a smaller key is an advantage because it saves storage—but that argument doesn't hold since nobody does data compression on the 64-bit keys in order to fit them into 56 bits. So what benefits are there to usurping 8 bits for parity that offset the loss in security?

People (not us, surely!) have suggested that our government consciously decided to weaken the security of DES just enough so that NSA would be able to break it. We would like to think there is an alternative explanation, but we have never heard a plausible one proposed.

Advances in semiconductor technology make the key-length issue more critical. Chip speeds have caught up so that DES keys can be broken with a bit of cleverness and exhaustive search. Perhaps a 64-bit key might have extended its useful lifetime by a few years. Given hardware price/performance improving about 40% per year, keys must grow by about 1 bit every 2 years. Assuming 56 bits was just sufficient in 1979 (when DES was standardized), 64 bits was about right in 1995, and 128 bits would suffice until 2123.

How secure is DES?

Suppose you have a single block of ⟨plaintext, ciphertext⟩. *Breaking* DES in this case would mean finding a key that maps that plaintext to that ciphertext. With DES implemented in software, it would take on the order of half a million MIP-years, through brute force, to find the key. (Is it possible to find the "wrong" key, given a particular pair? Might two different keys map the same plaintext to the same ciphertext? How many keys on the average map a particular pair? See Homework Problem 3.)

Often the attacker does not have a ⟨plaintext, ciphertext⟩ block. Instead the attacker has a reasonable amount of ciphertext only. It might be known, for example, that the encrypted data is likely to be 7-bit ASCII. In that case, it is still just about as efficient to do brute-force search. The ciphertext is decrypted with the guessed key, and if all the 8th bits are zero (which will happen with an incorrect key with probability 1 in 256), then another block is decrypted. After several (say ten) blocks are decrypted, and the result always appears to be 7-bit ASCII, the key has a high probability of being correct.

Current commercial DES chips do not lend themselves to doing exhaustive key search—they allow encrypting lots of data with a particular key. The relative speed of key loading is much less than the speed of encrypting data. However, it is straightforward to design and manufacture a key-searching DES chip.

In 1977, Diffie and Hellman [DIFF77] did a detailed analysis of what it would cost to build a DES-breaking engine and concluded that for $20 million you could build a million-chip machine that could find a DES key in twelve hours (given a ⟨plaintext, ciphertext⟩ pair). In 1998, EFF (Electronic Frontier Foundation) [EFF98] built a special-purpose DES-breaking engine, called the EFF DES Cracker, for under $250K. It was designed to find a DES key in 4.5 days. With the design done, the cost of replicating the engine was under $150K.

There are published papers [BIHA93] claiming that less straightforward attacks can break DES faster than simply searching the key space. However, these attacks involve the premise, unlikely in real-life situations, that the attacker can choose lots of plaintext and obtain the corresponding ciphertext.

Still it is possible to encrypt multiple times with different keys (see §4.4 *Multiple Encryption DES*). It is generally believed that DES with triple encryption is 2^{56} times as difficult to crack and therefore will be secure for the foreseeable future.

3.3.1 DES Overview

DES is quite understandable, and has some very elegant tricks. Let's start with the basic structure of DES (Figure 3-2).

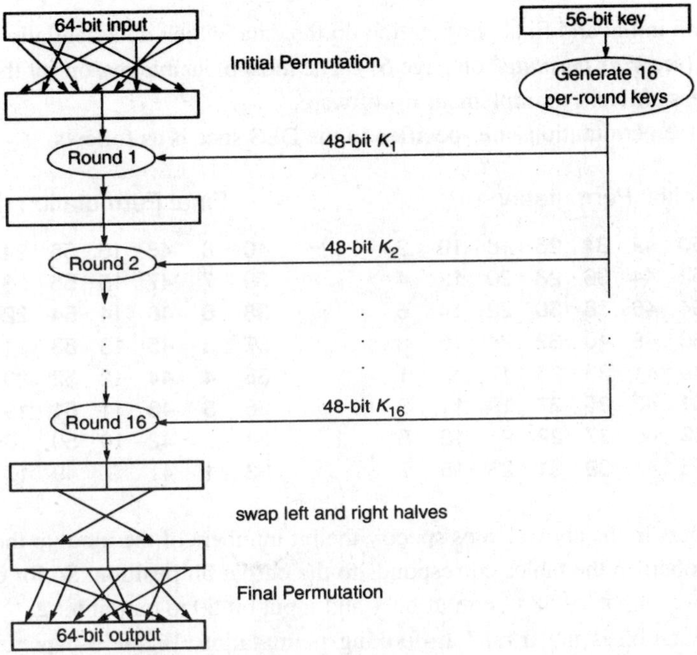

Figure 3-2. Basic Structure of DES

The 64-bit input is subjected to an initial permutation to obtain a 64-bit result (which is just the input with the bits shuffled). The 56-bit key is used to generate sixteen 48-bit per-round keys, by taking a different 48-bit subset of the 56 bits for each of the keys. Each round takes as input the 64-bit output of the previous round, and the 48-bit per-round key, and produces a 64-bit output. After the 16th round, the 64-bit output has its halves swapped and is then subjected to another permutation, which happens to be the inverse of the initial permutation.

That is the overview of how encryption works. Decryption works by essentially running DES backwards. To decrypt a block, you'd first run it through the initial permutation to undo the final permutation (the initial and final permutations are inverses of each other). You'd do the same key generation, though you'd use the keys in the opposite order (first use K_{16}, the key you generated last). Then you run 16 rounds just like for encryption. Why this works will be explained when we explain what happens during a round. After 16 rounds of decryption, the output has its halves swapped and is then subjected to the final permutation (to undo the initial permutation).

To fully specify DES, we need to specify the initial and final permutations, how the per round keys are generated, and what happens during a round. Let's start with the initial and final permutations of the data.

3.3.2 The Permutations of the Data

DES performs an initial and final permutation on the data, which do essentially nothing to enhance DES's security (see *Why permute?* on page 67). The most plausible reason for these permutations is to make DES less efficient to implement in software.

The way the permutations are specified in the DES spec is as follows:

Initial Permutation (IP)

58	50	42	34	26	18	10	2
60	52	44	36	28	20	12	4
62	54	46	38	30	22	14	6
64	56	48	40	32	24	16	8
57	49	41	33	25	17	9	1
59	51	43	35	27	19	11	3
61	53	45	37	29	21	13	5
63	55	47	39	31	23	15	7

Final Permutation (IP^{-1})

40	8	48	16	56	24	64	32
39	7	47	15	55	23	63	31
38	6	46	14	54	22	62	30
37	5	45	13	53	21	61	29
36	4	44	12	52	20	60	28
35	3	43	11	51	19	59	27
34	2	42	10	50	18	58	26
33	1	41	9	49	17	57	25

The numbers in the above tables specify the bit numbers of the input to the permutation. The order of the numbers in the tables corresponds to the output bit position. So for example, the initial permutation moves input bit 58 to output bit 1 and input bit 50 to output bit 2.

The permutation is not a random-looking permutation. Figure 3-3 pictures it. The arrows indicate the initial permutation. Reverse the arrows to get the final permutation. We hope you

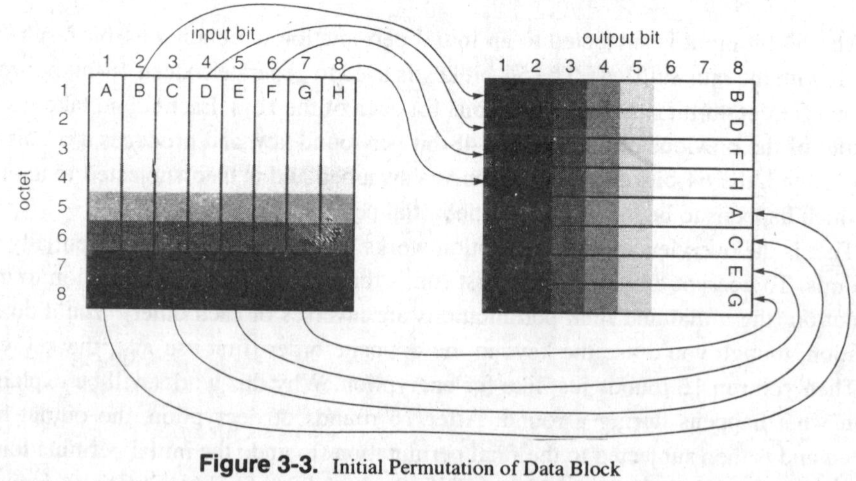

Figure 3-3. Initial Permutation of Data Block

appreciate the time we spent staring at the numbers and discovering this completely useless structure.

The input is 8 octets. The output is 8 octets. The bits in the first octet of input get spread into the 8th bits of each of the octets. The bits in the second octet of input get spread into the 7th bits of all the octets. And in general, the bits of the ith octet get spread into the $(9–i)^{th}$ bits of all the octets. The pattern of spreading of the 8 bits in octet i of the input among the output octets is that the even-numbered bits go into octets 1–4, and the odd-numbered bits go into octets 5–8. Note that if the data happens to be 7-bit ASCII, with the top bit set to zero, then after the permutation the entire 5th octet will be zero. Since the permutation appears to have no security value, it seems nearly certain that there is no security significance to this particular permutation.

Why permute?

Why can't the initial and final permutations of the data be of security value? Well, suppose they were important, i.e., if DES did not have them it would be possible to break DES. Let's call a modified DES that does not have the initial and final permutation **EDS**. Let's say we can break EDS, i.e., given a ⟨plaintext,ciphertext⟩ EDS pair, we can easily calculate the EDS key that converts the plaintext into the ciphertext. In that case, we can easily break DES as well. Given a DES ⟨plaintext,ciphertext⟩ pair $\langle m,c \rangle$, we simply do the inverse of the initial permutation (i.e. the final permutation) on m to get m', and the inverse of the final permutation (i.e. the initial permutation) on c to get c', and feed $\langle m',c' \rangle$ to our EDS-breaking code. The resulting EDS key will work as the DES key for $\langle m,c \rangle$.

Note that when multiple encryptions of DES are being performed, the permutation might have some value. However, if encryption with key_1 is followed by encryption with key_2, then the final permutation following encryption with key_1 will cancel the initial permutation for key_2. That is one of the reasons people discuss alternating encrypt operations with decrypt operations (see §4.4 *Multiple Encryption DES*).

In §3.3.3 *Generating the Per-Round Keys*, we'll see there is also a permutation of the key. It also has no security value (by a similar argument).

3.3.3 Generating the Per-Round Keys

Next we'll specify how the sixteen 48-bit per-round keys are generated from the DES key. The DES key looks like it's 64 bits long, but 8 of the bits are parity. Let's number the bits of the DES key from left to right as 1, 2,...64. Bits 8, 16,...64 are the parity bits. DES performs a function, which we are about to specify, on these 64 bits to generate sixteen 48-bit keys, which are $K_1, K_2, \ldots K_{16}$.

First it does an initial permutation on the 56 useful bits of the key, to generate a 56-bit output, which it divides into two 28-bit values, called C_0 and D_0. The permutation is specified as

C_0								D_0						
57	49	41	33	25	17	9		63	55	47	39	31	23	15
1	58	50	42	34	26	18		7	62	54	46	38	30	22
10	2	59	51	43	35	27		14	6	61	53	45	37	29
19	11	3	60	52	44	36		21	13	5	28	20	12	4

The way to read the table above is that the leftmost bit of the output is obtained by extracting bit 57 from the key. The next bit is bit 49 of the key, and so forth, with the final bit of D_0 being bit 4 of the key. Notice that none of the parity bits (8, 16,...64) is used in C_0 or D_0.

This permutation is not random. Figure 3-4 pictures it. Feel free to draw in any arrows or other graphic aids to make it clearer.

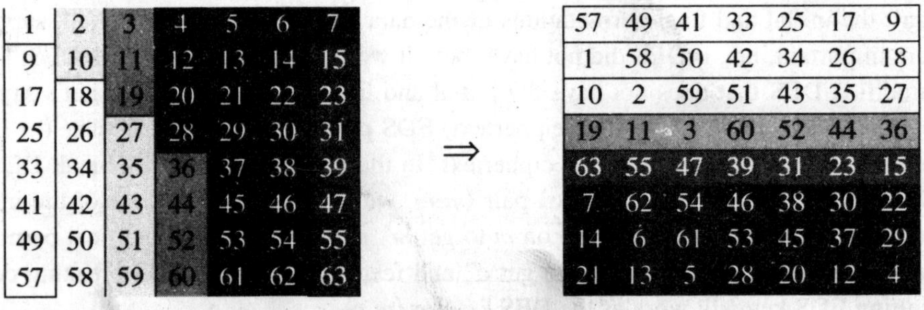

Figure 3-4. Initial Permutation of Key

The initial and final permutations of the bits in the key have no security value (just like the initial and final permutations of the data), so the permutations didn't have to be random—the identity permutation would have done nicely.

Now the generation of the K_i proceeds in 16 rounds (see Figure 3-5). The number of bits shifted is different in the different rounds. In rounds 1, 2, 9, and 16, it is a single-bit rotate left (with

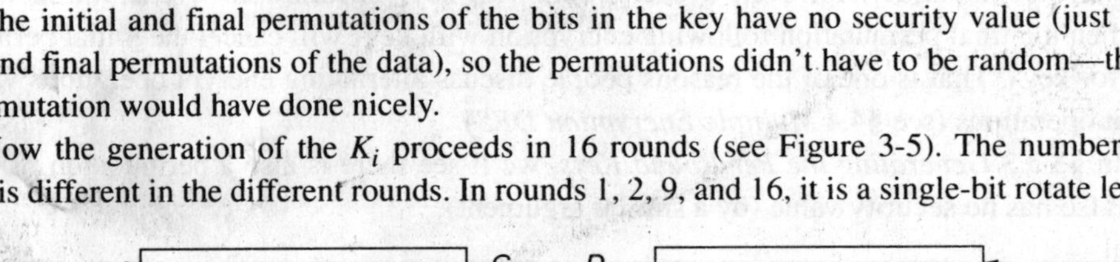

Figure 3-5. Round i for generating K_i

the bit shifted off the left end carried around and shifted into the right end). In the other rounds, it is a two-bit rotate left.

The permutations in this case are likely to be of some security value.

The permutation of C_i that produces the left half of K_i is the following. Note that bits 9, 18, 22, and 25 are discarded.

permutation to obtain the left half of K_i:

14	17	11	24	1	5
3	28	15	6	21	10
23	19	12	4	26	8
16	7	27	20	13	2

The permutation of the rotated D_{i-1} that produces the right half of K_i is as follows (where the bits of the rotated D_{i-1} are numbered 29, 30,...56, and bits 35, 38, 43, and 54 are discarded).

permutation to obtain the right half of K_i:

41	52	31	37	47	55
30	40	51	45	33	48
44	49	39	56	34	53
46	42	50	36	29	32

Each of the halves of K_i is 24 bits, so K_i is 48 bits long.

3.3.4 A DES Round

Now let's look at what a single round of DES does. Figure 3-6 shows both how encryption and decryption work.

In encryption, the 64-bit input is divided into two 32-bit halves called L_n and R_n. The round generates as output 32-bit quantities L_{n+1} and R_{n+1}. The concatenation of L_{n+1} and R_{n+1} is the 64-bit output of the round.

L_{n+1} is simply R_n. R_{n+1} is obtained as follows. First R_n and K_n are input to what we call a *mangler function*, which outputs a 32-bit quantity. That quantity is ⊕'d with L_n to obtain the new R_{n+1}. The mangler takes as input 32 bits of the data plus 48 bits of the key to produce a 32-bit output.

Given the above, suppose you want to run DES backward, i.e. to decrypt something. Suppose you know L_{n+1} and R_{n+1}. How do you get L_n and R_n?

Well, R_n is just L_{n+1}. Now you know R_n, L_{n+1}, R_{n+1} and K_n. You also know that R_{n+1} equals $L_n \oplus \text{mangler}(R_n, K_n)$. You can compute mangler(R_n, K_n), since you know R_n and K_n. Now ⊕ that with R_{n+1}. The result will be L_n. Note that the mangler is never run backwards. DES is elegantly designed to be reversible without constraining the mangler function to be reversible. This design is

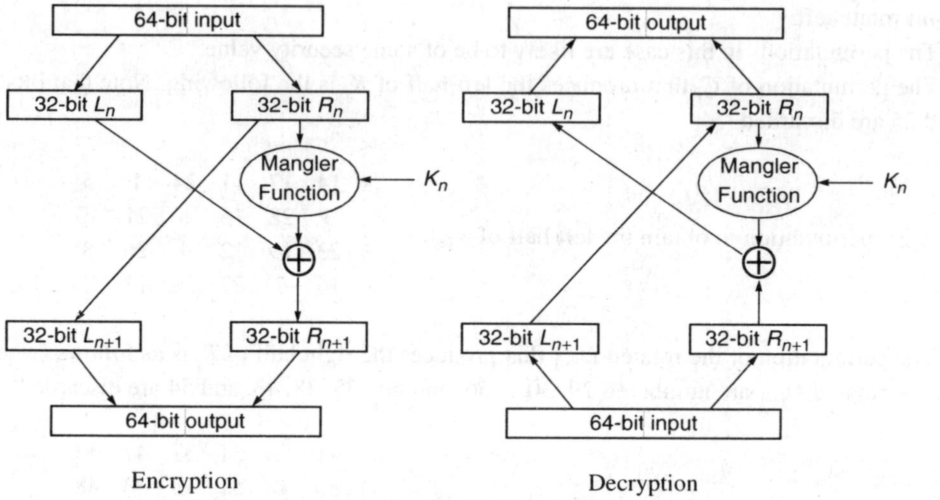

Figure 3-6. DES Round

due to Feistel [FEIS73]. Theoretically the mangler could map all values to zero, and it would still be possible to run DES backwards, but having the mangler function map all functions to zero would make DES pretty unsecure (see Homework Problem 5).

If you examine Figure 3-6 carefully, you will see that decryption is identical to encryption with the 32-bit halves swapped. In other words, feeding $R_{n+1}|L_{n+1}$ into round n produces $R_n|L_n$ as output.

3.3.5 The Mangler Function

The mangler function takes as input the 32-bit R_n, which we'll simply call R, and the 48-bit K_n, which we'll call K, and produces a 32-bit output which, when ⊕'d with L_n, produces R_{n+1} (the next R).

The mangler function first expands R from a 32-bit value to a 48-bit value. It does this by breaking R into eight 4-bit chunks and then expanding each of those chunks to 6 bits by taking the adjacent bits and concatenating them to the chunk. The leftmost and rightmost bits of R are considered adjacent.

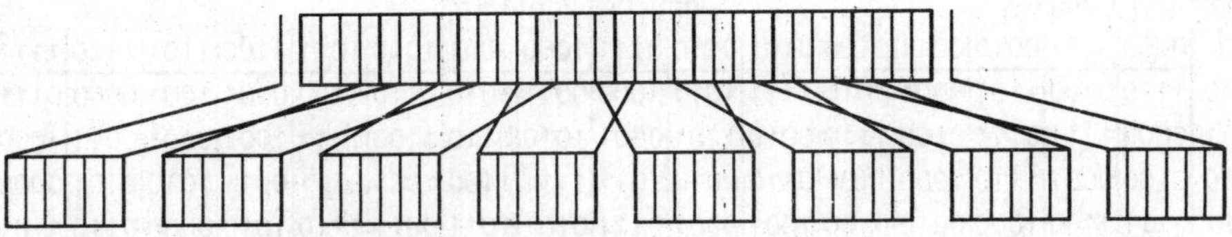

Figure 3-7. Expansion of R to 48 bits

The 48-bit K is broken into eight 6-bit chunks. Chunk i of the expanded R is ⊕'d with chunk i of K to yield a 6-bit output. That 6-bit output is fed into an **S-box**, a substitution which produces a

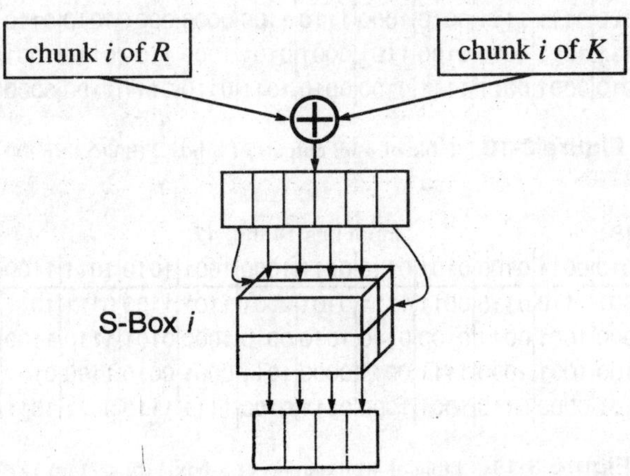

Figure 3-8. Chunk Transformation

4-bit output for each possible 6-bit input. Since there are 64 possible input values (6 bits) and only 16 possible output values (4 bits), the S-box clearly maps several input values to the same output value. As it turns out, there are exactly four input values that map to each possible output value. There's even more pattern to it than that. Each S-box could be thought of as four separate 4-bit to 4-

bit S-boxes, with the inner 4 bits of the 6-bit chunk serving as input, and the outer 2 bits selecting which of the four 4-bit S-boxes to use. The S-boxes are specified as follows:

Input bits 1 and 6 / Input bits 2 thru 5

↓	0000	0001	0010	0011	0100	0101	0110	0111	1000	1001	1010	1011	1100	1101	1110	1111
00	1110	0100	1101	0001	0010	1111	1011	1000	0011	1010	0110	1100	0101	1001	0000	0111
01	0000	1111	0111	0100	1110	0010	1101	0001	1010	0110	1100	1011	1001	0101	0011	1000
10	0100	0001	1110	1000	1101	0110	0010	1011	1111	1100	1001	0111	0011	1010	0101	0000
11	1111	1100	1000	0010	0100	1001	0001	0111	0101	1011	0011	1110	1010	0000	0110	1101

Figure 3-9. Table of 4-bit outputs of S-box 1 (bits 1 thru 4)

Input bits 7 and 12 / Input bits 8 thru 11

↓	0000	0001	0010	0011	0100	0101	0110	0111	1000	1001	1010	1011	1100	1101	1110	1111
00	1111	0001	1000	1110	0110	1011	0011	0100	1001	0111	0010	1101	1100	0000	0101	1010
01	0011	1101	0100	0111	1111	0010	1000	1110	1100	0000	0001	1010	0110	1001	1011	0101
10	0000	1110	0111	1011	1010	0100	1101	0001	0101	1000	1100	0110	1001	0011	0010	1111
11	1101	1000	1010	0001	0011	1111	0100	0010	1011	0110	0111	1100	0000	0101	1110	1001

Figure 3-10. Table of 4-bit outputs of S-box 2 (bits 5 thru 8)

Input bits 13 and 18 / Input bits 14 thru 17

↓	0000	0001	0010	0011	0100	0101	0110	0111	1000	1001	1010	1011	1100	1101	1110	1111
00	1010	0000	1001	1110	0110	0011	1111	0101	0001	1101	1100	0111	1011	0100	0010	1000
01	1101	0111	0000	1001	0011	0100	0110	1010	0010	1000	0101	1110	1100	1011	1111	0001
10	1101	0110	0100	1001	1000	1111	0011	0000	1011	0001	0010	1100	0101	1010	1110	0111
11	0001	1010	1101	0000	0110	1001	1000	0111	0100	1111	1110	0011	1011	0101	0010	1100

Figure 3-11. Table of 4-bit outputs of S-box 3 (bits 9 thru 12)

Input bits 19 and 24 / Input bits 20 thru 23

↓	0000	0001	0010	0011	0100	0101	0110	0111	1000	1001	1010	1011	1100	1101	1110	1111
00	0111	1101	1110	0011	0000	0110	1001	1010	0001	0010	1000	0101	1011	1100	0100	1111
01	1101	1000	1011	0101	0110	1111	0000	0011	0100	0111	0010	1100	0001	1010	1110	1001
10	1010	0110	1001	0000	1100	1011	0111	1101	1111	0001	0011	1110	0101	0010	1000	0100
11	0011	1111	0000	0110	1010	0001	1101	1000	1001	0100	0101	1011	1100	0111	0010	1110

Figure 3-12. Table of 4-bit outputs of S-box 4 (bits 13 thru 16)

Input bits 25 and 30 / Input bits 26 thru 29

↓	0000	0001	0010	0011	0100	0101	0110	0111	1000	1001	1010	1011	1100	1101	1110	1111
00	0010	1100	0100	0001	0111	1010	1011	0110	1000	0101	0011	1111	1101	0000	1110	1001
01	1110	1011	0010	1100	0100	0111	1101	0001	0101	0000	1111	1010	0011	1001	1000	0110
10	0100	0010	0001	1011	1010	1101	0111	1000	1111	1001	1100	0101	0110	0011	0000	1110
11	1011	1000	1100	0111	0001	1110	0010	1101	0110	1111	0000	1001	1010	0100	0101	0011

Figure 3-13. Table of 4-bit outputs of S-box 5 (bits 17 thru 20)

Input bits 31 and 36 / Input bits 32 thru 35

↓	0000	0001	0010	0011	0100	0101	0110	0111	1000	1001	1010	1011	1100	1101	1110	1111
00	1100	0001	1010	1111	1001	0010	0110	1000	0000	1101	0011	0100	1110	0111	0101	1011
01	1010	1111	0100	0010	0111	1100	1001	0101	0110	0001	1101	1110	0000	1011	0011	1000
10	1001	1110	1111	0101	0010	1000	1100	0011	0111	0000	0100	1010	0001	1101	1011	0110
11	0100	0011	0010	1100	1001	0101	1111	1010	1011	1110	0001	0111	0110	0000	1000	1101

Figure 3-14. Table of 4-bit outputs of S-box 6 (bits 21 thru 24)

Input bits 37 and 42 / Input bits 38 thru 41

↓	0000	0001	0010	0011	0100	0101	0110	0111	1000	1001	1010	1011	1100	1101	1110	1111
00	0100	1011	0010	1110	1111	0000	1000	1101	0011	1100	1001	0111	0101	1010	0110	0001
01	1101	0000	1011	0111	0100	1001	0001	1010	1110	0011	0101	1100	0010	1111	1000	0110
10	0001	0100	1011	1101	1100	0011	0111	1110	1010	1111	0110	1000	0000	0101	1001	0010
11	0110	1011	1101	1000	0001	0100	1010	0111	1001	0101	0000	1111	1110	0010	0011	1100

Figure 3-15. Table of 4-bit outputs of S-box 7 (bits 25 thru 28)

Input bits 43 and 48 / Input bits 44 thru 47

↓	0000	0001	0010	0011	0100	0101	0110	0111	1000	1001	1010	1011	1100	1101	1110	1111
00	1101	0010	1000	0100	0110	1111	1011	0001	1010	1001	0011	1110	0101	0000	1100	0111
01	0001	1111	1101	1000	1010	0011	0111	0100	1100	0101	0110	1011	0000	1110	1001	0010
10	0111	1011	0100	0001	1001	1100	1110	0010	0000	0110	1010	1101	1111	0011	0101	1000
11	0010	0001	1110	0111	0100	1010	1000	1101	1111	1100	1001	0000	0011	0101	0110	1011

Figure 3-16. Table of 4-bit outputs of S-box 8 (bits 29 thru 32)

The 4-bit output of each of the eight S-boxes is combined into a 32-bit quantity whose bits are then permuted. A permutation at this point is of security value to DES in order to ensure that the bits of the output of an S-box on one round of DES affects the input of multiple S-boxes on the next round. Without the permutation, an input bit on the left would mostly affect the output bits on the left.

The actual permutation used is very random looking (we can't find any nice patterns to make the permutation easy to visualize—it's possible a non-random looking permutation would not be as secure).

16	7	20	21	29	12	28	17	1	15	23	26	5	18	31	10	2	8	24	14	32	27	3	9	19	13	30	6	22	11	4	25

Figure 3-17. Permutation of the 32 bits from the S-boxes

The way to read this is that the 1st bit of output of the permutation is the 16th input bit, the 2nd output bit is the 7th input bit,...the 32nd output bit is the 25th input bit.

3.3.6 Weak and Semi-Weak Keys

We include this section mainly for completeness. There are sixteen DES keys that the security community warns people against using, because they have strange properties. But the probability of randomly generating one of these keys is only $16/2^{56}$, which in our opinion is nothing to worry about. It's probably equally insecure to use a key with a value less than a thousand, since an attacker might be likely to start searching for keys from the bottom.

Remember from §3.3.3 *Generating the Per-Round Keys* that the key is subjected to an initial permutation to generate two 28-bit quantities, C_0 and D_0. The sixteen suspect keys are ones for which C_0 and D_0 are one of the four values: all ones, all zeroes, alternating ones and zeroes, alternating zeroes and ones. Since there are four possible values for each half, there are sixteen possibilities in all. The four **weak keys** are the ones for which each of C_0 and D_0 are all ones or all zeroes. Weak keys are their own inverses.* The remaining twelve keys are the **semi-weak keys**. Each is the inverse of one of the others.

3.3.7 What's So Special About DES?

DES is actually quite simple, as is IDEA (which we'll explain next). One gets the impression that anyone could design a secret key encryption algorithm. Just take the bits, shuffle them, shuffle them some more, and you have an algorithm. In fact, however, these things are very mysterious. For example, the S-boxes seem totally arbitrary. Did anyone put any thought into exactly what substitutions each S-box should perform? Well, Biham and Shamir [BIHA91] have shown that with an incredibly trivial change to DES consisting of swapping S-box 3 with S-box 7, DES is about an order of magnitude less secure in the face of a specific (admittedly not very likely) attack.

*Two keys are inverses if encrypting with one is the same as decrypting with the other.

It is unfortunate that the design process for DES was not more public. We don't know if the particular details were well-chosen for strength, whether someone flipped coins, for instance, to construct the S-boxes, or even whether the particular details were well-chosen to have some sort of weakness that could only be exploited by someone involved in the design process. The claim for why the design process was kept secret, and it is a plausible claim, is that the DES designers knew about many kinds of cryptanalytic attacks, and that they specifically designed DES to be strong against all the ones they knew about. If they publicized the design process, they'd have to divulge all the cryptanalytic attacks they knew about, which would then further educate potential bad guys, which might make some cryptographic standards that were designed without this knowledge vulnerable.

In the hash algorithms designed by Ron Rivest (MD2, MD4, MD5), in order to eliminate the suspicion that they might be specifically chosen to have secret weaknesses, constants that should be reasonably random were chosen through some demonstrable manner, for instance by being the digits of an irrational number such as $\sqrt{2}$.

3.4 INTERNATIONAL DATA ENCRYPTION ALGORITHM (IDEA)

IDEA (International Data Encryption Algorithm) was originally called IPES (Improved Proposed Encryption Standard). It was developed by Xuejia Lai and James L. Massey of ETH Zuria.

IDEA was designed to be efficient to compute in software. It encrypts a 64-bit block of plaintext into a 64-bit block of ciphertext using a 128-bit key. It was published in 1991, so cryptanalysts have had time to find weaknesses. So far none has been found, at least by the good guys (the ones who would publish their results).

IDEA is similar to DES in some ways. Both of them operate in rounds, and both have a complicated mangler function that does not have to be reversible in order for decryption to work. Instead, the mangler function is run in the same direction for encryption as decryption, in both IDEA and DES. In fact, both DES and IDEA have the property that encryption and decryption are identical except for key expansion. With DES, the same keys are used in the reverse order (see Homework Problem 11); with IDEA, the encryption and decryption keys are related in a more complex manner.

3.4.1 Primitive Operations

Each primitive operation in IDEA maps two 16-bit quantities into a 16-bit quantity. (In contrast, each DES S-box maps a 6-bit quantity into a 4-bit quantity.) IDEA uses three operations, all easy to

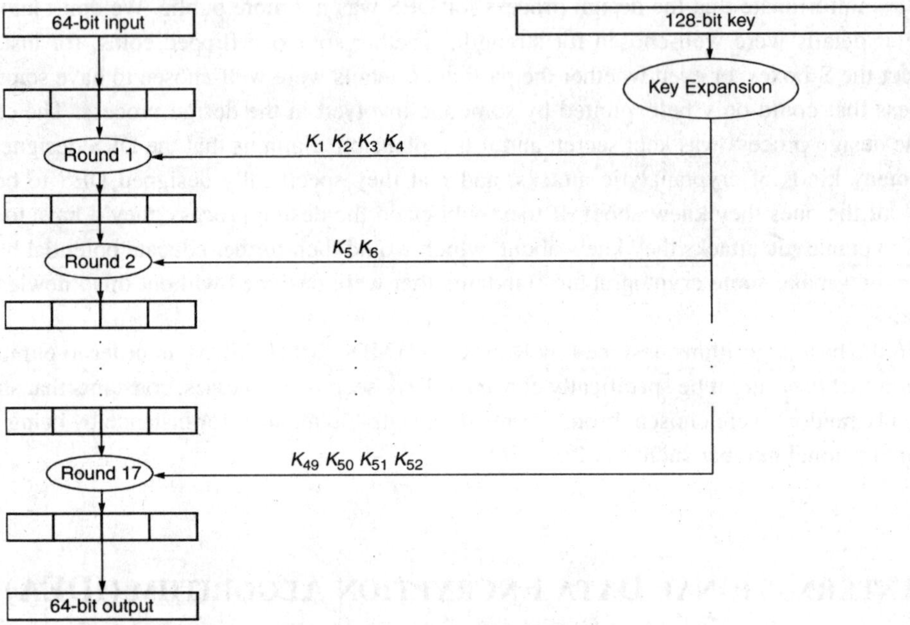

Figure 3-18. Basic Structure of IDEA

compute in software, to create a mapping. Furthermore, the operations are all reversible, which is important in order to run IDEA backwards (i.e., to decrypt).

The operations are bitwise exclusive or (⊕), a slightly modified add (+), and a slightly modified multiply (⊗). The reason add and multiply can't be used in the ordinary way is that the result has to be 16 bits, which won't always be the case when adding or multiplying two 16-bit quantities. Addition in IDEA is done by throwing away carries, which is equivalent to saying addition is mod 2^{16}. Multiplication in IDEA is done by first calculating the 32-bit result, and then taking the remainder when divided by $2^{16}+1$ (which can be done in a clever efficient manner). Multiplication mod $2^{16}+1$ is reversible, in the sense that every number x between 1 and 2^{16} has an inverse y (i.e., a number in the range 1 to 2^{16} such that multiplication by y will "undo" multiplication by x), because $2^{16}+1$ happens to be prime. There is one subtlety, though. The number 0, which can be expressed in 16 bits, would not have an inverse. And the number 2^{16}, which is in the proper range for mod $2^{16}+1$ arithmetic, cannot be expressed in 16 bits. So both problems are solved by treating 0 as an encoding for 2^{16}.

How are these operations reversible? Of course the operations are not reversible if all that is known is the 16-bit output. For instance, if we have inputs A and B, and perform ⊕ to obtain C, we can't find A and B from C alone. However, when running IDEA backwards we will have C and B, and will use that to obtain A. ⊕ is easy. If you know B and C, then you can simply do $B \oplus C$ to get

A. B is its own inverse with $\oplus$. $+$ is easy, too. You compute $-B$ (mod 2^{16}). If you know C and $-B$, then you can find A by doing $C + -B$. With $\otimes$ you find B^{-1} (mod $2^{16}+1$) using Euclid's algorithm—see §7.4 *Euclid's Algorithm*, and you perform $C \otimes B^{-1}$ to get A.

The only part of IDEA that isn't necessarily reversible is the mangler function, and it is truly marvelous to note how IDEA's design manages not to require a reversible mangler function (see §3.4.3.2 *Even Round*).

3.4.2 Key Expansion

The 128-bit key is expanded into 52 16-bit keys, $K_1, K_2, \ldots K_{52}$. The key expansion is done differently for encryption than for decryption. Once the 52 keys are generated, the encryption and decryption operations are the same.

The 52 encryption keys are generated by writing out the 128-bit key and, starting from the left, chopping off 16 bits at a time. This generates eight 16-bit keys (see Figure 3-19).

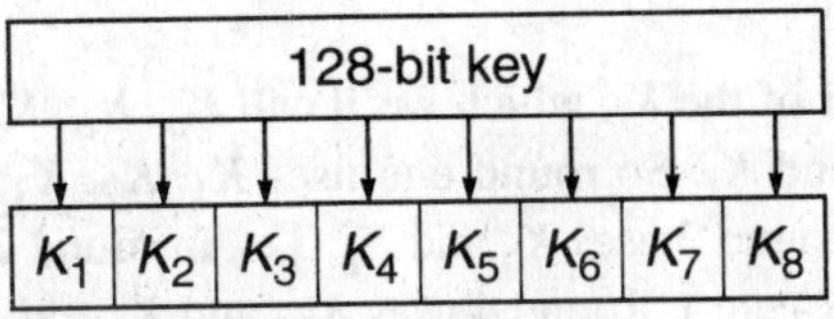

Figure 3-19. Generation of keys 1 through 8

The next eight keys are generated by starting at bit 25, and wrapping around to the beginning when the end is reached (see Figure 3-20).

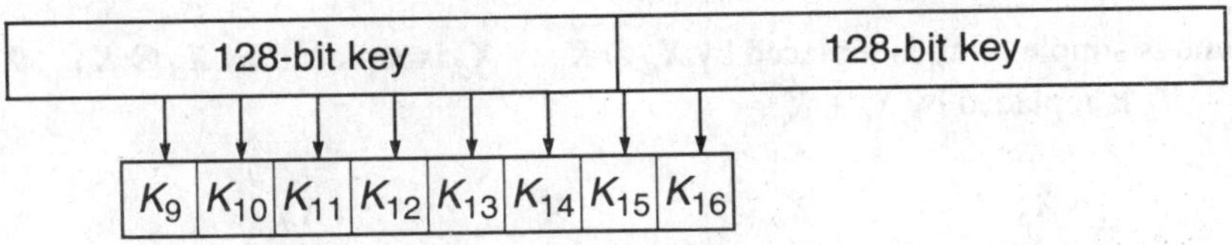

Figure 3-20. Generation of keys 9 through 16

The next eight keys are generated by offsetting 25 more bits, and so forth, until 52 keys are generated. The last offset starts at bit 23 and only needs 4 keys, so bits 1 thru 22 and bits 87 thru 128 get used in keys once less than bits 23 thru 86.

We'll discuss how to generate the 52 decryption keys after we finish describing IDEA.

Warning! If you're actually going to implement this, we lied a bit above because there's a strange quirk in IDEA. Possibly due to someone mixing up the labels on a diagram of IDEA, the keys K_{50} and K_{51} are swapped. That means that an implementation has to swap encryption keys K_{50} and K_{51} after generating them as described above.

3.4.3 One Round

Like DES, IDEA is performed in rounds. It has 17 rounds, where the odd-numbered rounds are different from the even-numbered rounds. (Note that in other descriptions of IDEA, it is described as having 8 rounds, where those rounds do the work of two of our rounds. Our explanation is functionally equivalent. It's just that we think it's clearer to explain it as having 17 rounds.)

Each round takes the input, a 64-bit quantity, and treats it as four 16-bit quantities, which we'll call X_a, X_b, X_c, and X_d. Mathematical functions are performed on X_a, X_b, X_c, X_d to yield new versions of X_a, X_b, X_c, X_d.

The odd rounds use four of the K_i, which we'll call K_a, K_b, K_c, and K_d. The even rounds use two K_i, which we'll call K_e and K_f. So round one uses K_1, K_2, K_3, K_4 (i.e., in round 1, $K_a = K_1$, $K_b = K_2$, $K_c = K_3$, $K_d = K_4$). Round 2 uses K_5 and K_6 (i.e., in round 2, $K_e = K_5$ and $K_f = K_6$). Round 3 uses K_7, K_8, K_9, K_{10} ($K_a = K_7$ etc.). Round 4 uses K_{11} and K_{12}, and so forth.

An odd round, therefore has as input X_a, X_b, X_c, X_d and keys K_a, K_b, K_c, K_d. An even round has as input X_a, X_b, X_c, X_d and keys K_e and K_f.

3.4.3.1 Odd Round

The odd round is simple. X_a is replaced by $X_a \otimes K_a$. X_d is replaced by $X_d \otimes K_d$. X_c is replaced by $X_b + K_b$. X_b is replaced by $X_c + K_c$.

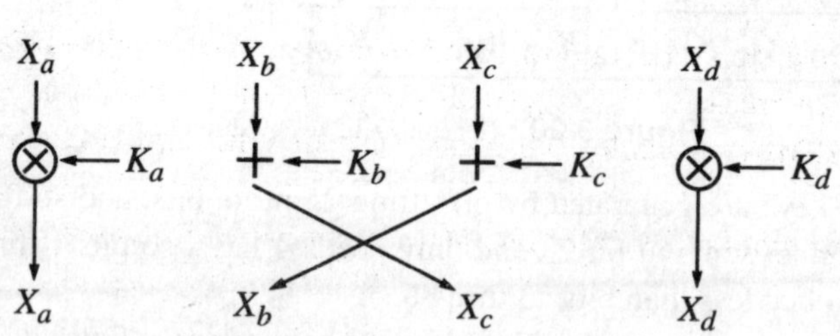

Figure 3-21. IDEA Odd Round

Note that this is easily reversible. To get from the new X_a to the old X_a, we perform $\otimes$ with the multiplicative inverse of K_a, mod $2^{16}+1$. Likewise with X_d. To get the old X_b, given the new X_c, we add the additive inverse of K_b, i.e., we subtract K_b.

So when decrypting, the odd rounds run as before, but with the mathematical inverses of the keys. This will undo the work that was done during that round in encryption.

3.4.3.2 Even Round

The even round is a little more complicated. Again, we have X_a, X_b, X_c, and X_d. We have two keys, K_e and K_f. We're going to first compute two values, which we'll call Y_{in} and Z_{in}. We'll do a function, which we'll call the *mangler function*, which takes as input Y_{in}, Z_{in}, K_e, and K_f and produces what we'll call Y_{out} and Z_{out}. We'll use Y_{out} and Z_{out} to modify X_a, X_b, X_c, and X_d.

$$Y_{in} = X_a \oplus X_b \qquad Z_{in} = X_c \oplus X_d$$

$$Y_{out} = ((K_e \otimes Y_{in}) + Z_{in}) \otimes K_f \qquad Z_{out} = (K_e \otimes Y_{in}) + Y_{out}$$

Now we compute the new X_a, X_b, X_c, and X_d.

$$\text{new } X_a = X_a \oplus Y_{out} \qquad \text{new } X_b = X_b \oplus Y_{out}$$

$$\text{new } X_c = X_c \oplus Z_{out} \qquad \text{new } X_d = X_d \oplus Z_{out}$$

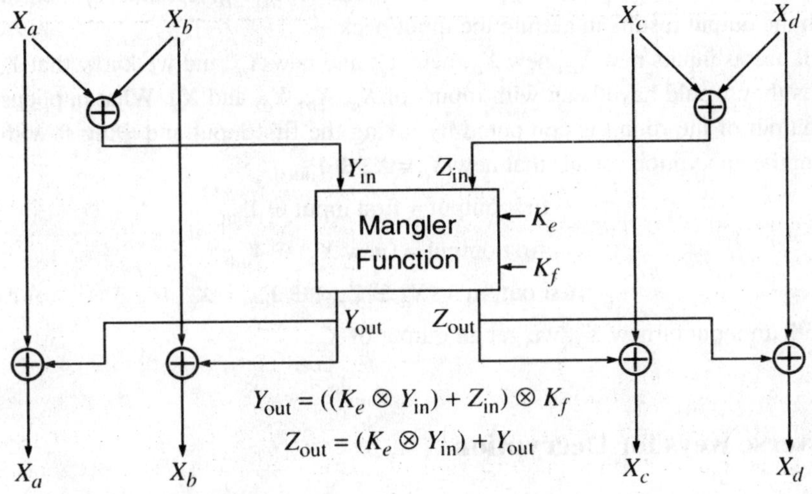

Figure 3-22. IDEA Even Round

How is the work of an even round reversed? This is truly spectacular (we don't get out much). The even round is its own inverse! When performing decryption, the same keys are used as when performing encryption (not the mathematical inverses of the keys, as in the odd rounds).

The even round takes as input the four quantities X_a, X_b, X_c, and X_d, together with keys K_e and K_f, and produces new X_a, new X_b, new X_c, and new X_d. If new X_a, new X_b, new X_c, and new X_d (with the same K_e and K_f) are fed into the even round, the output is the old X_a, X_b, X_c, and X_d. Why is this true?

Note that new $X_a = X_a \oplus Y_{out}$ and new $X_b = X_b \oplus Y_{out}$. In the beginning of the round, X_a and X_b are ⊕'d together, and the result is Y_{in}, the input to the mangler function. What if we use new X_a and new X_b instead of X_a and X_b? (new X_a) ⊕ (new X_b) $= (X_a \oplus Y_{out}) \oplus (X_b \oplus Y_{out}) = X_a \oplus X_b$. So Y_{in} will be the same, whether X_a and X_b are the inputs, or new X_a and new X_b are the inputs. The same is true for X_c and X_d. (Z_{in} is the same value whether the inputs X_c and X_d are used, or inputs new X_c and new X_d are used.) So we've shown that the input to the mangler function is the same whether the input is X_a, X_b, X_c, and X_d or whether the input is new X_a, new X_b, new X_c, and new X_d.

That means the output of the mangler function will be the same whether you're doing encryption (starting with X_a, etc.) or decryption (starting with new X_a, etc.). We called the outputs of the mangler function Y_{out} and Z_{out}. To get the first output of the round (new X_a, in the case of encryption), we take the first input (X_a) and ⊕ it with Y_{out}. We're going to show that with inputs of new X_a, new X_b, new X_c, and new X_d, the output of the round is X_a, X_b, X_c, and X_d, i.e., that running the round with the output results in getting the input back.

We'll use as inputs new X_a, new X_b, new X_c, and new X_d, and we know that Y_{out} and Z_{out} are the same as they would have been with inputs of X_a, X_b, X_c, and X_d. What happens in the round? The first output of the round is computed by taking the first input and ⊕ing it with Y_{out}. We also know (from the encryption round) that new $X_a = X_a \oplus Y_{out}$.

$$\text{first output} = \text{first input} \oplus Y_{out}$$

$$\text{first output} = (\text{new } X_a) \oplus Y_{out}$$

$$\text{first output} = (X_a \oplus Y_{out}) \oplus Y_{out} = X_a$$

Magic! With an input of new X_a, we get an output of X_a.

3.4.4 Inverse Keys for Decryption

IDEA is cleverly designed so that the same code (or hardware) can perform either encryption or decryption given different expanded keys. We want to compute inverse keys such that the encryption procedure, unmodified, will work as a decryption procedure. The basic idea is to take the inverses of the encryption keys and use them in the opposite order (use the inverse of the last-used encryption key as the first key used when doing decryption).

Remember that for encryption, we generated 52 keys, K_1 through K_{52}. We use four of them in each of the odd rounds, and two of them in each of the even rounds. And since we are working backwards, the first decryption keys should be inverses of the last-used encryption keys. Given that the final keys used are K_{49}, K_{50}, K_{51}, and K_{52}, in an odd round, the first four decryption keys will be inverses of the keys K_{49}–K_{52}. K_{49} is used in ⊗, so the decryption key K_1 will be the multiplicative inverse of K_{49} mod 2^{16}+1. And the decryption key K_4 is the multiplicative inverse of K_{52}. Decryption keys K_2 and K_3 are the additive inverses of K_{50} and K_{51} (meaning negative K_{50} and K_{51}).

In the even rounds, as we explained, the keys do not have to be inverted. The same keys are used for encryption as decryption.

3.4.5 Does IDEA Work?

The definition of "working" is that decryption really does undo encryption, and that is easy to see. Whether it is secure or not depends on the Fundamental Tenet of Cryptography, as nobody has yet published results on how to break it. Certainly, breaking IDEA by exhaustive search for the 128-bit key requires currently unbelievable computing resources.

3.5 ADVANCED ENCRYPTION STANDARD (AES)

The world needed a new secret key standard. DES's key was too small. Triple DES (3DES, see §4.4 *Multiple Encryption DES*) was too slow. IDEA was encumbered (i.e., had patent protection), suspect, and slow. The National Institute of Standards and Technology (NIST) decided it wanted to facilitate creation of a new standard, but it had at least as difficult a political problem as a technical problem. Years of some branches of the U.S. government trying everything they could to hinder deployment of secure cryptography was likely to raise strong skepticism if a branch of the government stepped forward and said *We're from the government, and we're here to help you develop and deploy strong crypto*. The following quote gives a hint as to the deep resentment and mistrust that previous crypto export policies and the threat of domestic controls on encryption created.

> *The NSA regularly lies to people who ask it for advice on export control. They have no reason not to; accomplishing their goal by any legal means is fine by them. Lying by government employees is legal.*
>
> —John Gilmore

NIST really did want to help create an excellent new security standard. The new standard should be efficient, flexible, secure, and unencumbered (free to implement). But how could it help create one? Staying out of the picture wouldn't help, since nobody else seemed to have the technical reputation and energy to lead the effort. Proposing an NSA-designed cipher, designed in secret, wouldn't work since everyone would speculate that there were trapdoors. So on January 2, 1997, NIST announced a contest to select a new encryption standard to be used for protecting sensitive, non-classified, U.S. government information. Proposals would be accepted from anyone, anywhere in the world. The candidate ciphers had to meet a bunch of requirements, including having a documented design rationale (and not just *Here's a bunch of transforms we do on the data*). Then there were several years in which conferences were held for presentation of papers analyzing the candidates. There was a group of highly motivated cryptographers (the authors of submitted entries) looking for flaws in the proposals. And NIST also ran tests of the candidates for performance and other characteristics.

After lots of investigation and discussion in the cryptographic community, NIST chose an algorithm called *Rijndael*, named after the two Belgian cryptographers who developed and submitted it—Dr. Joan Daemen of Proton World International and Dr. Vincent Rijmen, a postdoctoral researcher in the Electrical Engineering Department (ESAT) of Katholieke Universiteit Leuven [DAE99]. As of 26 November 2001, AES, a standardization of Rijndael, is a Federal Information Processing Standard [FIPS01].

Rijndael provides for a variety of block and key sizes. These two parameters can be chosen independently from 128, 160, 192, 224, and 256 bits. (in particular, key size and block size can be different). AES mandates a block size of 128 bits, and a choice of key size from 128, 192, and 256 bits*, with the resulting versions imaginatively called AES-128, AES-192, and AES-256, respectively. We'll describe Rijndael, mentioning the AES parameters explicitly from time to time.

Rijndael is based on some beautiful mathematics, but we'll leave the discussion of the mathematics to §8.5 *Mathematics of Rijndael*. Rijndael is similar to DES and IDEA in that there is a series of rounds which mangles a plaintext block into a ciphertext block, and a key expansion algorithm that takes the key and massages it into a bunch of round keys.

3.5.1 Basic Structure

Rijndael allows a certain amount of flexibility by use of two independent parameters, with a third parameter derived from the other two:

*We$_{1,2}$ can't imagine anyone using 192 bits. 256 is probably not necessary, since 128 bits is really long enough. 256 gives "bragging rights" to those who believe more must be better and are willing to take a performance hit to claim their product is more secure because of having a larger key than the competitors. Anyone willing to take a performance hit in order to advertise a larger key will use 256 bits rather than 192.

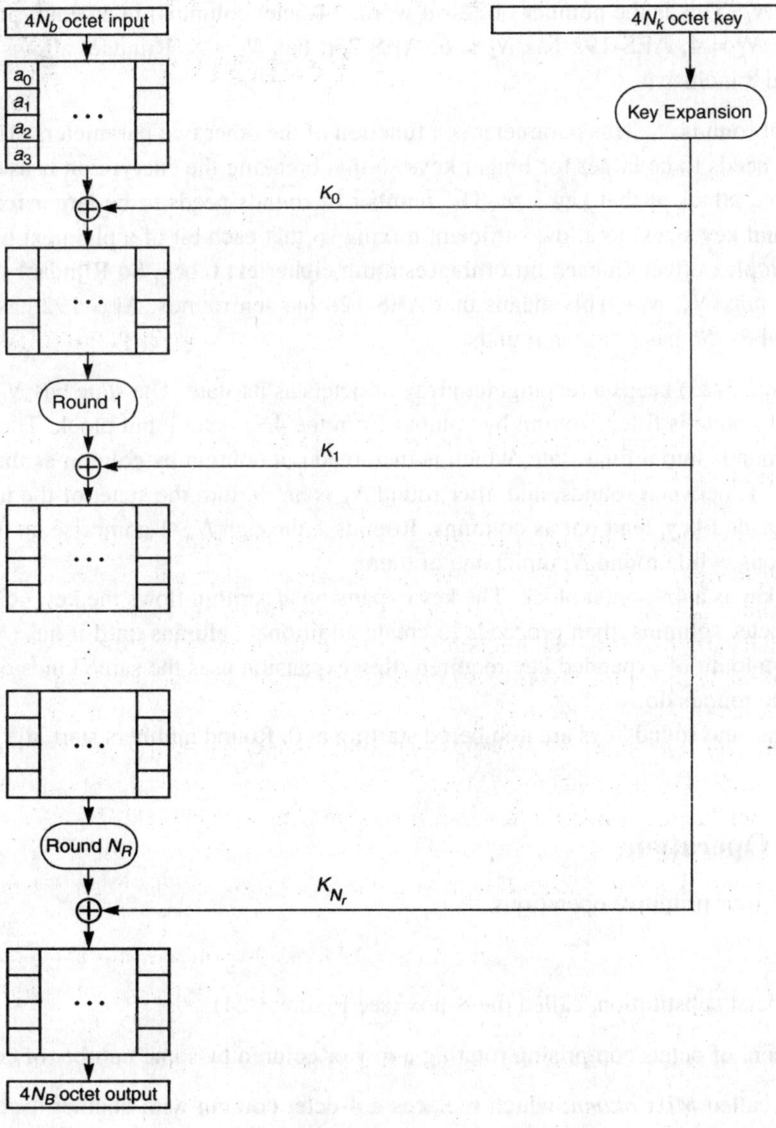

Figure 3-23. Basic Structure of Rijndael

- The block size, N_b. This is the number of 32-bit words (4-octet columns) in an encryption block. AES has $N_b = 4$, because its 128-bit block size is four 32-bit words.

- The key size, N_k. This is the number of 32-bit words (4-octet columns) in an encryption key. AES-128 has $N_k = 4$, AES-192 has $N_k = 6$, AES-256 has $N_k = 8$. Rijndael allows any N_k between 4 and 8 inclusive.
- The number of rounds N_r. This parameter is a function of the other two parameters. The number of rounds needs to be larger for longer keys so that breaking the encryption is as difficult as a brute-force attack at that key size. The number of rounds needs to be larger for bigger block sizes (and key sizes) to allow sufficient mixing so that each bit of a plaintext block (or key) has a complex effect on each bit of the resulting ciphertext block. So Rijndael specifies that $N_r = 6 + \max(N_b, N_k)$. This means that AES-128 has ten rounds, AES-192 has twelve rounds, and AES-256 has fourteen rounds.

Rijndael (Figure 3-23) keeps a rectangular array of octets as its state. The state has N_b 4-octet columns. Initially, the state is filled column by column from the $4N_b$-octet input block. The state is transformed in N_r rounds into a final state, which is then read out column by column as the output block. Before round 1, between rounds, and after round N_r is an ⊕, into the state, of the next $4N_b$ octets from the expanded key, read out as columns. Rounds 1 through N_r-1 comprise an identical sequence of operations, while round N_r omits one of them.

The Rijndael key is a $4N_k$-octet block. The key expansion algorithm flows the key, column by column, into N_k 4-octet columns, then proceeds to create additional columns until it has $(N_r+1)N_b$ columns, the exact amount of expanded key required. Key expansion uses the same kinds of primitive operations as the rounds do.

Rows, columns, and round keys are numbered starting at 0. Round numbers start at 1.

3.5.2 Primitive Operations

Rijndael is based on four primitive operations.

- ⊕
- An octet-for-octet substitution, called the S-box (see Figure 3-24)
- A rearrangement of octets comprising rotating a row or column by some number of cells
- An operation called *MixColumn*, which replaces a 4-octet column with another 4-octet column. *MixColumn* can be implemented with a single table (Figure 3-26) containing 256 4-octet columns. Each of the four octets in an input column is used as an index to retrieve a column from the table; each column retrieved from the table is rotated vertically so that its top octet is in the same row as the input octet; and the four rotated columns are ⊕'d together to produce the output column. (See Figure 3-25.) We'll describe *MixColumn* mathematically in §8.5 *Mathematics of Rijndael*.

right (low-order) nibble

left (high-order) nibble	0	1	2	3	4	5	6	7	8	9	a	b	c	d	e	f
0	63	7c	77	7b	f2	6b	6f	c5	30	01	67	2b	fe	d7	ab	76
1	ca	82	c9	7d	fa	59	47	f0	ad	d4	a2	af	9c	a4	72	c0
2	b7	fd	93	26	36	3f	f7	cc	34	a5	e5	f1	71	d8	31	15
3	04	c7	23	c3	18	96	05	9a	07	12	80	e2	eb	27	b2	75
4	09	83	2c	1a	1b	6e	5a	a0	52	3b	d6	b3	29	e3	2f	84
5	53	d1	00	ed	20	fc	b1	5b	6a	cb	be	39	4a	4c	58	cf
6	d0	ef	aa	fb	43	4d	33	85	45	f9	02	7f	50	3c	9f	a8
7	51	a3	40	8f	92	9d	38	f5	bc	b6	da	21	10	ff	f3	d2
8	cd	0c	13	ec	5f	97	44	17	c4	a7	7e	3d	64	5d	19	73
9	60	81	4f	dc	22	2a	90	88	46	ee	b8	14	de	5e	0b	db
a	e0	32	3a	0a	49	06	24	5c	c2	d3	ac	62	91	95	e4	79
b	e7	c8	37	6d	8d	d5	4e	a9	6c	56	f4	ea	65	7a	ae	08
c	ba	78	25	2e	1c	a6	b4	c6	e8	dd	74	1f	4b	bd	8b	8a
d	70	3e	b5	66	48	03	f6	0e	61	35	57	b9	86	c1	1d	9e
e	e1	f8	98	11	69	d9	8e	94	9b	1e	87	e9	ce	55	28	df
f	8c	a1	89	0d	bf	e6	42	68	41	99	2d	0f	b0	54	bb	16

Figure 3-24. Rijndael S-box

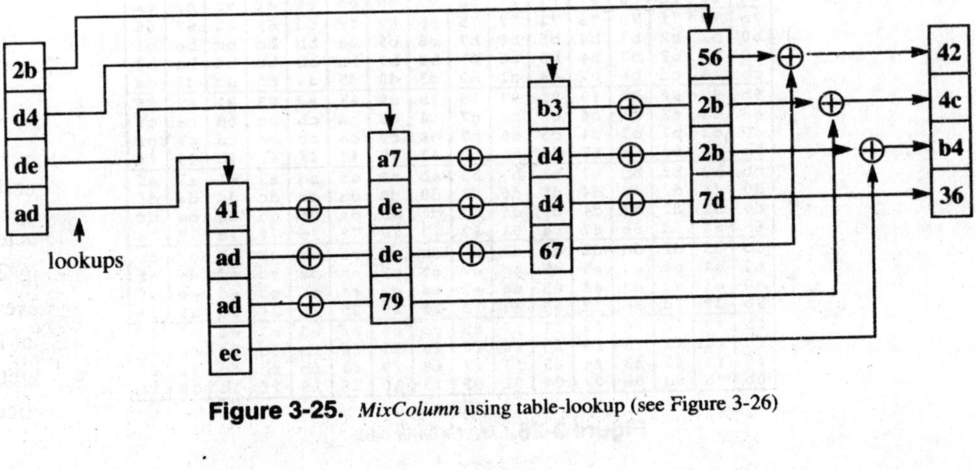

Figure 3-25. *MixColumn* using table-lookup (see Figure 3-26)

right (low-order) nibble

left (high-order) nibble	0	1	2	3	4	5	6	7	8	9	a	b	c	d	e	f
0	00 00 00 00	02 01 01 03	04 02 02 06	06 03 03 05	08 04 04 0c	0a 05 05 0f	0c 06 06 0a	0e 07 07 09	10 08 08 18	12 09 09 1b	14 0a 0a 1e	16 0b 0b 1d	18 0c 0c 14	1a 0d 0d 17	1c 0e 0e 12	1e 0f 0f 11
1	20 10 10 30	22 11 11 33	24 12 12 36	26 13 13 35	28 14 14 3c	2a 15 15 3f	2c 16 16 3a	2e 17 17 39	30 18 18 28	32 19 19 2b	34 1a 1a 2e	36 1b 1b 2d	38 1c 1c 24	3a 1d 1d 27	3c 1e 1e 22	3e 1f 1f 21
2	40 20 20 60	42 21 21 63	44 22 22 66	46 23 23 65	48 24 24 6c	4a 25 25 6f	4c 26 26 6a	4e 27 27 69	50 28 28 78	52 29 29 7b	54 2a 2a 7e	56 2b 2b 7d	58 2c 2c 74	5a 2d 2d 77	5c 2e 2e 72	5e 2f 2f 71
3	60 30 30 50	62 31 31 53	64 32 32 56	66 33 33 55	68 34 34 5c	6a 35 35 5f	6c 36 36 5a	6e 37 37 59	70 38 38 48	72 39 39 4b	74 3a 3a 4e	76 3b 3b 4d	78 3c 3c 44	7a 3d 3d 47	7c 3e 3e 42	7e 3f 3f 41
4	80 40 40 c0	82 41 41 c3	84 42 42 c6	86 43 43 c5	88 44 44 cc	8a 45 45 cf	8c 46 46 ca	8e 47 47 c9	90 48 48 d8	92 49 49 db	94 4a 4a de	96 4b 4b dd	98 4c 4c d4	9a 4d 4d d7	9c 4e 4e d2	9e 4f 4f d1
5	a0 50 50 f0	a2 51 51 f3	a4 52 52 f6	a6 53 53 f5	a8 54 54 fc	aa 55 55 ff	ac 56 56 fa	ae 57 57 f9	b0 58 58 e8	b2 59 59 eb	b4 5a 5a ee	b6 5b 5b ed	b8 5c 5c e4	ba 5d 5d e7	bc 5e 5e e2	be 5f 5f e1
6	c0 60 60 a0	c2 61 61 a3	c4 62 62 a6	c6 63 63 a5	c8 64 64 ac	ca 65 65 af	cc 66 66 aa	ce 67 67 a9	d0 68 68 b8	d2 69 69 bb	d4 6a 6a be	d6 6b 6b bd	d8 6c 6c b4	da 6d 6d b7	dc 6e 6e b2	de 6f 6f b1
7	e0 70 70 90	e2 71 71 93	e4 72 72 96	e6 73 73 95	e8 74 74 9c	ea 75 75 9f	ec 76 76 9a	ee 77 77 99	f0 78 78 88	f2 79 79 8b	f4 7a 7a 8e	f6 7b 7b 8d	f8 7c 7c 84	fa 7d 7d 87	fc 7e 7e 82	fe 7f 7f 81
8	1b 80 80 9b	19 81 81 98	1f 82 82 9d	1d 83 83 9e	13 84 84 97	11 85 85 94	17 86 86 91	15 87 87 92	0b 88 88 83	09 89 89 80	0f 8a 8a 85	0d 8b 8b 86	03 8c 8c 8f	01 8d 8d 8c	07 8e 8e 89	05 8f 8f 8a
9	3b 90 90 ab	39 91 91 a8	3f 92 92 ad	3d 93 93 ae	33 94 94 a7	31 95 95 a4	37 96 96 a1	35 97 97 a2	2b 98 98 b3	29 99 99 b0	2f 9a 9a b5	2d 9b 9b b6	23 9c 9c bf	21 9d 9d bc	27 9e 9e b9	25 9f 9f ba
a	5b a0 a0 fb	59 a1 a1 f8	5f a2 a2 fd	5d a3 a3 fe	53 a4 a4 f7	51 a5 a5 f4	57 a6 a6 f1	55 a7 a7 f2	4b a8 a8 e3	49 a9 a9 e0	4f aa aa e5	4d ab ab e6	43 ac ac ef	41 ad ad ec	47 ae ae e9	45 af af ea
b	7b b0 b0 cb	79 b1 b1 c8	7f b2 b2 cd	7d b3 b3 ce	73 b4 b4 c7	71 b5 b5 c4	77 b6 b6 c1	75 b7 b7 c2	6b b8 b8 d3	69 b9 b9 d0	6f ba ba d5	6d bb bb d6	63 bc bc df	61 bd bd dc	67 be be d9	65 bf bf da
c	9b c0 c0 5b	99 c1 c1 58	9f c2 c2 5d	9d c3 c3 5e	93 c4 c4 57	91 c5 c5 54	97 c6 c6 51	95 c7 c7 52	8b c8 c8 43	89 c9 c9 40	8f ca ca 45	8d cb cb 46	83 cc cc 4f	81 cd cd 4c	87 ce ce 49	85 cf cf 4a
d	bb d0 d0 6b	b9 d1 d1 68	bf d2 d2 6d	bd d3 d3 6e	b3 d4 d4 67	b1 d5 d5 64	b7 d6 d6 61	b5 d7 d7 62	ab d8 d8 73	a9 d9 d9 70	af da da 75	ad db db 76	a3 dc dc 7f	a1 dd dd 7c	a7 de de 79	a5 df df 7a
e	db e0 e0 3b	d9 e1 e1 38	df e2 e2 3d	dd e3 e3 3e	d3 e4 e4 37	d1 e5 e5 34	d7 e6 e6 31	d5 e7 e7 32	cb e8 e8 23	c9 e9 e9 20	cf ea ea 25	cd eb eb 26	c3 ec ec 2f	c1 ed ed 2c	c7 ee ee 29	c5 ef ef 2a
f	fb f0 f0 0b	f9 f1 f1 08	ff f2 f2 0d	fd f3 f3 0e	f3 f4 f4 07	f1 f5 f5 04	f7 f6 f6 01	f5 f7 f7 02	eb f8 f8 13	e9 f9 f9 10	ef fa fa 15	ed fb fb 16	e3 fc fc 1f	e1 fd fd 1c	e7 fe fe 19	e5 ff ff 1a

Figure 3-26. *MixColumn* table

3.5.2.1 What about the inverse cipher?

- ⊕ is its own inverse
- The inverse S-box is just given by a different table (see Figure 3-27)

right (low-order) nibble; left (high-order) nibble

	0	1	2	3	4	5	6	7	8	9	a	b	c	d	e	f
0	52	09	6a	d5	30	36	a5	38	bf	40	a3	9e	81	f3	d7	fb
1	7c	e3	39	82	9b	2f	ff	87	34	8e	43	44	c4	de	e9	cb
2	54	7b	94	32	a6	c2	23	3d	ee	4c	95	0b	42	fa	c3	4e
3	08	2e	a1	66	28	d9	24	b2	76	5b	a2	49	6d	8b	d1	25
4	72	f8	f6	64	86	68	98	16	d4	a4	5c	cc	5d	65	b6	92
5	6c	70	48	50	fd	ed	b9	da	5e	15	46	57	a7	8d	9d	84
6	90	d8	ab	00	8c	bc	d3	0a	f7	e4	58	05	b8	b3	45	06
7	d0	2c	1e	8f	ca	3f	0f	02	c1	af	bd	03	01	13	8a	6b
8	3a	91	11	41	4f	67	dc	ea	97	f2	cf	ce	f0	b4	e6	73
9	96	ac	74	22	e7	ad	35	85	e2	f9	37	e8	1c	75	df	6e
a	47	f1	1a	71	1d	29	c5	89	6f	b7	62	0e	aa	18	be	1b
b	fc	56	3e	4b	c6	d2	79	20	9a	db	c0	fe	78	cd	5a	f4
c	1f	dd	a8	33	88	07	c7	31	b1	12	10	59	27	80	ec	5f
d	60	51	7f	a9	19	b5	4a	0d	2d	e5	7a	9f	93	c9	9c	ef
e	a0	e0	3b	4d	ae	2a	f5	b0	c8	eb	bb	3c	83	53	99	61
f	17	2b	04	7e	ba	77	d6	26	e1	69	14	63	55	21	0c	7d

Figure 3-27. Rijndael inverse S-box

- The inverse of rotating a row or column is just rotating it the same amount in the opposite direction
- The inverse of *MixColumn*, called *InvMixColumn*, is just like *MixColumn*, but with a different table (Figure 3-28)

So the inverse cipher can clearly be implemented by applying the inverses of the primitive operations comprising the cipher in the opposite sequence from that in the cipher. But as it turns out, due to various mathematical properties (and by clever design), the inverse cipher can be made to look just like the forward cipher but with inverse operations, and with the round keys not just in reverse order, but having *InvMixColumn* applied to all but the first and last of them. This will be explained in §8.5 *Mathematics of Rijndael.*

right (low-order) nibble

left (high-order) nibble

	0	1	2	3	4	5	6	7	8	9	a	b	c	d	e	f
0	00 00 00 00	0e 09 0d 0b	1c 12 1a 16	12 1b 17 1d	38 24 34 2c	36 2d 39 27	24 36 2e 3a	2a 3f 23 31	70 48 68 58	7e 41 65 53	6c 5a 72 4e	62 53 7f 45	48 6c 5c 74	46 65 51 7f	54 7e 46 62	5a 77 4b 69
1	e0 90 d0 b0	ee 99 dd bb	fc 82 ca a6	f2 8b c7 ad	d8 b4 e4 9c	d6 bd e9 97	c4 a6 fe 8a	ca af f3 81	90 d8 b8 e8	9e d1 b5 e3	8c ca a2 fe	82 c3 af f5	a8 fc 8c c4	a6 f5 81 cf	b4 ee 96 d2	ba e7 9b d9
2	db 3b bb 7b	d5 32 b6 70	c7 29 a1 6d	c9 20 ac 66	e3 1f 8f 57	ed 16 82 5c	ff 0d 95 41	f1 04 98 4a	ab 73 d3 23	a5 7a de 28	b7 61 c9 35	b9 68 c4 3e	93 57 e7 0f	9d 5e ea 04	8f 45 fd 19	81 4c f0 12
3	3b ab 6b cb	35 a2 66 c0	27 b9 71 dd	29 b0 7c d6	03 8f 5f e7	0d 86 52 ec	1f 9d 45 f1	11 94 48 fa	4b e3 03 93	45 ea 0e 98	57 f1 19 85	59 f8 14 8e	73 c7 37 bf	7d ce 3a b4	6f d5 2d a9	61 dc 20 a2
4	ad 76 6d f6	a3 7f 60 fd	b1 64 77 e0	bf 6d 7a eb	95 52 59 da	9b 5b 54 d1	89 40 43 cc	87 49 4e c7	dd 3e 05 ae	d3 37 08 a5	c1 2c 1f b8	cf 25 12 b3	e5 1a 31 82	eb 13 3c 89	f9 08 2b 94	f7 01 26 9f
5	4d e6 bd 46	43 ef b0 4d	51 f4 a7 50	5f fd aa 5b	75 c2 89 6a	7b cb 84 61	69 d0 93 7c	67 d9 9e 77	3d ae d5 1e	33 a7 d8 15	21 bc cf 08	2f b5 c2 03	05 8a e1 32	0b 83 ec 39	19 98 fb 24	17 91 f6 2f
6	76 4d d6 8d	78 44 db 86	6a 5f cc 9b	64 56 c1 90	4e 69 e2 a1	40 60 ef aa	52 7b f8 b7	5c 72 f5 bc	06 05 be d5	08 0c b3 de	1a 17 a4 c3	14 1e a9 c8	3e 21 8a f9	30 28 87 f2	22 33 90 ef	2c 3a 9d e4
7	96 dd 06 3d	98 d4 0b 36	8a cf 1c 2b	84 c6 11 20	ae f9 32 11	a0 f0 3f 1a	b2 eb 28 07	bc e2 25 0c	e6 95 6e 65	e8 9c 63 6e	fa 87 74 73	f4 8e 79 78	de b1 5a 49	d0 b8 57 42	c2 a3 40 5f	cc aa 4d 54
8	41 ec da f7	4f e5 d7 fc	5d fe c0 e1	53 f7 cd ea	79 c8 ee db	77 c1 e3 d0	65 da f4 cd	6b d3 f9 c6	31 a4 b2 af	3f ad bf a4	2d b6 a8 b9	23 bf a5 b2	09 80 86 83	07 89 8b 88	15 92 9c 95	1b 9b 91 9e
9	a1 7c 0a 47	af 75 07 4c	bd 6e 10 51	b3 67 1d 5a	99 58 3e 6b	97 51 33 60	85 4a 24 7d	8b 43 29 76	d1 34 62 1f	df 3d 6f 14	cd 26 78 09	c3 2f 75 02	e9 10 56 33	e7 19 5b 38	f5 02 4c 25	fb 0b 41 2e
a	9a d7 61 8c	94 de 6c 87	86 c5 7b 9a	88 cc 76 91	a2 f3 55 a0	ac fa 58 ab	be e1 4f b6	b0 e8 42 bd	ea 9f 09 d4	e4 96 04 df	f6 8d 13 c2	f8 84 1e c9	d2 bb 3d f8	dc b2 30 f3	ce a9 27 ee	c0 a0 2a e5
b	7a 47 b1 3c	74 4e bc 37	66 55 ab 2a	68 5c a6 21	42 63 85 10	4c 6a 88 1b	5e 71 9f 06	50 78 92 0d	0a 0f d9 64	04 06 d4 6f	16 1d c3 72	18 14 ce 79	32 2b ed 48	3c 22 e0 43	2e 39 f7 5e	20 30 fa 55
c	ec 9a b7 01	e2 93 ba 0a	f0 88 ad 17	fe 81 a0 1c	d4 be 83 2d	da b7 8e 26	c8 ac 99 3b	c6 a5 94 30	9c d2 df 59	92 db d2 52	80 c0 c5 4f	8e c9 c8 44	a4 f6 eb 75	aa ff e6 7e	b8 e4 f1 63	b6 ed fc 68
d	0c 0a 67 b1	02 03 6a ba	10 18 7d a7	1e 11 70 ac	34 2e 53 9d	3a 27 5e 96	28 3c 49 8b	26 35 44 80	7c 42 0f e9	72 4b 02 e2	60 50 15 ff	6e 59 18 f4	44 66 3b c5	4a 6f 36 ce	58 74 21 d3	56 7d 2c d8
e	37 a1 0c 7a	39 a8 01 71	2b b3 16 6c	25 ba 1b 67	0f 85 38 56	01 8c 35 5d	13 97 22 40	1d 9e 2f 4b	47 e9 64 22	49 e0 69 29	5b fb 7e 34	55 f2 73 3f	7f cd 50 0e	71 c4 5d 05	63 df 4a 18	6d d6 47 13
f	d7 31 dc ca	d9 38 d1 c1	cb 23 c6 dc	c5 2a cb d7	ef 15 e8 e6	e1 1c e5 ed	f3 07 f2 f0	fd 0e ff fb	a7 79 b4 92	a9 70 b9 99	bb 6b ae 84	b5 62 a3 8f	9f 5d 80 be	91 54 8d b5	83 4f 9a a8	8d 46 97 a3

Figure 3-28. *InvMixColumn* table

3.5.3 Key Expansion

Key expansion starts with the key arranged as N_k 4-octet columns (see Figure 3-29) and iteratively

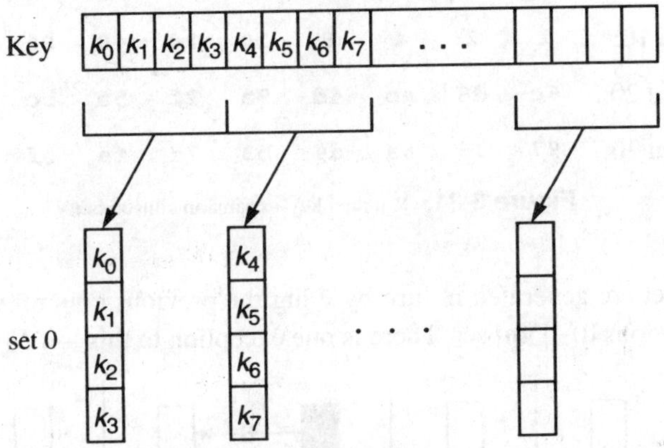

Figure 3-29. Rijndael key expansion, creation of set 0

generates the next N_k columns of the expanded key (see Figure 3-30). To generate the ith set of N_k

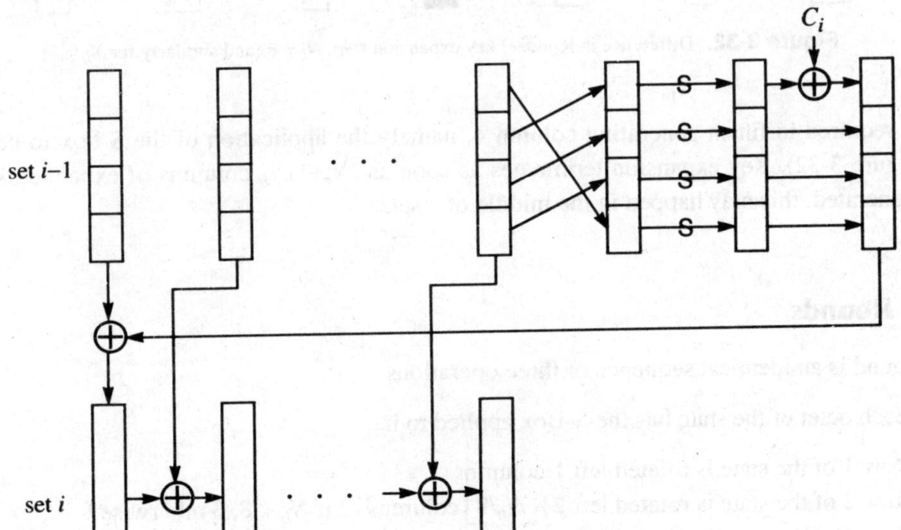

Figure 3-30. Rijndael key expansion, iteration step, $N_k \leq 6$

columns (i starts at 1; the 0th set is the supplied key), all that is needed is the (i–1)th set. Column 0 of the new set is gotten by rotating the last column of the (i–1)th set upward one cell, applying the S-box to each octet, and then ⊕ing a constant based on i (see Figure 3-31) into octet 0. The rest of

i = 1 thru 10:	1	2	4	8	10	20	40	80	1b	36
i = 11 thru 20:	6c	d8	ab	4d	9a	2f	5e	bc	63	c6
i = 21 thru 30:	97	35	6a	d4	b3	7d	fa	ef	c5	(91)

Figure 3-31. Rijndael key-expansion constants C_i

the columns in the set are generated in turn by ⊕ing the previous column with the corresponding column from the previous [(i–1)th] set. There is one exception to this—if $N_k > 6$, then an additional

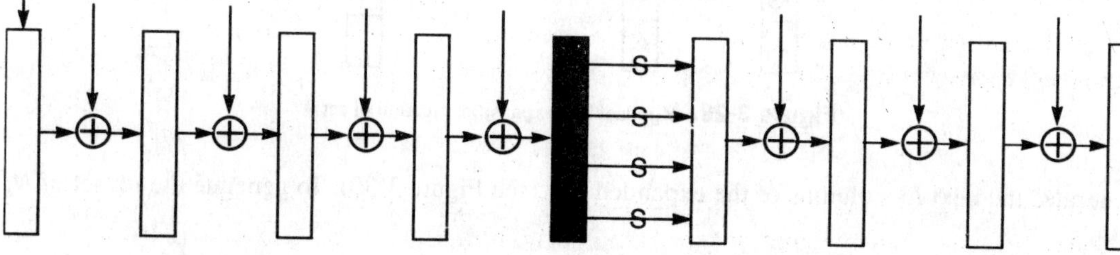

Figure 3-32. Difference in Rijndael key expansion step, $N_k = 8$ [and similarly for $N_k = 7$]

step is required to finish generating column 4, namely the application of the S-box to each octet (see Figure 3-32). Key expansion terminates as soon as $(N_r+1)N_b$ columns of expanded key have been generated; this may happen in the middle of a set.

3.5.4 Rounds

Each round is an identical sequence of three operations:

1. Each octet of the state has the S-Box applied to it.
2. Row 1 of the state is rotated left 1 column.
   Row 2 of the state is rotated left $2+\lfloor N_b/8 \rfloor$ columns (2 if $N_b < 8$, 3 otherwise).
   Row 3 of the state is rotated left $3+\lfloor N_b/7 \rfloor$ columns (3 if $N_b < 7$, 4 otherwise).
   (Note that for AES, this simplifies to rotating row i left i columns.)
3. Each column of the state has *MixColumn* applied to it. Round N_r omits this operation.

3.5.5 Inverse Rounds

Since each operation is invertible, decryption can be done by performing the inverse of each operation in the opposite order from that for encryption, and using the round keys in the reverse order.

But as we mentioned earlier, we can make decryption have the same structure as encryption. To do this, we not only have to use the round keys in the opposite order, but we have to apply *InvMixColumn* to each column of all but the initial and final round keys. Then each inverse round is an identical sequence of three operations:

1. Each octet of the state has the inverse S-Box applied to it.
2. Row 1 of the state is rotated right 1 column.
   Row 2 of the state is rotated right $2+\lfloor N_b/8 \rfloor$ columns (2 if $N_b < 8$, 3 otherwise).
   Row 3 of the state is rotated right $3+\lfloor N_b/7 \rfloor$ columns (3 if $N_b < 7$, 4 otherwise).
   (Note that for AES, this simplifies to rotating row *i* right *i* columns.)
3. Each column of the state has *InvMixColumn* applied to it. Round N_r omits this operation.

3.5.6 Optimization

In the straightforward implementation of a round, each octet of the state undergoes a table-lookup to apply the S-Box, and the resulting octet is later used for another table-lookup as part of *MixColumn*. We can combine these into a single table-lookup that transforms an octet into the column found by applying the S-Box and looking up the result in the *MixColumn* table.

We can further optimize a round by retaining the old state while we compute the new state. We initialize the new state to the round key. For each octet in the old state, we perform the combined table-lookup and ⊕ the resulting column (rotated downward by the old octet's row number) into the appropriate column of the new state. For the first row (row 0), this is the old octet's column. For the second row (row 1), it's the column one to the left.* For the third row (row 2), it's either two or three columns to the left (depending on whether or not $N_b < 8$); and for the last row (row 3), it's either three or four columns to the left (depending on whether or not $N_b < 7$). When we've processed all the old octets, we've completed the round (including the following ⊕).

The last round is a little different. We initialize the new state to the round key. For each octet in the old state, we apply the S-Box by table-lookup and ⊕ the result into the appropriate octet of the new state. The destination octet is in the same row as the source octet, and its column depends on the source row and column in the same manner as for the other rounds.

The inverse rounds can be optimized in the same manner (with *left* replaced by *right*).

*Think of the columns as residing on an upright cylinder—the rightmost column is immediately to the left of the leftmost.

3.6 RC4

A long random (or pseudo-random) string used to encrypt a message with a simple ⊕ operation is known as a **one-time pad**. A **stream cipher** generates a one-time pad and applies it to a stream of plaintext with ⊕.

RC4 is a stream cipher designed by Ron Rivest. RC4 was a trade secret, but was "outed" in 1994. As a result, it has been extensively analyzed and is considered secure as long as you discard the first few (say 256) octets of the generated pad.

The algorithm is an extremely simple (and fast) generator of pseudo-random streams of octets. The key can be from 1 to 256 octets. Even with a minimal key (a single null octet), the generated pseudo-random stream passes all the usual randomness tests (and so makes a fine pseudo-random number generator—I_3've used it for that purpose on numerous occasions). RC4 keeps 258 octets of state information, 256 octets of which are a permutation of 0, 1,…255 that is initially computed from the key and then altered as each pad octet is generated.

The box on page 93 gives a complete C implementation of RC4 one-time pad generation.

3.7 HOMEWORK

1. Come up with as efficient an encoding as you can to specify a completely general one-to-one mapping between 64-bit input values and 64-bit output values.

2. Token cards display a number that changes periodically, perhaps every minute. Each such device has a unique secret key. A human can prove possession of a particular such device by entering the displayed number into a computer system. The computer system knows the secret keys of each authorized device. How would you design such a device?

3. How many DES keys, on the average, encrypt a particular plaintext block to a particular ciphertext block?

4. Make an argument as to why the initial permutation of the bits of the DES key cannot have any security value.

5. Suppose the DES mangler function mapped every 32-bit value to zero, regardless of the value of its input. What function would DES then compute?

6. Are all the 56 bits of the DES key used an equal number of times in the K_i? Specify, for each of the K_i, which bits are not used.

RC4

```
typedef unsigned char uns8;
typedef unsigned short uns16;

static uns8 state[256], x, y;      /* 258 octets of state information */

void
rc4init (key, length)      /* initialize for encryption / decryption */
    uns8 *key;
    uns16 length;
{
    int i;
    uns8 t;
    uns8 j;
    uns8 k = 0;

    for (i = 256; i--; )
        state[i] = i;

    for (i = 0, j = 0; i < 256; i++, j = (j + 1) % length)
        t = state[i], state[i] = state[k += key[j] + t], state[k] = t;

    x = 0;
    y = 0;
}

uns8
rc4step ()     /* return next pseudo-random octet */
{
    uns8 t;

    t = state[y += state[++x]], state[y] = state[x], state[x] = t;
    return (state[state[x] + state[y]]);
}
```

7. What would change in the DES description if keys were input as 56-bit quantities rather than 64-bit quantities?

8. Why is a DES weak key (see §3.3.6 *Weak and Semi-Weak Keys*) its own inverse? Hint: DES encryption and decryption are the same once the per-round keys are generated.

9. Why is each DES semi-weak key the inverse of another semi-weak key?

10. Class project: design and implement an efficient DES breaking system. (Hint: Have your system take as input a ⟨plaintext, ciphertext⟩ pair and a starting key number, and searches from that starting key number for a DES key that will map the plaintext into that ciphertext.) Use your system to tell us what DES key mapped 0 to $5761b9ab9858b34b_{16}$. Free T-shirts to the first ten correct answers.

11. Show that DES encryption and decryption are identical except for the order of the 48-bit keys. Hint: running a round backwards is the same as running it forwards but with the halves swapped (see §3.3.4 *A DES Round*), and DES has a swap after round 16 when run forwards (see §3.3.1 *DES Overview*).

12. Verify the *MixColumn* result in Figure 3-25 by using the same method (in conjunction with Figure 3-28's table) to compute *InvMixColumn* of the *MixColumn* result and checking that you produce the *MixColumn* input.

13. Describe in detail the optimization of the Rijndael inverse round mentioned at the end of §3.5.6 *Optimization*.

14. Give an upper bound on the number of 258-octet states possible in RC4.

4 MODES OF OPERATION

4.1 INTRODUCTION

We've covered how to encrypt a 64-bit block with DES or IDEA, or a 128-bit block with AES, but that doesn't really tell how to use these algorithms. For instance, sometimes messages to be encrypted don't happen to be exactly one block long. We also mentioned in §2.4.5 *Integrity Check* that it was possible, using a secret key encryption scheme, to generate a MAC (message authentication code). This chapter will attempt to tie up these various loose ends.

4.2 ENCRYPTING A LARGE MESSAGE

How do you encrypt a message larger than 64 bits? There are several schemes defined in [DES81]. These schemes would be equally applicable to IDEA or any secret key scheme that encrypted fixed-length blocks, and no doubt one could come up with variant schemes as well. The ones defined in [DES81], and which we'll describe in detail, are:

1. Electronic Code Book (ECB)
2. Cipher Block Chaining (CBC)
3. *k*-Bit Cipher Feedback Mode (CFB)
4. *k*-Bit Output Feedback Mode (OFB)

A newer scheme that might be important in the future is:

5. Counter Mode (CTR)

4.2.1 Electronic Code Book (ECB)

This mode consists of doing the obvious thing, and it is usually the worst method. You break the message into 64-bit blocks (padding the last one out to a full 64 bits), and encrypt each block with the secret key (see Figure 4-1). The other side receives the encrypted blocks and decrypts each

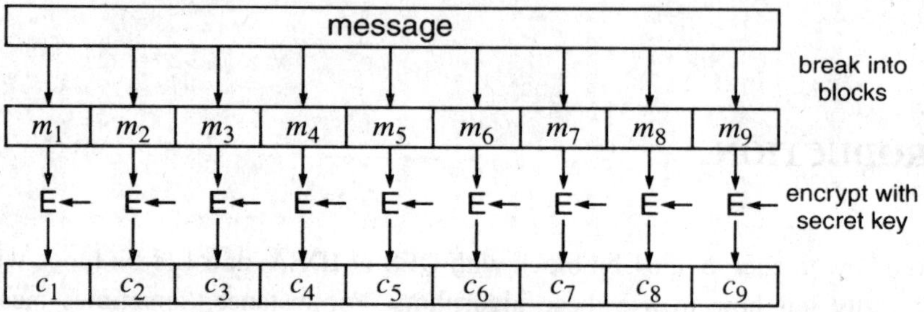

Figure 4-1. Electronic Code Book Encryption

block in turn to get back the original message (see Figure 4-2).

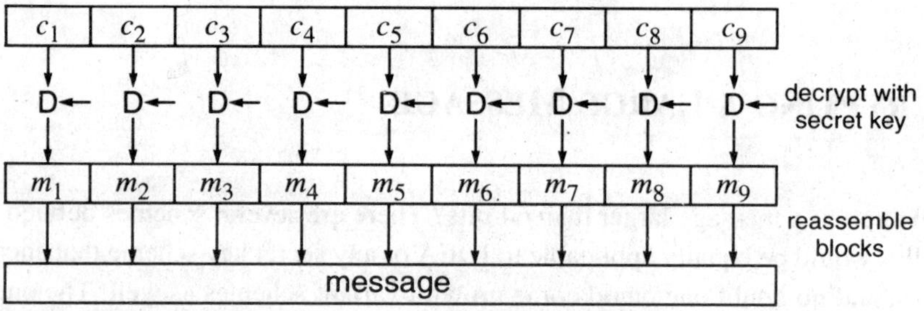

Figure 4-2. Electronic Code Book Decryption

There are a number of problems with this approach that don't show up in the single-block case. First, if a message contains two identical 64-bit blocks, the corresponding two blocks of ciphertext will be identical. This will give an eavesdropper some information. Whether it is useful or not depends on the context. We'll give an example where ECB would have a problem. Suppose that the eavesdropper knows that the plaintext is an alphabetically sorted list of employees and salaries being sent from management to payroll, tabularly arranged (see Figure 4-3).

Further suppose that, as luck would have it, each line is exactly 64 bytes long, and the blocks happen to be divided in the salary field between the 1,000's and the 10,000's digit. Since identical plaintext blocks produce identical ciphertext blocks, not only can an eavesdropper figure out which sets of employees have identical salaries, but also which sets of employees have salaries in the same

Name	Position	Salary
Adams, John	President	78,964.31
Bush, Neil	Accounting Clerk	623,321.16
Hoover, J. Edgar	Wardrobe Consultant	34,445.22
Stern, Howard	Affirmative Action Officer	38,206.51
Woods, Rosemary	Audiovisual Supervisor	21,489.15

Block boundaries

Figure 4-3. Payroll Data

$10,000 ranges. If he can guess a few relative salaries, he will have a pretty good idea of what all the salaries are from this "encrypted" message.

Furthermore, if the eavesdropper is one of the employees, he can alter the message to change his own salary to match that of any other employee by copying the ciphertext blocks from that employee to the corresponding blocks of his own entry. Even a human looking at the resulting message would see nothing awry.

So, ECB has two serious flaws. Someone seeing the ciphertext can gain information from repeated blocks, and someone can rearrange blocks or modify blocks to his own advantage. As a result of these flaws, ECB is rarely used to encrypt messages.

4.2.2 Cipher Block Chaining (CBC)

CBC is a method of avoiding some of the problems in ECB. Using CBC, even if the same block repeats in the plaintext, it will not cause repeats in the ciphertext.

First we'll give an example of how this might be accomplished. Our example is not CBC, but it helps for understanding CBC.

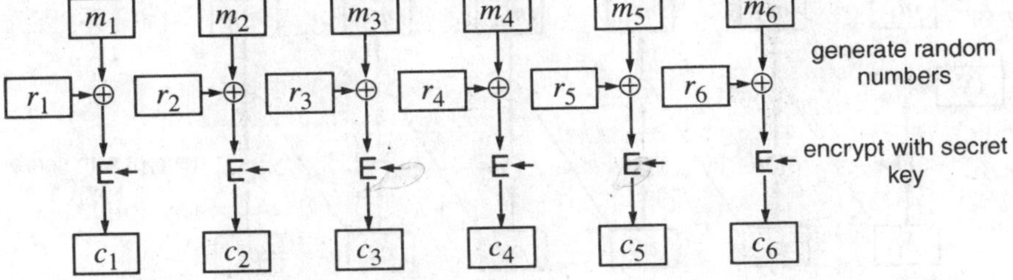

Figure 4-4. Randomized Electronic Code Book Encryption

Generate a 64-bit random number r_i for each plaintext block m_i to be encrypted. ⊕ the plaintext block with the random number, encrypt the result, and transmit both the unencrypted random number r_i and the ciphertext block c_i (see Figure 4-4). To decrypt this, you'd decrypt all the c_is, and for each c_i, after decrypting it, you'd ⊕ it with the random number r_i.

The main problem with this scheme is efficiency. It causes twice as much information to be transmitted, since a random number has to be transmitted along with each block of ciphertext. Another problem with it is that an attacker can rearrange the blocks and have a predictable effect on the resulting plaintext. For instance, if $r_2|c_2$ were removed entirely it would result in m_2 being absent in the decrypted plaintext. Or if $r_2|c_2$ were swapped with $r_7|c_7$, then m_2 and m_7 would be swapped in the result. Worse yet, an attacker knowing the value of any block m_n can change it in a predictable way by making the corresponding change in r_n.

Now we can explain CBC. CBC generates its own "random numbers". It uses c_i as r_{i+1}. In other words, it takes the previous block of ciphertext and uses that as the random number that will be ⊕'d into the next plaintext. To avoid having two plaintext messages that start the same wind up with the same ciphertext in the beginning, CBC does select one random number, which gets ⊕'d into the first block of plaintext, and transmits it along with the data. This initial random number is known as an **IV** (**initialization vector**).

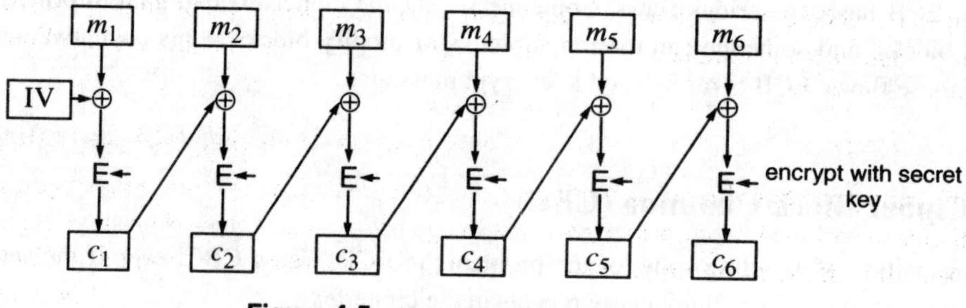

Figure 4-5. Cipher Block Chaining Encryption

Decryption is simple because ⊕ is its own inverse.

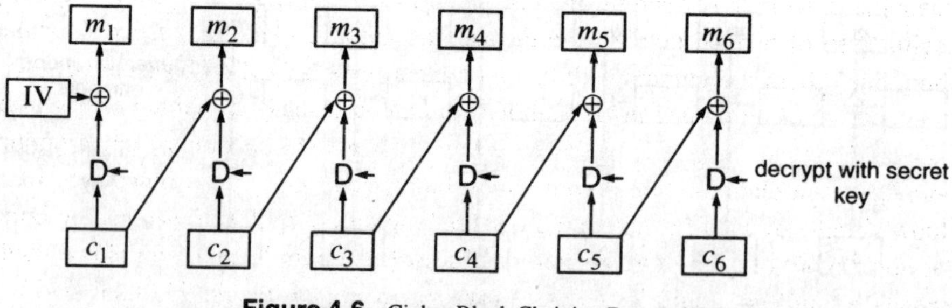

Figure 4-6. Cipher Block Chaining Decryption

Since the cost of the ⊕ is trivial compared to the cost of an encryption, CBC encryption has the same performance as ECB encryption except for the cost of generating and transmitting the IV.

In many cases the security of CBC would not be adversely affected by omitting the IV (or, equivalently, using the value 0 as the IV). However, we'll give one example where it would matter. Suppose the encrypted file of employees and salaries is transmitted weekly. If there were no IV, then an eavesdropper could tell where the ciphertext first differed from the previous week, and therefore perhaps determine the first person whose salary had changed.

Another example is where a general sends information each day saying continue holding your position. The ciphertext will be the same every day, until the general decides to send something else, like start bombing. Then the ciphertext would suddenly change, alerting the enemy.

A randomly chosen IV guarantees that even if the same message is sent repeatedly, the ciphertext will be completely different each time.

Finally, a randomly chosen IV prevents attackers from supplying chosen plaintext to the underlying encryption algorithm even if they can supply chosen plaintext to the CBC.

4.2.2.1 CBC Threat 1—Modifying Ciphertext Blocks

Using CBC does not eliminate the problem of someone modifying the message in transit; it does change the nature of the threat. Attackers can no longer see repeated values and simply copy or move ciphertext blocks in order to, say, swap the janitor's salary with the salary of the VP of marketing. But they certainly can still modify the ciphertext. What would happen if they changed a block of the ciphertext, say the value of ciphertext block c_n? c_n gets ⊕'d with the decrypted c_{n+1} to yield m_{n+1}, so changing c_n has a predictable effect on m_{n+1}. For instance, changing bit 3 of c_n changes bit 3 of m_{n+1}. c_n also gets decrypted, and then ⊕'d with c_{n-1} to produce m_n. Our attacker cannot know what a particular new value of c_n would decrypt to, so changing c_n will most likely garble m_n to some random 64-bit value.

For example, let's say our attacker knows that the plaintext corresponding to a certain byte range in the ciphertext is her personnel record:

```
Tacker, Jo A          System Security Officer          54,122.10
|         |        |        |        |        |        |        |
```

Let's say Jo wants to increase her salary by 20K. In this case she knows that the final byte of m_7 is the ten-thousands digit of her salary. The bottom three bits of the ASCII for 5 is 101. To give herself a raise of 20K, she merely has to flip the penultimate bit of c_6. Since c_6 gets ⊕'d into the decrypted c_7 (c_7 has not been modified, so the decrypted c_7 will be the same), the result will be the same as before, i.e. the old m_7, but with the penultimate bit flipped, which will change the ASCII 5 into a 7.

Unfortunately for Jo, as a side-effect a value she will not be able to predict will appear in her department field, since she cannot predict what the modified c_6 will decrypt to, which will affect m_6:

```
Tacker, Jo A          System Security Of#f8Ts9(*          74,122.10
     |       |       |       |       |       |       |       |
```

A human who reads this report and issues checks is likely to suspect something is wrong; however, if it's just a program, it would be perfectly happy with it. And a bank would most likely take the check even if some unorthodox information appeared in what to them is a comment field.

In the above example, Jo made a change she could control in one block at the expense of getting a value she could neither control nor predict in the preceding block.

4.2.2.2 CBC Threat 2—Rearranging Ciphertext Blocks

Suppose Jo knows the plaintext and corresponding ciphertext of some message. So she knows $m_1, m_2, \ldots m_n$. And she knows IV, $c_1, c_2, \ldots c_n$. She will also know what each of the c_i decrypt to,

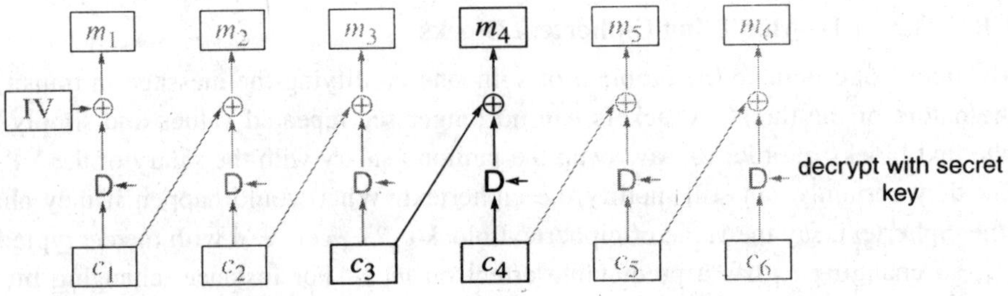

Figure 4-7. Cipher Block Chaining Decryption

since the decrypted version of c_i is $c_{i-1} \oplus m_i$ (see Figure 4-7).

Given this knowledge, she can consider each of the c_i as a *building block* and construct a ciphertext stream using any combination of c_i and she will be able to calculate what the corresponding plaintext would be.

How could this be useful? Well, admittedly it's stretching a bit, though people in the security field enjoy stretching. One of the ways to combat threat 1 is to attach a CRC to the plaintext before encrypting it with CBC. That way if Jo modifies any of the ciphertext blocks, the CRC will not match the message and a computer can verify that the message has been tampered with.

Still following? Well, suppose a 32-bit CRC is chosen. Then there is a 1 in 2^{32} chance that the CRC will happen to be correct after the message is tampered with. Suppose Jo doesn't care what she garbles the message to. She just wants the garbage accepted by the computer on the other side, knowing that it will check the CRC. Jo can try constructing lots of ciphertext streams out of c_1, $c_2, \ldots c_n$, calculate the resulting plaintext from each one, and then test the resulting plaintext to see if the CRC comes out correct. On the average she will only have to try 2^{31} arrangements before being able to find a message that will have a correct CRC.

What harm could Jo do by garbling a message into something she could not control the contents of, but would be accepted by the computer on the other side? Perhaps Jo is just being malicious, and wants to destroy some data being loaded across the network. But there is a subtle way in which Jo can actually control the garbling of the message to a small extent. Suppose she moves contiguous blocks; for instance, she might move c_n and c_{n+1} to some other place. Then the original m_{n+1} will appear in that other position. Perhaps if m_{n+1} contains the president's salary, Jo can swap blocks so that her salary will be changed to his, but then she'll be forced to pretty much totally garble the entire rest of the file in order to find an arrangement of blocks that will result in a correct CRC.

To prevent Jo from being able to rearrange blocks to find something that will have a correct CRC, a 64-bit CRC could be used. This would certainly suffice if the only attack on the CRC inside CBC encoding was a brute force attack such as we described. There have been some interesting attacks suggested in the theoretical community [JUEN84] though these attacks are not practical. An encryption mode that protects both the confidentiality and the authenticity of a message using a single cryptographic pass over the data has been the holy grail of cryptographic protocol design for many years, with many proposals subsequently discredited. There are some new ones that look promising (for example, see §4.3.5 *Offset Codebook Mode (OCB)*), but none has been formally standardized.

4.2.3 Output Feedback Mode (OFB)

Output feedback mode is a stream cipher. Encryption is performed by ⊕ing the message with the one-time pad generated by OFB.

Let's assume that the stream is created 64 bits at a time. To start, a random 64-bit number is generated, known as the IV (as in CBC mode). Let's call that b_0. Then b_0 is encrypted (using the secret key) to get b_1, which is in turn encrypted to get b_2, and so forth. The resulting one-time pad is $b_0|b_1|b_2|b_3|\ldots$.

To encrypt a message, merely ⊕ it with as many bits of $b_0|b_1|b_2|b_3|\ldots$ as necessary. The result is transmitted along with the IV. The recipient computes the same one-time pad based on knowledge of the secret key and the IV. To decrypt the message, the recipient merely ⊕s it with as many bits of $b_0|b_1|b_2|b_3|\ldots$ as necessary.

The advantages of a system like this are:

1. The one-time pad can be generated in advance, before the message to be encrypted is known. When the message arrives to be encrypted, no costly cryptographic operations are needed. Instead only ⊕ is required, and ⊕ is extremely fast.

2. If some of the bits of the ciphertext get garbled, only those bits of plaintext get garbled, as opposed to in CBC mode where if c_n is garbled then m_n will be completely garbled and the same portion of m_{n+1} as was garbled in c_n will be garbled.
3. A message can arrive in arbitrarily sized chunks, and each time a chunk appears, the associated ciphertext can be immediately transmitted. In contrast, with CBC, if the message is arriving a byte at a time, it cannot be encrypted until an entire 64-bit block of plaintext is available for encryption. This results in either waiting until 7 more bytes arrive, or padding the plaintext to a multiple of 8 bytes before encrypting it, which yields more ciphertext to be transmitted and decrypted.

The disadvantages of OFB are:

1. If the plaintext and ciphertext are known by a bad guy, he can modify the plaintext into anything he wants by simply ⊕ing the ciphertext with the known plaintext, and ⊕ing the result with whatever message he wants to transmit.

The FIPS document specifies OFB as being capable of being generated in *k*-bit chunks. The description above would be equivalent to 64-bit OFB as documented in [DES81]. The way *k*-bit OFB (see Figure 4-10) works is as follows. The input to the DES encrypt function is initialized to some IV. If the IV is less than 64 bits long, it is padded with 0's on the left (most significant portion). The output will be a 64-bit quantity. Only *k* bits are used, which happen to be specified in [DES81] as the most significant *k* bits. Cryptographically, any *k* bits would do, though it is nice to standardize which bits will be selected so that implementations will interoperate. So, we've generated the first *k* bits of the one-time pad. Now the same *k* bits are shifted into the rightmost portion of the input, and what was in that register is shifted *k* bits to the left. Now *k* more bits of one-time pad are selected, as before.

4.2.4 Cipher Feedback Mode (CFB)

CFB (see Figure 4-9) is very similar to OFB, in that *k* bits at a time are generated and ⊕'d with *k* bits of plaintext. In OFB the *k* bits that are shifted into the register used as the input to the DES encrypt are the output bits of the DES encrypt from the previous block. In contrast, in CFB, the *k* bits shifted in are the *k* bits of ciphertext from the previous block. So in CFB the one-time pad cannot be generated before the message is known (as it can be in OFB).

It is sensible to have *k*-bit CFB with *k* something other than 64, and in particular $k = 8$ makes sense. With OFB or CBC, if characters are lost in transmission, or extra characters are added to the ciphertext stream, the entire rest of the transmission is garbled. With 8-bit CFB, as long as the error is an integral number of bytes, things will resynchronize. If a byte is lost in transmission, one byte of plaintext will be lost and the next 8 bytes will be garbled. However, after that, the plaintext will

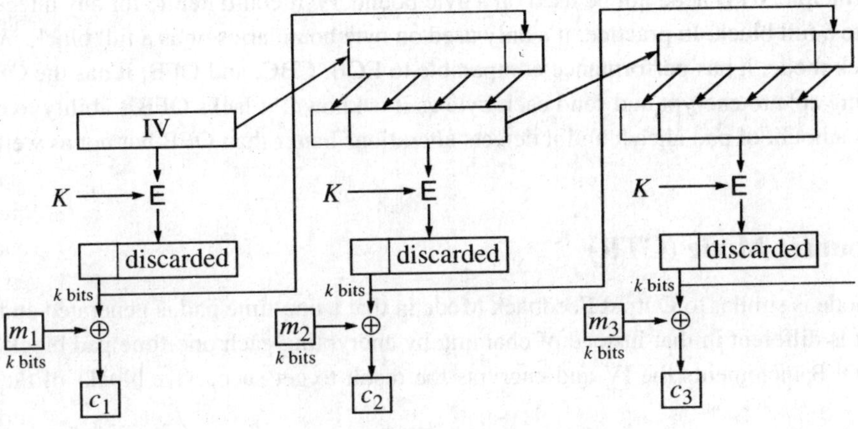

Figure 4-8. *k*-bit OFB

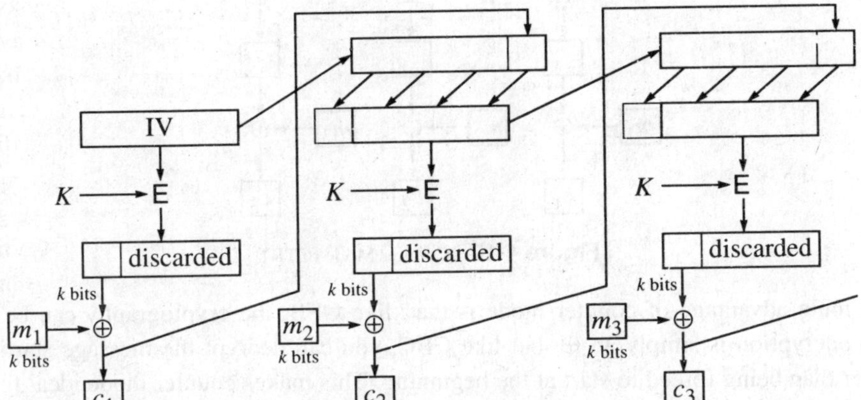

Figure 4-9. *k*-bit CFB

decrypt properly. If a byte is added to the ciphertext stream, then a byte of garbage will be added to the plaintext stream, and the following 8 bytes of plaintext will be garbled, but after that it will decrypt properly. It does have the disadvantage that every byte of input requires a DES operation.

CFB-encrypted messages are somewhat less subject to tampering than either CBC or OFB. With 8-bit CFB it is possible for an attacker to change any individual byte of plaintext in a predictable way at the cost of unpredictably garbling the next 8 bytes. With 64-bit CFB it is possible for an attacker to modify any 64-bit block in a predictable way at the cost of unpredictably garbling the next 64-bit block. There is no block-rearranging attack as with CBC, though whole sections of the message can be rearranged at the cost of garbling the splice points.

In principle, CFB need not be used on a byte boundary. It could iterate for any integer number of bits up to a full block. In practice, it's only used on byte boundaries or as a full block. When done in full-block mode, it has performance comparable to ECB, CBC, and OFB; it has the OFB advantage of being able to encrypt and send each byte as it is known; it lacks OFB's ability to compute a substantial amount of pad ahead; and it detects alterations better than OFB but not as well as CBC.

4.2.5 Counter Mode (CTR)

Counter mode is similar to Output Feedback Mode in that a one-time pad is generated and ⊕'d with the data. It is different in that instead of chaining by encrypting each one-time pad block to get the next one, OFB increments the IV and encrypts the result to get successive blocks of the one-time pad.

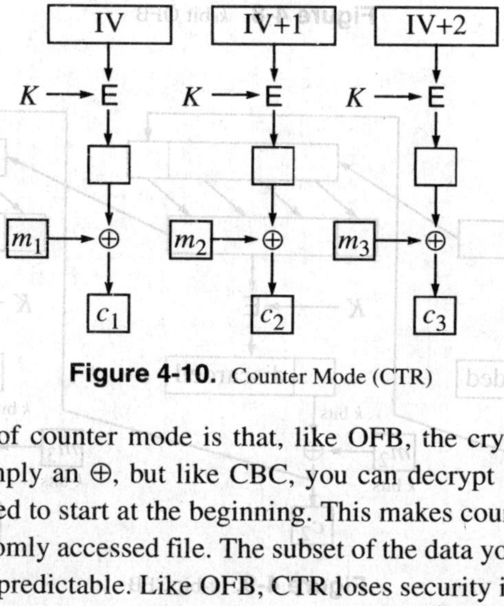

Figure 4-10. Counter Mode (CTR)

The main advantage of counter mode is that, like OFB, the cryptography can be pre-computed and encryption is simply an ⊕, but like CBC, you can decrypt the message starting at any point rather than being forced to start at the beginning. This makes counter mode ideal for applications like encrypting a randomly accessed file. The subset of the data you will need and the order in which you will need it is unpredictable. Like OFB, CTR loses security if different data is encrypted with the same key and IV. An attacker could get the ⊕ of two plaintext blocks by taking the ⊕ of the two corresponding ciphertext blocks.

4.3 GENERATING MACS

A secret key system can be used to generate a cryptographic checksum known as a MAC (message authentication code). A synonym for MAC is MIC (Message Integrity Code). The term MAC seems to be more popular though MIC is sometimes used, for instance in PEM (see §21.15.3 *MIC-ONLY or MIC-CLEAR, Public Key Variant*). While CBC, CFB, OFB, and CTR, when properly used, all offer good protection against an eavesdropper deciphering a message, none offers good protection against an eavesdropper who already knows the contents of the plaintext message modifying it undetected.

A standard way for protecting against undetected modifications is to compute the CBC but send only the last block along with the plaintext message. This last block is called the **CBC residue**. In order to compute the CBC residue, you have to know the secret key. If an attacker modifies any portion of a message, the residue will no longer be the correct value (except with probability 1 in 2^{64}). And the attacker will not be able to compute the residue for the modified message without knowing the secret key.

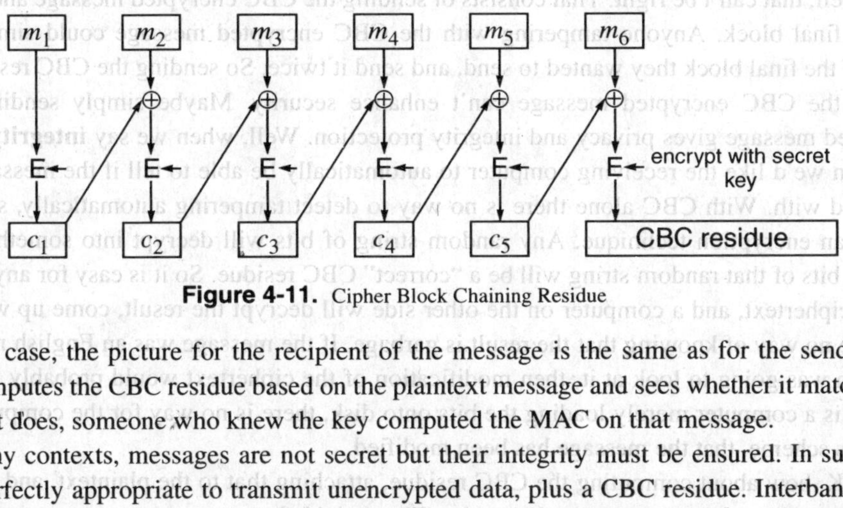

Figure 4-11. Cipher Block Chaining Residue

In this case, the picture for the recipient of the message is the same as for the sender. The recipient computes the CBC residue based on the plaintext message and sees whether it matches the one sent. If it does, someone who knew the key computed the MAC on that message.

In many contexts, messages are not secret but their integrity must be ensured. In such contexts it is perfectly appropriate to transmit unencrypted data, plus a CBC residue. Interbank transfers are a traditional example (there may be a desire for secrecy as well, but it is dwarfed by the requirement for accuracy). But more commonly, there is a desire to encrypt messages for both privacy and integrity. This can be done with a single encryption operation if the message is a single block. What is the equivalent transformation on a multiblock message? (Keep reading to find out!)

4.3.1 Ensuring Privacy and Integrity Together

To summarize, if we have a message and we want to ensure its privacy, we can CBC-encrypt the message. If we have a message and we want to ensure its integrity, then we can send the CBC residue along with the message. It is natural to assume that if we want to be secure against both modification and eavesdropping that we ought to be able to do something like Figure 4-12.

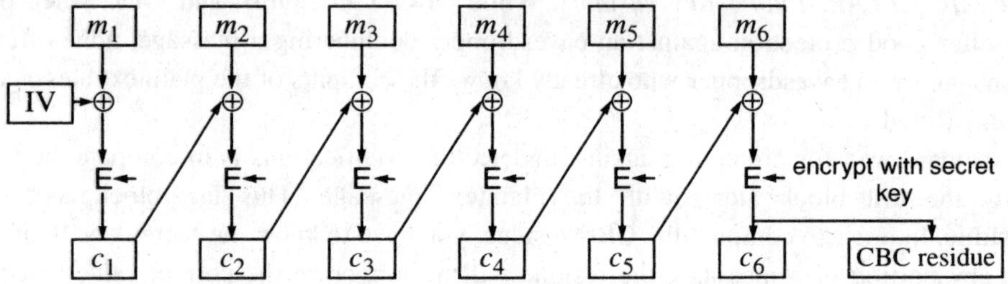

Figure 4-12. Cipher Block Chaining Encryption plus CBC Residue

Well, that can't be right. That consists of sending the CBC encrypted message and just repeating the final block. Anyone tampering with the CBC encrypted message could simply take the value of the final block they wanted to send, and send it twice. So sending the CBC residue in addition to the CBC encrypted message can't enhance security. Maybe simply sending the CBC encrypted message gives privacy and integrity protection. Well, when we say **integrity protection** we mean we'd like the receiving computer to automatically be able to tell if the message has been tampered with. With CBC alone there is no way to detect tampering automatically, since CBC is merely an encryption technique. Any random string of bits will decrypt into something, and the final 64 bits of that random string will be a "correct" CBC residue. So it is easy for anyone to modify the ciphertext, and a computer on the other side will decrypt the result, come up with garbage, but have no way of knowing that the result is garbage. If the message was an English message, and a human was going to look at it, then modification of the ciphertext would probably get detected, but if it is a computer merely loading the bits onto disk, there is no way for the computer to know, with this scheme, that the message has been modified.

OK, how about computing the CBC residue, attaching that to the plaintext, and then doing a CBC encryption of the concatenated quantity (Figure 4-13)?

It turns out that that doesn't work either. The last block is always the encryption of zero, since the ⊕ of anything with itself is always zero. An extra block that doesn't depend on the message can't offer any integrity protection.

Let's try one more. Suppose we compute a non-cryptographic checksum (e.g., a CRC) of the blocks of the message, append that to the end, and encrypt the whole thing (Figure 4-14).

This almost works. Subtle attacks are known if the CRC is short. Longer non-cryptographic checksums are suspect.

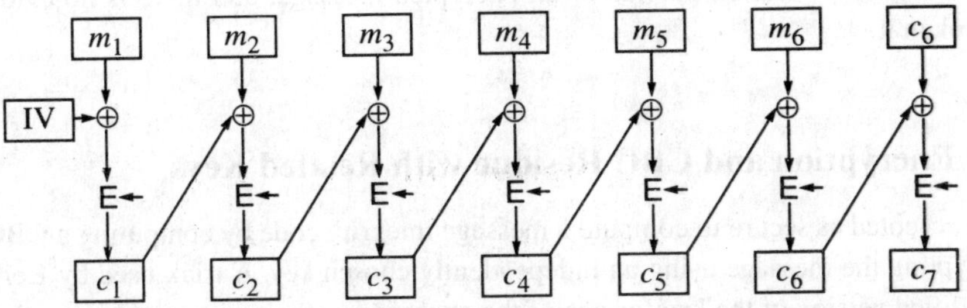

Figure 4-13. Cipher Block Chaining Encryption of Message with CBC Residue

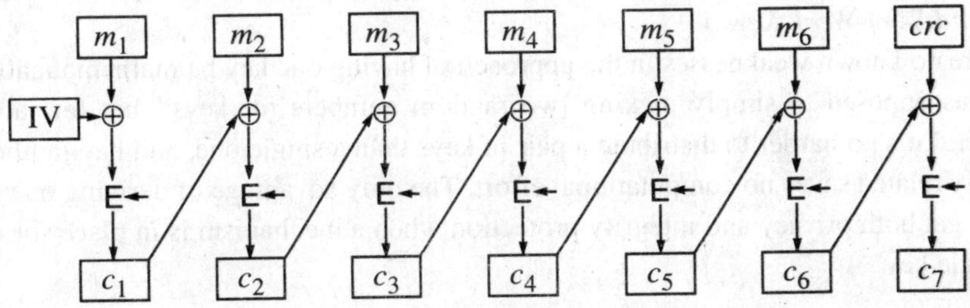

Figure 4-14. Cipher Block Chaining Encryption of Message with CRC

So, what can we do? It is generally accepted as secure to protect the privacy of a message with CBC encryption and integrity with a CBC residue as long as the two are computed with different keys. Unfortunately, this requires twice the cryptographic power of encryption alone. Various shortcuts have been proposed and even deployed, but generally they have subtle cryptographic flaws. Whether those flaws are serious depends on the application and the cleverness of the attacker. It's instructive to look at some of the techniques.

4.3.2 CBC with a Weak Cryptographic Checksum

Jueneman proposed [JUEN84, JUEN85] that since using non-cryptographic checksums inside CBC did not appear to be secure, and since quality cryptographic checksums were expensive to compute, perhaps a "weak" cryptographic checksum inside a CBC would provide good security on the basis that the computational complexity of breaking the weak checksum would be multiplied by the limitations of having to do it under the constraints of the CBC. He proposed a weak cryptographic checksum for this use.

There is no reason to believe that this approach would not be effective, but it has not caught on. Ironically, Kerberos V4 (see §13.10 *Encryption for Integrity Only*) uses a variant of his weak checksum for integrity protection outside of an encrypted message, and there is no evidence that anyone has broken it.

4.3.3 CBC Encryption and CBC Residue with Related Keys

It is generally accepted as secure to compute a message integrity code by computing a CBC residue and then encrypting the message using an independently chosen key. A trick used by Kerberos V5 is to use a modified version of the key for one of the operations. (Switching one bit should be sufficient, but Kerberos instead ⊕s the key with the constant $F0F0F0F0F0F0F0F0_{16}$. This has the nice properties of preserving key parity and never transforming a non-weak key into a weak key. See §3.3.6 *Weak and Semi-Weak Keys*.)

There are no known weaknesses in the approach of having one key be mathematically related to the other (as opposed to simply picking two random numbers for keys), but few advantages either. In general it's no harder to distribute a pair of keys than a single one, and having the keys be mathematically related saves no computational effort. The only advantage of deriving one key from the other is to get both privacy and integrity protection when a mechanism is in place for distributing only a single key.

4.3.4 CBC with a Cryptographic Hash

Another approach is to put a cryptographic hash of the message—typically 128 bits—inside, and CBC encrypt the whole thing. This is probably secure (though it hasn't gotten much use or scrutiny, since modern schemes use a keyed hash). It requires two cryptographic passes (just like doing CBC encryption and CBC residue with different keys), but it is more efficient than doing CBC twice if the hash function is faster than the encryption algorithm.

4.3.5 Offset Codebook Mode (OCB)

OCB is one of several modes that get both encryption and integrity protection while making only a single cryptographic pass over the data. This and similar schemes are too new to have stood the test of time, and there are patent issues hanging over them, but it seems likely that one or more will eventually become the standard way to achieving this effect.

4.4 MULTIPLE ENCRYPTION DES

The generally accepted method of making DES more secure through multiple encryptions is known as **EDE** (for encrypt–decrypt–encrypt) or **3DES**.

Actually, any encryption scheme might be made more secure through multiple encryptions. Multiple encryption, though, has specifically been discussed in the industry in order to arrive at a "standard" means of effectively increasing DES's key length. EDE could as easily be done with, say, IDEA. It is more important with DES than with IDEA, though, because of DES's key length (or lack thereof).

Remember that a cryptographic scheme has two functions, known as *encrypt* and *decrypt*. The two functions are inverses of each other, but in fact each one takes an arbitrary block of data and garbles it in a way that is reversed by the other function. So it makes sense to perform decrypt on the plaintext as a method of encrypting it, and then perform encrypt on the result as a method of getting back to the plaintext again. It might be confusing to say something like *encrypt with decryption*, so we'll just refer to the two functions as E and D.

How to do multiple encryption is not completely obvious, especially since there is also the problem of turning block encryption into stream encryption. The standard method for using EDE is:

1. Two keys are used: K_1 and K_2.
2. Each block of plaintext is subjected to E with K_1, then D with K_2, and then E with K_1. The result is simply a new secret key scheme—a 64-bit block is mapped to another 64-bit block.

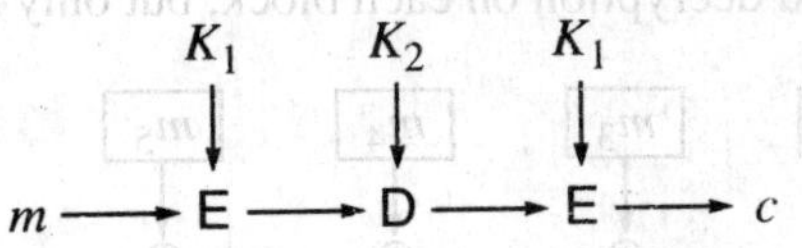

Decryption simply reverses the operation.

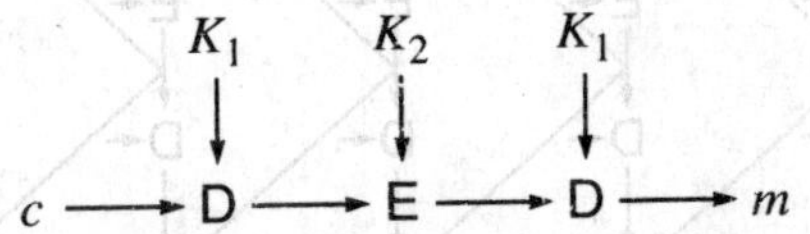

3. CBC is used to turn the block encryption scheme resulting from step 2 into a stream encryption (Figure 4-15).

Now we'll discuss why 3DES is defined this way. There are various choices that could have been made:

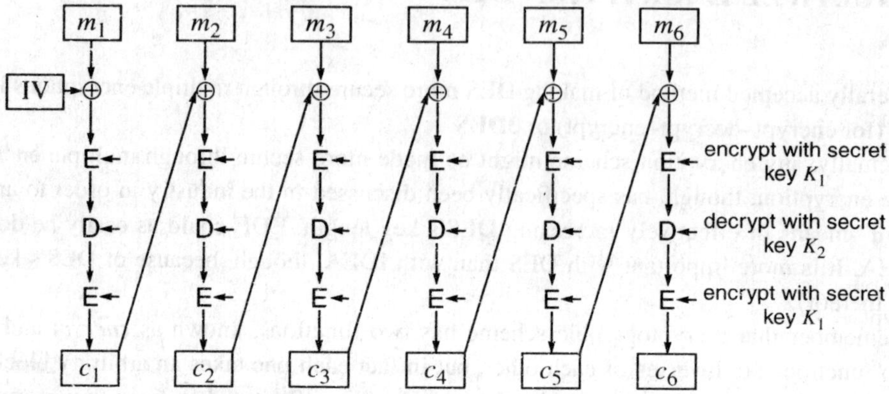

Figure 4-15. EDE with CBC on the Outside (3DES)

1. Three encryptions were chosen. It could have been 2 or 714. Is three the right number?
2. Why are the functions EDE rather than, say, EEE or EDD?
3. Why is the cipher block chaining done on the outside rather than on the inside? Doing CBC on the **inside** (Figure 4-16) means completely encrypting the message with CBC, then completely decrypting the result with CBC using a second key, and then completely CBC-encrypting the message again. Doing CBC on the **outside** (Figure 4-15) means performing the DES encryptions and decryption on each block, but only doing the CBC once.

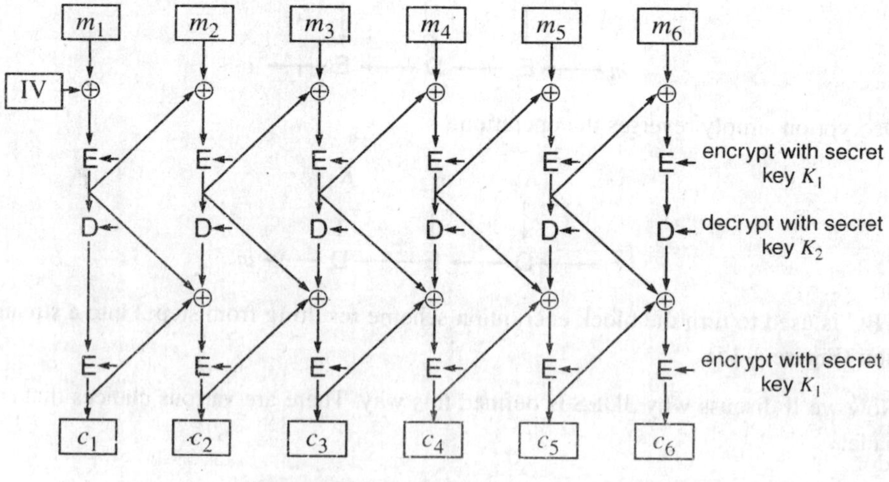

Figure 4-16. EDE with CBC on the Inside

4.4.1 How Many Encryptions?

Let's assume that the more times the block is encrypted, the more secure it is. So encrypting 749 times would therefore be some amount more secure than encrypting 3 times. The problem is, it is expensive to do an encryption. We don't want to do any more encryptions than are necessary for the scheme to be really secure.

4.4.1.1 Encrypting Twice with the Same Key

Suppose we didn't want to bother reading in two keys. Would it make things more secure if we encrypted twice in a row with the same key?

$$\text{plaintext} \xrightarrow{K} \xrightarrow{K} \text{ciphertext}$$

This turns out not to be much more secure than single encryption with K, since exhaustive search of the keyspace still requires searching only 2^{56} keys. Each step of testing a key is twice as much work, since the attacker needs to do double encryption, but a factor of two for the attacker is not considered much added security, especially since the good guys have their work doubled with this scheme as well.

(How about E followed by D using the same key? That's double the work for the good guy and no work for the bad guy, so that's generally not considered good cryptographic form.)

4.4.1.2 Encrypting Twice with Two Keys

If encrypting twice, using two different keys, were as secure as a DES-like scheme with a key length of 112 bits, then encrypting twice would have sufficed. However, it isn't, as we will show.

We'll use two DES keys, K_1 and K_2, and encrypt each block twice, first using key K_1 and then using key K_2. For the moment, let's ignore any block chaining schemes and assume we're just doing block encryption.

$$\text{plaintext} \xrightarrow{K_1} \xrightarrow{K_2} \text{ciphertext}$$

Is this as cryptographically strong as using a double-length secret key (112 bits)? The reason you might think it would be as strong as a 112-bit key is that the straightforward brute-force attack would have to guess both K_1 and K_2 in order to determine if a particular plaintext block encrypted to a particular ciphertext block.

However, there is a less straightforward attack that breaks double-encryption DES in roughly twice the time of a brute-force breaking of single-encryption DES. The attack is not particularly practical, but the fact that it exists makes double encryption sufficiently suspect that it's not generally done.

The threat involves the following steps:

1. Assume you have a few ⟨plaintext,ciphertext⟩ pairs $\langle m_1,c_1\rangle$, $\langle m_2,c_2\rangle$, $\langle m_3,c_3\rangle$ where c_i was derived from doubly encrypting m_i with K_1 and K_2. You want to find K_1 and K_2.
2. First make Table A with 2^{56} entries, where each entry consists of a DES key K and the result r of applying that key to encrypt m_1. Sort the table in numerical order by r.
3. Now make Table B with 2^{56} entries, where each entry consists of a DES key K and the result r of applying that key to decrypt c_1. Sort the table in numerical order by r.
4. Search through the sorted lists to find matching entries, $\langle K_A,r\rangle$ from table A and $\langle K_B,r\rangle$ from Table B. Each match provides K_A as a candidate K_1 and K_B as a candidate K_2 because K_A encrypts m_1 to r and K_B encrypts r to c_1.
5. If there are multiple intermediate values (which there almost certainly will be), test the candidate K_1 and K_2 against m_2 and c_2. If you've tested all the candidate $\langle K_1,K_2\rangle$ pairs and multiple of them work on m_2 and c_2, then try m_3 and c_3. The correct pair will always work, of course, and an incorrect pair will almost certainly fail to work on any particular $\langle m_i,c_i\rangle$ pair. (See below for exact numbers, if you care.)

This attack is not really practical, since a table of size 2^{56} is a bit daunting. The existence of the attack, though, is enough reason to bother doing triple DES encryption. It may be that double encryption would be good enough, but since triple encryption isn't that much harder, it will save you from defending yourself to management when they ask you why you're doing double encryption when they've heard that double encryption isn't secure.

How many matches should you expect to find after searching the two tables? Well, there are 2^{64} possible blocks, and only 2^{56} table entries in each table (because there are only 2^{56} keys). Therefore each 64-bit block has only a 1 in 256 chance of appearing in each of the tables. Of the 2^{56} blocks that appear in Table A, only 1/256 of them also appear in Table B. That means that there should be about 2^{48} entries which appear in both tables. One of those corresponds to the correct $\langle K_1,K_2\rangle$ pair and the others are imposters. We'll test them against $\langle m_2,c_2\rangle$. If $\langle K_1,K_2\rangle$ is an imposter, the probability that $D(c_2,K_2)$ will equal $E(m_2,K_1)$ is about $1/2^{64}$. There are about 2^{48} imposters, so the probability of one of them satisfying $D(c_2,K_2) = E(m_2,K_1)$ is about $2^{48}/2^{64}$, or roughly 1 in 2^{16}. Each test against an additional $\langle m_i,c_i\rangle$ reduces the probability by a factor of 2^{64}, so the probability that there will still be false matches after trying three $\langle m, c\rangle$ pairs is about $1/2^{80}$.

4.4.1.3 Triple Encryption with only Two Keys

3DES does triple encryption. Why does 3DES use only two keys? Presumably, security cannot possibly be enhanced because K_1 is used twice rather than using a third key. People believe using K_1 twice in this way is sufficiently secure that there's no reason to bother generating, transmitting, and storing a third key. For avoiding the brute-force exhaustive key space attack, 112 bits of key is considered sufficient, and no attacks other than the straightforward brute-force search is known for EDE. Some systems do implement 3DES with three independent keys, but this is not the standard.

An esoteric reason for using only two keys is that in some applications (like §5.2.4.1 *UNIX Password Hash*) an important property of a cryptosystem is that given a ⟨plaintext, ciphertext⟩ pair, it is impractical to find any key that maps the plaintext to the ciphertext. (With 64-bit blocks and 112-bit keys, there will be lots of such keys.) Using EDE with three keys, it is straightforward to find a triple of keys that maps a given plaintext to a given ciphertext (Homework Problem 4). There is no known practical way of finding such a triple with $K_1 = K_3$.

Why is K_2 used in decrypt mode? Admittedly, it is no more trouble to run DES in either mode, and either way gives a mapping. DES would be just as good always done backwards (i.e., swap *encrypt* and *decrypt*). One reason for the choice of EDE is that an EDE system with $K_1 = K_2$ is equivalent to simple DES, so that such a system can interoperate with a simple DES system. Another reason to do EDE rather than EEE is that if E is followed by E, then the initial permutation before the second E will reverse the final permutation after the first E. As we said in §3.3 2 *The Permutations of the Data*, there is no security value in the initial or final permutation, at least when a single encryption is done. However, there might conceivably be some security gained by having a permutation done between encryption steps. Doing E followed by D results in doing the final permutation twice, once after E and once at the beginning of D. Doing the final permutation twice results in some permutation (Homework Problem 7). Likewise, doing D followed by E results in doing the initial permutation twice.

4.4.2 CBC Outside vs. Inside

To review, the 3DES commonly used in the industry (and defined in §4.4 *Multiple Encryption DES*) does CBC on the outside, which means that each block is triply encrypted, and the CBC is done on the triply encrypted block (see Figure 4-15). The alternative would be to completely encrypt the message with K_1 and CBC, and then take the result and completely decrypt it with K_2 and CBC, and then take the result and completely encrypt it with K_1 (see Figure 4-16).

What are the implications of this choice?

As shown in §4.2.2.1 *CBC Threat 1—Modifying Ciphertext Blocks*, with CBC it is possible to make a predictable change to plaintext block n, for instance flipping bit x, by flipping bit x in ciphertext block n–1. There is a side-effect, though, of completely garbling plaintext block n–1. Whether an attacker can use this for nefarious purposes depends on the exact application.

With CBC done on the outside, an attacker can still do the same attack. The fact that the encryption scheme involves triple use of DES does not change the effects of CBC. An attacker that flips bit x in ciphertext block n–1 will completely and unpredictably (to the attacker) garble plaintext block n–1. However, plaintext block n will have bit x flipped. And all plaintext blocks other than n–1 and n will be unaffected.

With CBC done on the inside, any change to ciphertext block n completely and unpredictably garbles all plaintext blocks from n to the end of the message. This makes CBC done on the inside more secure, and perhaps would therefore have been a better choice. However, sometimes people would prefer if garbling of a ciphertext block did not garble the entire rest of the message. They'd prefer that the encryption scheme be **self-synchronizing**, which means that after some small number of garbled blocks, the plaintext will start decrypting properly again. There are also subtle security flaws with CBC on the inside if the attacker can supply chosen plaintext and IV and examine the output.

Another advantage of CBC on the inside is performance. With CBC on the inside it is possible to use three times as much hardware and pipeline the encryptions so that it is as fast as single encryption. With CBC on the outside, this is not possible.

One reason that people choose CBC on the outside despite its disadvantages is that EDE encryption can be considered a new secret key block encryption scheme that uses a 112-bit key. This can then be used with any of the chaining methods (OFB, ECB, CFB, CTR, as well as CBC).

4.5 HOMEWORK

1. What pseudo-random block stream is generated by 64-bit OFB with a weak DES key?
2. The pseudo-random stream of blocks generated by 64-bit OFB must eventually repeat (since at most 2^{64} different blocks can be generated). Will $K\{IV\}$ necessarily be the first block to be repeated?
3. Let's assume you do DES double encryption by encrypting with K_1 and doing DES in decrypt mode with K_2. Does the same attack work as with double encryption with K_1 and K_2? If not, how could it be made to work?
4. What is a practical method for finding a triple of keys that maps a given plaintext to a given ciphertext using EDE? Hint: It is like the meet-in-the-middle attack of §4.4.1.2 *Encrypting Twice with Two Keys*.
5. Let's assume that someone does triple encryption by using EEE with CBC on the inside. Suppose an attacker modifies bit x of ciphertext block n. How does this affect the decrypted plaintext?
6. Consider the following alternative method of encrypting a message. To encrypt a message, use the algorithm for doing a CBC decrypt. To decrypt a message, use the algorithm for doing

a CBC encrypt. Would this work? What are the security implications of this, if any, as contrasted with the "normal" CBC?

7. Give the first 16 values of the permutation formed by doing the DES initial permutation twice (as happens when ED is performed).

5 HASHES AND MESSAGE DIGESTS

5.1 INTRODUCTION

Random numbers should not be generated with a method chosen at random.
—Donald Knuth

A hash (also known as a **message digest**) is a **one-way function**. It is considered a **function** because it takes an input message and produces an output. It is considered **one-way** because it's not practical to figure out what input corresponds to a given output. For a message digest function to be considered cryptographically secure, it must be computationally infeasible to find a message that has a given prespecified message digest, and it similarly should be impossible to find two messages that have the same message digest. Also (which follows from the previous properties), given a message it should be impossible to find a different message with the same message digest.

We will use the terms *hash* and *message digest* interchangeably. The NIST message digest function is called **SHA-1**, which stands for **secure hash algorithm**, whereas the *MD* in the MD2, MD4, and MD5 algorithms stands for *message digest*. All of the digest/hash algorithms do basically the same thing, which is to take an arbitrary-length message and wind up with a fixed-length quantity.

There's an intuitive notion of **randomness** that is important to the understanding of message digest functions. We are not trying to create a math book, so our description will be mathematically imprecise. We are merely trying to capture the intuition. We explained before that with secret key cryptography, it is desirable for the mapping from input to output to appear randomly chosen. In other words, it should look (to someone who does not know the secret key) like someone flipped coins to determine, for each possible input, what the output should be. Examples of what this means are:

- If 1000 inputs are selected at random, any particular bit in the 1000 resulting outputs should be on about half the time.

- Each output should have, with high probability, about half the bits on.
- Any two outputs should be completely uncorrelated, no matter how similar the inputs are. So for instance, two inputs that differ by only one bit should have outputs that look like completely independently chosen random numbers. About half the bits in the two outputs should differ.

This sort of randomness is important for message digests as well. It is true that someone who knows the message and the digest function can calculate the output, and therefore the output is certainly provably not generated by flipping coins. But ignoring that, the output should look random. It should not be possible, other than by computing the message digest, to predict any portion of the output. And in particular it should be true that, for any subset of bits in the message digest, the only way of obtaining two messages with the same value in those bits would be to try messages at random and compute the message digest of each until two happened to have the same value. Given this property, a secure message digest function with n bits should be derivable from a message digest function with more than n bits merely by taking any particular subset of n bits from the larger message digest.

There certainly will be many messages that yield the same message digest, because a message can be of arbitrary length and the message digest will be some fixed length, for instance 128 bits. For instance, for 1000-bit messages and a 128-bit message digest, there are on the average 2^{872} messages that map to any one particular message digest. So certainly, by trying lots of messages, one would eventually find two that mapped to the same message digest. The problem is that "lots" is so many that it is essentially impossible. Assuming a good 128-bit message digest function, it would take trying approximately 2^{128} possible messages before one would find a message that mapped to a particular message digest, or approximately 2^{64} messages before finding two that had the same digest (see *The Birthday Problem*, below).

An example use of a message digest is to **fingerprint** a program or document to detect modification of it. If you know the message digest of the program (and store the message digest securely so that it can't be modified, and compute the message digest of the program before running it, and check to make sure that it matches the stored value), then nobody will be able to modify the program without being detected, because they will not be able to find a different program with the same message digest.

How many bits does the output of a message digest function have to be in order to prevent someone from being able to find two messages with the same message digest? Well, if the message digest has m bits, then it would take only about $2^{m/2}$ messages, chosen at random, before one would find two with the same value. So if there were a 64-bit message digest function, it would only take searching 2^{32} messages before one could find two with the same value, and it is feasible to search 2^{32} messages. That is why message digest functions have outputs of at least 128 bits, because it is not considered feasible to search 2^{64} messages given the current state of the art.

The Birthday Problem

If there are 23 or more people in a room, the odds are better than 50% that two of them will have the same birthday. Analyzing this parlor trick can give us some insight into cryptography. We'll assume that a birthday is basically an unpredictable function taking a human to one of 365 values (yeah yeah, 366 for you nerds).

Let's do this in a slightly more general way. Let's assume n inputs (which would be humans in the birthday example) and k possible outputs, and an unpredictable mapping from input to output. With n inputs, there are $n(n-1)/2$ pairs of inputs. For each pair there's a probability of $1/k$ of both inputs producing the same output value, so you'll need about $k/2$ pairs in order for the probability to be about 50% that you'll find a matching pair. That means that if n is greater than $\sqrt{k}$, there's a good chance of finding a matching pair.

If cryptographers were happy with message digest functions that merely made it infeasible to find a message with a particular prespecified digest (rather than being worried about being able to find any pair with the same digest), then a 64-bit digest would suffice.

Why are we worried about someone being able to find any two messages with the same message digest, instead of only worrying about finding a message with a particular prespecified message digest? In most applications, to subvert a system an attacker has to find a misleading message whose message digest matches that of a pre-existing message. However, there are cases where being able to find two messages with the same message digest is a threat to the security of the system.

Suppose Alice wants to fire Fred, and asks her diabolical secretary, Bob, who happens to be Fred's friend, to compose a letter explaining that Fred should be fired, and why. After Bob writes the letter, Alice will read it, compute a message digest, and cryptographically sign the message digest using her private key. Bob would like to instead write a letter saying that Fred is wonderful and his salary ought to be doubled. However, Bob cannot generate a message digest signed with Alice's key. If he can find two messages with the same message digest, one that Alice will look at and agree to sign because it captures what she'd like it to say, and one that says what Bob would like it to say, then Bob can substitute his own message after Alice generates the signed message digest.

Suppose the message digest function has only 64 bits, and is a good message digest function in the sense of its output looking random. Then the only way to find two messages with the same message digest would be by trying enough messages so that by the birthday problem two would have the same digest.

If Bob started by writing a letter that Alice would approve of, found the message digest of that, and then attempted to find a different message with that message digest, he'd have to try 2^{64}

different messages. However, suppose he had a way of generating lots of messages of each type (type 1—those that Alice would be willing to sign; type 2—those that Bob would like to send). Then by the birthday problem he'd only have to try about 2^{32} messages of each type before he found two that matched. (See Homework Problem 3.)

How can Bob possibly generate that many letters, especially since they'd all have to make sense to a human? Well, suppose there are 2 choices of wording in each of 32 places in the letter. Then there are 2^{32} possible messages he can generate. For example:

Type 1 message

I am writing {this memo | } to {demand | request | inform you} that {Fred | Mr. Fred Jones} {must | } be {fired | terminated} {at once | immediately}. As the {July 11 | 11 July} {memo | memoranaum} {from | issued by} {personnel | human resources} states, to meet {our | the corporate} {quarterly | third quarter} budget {targets | goals}, {we must eliminate all discretionary spending | all discretionary spending must be eliminated}.

{Despite | Ignoring} that {memo | memorandum | order}, Fred {ordered | purchased} {PostIts | nonessential supplies} in a flagrant disregard for the company's {budgetary crisis | current financial difficulties}.

Type 2 message

I am writing {this letter | this memo | this memorandum | } to {officially | } commend Fred {Jones | } for his {courage and independent thinking | independent thinking and courage}. {He | Fred} {clearly | } understands {the need | how} to get {the | his} job {done | accomplished} {at all costs | by whatever means nécessary}, and {knows | can see} when to ignore bureaucratic {nonsense | impediments}. I {am hereby recommending | hereby recommend} {him | Fred} for {promotion | immediate advancement} and {further | } recommend a {hefty | large} {salary | compensation} increase.

There are enough computer-generatable variants of the two letters that Bob can compute message digests on the various variants until he finds a match. It is within computational feasibility to generate and test on the order of 2^{32} messages, whereas it would not be feasible to deal with 2^{64} messages.

As we will see in Chapter 6 *Public Key Algorithms*, the math behind RSA and other public key cryptographic algorithms is quite understandable. In contrast, message digest functions are like alchemy. It's a bunch of steps that each mangle the message more and more. The functions sound like a bunch of people got together and each person had some idea for mangling the message further. "And now let's swap every bit with the complement of the bit 11 bits to the right!" "How about let's multiply every set of 12 adjacent bits by the constant 384729?" "How about we throw in *I*(*newt*)?" And every suggestion is adopted by the group. It is possible to follow all the steps, but the incomprehensible part is why this particular shuffling of the message is done, and why it couldn't be simpler and yet just as secure.

A plausible way of constructing a message digest function is to combine lots of perverse operations into a potential message digest function, and then play with it. If any patterns are detected in the output the function is rejected, or perhaps more perverse operations are folded into it.

Ideally, the message digest function should be easy to compute. One wonders what the "minimal" secure message digest function might be. It is safer for a function to be overkill, in the sense of shuffling beyond what it necessary, but then it is harder to compute than necessary. The designers would rather waste computation than discover later that the function was not secure. Just as with secret key algorithms, the digest algorithms tend to be computed in rounds. It is likely that the designers find the smallest number of rounds necessary before the output passes various randomness tests, and then do a few more just to be safe.

There is an interesting bit of folklore in the choice of constants in cryptographic algorithms. Often a "random number" is needed. If the designer of the algorithm chooses a specific number without explanation as to where that number came from, people are suspicious that there might be some hidden flaw that the designer of the algorithm wishes to exploit, and will be able to because the designer knows some hidden properties of that choice of number. Therefore, often the algorithm designers specify how they chose a particular random number. It is often done based on the digits of π or some other irrational number. There was also a book published in the 1930s of random numbers generated from a mechanically random source. People have used some of the numbers in that as well on the theory that cryptography was not well understood then so it is inconceivable that someone could have planted special numbers.

At the end of this chapter we'll describe the major hash functions which have been proposed as standards. Ron Rivest designed MD2, MD4, and MD5. These are all documented in RFCs (1319, 1320, and 1321). In MD2 all operations are done with octets (the microprocessors at the time operated on octets), whereas the other standards operate on 32-bit words (today's microprocessors efficiently compute with 32-bit quantities). In fact, now that there are 64-bit microprocessors, it's quite possible a new MD algorithm optimized for that architecture will be developed.

5.2 NIFTY THINGS TO DO WITH A HASH

Before we look at the details of several popular hash algorithms, let's look at some interesting uses of hash algorithms. Surprisingly, if there is a shared secret, the hash algorithms can be used in all the ways that secret cryptography is used. It is a little confusing calling the schemes in the next few sections "message digest" schemes, since they do involve a shared secret. By our definition in §2.3

Why are there so many message digest functions?

Surprisingly, the drive for message digest algorithms started with public key cryptography. RSA was invented, which made possible digital signatures on messages, but computing a signature on a long message with RSA was sufficiently slow that RSA would not have been practical by itself. A cryptographically secure message digest function with high performance would make RSA much more useful. Instead of having to compute a signature over a whole long message, the message could be compressed into a small size by first performing a message digest and then computing the RSA signature on the digest. So MD and MD2 were created. MD was proprietary and never published. It was used in some of RSADSI's secure mail products. MD2 is documented in RFC 1319.

Then Ralph Merkle of Xerox developed a message digest algorithm called SNEFRU [MERK90] that was several times faster than MD2. This prodded Ron Rivest into developing MD4 (RFC 1320), a digest algorithm that took advantage of the fact that newer processors could do 32-bit operations, and was therefore able to be even faster than SNEFRU. Then SNEFRU was broken [BIHA92] (the cryptographic community considered it broken because someone was able to find two messages with the same SNEFRU digest). Independently, [DENB92] found weaknesses in a version of MD4 with two rounds instead of three. This did not officially break MD4, but it made Ron Rivest sufficiently nervous that he decided to strengthen it, and create MD5 (RFC 1321), which is a little slower than MD4. NIST subsequently proposed SHA, which is very similar to MD5, but even more strengthened, and also a little slower. Probably after discovering a never published flaw in the SHA proposal, NIST revised it at the twelfth hour in an effort to make it more secure, and called the revised version SHA-1 (see §5.6.3 *SHA-1 Operation on a 512-bit Block*). MD2 and MD4 were subsequently broken (in the sense that collisions were found), though they remain secure for most uses. At the time of this writing, NIST was working on a new hash function (probably to be named SHA-2) to increase the number of bits of output to 256 in order to have security comparable to the AES encryption algorithm.

Yes, Virginia, there was an MD3, but it was superseded by MD4 before it was ever published or used.

Types of Cryptographic Functions in which we said something that had a single shared secret was a secret key algorithm, these might be considered secret key algorithms. Never take definitions too seriously. The significant difference between a secret key algorithm and a message digest algorithm is that a secret key algorithm is designed to be reversible and a message digest algorithm is designed to be impossible to reverse. In this section we'll use MD as a "generic" message digest (cryptographic hash) algorithm.

5.2.1 Authentication

In §2.4.4 *Authentication* we discussed how to use a secret key algorithm for authentication. A challenge is transmitted, and the other side has to encrypt the challenge with the shared key.

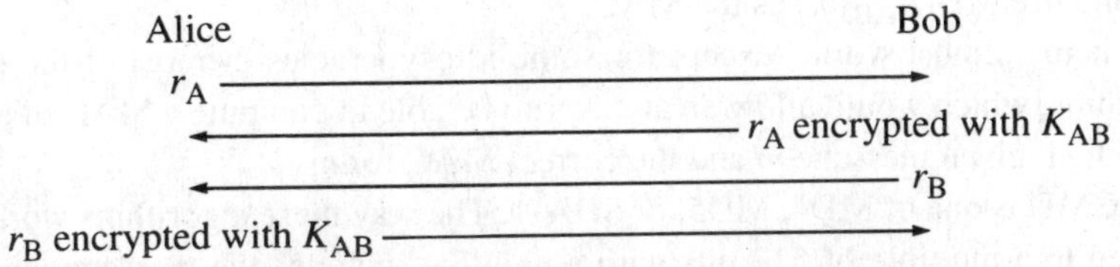

Imagine a world without secret key cryptography, but with cryptographic hash functions. So we can't use an algorithm like DES in the above example. This is not an entirely theoretical concern. Export controls may treat secret key algorithms more harshly than digest algorithms even if they are only used to compute MACs, especially when source code is provided. Could we use a message digest function in some way to accomplish the same thing? Bob and Alice will still need to share a secret. Message digest algorithms aren't reversible, so it can't work quite the same way. In the above example, in which secret key cryptography is used for authentication, Bob encrypts something, and Alice decrypts it to make sure Bob encrypted the quantity properly. A hash function will do pretty much the same thing. Alice still sends a challenge. Bob then concatenates the secret he shares with Alice with the challenge, takes a message digest of that, and transmits that message digest. Alice can't "decrypt" the result. However, she can do the same computation, and check that the result matches what Bob sends.

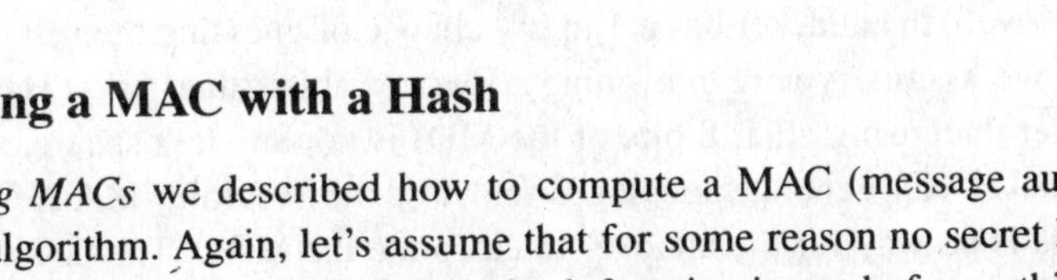

5.2.2 Computing a MAC with a Hash

In §4.3 *Generating MACs* we described how to compute a MAC (message authentication code) with a secret key algorithm. Again, let's assume that for some reason no secret key algorithms are available. Can we still compute a MAC, using a hash function instead of something like DES?

The obvious thought is that MD(m) is a MAC for message m. But it isn't. Anyone can compute MD(m). The point of the MAC is to send something that only someone knowing the secret can compute (and verify). For instance, if Alice and Bob share a secret, then Alice can send m, plus

MAC, and since nobody except Alice and Bob can compute a MAC with their shared key, nobody but Alice or Bob would be able to send a message to Bob with an appropriate MAC. If we just simply used MD, then anyone can send any message m' together with MD(m'). So we do roughly the same trick for the MAC as we did for authentication. We concatenate a shared secret K_{AB} with the message m, and use MD($K_{AB}|m$) as the MAC.

This scheme almost works, except for some idiosyncracies of most of the popular message digest algorithms, which would allow an attacker to be able to compute a MAC of a longer message beginning with m, given message m and the correct MAC for m.

Assume MD is one of MD4, MD5, or SHA-1. The way these algorithms work is that the message is padded to a multiple of 512 bits with a pad that includes the message length. The padded message is then digested from left to right in 512-bit chunks. In order to compute the message digest through chunk n, all that you need to know is the message digest through chunk $n-1$, plus the value of chunk n of the padded message.

Let's assume Carol would like to send a different message to Bob, and have it look like it came from Alice. Let's say that Carol doesn't care what's in the message. She only cares that the end of the message says P.S. Give Carol a promotion and triple her salary. Alice has transmitted some message m, and MD($K_{AB}|m$). Carol can see both of those quantities. She concatenates the padding and then whatever she likes to the end of m, and initializes the message digest computation with MD($K_{AB}|m$). She does not need to know the shared secret in order to compute the MAC.

How can we avoid this flaw? Lots of techniques have been proposed, all entirely effective as far as anyone can tell. But people came up with "improvements", each one a little more complex than the one before, with the apparent winner being HMAC. Some proposals with no known weaknesses are:

- Put the secret at the end of the message instead of at the beginning. This will work. This method can be criticized for an extremely unlikely security flaw. The complaint is that if the MD algorithm were weak, and it was therefore possible to find two messages with the same digest, then those two messages would also have the same MAC.
- Use only half the bits of the message digest as the MAC. For instance, take the low-order 64 bits of the MD5 digest. This gives an attacker no information with which to continue the message digest (well, the attacker has a 1 in 2^{64} chance of guessing the rest of the message digest correctly—we assume you're not going to worry about that risk). Having only 64 bits of MAC (rather than using all 128 bits of the MD) is not any less secure, since there is no way that an attacker can generate messages and test the resulting MAC. Without knowing the secret, there is no way for the attacker to calculate the MAC. The best that can be done is to generate a random 64-bit MAC for the message you'd like to send and hope that you'll be really really lucky.

- Concatenate the secret to both the front and the back of the message. That way you get the collision resistance of putting it in front and the protection from appending that comes from putting it in back.

HMAC concatenates the secret to the front of the message, digests the combination, then concatenates the secret to the front of the digest, and digests the combination again. The actual construction is a little more complicated than this, and is described in section §5.7 *HMAC*. HMAC has lower performance than the other alternatives because it does a second digest. But the second digest is only computed over the secret and a digest, so it does not add much cost to large messages. In the worst case, if the message concatenated with the key fit into a single (512-bit) block, HMAC would be four times as expensive as one of the other alternatives described above. However, if many small messages are to be HMAC'd with the same key, it is possible to reuse the part of the computation that digests the key, so that HMAC would only be twice as slow. With a large enough message, HMAC's performance is only negligibly worse.

We call any hash combining the secret key and the data a **keyed hash**.

5.2.3 Encryption with a Message Digest

"Encryption with a message digest algorithm is easy!" you say. "But let me see you do decryption!" Message digest algorithms are not reversible, so the trick is to design a scheme in which both encryption and decryption run the message digest algorithm in the forward direction. The schemes we'll describe are reminiscent of the chaining methods for a secret key algorithm (see §4.2 *Encrypting a Large Message*).

5.2.3.1 Generating a One-Time Pad

Just as OFB (§4.2.3 *Output Feedback Mode (OFB)*) generates a pseudorandom bit stream which then encrypts a message by simply being ⊕ed with the message, we can use a message digest algorithm to generate a pseudorandom bit stream.

Again, Alice and Bob need a shared secret, K_{AB}. Alice wants to send Bob a message. She computes MD(K_{AB}). That gives the first block of the bit stream, b_1. Then she computes MD($K_{AB}|b_1$) and uses that as b_2, and in general b_i is MD($K_{AB}|b_{i-1}$).

Alice and Bob can do this in advance, before the message is known. Then when Alice wishes to send the message, she ⊕s it with as much of the generated bit stream as necessary. Similarly, Bob decrypts the ciphertext by ⊕ing it with the bit stream he has calculated.

It is not secure to use the same bit stream twice, so, as with OFB, Alice starts with an IV. The first block is then MD(K_{AB}|IV). She must transmit the IV to Bob. Alice can generate the bit stream in advance of encrypting the message, but Bob cannot generate the bit stream until he sees the IV.

5.2.3.2 Mixing In the Plaintext

One-time pad schemes have the problem that if you are able to guess the plaintext, you can ⊕ the guessed text with the ciphertext, and then ⊕ any message you like. This is not too much of a problem. We just need to recognize that a one-time pad scheme gives privacy only, and integrity must be gained through a scheme such as using a MAC.

However, in a scheme similar to CFB (§4.2.4 *Cipher Feedback Mode (CFB)*), we can mix the plaintext into the bit stream generation. For instance, break the message into MD-length chunks p_1, p_2,.... We'll call the ciphertext blocks c_1, c_2,.... And we'll need intermediate values b_1, b_2,... from which we'll compute each ciphertext block.

$$\begin{array}{ll} b_1 = \mathrm{MD}(K_{\mathrm{AB}}|\mathrm{IV}) & c_1 = p_1 \oplus b_1 \\ b_2 = \mathrm{MD}(K_{\mathrm{AB}}|c_1) & c_2 = p_2 \oplus b_2 \\ \vdots & \vdots \\ b_i = \mathrm{MD}(K_{\mathrm{AB}}|c_{i-1}) & c_i = p_i \oplus b_i \\ \vdots & \vdots \end{array}$$

Decryption is straightforward. We leave it as Homework Problem 18.

5.2.4 Using Secret Key for a Hash

In case the previous sections make the secret key algorithms nervous about job security since they can be replaced by hash algorithms, we'll show that a hash algorithm can be replaced by a secret key algorithm. What we want to generate is a function with the properties of a hash algorithm. It should not require a secret. It should be publishable. It should be noninvertible.

5.2.4.1 UNIX Password Hash

UNIX uses a secret key algorithm to compute the hash of a password, which it then stores. It never has to reverse the hash to obtain a password. Instead, when the user types a password, UNIX uses the same algorithm to hash the typed quantity and compares the result with the stored quantity.

The hashing algorithm first converts the password into a secret key. This key is then used, with a DES-like algorithm, to encrypt the number 0. The method of turning a text string into a secret key is simply to pack the 7-bit ASCII associated with each of the first 8 characters of the password into a 56-bit quantity into which DES parity is inserted. (UNIX passwords can be longer than 8 characters, but the remaining octets are ignored.)

A 12-bit random number, known as *salt*, is stored with the hashed password. For an explanation of why salt is useful, see §10.3 *Off-Line Password Guessing*. A modified DES is used instead of standard DES to prevent hardware accelerators designed for DES from being used to reverse the password hash. The salt is used to modify the DES data expansion algorithm. The value of the salt determines which bits are duplicated when expanding R from 32 to 48 bits (see §3.3.5 *The Mangler Function*).

To summarize, each time a password is set, a 12-bit number is generated. The password is converted into a secret key. The 12-bit number is used to define a modified DES algorithm. The modified DES algorithm is used with the secret key as input to encrypt the constant 0. The result is stored along with the 12-bit number as the user's hashed password.

5.2.4.2 Hashing Large Messages

The UNIX password hash is a method of doing a message digest of a very short message (maximum length is the length of the secret key). Here's a method of converting a secret key algorithm into a message digest algorithm for arbitrary messages (see Figure 5-1).

A secret key algorithm has a key length, say k bits. It has a message block length, say b bits. In the case of DES, $k = 56$ and $b = 64$. In the case of IDEA, $k = 128$ and $b = 64$.

Divide the message into k-bit chunks $m_1, m_2, \ldots$. Use the first block of the message as a key to encrypt a constant. The result is a b-bit quantity. Use the second k-bit chunk of the message to encrypt the b-bit quantity to get a new b-bit quantity. Keep doing this until you run out of k-bit blocks of the message. Use the final b-bit result as the message digest.

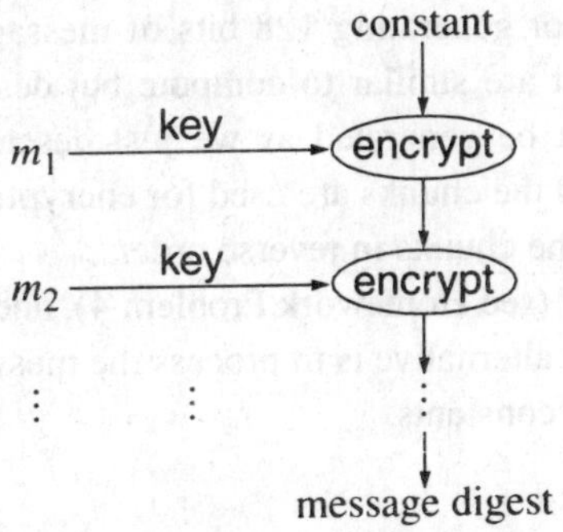

Figure 5-1. Message Digest Using Secret Key Cryptography

There's a serious problem with this, which is that the typical message block length b is 64 bits, which is too short to use as a message digest. To obtain two messages with the same message digest using this technique (and remembering the birthday problem), we'd only have to try about 2^{32} messages before finding two that had the same digest. And furthermore, if we want to find a message with a particular message digest, a technique similar to the one in §4.4.1.2 *Encrypting Twice with Two Keys* could find a message with a particular 64-bit message digest in about 2^{33} iterations.

A technique that works better (and in particular makes it a workfactor of 2^{63} to find a message matching a given hash) is to ⊕ the input to each round with the output as shown below:

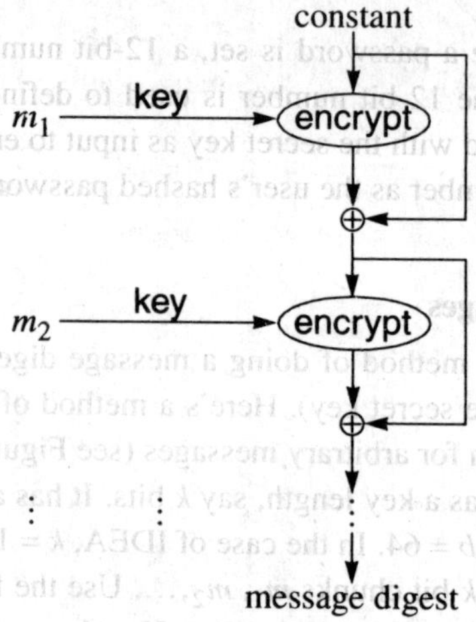

Figure 5-2. Improved Message Digest Using Secret Key Cryptography

One possible technique for generating 128 bits of message digest is to generate two 64-bit quantities using techniques that are similar to compute but designed to produce different values. The first 64-bit quantity might be generated as we just described—the message is broken into key-length chunks $b_1,b_2,\ldots$ and the chunks are used for encryption in that order. The second 64-bit quantity is generated by using the chunks in reverse order.

That technique has a flaw (see Homework Problem 4), and it's a little inconvenient to do two passes on the message. A better alternative is to process the message twice in the forward direction, and just start with two different constants.

5.3 MD2

MD2 takes a message equal to an arbitrary number of octets and produces a 128-bit message digest. It cannot handle a message that is not an integral number of octets, though it would be simple to modify MD2 (see Homework Problem 5), or to have a convention for bit-padding a message before feeding it to MD2.

The basic idea behind MD2 is as follows:

1. The input to MD2 is a message whose length is an arbitrary number of octets.
2. The message is padded, according to specified conventions, to be a multiple of 16 octets.
3. A 16-octet quantity, which MD2 calls a **checksum**, is appended to the end. This checksum is a strange function of the padded message defined specifically for MD2.
4. Final pass—The message is processed, 16 octets at a time, each time producing an intermediate result for the message digest. Each intermediate value of the message digest depends on the previous intermediate value and the value of the 16 octets of the message being processed.

Note that we describe the algorithm as if the message is processed three times, first to pad it, next to compute the checksum, and then to compute the actual message digest. However, it is possible to digest a message in a single pass. This is important for machines with limited memory.

5.3.1 MD2 Padding

The padding function (see Figure 5-3) is very simple. There must always be padding, even if the message starts out being a multiple of 16 octets. If the message starts out being a multiple of 16 octets, 16 octets of padding are added. Otherwise, the number of octets (1–15) necessary to make the message a multiple of 16 octets is added. Each pad octet specifies the number of octets of padding that was added.

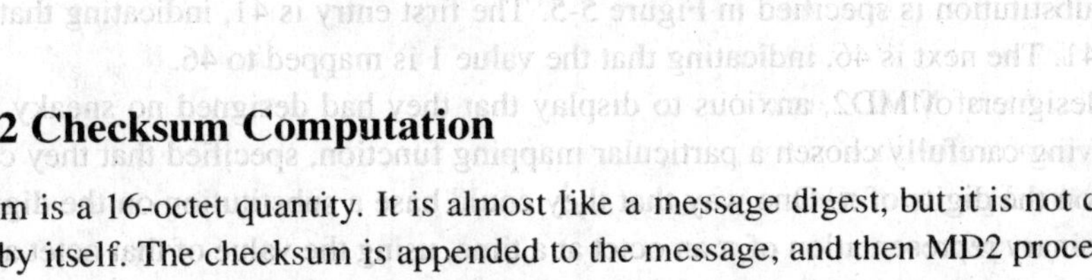

Figure 5-3. MD2 Padded Message

5.3.2 MD2 Checksum Computation

The checksum is a 16-octet quantity. It is almost like a message digest, but it is not cryptographically secure by itself. The checksum is appended to the message, and then MD2 processes the concatenated quantity to obtain the actual message digest.

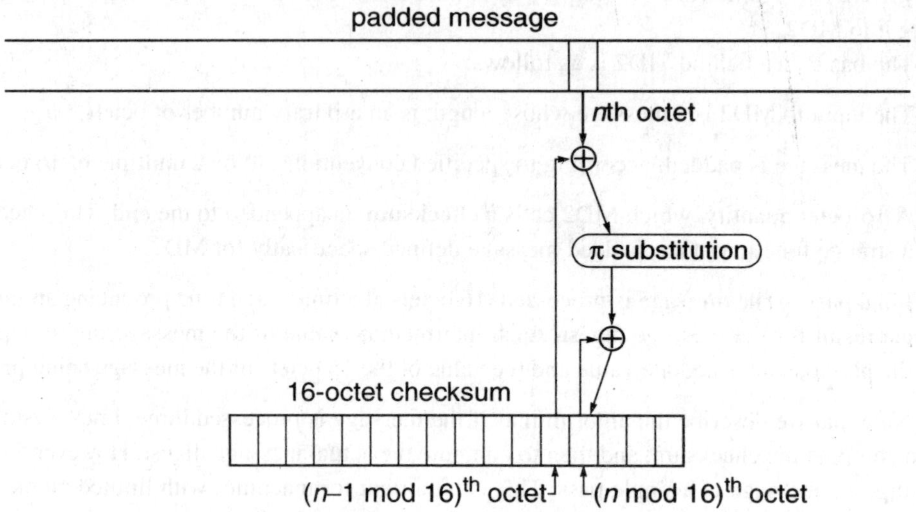

Figure 5-4. MD2 Checksum Calculation

The checksum starts out initialized to 0. Because of the padding mentioned in the previous section, the message is a multiple of 16 octets, say $k \times 16$ octets. The checksum calculation processes the padded message an octet at a time, so the calculation requires $k \times 16$ steps. Each step looks at one octet of the message and updates one octet of the checksum. After octet 15 of the checksum is updated, the next step starts again on octet 0 of the checksum. Therefore, each octet of the checksum will have been updated k times by the time the checksum computation terminates. At step n, octet (n mod 16) of the checksum is computed, but for simplicity we'll call it octet n of the checksum.

Octet n of the checksum depends on octet n of the message, octet $(n-1)$ of the checksum, and the previous value of octet n of the checksum (what it was updated to be in step $n-16$). (Think of the checksum as "wrapping around", so if $n = 0$, octet $n-1$ is octet 15.)

First, octet n of the message and octet $(n-1)$ of the checksum are ⊕'d together. This produces an octet having a value between 0 and 255. Then a substitution is done and the result is ⊕'d into the previous value of octet n of the checksum.

The substitution is specified in Figure 5-5. The first entry is 41, indicating that the value 0 is mapped to 41. The next is 46, indicating that the value 1 is mapped to 46.

The designers of MD2, anxious to display that they had designed no sneaky trapdoors into MD2 by having carefully chosen a particular mapping function, specified that they chose the mapping based on the digits of π. One way that they could base a substitution on the digits of π was to look at the binary representation of π an octet at a time, using the value of that octet as the next substitution value, unless it was already used, in which case they skipped it and went on to the next octet. We checked, and that isn't how they did it. We're willing to just take their word for it that somehow the numbers are based on the digits of π. We wonder whether anyone has ever bothered to verify their claim. We certainly hope none of you waste as much time as we did trying to figure out how the digits of π relate to the substitution. We could have asked the designers, but that seemed like cheating.

41	46	67	201	162	216	124	1	61	54	84	161	236	240	6	19
98	167	5	243	192	199	115	140	152	147	43	217	188	76	130	202
30	155	87	60	253	212	224	22	103	66	111	24	138	23	229	18
190	78	196	214	218	158	222	73	160	251	245	142	187	47	238	122
169	104	121	145	21	178	7	63	148	194	16	137	11	34	95	33
128	127	93	154	90	144	50	39	53	62	204	231	191	247	151	3
255	25	48	179	72	165	181	209	215	94	146	42	172	86	170	198
79	184	56	210	150	164	125	182	118	252	107	226	156	116	4	241
69	157	112	89	100	113	135	32	134	91	207	101	230	45	168	2
27	96	37	173	174	176	185	246	28	70	97	105	52	64	126	15
85	71	163	35	221	81	175	58	195	92	249	206	186	197	234	38
44	83	13	110	133	40	132	9	211	223	205	244	65	129	77	82
106	220	55	200	108	193	171	250	36	225	123	8	12	189	177	74
120	136	149	139	227	99	232	109	233	203	213	254	59	0	29	57
242	239	183	14	102	88	208	228	166	119	114	248	235	117	75	10
49	68	80	180	143	237	31	26	219	153	141	51	159	17	131	20

Figure 5-5. MD2 π Substitution Table

5.3.3 MD2 Final Pass

The final pass of the message digest computation is somewhat similar to the checksum computation. The message with padding and checksum appended is processed in chunks of 16 octets. Each time a new 16-octet chunk of the message is taken, a 48-octet quantity is constructed consisting of the (16-octet) current value of the message digest, the chunk of the message, and the ⊕ of those two 16-octet quantities. The 48-octet quantity is massaged octet by octet. After 18 passes over the 48-octet quantity, the first 16 octets of the 48-octet quantity are used as the next value of the message digest.

The message digest is initialized to 16 octets of 0.

At each stage, the next 16 octets of the message are taken to be processed. A 48-octet quantity is formed by appending the message octets to the current message digest, then appending the ⊕ of these two 16-octet quantities.

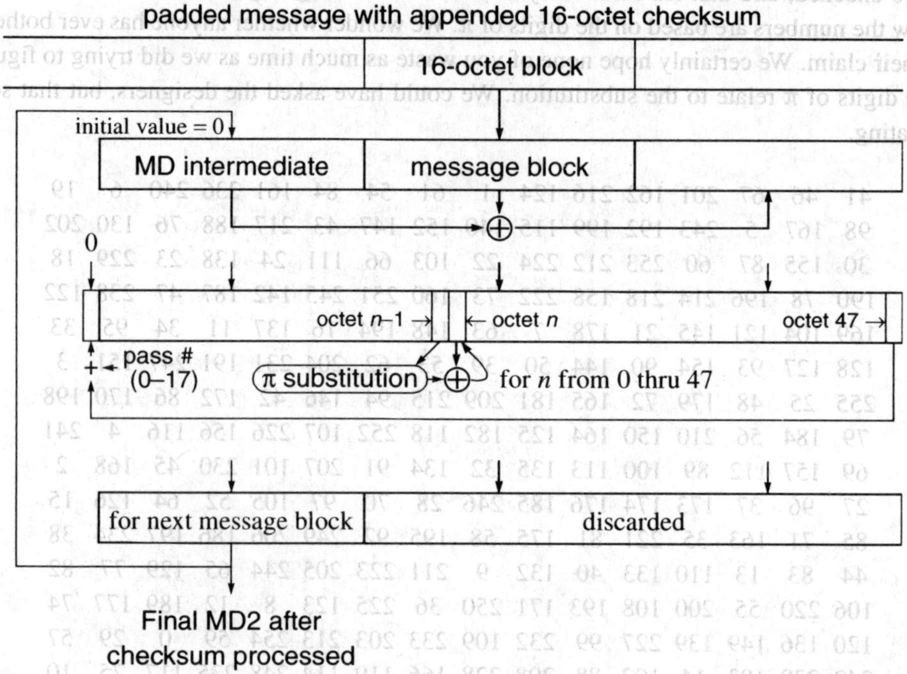

Figure 5-6. MD2 Final Pass

18 passes are made over the 48-octet quantity, and during a pass each step processes one octet, which means that 18×48 steps are made. It is necessary to know which pass is being made, since the pass number is used in the computation. Both passes and steps are numbered starting at zero. A phantom octet −1 appears before the first octet (octet 0) of the 48-octet quantity.

At the beginning of pass 0, octet −1 is set to 0. In step *n* of each pass we take octet *n*−1 and run it through the same substitution used for the checksum, then ⊕ the result into octet *n*. After step 47 of each pass, there is a step 48 which sets octet −1 to the mod 256 sum of octet 47 and the pass number. When we have completed pass 17, the first 16 octets of the 48-octet quantity are used as the value of the message digest for the next stage, and the next 16 octets of the message are processed. (So in pass 17, steps 16 through 48 are useless.)

After the entire message is processed, the 16 octets that come out of the last stage is the message digest value. The calculation requires only 16 octets (for the checksum) plus 48 octets of volatile memory plus a few indices and makes a single pass over the data. This is ideal for computation in a smart card (see §10.8 *Authentication Tokens*).

5.4 MD4

MD4 was designed to be 32-bit-word-oriented so that it can be computed faster on 32-bit CPUs than an octet-oriented scheme like MD2. Also, MD2 requires the message to be an integral number of octets. MD4 can handle messages with an arbitrary number of bits. Like MD2 it can be computed in a single pass over the data, though MD4 needs more intermediate state.

5.4.1 MD4 Message Padding

The message to be fed into the message digest computation must be a multiple of 512 bits (sixteen 32-bit words). The original message is padded by adding a 1 bit, followed by enough 0 bits to leave the message 64 bits less than a multiple of 512 bits. Then a 64-bit quantity representing the number of bits in the unpadded message, mod 2^{64}, is appended to the message. The bit order within octets is most significant to least significant, the octet order is least significant to most significant.

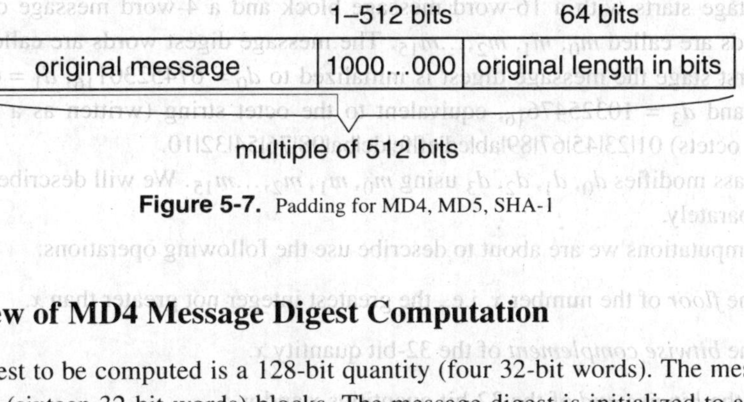

Figure 5-7. Padding for MD4, MD5, SHA-1

5.4.2 Overview of MD4 Message Digest Computation

The message digest to be computed is a 128-bit quantity (four 32-bit words). The message is processed in 512-bit (sixteen 32-bit words) blocks. The message digest is initialized to a fixed value, and then each stage of the message digest computation takes the current value of the message digest and modifies it using the next block of the message. The function that takes 512 bits of the message and digests it with the previous 128-bit output is known as the **compression function**. The final result is the message digest for the entire message.

Each stage makes three passes over the message block. Each pass has a slightly different method of mangling the message digest. At the end of the stage, each word of the mangled message digest is added to its pre-stage value to produce the post-stage value (which becomes the pre-stage value for the next stage). Therefore, the current value of the message digest must be saved at the beginning of the stage so that it can be added in at the end of the stage.

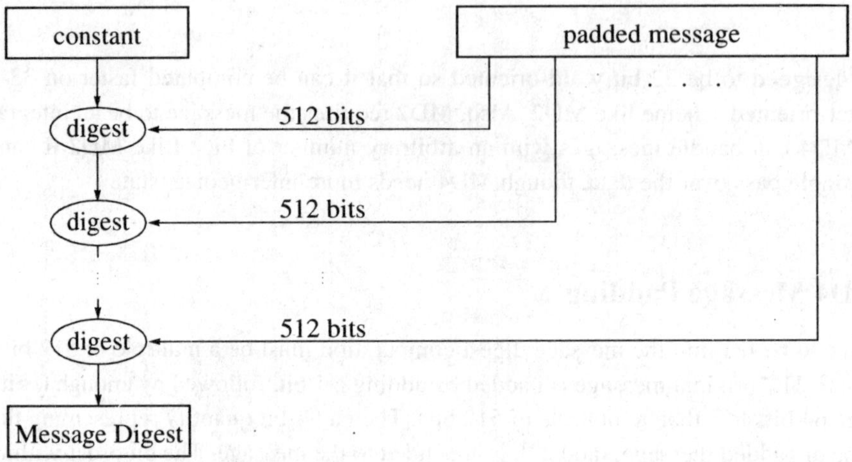

Figure 5-8. Overview of MD4, MD5, SHA-1

Each stage starts with a 16-word message block and a 4-word message digest value. The message words are called m_0, m_1, m_2,...m_{15}. The message digest words are called d_0, d_1, d_2, d_3. Before the first stage the message digest is initialized to $d_0 = 67452301_{16}$, $d_1 = \text{efcdab89}_{16}$, $d_2 = \text{98badcfe}_{16}$, and $d_3 = 10325476_{16}$, equivalent to the octet string (written as a concatenation of hex-encoded octets) 01|23|45|67|89|ab|cd|ef|fe|dc|ba|98|76|54|32|10.

Each pass modifies d_0, d_1, d_2, d_3 using m_0, m_1, m_2,...m_{15}. We will describe what happens in each pass separately.

The computations we are about to describe use the following operations:

- $\lfloor x \rfloor$ is the *floor* of the number x, i.e., the greatest integer not greater than x.
- $\sim x$ is the *bitwise complement* of the 32-bit quantity x.
- $x \wedge y$ is the *bitwise and* of the 32-bit quantities x and y.
- $x \vee y$ is the *bitwise or* of the two 32-bit quantities x and y.
- $x \oplus y$ is the *bitwise exclusive or* of the 32-bit quantities x and y.
- $x+y$ is the *binary sum* of the two 32-bit quantities x and y, with the carry out of the high order bit discarded.
- $x \lrcorner y$ is the 32-bit quantity produced by taking the 32 bits of x and shifting them one position left y times, each time taking the bit shifted off the left end and placing it as the rightmost bit. This operation is known as a **left rotate**.

5.4.3 MD4 Message Digest Pass 1

A function $F(x,y,z)$ is defined as $(x \wedge y) \vee (\sim x \wedge z)$. This function takes three 32-bit words x, y, and z, and produces an output 32-bit word. This function is sometimes known as the **selection function**, because if the nth bit of x is a 1 it selects the nth bit of y for the nth bit of the output. Otherwise (if the nth bit of x is a 0) it selects the nth bit of z for the nth bit of the output.

A separate step is done for each of the 16 words of the message. For each integer i from 0 through 15,

$$d_{(-i)\wedge 3} = (d_{(-i)\wedge 3} + F(d_{(1-i)\wedge 3}, d_{(2-i)\wedge 3}, d_{(3-i)\wedge 3}) + m_i) \lrcorner\ S_1(i \wedge 3)$$

where $S_1(i) = 3 + 4i$, so the $\lrcorner$s cycle over the values 3, 7, 11, 15.

If you don't find the previous sentence intimidating, you may go on to the next section. However, if you are a mere mortal, we'll explain, but just this once. The other passes in MD4 and MD5 are extremely similar, and we'll assume you'll understand their description with no further explanation.

The "$\wedge 3$" that appears several times in the above equation means that only the bottom two bits are used (because we're doing a *bitwise and* with 11_2). So $i \wedge 3$ cycles 0, 1, 2, 3, 0, 1, 2, 3, ... while $(-i) \wedge 3$ cycles 0, 3, 2, 1, 0, 3, 2, 1,... and $(1-i) \wedge 3$ cycles 1, 0, 3, 2, 1, 0, 3, 2,.... We can write out the first few steps of the pass as follows:

$$d_0 = (d_0 + F(d_1, d_2, d_3) + m_0) \lrcorner\ 3$$
$$d_3 = (d_3 + F(d_0, d_1, d_2) + m_1) \lrcorner\ 7$$
$$d_2 = (d_2 + F(d_3, d_0, d_1) + m_2) \lrcorner\ 11$$
$$d_1 = (d_1 + F(d_2, d_3, d_0) + m_3) \lrcorner\ 15$$
$$d_0 = (d_0 + F(d_1, d_2, d_3) + m_4) \lrcorner\ 3$$

5.4.4 MD4 Message Digest Pass 2

A function $G(x, y, z)$ is defined as $(x \wedge y) \vee (x \wedge z) \vee (y \wedge z)$. This function is sometimes known as the **majority function**, because the nth bit of the output is a 1 iff at least two of the three input words' n^{th} bits are a 1. As for pass 1, we'll write out the first few steps. Note that in pass 2 (and pass 3 as well), the words of the message are not processed in order. Also note that there's a strange constant thrown in. To show that the designers didn't purposely choose a diabolical value of the constant, the constant is based on the square root of 2. The constant is $\lfloor 2^{30}\sqrt{2} \rfloor = 5a827999_{16}$.

A separate step is done for each of the 16 words of the message. For each integer i from 0 through 15,

$$d_{(-i)\wedge 3} = (d_{(-i)\wedge 3} + G(d_{(1-i)\wedge 3}, d_{(2-i)\wedge 3}, d_{(3-i)\wedge 3}) + m_{X(i)} + 5a827999_{16}) \lrcorner\ S_2(i \wedge 3)$$

where $X(i)$ is the 4-bit number formed by exchanging the low order and high order pairs of bits in the 4-bit number i (so $X(i) = 4i - 15\lfloor i/4 \rfloor$), and $S_2(0) = 3$, $S_2(1) = 5$, $S_2(2) = 9$, $S_2(3) = 13$, so the ↲s cycle over the values 3, 5, 9, 13. We can write out the first few steps of the pass as follows:

$$d_0 = (d_0 + G(d_1, d_2, d_3) + m_0 + 5a827999_{16}) \hookleftarrow 3$$

$$d_3 = (d_3 + G(d_0, d_1, d_2) + m_4 + 5a827999_{16}) \hookleftarrow 5$$

$$d_2 = (d_2 + G(d_3, d_0, d_1) + m_8 + 5a827999_{16}) \hookleftarrow 9$$

$$d_1 = (d_1 + G(d_2, d_3, d_0) + m_{12} + 5a827999_{16}) \hookleftarrow 13$$

$$d_0 = (d_0 + G(d_1, d_2, d_3) + m_1 + 5a827999_{16}) \hookleftarrow 3$$

5.4.5 MD4 Message Digest Pass 3

A function $H(x,y,z)$ is defined as $x \oplus y \oplus z$. Pass 3 has a different strange constant based on the square root of 3. The constant is $\lfloor 2^{30}\sqrt{3} \rfloor = 6ed9eba1_{16}$.

A separate step is done for each of the 16 words of the message. For each integer i from 0 through 15,

$$d_{(-i)\wedge 3} = (d_{(-i)\wedge 3} + H(d_{(1-i)\wedge 3}, d_{(2-i)\wedge 3}, d_{(3-i)\wedge 3}) + m_{R(i)} + 6ed9eba1_{16}) \hookleftarrow S_3(i \wedge 3)$$

where $R(i)$ is the 4-bit number formed by reversing the order of the bits in the 4-bit number i (so $R(i) = 8i - 12\lfloor i/2 \rfloor - 6\lfloor i/4 \rfloor - 3\lfloor i/8 \rfloor$), and $S_3(0) = 3$, $S_3(1) = 9$, $S_3(2) = 11$, $S_3(3) = 15$, so the ↲s cycle over the values 3, 9, 11, 15. We can write out the first few steps of the pass as follows:

$$d_0 = (d_0 + H(d_1, d_2, d_3) + m_0 + 6ed9eba1_{16}) \hookleftarrow 3$$

$$d_3 = (d_3 + H(d_0, d_1, d_2) + m_8 + 6ed9eba1_{16}) \hookleftarrow 9$$

$$d_2 = (d_2 + H(d_3, d_0, d_1) + m_4 + 6ed9eba1_{16}) \hookleftarrow 11$$

$$d_1 = (d_1 + H(d_2, d_3, d_0) + m_{12} + 6ed9eba1_{16}) \hookleftarrow 15$$

$$d_0 = (d_0 + H(d_1, d_2, d_3) + m_2 + 6ed9eba1_{16}) \hookleftarrow 3$$

5.5 MD5

MD5 was designed to be somewhat more "conservative" than MD4 in terms of being less concerned with speed and more concerned with security. It is very similar to MD4. The major differences are:

1. MD4 makes three passes over each 16-octet chunk of the message. MD5 makes four passes over each 16-octet chunk.

2. The functions are slightly different, as are the number of bits in the shifts.

3. MD4 has one constant which is used for each message word in pass 2, and a different constant used for all of the 16 message words in pass 3. No constant is used in pass 1.

   MD5 uses a different constant for each message word on each pass. Since there are 4 passes, each of which deals with 16 message words, there are 64 32-bit constants used in MD5. We will call them T_1 through T_{64}. T_i is based on the sine function. Indeed, for any inquiring minds out there, $T_i = \lfloor 2^{32} |\sin i| \rfloor$. The 64 values (in hex) are:

T_{1} = d76aa478	T_{17} = f61e2562	T_{33} = fffa3942	T_{49} = f4292244
T_{2} = e8c7b756	T_{18} = c040b340	T_{34} = 8771f681	T_{50} = 432aff97
T_{3} = 242070db	T_{19} = 265e5a51	T_{35} = 6d9d6122	T_{51} = ab9423a7
T_{4} = c1bdceee	T_{20} = e9b6c7aa	T_{36} = fde5380c	T_{52} = fc93a039
T_{5} = f57c0faf	T_{21} = d62f105d	T_{37} = a4beea44	T_{53} = 655b59c3
T_{6} = 4787c62a	T_{22} = 02441453	T_{38} = 4bdecfa9	T_{54} = 8f0ccc92
T_{7} = a8304613	T_{23} = d8a1e681	T_{39} = f6bb4b60	T_{55} = ffeff47d
T_{8} = fd469501	T_{24} = e7d3fbc8	T_{40} = bebfbc70	T_{56} = 85845dd1
T_{9} = 698098d8	T_{25} = 21e1cde6	T_{41} = 289b7ec6	T_{57} = 6fa87e4f
T_{10} = 8b44f7af	T_{26} = c33707d6	T_{42} = eaa127fa	T_{58} = fe2ce6e0
T_{11} = ffff5bb1	T_{27} = f4d50d87	T_{43} = d4ef3085	T_{59} = a3014314
T_{12} = 895cd7be	T_{28} = 455a14ed	T_{44} = 04881d05	T_{60} = 4e0811a1
T_{13} = 6b901122	T_{29} = a9e3e905	T_{45} = d9d4d039	T_{61} = f7537e82
T_{14} = fd987193	T_{30} = fcefa3f8	T_{46} = e6db99e5	T_{62} = bd3af235
T_{15} = a679438e	T_{31} = 676f02d9	T_{47} = 1fa27cf8	T_{63} = 2ad7d2bb
T_{16} = 49b40821	T_{32} = 8d2a4c8a	T_{48} = c4ac5665	T_{64} = eb86d391

5.5.1 MD5 Message Padding

The padding in MD5 is identical to the padding in MD4.

5.5.2 Overview of MD5 Message Digest Computation

Like MD4, in MD5 the message is processed in 512-bit blocks (sixteen 32-bit words). (See Figure 5-8.) The message digest is a 128-bit quantity (four 32-bit words). Each stage consists of computing a function based on the 512-bit message chunk and the message digest to produce a new intermediate value for the message digest. The value of the message digest is the result of the output of the final block of the message.

Each stage in MD5 takes four passes over the message block (as opposed to three for MD4). As with MD4, at the end of the stage, each word of the modified message digest is added to the corresponding pre-stage message digest value. And as in MD4, before the first stage the message digest is initialized to $d_0 = 67452301_{16}$, $d_1 = \text{efcdab89}_{16}$, $d_2 = \text{98badcfe}_{16}$, and $d_3 = 10325476_{16}$.

As with MD4, each pass modifies d_0, d_1, d_2, d_3 using $m_0, m_1, m_2, \ldots m_{15}$. We will describe what happens in each pass separately.

5.5.3 MD5 Message Digest Pass 1

As in MD4, $F(x,y,z)$ is defined as the selection function $(x\wedge y)\vee(\sim x\wedge z)$. A separate step is done for each of the 16 words of the message. For each integer i from 0 through 15,

$$d_{(-i)\wedge 3} = d_{(1-i)\wedge 3} + (d_{(-i)\wedge 3} + F(d_{(1-i)\wedge 3}, d_{(2-i)\wedge 3}, d_{(3-i)\wedge 3}) + m_i + T_{i+1}) \lrcorner\, S_1(i\wedge 3)$$

where $S_1(i) = 7 + 5i$, so the $\lrcorner$s cycle over the values 7, 12, 17, 22. This is a different S_1 from that in MD4. We can write out the first few steps of the pass as follows:

$$d_0 = d_1 + (d_0 + F(d_1, d_2, d_3) + m_0 + T_1) \lrcorner\, 7$$
$$d_3 = d_0 + (d_3 + F(d_0, d_1, d_2) + m_1 + T_2) \lrcorner\, 12$$
$$d_2 = d_3 + (d_2 + F(d_3, d_0, d_1) + m_2 + T_3) \lrcorner\, 17$$
$$d_1 = d_2 + (d_1 + F(d_2, d_3, d_0) + m_3 + T_4) \lrcorner\, 22$$
$$d_0 = d_1 + (d_0 + F(d_1, d_2, d_3) + m_4 + T_5) \lrcorner\, 7$$

5.5.4 MD5 Message Digest Pass 2

A function $G(x,y,z)$ is defined as $(x\wedge z)\vee(y\wedge\sim z)$. Whereas the function F was the same in MD5 as in MD4, the function G is different in MD5 than the G function in MD4. In fact, MD5's G is rather like F—the nth bit of z is used to select the nth bit in x or the nth bit in y.

A separate step is done for each of the 16 words of the message. For each integer i from 0 through 15,

$$d_{(-i)\wedge 3} = d_{(1-i)\wedge 3} + (d_{(-i)\wedge 3} + G(d_{(1-i)\wedge 3}, d_{(2-i)\wedge 3}, d_{(3-i)\wedge 3}) + m_{(5i+1)\wedge 15} + T_{i+17}) \lrcorner\, S_2(i\wedge 3)$$

where $S_2(i) = i(i+7)/2 + 5$, so the $\lrcorner$s cycle over the values 5, 9, 14, 20. This is a different S_2 from that in MD4. We can write out the first few steps of the pass as follows:

$$d_0 = d_1 + (d_0 + G(d_1, d_2, d_3) + m_1 + T_{17}) \lrcorner\, 5$$
$$d_3 = d_0 + (d_3 + G(d_0, d_1, d_2) + m_6 + T_{18}) \lrcorner\, 9$$
$$d_2 = d_3 + (d_2 + G(d_3, d_0, d_1) + m_{11} + T_{19}) \lrcorner\, 14$$
$$d_1 = d_2 + (d_1 + G(d_2, d_3, d_0) + m_0 + T_{20}) \lrcorner\, 20$$

$$d_0 = d_1 + (d_0 + G(d_1, d_2, d_3) + m_5 + T_{21}) \hookleftarrow 5$$

5.5.5 MD5 Message Digest Pass 3

A function $H(x,y,z)$ is defined as $x \oplus y \oplus z$. This is the same H as in MD4.

A separate step is done for each of the 16 words of the message. For each integer i from 0 through 15,

$$d_{(-i)\wedge 3} = d_{(1-i)\wedge 3} + (d_{(-i)\wedge 3} + H(d_{(1-i)\wedge 3}, d_{(2-i)\wedge 3}, d_{(3-i)\wedge 3}) + m_{(3i+5)\wedge 15} + T_{i+33}) \hookleftarrow S_3(i \wedge 3)$$

where $S_3(0) = 4$, $S_3(1) = 11$, $S_3(2) = 16$, $S_3(3) = 23$, so the $\hookleftarrow$s cycle over the values 4, 11, 16, 23. This is a different S_3 from MD4. We can write out the first few steps of the pass as follows:

$$d_0 = d_1 + (d_0 + H(d_1, d_2, d_3) + m_5 + T_{33}) \hookleftarrow 4$$
$$d_3 = d_0 + (d_3 + H(d_0, d_1, d_2) + m_8 + T_{34}) \hookleftarrow 11$$
$$d_2 = d_3 + (d_2 + H(d_3, d_0, d_1) + m_{11} + T_{35}) \hookleftarrow 16$$
$$d_1 = d_2 + (d_1 + H(d_2, d_3, d_0) + m_{14} + T_{36}) \hookleftarrow 23$$
$$d_0 = d_1 + (d_0 + H(d_1, d_2, d_3) + m_1 + T_{37}) \hookleftarrow 4$$

5.5.6 MD5 Message Digest Pass 4

A function $I(x,y,z)$ is defined as $y \oplus (x \vee \sim z)$. A separate step is done for each of the 16 words of the message. For each integer i from 0 through 15,

$$d_{(-i)\wedge 3} = d_{(1-i)\wedge 3} + (d_{(-i)\wedge 3} + I(d_{(1-i)\wedge 3}, d_{(2-i)\wedge 3}, d_{(3-i)\wedge 3}) + m_{(7i)\wedge 15} + T_{i+49}) \hookleftarrow S_4(i \wedge 3)$$

where $S_4(i) = (i+3)(i+4)/2$, so the $\hookleftarrow$s cycle over the values 6, 10, 15, 21. We can write out the first few steps of the pass as follows:

$$d_0 = d_1 + (d_0 + I(d_1, d_2, d_3) + m_0 + T_{49}) \hookleftarrow 6$$
$$d_3 = d_0 + (d_3 + I(d_0, d_1, d_2) + m_7 + T_{50}) \hookleftarrow 10$$
$$d_2 = d_3 + (d_2 + I(d_3, d_0, d_1) + m_{14} + T_{51}) \hookleftarrow 15$$
$$d_1 = d_2 + (d_1 + I(d_2, d_3, d_0) + m_5 + T_{52}) \hookleftarrow 21$$
$$d_0 = d_1 + (d_0 + I(d_1, d_2, d_3) + m_{12} + T_{53}) \hookleftarrow 6$$

5.6 SHA-1

SHA-1 (**secure hash algorithm**) was proposed by NIST as a message digest function. SHA-1 takes a message of length at most 2^{64} bits and produces a 160-bit output. It is similar to the MD5 message digest function, but it is a little slower to execute and presumably more secure. MD4 made three passes over each block of data; MD5 made four; SHA-1 makes five. It also produces a 160-bit digest as opposed to the 128 of the MDs.

5.6.1 SHA-1 Message Padding

SHA-1 pads messages in the same manner as MD4 and MD5, except that SHA-1 is not defined for a message that is longer than 2^{64} bits. We don't consider that a problem. If there were such a message it would take several hundred years to transmit it at 10 Gigabits per second, and it would take even longer to compute the SHA-1 message digest for it at 1000 MIPS. As our grandmothers would surely have said, had the occasion arisen,

If you can't say something in less that 2^{64} bits, you shouldn't say it at all.

5.6.2 Overview of SHA-1 Message Digest Computation

Just like MD4 and MD5, SHA-1 operates in stages (see Figure 5-8). Each stage mangles the pre-stage message digest by a sequence of operations based on the current message block. At the end of the stage, each word of the mangled message digest is added to its pre-stage value to produce the post-stage value (which becomes the pre-stage value for the next stage). Therefore, the current value of the message digest must be saved at the beginning of the stage so that it can be added in at the end of the stage.

The 160-bit message digest consists of five 32-bit words. Let's call them A, B, C, D, and E. Before the first stage they are set to $A = 67452301_{16}$, $B = \text{efcdab89}_{16}$, $C = \text{98badcfe}_{16}$, $D = 10325476_{16}$, $E = \text{c3d2e1f0}_{16}$. After the last stage, the value of $A|B|C|D|E$ is the message digest for the entire message.

SHA-1 is extremely similar in structure to MD4 and MD5, even more so than their descriptions might indicate (see Homework Problem 7).

5.6.3 SHA-1 Operation on a 512-bit Block

At the start of each stage, the 512-bit message block is used to create a 5×512-bit chunk (see Figure 5-9). The first 512 bits of the chunk consist of the message block. The rest gets filled in, a 32-bit word at a time, according to the bizarre rule that the nth word (starting from word 16, since words 0 through 15 consist of the 512-bit message block) is the ⊕ of words n–3, n–8, n–14, and n–16. In SHA-1, the ⊕ of words n–3, n–8, n–14, and n–16 is rotated left one bit before being stored as word n; this is the only modification from the original SHA.

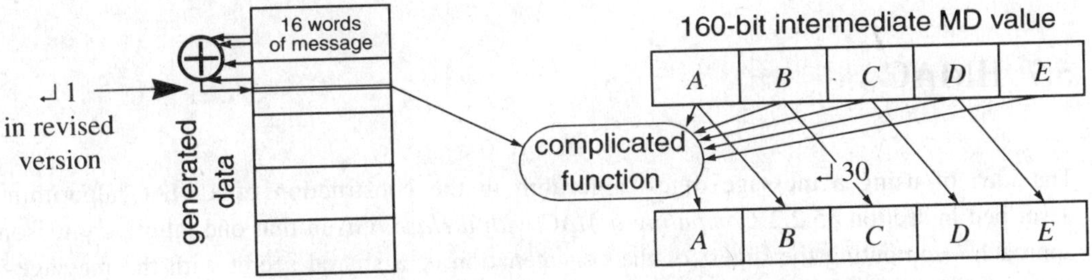

Figure 5-9. Inner Loop of SHA-1—80 Iterations per Block

Now we have a buffer of eighty 32-bit words (5×512 bits). Let's call the eighty 32-bit words $W_0, W_1, \ldots W_{79}$. Now, a little program:

For $t = 0$ through 79, modify A, B, C, D, and E as follows:

$B =$ old A $C =$ old B ↲ 30 $D =$ old C $E =$ old D

"Hmm," you're thinking. "This isn't too hard to follow." Well, we haven't yet said what the new A is! Since the new A depends on the old A, B, C, D, and E, a programmer would first compute the new A into a temporary variable V, and then after computing the new values of B, C, D, and E, set the new A equal to V. For clarity we didn't bother. In the following computation, everything to the right of the equal refers to the old values of A, B, C, D, and E:

$$A = E + (A ↲ 5) + W_t + K_t + f(t, B, C, D)$$

Let's look at each of the terms. E and A↲5 are easy. W_t is the tth 32-bit word in the 80-word block. K_t is a constant, but it varies according to which word you're on (do you like the concept of a variable constant?):

$$K_t = \lfloor 2^{30} \sqrt{2} \rfloor = 5a827999_{16} \quad (0 <= t <= 19)$$
$$K_t = \lfloor 2^{30} \sqrt{3} \rfloor = 6ed9eba1_{16} \quad (20 <= t <= 39)$$
$$K_t = \lfloor 2^{30} \sqrt{5} \rfloor = 8f1bbcdc_{16} \quad (40 <= t <= 59)$$
$$K_t = \lfloor 2^{30} \sqrt{10} \rfloor = ca62c1d6_{16} \quad (60 <= t <= 79)$$

$f(t,B,C,D)$ is a function that varies according to which of the eighty words you're working on:

$$f(t,B,C,D) = (B \wedge C) \vee (\sim B \wedge D) \qquad (0 <= t <= 19)$$
$$f(t,B,C,D) = B \oplus C \oplus D \qquad (20 <= t <= 39)$$
$$f(t,B,C,D) = (B \wedge C) \vee (B \wedge D) \vee (C \wedge D) \qquad (40 <= t <= 59)$$
$$f(t,B,C,D) = B \oplus C \oplus D \qquad (60 <= t <= 79)$$

5.7 HMAC

The idea of using a message digest algorithm in the construction of a MAC algorithm was described in section §5.2.2 *Computing a MAC with a Hash*. Given that one intuitively reasonable approach—computing the digest of the concatenation of a shared secret with the message—has flaws, cryptographers set out to find a construction that could be proven secure. Proving security of a cryptographic algorithm is difficult. First you have to start by defining "secure". Then the best you can do is prove that one algorithm is at least as secure as another.

HMAC resulted from an effort to find a MAC algorithm that could be proven to be secure if the underlying message digest's compression function (see §5.4.2 *Overview of MD4 Message Digest Computation*) was secure. They defined secure as having two properties:

- collision resistance (infeasible to find two inputs that yield the same output)
- an attacker that doesn't know the key K cannot compute the proper digest(K,x) for data x, even if the attacker can see the value of digest(K,y), for arbitrary numbers of inputs y, with y not equal to x.

So in the case of HMAC, they proved that HMAC was secure (had those 2 properties) provided that the underlying compression function was secure (had those 2 properties). Although there are likely other alternatives that are more efficient and just as secure, nobody has offered the same sort of proof of those alternatives. So HMAC seems likely to become the *de facto* standard.

In essence, HMAC prepends the key to the data, digests it, and then prepends the key to the result and digests that. This nested digest with secret inputs to both iterations prevents the extension attacks that would be possible if you simply digested the key and message once. In detail, HMAC function takes a variable-length key and a variable-sized message and produces a fixed-size output that is the same size as the output of the underlying digest. It first pads the key with 0 bits to 512 bits. If the key is larger than 512 bits, then HMAC first digests the key, resulting in 128 bits or 160 bits (depending on the size of output of the digest function) and pads the result out to 512 bits. It

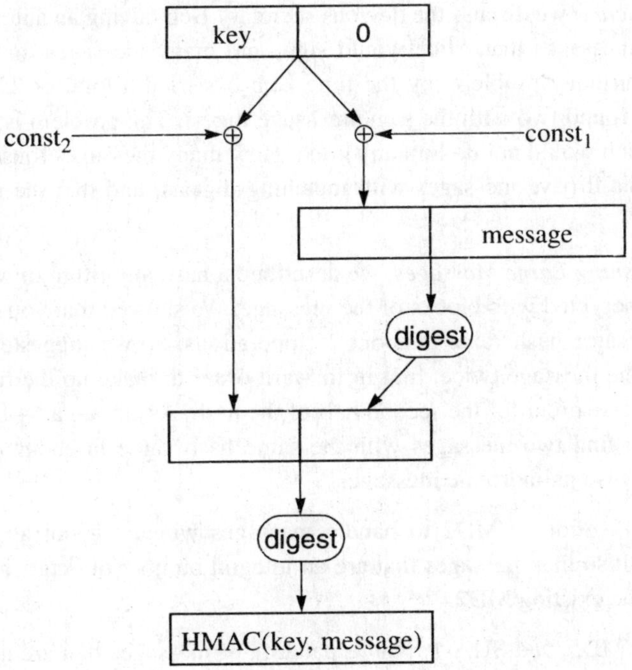

Figure 5-10. HMAC

then ⊕s the padded key with a constant string of octets of value 36_{16}, concatenates it with the message to be protected and computes a message digest. It ⊕s the padded key with a different constant string of octets of value $5c_{16}$, concatenates that with the result of the first digest, and computes a second digest on the result.

5.8 HOMEWORK

1. Doing a signature with RSA alone on a long message would be too slow (presumably using cipher block chaining). Suppose we could do division quickly. Would it be reasonable to compute an RSA signature on a long message by first finding what the message equals, mod n, and signing that?

2. Message digests are reasonably fast, but here's a much faster function to compute. Take your message, divide it into 128-bit chunks, and ⊕ all the chunks together to get a 128-bit result. Do the standard message digest on the result. Is this a good message digest function?

3. In §5.1 *Introduction* we discuss the devious secretary Bob having an automatic means of generating many messages that Alice would sign, and many messages that Bob would like to send. By the birthday problem, by the time Bob has tried a total of 2^{32} messages, he will probably have found two with the same message digest. The problem is, both may be of the same type, which would not do him any good. How many messages must Bob try before it is probable that he'll have messages with matching digests, and that the messages will be of opposite types?

4. In §5.2.4.2 *Hashing Large Messages*, we described a hash algorithm in which a constant was successively encrypted with blocks of the message. We showed that you could find two messages with the same hash value in about 2^{32} operations. So we suggested doubling the hash size by using the message twice, first in forward order to make up the first half of the hash, and then in reverse order for the second half of the hash. Assuming a 64-bit encryption block, how could you find two messages with the same hash value in about 2^{32} iterations? Hint: consider blockwise palindromic messages.

5. Design a modification to MD2 to handle messages which are not an integral number of octets. Design it so that messages that are an integral number of octets have the same digest value as with the existing MD2.

6. Why do MD4, MD5, and SHA-1 require padding of messages that are already a multiple of 512 bits?

7. Modify the specification of SHA-1 so that it looks a lot more like MD4 and MD5. Do this by having each of the words *A*, *B*, *C*, *D*, and *E* modified in place rather than (as SHA-1 specifies it) modifying *A* and then basically rotating the words. Alternatively, modify the specifications of MD4 and MD5 to make them look more like SHA-1. How would you choose which specification to base an implementation on in a particular underlying architecture?

8. Open-ended project: Implement one or more of the message digest algorithms and test how "random" the output appears. For example, test the percentage of 1 bits in the output, or test how many bits of output change with minor changes in the input. Also, design various simplifications of the message digest functions (such as reducing the number of rounds) and see how these change things.

9. What are the minimal and maximal amounts of padding that would be required in each of the message digest functions?

10. Assume $\wedge$, $\vee$, $\oplus$, $+$, $\sim$, and $\lrcorner$ all take about the same amount of time. Estimate the relative performance of MD2, MD4, MD5, and SHA-1.

11. Show that the checksum function in MD2 would not be a good message digest function by showing how to generate a message with a given checksum.

12. Assume a good 128-bit message digest function. Assume there is a particular value, *d*, for the message digest and you'd like to find a message that has a message digest of *d*. Given that there are many more 2000-bit messages that map to a particular 128-bit message digest than 1000-bit messages, would you theoretically have to test fewer 2000-bit messages to find one that has a message digest of *d* than if you were to test 1000-bit messages?

13. Why do we expect that a randomly chosen 100-bit number will have about the same number of 1 bits and 0 bits? (For you statistics fans, calculate the mean and standard deviation of the number of 1 bits.)

14. For purposes of this exercise, we will define **random** as having all elements equally likely to be chosen. So a function that selects a 100-bit number will be random if every 100-bit number is equally likely to be chosen. Using this definition, if we look at the function "+" and we have two inputs, *x* and *y*, then the output will be random if at least one of *x* and *y* are random. For instance, *y* can always be 51, and yet the output will be random if *x* is random. For the following functions, find sufficient conditions for *x*, *y*, and *z* under which the output will be random:

    $\sim x$
    $x \oplus y$
    $x \vee y$
    $x \wedge y$
    $(x \wedge y) \vee (\sim x \wedge z)$ [the selection function]
    $(x \wedge y) \vee (x \wedge z) \vee (y \wedge z)$ [the majority function]
    $x \oplus y \oplus z$
    $y \oplus (x \vee \sim z)$

15. Prove that the function $(x \wedge y) \oplus (x \wedge z) \oplus (y \wedge z)$ and the function $(x \wedge y) \vee (x \wedge z) \vee (y \wedge z)$ are equivalent. (Sorry—this isn't too relevant to cryptography, but we'd stumbled on two different versions of this function in different documentation and we had to think about it for a bit to realize they were the same. We figured you should have the same fun.)

16. We mentioned in §5.2.2 *Computing a MAC with a Hash* that using MD4($K_{AB}|m$) as a MAC is not secure. This is not a problem if MD2 is used instead of MD4. Why is that the case?

17. In §5.2.3.1 *Generating a One-Time Pad*, we generate a pseudo-random stream of MD-sized blocks. This stream must eventually repeat (since only $2^{\text{MD-size}}$ different blocks can be generated). Will the first block necessarily be the first to be repeated? How does this compare to OFB (see Chapter 4 *Modes of Operation* Homework Problem 2)?

18. How do you decrypt the encryption specified in §5.2.3.2 *Mixing In the Plaintext*?

19. Can you modify the encryption specified in §5.2.3.2 *Mixing In the Plaintext* so that instead of $b_i = \text{MD}(K_{AB}|c_{i-1})$ we use $b_i = \text{MD}(K_{AB}|p_{i-1})$? How do you decrypt it? Why wouldn't the modified scheme be as secure? (Hint: what would happen if the plaintext consisted of all zeroes?)

6 *PUBLIC KEY ALGORITHMS*

6.1 INTRODUCTION

This chapter describes public key cryptography. To really understand how and why the public key algorithms work, it is necessary to know some number theory. In this chapter we'll describe the number theory concepts necessary to understand the public key algorithms, but only in sufficient detail for an intuitive understanding. For instance, we won't give proofs, though we will explain things. And in the case of complex algorithms (like Euclid's algorithm), we'll merely state that the algorithm exists and what it does, rather than describing the algorithm in this chapter. Those desiring a more complete treatment of the subject matter can read Chapter 7 *Number Theory*.

Public key algorithms are a motley crew. All the hash algorithms do the same thing—they take a message and perform an irreversible transformation on it. All the secret key algorithms do the same thing—they take a block and encrypt it in a reversible way, and there are chaining methods to convert the block ciphers into message ciphers. But public key algorithms look very different from each other, not only in how they perform their functions, but in what functions they perform. We'll describe:

- RSA and ECC, which do encryption and digital signatures
- ElGamal and DSS, which do digital signatures
- Diffie-Hellman, which allows establishment of a shared secret but doesn't have any algorithms that actually use the secret (it would be used, for instance, together with a secret key scheme in order to actually use the secret for something like encryption)
- zero knowledge proof systems, which only do authentication

The thing that all public key algorithms have in common is the concept of a pair of related quantities, one secret and one public, associated with each principal. (A **principal** is anything or anyone participating in cryptographically protected communication.)

6.2 MODULAR ARITHMETIC

There was a young fellow named Ben
Who could only count modulo ten.
He said, "When I go
Past my last little toe
I shall have to start over again."

—Anonymous

Most of the public key algorithms are based on modular arithmetic. Modular arithmetic uses the non-negative integers less than some positive integer n, performs ordinary arithmetic operations such as addition and multiplication, and then replaces the result with its remainder when divided by n. The result is said to be **modulo** n or **mod** n. When we write "x mod n", we mean the remainder of x when divided by n. Sometimes we'll leave out "mod n" when it's clear from context.

6.2.1 Modular Addition

Let's look at mod 10 addition. $3 + 5 = 8$, just like in regular arithmetic. The answer is already between 0 and 9. $7 + 6 = 13$ in regular arithmetic, but the mod 10 answer is 3. Basically, one can perform mod 10 arithmetic by using the last digit of the answer. For example,

$$5 + 5 = 0$$

$$3 + 9 = 2$$

$$2 + 2 = 4$$

$$9 + 9 = 8$$

Let's look at the mod 10 addition table (Figure 6-1). Addition of a constant mod 10 can be used as a scheme for encrypting digits, in that it maps each decimal digit to a different decimal digit in a way that is reversible; the constant is our secret key. It's not a *good* cipher, of course, but it is a cipher. (It's actually a Caesar cipher.) Decryption would be done by subtracting the secret key modulo 10, which is an easy operation—just do ordinary subtraction and if the result is less than 0, add 10.

Just like in regular arithmetic, subtracting x can be done by adding $-x$, also known as x's **additive inverse**. An additive inverse of x is the number you'd have to add to x to get 0. For example, 4's inverse will be 6, because in mod 10 arithmetic $4 + 6 = 0$. If the secret key were 4, then to encrypt we'd add 4 (mod 10), and to decrypt we'd add 6 (mod 10).

+	0	1	2	3	4	5	6	7	8	9
0	0	1	2	3	4	5	6	7	8	9
1	1	2	3	4	5	6	7	8	9	0
2	2	3	4	5	6	7	8	9	0	1
3	3	4	5	6	7	8	9	0	1	2
4	4	5	6	7	8	9	0	1	2	3
5	5	6	7	8	9	0	1	2	3	4
6	6	7	8	9	0	1	2	3	4	5
7	7	8	9	0	1	2	3	4	5	6
8	8	9	0	1	2	3	4	5	6	7
9	9	0	1	2	3	4	5	6	7	8

Figure 6-1. Addition Modulo 10

6.2.2 Modular Multiplication

Now let's look at the mod 10 multiplication table (Figure 6-2). Multiplication by 1, 3, 7, or 9 works

·	0	1	2	3	4	5	6	7	8	9
0	0	0	0	0	0	0	0	0	0	0
1	0	1	2	3	4	5	6	7	8	9
2	0	2	4	6	8	0	2	4	6	8
3	0	3	6	9	2	5	8	1	4	7
4	0	4	8	2	6	0	4	8	2	6
5	0	5	0	5	0	5	0	5	0	5
6	0	6	2	8	4	0	6	2	8	4
7	0	7	4	1	8	5	2	9	6	3
8	0	8	6	4	2	0	8	6	4	2
9	0	9	8	7	6	5	4	3	2	1

Figure 6-2. Multiplication Modulo 10

as a cipher, because it performs a one-to-one substitution of the digits. But multiplication by any of the other numbers will not work as a cipher. For instance, if you tried to encrypt by multiplying by

5, half the numbers would encrypt to 0 and the other half would encrypt to 5. You've lost information. You can't decrypt the ciphertext 5, since the plaintext could be any of {1, 3, 5, 7, 9}. So multiplication mod 10 can be used for encryption, provided that you choose the multiplier wisely. But how do you decrypt? Well, just like with addition, where we undid the addition by adding the additive inverse, we'll undo the multiplication by multiplying by the multiplicative inverse. In ordinary arithmetic, x's multiplicative inverse is $1/x$. If x is an integer, then its multiplicative inverse is a fraction. In modular arithmetic though, the only numbers that exist are integers. The **multiplicative inverse** of x (written x^{-1}) is the number by which you'd multiply x to get 1. Only the numbers {1, 3, 7, 9} have multiplicative inverses mod 10. For example, 7 is the multiplicative inverse of 3. So encryption could be performed by multiplying by 3, and decryption could be performed by multiplying by 7. 9 is its own inverse. And 1 is its own inverse. Multiplication mod n is not a secure cipher, but it works, in the sense that we can scramble the digits by multiplying by x and get back to the original digits by multiplying by x^{-1}.

It is by no means obvious how you find a multiplicative inverse in mod n arithmetic, especially if n is very large. For instance if n was a 100-digit number, you would not be able to do a brute-force search for an inverse. But it turns out there is an algorithm that will efficiently find inverses mod n. It is known as Euclid's algorithm. §7.4 *Euclid's Algorithm* gives the details of the algorithm. For here, all you need to know is what it does. Given x and n, it finds the number y such that $x \cdot y \bmod n = 1$ (if there is one).

What's special about the numbers {1, 3, 7, 9}? Why is it they're the only ones, mod 10, with multiplicative inverses? The answer is that those numbers are all relatively prime to 10. **Relatively prime** means they do not share any common factors other than 1. For instance, the largest integer that divides both 9 and 10 is 1. The largest integer that divides both 7 and 10 is 1. In contrast, 6 is not one of {1, 3, 7, 9}, and it does not have a multiplicative inverse mod 10. It's also not relatively prime to 10 because 2 divides both 10 and 6. In general, when we're working mod n, all the numbers relatively prime to n will have multiplicative inverses, and none of the other numbers will. And mod n multiplication by any number x relatively prime to n will work as a cipher because we can multiply by x to encrypt, and then multiply by x^{-1} to decrypt. (Again let us hasten to reassure you that we're not claiming it's a *good* cipher, in the sense of being secure. What we mean by its being a cipher is that we can modify the information through one algorithm (multiplication by x mod n) and then reverse the process (by multiplying by x^{-1} mod n).

How many numbers less than n are relatively prime to n? Why would anyone care? Well, it turns out to be so useful that it's been given its own notation—$\phi(n)$. ϕ is called the **totient function**, supposedly from *total* and *quotient*. How big is $\phi(n)$? If n is prime, then all the integers $\{1, 2, \ldots n-1\}$ are relatively prime to n, so $\phi(n) = n-1$. If n is a product of two distinct primes, say p and q, then there are $(p-1)(q-1)$ numbers relatively prime to n, so $\phi(n) = (p-1)(q-1)$. Why is that? Well, there are $n = pq$ total numbers in $\{0, 1, 2, \ldots n-1\}$, and we want to exclude those numbers that aren't relatively prime to n. Those are the numbers that are either multiples of p or of q. There are p multiples of q less than pq and q multiples of p less than pq. So there are $p+q-1$ numbers less than

pq that aren't relatively prime to pq (we can't count 0 twice!). Thus $\phi(pq) = pq - (p+q-1) = (p-1)(q-1)$.

6.2.3 Modular Exponentiation

Modular exponentiation is again just like ordinary exponentiation. Once you get the answer, you divide by n and get the remainder. For instance, $4^6 = 6$ mod 10 because $4^6 = 4096$ in ordinary arithmetic, and $4096 = 6$ mod 10. Let's look at the exponentiation table mod 10. We are purposely putting in extra columns because in exponentiation, x^y mod n is not the same as x^{y+n} mod n. For instance, $3^1 = 3$ mod 10, but $3^{11} = 7$ mod 10 (it's 177147 in ordinary arithmetic).

Let's look at mod 10 exponentiation (Figure 6-3). Note that exponentiation by 3 would act as

x^y	0	1	2	3	4	5	6	7	8	9	10	11	12
0		0	0	0	0	0	0	0	0	0	0	0	0
1	1	1	1	1	1	1	1	1	1	1	1	1	1
2	1	2	4	8	6	2	4	8	6	2	4	8	6
3	1	3	9	7	1	3	9	7	1	3	9	7	1
4	1	4	6	4	6	4	6	4	6	4	6	4	6
5	1	5	5	5	5	5	5	5	5	5	5	5	5
6	1	6	6	6	6	6	6	6	6	6	6	6	6
7	1	7	9	3	1	7	9	3	1	7	9	3	1
8	1	8	4	2	6	8	4	2	6	8	4	2	6
9	1	9	1	9	1	9	1	9	1	9	1	9	1

Figure 6-3. Exponentiation Modulo 10

an encryption of the digits, in that it rearranges all the digits. Exponentiation by 2 would not, because both 2^2 and 8^2 are 4 mod 10. How would you decrypt? Is there an exponentiative inverse like there is a multiplicative inverse? Just like with multiplication, the answer is *sometimes*. (I bet people are going to hate our inventing the word *exponentiative*, but it's a useful word.)

Now we'll throw in an amazing fact about $\phi(n)$. Looking at the exponentiation table, we notice that columns 1 and 5 are the same, and 2 and 6 are the same, and 3 and 7 are the same. It turns out that x^y mod n is the same as $x^{(y \bmod \phi(n))}$ mod n. In the case of 10, the numbers relatively prime to 10 are {1, 3, 7, 9}, so $\phi(n) = 4$. So that's why the ith column is the same as the $i+4^{th}$ column. (Note for picky mathematicians—this fact isn't true for all n, but it's true for all n we care about. It's true for primes and it's true for any product of distinct primes, i.e. it's true for any n that doesn't have p^2 as a factor for any prime p—such an n is known as **square free**.)

What we'll find important is the special case of this where $y = 1 \bmod \phi(n)$, i.e. if $y = 1 \bmod \phi(n)$, then for any number x, $x^y = x \bmod n$. Armed with this knowledge, let's look at RSA.

6.3 RSA

RSA is named after its inventors, Rivest, Shamir, and Adleman. It is a public key cryptographic algorithm that does encryption as well as decryption. The key length is variable. Anyone using RSA can choose a long key for enhanced security, or a short key for efficiency. The most commonly used key length for RSA is 512 bits.

The block size in RSA (the chunk of data to be encrypted) is also variable. The plaintext block must be smaller than the key length. The ciphertext block will be the length of the key. RSA is much slower to compute than popular secret key algorithms like DES and IDEA. As a result, RSA does not tend to get used for encrypting long messages. Mostly it is used to encrypt a secret key, and then secret key cryptography is used to actually encrypt the message.

6.3.1 RSA Algorithm

First, you need to generate a public key and a corresponding private key. Choose two large primes p and q (probably around 256 bits each). Multiply them together, and call the result n. The factors p and q will remain secret. (You won't tell anybody, and it's practically impossible to factor numbers that large.)

To generate your public key, choose a number e that is relatively prime to $\phi(n)$. Since you know p and q, you know $\phi(n)$—it's $(p-1)(q-1)$. Your public key is $\langle e,n \rangle$.

To generate your private key, find the number d that is the multiplicative inverse of $e \bmod \phi(n)$. $\langle d,n \rangle$ is your private key.

To encrypt a message m ($< n$), someone using your public key should compute ciphertext $c = m^e \bmod n$. Only you will be able to decrypt c, using your private key to compute $m = c^d \bmod n$. Also, only you can sign a message m ($< n$) with signature $s = m^d \bmod n$ based on your private key. Anyone can verify your signature by checking that $m = s^e \bmod n$.

That's all there is to RSA. Now there are some questions we should ask.

- Why does it work? (E.g., will decrypting an encrypted message get the original message back?)

- Why is it secure? (E.g., given e and n, why can't someone easily compute d?)
- Are the operations encryption, decryption, signing, and verifying signatures all sufficiently efficient to be practical?
- How do we find big primes?

6.3.2 Why Does RSA Work?

RSA does arithmetic mod n, where $n = pq$. We know that $\phi(n) = (p-1)(q-1)$. We've chosen d and e such that $de = 1 \bmod \phi(n)$. Therefore, for any x, $x^{de} = x \bmod n$. An RSA encryption consists of taking x and raising it to e. If we take the result and raise it to the d (i.e., perform RSA decryption), we'll get $(x^e)^d$, which equals x^{ed}, which is the same as x. So we see that decryption reverses encryption.

In the case of signature generation, x is first raised to the d power to get the signature and then the signature is raised to the e power for verification; the result, x^{de}, will equal x.

6.3.3 Why Is RSA Secure?

We don't know for sure that RSA is secure. We can only depend on the Fundamental Tenet of Cryptography—lots of smart people have been trying to figure out how to break RSA, and they haven't come up with anything yet.

The real premise behind RSA's security is the assumption that factoring a big number is hard. The best known factoring methods are really slow. To factor a 512-bit number with the best known techniques would take about thirty thousand MIPS-years [ROBS95]. We suspect that a better technique is to wait a few years and *then* use the best known technique.

If you can factor quickly, you can break RSA. Suppose you are given Alice's public key $\langle e,n\rangle$. If you could find e's exponentiative inverse mod n, then you'd have figured out Alice's private key $\langle d,n\rangle$. How can you find e's exponentiative inverse? Alice did it by knowing the factors of n, allowing her to compute $\phi(n)$. She found the number that was e's multiplicative inverse mod $\phi(n)$. She didn't have to factor n—she started with primes p and q and multiplied them together to get n. You can do what Alice did if you can factor n to get p and q.

We do not know that factoring n is the only way of breaking RSA. We know that breaking RSA (for example, having an efficient means of finding d, given e and n) is no more difficult than factoring [CORM91], but there might be some other means of breaking RSA.

Note that it's possible to misuse RSA. For instance, let's say I'm going to send Alice a message divulging the name of the Cabinet member who allegedly once hired a kid to mow his/her lawn, and didn't fill out all the proper IRS forms. Bob knows that's what I'm going to transmit. I'll encrypt the text string which is the guilty person's name using Alice's public key. Bob can't possibly decrypt it, because we believe RSA is secure. So what can Bob learn from eavesdropping on the encrypted data?

Well, Bob can't decrypt, but he can encrypt. He knows I'm sending one of fourteen possible messages. He takes each Cabinet member's name and encrypts it with Alice's public key. One of them will match my message—unless I use RSA properly. In §6.3.6 *Public-Key Cryptography Standard (PKCS)* we'll discuss how to use RSA properly. For now, a simple thing I can do to prevent Bob from guessing my message, encrypting with Alice's public key, and checking the result, is to concatenate the name with a large random number, say 64 bits long. Then instead of fourteen possible messages for Bob to check, there are 14×2^{64}, and checking that many messages is computationally infeasible.

6.3.4 How Efficient Are the RSA Operations?

The operations that need to be routinely performed with RSA are encryption, decryption, generating a signature, and verifying a signature. These need to be very efficient, because they will be used a lot. Finding an RSA key (which means picking appropriate n, d, and e) also needs to be reasonably efficient, but it isn't as critical as the other operations, since it is done less frequently. As it turns out, finding an RSA key is substantially more computationally intensive than using one.

6.3.4.1 Exponentiating with Big Numbers

Encryption, decryption, signing, and verifying signatures all involve taking a large number, raising it to a large power, and finding the remainder mod a large number. For the sizes the numbers have to be for RSA to be secure, these operations would be prohibitively expensive if done in the most straightforward way. The following will illustrate some tricks for doing the calculation faster.

Suppose you want to compute 123^{54} mod 678. The straightforward thing to do (assuming your computer has a multiple-precision arithmetic package) is to multiply 123 by itself 54 times, getting a really big product (about 100 digits), and then to divide by 678 to get the remainder. A computer could do this with ease, but for RSA to be secure, the numbers must be on the order of 150 digits. Raising a 150-digit number to a 150-digit power by this method would exhaust the capacity of all existing computers for more than the expected life of the universe, and thus would not be cost-effective.

Luckily, you can do better than that.

If you do the modular reduction after each multiply, it keeps the number from getting really ridiculous. To illustrate:

$$123^2 = 123 \cdot 123 = 15129 = 213 \bmod 678$$

$$123^3 = 123 \cdot 213 = 26199 = 435 \bmod 678$$

$$123^4 = 123 \cdot 435 = 53505 = 621 \bmod 678$$

This reduces the problem to 54 small multiplies and 54 small divides, but it would still be unacceptable for exponents of the size used with RSA.

However, there is a much more efficient method. To raise a number x to an exponent which is a power of 2, say 32, you could multiply by x 32 times, which is reasonable if you have nothing better to do with your time. A much better scheme is to first square x, then square the result, and so on. Then you'll be done after 5 squarings (5 multiplies and 5 divides):

$$123^2 = 123 \cdot 123 = 15129 = 213 \bmod 678$$

$$123^4 = 213 \cdot 213 = 45369 = 621 \bmod 678$$

$$123^8 = 621 \cdot 621 = 385641 = 537 \bmod 678$$

$$123^{16} = 537 \cdot 537 = 288369 = 219 \bmod 678$$

$$123^{32} = 219 \cdot 219 = 47961 = 501 \bmod 678$$

What if you're not lucky enough to be raising something to a power of 2?

First note that if you know what 123^x is, then it's easy to compute 123^{2x}—you get that by squaring 123^x. It's also easy to compute 123^{2x+1}—you get that by multiplying 123^{2x} by 123. Now you use this observation to compute 123^{54}.

Well, 54 is 110110_2 (represented in binary). You'll compute 123 raised to a sequence of powers—1_2, 11_2, 110_2, 1101_2, 11011_2, 110110_2. Each successive power concatenates one more bit of the desired exponent. And each successive power is either twice the preceding power or one more than twice the preceding power:

$$123^2 = 123 \cdot 123 = 15129 = 213 \mod 678$$

$$123^3 = 123^2 \cdot 123 = 213 \cdot 123 = 26199 = 435 \mod 678$$

$$123^6 = (123^3)^2 = 435^2 = 189225 = 63 \mod 678$$

$$123^{12} = (123^6)^2 = 63^2 = 3969 = 579 \mod 678$$

$$123^{13} = 123^{12} \cdot 123 = 579 \cdot 123 = 71217 = 27 \mod 678$$

$$123^{26} = (123^{13})^2 = 27^2 = 729 = 51 \mod 678$$

$$123^{27} = 123^{26} \cdot 123 = 51 \cdot 123 = 6273 = 171 \mod 678$$

$$123^{54} = (123^{27})^2 = 171^2 = 29241 = 87 \mod 678$$

In other words, raising 123 to the 54 can be done by repeated squaring, together with sporadic multiplication by 123 for the bits that are 1:

$$54 = ((((1)2+1)2)2+1)2+1)2, \qquad \text{so}$$
$$123^{54} = (((((123)^2 123)^2)^2 123)^2 123)^2 = 87 \bmod 678.$$

The idea is that squaring is the same as multiplying the exponent by two, which in turn is the same as shifting the exponent left by one bit. And multiplying by the base is the same as adding one to the exponent.

In general, to perform exponentiation of a base to an exponent, you start with your value set to 1. As you read the exponent in binary bit by bit from high-order bit to low-order bit, you square your value, and if the bit is a 1 you then multiply by the base. You perform modular reduction after each operation to keep the intermediate results small.

By this method you've reduced the computation of 123^{54} to 8 multiplies and 8 divides. More importantly, the number of multiplies and divides rises linearly with the length of the exponent in bits rather than with the value of the exponent itself.

RSA operations using this technique are sufficiently efficient to be practical.

6.3.4.2 Generating RSA Keys

Most uses of public key cryptography do not require frequent generation of RSA keys. If generation of an RSA key is only done, for instance, when an employee is hired, then it need not be as efficient as the operations that use the keys. However, it still has to be reasonably efficient.

6.3.4.2.1. Finding Big Primes *p* and *q*

There is an infinite supply of primes. However, they thin out as numbers get bigger and bigger. The probability of a randomly chosen number n being prime is approximately $1/\ln n$. The natural logarithm function, ln, rises linearly with the size of the number represented in digits or bits. For a ten-digit number, there is about one chance in 23 of it being prime. For a hundred-digit number (a size that would be useful for RSA), there is about one chance in 230.

So, we'll choose a random number, and test if it is prime. On the average, we'll only have to try 230 of them before we find one that is a prime. So, how do we test if a number n is prime?

One naive method is to divide n by all numbers $\leq \sqrt{n}$ and see if the division comes out even. The problem is, that would take several universe lifetimes for each candidate prime. We said finding p and q didn't need to be as easy as generating or verifying a signature, but forever is too long.

It turns out there is no known practical way for absolutely determining that a number of this size is prime. Fortunately, there is a test for determining that a number is probably prime, and the more time we spend testing a number the more assured we can be that the number is prime.

We'll use **Euler's Theorem**: For any a relatively prime to n, $a^{\phi(n)} = 1 \bmod n$. (See §7.8 *Euler's Theorem* for a proof.)

In the case where n is a prime, $\phi(n) = n-1$. The theorem then takes on a simpler form and in fact another name:

Fermat's Theorem: If p is prime and $0 < a < p$, $a^{p-1} = 1 \bmod p$.

You might ask the question (somebody did)—does $a^{n-1} = 1 \bmod n$ hold even when n is not prime? The answer is—usually not! A primality test, then, for a number n is to pick a number $a < n$, compute $a^{n-1} \bmod n$, and see if the answer is 1. If it is not 1, n is certainly not prime. If it is 1, n may or may not be prime. If n is a randomly generated number of about a hundred digits, the probability that n isn't prime but $a^{n-1} \bmod n = 1$ is about 1 in 10^{13} [POME81, CORM91]. Most people would decide they could live with that risk of falsely assuming n was prime when it wasn't. The cost of such a mistake would be that (1) RSA might fail—they could not decrypt a message addressed to them, or (2) someone might be able to compute their private exponent with less effort than anticipated. There aren't many applications where a risk of failure of 1 in 10^{13} is a problem.

But if the risk of 1 in 10^{13} is unacceptable, the primality test can be made more reliable. A likely thing to try is using multiple values of a. If for any given n, each value of a had a probability of 1 in 10^{13} of falsely reporting primality, a few tests would assure even the most paranoid person. Unfortunately, there exist numbers n which are not prime, but which satisfy $a^{n-1} = 1 \bmod n$ for all values of a. They are called **Carmichael numbers**. Carmichael numbers are sufficiently rare that the chance of selecting one at random is nothing to lose sleep over. Nevertheless, mathematicians have come up with an enhancement to the above primality test that will detect non-primes (even Carmichael numbers) with high probability and negligible additional computation, so we may as well use it.

The method of choice for testing whether a number is prime is due to Miller and Rabin [RABI80]. We can always express $n-1$ as a power of two times an odd number, say $2^b c$. We can then compute $a^{n-1} \bmod n$ by computing $a^c \bmod n$ and then squaring the result b times. If the result is not 1, then n is not prime and we're done. If the result is 1, we can go back and look at those last few intermediate squarings. (If we're really clever, we'll be checking the intermediate results as we compute them.) If $a^c \bmod n$ is not 1, then one of the squarings took a number that was not 1 and squared it to produce 1. That number is a mod n square root of 1. It turns out that if n is prime, then the only mod n square roots of 1 are 1 and -1 (also known as $n-1$). Further, if n is not a power of a prime, then 1 has many square roots, and all are equally likely to be found by this test. For more on why, see §7.5 *Chinese Remainder Theorem*. So if the Miller-Rabin test finds a square root of 1 that is not ± 1, then n is not prime. Furthermore, if n is not prime (even if it is a Carmichael number), at least ¾ of all possible values of a will show n to be composite. By trying many values for a, we can make the probability of falsely identifying n as prime inconceivably small. In actual implementations, how many values of a to try is a trade-off between performance and paranoia.

To summarize, an efficient method of finding primes is:

1. Pick an odd random number n in the proper range.
2. Test n's divisibility by small primes and go back to step 1 if you find a factor. (Obviously, this step isn't necessary, but it's worth it since it has a high enough probability of catching some non-primes and is much faster than the next step).
3. Repeat the following until n is proven not prime (in which case go back to step 1) or as many times as you feel necessary to show that n is probably prime:

   Pick an a at random and compute a^c mod n (where c is the odd number for which $n-1 = 2^b c$). During the computation of a^c mod n, each time mod n squaring is performed, check if the result is 1; if so, check if the number that was squared (which is a square root of 1) is ± 1; if not, n is not prime.

   Next, if the result of the computation of a^c mod n is ± 1, n passes the primality test for this a. Otherwise, at most $b-1$ times, replace the result by its square and check if it is ± 1. If it is 1, n is not prime (because the previous result is a square root of 1 different from ± 1). If it is -1, n passes the primality test for this a. If you've done the squaring $b-1$ times, n is not prime (because $a^{(n-1)/2}$ is not ± 1).

6.3.4.2.2. Finding *d* and *e*

How do we find d and e given p and q? As we said earlier, for e we can choose any number that is relatively prime to $(p-1)(q-1)$, and then all we need to do is find the number d such that $ed = 1 \bmod \phi(n)$. This we can do with Euclid's algorithm.

There are two strategies one can use to ensure that e and $(p-1)(q-1)$ are relatively prime.

1. After p and q are selected, choose e at random. Test to see if e is relatively prime to $(p-1)(q-1)$. If not, select another e.
2. Don't pick p and q first. Instead, first choose e, then select p and q carefully so that $(p-1)$ and $(q-1)$ are guaranteed to be relatively prime to e. The next section will explain why you'd want to do this.

6.3.4.3 Having a Small Constant *e*

A rather astonishing discovery is that RSA is no less secure (as far as anyone knows) if e is always chosen to be the same number. And if e is chosen to be small, or easy to compute, then the operations of encryption and signature verification become much more efficient. Given that the procedure for finding a d and e pair is to pick one and then derive the other, it is straightforward to make e be a small constant. This makes public key operations faster while leaving private key operations unchanged. You might wonder whether it would be possible to select small values for d to make private key operations fast at the expense of public key operations. The answer is that you can't. If d were a constant, the scheme would not be secure because d is the secret. If d were small, an attacker could search small values to find d.

Two popular values of e are 3 and 65537.

Why 3? 2 doesn't work because it is not relatively prime to $(p-1)(q-1)$ (which must be even because p and q are both odd). 3 can work, and with 3, public key operations require only two multiplies. Using 3 as the public exponent maximizes performance.

As far as anyone knows, using 3 as a public exponent does not weaken the security of RSA if some practical constraints on its use are followed. Most dramatically, if a message m to be encrypted is small—in particular, smaller than $\sqrt[3]{n}$—then raising m to the power of three and reducing mod n will simply produce the value m^3. Anyone seeing such an encrypted message could decrypt it simply by taking a cube root. This problem can be avoided by padding each message with a random number before encryption, so that m^3 is always large enough to be guaranteed to need to be reduced mod n.

A second problem with using 3 as an exponent is that if the same message is sent encrypted to three or more recipients each of whom has a public exponent of 3, the message can be derived from the three encrypted values and the three public keys $\langle 3, n_1\rangle$, $\langle 3, n_2\rangle$, $\langle 3, n_3\rangle$.

Suppose a bad guy sees m^3 mod n_1, m^3 mod n_2, and m^3 mod n_3 and knows $\langle 3, n_1\rangle$, $\langle 3, n_2\rangle$, $\langle 3, n_3\rangle$. Then by the Chinese Remainder computation (see §7.5 *Chinese Remainder Theorem*), the bad guy can compute m^3 mod $n_1n_2n_3$. Since m is smaller than each of the n_is (because RSA can only encrypt messages smaller than the modulus), m^3 will be smaller than $n_1n_2n_3$, so m^3 mod $n_1n_2n_3$ will just be m^3. Therefore, the bad guy can compute the ordinary cube root of m^3 (which again is easy if you are a computer), giving m.

Now this isn't anything to get terribly upset about. In practical uses of RSA, the message to be encrypted is usually a key for a secret key encryption algorithm and in any case is much smaller than n. As a result, the message must be padded before it is encrypted. If the padding is randomly chosen (and it should be for a number of reasons), and if it is rechosen for each recipient, then there is no threat from an exponent of 3 no matter how many recipients there are. The padding doesn't really have to be random—for example, the recipient's ID would work fine.

Finally, an exponent of 3 works only if 3 is relatively prime to $\phi(n)$ (in order for it to have an inverse d). How do we choose p and q so that 3 will be relatively prime to $\phi(n) = (p-1)(q-1)$? Clearly, $(p-1)$ and $(q-1)$ must each be relatively prime to 3. To ensure that $p-1$ is relatively prime to 3, we want p to be 2 mod 3. That will ensure $p-1$ is 1 mod 3. Similarly we want q to be 2 mod 3. We can make sure that the only primes we select are congruent to 2 mod 3 by choosing a random number, multiplying by 3 and adding 2, and using that as the number we will test for primality. Indeed, we want to make sure the number we test is odd (since if it's even it is unlikely to be prime), so we should start with an odd number, multiply by 3 and add 2. This is equivalent to starting with any random number, multiplying by 6 and then adding 5.

Another popular value of e is 65537. Why 65537? The appeal of 65537 (as opposed to others of the same approximate size) is that $65537 = 2^{16}+1$ and it is prime. Because its binary representation contains only two 1s, it takes only 17 multiplies to exponentiate. While this is much slower than the two multiplies required with an exponent of 3, it is much faster than the 768 (on average) required with a randomly chosen 512-bit value (the typical size of an RSA modulus in practical use today). Also, using the number 65537 as a public exponent largely avoids the problems with the exponent 3.

The first problem with 3 occurs if $m^3 < n$. Unless n is much longer than the 512 bits in typical use today, there aren't too many values of m for which $m^{65537} < n$, so being able to take a normal 65537th root is not a threat.

The second problem with 3 occurs when the same message is sent to at least 3 recipients. In theory, with 65537 there is a threat if the same message is sent encrypted to at least 65537 recipients. A cynic would argue that under such circumstances, the message couldn't be very secret.

The third problem with 3 is that we have to choose n so that $\phi(n)$ is relatively prime to 3. For 65537, the easiest thing to do is just reject any p or q which is equal to 1 mod 65537. The probability of rejection is very small (2^{-16}), so this doesn't make finding n significantly harder.

6.3.4.4 Optimizing RSA Private Key Operations

There is a way to speed up RSA exponentiations in generating signatures and decrypting (the operations using the private key) by taking advantage of knowledge of p and q. Feel free to skip this section—it isn't a prerequisite for anything else in the book. And it requires more than the usual level of concentration.

In RSA, d and n are on the order of 512-bit numbers, or 150 digits. p and q are on the order of 256 bits, or 75 digits. RSA private key operations involve taking some c (usually a 512-bit number) and computing c^d mod n. It's easy to say "raise a 512-bit number to a 512-bit exponent mod a 512-bit number," but it's certainly processor-intensive, even if you happen to be a silicon-based computer. A way to speed up RSA operations is to do all the computation mod p and mod q, then use the Chinese Remainder Theorem to compute what the answer is mod pq.

So suppose you want to compute $m = c^d$ mod n.

Instead, you could take $c_p = c$ mod p and $c_q = c$ mod q and compute $m_p = {c_p}^d$ mod p and $m_q = {c_q}^d$ mod q, then use the Chinese Remainder Theorem to convert back to what m would equal mod n, which would give you c^d mod n. Also, it is not necessary to raise to the dth power mod p, given that d is going to be bigger than p (by a factor of about q). Since (by Euler's Theorem) any $a^{p-1} = 1$ mod p, we can take d's value mod p–1 and use that as the exponent instead. In other words, if $d = k(p-1) + r$, then c^d mod $p = c^r$ mod p.

So, let us compute $d_p = d \bmod (p-1)$ and $d_q = d \bmod (q-1)$. Then, instead of doing the expected RSA operation of $m = c^d \bmod n$ which involves 512-bit numbers, we'll compute both $m_p = c_p^{d_p} \bmod p$ and $m_q = c_q^{d_q} \bmod q$ and then compute m from the Chinese Remainder Theorem. To save ourselves work, since we'll be using d_p and d_q a lot (every time we do an RSA private key computation), we'll compute them once and remember them. Similarly, to use the Chinese Remainder Theorem at the end, we need to know $p^{-1} \bmod q$ and $q^{-1} \bmod p$, so we'll precompute and remember them as well.

All told, instead of one 512-bit exponentiation, this modified calculation does two 256-bit exponentiations, followed by two 256-bit multiplies and a 512-bit add. This might not seem like a net gain, but because the exponents are half as long, using this variant makes RSA about twice as fast.

Note that to do these optimizations for RSA operations, we need to know p and q. Someone who is only supposed to know the public key will not know p and q (or else they can easily compute d). Therefore, these optimizations are only useful for the private key operations (decryption and generating signatures). However, that's okay because we can choose e to be a convenient value (like 3 or 65537) so that raising a 512-bit number to e will be easy enough without the Chinese Remainder optimizations.

6.3.5 Arcane RSA Threats

Any number $x < n$ is a signature of $x^e \bmod n$. So it's trivial to forge someone's signature if you don't care what you're signing. The trick is to find a way to sign a specific number. Typically what is being signed is sufficiently constrained so that a random number has negligible probability of being a valid message. For example, often what is being signed is a message digest padded in a specific manner. If the pad is hundreds of zero bits, it is extremely unlikely that a random number will look like a padded message digest.

If you're not careful about how you pad your message data, you may allow an attacker without knowledge of your private key to forge your signature on valid messages.

Note: RSA deals with large numbers, and there is unfortunately more than one way to represent such numbers. In what follows, we have chosen to order the octets left to right from most significant to least significant.

6.3.5.1 Smooth Numbers

A **smooth number** is defined as one that is the product of reasonably small primes. There's no absolute definition of a smooth number, since there's no real definition of *reasonably small*. The more compute power the attacker has at her disposal, and the more signatures she has access to, the larger the primes can be.

The threat we are about to describe is known as the **smooth number threat**. It is really only of theoretical interest, because of the immense amount of computation, gathering of immense numbers of signed messages, and luck involved. However, it costs very little to have an encoding that avoids this threat. The smooth number threat was discovered by Desmedt and Odlyzko [DESM86].

The first observation is that if you have signed m_1 and m_2, and a bad guy Carol can see your signature on m_1 and m_2, she can compute your signature on $m_1 \cdot m_2$, and on m_1/m_2, and $m_1{}^j$, and on $m_1{}^j \cdot m_2{}^k$. For instance, if Carol sees $m_1{}^d$ mod n (which is your signature on m_1), then she can compute your signature on $m_1{}^2$ by computing $(m_1{}^d \bmod n)^2 \bmod n$ (see Homework Problem 8).

If Carol collects a lot of your signed messages, she will be able to compute your signature on any message that can be computed from her collection by multiplication and division. If the messages you sign are mostly smooth, there will be a lot of other smooth messages on which she will be able to forge your signature.

Suppose she collects your signatures on two messages whose ratio is a prime. Then she can compute your signature on that prime. If she's lucky enough to get many such message pairs, she can compute your signature on lots of primes, and then she can forge your signature on any message that is the product of any subset of those primes, each raised to any power. With enough pairs, she will be able to forge your signature on any message that is a smooth number.

Actually, Carol does not have to be nearly that lucky. With as few as k signatures on messages which are products of different subsets of k distinct primes, she will be able to isolate the signatures on the individual primes through a carefully chosen set of multiplications and divisions.

The typical thing being signed with RSA is a padded message digest. If it is padded with zeroes, it is much more likely to be smooth than is a random mod n number. A random mod n quantity is extremely unlikely to be smooth (low enough probability so that if you are signing random mod n numbers, we can assume Carol would have to have a lot of resources and a lot of luck to find even one smooth number you've signed, and she might need millions of them in order to mount the attack).

Padding on the left with zeroes keeps the padded message digest small and therefore likely to be smooth. Padding on the right with zeroes is merely multiplying the message digest by some power of 2, and so isn't any better.

Another tempting padding scheme is to pad on the right with random data. That way, since you are signing fairly random mod n numbers, it is very unlikely that any of the messages you sign will be smooth, so Carol won't have enough signed smooth messages to mount the threat. However, this leaves us open to the next obscure threat.

6.3.5.2 The Cube Root Problem

Let's say you pad on the right with random data. You chose that scheme so that there is a negligible probability that anything you sign will be smooth. However, if the public exponent is 3, this enables Carol to forge your signature on virtually any message she chooses!

Let's say Carol wants your signature on some message. The message digest of that message is h. Carol pads h on the right with zeroes. She then computes its ordinary cube root and rounds up to an integer r. Now she has forged your signature, because $r^e = r^3 =$ (h padded on the right with a seemingly random number).

6.3.6 Public-Key Cryptography Standard (PKCS)

It is useful to have some standard for the encoding of information that will be signed or encrypted through RSA, so that different implementations can interwork, and so that the various pitfalls with RSA can be avoided. Rather than expecting every user of RSA to be sophisticated enough to know about all the attacks and develop appropriate safety measures through careful encoding, RSADSI has developed a standard known as **PKCS** which recommends encodings. PKCS is actually a set of standards, called PKCS #1 through PKCS #15. There are also two companion documents, *An overview of the PKCS standards*, and *A layman's guide to a subset of ASN.1, BER, and DER*. (**ASN.1** = *Abstract Syntax Notation 1*, **BER** = *Basic Encoding Rules*, and **DER** = *Distinguished Encoding Rules*—aren't you glad you asked?).

The PKCS standards define the encodings for things such as an RSA public key, an RSA private key, an RSA signature, a short RSA-encrypted message (typically a secret key), a short RSA-signed message (typically a message digest), and password-based encryption.

The threats that PKCS has been designed to deal with are:

- encrypting guessable messages
- signing smooth numbers
- multiple recipients of a message when $e = 3$
- encrypting messages that are less than a third the length of n when $e = 3$
- signing messages where the information is in the high-order part and $e = 3$

6.3.6.1 Encryption

PKCS #1 defines a standard for formatting a message to be encrypted with RSA. RSA is not generally used to encrypt ordinary data. The most common quantity that would be encrypted with RSA is a secret key, and for performance reasons the ordinary data would be encrypted with the secret key.

The recommended standard is

0	2	at least eight random nonzero octets	0	data

The actual data to be encrypted, usually a secret key, is much smaller than the modulus. If it's a DES key, it's 64 bits. If multiple DES encryption is used, then there might be two DES keys there, or 128 bits.

The top octet is 0, which is a good choice because this guarantees that the message *m* being encrypted is smaller than the modulus *n*. (If *m* were larger than *n*, decryption would produce *m* mod *n* instead of *m*.) Note that PKCS specifies that the high-order octet (not bit!) of the modulus must be non-zero.

The next octet is 2, which is the format type. The value 2 is used for a block to be encrypted. The value 1 is used for a value to be signed (see next section).

Each octet of padding is chosen independently to be a random nonzero value. The reason 0 cannot be used as a padding octet is that 0 is used to delimit the padding from the data.

Let's review the RSA threats and see how this encoding addresses them:

- encrypting guessable messages—Since there are at least eight octets of randomly chosen padding, knowing what might appear in the data does not help the attacker who would like to guess the data, encrypt it, and compare it with the ciphertext. The attacker would have to guess the padding as well, and this is infeasible.
- sending the same encrypted message to more than three recipients (assuming 3 is chosen for *e*)—As long as the padding is chosen independently for each recipient, the quantities being encrypted will not be the same.
- encrypting messages that are less than a third the length of *n* when $e = 3$—Because the second octet is nonzero, the message will be guaranteed to be more than a third the length of *n*.

6.3.6.2 Encryption—Take 2

There was an attack on SSL (see Chapter 19 *SSL/TLS*) that could have been interpreted as a flaw in the design of SSL, but the world has come to see it as a flaw in the PKCS #1 encryption format, and there is a PKCS #1 version 2 format that fixes the "flaw". The attack is known as the **million message attack**, and occurs because SSL made some incorrect assumptions about the services PKCS #1 padding provides.

In the SSL protocol, the client sends the server a randomly chosen key padded according to PKCS #1 and encrypted using RSA. SSL decrypts the value, and, if the padding is correct, sends a response encrypted with the enclosed key. If after the decryption the padding is not correct, it sends an error message. The problem is that this allows an attacker to use the server as an oracle: it can send the server a message and the server will tell it whether the message (when decrypted) has proper PKCS #1 padding. Some SSL servers were particularly helpful and would say whether the padding was wrong because the first two octets were something other than 0 and 2 or whether it was wrong because the length of the encrypted quantity was something other than what was expected.

Daniel Bleichenbacher [BLEI98] figured out how an eavesdropper who picked up a key encrypted for a server could carefully craft variations of that encrypted key such that if the server would identify some of those variations which when decrypted began with the octets 0 and 2, the attacker could eventually figure out the encrypted key. The most helpful servers would identify one message in 2^{16} as having that form, allowing the eavesdropper to recover the encrypted key after sending about a million messages (most of them invalid).

Attacks of this sort can be avoided if the padding for encryption includes enough redundancy that the probability of a randomly chosen value decrypting into something that looks like it is properly padded is negligible. (*One in a million* is not considered negligible to cryptographers. To them "negligible" should be less than one in 2^{100} or so.) A particularly complex scheme for doing that is specified in PKCS #1 version 2, also known as OAEP [BELL94] and standardized in IEEE P1363.

Because this is an obscure attack easily avoided by other means (like not being so helpful when people send you invalid messages), the world has not scrambled to migrate to this new padding. But it will probably be mandated in newly defined protocols where backwards compatibility is not an issue.

6.3.6.3 Signing

PKCS #1 also defines a standard for formatting a message to be signed with RSA. Usually the data being signed is a message digest, typically 128 bits. As with encryption, padding is required.

0	1	at least eight octets of ff_{16}	0	ASN.1-encoded digest type and digest

As with encryption, the top octet of 0 ensures that the quantity to be signed will be less than n. The next octet is the PKCS type, in this case, a quantity to be signed. The padding ensures that the quantity to be signed is very large and therefore unlikely to be a smooth number.

Inclusion of the digest type instead of merely the digest serves two purposes. It standardizes how to tell the other party which digest function you used, and it prevents an obscure threat. The threat is that one of the message digest functions, say MD4, might be weak, so that bad guys with big budgets can generate a message with a particular MD4 message digest. Now suppose you were suspicious of MD4 and therefore used MD5. You signed the MD5 message digest of your message m. If the digest type were not included in the quantity that you RSA signed, then a bad guy could generate some message m' such that MD4(m') = MD5(m), and use the same signature you'd generated for m as the signature for m'. Including the digest type in the signature means you're at risk only for the cryptographic strength of the message digest functions you choose to use.

6.4 DIFFIE-HELLMAN

The Diffie-Hellman public key cryptosystem predates RSA and is in fact the oldest public key system still in use. It is less general than RSA (it does neither encryption nor signatures), but it offers better performance for what it does. If Diffie-Hellman neither encrypts nor signs, how can it be called a cryptosystem? What does it do?

Diffie-Hellman allows two individuals to agree on a shared key, even though they can only exchange messages in public. In other words, assume our famous two people, Alice and Bob, want to have a secret number that they share so that they can start encrypting messages to each other. But the only way they can talk is by some means of communication that lots of people can overhear. For instance, they might be sending messages across a network, or on a telephone that might be tapped, or they might be shouting at each other across a crowded room, or they might for some reason have to resort to communication by placing ads in the personals section of the local newspaper.

> Dear Bob, the magic number is 1890289304789234789279189028902.
> Wish you were here. Love, Alice.

In its original conception, the Diffie-Hellman algorithm has limited functionality, since the only thing it really accomplishes is having a secret number that both Alice and Bob know, and nobody else can figure out based on the messages they overhear between Alice and Bob. Neither Alice nor Bob start out with any secrets, yet after the exchange of two messages that the world can overhear, Alice and Bob will know a secret number. Once they know a secret number, they can use conventional cryptography (secret key cryptography like DES, for instance) for encryption. Diffie-Hellman is actually used for key establishment (getting two things to agree on a common secret key) in some applications, for instance data link encryption on a LAN.

A weakness of Diffie-Hellman is that although two individuals can agree on a shared secret key, there is no authentication, which means that Alice might be establishing a secret key with a bad guy. We will talk about this more after we force you to read through how Diffie-Hellman works.

To start out, there are numbers p and g, where p is a large prime and g is a number less than p with some restrictions that aren't too important for a basic understanding of the algorithm. p and g are known beforehand and can be publicly known. For instance, Alice could choose a p and g and send them (publicly) to Bob, for instance by publishing them in *The New York Times*.

> Dear Bob, I'd like our prime to be 128903289023 and our g to be 23489. Love, Alice.

Once Alice and Bob agree on a p and g, each chooses a 512-bit number at random and keeps it secret. Let's call Alice's secret number S_A and Bob's secret number S_B. Each raises g to their secret number, mod p. The result is that Alice computes some number T_A and Bob computes some number T_B. They exchange their Ts. Finally, each raises the received T to their secret number.

> Alice picks S_A at random. Bob picks S_B at random.
> Alice computes $T_A = g^{S_A} \bmod p$. Bob computes $T_B = g^{S_B} \bmod p$.
> They exchange Ts (in either order or simultaneously): $T_A \leftrightarrow T_B$
> Now each raises the number they receive to their private secret number:
> Alice computes ${T_B}^{S_A} \bmod p$. Bob computes ${T_A}^{S_B} \bmod p$.
> They will both come up with the same number. That is because
> ${T_B}^{S_A} = (g^{S_B})^{S_A} = g^{S_B S_A} = g^{S_A S_B} = (g^{S_A})^{S_B} = {T_A}^{S_B} \bmod p$.

Nobody else can calculate $g^{S_A S_B}$ in a reasonable amount of time even though they know g^{S_A} and g^{S_B}. If they could compute discrete logarithms, i.e. figure out S_A based on seeing g^{S_A}, then they could figure out the Alice/Bob shared key. But we assume they can't compute discrete logarithms, because of the Fundamental Tenet of Cryptography (mathematicians haven't figured out how to do that easily in spite of considerable effort, or at least they haven't told us they have).

6.4.1 The Bucket Brigade/Man-in-the-Middle Attack

If Alice receives T_B indirectly, there is no way for her to know for sure whether the number came from Bob. She will establish a secret key with whoever transmitted T_B, but it certainly might not be Bob. Let's assume Alice is talking to X, who may or may not be Bob. Once Alice and X establish a secret key, they can encrypt all their messages so that only Alice and X can read them. Let's say the first thing Alice and X exchange in their encrypted communication is a password that Alice and Bob have previously agreed upon, one password that Bob is to say to Alice, perhaps The fish are green, and one that Alice is to say to Bob, for instance The moon sets at midnight. If Alice receives the expected password from X, can she assume she is talking to Bob? (Think about this a bit before reading the next paragraph—it's fun. Hint: Obviously, there must be some subtle attack or we wouldn't claim it was an interesting question.)

Assume p and g are publicly known (if not, Alice can put them into her message). Alice places the ad Dear Bob. I'd like to talk to you. 8389. Love, Alice. Suppose there's a bad guy, Mr. X, who works for the newspaper. He makes one copy of the newspaper with Alice's ad printed as Alice wished, and bribes the newspaper deliverer to give that copy to Alice. Meanwhile, Mr. X picks his own S_X and computes g^{S_X} mod p. He edits the ad slightly by substituting this number instead of 8389, and has that version printed in the rest of the newspapers. Later, Bob replies, by ordering the ad So pleased to talk to you. My magic number is 9267. Love, Bob. Mr. X makes one copy of the newspaper with Bob's ad printed as Bob wished, and arranges for Bob to receive that copy. Mr. X edits Bob's ad slightly to substitute his own number for Bob's, and arranges for the newspaper with that version of the ad to get to Alice. Mr. X computes $K_{AX} = 8389^{S_X}$ and uses that for talking to Alice, and computes $K_{BX} = 9267^{S_X}$ and uses that for talking to Bob.

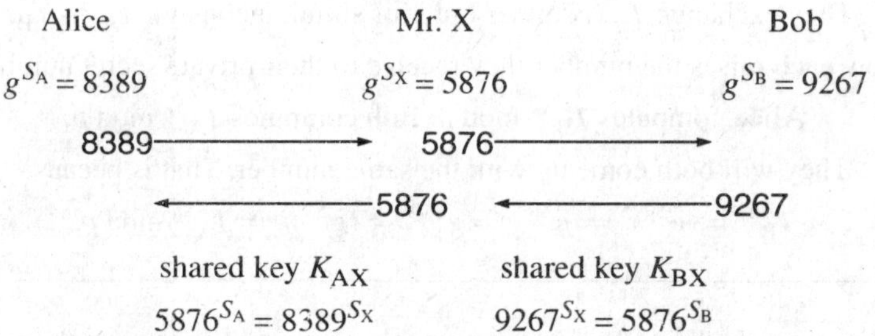

Figure 6-4. Bucket Brigade/Man-in-the-Middle Attack

Now suppose Alice sends an encrypted message (to Mr. X) which includes the password The fish are green. Mr. X can decrypt the message because it is encrypted using the key he shares with Alice. Mr. X reencrypts and transmits Alice's password to Bob, which reassures Bob that he is indeed talking to Alice, and Bob then transmits (encrypted, to Mr. X) The moon sets at midnight. Mr. X decrypts Bob's message, extracts the password, and reencrypts and transmits the password to Alice. Now both Alice and Bob think they are talking to each other.

To guard against this threat, perhaps Alice and Bob should transmit the actual secret number they think they are using, over the encrypted channel they have established? That won't work either. Alice sends the message I think we are using K_{AX}; however, Mr. X decrypts the message and edits it to be I think we are using K_{BX} before encrypting and forwarding it on to Bob.

Suppose instead Alice and Bob attempt to reassure themselves that they are indeed talking to each other by asking each other personal questions. If Bob asks What movie did we see the first night we met in Paris?, Mr. X merely decrypts the message with K_{BX}, encrypts it with K_{AX}, and forwards the message on to Alice. When Alice replies, Mr. X merely forwards the message on to

Bob. (We're assuming Alices's memory of past evenings makes it worthwhile for Mr. X to actually wait for her answer rather than making one up himself.)

The name **bucket brigade attack** comes from the way firefighters of old formed a line of people between a water source and a fire and passed full buckets toward the fire and empty buckets back. But the less politically correct term **man-in-the-middle** has become more common. After establishing the shared keys, Mr. X passes messages back and forth and can examine them and/or modify them as they go. Using Diffie-Hellman alone, there's really nothing Alice and Bob can do to detect the intruder through whom they are communicating. As a result, this form of Diffie-Hellman is only secure against passive attack where the intruder just watches the messages.

6.4.2 Defenses Against Man-in-the-Middle Attack

6.4.2.1 Published Diffie-Hellman Numbers

One technique by which Diffie-Hellman can be secure against active attacks is for each person to have a somewhat permanent public and secret number instead of inventing one for each exchange. For this to work, everyone (in the communicating set) has to agree on a common p and g. The public numbers are then all published by some means that is assumed reliable (for instance, through a PKI, see Chapter 15 *PKI (Public Key Infrastructure)*).

To the extent an intruder can't get in and modify the published public numbers, this makes Diffie-Hellman immune to active attacks. It has the additional advantage of eliminating the first two messages of the protocol. Knowing my own secret and looking up the public number of the person with whom I want to communicate, I can compute a key that the two of us will share for all messages we send to one another.

6.4.2.2 Authenticated Diffie-Hellman

If Alice and Bob know some sort of secret with which they can authenticate each other, either a shared secret key or knowledge of each other's public keys (and their own private keys), then they can use this secret to prove that it was they who generated their Diffie-Hellman values. We call such an exchange an **authenticated Diffie-Hellman exchange**. The proof can be done simultaneously with sending the Diffie-Hellman value, or after the Diffie-Hellman exchange. Examples are:

- Encrypt the Diffie-Hellman exchange with the pre-shared secret.
- Encrypt the Diffie-Hellman value with the other side's public key (see Homework Problem 2).
- Sign the Diffie-Hellman value with your private key.

- Following the Diffie-Hellman exchange, transmit a hash of the agreed-upon shared Diffie-Hellman value, your name, and the pre-shared secret.
- Following the Diffie-Hellman exchange, transmit a hash of the pre-shared secret and the Diffie-Hellman value you transmitted.

6.4.3 Encryption with Diffie-Hellman

We've described the lack of authentication with Diffie-Hellman. There's another disadvantage with classic Diffie-Hellman: in order for two individuals to communicate, they have to first have an active exchange. This is easy to remedy. Suppose Alice is working late and wants to send an encrypted message to Bob that Bob will be able to read when he shows up at work the next morning at 7 AM (and Alice has no intention of being around at 7 AM).

First everyone computes a public key, which consists of the three numbers $\langle p, g, T\rangle$, where $T = g^S \bmod p$, for the private key S. These public keys are displayed in a reliable and public place (like being published in *The New York Times*).

So Bob has published a $\langle p_B, g_B, T_B\rangle$.

If Alice wants to send Bob an encrypted message, she picks a random number S_A, computes $g_B{}^{S_A} \bmod p_B$ and computes $K_{AB} = T_B{}^{S_A} \bmod p_B$, and uses that as the encryption key to share with Bob. She uses K_{AB} to encrypt the message according to any secret key cryptographic technique, and sends the encrypted message, along with $g_B{}^{S_A} \bmod p_B$ to Bob. Bob raises $g_B{}^{S_A} \bmod p_B$ to his own secret S_B, and thereby calculates K_{AB} which enables him to decrypt the message.

6.4.4 ElGamal Signatures

Using the same sort of keys as Diffie-Hellman, ElGamal came up with a signature scheme [EFF98]. It is much harder to understand than signing with RSA. While it's important to know that it's possible and to understand the political and performance implications, the mathematics is tedious and unintuitive. We reluctantly recommend that all but true die-hards skip this section.

ElGamal signatures require each individual to have a long-term public/private key pair (the public key being $\langle g, p, T\rangle$ and the secret key being S, where $g^S \bmod p = T$, as described for Diffie-Hellman), and (surprisingly) require an individual to generate a new and different public/private key pair for each item that needs to be signed. Luckily the per-message public/private key pair is easy to compute. For a particular message m, choose a random number S_m and (using the same g and p as in the long-term key) compute $g^{S_m} \bmod p = T_m$. To use ElGamal, there has to be a message digest function that is well-known. Given a message m, to compute a signature, you first compute the message digest of $m|T_m$. Call that message digest d_m. Then you calculate $S_m + d_m S \bmod (p-1)$, which is the signature. Let's call that X (since we've already used S for the Secret number, and some people sign documents with an X).

m is transmitted, along with X and T_m. To verify this signature, you compute d_m and check that $g^X = T_m T^{d_m} \bmod p$. This will be true, assuming the signature is valid, because

$$g^X = g^{S_m + d_m S} = g^{S_m} g^{d_m S} = T_m T^{d_m} \bmod p.$$

This is not terrifically intuitive. The important things to try to convince oneself of are:

- If the signature is done correctly, the verification will succeed.
- If the message is modified after being signed, the inputs to the signature function will have changed and with overwhelming probability the signature will not match the modified message.
- Knowledge of the signature will not help divulge the signer's private key, S.
- Someone without knowledge of S will not be able to produce a valid signature.

6.4.5 Diffie-Hellman Details—Safe Primes

While Diffie-Hellman works with any prime p and any number g, it is less secure if p and g don't have additional mathematical properties.

It turns out that for obscure mathematical reasons it is particularly nice if $(p-1)/2$ is also prime. A prime p that satisfies this additional constraint is called a **safe prime**, or a Sophie Germain prime. It is also particularly nice if $g^x \neq 1 \bmod p$ unless $x = 0 \bmod p-1$. If p is a safe prime, this is satisfied by any $g \neq -1 \bmod p$ for which $g^{(p-1)/2} = -1 \bmod p$, which is true for almost half of all mod p numbers.

It is computationally expensive to choose p and g. Theoretically, one only needs to do it once. You could keep using the same p and g. It could even be a standard, and everyone could use the same p and g. However, that is not advisable. It turns out to be possible, though incredibly space- and computation-intensive, to calculate a large table based on a single p, which would allow you to compute discrete logarithms *for that* p. A similar scheme would allow you to break RSA, in the sense of being able to calculate someone's private key based on their public key, but there is not that much incentive to do so because that would only allow you to break one person's key. If the p for Diffie-Hellman were broken, then every key exchange based on Diffie-Hellman could be broken. Simply changing p occasionally will eliminate this threat.

6.5 DIGITAL SIGNATURE STANDARD (DSS)

NIST, the (U.S.) National Institute of Standards and Technology, has proposed an algorithm for digital signatures based on ElGamal. The algorithm is known as **DSA**, for **Digital Signature Algorithm**. As a proposed standard it is known as **DSS**.

The differences between it and ElGamal mainly have to do with performance. Instead of all calculations being done mod p (where p is a 512-bit prime), some are done mod q (where q is a 160-bit prime which divides p–1). This makes the exponents 160 bits rather than 512 bits, which makes signing three times faster. However, there are other differences that make DSS slower than it might have been. In particular, an inverse calculation is required by both the signer and the verifier. DSS could easily have been defined to require only the signer to calculate an inverse. Instead, DSS allows the signer to precalculate its inverse before it even has a message, at the expense of requiring the verifier to also calculate an inverse.

But why should we make it more convenient for the signer, given that it's less convenient for the verifier? Presumably there is at least one verification for each signature—otherwise why would one bother signing anything?

There is one important application in which DSS's approach might be an important optimization: smart cards (see §10.8 *Authentication Tokens*). A smart card is likely to have a very low-performance processor. It will have to do a signature in order for a user to successfully log in. If the operation of signing takes a long time, say two minutes or more, it will annoy the human who is trying to use the network.

Taking inverses is one of the most computationally expensive parts of generating a DSS signature. If it had to be done on a smart card at the time the user logged in, the user would be forced to wait many seconds. However, if the smart card generated some $\langle S_m, S_m^{-1}\rangle$ pairs while the user was logged in, then when the user next wants to log in, the smart card will have already done the requisite inverse operation.

The machines doing verifications, the DSS designers believe, will be fast machines, so doing an extra inverse operation will not be annoying.

6.5.1 The DSS Algorithm

- Generate p and q (which will be public).

  Find 160-bit prime q. Find a 512-bit prime p of the form $kq+1$. This is a very expensive operation, but it need not be done often. As a matter of fact it can be done once and the p can be published in the standard. Everyone can use the same p, with some caveats. It is rumored to be possible for someone to generate a p in such a way that someone can break cryptographic operations based on that p, but no other someone would be able to tell that there was anything wrong with using that p. So having a particular p published in the standard as the one everyone should use is controversial. In addition, if there is a p that everyone uses, there is an efficiency gain (because you don't have to generate new ps and qs), but the chosen p presents a target for attacking the algorithm.

- Generate g (which will be public).

  Find a number g such that $g^q = 1 \bmod p$.
  This is done by taking any random number $h > 1$ and raising it to $(p-1)/q$ to get g. Then, since $g = h^{(p-1)/q}$, $g^q = h^{p-1} = 1$ by Fermat's theorem.
  (Actually, h can't be just *any* old random number. It is important that g not be 1, or else things will not be secure at all. So a new h is tried if $g = h^{(p-1)/q}$ turns out to be 1.)

- Choose a long-term public/private key pair $\langle T, S\rangle$.

  This is done by choosing a random $S < q$ and setting $T = g^S \bmod p$.

- Choose a per message public/private key pair $\langle T_m, S_m\rangle$.

  This is done by choosing a random S_m and setting $T_m = ((g^{S_m} \bmod p) \bmod q)$.
  While you're at it, calculate $S_m^{-1} \bmod q$ so it won't need to be done in real time when signing the message.

- Calculate a message digest d_m of the message.

  The DSS has a sister function, **SHS**, that is a hashing algorithm recommended by NIST for use with DSS. SHS happens to hash to 160 bits, but it is only coincidence that the size of the hash matches the size of q. 160 bits seemed a logical number for both because it's about the right size and it's a multiple of 32, so it's conveniently stored on machines with 32-bit words. DSS could be used with any hash function, though no security would be gained by using one longer than 160 bits.

- Compute the signature $X = S_m^{-1}(d_m + ST_m) \bmod q$.

- Transmit all relevant information:

  the message m;
  the per-message public number T_m;
  the signature X.

  The public key information, consisting of T, p, q, and g, is known beforehand and doesn't need to be transmitted with the message.

- Verify the signature:

Calculate the mod q inverse of the signature, X^{-1}.
Calculate d_m.
Calculate $x = d_m \cdot X^{-1}$ mod q.
Calculate $y = T_m \cdot X^{-1}$ mod q.
Calculate $z = (g^x \cdot T^y \bmod p) \bmod q$.
If $z = T_m$, then the signature is verified.

6.5.2 Why Does the Verification Procedure Work?

Let $v = (d_m + ST_m)^{-1} \bmod q$. Then,

$$X^{-1} = (S_m{}^{-1}(d_m + ST_m))^{-1} = S_m(d_m + ST_m)^{-1} = S_m v \bmod q,$$
$$x = d_m \cdot X^{-1} = d_m S_m v \bmod q,$$
$$y = T_m \cdot X^{-1} = T_m S_m v \bmod q,$$
$$z = g^x \cdot T^y = g^{d_m S_m v} g^{S T_m S_m v} = g^{(d_m + ST_m)S_m v} = g^{S_m} = T_m \bmod p \bmod q.$$

(We're not worried about the mod q in the exponents of g since $g^q = 1 \bmod p$.)

6.5.3 Why Is This Secure?

What does it mean to be secure? It means several things.

- Signing something does not divulge the private key S.
- Nobody should be able to generate a signature for a given message without knowing S.
- Nobody should be able to generate a message that matches a given signature.
- Nobody should be able to modify a signed message in a way that keeps the same signature valid.

Why does DSS have all these properties? The Fundamental Tenet of Cryptography (nobody knows how to break it). DSS also has the blessing of the NSA, arguably the best cryptographers in the world. Unfortunately it's a mixed blessing, since some cynics believe NSA would never propose an algorithm it couldn't break.

6.5.4 The DSS Controversy

DSS was published by NIST on August 30, 1991 as a proposed standard for digital signatures. NIST announced a 90-day comment period, which sparked a flurry of debate and an extension of the comment period. At the time of this writing the debate continues with no end in sight.

The hidden (or sometimes not hidden) question in the debate over DSS is why NIST chose a variant of ElGamal rather than standardizing on RSA, which had become the de facto industry standard. The arguments about standardizing on DSS are:

- Test of time—DSS may have undetected flaws, since it has not be subjected to the intense scrutiny of RSA.
- Mandated 512-bit/160-bit moduli—DSS fixes the key length at 512 bits for p and 160 bits for q. It is true that a DSS key of 512 bits might be a little more secure than a 512-bit RSA key, because the RSA key is a composite number and the DSS key is a prime, but it certainly won't be as secure as a 600-bit RSA key. According to calculations made by Ron Rivest [RIVE91b], a determined and well-financed attacker, say with a budget of $25 million, could break DSS with a 512-bit modulus in a year. [NIST has responded by allowing key lengths up to 1024 bits for p.]
- Since choosing a DSS $\langle p, q, g \rangle$ triple is computationally expensive, it is likely that many people will base their own key on parameters that have been published. With RSA, an attacker that breaks a key breaks only a single key. With DSS, an attacker that breaks a $\langle p, q, g \rangle$ triple breaks all keys upon which it is based.
- Trapdoor primes—Another problem with using a published $\langle p, q, g \rangle$ triple is that you have to trust the source. It is possible for the source to generate a triple that is "pre-broken" in the sense that the source knows how to forge signatures for any key based on that triple. It's been claimed that the sample $\langle p, q, g \rangle$ published in the DSS document is suspicious, in that it has interesting mathematical properties which make it unlikely that it was chosen at random. This does not by any means prove that it is pre-broken, but it does make people nervous.
- Performance—DSS is about a hundred times slower for signature verification than RSA with $e = 3$, and in many applications, signature verification happens frequently and is performance-sensitive. In terms of the other operations, DSS is much faster for key generation, though for most applications the performance of key generation is not an issue since it is not done frequently. RSA and DSS are similar in performance for generating signatures, though DSS has the advantage that some of the signature computation can be precomputed before seeing the message. The NIST reasoning is that for the application of smart cards, this ability to precompute for signatures makes DSS superior, since a human will not need to wait as long when logging into a system.

- DSS requires choosing a unique secret number for each message. There are several ways of doing this, but they all have problems (see next section).
- Patents—One of the advantages of DSS was that it was not owned by RSADSI or PKP (which own exclusive rights to most other public key techniques) and could be used royalty-free. PKP subsequently acquired a patent by Schnorr, which it claims covers DSS. NIST has never conceded that Schnorr covers DSS, and at this time the issue remains unresolved.

6.5.5 Per-Message Secret Number

Anyone who considers arithmetical methods of producing random digits is, of course, in a state of sin.

—John Von Neumann (1951)

Both DSS and ElGamal require that the signer generate a unique secret number for each message. If the same secret number were used for two different messages, it would expose the signer's private key. Likewise, if a secret number were predictable or guessable, the signer's private key would be exposed.

How is the private key exposed if the secret number for a message is known? In DSS, the signature is $X_m = S_m^{-1}(d_m + ST_m) \bmod q$. Remember that S_m is the secret number, d_m is the message digest, T_m is $g^{S_m} \bmod p \bmod q$, and S is the signer's private key. So if S_m is known, then we can compute

$$(X_m S_m - d_m)T_m^{-1} \bmod q = S \bmod q$$

This is all we need to forge DSS signatures.

How is the private key exposed when two messages share the same secret number? In DSS, if m and m' are signed using the same secret number S_m, then we can compute

$$(X_m - X_{m'})^{-1}(d_m - d_{m'}) \bmod q = S_m \bmod q$$

This is enough to compute $S \bmod q$ as we did above, allowing us to forge signatures.

Similar arguments exist for ElGamal signatures. See Homework Problem 10.

There are several ways of generating a unique secret number for each message. Keep in mind that signatures might be done with a device with minimal computational ability.

- Use truly random numbers. The problem with this is that it requires special hardware. It's difficult enough to make hardware predictable, but it's even harder to make it predictably unpredictable.

- Use a cryptographic pseudo-random number generator. The problem with this is that it requires nonvolatile storage in order to store its state.
- Use a cryptographic hash of a combination of the message and the signer's private key. The problem with this is that it can't be computed until the message is known, eliminating a claimed advantage of DSS and ElGamal over RSA.

6.6 How Secure Are RSA and Diffie-Hellman?

A brute force attack (trying all possible keys) requires an exponential amount of overhead. The security of RSA is based on the difficulty of factoring. The security of Diffie-Hellman is based on the difficulty of solving the discrete log problem. These problems have been proven to be equivalently difficult. The best known algorithms for solving them are subexponential (less than exponential), but superpolynomial, (more than any fixed degree polynomial). Because the difficulty is subexponential, the required size of the keys in these public key algorithms is much larger (say 1024 bits) than a corresponding secret key (say 80 bits). At the RSA patent expiration party, Eric Hughes created and performed the following, sung to the tune of *Supercalifragilisticexpialidocious*.

Superpolynomial subexponential runtimes.
Even though in practice it would take you several lifetimes,
If you ran it long enough you'd always find those two primes.
Superpolynomial subexponential runtimes

E to the root-log root-log-log [4×]

When I was but a naive lad first coding two's and three's
I thought the only "orders of" were trivialities.
But when I saw this function something opened up to me
The elegance of computational complexity.

[Chorus]

I was at a meeting when up came a man in black
Who told me that his agency had mounted an attack.
Convincing him was fruitless that his budget would collapse
All I know his trumpeter will soon be playing Taps.

[Chorus]

In virtual environments has grown up a debate
Of whether strong cryptography can overthrow the state.
But several such technologies including public key
Shall herald in the coming age of crypto-anarchy.

6.7 ELLIPTIC CURVE CRYPTOGRAPHY (ECC)

As we said in §6.6 *How Secure Are RSA and Diffie-Hellman?*, there are known subexponential (but superpolynomial) algorithms for breaking RSA and Diffie-Hellman based on modular arithmetic. Elliptic curve cryptography (ECC) is important because the mathematicians do not (yet?) have subexponential algorithms for breaking it. Therefore, it is believed to be secure with much smaller key sizes, which is important for performance. ECC is a candidate replacement for public key cryptographic schemes like RSA, Diffie-Hellman, ElGamal, DSS, etc. For some of these crytographic schemes, one can replace modular multiplication by elliptic curve multiplication directly, resulting in algorithms referred to as ECC Diffie-Hellman, ECC ElGamal, etc.

An elliptic curve is a set of points on the coordinate plane satisfying an equation of the form $y^2 + axy + by = x^3 + cx^2 + dx + e$. In order to use elliptic curves for, say, Diffie-Hellman, there needs to be some mathematical operation on two points in the set that will always produce a point also in the set. Let's call that operation multiplication, although in ECC it will not look like the multiplication you are used to. And the operation has to be associative, so that you can use the repeated squaring trick to raise a number to a large power in time linear with the length of the exponent. In other words, to "exponentiate" a point by 128, you should be able to "multiply" the point by itself (you've now raised it to the power 2), then multiply the result by itself (you've now raised it to the power 4), multiply the result by itself (to have raised it to the power 8), etc. Since "multiplication" is associative, it will be true that $(g^x)^y = g^{xy} = (g^y)^x$. And it is also important that doing discrete logs is hard (knowing g and g^x, it is disproportionately difficult to compute x).

ECC can be done with at least two types of arithmetic, each of which gives different definitions of multiplication. When you do regular Diffie-Hellman, you have to specify p and g. When you do ECC-Diffie-Hellman, you have to specify the constants in the elliptic curve equation and the type of arithmetic you are using (to take the place of p), and a point on the elliptic curve (to take the place of g).

The two types of arithmetic are

- $\mathbf{Z}_p$ arithmetic (modular arithmetic with a large prime p as the modulus)
- GF(2^n) arithmetic, which can be done with shifts and ⊕s. This can be thought of as modular arithmetic of polynomials with coefficients mod 2.

While more complex to understand, the code to implement ECC is no more complex than one that efficiently does modular arithmetic with big integers. And it is faster, at least for private key operations, since until someone comes up with a subexponential algorithm for breaking ECC, the keys can be smaller. For public key operations, such as signature verification, RSA is likely to be faster, even with larger keys, because it can use a small public exponent. See Chapter 8 *Math with AES and Elliptic Curves* or ROSI99 for more information on ECC.

6.8 ZERO KNOWLEDGE PROOF SYSTEMS

A zero knowledge proof system only does authentication. It allows you to prove that you know a secret (something associated with your public key) without actually revealing the secret. RSA is a zero knowledge proof system, in the sense that you can prove you know the secret associated with your public key without revealing your private key. However, there are zero knowledge proof systems with much higher performance than RSA, although they do not have the ability to do signatures or encryption.

The classic example of a zero knowledge authentication scheme is based on graphs. A graph is a bunch of vertices connected by a bunch of edges. Typically, we name the vertices and specify the edges as pairs of vertices. We consider two graphs **isomorphic** if we can rename the vertices of one to get a graph identical to the other. Nobody knows how to efficiently determine whether two arbitrary graphs are isomorphic. The assumption that this is hard forms the basis of the authentication scheme.

Alice specifies a large graph (say 500 vertices). She renames the vertices to produce an isomorphic graph. Call the two graphs Graph A and Graph B. Alice knows the mapping that will transform Graph A into Graph B. Nobody else can compute it (in reasonable time). Her public key is the specification of the two graphs. Her private key is the mapping between the two graphs.

To prove to Bob that she is Alice, she renames the vertices to find a new set of graphs, say $G_1, G_2, \ldots G_k$, which she sends to Bob. Then Bob asks, for each i, for Alice to show him the mapping between G_i and one of Graph A or Graph B. Bob can choose which one, but he can't ask Alice to show both mappings for any i (or else Bob could piece the two mappings together to get a mapping from Graph A to Graph B). If Fred tries to impersonate Alice, he can make some graphs that are mapped from Graph A and some graphs that are mapped from Graph B, but he won't be able to find any graph for which he could show a map for both. So for each graph he sends to Bob, he will have only a 50% chance of successfully showing the requested mapping. For 30 graphs, the odds of Fred successfully impersonating Alice are only 1 in 2^{30}, or one in ten billion.

Why is this zero knowledge? After Alice proves herself to Bob, Bob knows some graphs with mappings to Graph A, and some with mappings to Graph B. He could have generated these himself, so Alice can't have given him any actual information.

The graph-based authentication scheme is unfortunately too inefficient for practical use. The following authentication protocol, while not quite zero knowledge, is extremely efficient. It is a variant of Fiat-Shamir [FEIG87].

Alice establishes a public key consisting of $\langle n,v \rangle$, where n is the product of two large primes (just like the n in RSA), and v is a number for which only Alice knows the square root mod n. Finding such an n is done just like in RSA. Finding v is really easy. Alice merely selects any random number s and squares it mod n to obtain v. After doing so, Alice can forget n's factors and only remember s as her secret, and divulge $\langle n,v \rangle$ as her public key.

To prove to Bob that she is Alice, she does the following:

1. Alice chooses k random numbers, $r_1, r_2, \ldots r_k$. For each r_i, she sends $r_i^2 \bmod n$ to Bob.
2. Bob chooses a random subset of the r_i^2 and tells Alice which subset he has selected to be known as subset 1. The others will be known as subset 2.
3. Alice sends $sr_i \bmod n$ for each r_i^2 of subset 1, and sends $r_i \bmod n$ for each r_i^2 of subset 2.
4. Bob squares Alice's replies mod n. For those r_i^2 in subset 1 he checks that the square of the reply is $vr_i^2 \bmod n$. For those r_i^2 in subset 2 he checks that the square of the reply is $r_i^2 \bmod n$.

Why does this work?

- Finding square roots mod n is at least as hard as factoring n. This means that if you knew an easy way to find square roots mod n, you'd be able to factor n. And we all hope that factoring is difficult.

> How to factor n if you can compute square roots mod n
>
> We'll assume n is odd and not the power of a prime. (If n is even, you can factor out all the factors of 2. If n is a power of a prime, you can try computing its kth root using ordinary arithmetic, and you'll only need to try for $k \leq \log_p n$ where p is the smallest prime you're not willing to try dividing into n directly.)
>
> Assume you have a method to compute square roots mod n. You choose a random x and compute $s = x^2 \bmod n$. Then you use your method of computing square roots mod n to compute the square root of $s \bmod n$, say y. This gives you two numbers, x and y, with the same square mod n. So $(x + y)(x - y) = x^2 - y^2 = 0 \bmod n$. If n has k distinct prime factors, then x^2 has 2^k square roots mod n (see §7.5 *Chinese Remainder Theorem*). So if n has at least 2 distinct prime factors, there is at least a 50% chance that y isn't x or $-x \bmod n$. In that case, neither $x + y \bmod n$ nor $x - y \bmod n$ is 0 mod n. And so the gcd of either of them with n must be a nontrivial factor of n.

- Suppose Fred wants to impersonate Alice. Anyone (including Fred) can compute squares mod n. Fred cannot take square roots mod n, but if he starts with a random r, he can compute r^2. Fred can give the correct answers for subset 2. But he cannot give the correct answers for subset 1, since he does not know s. So, what is the purpose of subset 2? Why isn't the protocol simply that Alice sends pairs $\langle r_i^2, sr_i \rangle$?

  The problem with the simpler protocol is that once Alice sends a list of values to Bob, Bob can send the same values to Carol and successfully impersonate Alice. With the protocol as specified, the only information Bob can get is some numbers z_i for which Alice tells him the square root of z_i (those in subset 2), and some numbers z_i for which Alice tells him the square root of vz_i. He doesn't need Alice in order to find numbers for which he knows the square root—he can get such numbers himself by taking random numbers and squaring them. But he does need Alice for finding pairs $\langle r_i^2, sr_i \rangle$. However, for any $\langle r_i^2, sr_i \rangle$ he obtains from Alice rather than starting with r_i and squaring it himself, he will not know r_i—he will only know sr_i.

So, assuming Fred has overheard Alice proving her identity to some people (maybe even Fred), Fred may have collected some values of $\langle r_i^2, sr_i \rangle$. When Fred attempts to impersonate Alice he has a choice for each number of taking one of the values he has overheard from Alice, and for those he will be able to know the answer if they are selected to be in subset 1, or he can choose a random r and square it, and for those he will know the answer if they are selected to be in subset 2. But there will be no number for which he'll know both answers. That means there is a 50% probability, for each i, that Fred will be unlucky, and Carol will ask for the answer Fred does not know. If the protocol demands that Fred sends enough values (say 30), then the probability is overwhelming that his impersonation will be discovered.

This scheme is much less work than RSA. Work for Alice is 45 modular multiplies (30 squarings plus an average 15 multiplies by s). Work for Bob is the same. By contrast, using RSA Alice must do a modular exponentiation with an average 768 modular multiplies, while Bob would get off easier with three (assuming a public exponent of 3).

6.8.1 Zero Knowledge Signatures

Any zero knowledge system can be transformed into a public key signature scheme, though the performance in terms of bandwidth and CPU power usually makes the resulting scheme unattractive. Let's assume a typical sort of zero knowledge system. Alice has some sort of secret that enables her to transmit something and compute any answer to a question Bob might pose about that something, whereas an impostor can answer only one specific question Bob might pose. For example, in the case of the graph isomorphism scheme, Alice's secret is the mapping between graphs G_1 and G_2. The "something" that Alice transmits is a new graph, G_i. Bob's challenges are binary values. Only Alice can answer both 0 (show me the mapping from G_i to G_1) and 1 (show me the mapping from G_i to G_2). An impostor, say Trudy, can only answer one of the values (if she derived G_i from G_1, she'll be lucky if Bob asks 0 but be unable to respond if Bob asks 1).

In some other zero knowledge proof schemes Bob's challenge is a larger number (say 16 bits). Alice can answer any value Bob supplies, whereas impostor Trudy can only know a single value. So Trudy in that case would have only a 1 in 2^{16} chance (per challenge) of being lucky enough for Bob to supply the question she can answer.

A signature scheme is not interactive. Bob cannot supply a challenge, or set of challenges. Instead, Alice has a message m that she wishes to sign. We're going to use a message digest function as a Bob surrogate. The message digest function will create a set of challenges that Alice cannot predict, and the fact that she can answer all the queries will reassure someone that Alice did produce the signature.

Let's use Fiat-Shamir as an example. If Alice were proving her identity to Bob using Fiat-Shamir, her public key would be $\langle n,v \rangle$ and she'd transmit r_i^2 mod n (for randomly chosen $r_1,\ldots r_k$). Then Bob would send her k binary challenges. Now let's transform it into a signature scheme. Alice (and someone verifying Alice's signature) will take the message m, concatenated with the k values r_i^2 mod n. The result is message digested, and the resulting message digest is used as the surrogate Bob. For a 128-bit message digest, if k is 128, then each bit in the message digest corresponds to the challenge for the corresponding r_i. The signature on m consists of the k values r_i^2 mod n and the k responses to the calculated challenges.

Why can't impostor Trudy forge a signature? She can choose any k values of r_i, but until she chooses them, she cannot predict the generated challenge for each one. She can spend a lot of off-line searching for a set of r_i that will happen to generate the challenges she can answer, so k probably needs to be a bit larger than it would be in an interactive zero knowledge proof. For instance, it might be acceptable for an impostor to have only a one in a billion chance of fooling an interactive Bob, but an impostor that was constructing a signature might be able to test a billion signatures for one that wound up asking the right questions. If there's a 1 in 2^{64} chance, then a signature verifier can be reasonably certain that an impostor could not have been lucky enough, even with an off-line search, to find an appropriate set of r_i.

6.9 HOMEWORK PROBLEMS

1. In mod n arithmetic why does x have a multiplicative inverse if and only if x is relatively prime to n?
2. In section §6.4.2 *Defenses Against Man-in-the-Middle Attack*, it states that encrypting the Diffie-Hellman value with the other side's public key prevents the attack. Why is this the case, given that an attacker can encrypt whatever it wants with the other side's public key?
3. In RSA, is it possible for more than one d to work with a given e, p, and q?
4. In RSA, given that the primes p and q are approximately the same size, approximately how big is $\phi(n)$ compared to n?

5. In DSS, other than saving users the trouble of calculating their own p, q, and g, why is there an efficiency gain if the value of p, q, and g are constant, determined in the specification?

6. What is the probability that a randomly chosen number would not be relatively prime to some particular RSA modulus n? What threat would finding such a number pose?

7. How would you modify ElGamal to operate with a smaller exponent like DSS?

8. Suppose Fred sees your RSA signature on m_1 and on m_2 (i.e. he sees $m_1{}^d$ mod n and $m_2{}^d$ mod n). How does he compute the signature on each of $m_1{}^j$ mod n (for positive integer j), $m_1{}^{-1}$ mod n, $m_1 \cdot m_2$ mod n, and in general $m_1{}^j \cdot m_2{}^k$ mod n (for arbitrary integers j and k)?

9. Suppose we have the encoding that enables Carol to mount the cube root attack (see §6.3.5.2 *The Cube Root Problem*). If Carol sends a message to Bob, supposedly signed by you, will there be anything suspicious and noticeable about the signed message, so that with very little additional computation Bob can detect the forgery? Is there anything Carol can do to make her messages less suspicious?

10. In ElGamal, how does knowing the secret number used for a signature reveal the signer's private key? How do two signatures using the same secret number reveal the signer's private key? [Hint: p–1 is twice a prime. Even though not all numbers have inverses mod p–1, division can still be performed if one is willing to accept two possible answers. (We're neglecting the case where the divisor is $(p–1)/2$, since it is extremely unlikely.)]

11. Transform the graph isomorphism scheme described in §6.8 *Zero Knowledge Proof Systems* into a signature scheme. Make an estimate of how large a signature would need to be.

7 NUMBER THEORY

7.1 INTRODUCTION

This chapter describes enough of number theory to understand not only the mathematical operations necessary to perform cryptographic algorithms such as RSA, but to understand why they work. The chapter requires no background other than intellectual curiosity, a vague remembrance of high school algebra, a certain amount of trust that it will all be understandable with just a little bit of thought, and a reasonable night's sleep in the recent past.

Some of this material has been covered in previous chapters with a large waving of hands. Other material in here has merely been referenced. If you're happy to take the results on faith, don't bother reading this chapter.

7.2 MODULAR ARITHMETIC

We were rather imprecise when we discussed modular arithmetic in previous chapters. While we didn't lie, we didn't tell the whole truth either. What we did was good enough for a vague intuitive grasp, but not really good enough for a deep understanding. Armed with a vague intuitive grasp, this should be fairly painless.

First we need to define *remainder*. (You may think you know what a remainder is, but if you've been using computers for too long you may have assimilated their strange ideas associated with negative numbers.) If m and n are two integers and $n > 0$, the **remainder** of m divided by n is the smallest non-negative integer that differs from m by a multiple of n. For example, 3, 13, and –7 each have remainder 3 when divided by 10.

In arithmetic modulo n, two integers are **equivalent** if their difference is a multiple of n. Another way of saying this is that two integers are equivalent if they have the same remainder when divided by n. Among other things, this means that there are only n different integers mod n. Normally we represent a mod n number by its remainder when divided by n, but any equivalent number would do. For example, 3, 13, and −7 all represent the same mod 10 number.

While it is fairly conventional to use the symbol "≡" for equivalence, we have chosen to use the symbol "=" to emphasize that in modular arithmetic two equivalent numbers are really just two different names for the same mod n number.

It turns out that we can define mod n addition using ordinary addition—if a and b are names for two mod n numbers, then $a+b$ (ordinary addition) is a name for the mod n sum. This wouldn't make any sense if, by choosing different names for the two mod n numbers, we could get a sum (by ordinary addition) which was a name for a different mod n sum. But we can't:

Suppose we chose different names for a and b, say $a+kn$ and $b+ln$. Then the new sum would be $(a+kn)+(b+ln) = (a+b)+(k+l)n$, which is just another name for $a+b$.

Similarly, we can define mod n multiplication using ordinary multiplication—if a and b are names of two mod n numbers, then ab (ordinary multiplication) is a name for the mod n product. Again, if we chose different names, we'd just get a different name for the same mod n result: $(a+kn)(b+ln) = ab+(al+kb+kln)n$.

We have to be careful about exponentiation. Exponentiation is repeated multiplication, with the repeat count being the exponent. So when we do mod n exponentiation, the exponent is not a mod n number; it is a real positive integer. It turns out that in certain cases we will be able to treat the exponent as a mod $\phi(n)$ number, but we'll discuss that later in the chapter.

7.3 PRIMES

(Yeah, I know you already know this…) A positive integer p is prime iff it is evenly divisible by exactly two positive integers (itself and 1). (Remember—**iff** means *if and only if*.) The smallest primes are

$$2, 3, 5, 7, 11, 13, 17, 19, 23, 29, 31, 37, 41, 43, 47, \ldots$$

There are infinitely many primes. The proof of this is very interesting: Suppose you have a finite set of primes. Multiply them together and add one. The result will not be divisible by any of the primes in your set (the remainder would be one when you divided by any one of them). So the result has a prime factor not in your set—you've found another prime. In other words, you can always find another prime, so the set of all primes is infinite.

While there are infinitely many of them, primes do thin out as numbers get bigger. There are 25 primes less than 100, so the density of the primes is 1 in 4 for the first hundred integers. By the time you get up to ten-digit numbers, the density of primes is only 1 in 23. For hundred-digit numbers, the density is 1 in 230. While there is a lot of variation in small ranges, in general the density of primes is inversely proportional to their length in digits.

Why do we care how many primes there are? Well, many of the cryptographic algorithms (including RSA) require finding large primes. This is done by choosing numbers at random and testing whether they are prime (we discussed how this is done in §6.3.4.2.1 *Finding Big Primes p and q*). If only one in a zillion numbers of the appropriate size were prime, then it would take too long to find an appropriate prime for such cryptographic algorithms to be practical. Luckily, a common-sized prime to look for is about a hundred digits, and a random hundred-digit number has a 1 in 230 chance of being prime. With such slim odds, it may sound unlikely that one would be lucky enough to select a prime, but a computer doesn't mind checking a few hundred numbers before finding one that is prime. On the average, it will be necessary to select 230 hundred-digit numbers before a prime is found. If you do select 230 random hundred-digit numbers, the probability that none of them is prime is about 1/e (≈ 0.37).

7.4 EUCLID'S ALGORITHM

One of the earliest algorithms was Euclid's Algorithm, invented by Euclid (yeah, I bet you guessed). It finds the greatest common divisor of two integers. It can also be used to efficiently find multiplicative inverses mod n. (The **multiplicative inverse** of x is the number by which you need to multiply x to get 1.) In RSA the numbers d and e are inverses. We choose one and then calculate the other using Euclid's algorithm.

The **greatest common divisor** (**gcd**) of two integers is the largest integer that evenly divides both of them. Two integers are **relatively prime** iff their gcd is 1. For example, $\gcd(12,8) = 4$, $\gcd(12, 25) = 1$, $\gcd(12, 24) = 12$, so 12 and 25 are relatively prime but the other pairs are not.

Note that by the above definitions, for any positive integer x, 1 is relatively prime to x and $\gcd(0,x) = x$.

Euclid's algorithm is a method of finding the gcd of two numbers x and y. The idea is to repeatedly replace the original numbers with smaller numbers that have the same gcd until one of the numbers is zero. Then the remaining number is the gcd.

We first note that $\langle x,y\rangle$ and $\langle x-y, y\rangle$ have the same common divisors (and so the same greatest common divisor), because if d is a divisor of both x and y, then $y = kd$ and $x = jd$, so $x-y = jd-kd = (j-k)d$; while if d is a divisor of both y and $x-y$, then $y = kd$ and $x-y = ld$, so $x = (k+l)d$.

So we can subtract y from x and still have the same gcd. But since we would like to get our new numbers as small as possible, we may as well subtract as many ys as we can from x, so we replace x with its remainder when divided by y. Since this won't get us anywhere once x is smaller than y, we now switch our new x and y, then repeat the process. Each step now looks like

$$\langle x,y\rangle \rightarrow \langle y, \text{remainder}(x/y)\rangle$$

Since at each step one of the numbers gets smaller, eventually one of the numbers will be zero, and so the other will be the gcd.

For example, to find the gcd of 408 and 595:

$$595/408 = 1 \text{ remainder } 187$$
$$408/187 = 2 \text{ remainder } 34$$
$$187/34 = 5 \text{ remainder } 17$$
$$34/17 = 2 \text{ remainder } 0$$

Therefore, $\gcd(408,595) = 17$.

We describe Euclid's algorithm elegantly as follows. (Mathematicians are very big on elegance!)

- Initial setup:
  Let $r_{-2} = x$ and $r_{-1} = y$.
  [We're using the subscripts −2 and −1 just to show you that these two rs aren't really remainders—they just get us started.]
  Set $n = 0$.

- Step n:
  [This is where we replace the larger number (r_{n-2}) by its remainder when divided by the smaller number (r_{n-1}).]
  If $r_{n-1} = 0$, $\gcd(x,y) = r_{n-2}$.
  Otherwise, divide r_{n-2} by r_{n-1} to get quotient q_n and remainder r_n.
  Set $n = n + 1$.
  Repeat.

If we do a little extra bookkeeping, we can keep track of numbers u_n and v_n such that $r_n = u_n x + v_n y$:

- In the initial setup, set $u_{-2} = 1$, $v_{-2} = 0$ and $u_{-1} = 0$, $v_{-1} = 1$.
  [Notice that this makes $r_n = u_n x + v_n y$ for $n = -2$ and $n = -1$.]

- At step n, set $u_n = u_{n-2} - q_n u_{n-1}$ and $v_n = v_{n-2} - q_n v_{n-1}$.
  [Since $r_n = r_{n-2} - q_n r_{n-1}$, $r_{n-2} = u_{n-2}x + v_{n-2}y$, and $r_{n-1} = u_{n-1}x + v_{n-1}y$, this ensures $r_n = u_n x + v_n y$.]

So when we are done we have found u and v such that $\gcd(x,y) = ux + vy$. This is a remarkable fact—the gcd of two numbers can be expressed as the sum of some multiple of each. And of course any such sum must be a multiple of the gcd since each of the numbers is. In particular, two numbers x and y are relatively prime iff there are integers u and v such that $ux + vy = 1$.

For example, if $x = 408$ and $y = 595$,

n	q_n	r_n	u_n	v_n
−2		408	1	0
−1		595	0	1
0	0	408	1	0
1	1	187	−1	1
2	2	34	3	−2
3	5	17	−16	11
4	2	0	35	−24

Since $r_4 = 0$, we can read the $n = 3$ line to see that

$$\gcd(408,595) = r_3 = 17 = -16 \cdot 408 + 11 \cdot 595$$

7.4.1 Finding Multiplicative Inverses in Modular Arithmetic

How does Euclid's Algorithm find multiplicative inverses? Suppose we want to find a multiplicative inverse of m mod n. This means we want to find a number u such that $um = 1 \bmod n$. Another way of saying this is that um differs from 1 by a multiple of n, so there is an integer v such that $um + vn = 1$. From the previous section, we see that using Euclid's Algorithm to calculate $\gcd(m,n)$ finds u and v provided $\gcd(m,n) = 1$, i.e. provided m and n are relatively prime. Furthermore, if m and n are not relatively prime, we can't find such u and v, so in that case m doesn't have a multiplicative inverse mod n.

Could there be more than one u mod n for which $um = 1 \bmod n$? Well, suppose $xm = 1 \bmod n$. Multiplying both sides by u gives $xmu = u \bmod n$, and noticing that $mu = um = 1 \bmod n$, we get $x = u \bmod n$. So there is at most one multiplicative inverse of m mod n.

Summarizing, if m and n are relatively prime, we can use Euclid's algorithm to find u (and v) such that $um + vn = 1$. Mod n, the number u behaves just like $1/m$, so we will call it the mod n **inverse** of m, and represent it by m^{-1}. (The conclusion of the previous paragraph allows us to say *the* mod n inverse.) If m and n are not relatively prime, m^{-1} mod n doesn't exist.

For example, say we wanted to find the inverse of 797 mod 1047.

n	q_n	r_n	u_n	v_n
−2		797	1	0
−1		1047	0	1
0	0	797	1	0
1	1	250	−1	1
2	3	47	4	−3
3	5	15	−21	16
4	3	2	67	−51
5	7	1	−490	373

From the last line we see that $1 = -490 \cdot 797 + 373 \cdot 1047$. This gives $797^{-1} = -490 = 557 \pmod{1047}$.

7.5 CHINESE REMAINDER THEOREM

The Chinese Remainder Theorem states that if $z_1, z_2, z_3, \ldots, z_k$ are relatively prime, and you know that some number is x_1 mod z_1, and is x_2 mod z_2, and in general is x_k mod z_k, then you can calculate what the number is mod $z_1 z_2 z_3 \cdots z_k$. Likewise, if something equals x mod $z_1 z_2 z_3 \cdots z_k$, then you can calculate what the number is mod z_1, mod $z_2, \ldots$. In other words, there are two representations of a number. These representations are equivalent in the sense that they define the same number, and it is easy to convert from one representation to the other.

Standard Representation: x mod $z_1 z_2 z_3 \cdots z_k$ (all the zs relatively prime)

Decomposed Representation: x_1 mod z_1, x_2 mod $z_2, \ldots, x_k$ mod $z_k \rangle$

Why is it true? Well, it's pretty easy to see that if you have a number x, you can calculate what it is mod z_i simply by dividing by z_i and taking the remainder. Therefore going from the standard representation to the decomposed representation is very easy.

Euclidean Algorhyme

You're given two numbers, and now you desire
a method for finding their common divisor.
(The greatest, of course, is the one you must name.)
To do it, you'll keep shared divisors the same
while repeatedly shrinking each number in turn
'til one of them's zero, and then you discern
that the other's the greatest divisor they share.
So how do you manage to lessen the pair?
You divide large by small, then large is ejected,
small becomes large, as remainder's injected.

Multiplicative inVerse

Now if clever you are you can take this lots farther,
by some bookkeeping work which is not much a bother.
Each number you deal with, depict as a duple
to dot-product with the original couple.
You start with one-zero, and then zero-one,
then each new remainder's the combination
of the smaller one's duple times minus the quotient
plus one times the larger one's duple. The notion?
If the numbers you're given are relative primes,
then gcd's duple holds inverses (times).

—Mike Speciner

To go from the decomposed representation to the standard representation is not as obvious, but it is still fairly easy. We'll do the special case where $k = 2$. You can do the general case (Homework Problem 5).

We know that the number is x_1 mod z_1 and x_2 mod z_2. We want to find out what it is mod z_1z_2. We also know that z_1 and z_2 are relatively prime. And to get rid of subscripts, and to match the notation used for RSA, we'll call the two *z*s *p* and *q*. So we know that something equals x_1 mod *p* and x_2 mod *q*, and we want to know what it equals mod *pq*. Call this mod *pq* value *x*.

Given that *p* and *q* are relatively prime, we can use Euclid's algorithm to find *a* and *b* such that $ap + bq = 1$. (Note that $a = p^{-1}$ mod *q* and $b = q^{-1}$ mod *p*.) If we multiply this equation by *x*, we get $x = xap + xbq$. Since *x* differs from x_1 by a multiple of *p* and *x* differs from x_2 by a multiple of *q*, taking both sides mod *pq* gives $x = x_2ap + x_1bq$ mod *pq*.

The Chinese Remainder Theorem will help us compute Euler's totient function and generalize Euler's Theorem. It also gives us some other interesting results that we used in Chapter 6 *Public Key Algorithms*:

- an explanation of why 1 has more than two square roots mod n if n has two relatively prime factors > 2
- a way to speed up RSA exponentiations in generating signatures and decrypting (the operations using the private key)
- an amusing reason not to use 3 as the public exponent, since seeing a message m encrypted according to three different public keys will enable you to figure out what m is

Why does 1 have more than two square roots mod n if n has two relatively prime factors > 2? Suppose $n = pq$ where p and q are relatively prime and > 2.

1 mod n will equal 1 mod p and 1 mod q. Also, –1 mod n will equal –1 mod p and –1 mod q. Both –1 and 1 are square roots of n.

However, look at the number z which is –1 mod p and 1 mod q. It won't be 1 or –1 mod n (since by the Chinese Remainder Theorem, there can't be two different values of the form $\langle x_1 \text{ mod } p, x_2 \text{ mod } q\rangle$ that equal the same value mod pq.) However, if you square z mod p you'll get 1 (since $-1 \cdot -1 = 1$ mod p). And if you square z mod q you'll also get 1. So $z^2 = 1$ mod n, which means z is a square root of n different from 1 or –1. And the number $\langle 1 \text{ mod } p, -1 \text{ mod } q\rangle$ also is a square root of 1. So 1 will have at least four square roots. If n has k relatively prime factors > 2, 1 will have at least 2^k square roots! (every combination of 1's and –1's mod each of the factors).

In general, if $n = 2^{\alpha_0} p_1^{\alpha_1} p_2^{\alpha_2} p_3^{\alpha_3} \ldots p_k^{\alpha_k}$ where p_i are distinct odd primes and $\alpha_i > 0$ for $i > 0$, then, mod n, 1 will have 2^k square roots if $\alpha_0 \leq 1$, 2^{k+1} square roots if $\alpha_0 = 2$, and 2^{k+2} square roots if $\alpha_0 \geq 3$. The number of square roots of 1 mod n is important, as we saw in §6.3.4.2.1 *Finding Big Primes p and q*, because of the Miller-Rabin primality test.

7.6 $\mathbf{Z}_n$*

First we'll define some notation. **Z** is used as the symbol for the set of all integers. $\mathbf{Z}_n$ is the symbol for the set of integers mod n. So, for instance, $\mathbf{Z}_{10} = \{0,1,2,3,4,5,6,7,8,9\}$.

$\mathbf{Z}_n$* is defined as the set of mod n integers that are relatively prime to n. So $\mathbf{Z}_{10}$* is $\{1,3,7,9\}$. Notice that 0 is missing from $\mathbf{Z}_{10}$*. That is because $\gcd(0,10) = 10$, so 0 is not relatively prime to 10. It turns out that the multiplication table for $\mathbf{Z}_{10}$* (Figure 7-1) has some surprising properties.

One interesting observation is that all the entries are either 1, 3, 7, or 9. If you multiply any two numbers in $\mathbf{Z}_{10}$*, you get another number in $\mathbf{Z}_{10}$*. Even more surprising, each row and column contains all the elements of $\mathbf{Z}_{10}$*, with no repeats. You might wonder whether this is a coincidence having to do with the number 10, particularly if you weren't paying attention earlier in this chapter.

·	1	3	7	9
1	1	3	7	9
3	3	9	1	7
7	7	1	9	3
9	9	7	3	1

Figure 7-1. $\mathbf{Z}_{10}$* multiplication

Let's try the same thing with 15 (Figure 7-2). The integers smaller than 15 that are relatively prime to 15 are {1,2,4,7,8,11,13,14}.

·	1	2	4	7	8	11	13	14
1	1	2	4	7	8	11	13	14
2	2	4	8	14	1	7	11	13
4	4	8	1	13	2	14	7	11
7	7	14	13	4	11	2	1	8
8	8	1	2	11	4	13	14	7
11	11	7	14	2	13	1	8	4
13	13	11	7	1	14	8	4	2
14	14	13	11	8	7	4	2	1

Figure 7-2. $\mathbf{Z}_{15}$* multiplication

It turns out to be true in all cases that if you construct the multiplication table for $\mathbf{Z}_n$*, each row and column contains the elements of $\mathbf{Z}_n$* rearranged. (Homework Problem 6.)

Theorem: $\mathbf{Z}_n$* is closed under multiplication mod *n*.

Proof: $\mathbf{Z}_n$* is closed under multiplication mod *n* means that if *a* and *b* are in $\mathbf{Z}_n$*, then so is their product *ab* mod *n*. We know that *m* is relatively prime to *n* iff there are integers *u* and *v* such that $um + vn = 1$. So if *a* and *b* are in $\mathbf{Z}_n$*, there are integers u_a, v_a, u_b, and v_b such that

$$u_a a + v_a n = 1 \quad \text{and} \quad u_b b + v_b n = 1.$$

Multiplying these two equations together gives

$$(u_a u_b)\, ab + (u_a v_b a + v_a u_b b + v_a v_b n) n = 1,$$

so *ab* is in $\mathbf{Z}_n$*.

7.7 EULER'S TOTIENT FUNCTION

The symbol $\phi(n)$ is known as Euler's totient function and is defined as the number of elements in Z_n*. For instance, $\phi(10)$ is 4, since $\mathbf{Z}_{10}$* is {1,3,7,9}. You may remember how pervasive the totient function was in Chapter 6 *Public Key Algorithms*.

Given n, can we calculate $\phi(n)$? Suppose n is prime. What is $\phi(n)$? That's fairly easy—$\mathbf{Z}_n$* is $\{1,2,\ldots,n-1\}$. So $\phi(n)$ is $n-1$.

What is $\phi(n)$ when $n = p^\alpha$, where p is prime and $\alpha > 0$? Only multiples of p are not relatively prime to p^α, and every pth number is a multiple of p, so there are $p^{\alpha-1}$ of them less than p^α. So $\phi(p^\alpha) = p^\alpha - p^{\alpha-1} = (p-1)\cdot p^{\alpha-1}$.

What is $\phi(n)$ when $n = pq$ and p and q are relatively prime? Here's where we get to use the Chinese Remainder Theorem. The Chinese Remainder Theorem says there is a one-to-one correspondence between numbers m in $\mathbf{Z}_{pq}$ and pairs of numbers m_p in $\mathbf{Z}_p$ and m_q in $\mathbf{Z}_q$ for which $m_p = m \bmod p$ and $m_q = m \bmod q$. We'll show that m is relatively prime to pq iff m_p is relatively prime to p and m_q is relatively prime to q.

If m in $\mathbf{Z}_{pq}$ is relatively prime to pq, then there are integers u and v such that $um + vpq = 1$. Substituting $m = m_p + kp$, we get $um_p + (uk + vq)p = 1$, so m_p is relatively prime to p. Similarly, m_q is relatively prime to q.

Conversely, if m_p in $\mathbf{Z}_p$ is relatively prime to p and m_q in $\mathbf{Z}_q$ is relatively prime to q, then there are integers u_p, v_p, u_q, v_q such that $u_pm_p + v_pp = 1$ and $u_qm_q + v_qq = 1$. Since $m_p = m - kp$ for some k, and $m_q = m - lq$ for some l, we have $u_pm + (v_p - u_pk)p = 1$ and $u_qm + (v_q - u_ql)q = 1$. Multiplying these together gives $(u_pu_qm + u_p(v_q - u_ql)q + u_q(v_p - u_pk))m + (v_p - u_pk)(v_q - u_ql)pq = 1$, so m is relatively prime to pq.

So there is a one-to-one correspondence between numbers m in $\mathbf{Z}_{pq}$* and pairs of numbers m_p in $\mathbf{Z}_p$* and m_q in $\mathbf{Z}_q$*. So $\phi(pq) = \phi(p)\phi(q)$.

7.8 EULER'S THEOREM

Theorem: For all a in $\mathbf{Z}_n$*, $a^{\phi(n)} = 1 \bmod n$.

Proof: Multiply all $\phi(n)$ elements of $\mathbf{Z}_n$* together, and call the product x. Notice that since $\mathbf{Z}_n$* is closed under multiplication, x is in $\mathbf{Z}_n$* and so has an inverse x^{-1}. Now multiply each element of $\mathbf{Z}_n$* by a, and multiply all those together. The result will be $a^{\phi(n)}x$. But remember that multiplying the elements of $\mathbf{Z}_n$* by a merely rearranges them (see Homework Problem 6), so the product must also be x. In other words, $a^{\phi(n)}x = x$. Multiplying both sides by x^{-1} gives the desired result.

Euler's Theorem Variant: For all a in $\mathbf{Z}_n{}^*$, and any non-negative integer k, $a^{k\phi(n)+1} = a \bmod n$.

Proof: $a^{k\phi(n)+1} = a^{k\phi(n)}a = a^{\phi(n)k}a = 1^k a = a$.

The variant doesn't tell us that raising any number m to the power $k\phi(n) + 1$ gets m back mod n. It only works for m in $\mathbf{Z}_n{}^*$, which means m must be relatively prime to n. It turns out that for numbers n of the form we are interested in for RSA (the product of two primes), it is still the case that $m^{k\phi(n)+1} = m \bmod n$, even if m was not relatively prime to n.

Do we really care? What is the probability that we'll ever find a number to encrypt that isn't relatively prime to n? (See Homework Problem 11.) Well, in case we care, RSA will still work even if the message is not relatively prime to n. And the proof isn't very hard.

7.8.1 A Generalization of Euler's Theorem

We will show that for numbers n of the form used in RSA, namely $n = pq$, where p and q are distinct primes, $a^{k\phi(n)+1} = a \bmod n$ for all a in $\mathbf{Z}_n$ (not just for a in $\mathbf{Z}_n{}^*$) as long as k is a non-negative integer. We will use the Chinese Remainder Theorem.

If a is relatively prime to n, the result is true by Euler's Theorem Variant. So our only problem is if a is not relatively prime to n, which means a is a multiple of p or q. Let's say a is a multiple of q. Let's compute the decomposed representation for $a^{k\phi(n)+1} \bmod n$. In other words, we want to find out what $a^{k\phi(n)+1}$ is mod p and mod q. Then, by the Chinese Remainder Theorem, we'll know what it is mod n.

Since a is a multiple of q, it must be relatively prime to p (or else a is a multiple of n, in which case it is 0 and the result is trivially true). Since a is relatively prime to p, by Euler's Theorem $a^{\phi(p)} = 1 \bmod p$. Since $\phi(n) = \phi(p)\phi(q)$, we find that, mod p, $a^{k\phi(n)+1} = a^{k\phi(n)}\cdot a = a^{k\phi(p)\phi(q)}\cdot a = 1^{k\phi(q)}\cdot a = a$. And mod q, $a = 0$, so $a^{k\phi(n)+1} = 0^{k\phi(n)+1} = 0 = a$.

So $a^{k\phi(n)+1} = a \bmod p$ and $a^{k\phi(n)+1} = a \bmod q$, so by the Chinese Remainder Theorem, $a^{k\phi(n)+1} = a \bmod n$.

7.9 HOMEWORK PROBLEMS

1. If m and n are any two positive integers, show that $m/\gcd(m,n)$ and $n/\gcd(m,n)$ are relatively prime. [Hint: use the result of Euclid's algorithm.]
2. If a and b are relatively prime, and bc is a multiple of a, show that c is a multiple of a. [Hint: use the result of Euclid's algorithm.]

3. In mod n arithmetic, the quotient of two numbers r and m is a number q such that $mq = r$ mod n. Given r, m, and n, how can you find q? How many qs are there? Under what conditions is q unique? [Hint: $mq = r$ mod n iff there is an integer k such that $qm + kn = r$. Divide by gcd(m,n).]

4. In the final step of Euclid's algorithm for finding gcd(m,n), we get u and v such that $um + vn = 0$. Is $|um|$ (which = $|vn|$) the least common multiple of m and n?

5. Prove the general case of the Chinese Remainder Theorem. [Hint: z_1 is relatively prime to $z_2 z_3 \cdots z_k$.]

6. Show that each row of the $\mathbf{Z}_n$* multiplication table is a rearrangement of the 1 row. [Hint: multiply the row by the inverse of its first element.]

7. For what type of number n is $\phi(n)$ largest (relative to n)?

8. For what type of number n is $\phi(n)$ smallest (relative to n)?

9. Is it possible for $\phi(n)$ to be bigger than n?

10. If $n = p_1^{\alpha_1} p_2^{\alpha_2} p_3^{\alpha_3} \ldots p_k^{\alpha_k}$ where p_i is prime, what is $\phi(n)$?

11. In RSA, what is the probability that something to be encrypted will not be in $\mathbf{Z}_n$*?

12. Euler's Theorem Variant states that for all a in $\mathbf{Z}_n$*, $a^{k\phi(n)+1} = a$ mod n. As stated in §7.8.1 *A Generalization of Euler's Theorem*, if n is the product of two distinct primes, $a^{k\phi(n)+1} = a$ mod n for all a in $\mathbf{Z}_n$. For what other forms of n will this be true? For what forms of n does it fail?

13. Prove that if $n = 2^{\alpha_0} p_1^{\alpha_1} p_2^{\alpha_2} p_3^{\alpha_3} \cdots p_k^{\alpha_k}$ where p_i are distinct odd primes and $\alpha_i > 0$ for $i > 0$, then, mod n, 1 will have 2^k square roots if $\alpha_0 \le 1$, 2^{k+1} square roots if $\alpha_0 = 2$, and 2^{k+2} square roots if $\alpha_0 \ge 3$. [Hints: use the Chinese Remainder Theorem to show that a number is a square root of 1 mod n iff it is a square root of 1 mod each of the prime power factors; show that 1 and -1 are the only square roots of 1 mod a power of an odd prime; finally, find the square roots of 1 mod a power of 2.]

8 Math with AES and Elliptic Curves

8.1 Introduction

We've seen a plethora of techniques for performing secret key and public key cryptography, and the number theory behind some of the public key algorithms. These public key schemes are based on the difficulty of factoring large integers, or the difficulty of calculating discrete logarithms over $\mathbf{Z}_p$*. While these problems still seem intractable, some significant progress has been made, and that makes cryptographers nervous.

So cryptographers have started exploiting somewhat different mathematical structures to use as the basis for cryptographic schemes. In this chapter we'll explore the mathematics needed to properly understand Rijndael/AES (described algorithmically in §3.5 *Advanced Encryption Standard (AES)*) and to vaguely understand elliptic curve cryptography. As with the previous chapter, this chapter requires no background other than intellectual curiosity, a more than vague remembrance of high school algebra, and trust that it's all understandable with a fair bit of thought, lots of patience, and several nights' sleep. We cover a great deal of material in a very few pages, so don't expect to skim through it all. We suggest you do the homework problems at the point they are referenced in the text.

If you skipped the last chapter, and not because you already knew it all, you almost certainly want to skip this chapter, or go back and read the previous chapter first.

8.2 Notation

In order to avoid cumbersome long formulas with lots of ellipses ("…"s, not conic sections), we'll be using Σ notation for sums and Π notation for products:

$$\sum_{i=m}^{n} a_i = a_m + a_{m+1} + \cdots + a_{n-1} + a_n$$

$$\prod_{i=m}^{n} a_i = a_m a_{m+1} \cdots a_{n-1} a_n$$

As an example, we can define exponentiation (for non-negative integer exponents) in Π notation as

$$a^n = \prod_{i=1}^{n} a$$

(A sum with no components is 0, a product with no components is 1.) Sometimes, instead of low and high limits, we'll specify the components of a sum or product with a condition, e.g., $a^n = \prod_{1 \le i \le n} a$. When not otherwise specified, the index variable (i in the previous examples) takes on integer values satisfying the condition or limits. Within this chapter, if a low limit is not specified, it is assumed to be 0. Sometimes we'll leave out the index variable altogether when it's clear what it is.

We'll also use a bit of set notation. A set is a collection of elements. We write $s \in S$ to indicate that s is an element of the set S. If we know all the elements of a set, we can write it by listing its elements separated by commas and enclosed in curly braces, e.g. $\{0,1,2\}$ is a notation for the set comprising the first three non-negative integers. Listing an element more than once is the same as listing it once. If we know some property of the elements of a set, we can write it in terms of that property: $\{x \mid property(x)\}$ is the set of elements x for which $property(x)$ is true. More generally, $\{expression \mid condition\}$ is the set of elements which can be written as *expression* subject to *condition*, e.g. $\{x^2+y^2 \mid x \in \mathbf{Z} \text{ and } y \in \mathbf{Z}\}$ is the set of numbers that can be expressed as the sum of two squares of integers. The difference of two sets A and B, written $A-B$, is the set of elements in A that are not in B.

8.3 GROUPS

Sometimes it's easier to understand something by generalizing it. So it is with $\mathbf{Z}_n$ (the integers mod n), which is the basis for so much of public key cryptography. Let's start by listing some of the properties we've seen while investigating $\mathbf{Z}_n{}^*$ (the integers relatively prime to n, mod n).

(A) **Associativity.** $(ab)c = a(bc)$.

(I) Existence of **identity**. There exists an element e such that, for each a, $ea = ae = a$. In the case of $\mathbf{Z}_n{}^*$, this identity element is 1.

(N) Existence of **inverse**. For each a, there is an a^{-1} such that $a^{-1}a = aa^{-1} = e$.

(C) **Commutativity**. For each pair of elements a and b, $ab = ba$.

We'll define any structure $\langle G, \cdot \rangle$, a set of elements (G) and an operation ($\cdot$) taking two elements of G and producing a single element of G, that satisfies properties A, I, and N to be a **group**. If the structure also satisfies property C, we'll call it a **commutative group**, also known as an **Abelian group**. Most groups used in cryptography are commutative groups.

When there is ambiguity, we'll specify the group operator explicitly; normally we'll use the same terminology and notation for the group operator as we use for multiplication, including exponentiation for repeated multiplication, where $a^0 = e$, a^{-1} is the inverse of a, and $a^{-n} = (a^{-1})^n$.

Some examples of groups:

- $\mathbf{Z}_n$* (with multiplication mod n).
- $\mathbf{Z}_n$ with addition (mod n).
- $\mathbf{Z}$ with addition. (This is the simplest infinite group.)
- Permutations (i.e. rearrangements) of three objects, with the composition operator. (This is the simplest non-Abelian group.) See Homework Problem 1.

A **subgroup** of a group G is a subset of G that is a group under G's operator. It is always the case that the identity element is a subgroup of any group, as is the group itself. It is also the case that the powers $\{g^n \mid n \in \mathbf{Z}\}$ of any element g of the group is a subgroup, called the **cyclic subgroup** generated by g. If G is finite, then we only need to include non-negative powers of g. A group G is **cyclic** if it is its own cyclic subgroup, i.e. there is a $g \in G$ such that $G = \{g^n \mid n \in \mathbf{Z}\}$; g is called a **generator** of G. A cyclic group can have many generators.

Some examples of subgroups:

- $\{1,9\}$ is a cyclic subgroup of $\mathbf{Z}_{10}$*; 9 is the only generator.
- The even numbers form a cyclic subgroup of $\mathbf{Z}$ with addition. 2 is a generator.
- Permutations of the first three of four objects is a subgroup of the four-object permutations.

The **order** of a group is the number of elements in the group. We write the order of G as $|G|$.

If G is a finite group, and H is a subgroup of G, then $|H|$ divides $|G|$. The proof involves creating a multiplication table, where the top row comprises the elements of H, starting with the identity. Successive rows consist of elements of the form gh, where g is any element of G not in any previous row of the table, and h is in H. No two elements in the same row can be equal, because if $gh_1 = gh_2$, $h_1 = g^{-1}gh_1 = g^{-1}gh_2 = h_2$. (Notice how we just used the group properties of G.) It is easy to see that if g is not already in the table, neither are any of the gh: if gh is in the table, it is g_0h_0 for some g_0 in the first column and some h_0 in H; then $gh = g_0h_0$ so $g = g_0h_0h^{-1}$, so g is in the g_0 row.

(Notice how we just used the group properties of H.) So all we have to do is fill the table row by row, each time choosing for the first column a g in G not already in the table. When there is no remaining g, we have a complete table, with each element of G appearing exactly once, and each row containing $|H|$ elements. The number of rows is called the **index** of H in G. So $|G|$ is the product of $|H|$ and the index of H in G.

The **order** of an element is the order of the cyclic subgroup it generates. If g has finite order, it is clear that the order of g is the smallest positive integer λ for which $g^\lambda = e$. Note that if $g^k = e$, then λ divides k: if $k = q\lambda + r$ with $0 \leq r < \lambda$, $g^r = g^{-q\lambda} g^k = e$, so $r = 0$.

For the rest of this chapter, all the groups will be commutative.

Pay attention to how we use this fact in the next paragraph (and see Homework Problem 2).

If we have two elements with finite order, we can find an element whose order is the least common multiple of those orders as follows. First, suppose a and b have orders λ and μ, respectively, and $\gcd(\lambda, \mu) = 1$. Since $\gcd(\lambda, \mu) = 1$, there are integers u and v such that $u\lambda + v\mu = 1$. Consider the cyclic group generated by ab. $(ab)^{u\lambda} = a^{u\lambda} b^{u\lambda} = eb^{u\lambda} = eb^{u\lambda} e = eb^{u\lambda} b^{v\mu} = b^{u\lambda + v\mu} = b$, so b is in the cyclic group. Similarly, $(ab)^{v\mu} = a$, so a is in the cyclic group. Since the order of each element of a group divides the order of the group, the order of the cyclic group (which is the order of ab) must be a multiple of $\lambda\mu$. And $(ab)^{\lambda\mu} = a^{\lambda\mu} b^{\lambda\mu} = ee = e$, so ab has order $\lambda\mu$. Now if a and b have orders λ and μ, respectively, and $\gcd(\lambda, \mu) = \gamma$, let $\delta = \gcd(\gamma, \mu/\gamma)$ and $\varepsilon = \gamma/\delta$. Consider a^δ and b^ε. These have orders λ/δ and $\mu/\varepsilon = \mu\delta/\gamma$, respectively, and $\gcd(\lambda/\delta, \mu\delta/\gamma) = 1$, so the order of $a^\delta b^\varepsilon$ is $\lambda\mu/\gamma = \mathrm{lcm}(\lambda, \mu)$.

A corollary of this result is that for any finite Abelian group, there is an element whose order is the least common multiple of the orders of all the elements. We can produce such an element as follows: set our candidate to the identity, then repeatedly choose an element whose order is not a divisor of the order of the current candidate and replace the candidate with an element whose order is the lcm of the orders of the candidate and the newly chosen element; eventually we'll run out of elements and the candidate will have the desired order. We'll make use of this corollary in §8.4.2 *Finite Fields*.

8.4 FIELDS

We'll now consider two operators (+ and ·) at the same time, as we do with normal arithmetic on real numbers. The property we'd most like, because we're so used to it, and because it is so useful, is

(D) **Distributivity** of · over +. For all a, b, c, $a \cdot (b + c) = a \cdot b + a \cdot c$.

Now we can define a **field** as a structure comprising a set F and two operators, + and ·, satisfying property D and for which $\langle F, +\rangle$ is a commutative group with identity 0 and $\langle F-\{0\}, \cdot\rangle$ is a commutative group with identity 1. Examples of fields are

- $\mathbf{Z}_p$, the integers mod p, where p is a prime (see Homework Problem 5)
- **Q**, the rational numbers
- **R**, the real numbers
- **C**, the complex numbers

Intuitively, you can think of a field as something like **Q**, but without any notion of order. We'll use a lot of the same notation as we use for **Q**, including unary minus (–) for additive inverse ($a + -a = 0$), $a - b$ for $a + -b$, and a/b for $a \cdot b^{-1}$.

For cryptography, it turns out that the most useful fields are finite—fields such as $\mathbf{Z}_p$. As we'll see after of bit of investigation, there are other finite fields.

A **subfield** of a field F is a subset of F that is a field under F's operators. If E is a subfield of F, then we say F is a **field extension** of E.

8.4.1 Polynomials

One of the most useful ways of investigating fields is to consider polynomials $c(x) = \Sigma c_i x^i$ with **coefficients** c_i in some field. You probably remember this sort of thing from high school algebra. We define the **degree** of a non-zero polynomial to be the highest exponent of x having a non-zero coefficient. (This coefficient is called the **leading coefficient**.) By convention, the degree of the zero polynomial is $-\infty$ (negative infinity). A polynomial of degree less than 1 is called a **constant**. A polynomial with leading coefficient 1 is called **monic**.

We define polynomial addition and multiplication in the usual way:

$$\sum_i c_i x^i + \sum_i d_i x^i = \sum_i (c_i + d_i) x^i$$

$$\sum_i c_i x^i \cdot \sum_i d_i x^i = \sum_i \sum_{j=0}^{i} c_{i-j} d_j x^i$$

Note that when multiplying polynomials, the degrees add. (See Homework Problem 6 for an example.) And that's why we had to define the degree of the zero polynomial to be $-\infty$.

We can also note that polynomials satisfy properties A, C, and D, i.e., if $a(x)$, $b(x)$, and $c(x)$ are polynomials over some field, then property A: $a(x) + (b(x) + c(x)) = (a(x) + b(x)) + c(x)$ and $a(x)(b(x)c(x)) = (a(x)b(x))c(x)$, property B: $a(x) + b(x) = b(x) + a(x)$ and $a(x)b(x) = b(x)a(x)$, and property C: $a(x) \cdot (b(x) + c(x)) = a(x)b(x) + a(x)c(x)$. (See Homework Problem 7.)

Polynomial division is a bit more complicated, but suffice it to say that if we have two polynomials $p(x)$ and $d(x)$, with $d(x)$ non-zero, there are unique polynomials $q(x)$ and $r(x)$, called the **quotient** and **remainder**, respectively, such that $r(x)$ has degree smaller than $d(x)$, and $p(x) = q(x)d(x) + r(x)$. If $r(x)$ is zero, we say that $d(x)$ is a **factor** of $p(x)$, or that $d(x)$ **divides** $p(x)$. There is a simple algorithm, which we're sure you learned in high school algebra, for computing polynomial quotients and remainders (it's a lot like integer long division):

- Initialize $q(x) \leftarrow 0$, $r(x) \leftarrow p(x)$.
- Repeat:
  If degree($r(x)$) < degree($d(x)$), terminate.
  $s(x) \leftarrow (\text{leading\_coefficient}(r(x))/\text{leading\_coefficient}(d(x)))x^{\text{degree}(r(x))-\text{degree}(d(x))}$
  $q(x) \leftarrow q(x) + s(x)$
  $r(x) \leftarrow r(x) - s(x)d(x)$

Sample Polynomial Division

(polynomials over $\mathbf{Z}_5$)

$$
\begin{array}{rr|l}
 & & \quad\quad\quad\quad 3x^2 + 3x + 1 \quad \leftarrow\text{quotient} \\
\text{divisor}\rightarrow & 2x^3+3x+1 & x^5 + x^4 + x^3 + x^2 + x + 1 \quad \leftarrow\text{dividend} \\
 & & \underline{x^5 \quad\quad + 4x^3 + 3x^2} \\
 & & \quad\quad x^4 + 2x^3 + 3x^2 + x + 1 \\
 & & \quad\quad \underline{x^4 \quad\quad + 4x^2 + 3x} \\
 & & \quad\quad\quad\quad 2x^3 + 4x^2 + 3x + 1 \\
 & & \quad\quad\quad\quad \underline{2x^3 \quad\quad + 3x + 1} \\
 & & \quad\quad\quad\quad\quad\quad 4x^2 \quad \leftarrow\text{remainder}
\end{array}
$$

(See Homework Problem 8.)

Just as we did with integers in §7.2 *Modular Arithmetic*, we can do modular arithmetic with polynomials. Given a non-zero polynomial $m(x)$ as the **modulus**, we represent each polynomial $p(x)$ by its remainder when divided by $m(x)$, writing $p(x)$ mod $m(x)$ for that remainder. And just as with integers, we can do addition and multiplication mod $m(x)$ by doing regular addition and multiplication and then taking the remainder. (See Homework Problem 9.) And we can sometimes do division mod $m(x)$—by use of multiplicative inverses when they exist.

We can define the **greatest common divisor (gcd)** of two polynomials as the monic polynomial of highest degree that divides both of them. To compute the gcd, we can perform Euclid's algorithm on polynomials in exactly the same way as we did for integers. We have to perform one final step—we divide by the leading coefficient of the last non-zero remainder to make the gcd monic. So, to compute the gcd of $a(x)$ and $b(x)$, together with $u(x)$ and $v(x)$ such that $\gcd(a(x),b(x)) = u(x)a(x) + v(x)b(x)$:

- Initial setup:
  $r_{-2}(x) \leftarrow a(x) \quad u_{-2}(x) \leftarrow 1 \quad v_{-2}(x) \leftarrow 0$
  $r_{-1}(x) \leftarrow b(x) \quad u_{-1}(x) \leftarrow 0 \quad v_{-1}(x) \leftarrow 1$
  $n \leftarrow 0$

- Step n:
  If $r_{n-1}(x) = 0$, go to final step.
  Otherwise, divide $r_{n-2}(x)$ by $r_{n-1}(x)$ to get quotient $q_n(x)$ and remainder $r_n(x)$.
  $u_n(x) \leftarrow u_{n-2}(x) - q_n(x)u_{n-1}(x) \qquad v_n(x) \leftarrow v_{n-2}(x) - q_n(x)v_{n-1}(x)$
  $n \leftarrow n+1$
  Repeat.

- Final step:
  $t \leftarrow (\text{leading\_coefficient}(r_{n-2}(x)))^{-1}$
  $\gcd(a(x),b(x)) \leftarrow t \cdot r_{n-2}(x) \qquad u(x) \leftarrow t \cdot u_{n-2}(x) \qquad v(x) \leftarrow t \cdot v_{n-2}(x)$

For example, if $a(x) = 2x^4+3x^3+4x^2+2x+1$ and $b(x) = 4x^3+1$ (polynomials over $\mathbf{Z}_5$):

n	$q_n(x)$	$r_n(x)$	$u_n(x)$	$v_n(x)$
−2		$2x^4+3x^3+4x^2+2x+1$	1	0
−1		$4x^3+1$	0	1
0	$3x+2$	$4x^2+4x+4$	1	$2x+3$
1	$x+4$	0	$4x+1$	$3x^2+4x+4$
2	$t = 4$	$\gcd = x^2+x+1$	$u(x) = 4$	$v(x) = 3x+2$

We can **evaluate** a polynomial $p(x)$ at a value v in the field by substituting the value v for each occurrence of x and doing the arithmetic (in the field, of course). Because of the way polynomial addition and multiplication are defined, any equation involving polynomial addition and multiplication will continue to be valid when all the polynomials are evaluated at any particular value v.

We define v to be a **root** of the polynomial $p(x)$ if $p(v) = 0$. It's not hard to see that v will be a root iff the degree 1 polynomial $(x-v)$ is a factor of $p(x)$: $p(x) = q(x)(x-v) + r(x)$ with $r(x)$ a constant, say k, by polynomial division, so $p(v) = q(v)(v-v) + k = k$. Since a degree n polynomial can have at most n degree 1 factors, it can have at most n roots. (See Homework Problem 16.)

Euclidean Algorhyme #2

Numberlike objects *a* and *b*
reveal to us their gcd—
a linear combo of the two
with coeffs found from Euclid's brew.

We'll build a table row by row
with columns three. Now here's the flow.
The first two rows will start the run:
first *a*, one, ought; then *b*, ought, one.
Discarding rows as we proceed,
The last two rows are all we need.
On these last rows we'll set our sight
and name the objects left to right.
The penult row is *j*, *s*, *t*;
the final row's then *k*, *u*, *v*.
When *k* is nought, then *j* will be
the long-sought-after gcd.
This gcd, inversefully,
is *s* times *a* plus *t* times *b*.
Now Euclid tells us how to step
from two last rows down to the next:
Compute the quotient *j* slash *k*;
remainder can be thrown away.
Subtract from the penfinal row
the quotient times the last, and so
a new row forms, and we delete
the first of three, now obsolete.
That's all there is; Euclid we thank.
So this line left intentionally blank.

—Mike Speciner*

*$I_{1,2}$ let me_3 put this poem in in exchange for a number of questionable jokes.

8.4.2 Finite Fields

If F is a finite field with q elements, then every element of F is a root of $x^q - x$. Why? Well $x^q - x = x(x^{q-1} - 1)$, so clearly 0 is a root. Now, remember that $F - \{0\}$ is a group under multiplication, and it has order $q-1$. Since the order of any group element divides the order of the group, each $a \in F-\{0\}$ satisfies $a^{q-1} = 1$. So each non-zero element is a root of $x^{q-1}-1$. Since there are q elements of F, and $x^q - x$ has degree q, we can conclude that $x^q - x = \Pi_{a \in F}(x-a)$.

In fact, $F-\{0\}$ is cyclic. Why? Consider the order of each element. We know there is some element g whose order is the least common multiple λ of all those orders. We know that each of the $q-1$ elements a in $F-\{0\}$ satisfies $a^\lambda = 1$ (because λ is a multiple of the order of a), and so are roots of $x^\lambda - 1$. But $x^\lambda - 1$ has degree λ, so there can be at most λ roots. Thus $\lambda \geq q-1$. And we know $\lambda \mid q-1$, so $\lambda = q-1$, and $F-\{0\}$ is cyclic with generator g.

8.4.2.1 What Sizes Can Finite Fields Be?

For a finite field, if we start at 0 and continually add 1, we must eventually get back to 0. The number of times we can add 1 before getting back to 0 is called the **characteristic** of the field. Notationally, we'll write the sequence as $0, 1, 2, \ldots$. Property D (distributivity) allows us to conclude that the characteristic is a prime: if the characteristic were ab with each of a and b smaller than the characteristic, then $ab = (\Sigma_{a \text{ times}} 1)(\Sigma_{b \text{ times}} 1) = \Sigma_{ab \text{ times}} 1 = 0$; so $F-\{0\}$ would contain a and b but not ab. Distributivity also allows us to conclude that if F has characteristic p, then for any $c \in F$, $\Sigma_{p \text{ times}}\, c = (\Sigma_{p \text{ times}} 1)c = 0 \cdot c = 0$.

Now we'll enumerate the elements of a finite field F of characteristic p. We'll pick a sequence of elements a_i of F so that each new element can't be expressed as a linear combination $\Sigma c_i a_i$ (with coefficients $c_i \in \mathbf{Z}_p$) of the previously selected elements. Eventually, we'll run out of new elements. Then each element of F will be representable as a linear combination of elements of the sequence, with coefficients in $\mathbf{Z}_p$. If there are n elements in the sequence, then there are p^n linear combinations $\Sigma_{i<n} c_i a_i$ where $c_i \in \mathbf{Z}_p$. No two of these can be equal because we could then solve for the last a_i for which the coefficients differ, as a linear combination of the earlier a_is, contrary to our choice of a_is.

So $|F| = p^n$.

8.4.2.2 Representing a Field

It turns out that, for a given prime p and positive integer n, there is exactly one field of order $q = p^n$. It is the **splitting field** of $x^q - x$ (considered as a polynomial over $\mathbf{Z}_p$), the smallest field extension of $\mathbf{Z}_p$ in which $x^q - x$ factors completely into degree 1 polynomials. It is called the **Galois field** of order q, written GF(q). But there are many ways to represent this field. We now have a sufficient handle on finite fields to be able to represent them in a way that allows us to compute with them. We'll choose a prime p and a positive integer n, thus determining the field F of order $q = p^n$. Pick a (multiplicative) generator g of $F-\{0\}$. Consider $g^0, g^1, \ldots, g^{n-1}$. These must be linearly independent over $\mathbf{Z}_p$, i.e. there's no non-trivial linear combination of them that equals 0, because otherwise we'd have $g^k = \Sigma_{i<k} c_i g^i$ for some $k < n$, and so, since every non-zero element of F is g^m for some

m, we could express every element of F as a linear combination of $g^0, g^1, \ldots, g^{k-1}$ with coefficients from $\mathbf{Z}_p$, but there are only p^k such linear combinations. Conversely, by the proof of $|F| = p^n$, there can be no more than n linearly independent elements of F, so $g^n = \Sigma_{i<n} c_i g^i$ for some (unique) set of coefficients $c_0, \ldots, c_{n-1}$ determined by the generator we chose.

So we can represent any element a of F as a sequence of n elements of $\mathbf{Z}_p$, namely the coefficients a_i of $g^0, g^1, \ldots, g^{n-1}$ for which $a = \Sigma_{i<n} a_i g^i$. Addition is just componentwise addition in $\mathbf{Z}_p$. Multiplication is like polynomial multiplication, but we have to convert terms with exponents $\geq n$ by use of $g^n = \Sigma_{i<n} c_i g^i$. The most straightforward technique (but by no means the most efficient) is to decompose the multiplication into a sequence of multiplications by g, multiplications by elements of $\mathbf{Z}_p$, and componentwise additions. Multiplying by g is easy: $g\Sigma_{i<n} a_i g^i = \Sigma_{i<n}(a_{i-1}+c_i a_{n-1})g^i$, where $a_{-1}=0$. Multiplication by b_j is trivial: $b_j \Sigma_{i<n} a_i g^i = \Sigma_{i<n} a_i b_j g^i$. So to multiply $a = \Sigma_{i<n} a_i g^i$ by $b = \Sigma_{j<n} b_j g^j$, we multiply a by b_{n-1}, then for $j = n-2$ to 0, multiply the result by g and add ab_j.

We also need to be able to compute negation (additive inverse) and (multiplicative) inverse. Negation is just componentwise negation in $\mathbf{Z}_p$. Inverse is more difficult, but as we commented before, we can make use of the Euclidean algorithm for polynomials over $\mathbf{Z}_p$. (Alternatively, we could exponentiate to the power $q-2$, since for $a \in F-\{0\}$, $a \cdot a^{q-2} = a^{q-1} = 1$.) If $a = \Sigma_{i<n} a_i g^i$, let $\alpha(x) = \Sigma_{i<n} a_i x^i$. Let $\gamma(x) = x^n - \Sigma_{i<n} c_i x^i$. Note $\gamma(g) = 0$. If we perform Euclid's algorithm on $\alpha(x)$ and $\gamma(x)$, we get polynomials $\mu(x)$ and $\nu(x)$ such that $\alpha(x)\mu(x) + \gamma(x)\nu(x) = \gcd(\alpha(x), \gamma(x))$. Note that, since $\gamma(g) = 0$, $\alpha(g)\mu(g) = \gcd(\alpha(x), \gamma(x))(g)$. If the gcd of $\alpha(x)$ and $\gamma(x)$ is 1, then $\mu(g)$ is a^{-1}. But if the gcd is not 1, then a has no inverse. Since $F-\{0\}$ is a group under $\cdot$, every nonzero a has an inverse, so no non-constant $\alpha(x)$ can divide $\gamma(x)$, i.e. $\gamma(x)$ has no non-trivial factors. A polynomial with no non-trivial factors is called **irreducible**. So the field can be thought of as polynomials over $\mathbf{Z}_p$ modulo the irreducible polynomial $\gamma(x)$.

We could equally well have started with the irreducible polynomial $\gamma(x)$ instead of the element g. Any choice of an irreducible nth degree polynomial $\gamma(x)$ over $\mathbf{Z}_p$ will produce a representation of GF(p^n).

8.5 MATHEMATICS OF RIJNDAEL

Rijndael is based on arithmetic in GF(2^8). The nice thing about this is that each element of the field can be represented by an octet. The bits in this octet are the coefficients of a polynomial over $\mathbf{Z}_2$ modulo the irreducible $\mathbf{Z}_2$ polynomial $m(x) = x^8 + x^4 + x^3 + x + 1$ (see Homework Problem 10), with the least significant bit being the coefficient of 1 and the most significant bit the coefficient of x^7. Addition in this representation is just bitwise $\oplus$, since addition modulo 2 is the same as $\oplus$. Also note that each element is its own negation. Multiplicative inverse is most easily done by table lookup. The multiplicative inverse table has only 256 1-octet entries (well really 255, since 0 doesn't have an inverse). (See Homework Problem 11.) A multiplication table would have 65536 1-octet entries—one entry per pair of octets. Fortunately, Rijndael only requires multiplication by six different constants (elements of GF(2^8)) not counting 0 and 1. Rijndael key expansion uses a sequence of constants C_i tabulated in Figure 3-31; these are obtained by the formula $C_i = x^{i-1} \bmod m(x)$. (See Homework Problem 14.)

Rijndael also uses polynomials over GF(2^8). These polynomials are taken modulo the GF(2^8) polynomial $x^4 + 1$. These polynomials are represented as 4-vectors of octets, with the coefficient of 1 being the first octet in the 4-vector. With this representation, multiplication by x is just a rotation, with the last octet becoming the first. Rijndael's *MixColumn* operation is multiplication by the fixed polynomial $c(x) = 03x^3 + 01x^2 + 01x + 02$, which we'll call the **MixColumn polynomial**. *InvMixColumn* is multiplication by $d(x) = 0Bx^3 + 0Dx^2 + 09x + 0E$, which we may as well call the **InvMixColumn polynomial**. (See Homework Problem 13.)

Finally, for one of the operations composing its S-box, Rijndael treats octets as polynomials over $\mathbf{Z}_2$ modulo the non-irreducible $\mathbf{Z}_2$ polynomial $x^8 + 1$, again with the least significant bit being the coefficient of 1 and the most significant bit the coefficient of x^7. This S-box component consists of multiplying by $x^4 + x^3 + x^2 + x + 1$ and then adding $x^6 + x^5 + x + 1$. Its inverse consists of multiplying by $x^6 + x^3 + x$ and then adding $x^2 + 1$. (See Homework Problem 12.)

In fact, Rijndael's S-box is composed of a sequence of three invertible operations in which octets are interpreted as $\mathbf{Z}_2$ polynomials:

1. a permutation in which each octet maps to its multiplicative inverse mod $m(x)$ (except for 0 which maps to itself)
2. multiplication by $x^4 + x^3 + x^2 + x + 1 \bmod x^8 + 1$
3. addition of $x^6 + x^5 + x + 1$

Rijndael's *MixColumn* is just multiplication by the MixColumn polynomial $c(x) \bmod x^4 + 1$, and its inverse is just multiplication by the InvMixColumn polynomial $d(x) \bmod x^4 + 1$.

The rotation of the columns performed in Rijndael's key expansion can be thought of as multiplication by $x^3 \bmod x^4 + 1$.

8.5.1 A Rijndael Round

The actual description of a Rijndael round, as found in the spec, is as follows. Recall that each round operates on a state consisting of N_b 4-octet columns.

1. The S-box is applied to each octet in the state.

2. Row 0 (the top row) of the state is left alone.
   Row 1 of the state is rotated left 1 column.
   Row 2 of the state is rotated left $2+\lfloor N_b/8 \rfloor$ columns (2 if $N_b < 8$, 3 otherwise).
   Row 3 of the state is rotated left $3+\lfloor N_b/7 \rfloor$ columns (3 if $N_b < 7$, 4 otherwise).
3. *MixColumn* is applied to each column.
4. The round key is ⊕'d into the state.

We can think of the initial ⊕ as an initial round (round 0) which only has step 4. The final round (round N_r) is missing step 3.

You might think that the inverse of encryption would just run encryption backwards, with each operation replaced by its inverse. And this, of course, works fine. But by regrouping and reordering the operations, decryption can look much more like encryption. The key observations for this are that steps 1 and 2 can be exchanged without changing the result, and that *InvMixColumn* is polynomial multiplication, and so it distributes over addition (⊕): if $s(x)$ is a column of the state, and $k(x)$ is the corresponding column of the round key, and $d(x)$ is the InvMixColumn polynomial, then $(s(x) \oplus k(x)) \cdot d(x) = s(x)d(x) \oplus k(x)d(x)$, and of course this stays true mod $x^4 + 1$.

So if we group steps 3 and 4 from one round with steps 1 and 2 from the next, then interchange steps 1 and 2, and interchange steps 3 and 4 by applying *InvMixColumn* to each column of the round key, then, when we run this backwards with the operations inverted, we get the following description of an inverse round.

1. The Inverse S-box is applied to each octet in the state.
2. Row 0 (the top row) of the state is left alone.
   Row 1 of the state is rotated right 1 octet.
   Row 2 of the state is rotated right $2+\lfloor N_b/8 \rfloor$ columns (2 if $N_b < 8$, 3 otherwise).
   Row 3 of the state is rotated right $3+\lfloor N_b/7 \rfloor$ columns (3 if $N_b < 7$, 4 otherwise).
3. *InvMixColumn* is applied to each column.
4. The (modified) round key is ⊕'d into the state.

This is the way decryption rounds 1 through N_r-1 work. Decryption round 0 is just the inverse of step 4 from encryption round N_r (remember that there is no step 3 in that round—now you know why), namely ⊕ of the (unmodified) round key. Decryption round N_r is the inverse of step 4 (the only step) of encryption round 0 followed by steps 1 and 2 from encryption round 1. So it is missing inverse step 3 (there's the other side of the reason for the final round being the way it is), and its round key is unmodified (i.e. it's just encryption round key 0).

8.6 ELLIPTIC CURVE CRYPTOGRAPHY

An elliptic curve is a set of points on the coordinate plane satisfying an equation of the form $y^2 = x^3 + ax^2 + bx + c$. If you have two points on such a curve, and draw a line through both of them, the line will intersect the curve at a unique third point, basically because in a field, if a polynomial of degree 3 has two roots (say r and s), you can divide the polynomial by the product $(x-r)(x-s)$ and you end up with a degree-1 polynomial from which you can read off the third root. (There are a couple of special cases. If the two points are the same, the line we draw is the tangent to the curve. If the two points are opposite each other about the x axis, i.e. their abscissas (x coordinates) are the same and their ordinates (y coordinates) are additive inverses, the third point is at infinity, and we'll call it **I**.

So you can define a weird kind of multiplication* of points on an elliptic curve. The product of two points is the point you get by drawing a line through the two points, finding the third intersection point of the curve and the line, and reflecting that point across the x axis (by negating its ordinate). What's so amazing about this multiplication is that it is associative! We just have to define the inverse of a point as the opposite point about the x axis, and then **I** is the identity, and we have a group.

If our coordinate plane is not the real plane, but instead the coordinate plane of a finite field, then this elliptic curve group is finite. One can then pick an element from this group and use the resulting cyclic subgroup for cryptography. For example, Diffie-Hellman works for this group the same way it does for $\mathbf{Z}_p$*. The discrete logarithm problem for elliptic curve groups appears to be harder than for $\mathbf{Z}_p$*.

In common usage, coefficient a is chosen to be zero. There is no loss of generality in doing this, because a is minus the sum of the roots of the cubic, so a horizontal translation of the curve by a third of that sum puts it in the restricted form. (Of course, if the field has characteristic 3, you can't do that, but no one uses fields of characteristic 3 for elliptic curve cryptography.)

There is a slight complication for some of the (computationally) best finite groups, namely GF(2^n). Because these groups have characteristic 2, $x = -x$ and so there is only one square root of each square, which pretty much wrecks the scheme described above. But all is not lost. If we skew the coordinate system by a linear transformation so that each point $\langle x, y\rangle$ becomes $\langle x, y-½x\rangle$, then iff the original point satisfied $y^2 = x^3 + ax^2 + bx + c$, the new point satisfies $(y+½x)^2 = x^3 + ax^2 + bx + c$ or $y^2 + xy = x^3 + (a-¼)x^2 + bx + c$. So this suggests that we can look at skewed elliptic curves of the form $y^2 + xy = x^3 + ax^2 + bx + c$, and points on these curves will have the same group properties. But over a field of characteristic two, we see that if $\langle x, y\rangle$ is on such a curve, so is $\langle x, y+x\rangle$, because $(y+x)^2 + x(y+x) = y^2 + x^2 + xy + x^2 = y^2 + xy$ (remember that for characteristic 2, $2 = 0$). So

*Typical descriptions of elliptic curve groups show the group operation as addition, and the identity as **O**. As a consequence, exponentiation is instead written as left-multiplication by an integer. We've chosen to use the multiplicative paradigm to emphasize the similarity with cryptography based on $\mathbf{Z}_p$*, such as Diffie-Hellman.

this allows us to use GF(2^n), which is one of the two common finite field categories used for elliptic curve cryptography. The other common choice is $\mathbf{Z}_p$, for large primes p.

8.7 HOMEWORK

1. A) A finite permutation, π, is a rearrangement of a finite sequence of objects, which we might as well number 1, 2,…*n*. If we have a permutation, we can look at where 1 goes (π(1)), and then look at where the number at that position goes (π(π(1))), and so forth until we get back to 1. Why do we have to get back to 1?
   B) We show this cycle as (1 π(1) π(π(1)) …). (We don't bother listing 1 twice; the understanding is that the last listed element goes to the first.) We then look for the next object that's not in the cycles we've already listed, say *k*, and find its cycle (*k* π(*k*) π(π(*k*)) …), and so forth until we have accounted for all the objects 1, 2,…*n*. As an optimization, we don't bother listing length-1 cycles; the understanding is that any object that is not listed is not moved. But just so we have a notation for the permutation that doesn't move anything, we write it as (). Some of the permutation of four objects are thus (), (1 2), (1 2) (3 4). List all the permutations of three objects.
   C) Composition. As long as two permutations in this cycle notation don't share any elements, it doesn't matter what order we compose them in. But otherwise it does. And unfortunately, there are two ways to do it: left to right and right to left. Religious wars amongst mathematicians have been fought over this, much like big-endian and little-endian in the computer field. The problem is that if π and ρ are two permutations, we might want the permutation specified by π(ρ(*k*)) to be the composition (π·ρ)(*k*). But this means we have to apply the cycles right to left, even though within a cycle the notation is clearly left to right. We could just redefine the cycle notation so that each successive object in the list tells from where the object immediately to its left came, and then it would make sense to read the cycles from right to left. Another approach, fairly common amongst algebraists, is to write arguments to the right of the function, as in (*k*)π. Then ((*k*)π)ρ would be (*k*)(π·ρ) with the cycles just concatenated. This is also consistent with multiplication of row vectors by square matrices. Anyway, for purposes of this book, we'll specify that (π·ρ) means first apply ρ and then π. Write out the composition table for the permutations of three objects, and verify that this is a non-commutative group.

2. Show that in the permutation group of three objects, there are elements of orders 2 and 3, but no element of order lcm(2,3) = 6.

3. Show that the group of permutations of $n > 2$ objects does not have a generator. But show that any permutation of n objects is the composition of a sequence of instances of the permutations (1 2) and (1 2 ... n).

4. This is one of my₃ favorite problem. It shows the power of associativity. See §8.3 *Groups*. Consider the following properties:

   (LI) Existence of **left identity**. There exists an element e such that, for each a, $ea = a$.

   (LN) Existence of **left inverse**. For each a, there is an a^{-1} such that $a^{-1}a = e$.

   (RI) Existence of **right identity**. There exists an element e such that, for each a, $ae = a$.

   (RN) Existence of **right inverse**. For each a, there is an a^{-1} such that $aa^{-1} = e$.

   Show that if $\langle G, \cdot \rangle$ has properties A, LI, and LN (or properties A, RI, and RN), it is a group.
   Nonhint: This would be trivial if you could assume property C. So don't!
   Hint: Consider $(a^{-1})^{-1}a^{-1}aa^{-1}$.
   Find a non-group with properties A, LI, and RN.

5. Why isn't $\mathbf{Z}_n$ a field when n isn't prime? Which property fails?

6. Multiply the polynomials $2x^3 + 3x + 1$ and $3x^2 + 3x + 1$.

7. Show that polynomials satisfy properties A, C, and D. You may first want to notice that

$$\sum_i a_i x^i \cdot \sum_i b_i x^i = \sum_i \sum_{j+k=i} b_j c_k x^i$$

   and then use properties A, C, and D of the coefficients' field.

8. Divide the $\mathbf{Z}_5$ polynomial $x^5 + x^3 + 1$ by the $\mathbf{Z}_5$ polynomial $3x^2 + 2x + 1$.

9. In an analogous manner to §7.2 *Modular Arithmetic*, define polynomial addition and multiplication modulo a non-zero polynomial $m(x)$. Show that each definition makes sense in that it produces the same value (mod $m(x)$) when you replace either of the operands with an equivalent (mod $m(x)$) polynomial.

10. Show that the $\mathbf{Z}_2$ polynomial $m(x) = x^8 + x^4 + x^3 + x + 1$ is irreducible. Hint: If not, it would have a factor of degree 4 or less, so try all 32 possibilities. You can quickly eliminate half of these because x isn't a factor, so neither is any multiple of x.

11. Compute the inverse of all the nonzero $\mathbf{Z}_2$ polynomials mod $m(x)$, where $m(x) = x^8 + x^4 + x^3 + x + 1$. Represent each polynomial as an octet, with the most significant bit being the coefficient of x^7 and the least significant bit being the coefficient of x^0.

12. The Rijndael S-box is the composition of two permutations. The first is the inverse just described, but with 0 mapping to itself (since it doesn't have an inverse). This permutation is clearly its own inverse. The second permutation is multiplication by $x^4 + x^3 + x^2 + x + 1$ mod $x^8 + 1$ followed by addition of $x^6 + x^5 + x + 1$. What is its inverse? Verify the S-box and inverse S-box tables (see Figure 3-24 and Figure 3-27).

13. Verify that the MixColumn polynomial $c(x) = \mathsf{03}x^3 + \mathsf{01}x^2 + \mathsf{01}x + \mathsf{02}$ and the InvMixColumn polynomial $d(x) = \mathsf{0B}x^3 + \mathsf{0D}x^2 + \mathsf{09}x + \mathsf{0E}$ are multiplicative inverses mod $x^4 + 1$, with all polynomials over GF(2^8) as represented in Rijndael. Extra credit: Find the inverse of $c(x)$ by using the Euclidean algorithm.

14. Verify that the key expansion constants C_i tabulated in Figure 3-31 are just x^{i-1} mod $m(x)$, using the same representation as in Homework Problem 11.

15. Verify that the description of Rijndael rounds in §3.5 *Advanced Encryption Standard (AES)* is equivalent to that in §8.5 *Mathematics of Rijndael*, and that the decryption described in §3.5.5 *Inverse Rounds* truly undoes the encryption described in §3.5.4 *Rounds*.

16. Show that polynomials over a field form a unique factorization domain (in that every monic polynomial can be expressed uniquely as a product of powers of monic irreducible polynomials) by using the Euclidean algorithm to prove that if $a|bc$ and a is irreducible, then $a|b$ or $a|c$. Big hint: if not $a|b$, then $\gcd(a,b)=1$, so $xa+yb=1$, so $c=1c=xac+ybc=a(xc+y(bc/a))$.

PART 2

AUTHENTICATION

9 OVERVIEW OF AUTHENTICATION SYSTEMS

Authentication is the process of reliably verifying the identity of someone (or something). There are lots of examples of authentication in human interaction. People who know you can recognize you based on your appearance or voice. A guard might authenticate you by comparing you with the picture on your badge. A mail order company might accept as authentication the fact that you know the expiration date on your credit card.

This chapter gives an overview of authentication systems, and subsequent chapters deal with the issues in more detail. There are two interesting cases. One case is when a computer is authenticating another computer, such as when a print spooler wants to authenticate a printer. The other case occurs when a person is using a public workstation, for instance a workstation installed in a public area (like a roomful of workstations set up for the convenience of attendees at a convention). Such a workstation can perform sophisticated operations, but it will not store secrets for every possible user. Instead, the user's secret must be remembered by the user. A person is most likely to remember a secret if it is a text string (a password) and the user is allowed to choose it. Many users will not choose passwords wisely, and therefore the secret is a low-quality secret (one vulnerable to guessing). In this chapter we'll discuss various forms of authentication: password-based, address-based, and cryptographic. In subsequent chapters we cover authentication system concepts and standards in more depth.

9.1 PASSWORD-BASED AUTHENTICATION

It's not who you know. It's what you know.

Everyone knows what a password is, right? We thought so, too, until we tried to define it. When we use the phrase **password-based authentication** we are referring to a secret quantity (the **password**) that you state to prove you know it. The big problem with password-based authentication is eavesdropping.

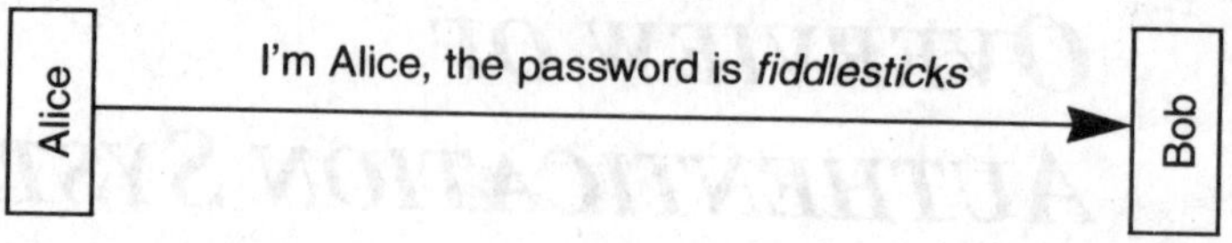

There are certain types of systems that might be thought of as password-based that we are excluding from our definition. For instance, in some systems a user has a secret word or phrase that the user thinks of as a password, but the string known by the user is converted into a cryptographic key. We consider such a system a cryptographic rather than a password-based authentication system.

Why does anyone use password-based authentication when cryptographic authentication is more secure? When dealing with people unaided by a workstation (e.g. the declining fraction of people at "dumb terminals"), it's difficult to avoid basing protocols on passwords, though as we will see (§10.8 *Authentication Tokens*), there are some clever devices being manufactured today that make cryptographic solutions compatible with human beings.

Unfortunately, even computer-computer authentication is often based on passwords. Sometimes cryptography is not used because the protocol started out as a human-computer protocol and was not redesigned when its use got expanded to computer-computer communication. Sometimes it isn't used because the protocol designers assumed (perhaps correctly) that cryptography would be overly expensive in implementation time or processing resources. And sometimes cryptography is avoided because of legal issues.

There are some cases in which it is really annoying that the designers opted for a simple password-based scheme. For instance, some older cellular phones transmit the telephone number of the phone and a password when making a call, and if the password corresponds to the telephone number, the phone company lets the call go through and bills that telephone number. The problem is, anyone can eavesdrop on cellular phone transmissions and **clone** such a phone, meaning they can make a phone that uses the overheard ⟨telephone number, password⟩ pair. Indeed, this *is* a problem—criminals do clone phones for stealing phone service and/or making untraceable calls. It would have been technologically easy to implement a simple cryptographic challenge-response protocol in the phone, and indeed the newer cell phones do this.

There are other issues involved in using passwords. If you are using a workstation, accessing lots of resources across the network, it would be inconvenient for you to have to do a remote login, typing a name and password, every time you accessed a resource such as a file server. For a distributed system to be as convenient to use as a centralized one, you should only need a single password and should only need to enter it once per session. Your workstation could remember your name and password and transmit them on your behalf every time you accessed a remote resource, but this assumes you have the same password on every remote system. How could it be possible to have the same password on many systems? You could individually set your password to the same value on all the systems, but how would you manage to change your password and have the stored password information change simultaneously on all the systems?

9.1.1 Off- vs. On-Line Password Guessing

One way of guessing passwords is simply to type passwords at the system that is going to verify the password. To thwart such an **on-line attack**, the system can make it impossible to guess too many passwords in this manner. For instance, ATM machines eat your card if you type three incorrect passwords. Alternatively, the system can be designed to be slow, so as not to allow very many guesses per unit time. Also, with an on-line attack, the system can become suspicious that someone might be attempting to break in, based on noticing an unusually large number of incorrect passwords. The system might then dispatch a human to investigate.

In contrast, in an **off-line attack**, an intruder can capture a quantity X that is derived from a password in a known way. Then the intruder can, in complete privacy, use an arbitrary amount of compute power to guess passwords, convert them in the known way, and see if X is produced. Because a source of good password guesses is a dictionary, an off-line password guessing attack is sometimes referred to as a **dictionary attack**.

If it is possible for an intruder to do off-line guessing, the secret must be chosen from a much larger space (see §10.3 *Off-Line Password Guessing*).

9.1.2 Storing User Passwords

How does a server know Alice's password? There are several possibilities.

1. Alice's authentication information is individually configured into every server Alice will use.
2. One location, which we'll call an **authentication storage node,** stores Alice's information, and servers retrieve that information when they want to authenticate Alice.
3. One location, which we'll call an **authentication facilitator node**, stores Alice's information, and a server that wants to authenticate Alice sends the information received from Alice to the authentication facilitator node, which does the authentication and tells the server yes or no.

In cases 2 and 3, it's important for the server to authenticate the authentication storage or facilitator node, since if the server were fooled into thinking a bad guy's node was the authentication storage or facilitator node, the server could be tricked into believing the wrong authentication information, and therefore let bad guys impersonate valid users.

Regardless of where authentication information is stored, it is undesirable to have the database consist of unencrypted passwords because anyone who captured the database could impersonate all the users. Someone could capture the database by breaking into the node with the database, or by stealing a backup tape. In the first case above (authentication information individually configured into every server), capturing a server's database (of unencrypted passwords) would enable someone to impersonate all the users of that server. Also, if a user had the same password on multiple servers, that user could then be impersonated at the other servers as well. In the second and third cases, many servers would use the one location, and capturing its database would enable someone to impersonate the users of all those servers. There's a trade-off, though. It might be difficult to physically protect every server, whereas if all the security information is in one location, it is only necessary to protect that one location.

Put all your eggs in one basket, and then watch that basket very carefully.

—Anonymous

An alternative to storing unencrypted passwords is to store hashes of passwords, as is done in UNIX and VMS (see §10.3 *Off-Line Password Guessing*). Then if anyone were to read the password database they could do off-line password-guessing attacks, but would not be able to obtain passwords of users who chose passwords carefully.

Alternatively, we could have the node that stores the password information encrypt the stored passwords (so that the server could decrypt a given password when needed). With hashed passwords an intruder who can read the hashed password database can do a password-guessing attack because the intruder will likely know the hash function (the function itself would not be secret). But with encrypted passwords the intruder can't get the passwords without knowledge of the node's key. Since the node would be a computer, the node's key would be a high-quality key, not derived from a password a human might be able to remember, and therefore invulnerable to guessing. Seemingly, then, encrypting (rather than hashing) the password database would be more secure, since an intruder would not only have to be able to read the node's database of encrypted passwords, but also acquire the node's key.

Encryption of the password database is indeed fairly secure for storage of the database on backup media, but it really isn't much protection against an intruder compromising the node itself, since the node's key is probably easily obtainable once inside the system. Most likely the node's key would be stored in some easily accessible place, readable by anyone with privileges (intruders always seem to obtain privileges). Worse yet, if the key isn't stored in nonvolatile memory somewhere, it likely would have to be typed in by the system manager every time the node was rebooted, in which case the key would most likely be handwritten and pasted to the keyboard.

It is possible to combine both techniques by encrypting the database of hashed passwords. Then you get the security benefits of both.

Sun Microsystems' NIS (Network Information Service), formerly known as YP (Yellow Pages), uses the directory service as an authentication storage node and stores the user's hashed password there. Like the original UNIX password file, the directory service information is world-readable, which means that anything can claim to be a server needing to see some user's authentication information. As generally deployed, the NIS directory service does not prove its identity to the server requesting the user's authentication information, so impersonation of the directory service is somewhat of a security hole. NIS does make authentication across a network more convenient, but we suspect its availability will not convince NSA that it is safe to hook all its computers to the Internet.

9.2 ADDRESS-BASED AUTHENTICATION

It's not what you know. It's where you are.

Address-based authentication does not rely on sending passwords around the network, but rather assumes that the identity of the source can be inferred based on the network address from which packets arrive. It was adopted early in the evolution of computer networks by both UNIX and VMS. The basic idea is that each computer stores information which specifies accounts on other computers that should have access to its resources. For instance, suppose account name Smith on the machine residing at network address *N* is allowed access to computer *C*. Requests for resources are commands like copy a specified file, log in, or execute the following command at the specified remote machine. If a request arrives from address *N* claiming to be sent on behalf of user Smith, then *C* will honor the request.

On UNIX, the *Berkeley rtools* support such access; on VMS, similar functionality is called *PROXY.* The general idea can be implemented in various ways.

- Machine *B* might have a list of network addresses of "equivalent" machines. If machine *A* is listed, then any account name on *A* is equivalent to the same account name on *B*. If a request from *A* arrives with the name JohnSmith, then the request will be honored if it is for anything that the account JohnSmith on *B* was allowed to do. This has the problem that the user has to have the identical account name on all systems.
- Machine *B* might instead have a list of ⟨address, remote account name, local account name⟩. If a request arrives from address *A* with the name Jekyll, then the database is scanned for the matching entry, say ⟨*A*, Jekyll, Hyde⟩. Then the request is honored provided the local account Hyde is authorized to do the request.

UNIX implements two account mapping schemes:

- /etc/hosts.equiv file. There is a global file (named /etc/hosts.equiv) which implements the first scheme above. The file /etc/hosts.equiv on machine *A* contains a list of computers that have identical user account assignments. Suppose a computer *B* is listed in /etc/hosts.equiv. Suppose *A* receives a request with account name Smith, and *B*'s address in the source address field of the network header. If an account with the name Smith exists on machine *A*, the request will be given the same privileges as the local user Smith. (Actually, an exception is made for the privileged account root; it will not be given access by virtue of an entry in /etc/hosts.equiv). The /etc/hosts.equiv file is useful for managing corresponding accounts in bulk on machines with common accounts and common management.

- Per-user .rhosts files. In each UNIX user's home directory, there can be a file named .rhosts, which contains a list of ⟨computer, account⟩ pairs that are allowed access to the user's account. Any user Bob can permit remote access to his account by creating a .rhosts file in his home directory. The account names need not be the same on the remote machine as they are on this one, so Bob can handle the case where he has different account names on different systems. Because of the way the information is organized, any request that is *not* for an account named the same as the source account must include the name of the account that should process the request. For instance, if the local account name on system *A* is Bob and the request is from computer *B*, account name Smith, the request has to specify that it would like to be treated with the privileges given account name Bob. (See Homework Problem 1.)

On VMS, individual users are not permitted to establish their own proxy access files. (This is considered a security feature to prevent users from giving access to their friends). Instead, there is a centrally managed **proxy database** that says for each remote ⟨computer, account⟩ pair what account(s) that pair may access, usually with one of them marked as the default. For example, there might be an entry specifying that account Smith from address *B* should have access to local accounts Bob and Alice, where the account Bob might be marked as the default.

The VMS scheme makes access somewhat more user-friendly than the UNIX scheme in the case where a user has different account names on different systems. Generally (in VMS) the user need not specify the target account in that case. In the rare case where a user is authorized to access multiple accounts on the remote computer, a target account can be specified in the request to access an account other than the default. (In UNIX, it is always necessary to specify the target account in the request if the account name is different.)

Address-based authentication is safe from eavesdropping, but is subject to two other threats:

- If someone, say Trudy, gains privilege on a node FOO, she can access all users' resources of FOO—there's nothing authentication can do about that. But in addition, she can access the network resources of any user with an account on FOO by getting FOO to claim the request comes from that user. Theoretically, it is not obvious how Trudy, once she gains access to FOO, would know which other machines she could invade, since the ⟨machine, account⟩ pairs reachable from ⟨FOO, Smith⟩ are not listed at FOO, but are instead listed at the remote machine. However, in a lot of cases, if ⟨FOO, Smith⟩ allows proxy access from ⟨BAR, JohnS⟩, then it is likely that node BAR specifically allows account Smith at node FOO access to account JohnS at BAR. So Trudy, once she has privileges on FOO, can scan the proxy database (in the case of VMS) or the /etc/hosts.equiv file and the .rhosts files of each of the users (in the case of UNIX), and make a guess that any ⟨node, account name⟩ pairs she finds are likely to let her in from node FOO with the specified account name.

- If someone on the network, say Trudy, can impersonate network addresses of nodes, she can access all the network resources of all users who have accounts on any of those nodes. It is often relatively easy to impersonate a network address. For instance, on broadcast LANs (like Ethernet and Token Ring), it is easy not only to send traffic with the address of a different node on that LAN, but also to receive traffic destined for that node. In many other cases, although it is easy to transmit a packet that has a false source address, the returning traffic would be delivered to the real node rather than the impersonating node.

Depending on the environment, therefore, address-based authentication may be more or less secure than sending passwords in the clear. It is unquestionably more convenient and is the authentication mechanism of choice in many distributed systems deployed today.

9.2.1 Network Address Impersonation

The wire protocol guys don't worry about security because that's really a network protocol problem. The network protocol guys don't worry about it because, really, it's an application problem. The application guys don't worry about it because, after all, they can just use the IP address and trust the network.

—Marcus Ranum

How can Trudy impersonate Alice's network address? Generally it is easy to transmit a packet claiming any address as the source address, either at the network layer or the data link layer. Sometimes it is more difficult. For instance, due to the design of token rings, if Trudy and Alice were on the same ring and Trudy were to transmit a packet using Alice's data link address, then Alice might remove Trudy's packet from the ring or raise a duplicate address error. Another example is star-topology LANs, where each node is connected via a point-to-point link to a central hub. A hub might learn (or be configured with) the data link address of the node on each link, and refuse to forward a packet if the data link source address is not correct for that line, though a hub (being a layer 2 device) is unlikely to check the network layer (layer 3) source address.

A router could also have features to make it difficult for someone to claim to be a different network address. If a router has a point-to-point link to an endnode, it could (like the hub) refuse to accept a packet if the network layer source address is not correct according to the router's configuration. A router could also be configured, on a per-link basis, with a set of addresses that it should expect to appear on each link, and refuse packets with unexpected source addresses. Perhaps if the routers were all trusted, and authentication were added to routing messages to prevent someone from injecting bad routing messages, then a router would not need to be configured on a per-link basis with a set of expected source addresses, but instead could derive the per-link expected source addresses from the routing database.

It is often more difficult for Trudy to receive messages addressed to Alice's network address than for Trudy to claim Alice's address as the source address. If Trudy is on the same LAN as Alice, it is trivial—Trudy just needs to listen to packets addressed to Alice's data link address. If Trudy is not on the same LAN as Alice, but is on one of the LANs in the path between the source and Alice, it's a little harder but still easy. The reason it's a little harder is that Trudy would need to listen to all packets address to the data link address of the router that forwards packets towards Alice from the LAN on which Trudy resides. This is harder than listening to Alice's data link address because a router will probably be receiving packets for many destinations, and Trudy will have to be fast enough to ignore the messages that aren't specifically for Alice.

If Trudy is not on the same LAN as Alice, and not on the path between the source and Alice, then it is more difficult for Trudy to receive packets addressed to Alice. Trudy could potentially inject routing messages that would trick the routers into sending traffic for Alice's address to Trudy. It is possible to add a cryptographic authentication mechanism to router messages which would prevent Trudy from injecting routing information.

Even with cryptographic authentication of routers, it may be possible for Trudy to be able to both transmit from and receive packets for Alice's network address. For instance, in IP, there is a feature known as *source routing*, in which Trudy can inject an IP packet containing not just a source address (Alice's network address) and destination address D, but also a *source route* that gives intermediate destinations. IP will route to each intermediate destination in turn. Assume Trudy uses the source route ⟨Alice, Trudy, D⟩. The applications that run on IP that do address-based authentication will use the field Alice for the address check. When D receives a packet from Alice via source route ⟨Alice, Trudy, D⟩, then D, following the IP host requirements document (RFC 1122), will reply with source route ⟨D, Trudy, Alice⟩. The return traffic will go to Trudy.

9.3 CRYPTOGRAPHIC AUTHENTICATION PROTOCOLS

It's not what you know or where you are, it's
%zPy#bRw Lq(ePAoa&N5nPk9W7Q2EfjaP!yDB$S

Cryptographic authentication protocols can be much more secure than either password-based or address-based authentication. The basic idea is that Alice proves her identity to Bob by performing a cryptographic operation on a quantity Bob supplies. The cryptographic operation performed by Alice is based on Alice's secret. We talked in Chapter 2 *Introduction to Cryptography* about how hashes, secret key cryptography, and public key cryptography could all be used for authentication. The remainder of this chapter discusses some of the more subtle aspects of making these protocols work.

9.4 WHO IS BEING AUTHENTICATED?

Suppose user Bob is at a workstation and wants to access his files at a file server. The purpose of the authentication exchange between the workstation and the file server is to prove Bob's identity. The file server generally does not care which workstation Bob is using.

There are other times when a machine is acting autonomously. For instance, directory service replicas might coordinate updates among themselves and need to prove their identity to each other.

Sometimes it might be important to authenticate both the user and the machine from which the user is communicating. For example, a bank teller might be authorized to do some transactions, but only from the terminal at the bank where that teller is employed.

What's the difference between authenticating a human and authenticating a computer? A computer can store a high-quality secret, such as a long random-looking number, and it can do cryptographic operations. A workstation can do cryptographic operations on behalf of the user, but the system has to be designed so that all the person has to remember is a password. The password can be used to acquire a cryptographic key in various ways:

- directly, as in doing a hash of the password
- using the password to decrypt a higher-quality key, such as an RSA private key, that is stored in some place like a directory service

9.5 PASSWORDS AS CRYPTOGRAPHIC KEYS

Cryptographic keys, especially public key based cryptographic keys, are specially chosen very large numbers. A normal person would not be able to remember such a quantity. But a person can remember a password. It is possible to convert a text string memorizable by a human into a cryptographic key. For instance, to form a DES secret key, a possible transformation of the user's password is to do a cryptographic hash of the password and take 56 bits of the result. It is much more tricky (and computationally expensive) to convert a password into something like an RSA private key, since an RSA key has to be a carefully constructed number.

Jeff Schiller proposed a method of converting a password into an RSA key pair that has plausible efficiency. The basic idea is to convert the user's password into a seed for a random number generator. Choosing an RSA key pair involves testing a lot of randomly chosen numbers for primality to obtain two primes. And the primality tests involve choosing random numbers with which to test the randomly chosen primes. If the RSA key pair generator is run twice, and if for each run the sequence of the random numbers selected by the random number generator is the same, the RSA key pair generator will find the same RSA key pair. So if the user's password is the seed for the random number generator, the RSA key pair generator will always generate the same RSA key pair for the user.

Running the RSA key pair generator from the beginning, seeded with the user's password, is likely to take an unacceptable amount of computation, since typically the RSA key generator will find many non-primes before it finally finds two primes. If it had to be done every time the user logged in, it would be prohibitively expensive. But after the workstation successfully finds the RSA key pair derived from the user's password, it can give the user something to remember that would enable it to complete its work more quickly. For example, if (starting with the user's password as seed) the first prime was found after 857 guesses and the second after 533 guesses, then the user might be told to remember ⟨857, 533⟩. It is an interesting problem to come up with a scheme that minimizes the amount of information the user needs to remember while still significantly lowering the work necessary for the computer. Note that since the ⟨857, 533⟩ quantity is not particularly security-sensitive, it could be posted on the user's workstation without significant loss of security.

Schemes based on this idea (direct conversion of the user's password to a public key pair) are not used because they perform poorly and because knowledge of the public key alone gives enough information for an off-line password-guessing attack. So the usual practice when using public keys with humans is to encrypt the user's private key with the user's password and store it somewhere (e.g., the directory service) from which it can be retrieved by the user's workstation and decrypted. In order for Alice's workstation, on behalf of Alice, to prove Alice's identity, it must first retrieve her encrypted private key from the directory service. Then it takes the password as typed by Alice, converts it into a secret key, and uses that secret key to decrypt the encrypted private key. There are clever schemes for doing this described in §12.4 *Strong Password Credentials Download Protocols*.

9.6 EAVESDROPPING AND SERVER DATABASE READING

Public key technology makes it easy to do authentication in a way that is both secure from eavesdropping and from an intruder reading the server database. Alice knows her own private key. Bob stores Alice's public key. An intruder who reads Bob's database (and therefore obtains Alice's public key) will not be able to use the information to impersonate Alice. Authentication is done by

Alice using her private key to perform a cryptographic operation on a value Bob supplies, and then transmitting the result to Bob. Bob checks the result using Alice's public key.

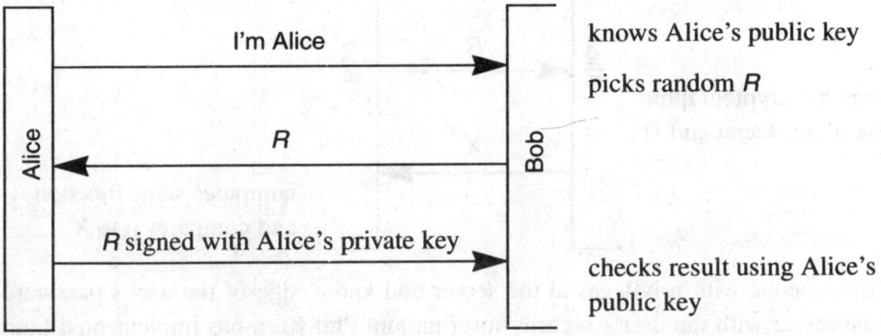

Without public key cryptography, it's difficult to protect against both eavesdropping and server database reading with a single protocol, although it is easy to do one or the other. For instance, let's try a protocol such as is used when a person logs into a system such as UNIX. Bob (the computer authenticating the user Alice) stores a hash of Alice's password. Let's say Alice's password is fiddlesticks. In this protocol someone, say Trudy, who accessed Bob's database would

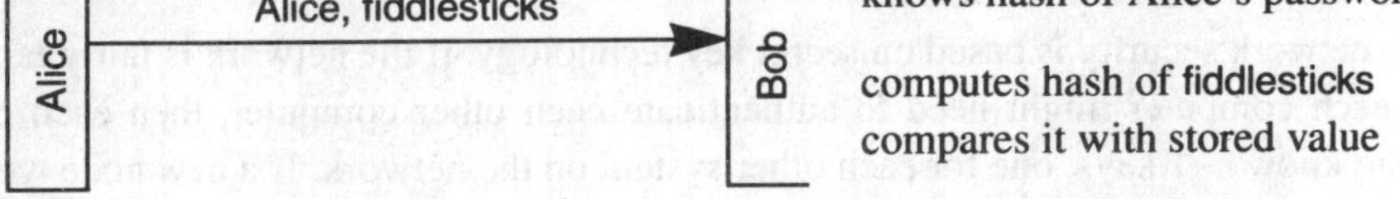

not be able to impersonate Alice. She could do an off-line password-guessing attack if she were to obtain Alice's hashed password from Bob's database, but that would not help her if Alice had chosen a good password. But if Trudy were to eavesdrop when Alice was proving her identity to Bob, Trudy would obtain Alice's password. So this protocol is secure against server database disclosure but not against eavesdropping.

Now consider another protocol (see below). Let's assume that Bob stores Alice's actual secret. In this case Trudy, if she were to eavesdrop, would not be able to obtain information to allow her to impersonate Alice (except by an off-line password-guessing attack). But if she were to read Bob's database, she'd obtain Alice's secret. We'd almost claim it was impossible to simultaneously protect against eavesdropping and server database disclosure without using public key cryptography. However, an elegant protocol invented by Leslie Lamport can claim to accomplish this feat. Lamport's scheme does have a serious drawback, though. A user can only be authenticated a small finite number of times (such as 1000) before it is necessary to reinstall the user's information at the

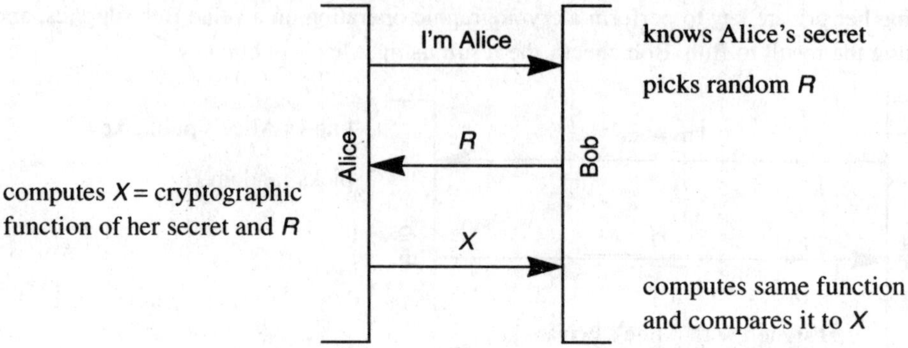

server; that is, someone with privileges at the server and knowledge of the user's password must reconfigure the server with the user's security information. Phil Karn has implemented Lamport's scheme in his S/Key software, and it is being used in the Internet. Lamport's scheme is described in §12.2 *Lamport's Hash*.

9.7 TRUSTED INTERMEDIARIES

Assume that network security is based on secret key technology. If the network is fairly large, say *n* nodes, and each computer might need to authenticate each other computer, then each computer would need to know *n*–1 keys, one for each other system on the network. If a new node were added to the network, then *n* keys would need to be generated, enough for that new node to have a shared secret with each of the other nodes. Somehow the keys would have to be securely distributed to all the other nodes in the network. This is clearly unworkable in any but very small networks.

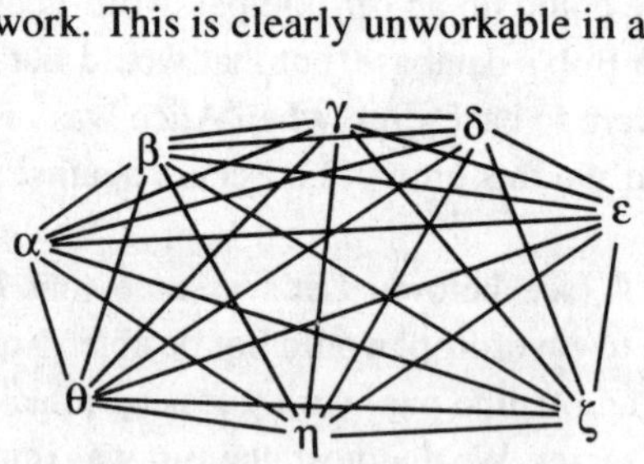

9.7.1 KDCs

One way to make things manageable is to use a trusted node known as a **Key Distribution Center** (**KDC**). The KDC knows keys for all the nodes. If a new node is installed in the network, only that

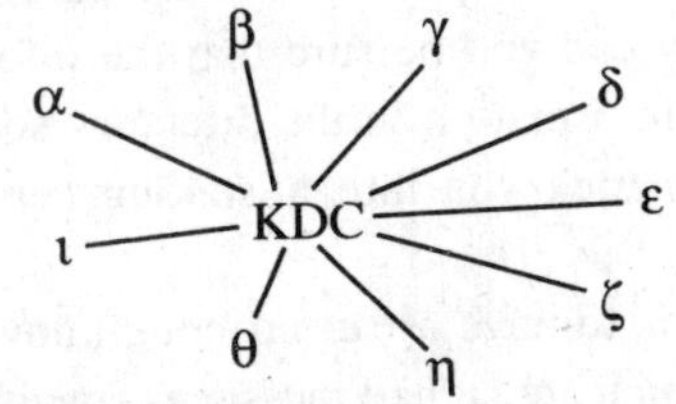

new node and the KDC need to be configured with a key for that node. If node α wants to talk to node β, α talks to the KDC (securely, since α and the KDC share a key), and asks for a key with which to talk to β. The KDC authenticates α, chooses a random number $R_{\alpha\beta}$ to be used as a key to be shared by α and β for their conversation, encrypts $R_{\alpha\beta}$ with the key the KDC shares with α and gives that to α. The KDC also encrypts $R_{\alpha\beta}$ with the key the KDC shares with β and gives that to β, with the instruction that it is to be used for conversing with α. (Usually, the KDC will not bother to actually transmit the encrypted $R_{\alpha\beta}$ to β but rather will give it to α to forward to β.) The encrypted message to β that the KDC gives to α to forward is often referred to as a **ticket**. Besides containing $R_{\alpha\beta}$, the ticket generally contains other information such as an expiration time and α's name. We'll discuss protocols involving KDCs in §11.4 *Mediated Authentication (with KDC)*.

KDCs make key distribution much more convenient. When a new user is being installed into the network, or when a user's key is suspected of having been compromised, there's a single location (the KDC) that needs to be configured. The alternative to using a KDC is installing the user's information at every server to which the user might need access. There are some disadvantages to KDCs, though:

- The KDC has enough information to impersonate anyone to anyone. If it is compromised, all the network resources are vulnerable.
- The KDC is a single point of failure. If it goes down, nobody can use anything on the network (or rather, nobody can start using something on the network—keys previously distributed can continue to be used). It is possible to have multiple KDCs which share the same database of keys, but that means added complexity and cost for extra machines and replication protocols, and added vulnerability, since there are now more targets that need to be protected.
- The KDC might be a performance bottleneck, since everyone will need to frequently communicate with it. Having multiple KDCs can alleviate this problem.

9.7.2 Certification Authorities (CAs)

Key distribution is easier with public key cryptography. Each node is responsible for knowing its own private key, and all the public keys can be accessible in one place. But there are problems with public keys as well. If, for instance, all the public keys are published in *The New York Times*, or stored in the directory service, how can you be sure that the information is correct? An intruder, Trudy, might have overwritten the information in the directory service or taken out her own ad in *The New York Times*. If Trudy can trick you into mistaking her public key for Alice's, she can impersonate Alice to you.

The typical solution for this is to have a trusted node known as a **Certification Authority (CA)** that generates **certificates**, which are signed messages specifying a name (Alice) and the corresponding public key. All nodes will need to be preconfigured with the CA's public key so that they can verify its signature on certificates, but that is the only public key they'll need to know *a priori*. Certificates can be stored in any convenient location, such as the directory service, or each node can store its own certificate and furnish it as part of the authentication exchange. CAs are the public key equivalent of KDCs. A CA or a KDC is the single trusted entity whose compromise can destroy the integrity of the entire network. The advantages of CAs over KDCs are:

- The CA does not need to be on-line. It might be in a locked room protected by a scary-looking guard. Perhaps only a single very trusted individual has access to the CA. That person types the relevant information at the CA, and the CA writes a floppy disk with the new user's certificate, and the floppy disk can be hand-carried to a machine that's on the network. If the CA is not on-line it cannot be probed by curious intruders.
- Since the CA does not have to be on-line or perform network protocols, it can be a vastly simpler device, and therefore it might be more secure.
- If the CA were to crash, the network would not be disabled (as would be the case with a KDC). The only operation that would be impacted is installing new users (until things start expiring, such as certificates or Certificate Revocation Lists—see §9.7.3 *Certificate Revocation*). So it's not as essential to have multiple CAs.
- Certificates are not security-sensitive. If they are stored in a convenient, but potentially insecure, location like the directory service, a saboteur might delete certificates, which might prevent network access by the owners of those certificates, but the saboteur cannot write bogus certificates or modify certificates in any way, since only the CA can generate signatures.
- A compromised CA cannot decrypt conversations, whereas a compromised KDC that sees a conversation between any two parties it serves can decrypt the conversation. A compromised CA can fool Alice into accepting an incorrect public key for Bob, and then the CA can impersonate Bob to Alice, but it will not be able to decrypt a conversation between the real Alice

and the real Bob. (It's still really bad for a CA to be compromised, but we're just saying it's not quite as bad as compromise of a KDC.)

> *Why do you security people always speak of compromise as if it's a bad thing? Good engineering is all about compromise.*
>
> —overheard at a project review

9.7.3 Certificate Revocation

There is a potential disadvantage with CAs. Suppose Fred is given a certificate with an expiration time a year in the future, and then Fred is fired. Since Fred is now a disgruntled ex-employee, it would be nice to alert the network not to allow him access. With KDCs it's easy—merely delete his key from the KDC. With CAs, though, it's not as straightforward to deny access to someone once he is given a certificate. It is common practice to put an expiration date in a certificate. The certificate becomes invalid after that date. The typical validity interval is about a year. A disgruntled ex-employee can do a lot of damage in a year, even without a machine gun. But you wouldn't want validity intervals much smaller than that, because renewing certificates is a nuisance.

The solution is similar to what was done for credit cards. When the bank issues a credit card, it prints an expiration date, perhaps a year in the future. But sometimes a card is reported stolen, or the bank might for some other reason like to revoke it. The credit card company publishes a book of credit card numbers that stores should refuse to honor. These days, most stores are hooked to computer networks where they check the validity of the card, but in ancient times merchants needed to rely on the book of bad credit card numbers, which was presumably published frequently.

X.509 [ISO97] has a defined format for a certificate, as well as of a **Certificate Revocation List (CRL)**. We document the formats in §15.6 *PKIX and X.509*. A CRL lists serial numbers of certificates that should not be honored. A new CRL is posted periodically, and lists all revoked and unexpired certificates. A certificate is valid if it has a valid CA signature, has not expired, and is not listed in the CA's most recent CRL. The CRL has an issue time. If an application wants to ensure that none of the certificates it honors has been revoked in the last hour, say, then the application will need to see a CRL issued within the last hour before it will honor any certificates. This means, in this case, that a new CRL must be posted at least once an hour. An intruder might delete the latest CRL, in which case applications that want to see a CRL posted within the last hour will refuse to honor any certificates, but the intruder cannot impersonate a valid user by destroying the CRL or overwriting it with a CRL issued longer ago than the application's tolerance.

A certificate includes the user's name, the user's public key, an expiration time, a serial number, and the issuing CA's signature on the entire contents of the certificate. An X.509 CRL includes a list of serial numbers of unexpired revoked certificates and an issue time for the CRL.

Suppose Bob is an application that needs to authenticate the user Alice. Bob needs Alice's certificate and a recent CRL. Bob can obtain them from the directory service, or perhaps Alice transmits them to Bob. Armed with the certificate and CRL, Bob decides what public key is associated with the name Alice. If the certificate is validly signed by the CA and has not expired, and the CRL is validly signed by the CA and is sufficiently recent and does not list Alice's certificate, then Bob will assume that Alice's public key is as stated in the certificate. Then Bob will go through an authentication handshake whereby Alice proves she knows the private key that corresponds to the public key listed in her certificate. Revocation schemes are discussed in more detail in §15.4 *Revocation*.

9.7.4 Multiple Trusted Intermediaries

A problem with both KDCs and CAs as described so far is that they require that there be a single administration trusted by all principals in the system. Anyone who compromises the KDC or the CA can impersonate anyone to anyone. As you try to scale authentication schemes up to international or intercorporate scale, you discover that there is no one who everyone trusts (and if there were, they would be too busy with more important tasks to operate and manage a KDC or CA).

The solution is to break the world into **domains**. Each domain has one trusted administration (one logical KDC or one CA—there might be replicas for availability, but they are all are functionally equivalent). If Alice and Boris are in the same domain, they authenticate as described above. If they are in different domains, then authentication is still possible, but a little more complicated.

9.7.4.1 Multiple KDC Domains

How does key distribution work with multiple KDC domains? Let's say Alice is in the CIA and Boris is in the KGB. The CIA will manage a KDC, and the CIA's KDC will know Alice's key. Boris's key is known to the KGB's KDC. Given that the two organizations want to be able to exchange secure electronic mail (perhaps so they can express outrage that the other organization is

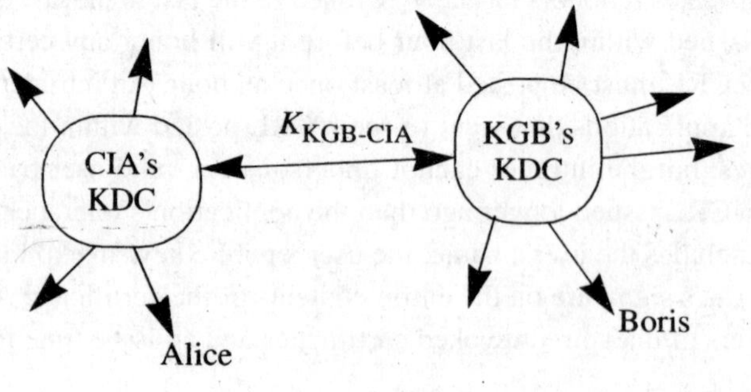

engaged in, gasp, *spying*), they can make this possible by having a key that the two KDCs share. So the CIA's KDC, in addition to having keys for all its users, will also have configured a key which it shares with the KGB's KDC. Let's call that shared key $K_{KGB\text{-}CIA}$.

$K_{KGB\text{-}CIA}$ is used when a user in the CIA wants to have a secure communication with a user in the KGB. Alice, knowing Boris is in the KGB, tells her KDC that she wants to talk to the KGB's KDC. Her KDC facilitates this the same way it would facilitate communication between two CIA users. It generates a new random key, K_{new}, and encrypts a message containing K_{new} using Alice's key. This message is to inform Alice of K_{new}. It separately encrypts a message containing K_{new} using the key $K_{KGB\text{-}CIA}$. That message, which also contains Alice's name, will be sent to the KGB's KDC. The fact that the message is encrypted with $K_{KGB\text{-}CIA}$ lets the KGB's KDC know that Alice is from the CIA's domain. (Note that the KGB's KDC will probably have many KDCs with which it shares keys. For performance reasons, a cleartext clue that the message is coming from the CIA's KDC will have to be sent along with the encrypted message so that the KGB's KDC will know to try the key $K_{KGB\text{-}CIA}$.) After verifying that the message is encrypted with $K_{KGB\text{-}CIA}$, the KGB's KDC will generate a key $K_{Alice\text{-}Boris}$ and send that to Alice, encrypted with K_{new}. It will also generate a message for Boris (which it gives to Alice to deliver) that will be encrypted with Boris's key. The message will contain $K_{Alice\text{-}Boris}$ and the information that Alice is from the CIA domain.

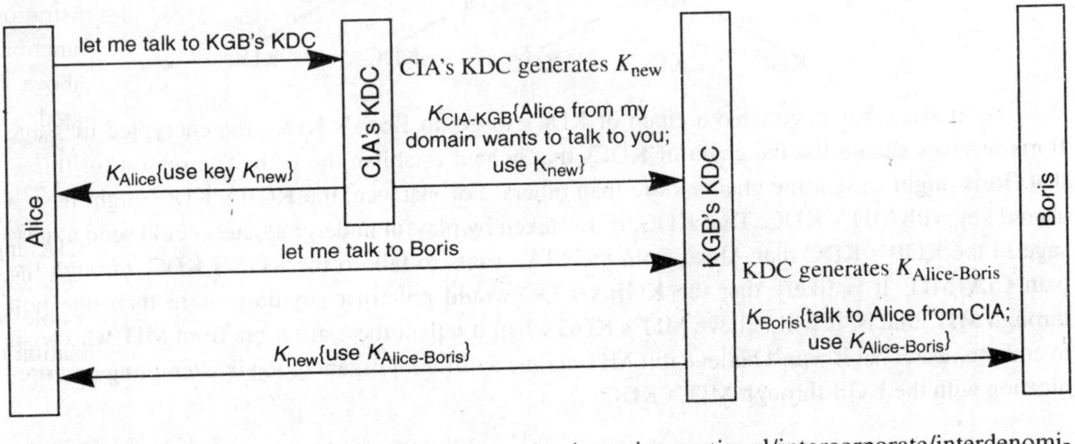

There would likely be thousands of domains in an international/intercorporate/interdenominational internetwork. The conceptually simplest method of allowing users from one domain to talk to users in another domain securely is to have every pair of KDCs configured with a shared key. So the CIA KDC would have a shared key, not only with the KGB's KDC, but with Greenpeace's KDC, and MIT's KDC, and IBM's KDC. Perhaps someone (either in Greenpeace or the CIA) might decide that there was no reason for traffic between the two domains, in which case those KDCs would not need to share a key. But most likely there would be so many domains that it would be unworkable to have every pair of domains configured with a shared key. So there would likely be either a tree of KDCs, or some perhaps less structured logical interconnection of KDCs.

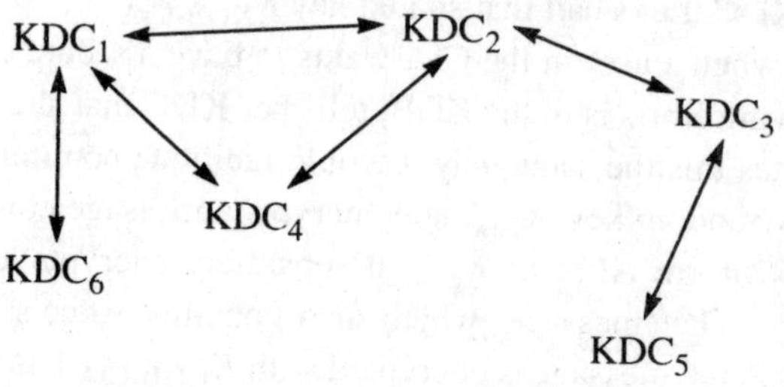

Users can securely authenticate even if their KDCs are not directly linked, if a chain of KDCs can be found. It isn't obvious how one would find an appropriate chain of KDCs. For instance, as we will discuss in the Kerberos chapters, Kerberos V4 does not allow chains of KDCs; to have interdomain communication between two KDCs, they have to have a shared key. Kerberos V5 allows arbitrary connectivity, but assumes there is a default hierarchy, with perhaps additional links (shared keys) between pairs of KDCs that are not directly connected in the default hierarchy.

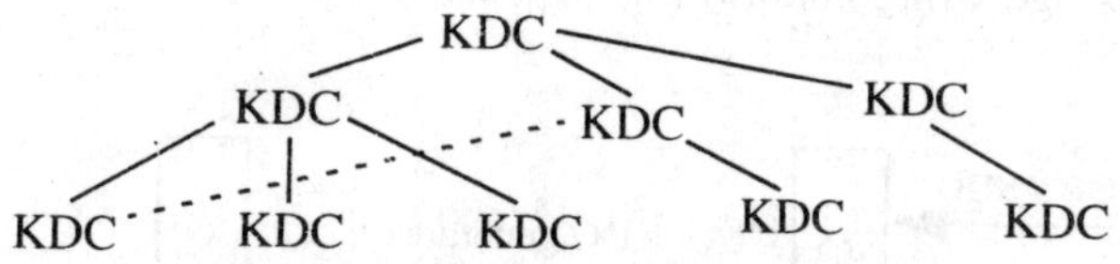

After Alice has negotiated a chain of KDCs to get to Boris's KDC, the encrypted message Boris receives should list the chain of KDCs that helped establish the path. The reason for this is that Boris might trust some chains more than others. For instance, the KGB's KDC might have a shared key with MIT's KDC. That KDC, if overtaken by playful undergraduates, could send a message to the KGB's KDC that Alice, from the CIA, wants to talk to the KGB's KDC, through the path CIA–MIT. It is likely that the KGB's KDC would not trust anything more than one hop through MIT; that is, it will believe MIT's KDC when it tells it there are users from MIT who wish to communicate, but it won't believe it if MIT claims a different organization is attempting communication with the KGB through MIT's KDC.

9.7.4.2 Multiple CA Domains

The situation is similar with CAs. Each CA services a set of users, and issues certificates for those users. This is functionally similar to a KDC having a shared key with a user. The users of a particular CA can verify each other's certificates, since all users of a particular CA know its public key.

How can Alice be sure she knows Boris's public key if Alice's CA is different from Boris's CA? This is accomplished by having the two CAs issue certificates for each other. Alice obtains a certificate, signed by her own CA, stating the public key of Boris's CA. Then, using that certificate plus Boris's certificate (which has been signed by Boris's CA), she can verify Boris's public key.

- Alice obtains Boris's CA's certificate stating that its public key is P_1, signed by her own CA.
- Alice obtains Boris's certificate stating that his public key is P_2, signed with key P_1.

Because she has both of those certificates, she now can verify Boris's public key.

As with chains of KDCs, it is possible that some CAs will not have certificates for each other, but there will be a chain of CAs which works. In Chapter 15 *PKI (Public Key Infrastructure)*, we discuss various strategies for finding appropriate chains of certificates. It is really no different from the problem of navigating through logically interconnected KDCs, and there is really no universally accepted wonderful answer, though there are several workable schemes.

9.8 SESSION KEY ESTABLISHMENT

If all that was done about computer network security was to replace all the cleartext password exchanges with cryptographic authentication, computer networks would be a lot more secure than they are today. But there are security vulnerabilities that occur after authentication. An eavesdropper might steal information by seeing your conversation. Something along the path (e.g., a router) might intercept messages in transit and modify them or replay them. Or someone on the path might "hijack" the entire session by impersonating the network address of one of the parties after the initial authentication is complete. We can protect against eavesdroppers, session hijackers, and message manglers by using cryptography throughout the conversation. But cryptography, of course, involves keys. What should we use for a key?

One possibility is that our authentication exchange is based on public keys. In theory, in a conversation between Alice and Bob, Alice could encrypt all of the data she sends to Bob with Bob's public key (for privacy), and sign each message with her own private key (for integrity). Bob could similarly encrypt all the data he sends to Alice with Alice's public key, and sign the data with his private key. This isn't generally done because public key operations are computationally expensive. It is far more practical to have Alice and Bob somehow agree on a secret key, and protect the remainder of the conversation with the secret key. It would be nice if the authentication protocol helped them agree on a secret key, in addition to having Alice and Bob authenticate each other.

When Alice and Bob are using a shared secret key to authenticate each other they could continue to use that key to protect their conversation. However, it is a good idea to generate a separate session key:

- Keys sort of "wear out" if used a lot. If you're an intruder trying to find a key, the more encrypted data you have the more likely you'll succeed. Since establishing a shared authentication key is usually an expensive operation involving out-of-band mechanisms, it is desirable that the authentication key be used only for the initial exchange. A secret per-session key can be generated at the time of authentication and used for integrity protection and encryption for the remainder of the session.
- If Alice and Bob were to use the same secret key for authentication as for integrity-protecting their data, it might be possible for an intruder to record messages from a previous Alice-Bob conversation and inject those packets into a current Alice-Bob conversation, tricking them into thinking the messages were part of the current session. Within a session there is generally a sequence number to prevent an intruder from adding, deleting, or reordering messages. But there might be nothing in the packet to distinguish packets transmitted a month ago from packets transmitted today. For instance, the transport protocol might always start with sequence number 1. If the authentication protocol agreed upon a new session key for each conversation, then replayed messages from previous conversations would not be accepted as valid.
- If the long-term shared secret key is compromised, it would be nice to prevent an old recorded conversation from being decryptable. If every conversation is encrypted with a different per-session key, then a suitable authentication protocol can prevent old conversations from being decrypted.
- You may want to establish a session and give a relatively untrusted piece of software the session key, which is good only for that conversation, rather than giving it your long-term secret key, which the untrusted software could store away for future use.

For these reasons, authentication protocols usually establish a session key, in addition to providing authentication. We'll describe the subtleties of authentication protocols in Chapter 11 *Security Handshake Pitfalls*.

9.9 DELEGATION

It's not who you are. It's who you're working for.

Sometimes it is necessary to have things act on your behalf. For instance, you might be logged into system Bob, and then need to access remote files from Bob. In that case, Bob will need to retrieve the files on your behalf, and will need to have the same privileges for those files as you have. Similarly you might tell a printserver to print a remote file that you are authorized to read. You could allow the required access by explicitly being available to log in to each resource that is ever needed on your behalf. That would be inconvenient at best, and sometimes impossible, for instance when you run a batch job when you aren't around.

One possible means of allowing access is to give your password to everything that might need to act on your behalf (printservers, foreign systems). This might be reasonable if you changed your password immediately after the work was completed. But most users would not change their password that frequently. Another possibility is that you could explicitly add every system to every ACL for every resource that they need to access on your behalf, and then, if you are conscientious, delete them from the ACL when the operation completes. These mechanisms are far too inconvenient, and most users would opt for no security at all if that was the alternative. Therefore it is advisable to have some more convenient mechanism for giving something permission to act on your behalf. This permission is known as **delegation** or **authentication forwarding**. The best mechanism for delegation in a computer network is to generate a special message, signed by you, specifying to whom you are delegating rights, which rights are being delegated, and for how long. Once the duration specified in the message has expired, the message no longer grants any permissions.

Using public key cryptography, the usual approach is for you to sign the delegation message with your own private key. Using KDCs, the usual approach is for you to ask the KDC to give Fred certain permissions. The KDC constructs a message listing the permissions you'd like to grant Fred, encrypts the message with a key known only to the KDC, and Fred is given the encrypted message. Fred cannot decrypt the message, but he can present it to the KDC when asking for access; the KDC can decrypt it and then see the rights that have been delegated to Fred.

Why is it necessary for the delegation message to expire? If you are delegating rights to a printserver and it can be trusted for the hour it takes to finish printing all the documents ahead of yours, and then print your document, can't it always be trusted? If it were untrustworthy, surely it could have retrieved all your documents during the one hour in which you gave it access rights to your files. In theory this argument is true. You can't necessarily know that the printserver hasn't had some Trojan horse software installed which will steal all your files during the limited time you give it access, but limiting the delegation in time limits the window of vulnerability. You can further limit the vulnerability by limiting the scope of the delegation. Instead of specifying that the printserver has rights to see all your files, you might specify only the single file that you'd like printed.

The need for delegation in some form is generally recognized, and various systems implement crude forms of it. However, designing a user interface and corresponding data structure where a user specifies what rights are delegated and to whom is an open research problem.

9.10 HOMEWORK

1. As stated in §9.2 *Address-Based Authentication*, UNIX requires a request from system *A* for a resource at *B* to explicitly state the desired account name at *B* if it is not identical to the account name at *A*. Why do you suppose it makes that requirement? How would one implement this feature without the requirement?

2. In §9.6 *Eavesdropping and Server Database Reading* we asserted that it is extremely difficult, without public key cryptography, to have an authentication scheme which protects against both eavesdropping and server database disclosure. Consider the following authentication protocol (which is based on Novell version 3 security). Alice knows a password. Bob, a server that will authenticate Alice, stores a hash of Alice's password. Alice types her password (say fiddlesticks) to her workstation. The following exchange takes place:

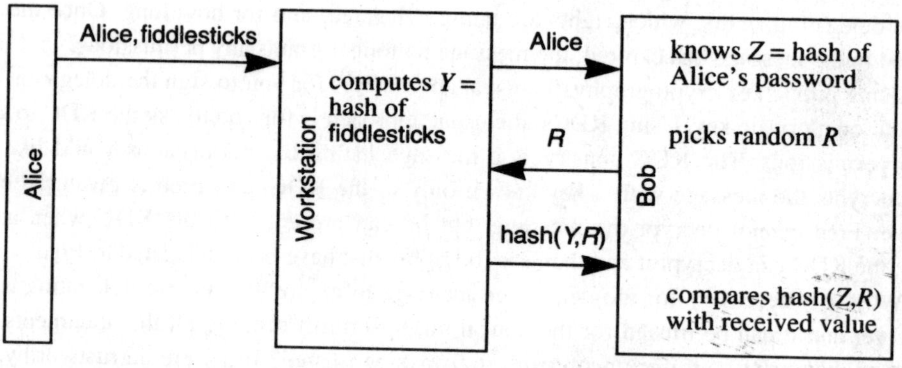

Is this an example of an authentication scheme that isn't based on public key cryptography and yet guards against both eavesdropping and server database disclosure?

3. Extend the scenario in §9.7.4.1 *Multiple KDC Domains* to a chain of three KDCs. In other words, assume that Alice wants to talk to Boris through a chain of three KDCs (Alice's KDC, a KDC that has shared keys with both Alice's KDC and Boris's KDC, and finally, Boris's KDC). Give the sequence of events necessary to establish communication.

10 AUTHENTICATION OF PEOPLE

In the previous chapter we discussed in general how a computer authenticates a computer across a network. This chapter deals with the special issues involved when a computer is authenticating a human. We use the terms *user* and *human* interchangeably. This chapter deals with password-related issues like how to force users to choose unguessable passwords, how to store password information securely at the system being logged into, and how to avoid divulging information to eavesdroppers.

Authentication is done somewhat differently depending on the capabilities of the thing being authenticated. The two most important capabilities are the ability to store a high-quality cryptographic key and the ability to perform cryptographic operations. (A **high-quality key** is a secret chosen from a very large space so that it is computationally infeasible to guess the secret by exhaustive search.)

A computer has both of these capabilities; a person has neither of them. Humans are incapable of securely storing high-quality cryptographic keys, and they have unacceptable speed and accuracy when performing cryptographic operations. (They are also large, expensive to maintain, difficult to manage, and they pollute the environment. It is astonishing that these devices continue to be manufactured and deployed. But they are sufficiently pervasive that we must design our protocols around their limitations.)

User authentication consists of a computer verifying that you are who you claim to be. There are three main techniques:

- *what you know*
- *what you have*
- *what you are*

Passwords are one method of reassuring someone that you are who you claim to be, and fit into the *what you know* category. Physical keys or ATM cards fit into the *what you have* category. Biometric devices, such as voice recognition systems or fingerprint analyzers, fit into the *what you are* category.

10.1 PASSWORDS

Passwords predate computers. The concept is simple: if Alice needs to prove to Bob that she is Alice, and Bob does not know Alice by sight, they can prearrange a special greeting (a password), and Bob can assume that someone who says the magic word is Alice. As with many aspects of security, the classic uses of passwords are in the military. All members of a group are given the password of the day, and when they return to the fort after dark they state the password to prove they are not the enemy.

Most readers have undoubtedly logged into a system by typing their user name and password so often that they no longer think about it. There are a lot of problems with using passwords for authentication:

- An eavesdropper might see the password when Alice is using it to log in.
- An intruder might read the file where the computer stores password information.
- Alice's password might be easy to guess by someone making direct login attempts to the computer.
- Alice's password may be crackable by an off-line computer search, given information such as a recognizable quantity encrypted with the password. (The difference between this off-line attack and the on-line attack above is in the number of password guesses that can be practically tried.)
- In attempting to force users to choose unguessable passwords, the system might become so inconvenient that it becomes unusable, or users might resort to writing passwords down.

This chapter describes the mechanisms in use to prevent unauthorized people from gaining access to passwords. The main lines of defense are keeping transmission of the password from being overheard, limiting the number of incorrect guesses, and making passwords difficult to guess. However, the intruder isn't the only bad guy. The authorized users will become the enemy, too, if the security mechanism becomes too inconvenient to deal with.

10.2 ON-LINE PASSWORD GUESSING

I can impersonate you if I can guess your password. And that might not be hard. I_2 once heard someone remark, about a faculty member at a major university, that "although in all other respects she appears to be a sentient human being, she insists on using her first name as her password." On some systems, passwords are administratively set to a fixed attribute of a person, such as their birthday or their badge number. This makes passwords easy to remember and distribute, but it also makes them easy to guess. I_1 once worked on a system where students' passwords were administratively set to their first and last initials. Faculty accounts were considered more sensitive, so they were protected with *three* initials.

An astonishing number of banks allow Internet access based on your account number and a password, and they set initial passwords to the last four digits of your Social Security Number. In many states in the U.S., it is the local custom to use your Social Security Number as your driver's license number, and to use your driver's license as identification for cashing checks. That means cashiers can easily get your account number (from the front of the check) and your social security number (from the driver's license). It is surprising there has been so little fraud based on this poor design.

Even if passwords are chosen so they are not obvious, they may be guessable if the impostor gets enough guesses. In fact, given enough guesses, any password, no matter how carefully chosen, can be guessed (by enumerating all finite character sequences until you hit on the correct password). Whether this is feasible depends on how many guesses it takes and how rapidly passwords can be tested.

In the military use of passwords, guessing is not a problem. You show up at the door. You utter a word. If it's the right word, they let you in; if it's the wrong word, they shoot you. Even if you know the password is the month in which the general was born, guessing is not an attractive pursuit.

Most terminals do not have an "execute user" function controllable from the remote end (as useful as that might be), so this mechanism for limiting password guessing is not available. Given that people's fingers slip or they forget that they changed their password, it's important that they get more than one chance anyway. There are ways to limit the number or rate of guesses. The first is to design the system so that guesses have to actually be typed by a human. Computers are much faster and more patient than people at making guesses, so the threat is much greater if the impostor can get a computer to do the dirty work. Before the days of networks and PCs, this just meant that operating systems needed to ensure that they got passwords from terminals rather than programs. But now that login requests can come in over networks and lots of terminals are really PCs emulating terminals, there's really no way to prevent this.

One seemingly attractive mechanism for preventing password guessing is to keep track of the number of consecutive incorrect passwords for an account and when the number exceeds a threshold, say five, "lock" the account and refuse access, even with a correct password, until the system is administratively reset. This technique is used with PINs on ATM cards—three wrong guesses and the machine eats your card. You have to show up at the bank with ID to get it back. An important downside of this approach is that a computer vandal (someone who simply wants to annoy people and disrupt operations) can, possibly with the aid of a computer, guess five bad passwords against all the accounts on a system and lock them all up, effectively shutting the system down until it is administratively reset (assuming it can be administratively reset when all of the administrators' accounts are locked!). This represents little work for the vandal and can cause serious disruption. So this approach is unacceptable in most environments.

Another approach to slow down a guesser is to only allow a limited number of account/password guesses per connection attempt. If the system is based on dialing in via modem or restarting a big slow application, the overhead of having to restart for each five attempts can slow down the guessing rate considerably (even with an auto-dial modem). A variant on this theme is simply to have incorrect passwords (or even all passwords) be processed s l o w l y .

If you can't prevent guessing, maybe you can catch the guesser. By auditing invalid password attempts, a system manager can be alerted to the fact that an attempt is being made to penetrate the system. It might then be possible to try to trace the connection or take other corrective action. False alarms in audit logs can be prevented by filtering out the common case where a user mistypes a password and then immediately thereafter types it correctly. Events where a password fails and the connection then switches to a different account or disconnects are substantially more suspicious. A method for distributing the detective work is for systems to report to users when they log in the time of their previous login and the number of unsuccessful password attempts since the last successful login. In practice, few users will check the time of last successful login to see whether it looks right, but most will notice reports of failed login attempts if they did not mistype the password themselves. This doesn't work for "stale" accounts that the user never logs into. Such accounts are subject to other threats as well; it's good security policy to eliminate accounts not in regular use.

The expected time to guess a password is the expected number an impostor has to guess before getting it right divided by the guess rate. So far, we've concentrated on limiting the rate of password guesses. Another promising approach is to ensure that the number of passwords an attacker would need to search is large enough to be secure against an off-line, unaudited search with a lot of CPU power. If passwords are randomly chosen eight-character strings made from the characters a–z, then even if an attacker could guess a password every millisecond, it would take (on average) over three years to guess it. This would make all the more obtrusive and expensive preventive mechanisms unnecessary. Some administrations assign such passwords (randomly chosen 8-character strings). These systems have another problem:

Users hate them…and forget them…and write them down. As discussed later, when users write down passwords rather than memorizing them, a whole new class of threats open up. Many otherwise fine minds are genetically incapable of memorizing randomly chosen eight-character passwords. Sometimes the random password generator is clever enough to generate pronounceable strings, which makes it a little easier for the human to remember the password. Constraining the generated passwords to pronounceable strings of the same length limits the number of possible passwords by at least an order of magnitude, but since a 10-character pronounceable string is probably easier to remember than an 8-character completely random string, and is about as secure, generating pronounceable strings is a good idea if the administrator wants to impose passwords.

A better approach is to let users choose their own passwords but to warn them to choose "good" ones and enforce that choice where possible. Usually the best combination of memorability and difficulty of guessing is a "pass-phrase" with intentional misspelling or punctuation and odd capitalization, like GoneFi$hing or MyPassworDisTuff!, or the first letter of each word of a phrase, like Mhall;Ifwwas (Mary had a little lamb; Its fleece was white as snow).

The program that lets users set passwords should check for easy-to-guess passwords and disallow them. It might, for example, run them through a spell-checking dictionary and reject them if they are spelled correctly! (A favorite attack is to guess all the words in a dictionary as passwords; a large dictionary might contain 500000 words, and it is not difficult to check that many.) If possible, the dictionary should be extended with common first and last names. The program could also require mixed cases, non-alphabetic characters, a minimum length, and a minimum number of different characters.

Surprisingly, most variants of UNIX limit password length to eight characters (or more precisely, they only check the first eight). VMS allows long passwords, and allows the administrator to set policies such as how long they must be, how often they must be changed, and how many old passwords the system remembers in order to prevent a user from reusing an old password.

10.3 OFF-LINE PASSWORD GUESSING

In the previous section, we discussed on-line password guessing, where guessing can be slowed down and audited. Passwords do not have to be very strong if the only threat is on-line password guessing. But sometimes it is possible for an attacker, through either eavesdropping or reading a database, to obtain a cryptographic hash of the password or a quantity encrypted with the password. In such a case, even though the attacker cannot reverse the hash of the password, the attacker can guess a password, perform the same hash, and compare it with the stolen quantity. Once the attacker has obtained the hash of the password, the attacker can perform password guessing without anyone knowing it, and at a speed limited only by procurable compute power.

We've talked a lot about how users should protect their passwords. Remember that passwords must be stored in two places—users must know their own, and systems must be able to verify passwords. If the system simply directly stores passwords, the password list on a system must be protected at least as well as anything else on the system. Even that is not sufficient. Most systems keep backup tapes for use in the case where a disk fails or a user accidentally destroys a file. If those tapes contain password lists, they must be protected as carefully as the system; anyone who can read them will subsequently be able to impersonate all users.

Several techniques can lessen this threat. Some operating systems, for instance UNIX and VMS, do not store actual user passwords. They take passwords as typed, run them through a one-way algorithm such as a cryptographic hash, and store the results. With such a system, the password file needs to be carefully protected from modification, but disclosure of the file is not immediately of use to an attacker. Standard UNIX systems, in fact, place such confidence in this technique that they make the password file publicly readable. This turns out to be a bad idea. Even though it is impossible to compute the password from the hash, it is possible to guess a password and verify whether you got it right by hashing it and comparing it to the stored value. This gives attackers an unaudited and fairly high-performance way of guessing passwords. Many systems have now been modified to prevent unprivileged programs from reading the password file. Another interesting downside of this technique is that if a user forgets a password, the system administrator can't look it up. Instead, the user must choose a new password and the system administrator must install it. The only time this is a problem is when an attacker has changed the user's password but the user isn't sure whether it was changed nefariously or merely forgotten. Being able to read the old value might make it easier to tell the difference.

Password Hash Quirk

There was an operating system (which we'll allow to remain nameless) that stored hashes of passwords, and the password hash used by that operating system had an interesting property. We are purposely not giving the exact details, but the general idea is that there was a magic character sequence *X* such that the hash of any string *S* was the same as the hash of *X* concatenated with *S*. This is not exactly a security flaw, but instead is a wonderfully user-friendly feature. How can this odd feature be useful?

Suppose the system administrator made the common policy decision that user passwords had to be some minimum length. This particular operating system enforced the policy only when you set your password (as opposed to when you logged in). Now suppose you wanted a password you could type quickly, like FOO. The operating system would not let you set your password to FOO because it's not long enough. But it would let you set it to *X* concatenated with FOO. Let's say the magic string was %#v27dR678riwueyru3ir3. You'd set your password to %#v27dR678riwueyru3ir3FOO. That would be the last time you'd have to type %#v27dR678riwueyru3ir3FOO. From then on, FOO would work just fine, since the hash of FOO is the same as the hash of %#v27dR678riwueyru3ir3FOO.

When disclosure of whole files full of hashed passwords is a concern, another useful technique is to apply *salt*. Rather than guessing passwords against a single user account, an attacker with a file full of hashed passwords might hash all the words in a dictionary and check to see whether any of the passwords match any of the stored hashed values. This would be a much more efficient means of attack, particularly when the attacker just wanted any account on the system or, more likely, as many accounts as possible on the system. Tests at universities have shown 30% hit rates with fairly small dictionaries. A way to slow down such an attacker is as follows:

When a user chooses a password, the system chooses a random number (the **salt**). It then stores both the salt and a hash of the combination of the salt and the password. When the user supplies a password during authentication, the system computes the hash of the combination of the stored salt and the supplied password, and checks the computed hash against the stored hash. The presence of the salt does not make it any harder to guess any one user's password, but it makes it impossible to perform a single cryptographic hash operation and see whether a password is valid for any of a group of users.

user ID	salt value	password hash
Mary	2758	hash(2758|$\text{password}_{\text{Mary}}$)
John	886d	hash(886d|$\text{password}_{\text{John}}$)
Ed	5182	hash(5182|$\text{password}_{\text{Ed}}$)
Jane	1763	hash(1763|$\text{password}_{\text{Jane}}$)

Another technique is to encrypt the password file. This doesn't eliminate the problem of keeping passwords secret; it just reduces it to the problem of protecting the key that decrypts the password file. This might be done by having the key held in operating system memory, not backed up to disk or tape, and having it either stored in special nonvolatile memory in the machine or reentered by the operator on boot-up.

10.4 HOW BIG SHOULD A SECRET BE?

From how big a space must a secret be chosen in order to be secure? To thwart an on-line attack the secret does not have to be chosen from a large space, because the intruder is detected after a small number of guesses or because the amount of time the intruder needs to guess correctly is worth much more than the payoff. For instance, many ATM systems have only four decimal digits worth of secret, which means there are only 10000 different secrets, and this is really sufficiently secure because you only get three guesses.

If there's the opportunity to do off-line password guessing, the secret must be chosen from a much larger space. The general rule of thumb is that a secret needs about 64 bits of randomness, since it is considered computationally infeasible to search 2^{64} possibilities. Therefore a 64-bit secret cryptographic key is reasonably secure.

Humans aren't usually willing to remember or type 64-bit (about 20-digit) random numbers (though one of our children is perfectly happy to remember dozens of digits of $\sqrt{2}$, and another of our children seems to know innumerable 7-digit phone numbers). How big does a password have to be in order to have the equivalent security of a 64-bit random number? If the text string is truly randomly chosen from upper- and lower-case letters, the 10 digits, plus a couple of punctuation marks, there are 64 possibilities per keystroke (6 bits), so an 11-character password would be necessary. A human will not remember a randomly chosen 11-character string.

What about a randomly chosen pronounceable password? If a computer were to generate such strings (as opposed to allowing a human to choose), the pronounceability constraint means that about every third character must be a vowel. To be memorizable, the password should be a case-insensitive string of letters, giving only about 4½ bits per character, and only about 2½ bits per vowel (since there are 6 vowels in English). The combination of limiting characters to case-insensitive letters and having a reasonable percentage of vowels yields randomness of about 4 bits per character. This would require a 16-character computer-generated pronounceable string, which is also too long for a person to willingly memorize or type.

What about if people are allowed to choose their own passwords? The general wisdom is that the randomness achievable in human-generated passwords is about 2 bits per character, which would result in a 32-character password, which is also too long.

The conclusion is that a secret a person would be willing to memorize and type will not be as good as a 64-bit random number, and therefore passwords will be open to off-line password-guessing attacks.

10.5 EAVESDROPPING

A second important weakness in using passwords is that they must be "uttered" to be used, and there is always a chance of eavesdropping when they are uttered. The lowest-tech form of eavesdropping is to watch as someone types a password. There is an etiquette around the operation of ATMs. Even when there is a substantial line, the second person stands a discreet distance behind the person operating the machine and looks away. The etiquette is not so highly evolved in an office environment, and it often isn't difficult to pick up passwords this way. The only prevention beyond training people to be more paranoid is to pick passwords involving shift and control characters so more fingers are involved.

Of course, it's easier to watch the screen than fingers. Most systems have the sophistication to not display passwords as they are being typed.

A more high-tech method of eavesdropping is to place a wiretap on the communications line and watch all the passwords (and everything else, for that matter) go by. Whether this is easy or hard depends on the environment. There are also software-based keystroke logs that can be covertly installed on PCs and even hardware logging devices that can be embedded in keyboards or cables.

If you're going to give up on memorization and accept the risks of written-down passwords, an effective mechanism is **one-time passwords**. Here, the user and the system have a list of valid passwords, but each one is only valid once. After it's used, it is crossed off the list (at both ends). Periodically, the user must get a new list from the system administrator. This mechanism is nearly impervious to eavesdropping.

A variant is to have a numbered list of passwords and have the system ask for specific ones on each authentication. An attacker would have to eavesdrop on many authentications before obtaining enough information to impersonate the user. With this technique, the list can be somewhat shorter and can be used for longer than the one-time password list, but at some loss of security and convenience. (See Homework Problem 2.)

10.6 PASSWORDS AND CARELESS USERS

At a lecture on computer security, a professor asked, "Are there any advantages of passwords over biometric devices?" A helpful student replied "When you want to let someone use your account, with a password you just give it to them, while with a biometric device you have to go with them until they are logged in." This is the sort of remark that sends chills down the back of security administrators and makes them think of their users as adversaries rather than the customers they are trying to protect. Security people need to remember that most people regard security as a nuisance rather than as needed protection, and left to their own devices they often carelessly give up the security that someone worked so hard to provide. The solution is to educate users on the importance of security, helping them to understand the reasons for the procedures they are asked to follow, and making those procedures sufficiently tolerable that they don't develop contempt for the process.

Passwords are particularly easy to abuse. The classic tale is one where the system manager's password is posted on the console because it is too long and complex to remember.

One particular danger is users' including passwords on-line in accessible places. In addition to doing this as a substitute for little black books, users might find it convenient to include passwords in scripts used to automate access to other systems, or they might include passwords in messages sent via electronic mail. Electronic mail messages are frequently archived. Both schemes allow an attacker who has gotten into one account to cascade those rights into other accounts on other systems.

10.6.1 Using a Password in Multiple Places

One of the tough trade-offs is whether to recommend that users use the same password in multiple places or keep their passwords different for different systems. All things being equal, use of different passwords is more secure because if one password is compromised it only gives away the user's rights on a single system. Things are rarely equal, however. When weighed against the likelihood that users will resort to writing passwords down if they need to remember more than one, the trade-off is less clear.

An issue that weighs in favor of different passwords is that of a cascaded break-in. An attacker that breaks in to one system may succeed in reading the password database. If users have different passwords on different systems, this information will be of no use. But if passwords are common, a break-in to a system that was not well protected because it contained no "important" information might in fact leak passwords that are useful on critical systems.

10.6.2 Requiring Frequent Password Changes

Security is a wet blanket. —apologies to Charles Schulz

A technique that offers some security but is probably overused, is requiring frequent password changes. The idea behind frequent password changes is that if someone does learn your password, it will only be useful until it next changes. This protection may not be worth much if a lot of damage can be done in a short time.

The problem with requiring frequent password changes is that users are more likely to write passwords down and less likely to give much thought or creativity to choosing them. The result is observable and guessable passwords. It's also true that users tend to circumvent password change policy unless enforcement is clever. In a spy-vs.-spy escalation, the following is a common scenario:

1. The system administrator decides that passwords must be changed every 90 days, and the system enforces this.
2. The user types the change password command, resetting the password to the same thing as before.
3. The system administrator discovers users are doing this and modifies the system so that it makes sure the password, when changed, is set to a different value.
4. The user then does a change password procedure that sets the password to something new, and then immediately sets it back to the old, familiar value.

5. The system administrator then has the system keep track of the previous *n* password values and does not allow the password to be set to any of them.

6. The user then does a change password procedure that goes through *n* different password values and finally, on the $n+1^{st}$ password change, returns the password to its old familiar value.

7. The system is modified to keep track of the last time the password was changed and does not allow another password change for some number of days.

8. The user, when forced to change passwords, constructs a new password by appending '1' to the end of the previous password. Next time the user replaces the '1' with a '2', ...

9. The system, in looking for guessable passwords, looks for passwords that look "too much like" one of the previous *n* passwords.

10. The users throw up their hands in disgust, accept impossible-to-remember passwords, and post them on their terminals.

All of these techniques have been tried on some system or another. In general, it's impossible to make systems secure without the cooperation of the legitimate users. If frequent password changes address a real threat, users must be educated to fear that threat so they will strive for good passwords. If the threat cannot be made real to the users, the inconvenience won't be worth the trouble.

10.6.3 A Login Trojan Horse to Capture Passwords

A threat as old as timesharing is to leave a program running on a public terminal that displays a login prompt. An unsuspecting user then enters a user name and password. The Trojan horse program logs the name and password to a file before the program terminates in some way designed to minimize suspicion. There is no protection from this threat given a sufficiently naive user. Approaches toward minimizing it are based on making it difficult for a program to "look like" a normal login prompt. For example:

- On some systems, any program request for input is preceded by an automatically inserted '?'. If the real login prompt is made to have no '?', a program can't produce a believable counterfeit.
- On the bit-mapped screens associated with workstations and X-windows terminals, the login screen takes up the entire screen and has no border. If the protocol prevents ordinary programs from displaying such a screen, they can't counterfeit a login prompt very reasonably.
- On most systems, there is some way to interrupt running programs. Training users to enter the interrupt key sequence before logging in would then thwart such Trojan horses. For exam-

ple, newer Windows systems require the user to type Ctrl-Alt-Delete as part of the login sequence. In (almost) any scenario other than a login prompt, this key sequence would interrupt a running program. Unfortunately, many systems allow programs to disable interrupts; for those systems, this technique would not be useful.

Even if the Trojan horse program can do the login prompt exactly, it might not be able to exactly duplicate the way the system behaves after a user logs in. This will make an alert user suspicious. For example:

- A reasonable action following the capture of a password is to log it, put out the message the user would get if the password were mistyped, and then terminate and return to a regular login prompt. The user will assume the password was mistyped the first time and try again. This can be prevented if a program can't end its session without a logout banner. Such a banner before the second login message is a dead giveaway. Mentioned earlier was having a message displayed at login telling users the number of unsuccessful login attempts to the account since the last successful attempt. This doubles as Trojan horse protection because the successful login would not report that there had just been a failed login attempt.
- Another thing the Trojan horse program can do is hang after accepting the user's name and password, as if the system had gotten into a wedged state. If the program can prevent the user from using any escape characters, the user will just get frustrated and reboot or reconnect. Given how accustomed we all have become to the flakiness of our computers, very few users would find this behavior suspicious.
- An optimally designed Trojan horse would actually use the username and password to log the user in and run a session. Some operating systems offer sufficient modularity and generality to make this possible. It would be a security feature to make this evident to processes started in non-standard ways so that some sort of warning banner could be displayed.

10.6.4 Non-Login Use of Passwords

Entering a single password to log into a system and subsequently having access to all the user's resources is, in most environments, a reasonable mix of security and convenience. It's not the only way to do it. Some systems permit password protection on individual files. A user could specially protect certain files so that someone learning the user's login password still couldn't get at those files.

Similarly, applications could require their own authentication of a user before permitting access to certain databases (even after the user has logged in).

10.7 INITIAL PASSWORD DISTRIBUTION

Everything we've discussed so far describes how systems work once users have passwords and the systems know them. Another opportunity to get it wrong exists in the administrative procedures involved in getting to that state. After all, if you can impersonate the user to the system administrator, you can get the password by whatever mechanism the user could.

A secure method for the initial distribution of passwords is for the user to appear at the terminal of the system administrator and authenticate by whatever means humans use to authenticate (driver's license, student ID, birth certificate and two major credit cards, whatever). The system administrator then sets up all the particulars of the account for the user except the password (name, rights, quotas, choice of shell, ...) and then lets the user choose a password. This method has two drawbacks: it may be inconvenient for the user to meet the system administrator; and it's a little scary to let this new user type to this highly privileged terminal session while the system administrator discreetly looks away. A skilled user could probably do substantial damage in a short time. Even this problem could be circumvented by giving the user access to a special keyboard that only accepts passwords. This mechanism is sometimes used in special-case environments like establishing the PIN for an ATM. For a bank this is a sufficiently high-volume and security-sensitive application to justify special hardware.

Another variant on this theme is for the system administrator to create the account and an initial **strong** (randomly chosen from a large space) password, give it to the user, and instruct the user to use the password only for an initial login and then change it to something more easily remembered. Some systems support the notion of **pre-expired** passwords that require the user to change them as part of the login process. Even if the initial strong password is written down and the paper handed to a user, little security is lost because the password is no good after it is used and the user is likely to keep it safe that long.

In the name of convenience, there are weaker versions of this protocol. The administrator could set up the account and distribute the password by (paper) mail, in which case the security is as good as the security of mail. A common but insecure practice is to have the initial password be either a constant or an easily determined property of the user. A school might, for example, set all student passwords initially to their student IDs. Then they could communicate passwords to students with a broadcast (published) message rather than sending individualized notes. The security of this might be vaguely acceptable if the only thing a student account password protects is the work of the student, which is presumably nothing until the student uses the account for the first time. Even so, an attacker could log into the student's account ahead of time and plant Trojan horses.

The following story is true (or rather was told to me_1 as true by a person supposedly involved). Names are omitted to protect the guilty. See how many things you can find wrong with the way security was administered.

At a large commercial timesharing service bureau, security of privileged accounts (those that could access other users' data) was considered paramount. One of the security measures used to protect these accounts was that the passwords were randomly chosen and changed weekly. Every Sunday afternoon a batch job was run, selecting new random passwords and changing all the privileged accounts. Part of the batch job was to print a list of all the accounts and their passwords. This list was posted on a bulletin board so that as people came in Monday morning they could get their new passwords.

This worked fine until one Sunday the printer was broken. All the passwords were changed, but they weren't printed. Monday morning the printer was fixed, but no one could log in to request that the list be printed. In fact, no one could log in at all (except the commercial users, who saw no disruption). Some systems have a way to perform a privileged login given physical access to the machine, but this operating system didn't—it would support such an override only upon also erasing the disks, which by that time included unbacked-up commercial data. Many systems that do have such an override require that the system be rebooted in single-user mode, which would have been an unacceptable interruption of commercial service.

After thinking hard, some bright fellow noticed that the space from which the passwords were randomly selected was not unmanageably large, so they got all the people who couldn't do any work anyway (about 50) to repeatedly attempt logins to a single account with each of them assigned a range of passwords. By the end of the day Monday, one of them had succeeded and they were able to return to business as usual.

10.8 AUTHENTICATION TOKENS

An authentication token is a physical device that a person carries around and uses in authenticating. In the breakdown of security according to *what you know*, *what you have*, and *what you are*, authentication tokens fall in the middle category (passwords are in the first, and biometric devices the third). Generally, authentication tokens offer security advantages and disadvantages over other mechanisms. Unless they are physically attached to users (which is unacceptable in our culture), they are subject to theft. Generally they must be coupled with one of the other two mechanisms to be secure.

There are several forms of authentication token in use today. The most ubiquitous is the key that people use to unlock their home or car. Another common form of authentication token is the credit card. If a credit card includes a picture or a signature, it combines an authentication token with a primitive biometric device (the person who compares signatures or sees whether you look like the picture).

Credit cards these days contain a magnetic strip that contains information. The advantage that magnetic strip cards offer over simple passwords is that they are not trivial to reproduce and they can conveniently hold a secret larger than most people are willing to memorize. Perhaps the biggest advantage is psychological—people tend to be less willing to "loan" a token to a friend than to share a password. There are a number of disadvantages:

- Use of these tokens requires custom hardware (a key slot or card reader) on every access device. This may be expensive and it requires standardization.
- Tokens can be lost or stolen. For reasonable security, tokens must be supplemented with a PIN or password. In most environments, a convenient override must be available for when "I forgot my card at home." That override should not be substantially less convenient than the one for "I forgot my password."

These devices offer little or no protection against communications eavesdropping. Whatever information is sent "over the wire" can be collected just like a password and replayed later. To make use of the information using a "standard terminal" requires that a card be manufactured to regurgitate the stolen information, but someone who can eavesdrop can likely connect a nonstandard terminal to the network and replay the information without making a card. There is nothing conceptually difficult about copying a key or mag-stripe card; devices for doing so are readily available.

A better form of authentication token is the **smart card**. This is a device about the size of a credit card but with an embedded CPU and memory. When inserted in a (misleadingly named) **smart card reader**, the card carries on a conversation with the device (as opposed to a magnetic strip, which simply dumps its contents). There are various forms of smart cards:

- **PIN protected memory card**. With this card, there is information in the memory of the card that can only be read after a PIN is input to the card. Usually, after some number of wrong PIN guesses, the card "locks" itself and will not give the information to anyone. Information stored on such a smart card is safer than that stored on a magnetic strip card because a stolen card is useless without the PIN. These cards are more difficult to duplicate than magnetic strip cards, but it's still possible given the PIN.
- **Cryptographic challenge/response cards**. With this card, there is a cryptographic key in memory, and the card is willing to encrypt or decrypt using the key but will not reveal the key even after the PIN is entered. A computer that knows the key in the card can authenticate the user by creating a random challenge and "challenging" the card to encrypt or decrypt it. If the correct answer is returned, the computer can have confidence that the smart card is present and the correct PIN was entered. These cards can be constructed so as to be nearly impossible to duplicate or to extract the key from. Since there is no way to directly extract the key, it can only be done by disassembling or inserting probes into the card. There is a reciprocating esca-

lation in the technologies for probing the card and for packaging it to be unreadable. For most practical purposes, the cards are unreadable. Like keys and magnetic strip cards, the serious practical problems with smart cards are the need for readers at every access point and the need for recovery when a card is lost or forgotten. The cryptographic card offers substantial protection against eavesdropping.

- **Cryptographic calculator** (sometimes called a **readerless smart card**). A cryptographic calculator is like a smart card in that it performs cryptographic calculations using a key that it will not disclose. It is unlike a smart card in that it requires no electrical connection to the terminal. It has a display and usually a keyboard, and all interaction is through the user. One way it could work is by simulating a smart card: The user enters a PIN to unlock the device; the computer wishing to authenticate the user generates a random challenge and displays it to the user; the user types it into the calculator; the calculator encrypts the value and displays the result; the user enters the result on the terminal; the computer does the same calculation and compares the results.

  An alternative protocol that cuts the typing in half is for the calculator to encrypt the current time and display the result. The user types in this number in place of a password. There's a little more work for the computer since it will not be sure of the exact time that the calculator thinks it is (clocks drift); it will have to do the calculation on several candidate time values to verify what the device said. It might then record the accumulated clock skew to make the next such calculation easier. It's possible to eliminate the keyboard (needed for entering the PIN) from the calculator by having a PIN or password sent to the computer instead. It is important to have some form of PIN to prevent someone who steals the calculator from impersonating its owner. In addition to saving typing, another advantage of the time encryption protocol is that it fits the "form factor" of protocols designed for passwords. If a protocol has a "password" field and no way for the authenticating application to send a challenge, the encrypted time variant can still be made to work.

  The biggest advantage of these readerless smart cards is that they can be used from ordinary terminals with no special hardware. Their popularity is growing among companies that want to let their employees log in from home using laptops and modems but are afraid of opening their networks up to intruders.

10.9 PHYSICAL ACCESS

A low-tech way of performing user authentication is to have human guards do it "at the door". If a system is only accessible from protected areas, and it requires some form of person-to-person authentication to enter those areas, then any authentication the system does is for purposes of differentiating legitimate users from each other as opposed to differentiating legitimate users from illegitimate users. For high-security applications, this may be perfectly reasonable. Many bank transactions, for example, can only be initiated at tellers' terminals inside the bank.

Alternatively, the location from which access is requested can be part of the authentication process, where fewer rights are granted from less secure access points. For instance, ATMs and the tellers' terminals connect to the same computer, but support different transaction types.

10.10 BIOMETRICS

> *Biometric devices sell best in places where users aren't afraid of technology or don't have a choice.*
>
> —*Wall Street Journal*, Oct 13, 1992, William M. Bulkeley

In dividing authentication mechanisms into *what you know*, *what you have*, and *what you are*, biometric devices authenticate you according to *what you are*. They measure your physical characteristics and match them against a profile. You can't "loan out" anything that would help someone fool a biometric authentication device; nor can anything be stolen.

There are a variety of biometric devices available. All are too expensive to be in everyday use, but in some cases the costs are coming down to where we may see these. Technology available today includes:

- **Retinal scanner.** This is a device that examines the tiny blood vessels in the back of your eye. The layout is as distinctive as a fingerprint and apparently easier to read. These devices are quite expensive and have a "psychologically threatening" user interface.
- **Fingerprint readers.** This would seem an obvious technology since fingerprints have been used as a method of identification for many years. For some reason, automating this technology has never been very successful, though there are devices available.

- **Face recognition.** Looking at a digitized picture of a person, a computer can measure facial dimensions and do a good job of recognizing people. Just don't show up at work with a black eye and a swollen jaw.
- **Iris scanner**. Like a retinal scanner, this maps the distinctive layout of the iris of your eye. It has the major advantage of having a less intimidating user interface—rather than requiring you to look into a laser device, iris scans can be done with a camera several feet away and might even be done covertly.
- **Handprint readers**. These are more widely used than fingerprint readers. They measure the dimensions of the hand: finger length, width, and so on. They are not as accurate as fingerprints (more false positives), but they are less expensive and less problem-prone.
- **Voiceprints**. It turns out that it's possible to do a frequency spectrum analysis of someone's voice and get identification nearly as accurate as a fingerprint. This technology is in use, but has not caught on in spite of the fact that it should be fairly cheap. It can be defeated with a tape recording, and it may refuse to authenticate someone whose voice has shifted due to illness.
- **Keystroke timing**. The exact way in which people type is quite distinctive, and experiments have been done with identification based on the way people type. There is a problem that various injuries can throw off timing, and the networks that connect terminals and computers tend to lose the keystroke timing information before it reaches a processor that can use it.
- **Signatures**. These are a classic human form of authentication, and there are human experts quite adept at determining whether two signatures were produced by the same person. Machines thus far have not been able to duplicate that ability. However, when not just the signature is recorded, but the actual timing of the movements that go into scribing the signature, there is sufficient information for authentication, and some systems use this method, with the user signing on an electronic tablet.

It might seem tempting to build a portable fingerprint reader as a peripheral to a laptop or PC that lets you stick your finger in and turns it into bits. Such devices are commercially available. The bits are then sent to a remote computer as a form of authentication. The problem with this approach is that the biometric properties cannot reasonably be kept secret. Anyone who knows your fingerprint can transmit the relevant fingerprint data. The only way in which a remote biometric device can be secure is if the device possesses a tamper-resistant secret and communicates with the remote computer via a cryptographically protected exchange.

10.11 HOMEWORK

1. Design a password hash algorithm with the property stated in *Password Hash Quirk* on page 242. It should be impossible to reverse, but for any string *S* it should be easy to find a longer string with the same hash.

2. In §10.5 *Eavesdropping* we described a scheme in which a user has a numbered list of passwords and the system asks for some small subset on each login. Is there any advantage in asking for more than one password per login? Note that the more passwords requested, the more information an eavesdropper will get. On the other hand, when the eavesdropper attempts to impersonate the user, the more passwords requested, the less likely the eavesdropper will know all of them.

11 Security Handshake Pitfalls

Knock Knock!
Who's there?
Alice.
Alice who?

and you'll have to read on to find secure ways of continuing…

Security in communications almost always includes an initial authentication handshake, and sometimes, in addition, integrity protection and/or encryption of the data. Let's assume Alice and Bob wish to communicate. In order to communicate, they need to know some information about themselves and about the other party. Some of this information is secret. Some usually isn't, such as the names Alice and Bob.

In §9.3 *Cryptographic Authentication Protocols* we described some example security handshakes. Although they may seem straightforward, minor variants of secure protocols can have security holes. As a matter of fact, many deployed protocols have been designed with security flaws.

This stuff just isn't that hard. How come nobody gets it right?

—Al Eldridge

This book does not tell you the one "best" protocol. Different protocols have different tradeoffs. Some threats are more likely in some situations, and different resources are available in terms of computational power, specialized hardware, money to pay off patent holders, humans willing and able to be careful, and so forth. We mortals should never need to design our own cryptographic algorithms (like DES, RSA, or MD5)—we can leave that in the able hands of Ron Rivest and a handful of other specialists. But it is often the case that people outside the security community, such as implementers or protocol designers, have to design security features into protocols—including authentication handshakes. It is crucial that potential flaws be well understood. Even when a protocol is patterned after known protocols, the slightest alteration, even in something that "couldn't conceivably matter", can introduce subtle security flaws. Or even if a new flaw is not introduced, a weakness that was not important in the original protocol might be serious in a different environment.

In practice, the way that security protocols are designed is by starting with some design, which is almost certainly flawed, and then checking for all the weaknesses one can imagine, and fixing them. So the more educated we can become about the types of flaws likely to be in a protocol, the more likely it is that we'll understand all the properties of a protocol we deploy.

In this chapter we describe some typical protocols and evaluate them according to performance (number of messages, processing power required, compactness of messages) and security.

11.1 LOGIN ONLY

A lot of existing protocols were designed in an environment where eavesdropping was not a concern (rightly or wrongly), and bad guys were (rightly or wrongly) not expected to be very sophisticated. The authentication in such protocols generally consists of:

- Alice (the initiator) sends her name and password (in the clear) across the network to Bob.
- Bob verifies the name and password, and then communication occurs, with no further attention to security—no encryption, no cryptographic integrity protection.

A very common enhancement to such a protocol is to replace the transmission of the cleartext password with a cryptographic challenge/response. First we'll discuss protocols based on shared secrets, using either secret key cryptographic algorithms or message digest algorithms. Then we'll discuss similar protocols using public key technology.

11.1.1 Shared Secret

The notation $f(K_{\text{Alice-Bob}},R)$ means that R is cryptographically transformed, somehow, with Alice and Bob's shared secret $K_{\text{Alice-Bob}}$. This could be done by using $K_{\text{Alice-Bob}}$ as a secret key in some algorithm such as DES or AES, and using $K_{\text{Alice-Bob}}$ to encrypt R. Or it could be done by hashing R and $K_{\text{Alice-Bob}}$, for instance by concatenating R and $K_{\text{Alice-Bob}}$ and computing a message digest on the result. When we explicitly mean encryption with $K_{\text{Alice-Bob}}$ we'll write $K_{\text{Alice-Bob}}\{R\}$. When we explicitly mean a hash, we'll write $\text{h}(K_{\text{Alice-Bob}},R)$ or $\text{hash}(K_{\text{Alice-Bob}},R)$.

Consider Protocol 11-1. An eavesdropper will see both R and $f(K_{\text{Alice-Bob}},R)$. It is essential that seeing the pair does not enable the eavesdropper to derive $K_{\text{Alice-Bob}}$.

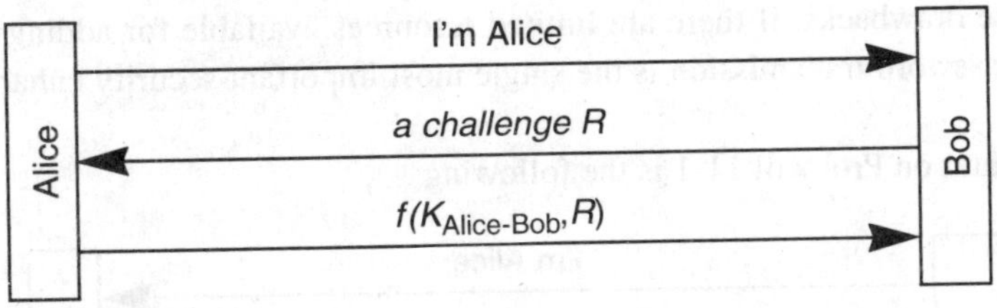

Protocol 11-1. Bob authenticates Alice based on a shared secret $K_{\text{Alice-Bob}}$

This protocol is a big improvement over passwords in the clear. An eavesdropper cannot impersonate Alice based on overhearing the exchange, since next time there will be a different challenge. However, there are some weaknesses to this protocol:

- Authentication is not mutual. Bob authenticates Alice, but Alice does not authenticate Bob. If Trudy can receive packets transmitted to Bob's network address, and respond with Bob's network address (or through other means convince Alice that Trudy's address is Bob's), then Alice will be fooled into assuming Trudy is Bob. Trudy doesn't need to know Alice's secret in order to impersonate Bob—she just needs to send any old number R to Alice and ignore Alice's response.
- If this is the entire protocol (i.e., the remainder of the conversation is transmitted without cryptographic protection), then Trudy can hijack the conversation after the initial exchange, assuming she can generate packets with Alice's source address. It's also useful to Trudy, but not absolutely essential, that she be able to receive packets transmitted to Alice's network layer address. (See Homework Problem 1.)
- An eavesdropper could mount an off-line password-guessing attack (assuming $K_{\text{Alice-Bob}}$ is derived from a password), knowing R and $f(K_{\text{Alice-Bob}}, R)$. (Recall that an off-line password-guessing attack is one in which an intruder captures information against which passwords can be tested in private, so in this context it means guessing a password, turning that password into a key K, and then seeing whether $f(K,R)$ equals $f(K_{\text{Alice-Bob}}, R)$.)
- Someone who reads the latabase at Bob can later impersonate Alice. In many cases it is difficult to protect the database at Bob. There might be many servers where Alice uses the same password, and although the administrators of most of the servers might be very conscientious about security (not letting unauthorized people get near their machines, and enforcing unguessable passwords), it only takes one unprotected server for an intruder to read the relevant information. Furthermore, protecting the database implies protecting all the backup media as well, by either preventing access to it (locking it in a safe) or encrypting the contents and somehow protecting the key with which it was encrypted.

Despite these drawbacks, if there are limited resources available for adding security, replacing the cleartext password transmission is the single most important security enhancement that can be done.

A minor variant on Protocol 11-1 is the following:

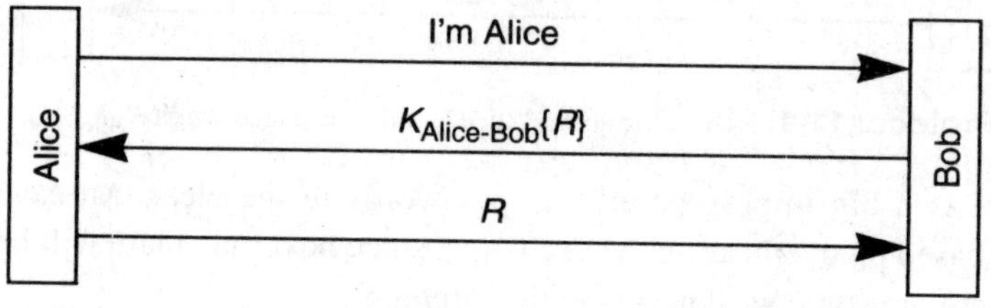

Protocol 11-2. Bob authenticates Alice based on a shared secret key $K_{Alice\text{-}Bob}$

In this protocol Bob chooses a random challenge R, encrypts it, and transmits the result. Alice then decrypts the received quantity, using the secret key $K_{Alice\text{-}Bob}$ to get R, and sends R to Bob. This protocol has only minor security differences from Protocol 11-1:

- This protocol requires reversible cryptography, for example a secret key cryptographic algorithm. Protocol 11-1 can be done using a hash function. For example, $f(K_{Alice\text{-}Bob}, R)$ could be the message digest of $K_{Alice\text{-}Bob}$ concatenated with R. But in Protocol 11-2, Alice has to be able to reverse what Bob has done to R in order to retrieve R. Sometimes there is a performance advantage to being able to use one of the message digest functions rather than having to use, say, DES. Sometimes there are export issues involved in having code for encryption available, even if it's only used for authentication, whereas using a message digest function would be less likely to create export problems.

- Suppose $K_{Alice\text{-}Bob}$ is derived from a password and therefore vulnerable to a dictionary attack. If R is a recognizable quantity, for instance a 32-bit random number padded with 32 zero bits to fill out an encryption block, then Trudy can, without eavesdropping, mount a dictionary attack by merely sending the message I am Alice and obtaining $K_{Alice\text{-}Bob}\{R\}$. If Trudy is eavesdropping, however, and sees both R and $K_{Alice\text{-}Bob}\{R\}$, she can mount a dictionary attack with either protocol. It is often the case that eavesdropping is more difficult than merely sending a message claiming to be Alice. Kerberos V4 (see Chapter 13 *Kerberos V4*) is an example of a protocol that has this security weakness.

- If R is a recognizable quantity with limited lifetime, such as a random number concatenated with a timestamp, Alice authenticates Bob because only someone knowing $K_{Alice\text{-}Bob}$ could generate $K_{Alice\text{-}Bob}\{R\}$. To accomplish mutual authentication, R must be limited lifetime to foil the replaying of an old $K_{Alice\text{-}Bob}\{R\}$.

Another variant on Protocol 11-1 is to shorten the handshake to a single message by having Alice use a timestamp instead of an *R* that Bob supplies:

Protocol 11-3. Bob authenticates Alice based on synchronized clocks and a shared secret $K_{\text{Alice-Bob}}$

This modification requires that Bob and Alice have reasonably synchronized clocks. Alice encrypts the current time. Bob decrypts the result and makes sure the result is acceptable (i.e., within an acceptable clock skew). The implications of this modification are:

- This modification can be added very easily to a protocol designed for sending cleartext passwords, since it does not add any additional messages—it merely replaces the cleartext password field with the encrypted timestamp in the first message transmitted by Alice to Bob.
- The protocol is now more efficient. It goes beyond saving two messages. It means that a server, Bob, does not need to keep any volatile state (such as *R* in Protocol 11-1) regarding Alice (but see next bullet). This protocol can be added to a request/response protocol (such as RPC) by having Alice merely add the encrypted timestamp into her request. Bob can authenticate the request, generate a reply, and forget the whole thing ever happened.
- Someone eavesdropping can use Alice's transmitted $K_{\text{Alice-Bob}}\{timestamp\}$ to impersonate Alice, if done within the acceptable clock skew. This threat can be foiled if Bob remembers all timestamps sent by Alice until they "expire" (i.e., they are old enough that the clock skew check would consider them invalid).
- Another potential security pitfall occurs if there are multiple servers for which Alice uses the same secret $K_{\text{Alice-Bob}}$. Then an eavesdropper who acts quickly can use the encrypted timestamp field Alice transmitted, and (if still within the acceptable time skew) impersonate Alice to a different server. This can be foiled by concatenating the server name in with the timestamp. Instead of sending $K_{\text{Alice-Bob}}\{timestamp\}$, Alice sends $K_{\text{Alice-Bob}}\{\text{"Bob"} \mid timestamp\}$. That quantity would not be accepted by a different server.
- If our bad guy Trudy can convince Bob to set his clock back, she can reuse encrypted timestamps she had overheard in what is now Bob's future. In practice there are systems that are vulnerable to an intruder resetting the clock. Although it might be obvious that a password file would be something that needed to be protected, if the security protocols are not completely understood, it might not be obvious that clock-setting could be a serious security vulnerability.

- If security relies on time, then setting the time will be an operation that requires a security handshake. A handshake based on time will fail if the clocks are far apart. If there's a system with an incorrect time, then it will be impossible to log into the system in order to manage it (in order to correct its clock). A plausible solution to this is to have a different authentication handshake based on challenge/response (i.e., not dependent on time) for managing clock setting.

In Protocol 11-1, computing $f(K_{\text{Alice-Bob}},R)$. may be done with a secret key encryption scheme using $K_{\text{Alice-Bob}}$ as a key, or by concatenating $K_{\text{Alice-Bob}}$ with R and doing a hash. When we're using timestamps the same is true (a message digest works), except for a minor complication. How does Bob verify that hash($K_{\text{Alice-Bob}}$,R) is reasonable? Suppose the timestamp is in units of minutes, and the believable clock skew is 10 minutes. Then Bob would have to compute hash($K_{\text{Alice-Bob}}$, *timestamp*) for each of the twenty possible valid timestamps to verify the value Alice sends (though he could stop as soon as he found a match). With a reversible encryption function, all he had to do was decrypt the quantity received and see if the result was acceptable. While checking twenty values might have acceptable performance, this approach would become intolerably inefficient if the clock granularity allows a lot more legal values within the clock skew. For instance, the timestamp might be in units of microseconds. There are 600 million valid timestamps within a five-minute clock skew. This would be unacceptably inefficient for Bob to verify. The solution (assuming you wanted to use a microsecond clock and a hash function rather than a reversible encryption scheme) is to have Alice transmit the actual timestamp unencrypted, in addition to transmitting the hashed value. So the protocol would be:

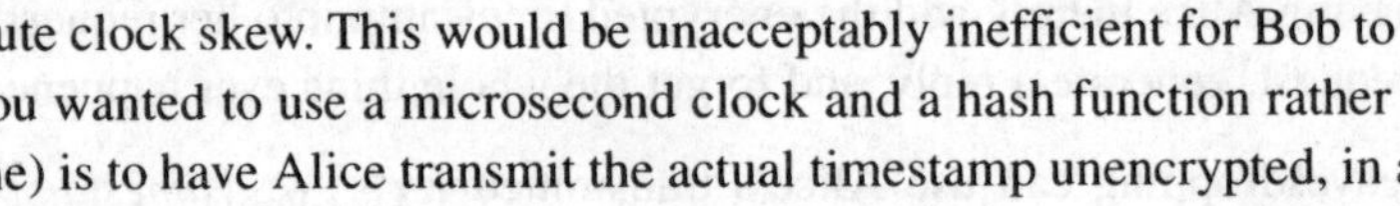

Protocol 11-4. Bob authenticates Alice based on hashing a high-resolution time and a shared secret $K_{\text{Alice-Bob}}$

11.1.2 One-Way Public Key

With protocols in the previous section, which are based on shared secrets, Trudy can impersonate Alice if she can read Bob's database. If the protocols are based on public key technology instead, this can be avoided, as in Protocol 11-5.

In this case $[R]_{\text{Alice}}$ means that Alice signs R (i.e. transforms R using her private key). Bob will verify Alice's signature $[R]_{\text{Alice}}$ using Alice's public key, and accept the login if the result matches R. This is very similar to Protocol 11-1. The advantage of this protocol is that the database at Bob is no longer security-sensitive to an attacker reading it. Bob's database must be protected from unauthorized modification, but not from unauthorized disclosure.

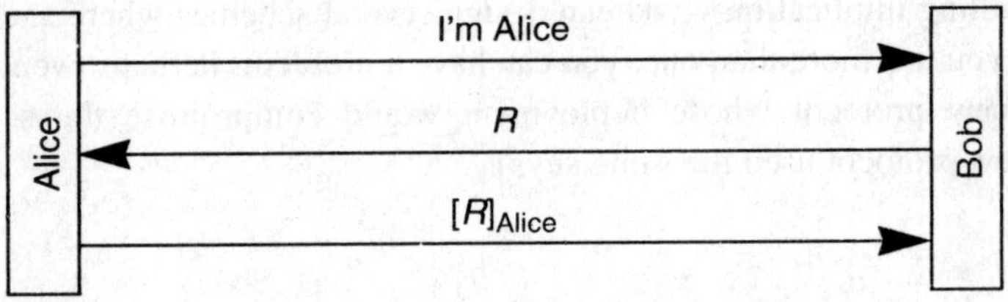

Protocol 11-5. Bob authenticates Alice based on her public key signature

And as before, the same minor variant works:

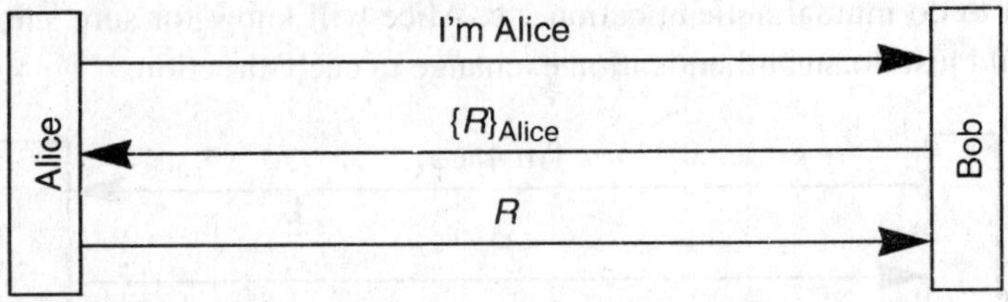

Protocol 11-6. Bob authenticates Alice if she can decrypt a message encrypted with her public key

In this variant, Bob chooses *R*, encrypts it using Alice's public key, and Alice proves she knows her private key by decrypting the received quantity to retrieve *R*. A problem with this variant is that some public key schemes (such as DSS) can only do signatures, not reversible encryption. So in those cases this variant cannot be used.

In both Protocol 11-5 and Protocol 11-6 there is a potential serious problem. In Protocol 11-5 you can trick someone into signing something. That means, if you have a quantity on which you'd like to forge Alice's signature, you might be able to impersonate Bob's network address, wait for Alice to try to log in, and then give her the quantity as the challenge. She'll sign it, and now you know her signature on that quantity. Protocol 11-6 has Alice decrypting something. So, if there's some encrypted message someone sent to Alice and you're wondering what's in it, you might again impersonate Bob's address, wait for Alice to log in, and then have Alice decrypt it for you.

How can we avoid getting in trouble? The general rule is that you should not use the same key for two different purposes unless the designs for all uses of the key are coordinated so that an attacker can't use one protocol to help break another. An example method of coordination is to ensure that *R* has some structure. For instance, if you sign different types of things (say an *R* in a challenge/response protocol versus an electronic mail message), each type of thing should have a structure so that it cannot be mistaken for another type of thing. For example, there might be a type field concatenated to the front of the quantity before signing, with different values for *authentication challenge* and *mail message*. Part of the purpose of the PKCS standards (see §6.3.6 *Public-Key Cryptography Standard (PKCS)*) is to impose enough structure to prevent this sort of problem when the same RSA key is used for different purposes.

Note the chilling implication—you can design several schemes where each is independently secure, but when you use more than one, you can have a problem. Perhaps even more chilling, you could design a new protocol whose deployment would compromise the security of existing schemes (if the new protocol used the same keys).

11.2 MUTUAL AUTHENTICATION

Suppose we want to do mutual authentication, i.e. Alice will know for sure she is communicating with Bob. We could just do an authentication exchange in each direction:

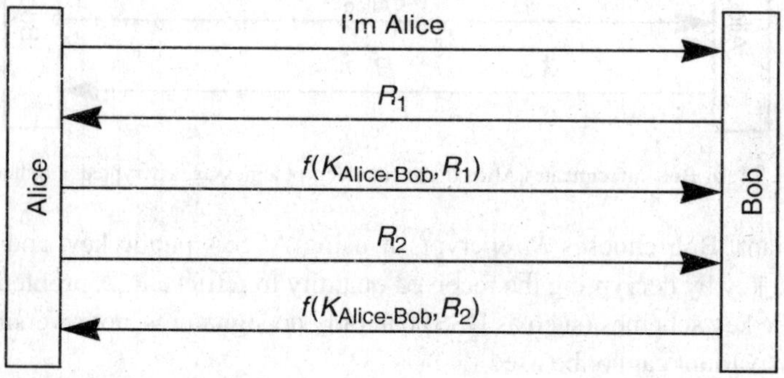

Protocol 11-7. Mutual authentication based on a shared secret $K_{Alice-Bob}$

11.2.1 Reflection Attack

The first thing we might notice is that the protocol is inefficient. We can reduce the protocol down to three messages (instead of five used above) by putting more than one item of information into each message:

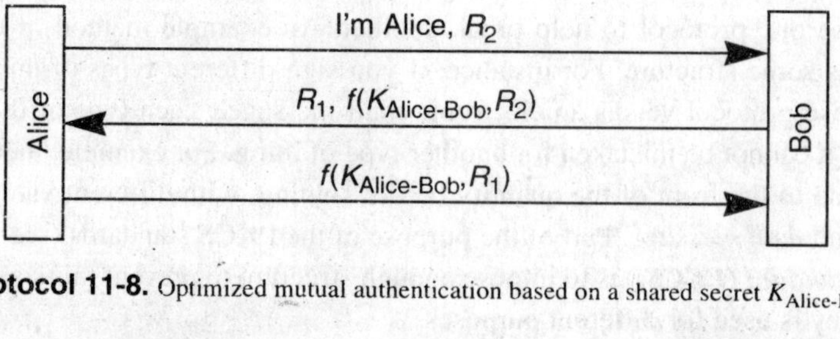

Protocol 11-8. Optimized mutual authentication based on a shared secret $K_{Alice-Bob}$

This version of the protocol has a security pitfall known as the **reflection attack**. Suppose Trudy wants to impersonate Alice to Bob. First Trudy starts Protocol 11-8, but when she receives the challenge from Bob, she cannot proceed further, because she can't encrypt R_1.

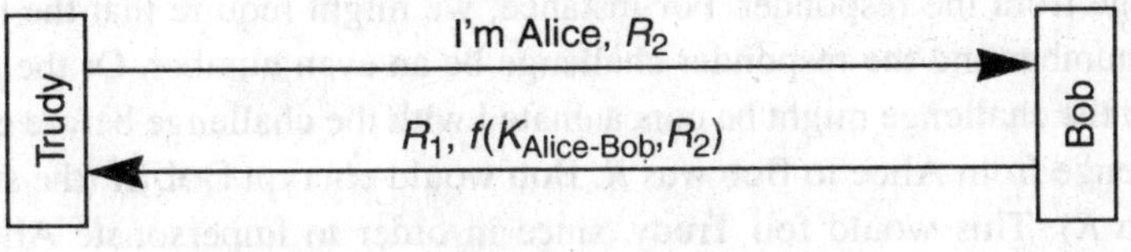

Figure 11-9. Beginning of reflection attack

"I can't explain myself, *I'm afraid sir," said Alice, "because I'm not myself, you see."*

Alice in Wonderland

However, note that Trudy has managed to get Bob to encrypt R_2. So at this point Trudy opens a second session to Bob. This time she uses R_1 as the challenge to Bob:

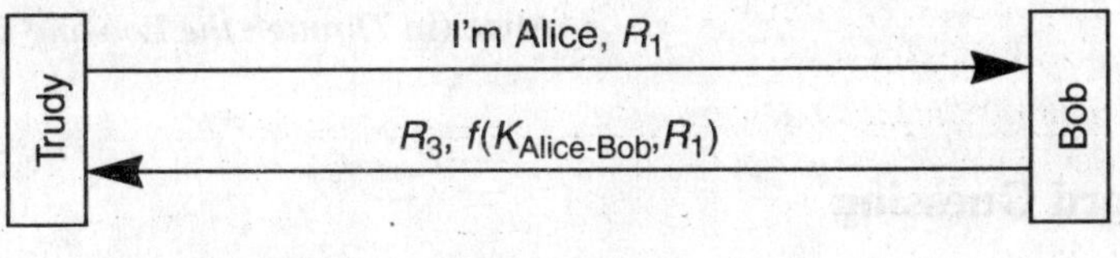

Figure 11-10. Second session in reflection attack

Trudy can't go any further with this session, because she can't encrypt R_3. But now she knows $K_{\text{Alice-Bob}}\{R_1\}$, so she can complete the first session.

This is a serious security flaw, and there are deployed protocols that contain this flaw. In many environments it is easy to exploit this, since it might be possible to open multiple simultaneous connections to the same server, or there might be multiple servers with the same secret for Alice (so Trudy can get a different server to compute $f(K_{\text{Alice-Bob}}, R_1)$ so that she can impersonate Alice to Bob).

We can foil the reflection attack if we are careful and understand the pitfalls. Here are two methods of fixing the protocol, both of which are derived from the general principle *don't have Alice and Bob do exactly the same thing*:

- different keys—Have the key used to authenticate Alice be different from the key used to authenticate Bob. We could use two totally different keys shared by Alice and Bob at the cost of additional configuration and storage. Alternatively we could derive the key used for authenticating Bob from the key used to authenticate Alice. For instance, Bob's key might be $-K_{\text{Alice-Bob}}$, or $K_{\text{Alice-Bob}}+1$, or $K_{\text{Alice-Bob}} \oplus \text{F0F0F0F0F0F0F0F0}_{16}$. Any of these would foil

Trudy in her attempt to impersonate Alice to Bob since she would not be able to get Bob to encrypt anything using Alice's key.

- different challenges—Insist that the challenge from the initiator (Alice) look different from the challenge from the responder. For instance, we might require that the initiator challenge be an odd number and the responder challenge be an even number. Or the name of the party that created the challenge might be concatenated with the challenge before encryption, so that if the challenge from Alice to Bob was *R*, Bob would encrypt Bob|*R* (the string Bob concatenated with *R*). This would foil Trudy, since in order to impersonate Alice to Bob, Trudy would need to get Bob to encrypt the string Alice concatenated with some number.

Notice that Protocol 11-7 did not suffer from the reflection attack. The reason is that it follows another good general principle of security protocol design: *the initiator should be the first to prove its identity.* Ideally, you shouldn't prove your identity until the other side does, but since that wouldn't work, the assumption is that the initiator is more likely to be the bad guy.

> *...if you only spoke when you were spoken to, and the other person always waited for you to begin, you see nobody would ever say anything...*
>
> —Alice (in *Through the Looking Glass*)

11.2.2 Password Guessing

Another security weakness of Protocol 11-8 (which doesn't exist in Protocol 11-7) is that Trudy can mount an off-line password-guessing attack without needing to eavesdrop. All she needs to do is send a message to Bob claiming to be Alice and enclosing a number to be encrypted, and Bob will obligingly return the encrypted value. Then Trudy has the pair $\langle R, f(K_{\text{Alice-Bob}}, R)\rangle$ which she can use to check password guesses. We could fix that by making the protocol one message longer (Protocol 11-11).

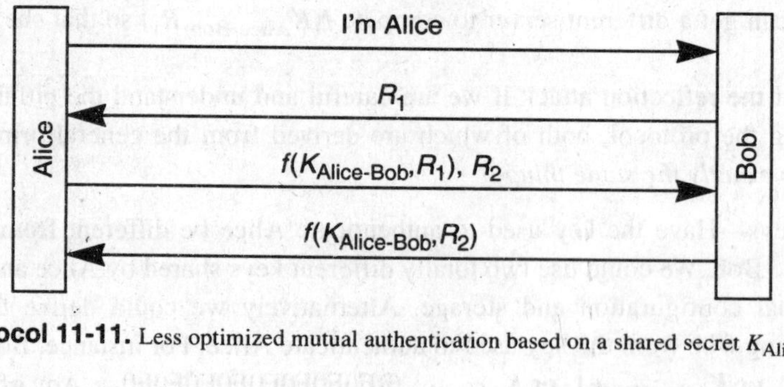

Protocol 11-11. Less optimized mutual authentication based on a shared secret $K_{\text{Alice-Bob}}$

Now Trudy can't obtain a quantity with which to do off-line password guessing by claiming to be Alice, but she can by impersonating Bob's address and tricking Alice into attempting a connection to her. The threat of having Trudy impersonate Bob should not be ignored, but it is much more difficult than impersonating Alice.

11.2.3 Public Keys

Mutual authentication can also be done with public key technology, assuming that Bob and Alice know each other's public keys. It can be done with three messages:

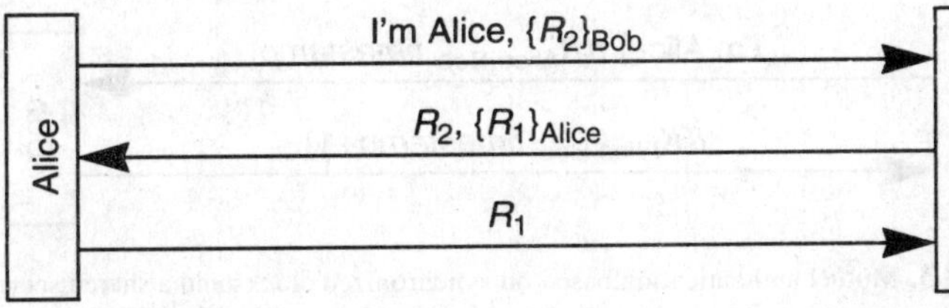

Protocol 11-12. Mutual authentication with public keys

A variant is for Alice to send R_2 and for Bob to return it signed (and similarly for Alice to sign R_1).

Public key mutual authentication presents some special challenges. How does Alice (or Alice's workstation) know Bob's public key? Often the situation is that Alice is a human, working on a generic workstation. In such cases Alice isn't going to remember Bob's public key, nor is Alice's workstation likely to have it stored. It could be done by having Alice attach to something, hoping it's Bob, and having the thing she's talking to send its public key. But that would not be secure if Trudy is impersonating Bob.

We also have the problem of having Alice's workstation obtain Alice's private key when all Alice knows is a password. It is generally straightforward to convert a password into a secret key, because most secret key algorithms will accept any value of the right size as a key. Some public key algorithms—notably RSA—have private keys that take special forms and cannot easily be derived from passwords. The usual method of dealing with this is to have Alice's workstation retrieve Alice's private key, encrypted with her password, from a directory service, or perhaps from Bob. It is not much more trouble to store, in the same place, information that would allow Alice to reliably learn Bob's public key. Two possible techniques:

- Store Bob's public key encrypted with Alice's password. If anyone is impersonating Bob, they will not be able to give Alice a quantity encrypted with her password for which they'd know a corresponding private key.

- Store a certificate for Bob's public key, signed with Alice's private key. Once her workstation obtains her private key, it can validate the certificate for Bob's public key.

For more information on this, see Chapter 15 *PKI (Public Key Infrastructure)* and §12.4 *Strong Password Credentials Download Protocols*.

11.2.4 Timestamps

We can reduce the mutual authentication down to two messages by using timestamps instead of random numbers for challenges:

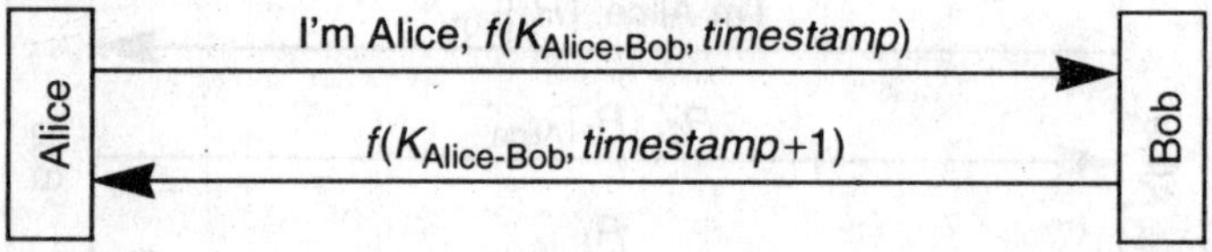

Protocol 11-13. Mutual authentication based on synchronized clocks and a shared secret $K_{\text{Alice-Bob}}$

This two message variant is very useful because it is easy to add onto existing protocols (such as request/response protocols), since it does not add any additional messages. But it has to be done carefully. In the diagram we have Bob encrypt a timestamp later than Alice's timestamp. Obviously Bob can't send the same timestamp back to Alice, since that would hardly be mutual authentication. (Alice would be assured that she was either talking to Bob or someone smart enough to copy a field out of her request!) So in the exchange, Alice and Bob have to encrypt different timestamps, use different keys for encrypting the timestamp, concatenate their name to the timestamp before encrypting it, or use any other scheme that will cause them to be sending different things. And the issues involved with the one-way authentication done with timestamps apply here as well (time must not go backwards, they must remember values used within the clock skew, etc.).

Note that any modification to the timestamp would do. The idea of *timestamp*+1 comes from Needham-Schroeder, where they have one side use the incremented challenge of the other. We use *timestamp*+1 in our example because that's what Kerberos V4 uses, but *timestamp*+1 is probably not the best choice. *timestamp*+1 has the potential problem that Trudy eavesdropping could use $K_{\text{Alice-Bob}}\{timestamp+1\}$ to impersonate Alice. A better choice would be a flag concatenated with the timestamp indicating whether the initiator or responder is transmitting. Although the threat of Trudy using $K_{\text{Alice-Bob}}\{timestamp+1\}$ can be avoided if Bob keeps both *timestamp* and *timestamp*+1 in his replay cache, in general it is poor security practice to use something like +1, where there isn't anything intrinsically different between what Bob does and what Alice does. Also, if service Bob consists of multiple replicas all with the same key, where it would be difficult for a replica to keep track of timestamps used at other replicas, then the quantity Alice encrypts should include something unique to the replica she's talking to, such as its name or IP address.

11.3 INTEGRITY/ENCRYPTION FOR DATA

In order to provide integrity protection and/or encryption of the data following the authentication exchange it is necessary for Alice and Bob to use cryptography to encrypt and/or add integrity checks to the data messages. We described several bases for the authentication exchange:

- §11.1.1 *Shared Secret*—Alice and Bob share a secret key $K_{\text{Alice-Bob}}$.
- §11.2.3 *Public Keys*—Alice and Bob know each other's public keys, as well as their own private keys.
- §11.1.2 *One-Way Public Key*—only one side has a public key pair; authentication is one-way.

As we discussed in §9.8 *Session Key Establishment*, it is desirable for Alice and Bob to establish a shared secret per-conversation key (known as the **session key**) to be used for integrity protection and encryption, even if they already know enough long-term secrets to be able to encrypt and add integrity checks to messages. So we'll want to enhance the authentication exchange so that after the initial handshake both Alice and Bob will share a session key. It is important that an eavesdropper not be able to figure out what the session key is. Once a session key is established, the workstation can forget the user's password, or at least a piece of untrusted software can proceed with a cryptographically protected conversation without being told any long-term secrets. First we'll discuss how to establish a session key for each of the three cases above. Then we'll discuss how to use the session key for encryption and/or integrity protection.

11.3.1 Shared Secret

Alice and Bob have a shared secret key $K_{\text{Alice-Bob}}$. The authentication exchange is shown in Protocol 11-14. Perhaps mutual authentication was done, in which case there are two *R*s, R_1 and R_2. Perhaps authentication was done using timestamps instead of random *R*s. At any rate, there is sufficient information in this protocol so that Alice and Bob can establish a shared session key at this point in the conversation. They can, for example, use $(K_{\text{Alice-Bob}}+1)\{R\}$ as the session key. More generally, they can take the shared secret $K_{\text{Alice-Bob}}$ and modify it in some way, then encrypt the challenge R using the modified $K_{\text{Alice-Bob}}$ as the key, and use the result as the session key.

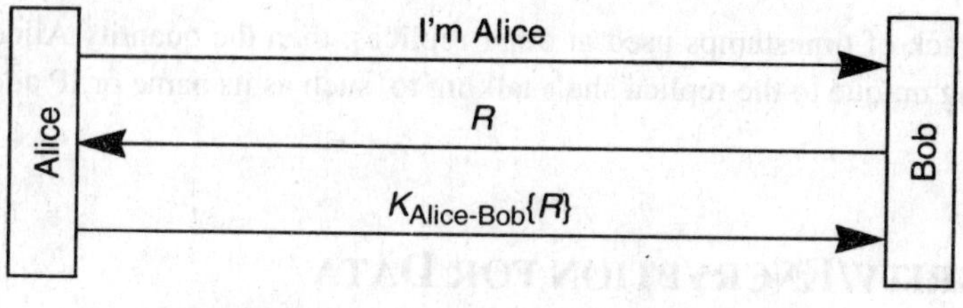

Protocol 11-14. Authentication with shared secret

Why do they need to modify $K_{\text{Alice-Bob}}$? Why can't they use $K_{\text{Alice-Bob}}\{R\}$ as the key? The reason they can't use $K_{\text{Alice-Bob}}\{R\}$ is that $K_{\text{Alice-Bob}}\{R\}$ is transmitted by Alice as the third message in the authentication handshake, so an eavesdropper would see that value, and it certainly would not be secure as a session key.

How about using $K_{\text{Alice-Bob}}\{R+1\}$ as the session key? There's a more subtle reason why that isn't secure. Suppose Alice and Bob have started a conversation in which Bob used R as the challenge. Perhaps Trudy recorded the entire subsequent conversation, encrypted using $K_{\text{Alice-Bob}}\{R+1\}$. Later, Trudy can impersonate Bob's network layer address to Alice, thereby tricking Alice into attempting to communicate with Trudy instead of Bob, and Trudy (pretending to be Bob) can send $R+1$ as a challenge, to which Alice will respond with $K_{\text{Alice-Bob}}\{R+1\}$:

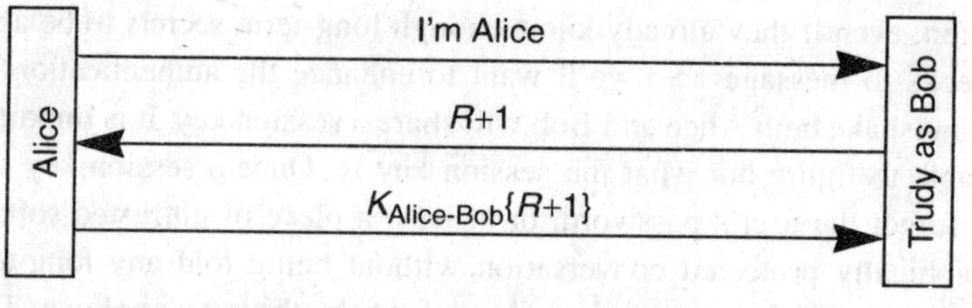

Figure 11-15. Trudy impersonates Bob

Then Trudy will be able to decrypt the previous Alice-Bob conversation.

So, Alice and Bob, after the authentication exchange, know $K_{\text{Alice-Bob}}$ and R, and there are many combinations of the two quantities that would be perfectly acceptable as a session key, but there are also some that are not acceptable as a session key. What makes a good session key? It must be different for each session, unguessable by an eavesdropper, and should not consist of a quantity X encrypted with $K_{\text{Alice-Bob}}$, where X is a value that can be predicted or extracted by an intruder (as just discussed for $X = R+1$). See Homework Problem 3.

11.3.2 Two-Way Public Key Based Authentication

Suppose we are doing two-way authentication using public key technology, so that Alice and Bob know their own private keys and know each other's public keys. How can they establish a session key? We'll discuss various possibilities, with their relative security and performance strengths and weaknesses.

1. One side, say Alice, could choose a random number R, encrypt it with Bob's public key, and send $\{R\}_{\text{Bob}}$ to Bob attached to one of the messages in the authentication exchange. This scheme has a security flaw. Our intruder, Trudy, could hijack the conversation by picking her own R, encrypting it with Bob's public key, and send that to Bob (while impersonating Alice's network layer address) in place of the encrypted key supplied by Alice.

2. Alice could, in addition to encrypting R with Bob's public key, sign the result. So she'd send $[\{R\}_{\text{Bob}}]_{\text{Alice}}$ to Bob. Bob would take the received quantity, first verify Alice's signature using Alice's public key, and then use his private key on the result to obtain R. If Trudy were to attempt the same trick as in scheme 1, namely choosing her own R and sending it to Bob, she wouldn't be able to forge Alice's signature on the encrypted R.

   This scheme is reasonable. It has a minor security weakness that can be fixed partially (in 3, below) or completely (in 4, below). The flaw is that if Trudy records the entire Alice-Bob conversation, and then later **overruns** Bob (i.e., manages to take over node Bob and learn all Bob's secrets), she will be able to decrypt the conversation she'd recorded. It seems like the kind of threat that only a very energetic paranoid would bother worrying about, but we'll show how to fix it. First note that if Alice is careful to forget R after terminating the conversation with Bob, then overrunning Alice will not enable Trudy to decrypt the recorded conversation, since Trudy needs Alice's public key and Bob's private key to retrieve the session key R. She can only get that by overrunning Bob.

3. This is like 2, above, but Alice picks R_1 and Bob picks R_2. Alice sends $\{R_1\}_{\text{Bob}}$ to Bob. Bob sends $\{R_2\}_{\text{Alice}}$ to Alice. The session key will be $R_1 \oplus R_2$. Overrunning Alice will enable Trudy to retrieve R_2. Overrunning Bob will enable Trudy to retrieve R_1. But in order to retrieve $R_1 \oplus R_2$, she'll need to overrun them both.

   In 2 we had Alice sign her quantity (i.e., she sent $[\{R\}_{\text{Bob}}]_{\text{Alice}}$ instead of merely $\{R\}_{\text{Bob}}$). Why isn't it necessary for Bob and Alice to sign their quantities here? Alice and Bob don't need to sign their quantities because although Trudy is perfectly capable of inserting her own $\{R_1\}_{\text{Bob}}$, she cannot decrypt $\{R_2\}_{\text{Alice}}$. Trudy might therefore be able to inject confusion into the system by having Bob think $R_1 \oplus R_2$ is a key he shares with Alice, but since Trudy only knows R_1, she can't actually see any data intended for Alice.

4. Alice and Bob can do a Diffie-Hellman key establishment exchange (see §6.4 *Diffie-Hellman*), where each signs the quantity they are sending. In Diffie-Hellman, Alice chooses a random R_A. Bob chooses a random R_B. They have already agreed on public numbers g and p. Alice transmits $g^{R_A} \bmod p$. Bob transmits $g^{R_B} \bmod p$. They will use $g^{R_A R_B} \bmod p$ as their session key. When we say they each sign the quantity they send, we mean that Alice doesn't simply transmit $g^{R_A} \bmod p$. She actually transmits $[g^{R_A} \bmod p]_{\text{Alice}}$. And Bob actually transmits $[g^{R_B} \bmod p]_{\text{Bob}}$. In this scheme, even if Trudy overruns both Alice and Bob, she won't be able to decrypt recorded conversations because she won't be able to deduce either R_A or R_B.

11.3.3 One-Way Public Key Based Authentication

In some cases only one of the parties in the conversation has a public/private key pair. Commonly, as in the case of SSL, it is assumed that servers will have public keys, and clients will not bother obtaining keys and certificates. Cryptographic authentication is one-way. The protocol assures the client that she is talking to the right server Bob, but if Bob wants to authenticate Alice, after the cryptographic session is established, Alice will send a name and password. Here are some ways of establishing a shared session key in this case.

1. Alice could choose a random number R, encrypt it with Bob's public key, send $\{R\}_{\text{Bob}}$ to Bob, and R could be the session key. A weakness in this scheme is that if Trudy records the conversation and later overruns Bob, she can decrypt the conversation (since she can retrieve R once she steals Alice's private key).

2. Bob and Alice could do a Diffie-Hellman exchange, where Bob signs his Diffie-Hellman quantity. Alice can't sign hers because she doesn't have a public key. This is slightly more secure than scheme 1 because Trudy can't later overrun Bob and retrieve the session key (assuming Bob has diligently forgotten the session key after terminating the conversation with Alice).

Note that neither of these schemes assure Bob he's really talking to Alice, but in either scheme Bob is assured that the entire conversation is with a single party.

11.3.4 Privacy and Integrity

In §4.3 *Generating MACs* we discuss various methods of computing a MAC with secret key cryptography. In §5.2.2 *Computing a MAC with a Hash* we discuss how to do it with a message digest function. As noted in §4.3.1 *Ensuring Privacy and Integrity Together*, there is currently no standard algorithm for providing both privacy and integrity with a single key and a single cryptographic pass over the data. But see §4.3.5 *Offset Codebook Mode (OCB)*. Until a standard is adopted, plausible solutions are: develop two keys in the authentication exchange and do the two operations independently; make a second key by modifying the first (by changing a few bits in a predictable way); use different cryptographic algorithms so a common key is (presumably) irrelevant; or use a weak checksum for integrity inside a strong algorithm for privacy.

The messages exchanged on a connection once the keys are known are likely to be in the form of discrete messages, where the authenticity of each must be determined before the conversation can proceed. Even if a message is authentic, it could be misinterpreted if played out of order. An attacker might, for example, record a message and then replay it later on in the exchange. This can be prevented by having all of the messages contain sequence numbers so that an out-of-order message is detected. Sequence numbers are used in both versions of Kerberos. Alternatively, the integrity code can be computed using not just the current message, but information about all previous messages, so that a replayed message will not be valid. This technique is used by Novell (see §24.1 *NetWare V3*).

Another form of attack is reflection. Here the attacker records a message going in one direction and replays it in the other. If the same sequence number could be valid in both directions, such a message could be misinterpreted. This can be avoided by using sequence numbers in different ranges for the two directions, by having a DIRECTION BIT somewhere in the message, or by having the integrity code computed by some subtly different algorithm in the two directions.

Sequence numbers have to be very large or you face the possibility of running out during a conversation. If you reuse sequence numbers during a conversation (i.e. while using the same session key), an attacker can replay an old recorded message when its sequence number recurs. This is an unlikely threat, but it is good form to prevent it. The best method is to change keys periodically during the conversation. (This also limits the amount of material a cryptanalyst can gather all encrypted under one key.) Changing keys in the middle of a conversation is known as **key rollover**. The simplest method of rolling over a key is to have one end choose a random key, encrypt it under the existing key, and send it to the other end. Because an attacker might cryptanalyze one key and use it to decrypt the subsequent keys, a stronger design would periodically repeat the authentication protocol or roll over keys by doing a Diffie-Hellman exchange to get the new key and integrity-protecting the public numbers with the old key.

Sequence number maintenance and key rollover can be significantly complicated if encryption is done using a communications protocol that does not automatically retry transmissions after errors and put messages back in order before decrypting them.

11.4 MEDIATED AUTHENTICATION (WITH KDC)

In Chapter 9 *Overview of Authentication Systems*, we discussed the concept of a KDC, which has a database consisting of keys for all users. Any user Alice registered with the KDC can securely communicate with the KDC. Alice and the KDC can authenticate each other and encrypt their communication to one another because they each know Alice's key:

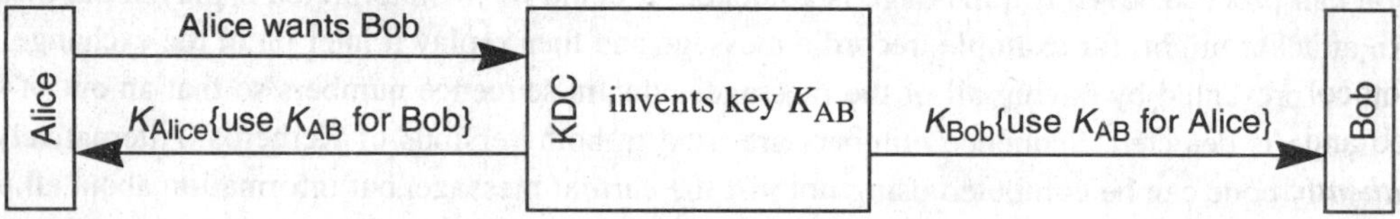

Protocol 11-16. KDC operation (in principle)

In the above exchange, the KDC does not know whether it was really Alice that asked to talk to Bob. Some bad guy, Trudy, could send the message to the KDC saying I am Alice, I'd like to talk to Bob. But that won't do Trudy any good because she cannot decrypt the encrypted K_{AB}. Trudy is causing Bob to get a spurious message that Alice wants to talk to him using key K_{AB}, but it doesn't do any harm. The only parties that can know K_{AB} after this exchange are the KDC, Bob, and Alice, so after this exchange Alice and Bob can mutually authenticate using key K_{AB} (using a protocol such as discussed in §11.2 *Mutual Authentication*).

Protocol 11-16 is not the way it is done in practice. That protocol has some practical problems, the most important of which is that if Alice immediately sends a message to Bob based on the new shared key, it's possible, given the vagaries of networks, for Alice's message to arrive first, in which case Bob would not know how to decrypt it. It also is a lot of trouble for the KDC to initiate a connection to Bob. Instead, since Alice is going to communicate with Bob anyway, the KDC gives Alice the information the KDC would have sent to Bob. The Kerberos protocol, which we'll describe in Chapter 13 *Kerberos V4* and Chapter 14 *Kerberos V5*, refers to the encrypted piece of information that the KDC gives to Alice to pass along to Bob as a **ticket** to Bob. The ticket is information that will allow Alice to access Bob:

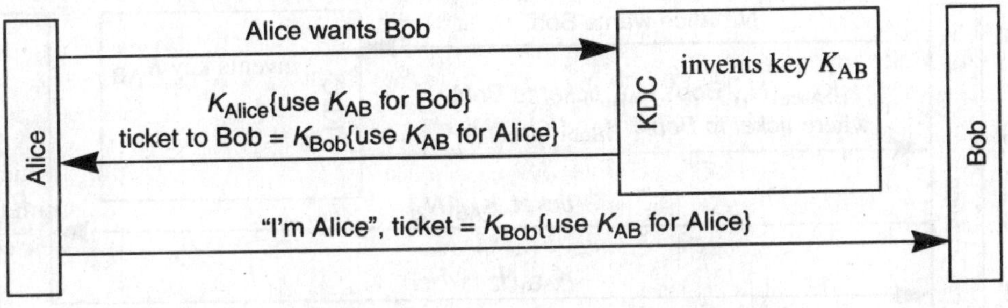

Protocol 11-17. KDC operation (in practice)

Protocol 11-17 is incomplete. It has to be followed by a mutual authentication exchange between Bob and Alice in which they prove to each other that they know key K_{AB}. But in §11.2 *Mutual Authentication* we've described how they can do that.

11.4.1 Needham-Schroeder

A classic protocol for authentication using KDCs was designed by Needham and Schroeder. It is very similar to the protocol we just described, and it completes the exchange by doing the mutual authentication between Alice and Bob. [NEED78]. The Needham Schroeder protocol is important because it is a classic KDC-arbitrated authentication protocol and many others have been modeled after it. The Kerberos protocol is based on it, and it is instructive to understand its strengths and weaknesses.

The paper gives a few variants, but the basic Needham-Schroeder protocol is shown as Protocol 11-18. Let's analyze this protocol. First we must apologize for the arcaneness of the analysis. It's unfortunately necessary to go into this depth in order to really understand a protocol. Without a thorough understanding, there might be subtle security flaws.

The terminology **nonce** refers to a number that is used only once. A nonce could be a sequence number (provided that state is not lost during crashes), or a large random number. It also could be a timestamp, if you believe that your clock never goes backwards, but Needham and Schroeder specifically wanted to avoid dependence on timestamps (see §11.5 *Nonce Types* for more detail on nonces).

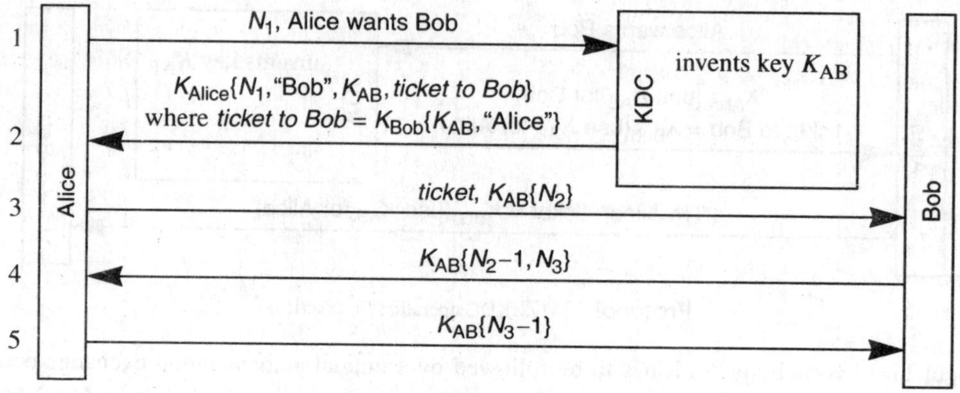

Protocol 11-18. Needham-Schroeder

Message 1 tells the KDC that Alice wants to talk to Bob. The purpose of the nonce N_1 is to assure Alice that she is really talking to the KDC. The (admittedly far-fetched) threat the protocol is trying to avoid is where Trudy has stolen an old key of Bob's, and stolen the message where Alice had previously requested a key for Bob. Bob, realizing Trudy has stolen his key, has changed his key. Trudy waits around until Alice makes a request to the KDC to talk to Bob. Trudy then replays the stolen message, which looks like an ordinary reply from the KDC. Then Trudy successfully impersonates Bob to Alice, because Trudy knows the key that Alice thinks the KDC just created for Alice and Bob. As we've already said, it is hard to imagine a circumstance where this would be a practical threat, but adding the nonce costs virtually nothing, and it removes the need to think about whether the threat might be practical in any particular circumstance.

In message 2, the KDC securely (i.e. encrypted and integrity-protected) gives Alice the key K_{AB} it has generated for Alice and Bob to share. It puts in the string "Bob" to make it impossible for Trudy to tamper with Alice's request, substituting the string "Trudy" for "Bob" and then being able to trick Alice into talking to Trudy and thinking that Trudy is Bob. If Trudy were to tamper with message 1 by substituting her name for Bob's, then Alice will discover, in message 2, that the KDC has just given her a key to communicate with Trudy, not Bob. In message 2, along with the encrypted key K_{AB} and Bob's name, the KDC also gives Alice a ticket to Bob. The ticket to Bob consists of the key K_{AB} and Alice's name, encrypted with Bob's key. To Alice, the ticket will just be a pile of unintelligible bits. The Needham-Schroeder protocol has been criticized for doubly encrypting the ticket. The ticket is sent encrypted with Alice's key, though it would have been just as secure to send it in the clear.

In message 3, Alice sends a challenge (N_2) to Bob, encrypted with K_{AB}, along with the ticket. Bob decrypts the ticket to find the shared key K_{AB}. He uses K_{AB} to extract N_2. Alice knows that only someone who knows Bob's key can decrypt the ticket and thereby discover the shared key K_{AB}. In message 4, Bob proves he knows K_{AB}, since he was able to find N_2. Likewise, Bob assumes that it must be Alice if she knows K_{AB} because the KDC puts Alice's name in the ticket with K_{AB}. In message 4, in addition to sending back N_2 (actually a decremented version of N_2), he includes a challenge N_3 encrypted with K_{AB}, and Alice sends back (in message 5) a message proving she knows K_{AB}.

There is an interesting reflection attack to which the protocol would be vulnerable if the encryption in message 4 were done using, say, DES in ECB mode. Suppose each of the nonces were 64 bits long. Because of the nature of ECB, N_2-1 and N_3 would each be separately encrypted. Suppose Trudy wants to impersonate Alice to Bob. First she eavesdrops on an authentication handshake where Alice talks to Bob. So Trudy sees messages 3 and 4. Later, she replays message 3 to Bob. Bob will respond with $K_{AB}\{N_2-1,N_4\}$ (where N_4 is a nonce different from the one Bob chose last time he talked to Alice). Trudy can't return $K_{AB}\{N_4-1\}$, but she can open a new connection to Bob, this time splicing in $K_{AB}\{N_4\}$ instead of $K_{AB}\{N_2\}$. Bob will return $K_{AB}\{N_4-1,N_5\}$. Then Trudy can take the first encrypted block, which will be $K_{AB}\{N_4-1\}$ and return that as message 5 of her first connection. In fact she will never have found out what N_4 was, but she didn't need to know N_4. She just needed to know $K_{AB}\{N_4-1\}$.

If encryption were done in CBC mode instead of ECB mode, Trudy would not be able to accomplish this, because she couldn't splice pieces of messages. But if encryption were done in CBC mode, there would be no reason to have Bob and Alice decrement each other's nonces. Message 4 could just as securely be $K_{AB}\{N_2,N_3\}$, and message 5 could just as securely be $K_{AB}\{N_3\}$.

The lesson to be learned is that if pieces of a message must, for security reasons, be sent together, then the entire message must be integrity-protected so that parts of it cannot be modified by an attacker.

11.4.2 Expanded Needham-Schroeder

There is a remaining security vulnerability with Protocol 11-18. Suppose Trudy finds out Alice's key. Trudy can of course, at that point, claim to be Alice and get the KDC to give Trudy (which the KDC thinks is Alice), a shared key to Bob and a ticket to Bob. There's really nothing we can do about Trudy impersonating Alice if Trudy steals Alice's key. But we'd like it to be possible to prevent Trudy from doing any more damage once Alice changes her key. The problem is, with the protocol we've just described, the ticket to Bob stays valid even if Alice changes her key.

The vulnerability can occur even if Trudy only manages to capture a previous key used by Alice, say J_{Alice}, and not the key Alice is using now. Suppose that when Alice was using J_{Alice}, Trudy had overheard (and recorded) Alice asking the KDC for a ticket for Bob. At that time, the KDC would have generated a shared key J_{AB}, and Trudy would have seen $J_{Alice}\{N_1,\text{"Bob"},J_{AB},K_{Bob}\{J_{AB},\text{"Alice"}\}\}$. At the time, Trudy could not decrypt the message, but we'll assume she's stored it away, hoping to capture an old key of Alice's. Once Trudy does discover J_{Alice}, she can interpret the messages she's recorded, discover J_{AB}, and, using the ticket

$K_{Bob}\{J_{AB}$, "Alice"}, she can convince Bob that Alice will be talking to him using J_{AB}. The fact that the KDC knew Alice's key changed is irrelevant; the KDC doesn't participate in this new authentication.

A paper [DENN81] pointed out this weakness, and in [NEED87], a suggested fix was proposed by adding two additional messages. Alice requests a nonce N_B from Bob, which Alice will send to the KDC, and the KDC will package N_B in the ticket to Bob. This will reassure Bob that whoever is talking to him has talked to the KDC since Bob generated N_B. Once Alice changes her key, Trudy will not be able to talk to the KDC using Alice's old key, and any recorded messages from the KDC using an old key of Alice's will also not be useful. The proposed protocol added 2 messages, and therefore uses 7 messages. The protocol can, however, be reduced to 6 messages (see Homework Problem 9).

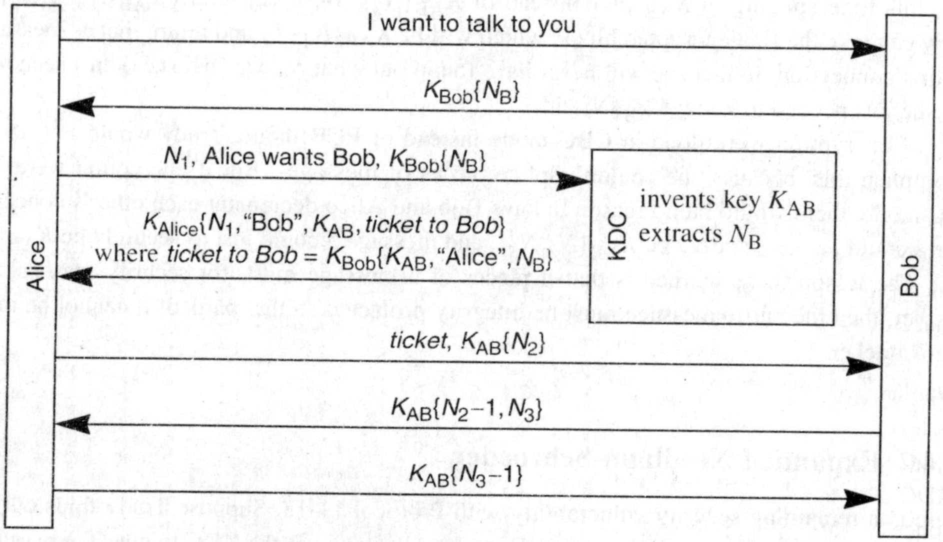

Protocol 11-19. Expanded Needham-Schroeder

11.4.3 Otway-Rees

In [OTWA87], an improved authentication protocol is given. It also solves the ticket invalidation problem, and it does mutual authentication in 5 messages.

Otway and Rees mention that they were inspired by a remark from Needham that *the suspicious party should always generate a challenge*. Let's look at their protocol (Protocol 11-20). Alice generates two nonces. One, N_C, is sent in the clear to Bob. In addition N_C is included (along with

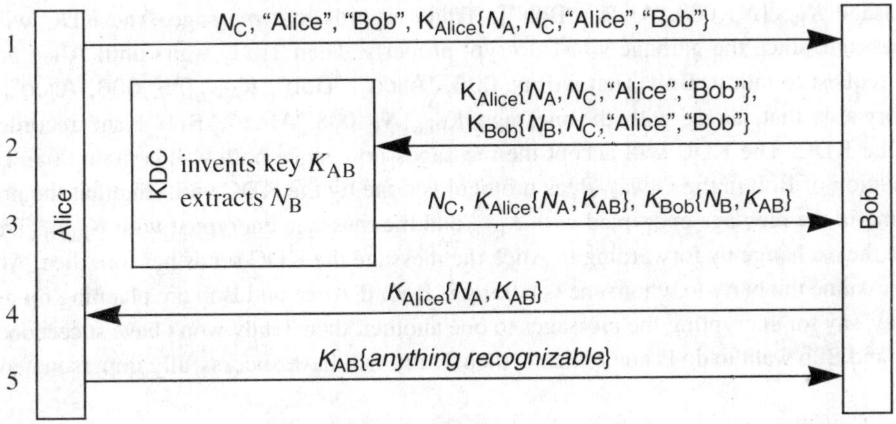

Protocol 11-20. Otway-Rees

the other nonce, N_A) in a message encrypted by Alice that Bob cannot interpret. It just looks like a pile of bits, and he will simply forward $K_{Alice}\{N_A, N_C,$"Alice","Bob"$\}$ to the KDC.

In message 2, Bob forwards the encrypted message Alice sent, along with a message Bob encrypts which includes his own nonce N_B, the nonce N_C that Alice sent in the clear, "Alice", and "Bob", to the KDC. The KDC checks to make sure that the common nonce N_C is the same in both encrypted messages. If not, the KDC will reject the message. The fact that they are the same proves that Bob is really Bob, since only someone knowing K_{Bob} can encrypt N_C inside a message.

In message 3, the KDC gives Bob a message to forward to Alice. That message, when forwarded to Alice, reassures Alice that both the KDC and Bob are legitimate. (Alice knows the KDC is legitimate because it encrypts N_A with key K_{Alice}. Alice knows Bob is legitimate because the KDC would not have continued the protocol if it hadn't already verified that Bob was legit.) The KDC also tells Bob the common key, and reassures Bob that it is really the KDC by putting Bob's nonce N_B inside the message to Bob.

Message 4 is merely having Bob forward $K_{Alice}\{N_A, K_{AB}\}$ to Alice. In message 5, Alice proves her identity to Bob by showing that she knows K_{AB}. Bob does not need to prove his identity explicitly to Alice because Alice will assume that the KDC authenticated Bob.

In fact, this protocol could be simplified by getting rid of one of Alice's nonces (see Homework Problem 4).

If we want to be really paranoid, then for subtle reasons it is necessary in the Otway-Rees protocol that N_C be not just a nonce but also unpredictable. Otherwise Trudy, in a rather involved scenario, could impersonate Bob to Alice. This is the way it would work: Suppose Alice is using a sequence number for N_C. Trudy watches and sees that Alice is currently using, say, 007 for N_C. So Trudy sends a message to Bob claiming to be Alice. She sends 008, "Alice", "Bob", *garbage*. Bob can't tell that the fourth element in the message is garbage. He forwards *garbage* on, along with his own message $K_{Bob}\{N_B, 008, \text{"Alice"}, \text{"Bob"}\}$. Trudy records that message. The KDC will reject Bob's message, since the garbage won't decrypt properly. Then Trudy waits until Alice generates her next request to talk to Bob. That will be 008, "Alice", "Bob", $K_{Alice}\{N_A, 008, \text{"Alice"}, \text{"Bob"}\}$. Trudy forwards that, along with the message $K_{Bob}\{N_B, 008, \text{"Alice"}, \text{"Bob"}\}$ she recorded from Bob, to the KDC. The KDC will accept the messages now since both will contain 008. The only authentication of Bob in the Otway-Rees protocol is done by the KDC verifying that the nonce N_C is the same in the message encrypted with K_{Bob} and the message encrypted with K_{Alice}. Trudy can complete the exchange by forwarding to Alice the message the KDC sends her for Alice. Alice will wrongly assume the party to whom she is talking is Bob. If Alice and Bob are planning on using the shared key, say for encrypting the messages to one another, then Trudy won't have succeeded. But if all Alice and Bob want to do is authenticate, then Trudy will have successfully impersonated Bob to Alice.

The Kerberos authentication service (see Chapter 13 *Kerberos V4*) is roughly based on the Needham-Schroeder protocol. It looks a lot simpler than these protocols because it assumes a universal idea of time, and includes expiration dates in messages. The basic Kerberos protocol is:

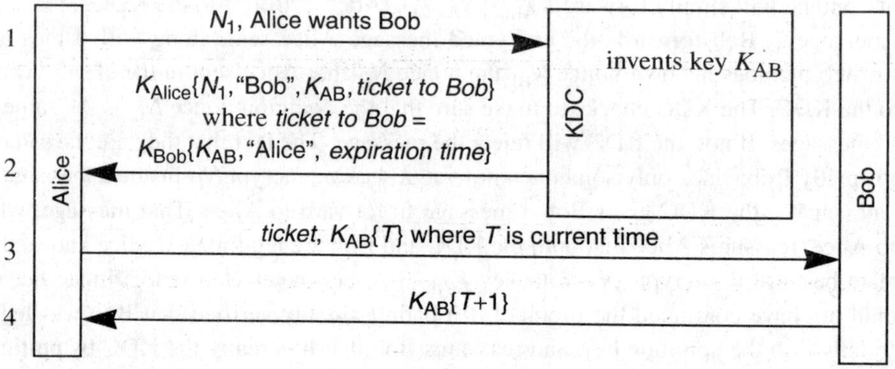

Protocol 11-21. Kerberos

11.5 NONCE TYPES

A **nonce** is a quantity which any given user of a protocol uses only once. Many protocols use nonces, and there are different types of nonces with different sorts of properties. It is possible to introduce security weaknesses by using a nonce with the wrong properties. Various forms of nonce are a timestamp, a large random number, or a sequence number. What's different about these quantities? A large random number tends to make the best nonce, because it cannot be guessed or predicted (as can sequence numbers and timestamps). This is somewhat unintuitive, since non-reuse is only probabilistic. But a random number of 128 bits or more has a negligible chance of being reused. A timestamp requires reasonably synchronized clocks. A sequence number requires nonvolatile state (so that a node can be sure it doesn't use the same number twice even if it crashes and restarts between attempts). When are these properties important?

Protocol 11-22 is a protocol in which the unpredictability of the challenge is important. Let's

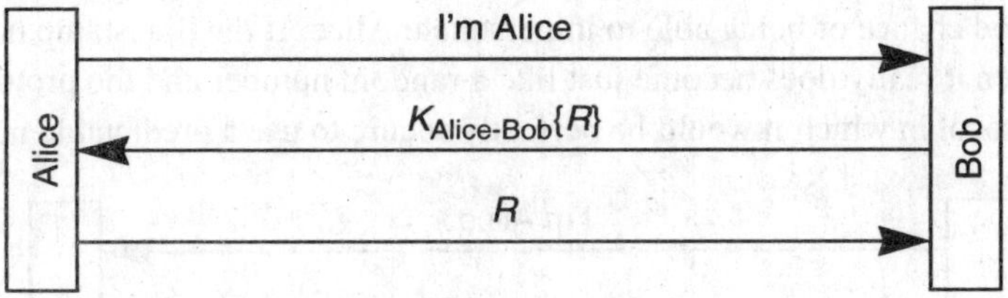

Protocol 11-22. Protocol in which *R* must be unpredictable

say Bob is using a sequence number, and when Alice attempts to log in, Bob encrypts the next sequence number and transmits it to Alice, Alice decrypts the challenge and transmits it to Bob. Let's say our eavesdropper Eve watches Alice's authentication exchange, and sees Alice return an *R* of 7482. If Eve knows Bob is using sequence numbers for the challenge, she can then claim to be Alice, get an undecipherable pile of bits from Bob (the encrypted challenge), and return 7483. Bob will be suitably impressed and assume he's talking to Alice. So it is obvious in this protocol that Bob's challenge has to be unpredictable.

How about if we do it the other way, i.e., make Alice do the encryption as in Protocol 11-23?

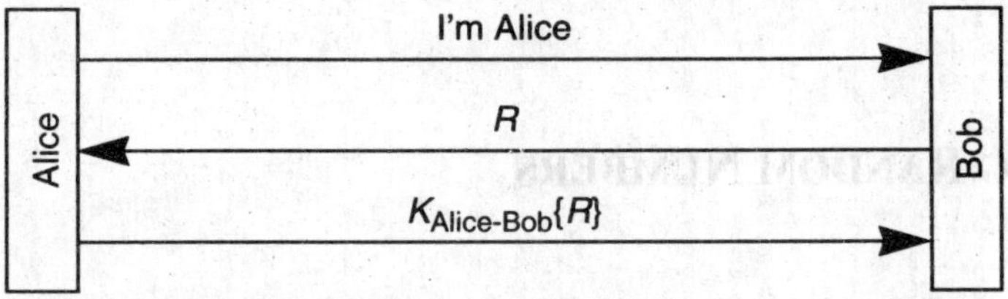

Protocol 11-23. Another protocol in which *R* must be unpredictable

Must the challenge then be unpredictable? Let's say again that Bob is using sequence numbers. Eve watches Alice's authentication exchange and sees that *R* is 7482. Then Eve lies in wait, impersonating Bob's network address, hoping to entrap Alice into authenticating herself to Eve. When she does, Eve sends her the challenge 7483, and Alice will return the encrypted 7483. Now Eve can impersonate Alice to Bob, since Bob's challenge will be 7483, and Eve will know how to encrypt that. This is a lot like a bucket brigade attack (see §6.4.1 *The Bucket Brigade/Man-in-the-Middle Attack*), to which any authentication-only protocol is vulnerable, but this is somewhat worse. In the bucket brigade attack, Eve has to impersonate Bob's address to Alice and Alice's address to Bob while both Alice and Bob are available on the network. In contrast this attack allows Eve to impersonate Bob's address to Alice when Bob is down (and likewise Alice's address when Alice is down). In many cases it is easier to impersonate someone's address if that someone is not available on the network.

These protocols are also insecure if timestamps are used. Eve has to guess the timestamp Bob will use, and she might be off by a minute or two. If the timestamp has coarse granularity, say seconds, Eve has a good chance of being able to impersonate Alice. If the timestamp has, say, nanosecond granularity, then it really does become just like a random number and the protocol is secure.

Here's a protocol in which it would be perfectly secure to use a predictable nonce for *R*. Even

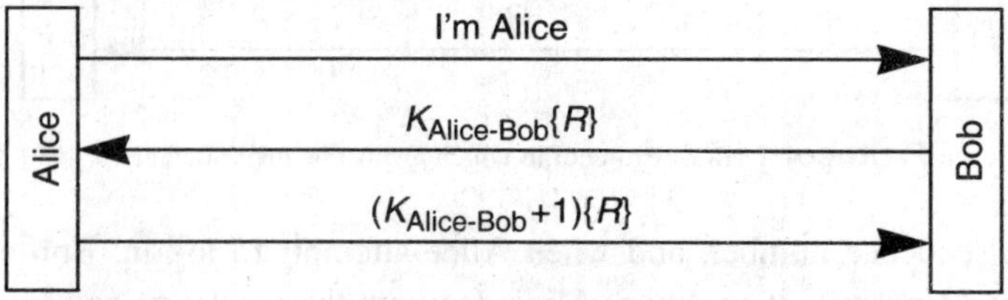

Protocol 11-24. Protocol in which *R* need not be unpredictable

if Eve could predict what *R* would be, she can't predict either the value sent by Bob or the appropriate response from Alice.

Getting truly random numbers can be expensive. A common method of obtaining pseudorandom numbers is by using a key known only to the node generating the numbers, and encrypting any sort of nonce, say a sequence number or timestamp.

11.6 PICKING RANDOM NUMBERS

> *The use of pseudo-random processes to generate secret quantities can result in pseudo-security.*
> —Richard Pitkin

You can have perfect cryptographic algorithms, and perfectly designed protocols, but if you can't select good random numbers, your system can be remarkably insecure. Random numbers may be required in choosing cryptographic keys, challenges, IVs, or per-message secrets for ElGamal/DSS signatures (see §6.5.5 *Per-Message Secret Number*).

Although I_3'd love to rigorously define "random", I_2 won't let me_3 because a really rigorous definition is beyond the scope and spirit of the book. For instance, in [KNUT69], fifteen pages are devoted to coming up with a definition of a random sequence. For those readers who are not intimidated by notions such as (m,k)-distributed, serial correlation coefficients, and Riemann-integrability (don't try to find those terms in our glossary), the discussion of randomness in [KNUT69] is actually very interesting.

The distinction is often made between *random* and *pseudorandom*. A *pseudorandom* number generator is a deterministic algorithm. The entire sequence it will generate is determined by its initial state. A *random* number generator is one that truly picks numbers unpredictably. It is difficult to have a source of true randomness. It can be done with special hardware that does something like measure the low order bits of a counter that counts radioactive particles per unit time. Although such hardware would not be difficult or expensive to provide [DAVI84b], most computers do not have it, so the typical technique is to use a pseudorandom number generator. Sometimes computers use the people they interact with as a source of randomness, for instance, by timing their keystrokes. Such a technique is useful to obtain a few bits of randomness, perhaps to seed a pseudorandom number generator.

Applications that use random numbers have different requirements. For most applications, for instance one that generates test cases for debugging a computer program, all that might be required is that the numbers are spread around with no obvious pattern. For such applications it might be perfectly reasonable to use something like the digits of π. However, for cryptographic applications such as choosing a key, it is essential that the numbers be unguessable.

Consider the following pseudorandom number generator. It starts with a truly random seed, say by timing a human's keystrokes. Then it computes a hash of the seed, then at each step it computes a hash of the output of the previous step. Assuming a good hash function, the output will pass any sort of statistical tests for randomness, but an intruder that captures one of the intermediate quantities will be able to compute the rest.

It is possible to make a pseudorandom number generator that is as good as a source of true random numbers provided that it can be provided with an adequately unguessable seed. For example, a generator that outputs the hash of the seed, and thereafter outputs the hash of the previous output concatenated with the seed would be adequate provided, of course, that the seed was sufficiently unguessable.

Implementations have made some amusing mistakes. Typical mistakes are:

- seeding the generator with a seed that is from too small a space, say 16 bits. Suppose each time a cryptographic key needed to be chosen the application obtained 16 bits worth of true randomness from special purpose hardware and used those 16 bits to seed a pseudorandom number generator. The problem is, there would be only 65536 possible keys it would ever choose, and that is a very small space for an adversary (equipped with a computer) to search. Jeff Schiller found an application that used this technique with a seed that was only 8 bits! (The application has since been fixed.)

- using a hash of the current time when an application needs a random value. The problem is, some clocks do not have fine granularity, so an intruder that knew approximately when the program was run would not need to search a very large space to find the exact clock value for the seed. For instance, if a clock has 1/60 second granularity and the intruder knew the program chose the user's key somewhere within a particular hour, there would only be 60×60×60 = 216000 possible values.
- divulging the seed value. An implementation, again discovered by Jeff Schiller (who warned the implementers so that the implementation has been fixed), used the time of day to choose a per-message encryption key. The time of day in this case may have had sufficient granularity, but the problem was that the application included the time of day in the unencrypted header of the message!

In general the subroutines provided in programming languages for "random numbers" are not designed to be unguessable. Instead they are designed merely to pass statistical tests.

A good strategy for finding a suitable seed for a pseudorandom number generator is to hash together all the sources of randomness you can find, e.g., timing of keystrokes, disk seek times, count of packet arrivals, etc. If any of the sources are unguessable the result will be. Even better, if there is any access to a good quality secret, hashing in the secret will make the seed unguessable. Note that if the secret is not of good quality, this strategy can backfire and give the attacker who learns one of your random numbers (say for an IV) enough information to do off-line password guessing.

For more reading on the subject of randomness, see RFC 1750.

> *The generation of random numbers is too important to be left to chance.*
> Robert Coveyou, Oak Ridge National Laboratory

11.7 PERFORMANCE CONSIDERATIONS

In addition to the security issues in the design of authentication protocols, there are also performance considerations. As CPUs get faster, performance becomes less important, but we haven't yet reached the point where it can be ignored. Metrics to be considered in evaluating the performance of an authentication protocol include:

- number of cryptographic operations using a private key
- number of cryptographic operations using a public key
- number of bytes encrypted or decrypted using a secret key

- number of bytes to be cryptographically hashed
- number of messages transmitted

Note that public key operations are typically counted in blocks, while secret key and message digest operations are counted in bytes. The reason for this is that public key operations are so expensive that large amounts of data are not processed with public key operations. Public key operations are typically done on something that fits within a block, such as a secret key or a message digest of a message.

For RSA, the de facto standard public key cryptographic algorithm, private key operations are much more expensive than public key operations. Other public key algorithms have different rules. Most secret key algorithms have similar performance for encrypting and decrypting. As a general rule, computing a message digest has somewhat better performance (per byte) than secret key encryption, but there is not a dramatic difference.

Besides the processing power cost of cryptographic operations, there is also the real-time cost of performing an authentication. If an authentication protocol is running over a link to Mars, the number of round-trip message exchanges will certainly be the dominant factor in authentication time (as opposed to the processing time required to do the cryptographic operations). As processors get faster and the speed of light stays the same, the number of round-trip exchanges grows in relative importance as a factor in authentication time. Another consideration in real-time calculations is that if cryptographic operations can go on in parallel at the two ends of a connection, they will take less real time to complete. Some protocols are designed with this in mind (see §24.5.5 *Lotus Notes Authentication*, for example).

Perhaps the most important optimization that can be added to a protocol is the ability to cache state from a previous authentication to make it easier for the same two parties to authenticate a second time. If a public key based authentication establishes a shared secret key as a side effect, that shared secret key can be used to do a more efficient authentication protocol on a second round if both ends remember it (see §16.9 *Session Resumption*). In a KDC-based scheme, it may be possible for one of the parties to remember a ticket from a previous authentication and thus avoid having to interact with the KDC on a second authentication (see §13.2 *Tickets and Ticket-Granting Tickets*).

11.8 AUTHENTICATION PROTOCOL CHECKLIST

By way of review, the following is a checklist of things to consider when designing or evaluating an authentication protocol. Assume that Alice initiates conversations with Bob, and that Alice and Bob each have a database of information (some secret, some not) used in running the protocol. The list is organized around what intruder Trudy might attempt to do and what the protocol being designed should protect against.

- *Eavesdrop*. Even if Trudy can watch the messages between Alice and Bob pass over the network, she shouldn't be able to
  - learn the contents of the messages between Alice and Bob
  - learn information that would enable her to impersonate either Alice or Bob in a subsequent exchange
  - learn information that would enable her to impersonate Alice to another replica of Bob
  - learn information that would permit her to do an off-line password-guessing attack against either Alice's or Bob's secret information
- *Initiate a conversation pretending to be Alice*. Trudy can send a message to Bob and claim to be Alice and proceed at least partway through an authentication exchange. In doing so, she shouldn't be able to
  - convince Bob she is Alice
  - learn information that would enable her to do an off-line password-guessing attack against either Alice's or Bob's secret information
  - learn information that would enable her to impersonate Alice on a subsequent (or interleaved) attempt
  - learn information that would enable her to impersonate Bob to Alice
  - trick Bob into signing or decrypting something
- *Lie in wait at Bob's network address and accept a connection from Alice*. Trudy can get at least partway through an authentication exchange. In doing so, she shouldn't be able to
  - convince Alice that Trudy is Bob
  - learn information that would enable her to do an off-line password-guessing attack against either Alice's or Bob's secret information
  - learn information that would enable her to impersonate Bob on a subsequent attempt
  - learn information that would enable her to impersonate Alice to Bob
  - trick Alice into signing or decrypting something
- *Read Alice's database*. If Trudy can get all of Alice's secrets, she can convince Bob she is Alice; she can also conduct an off-line password-guessing attack against Bob's secret information (assuming Bob's secret is derived from a password), since Alice must have enough information to know if someone is really Bob. She should not, however, be able to

    - impersonate Bob to Alice
    - decrypt old recorded conversations between Alice and Bob

- *Read Bob's database*. If Trudy can get all of Bob's secrets, she can convince Alice she is Bob; she can also conduct an off-line password-guessing attack against Alice's secret information since Bob must have enough information to know if someone is really Alice. She should not, however, be able to
    - impersonate Alice to Bob
    - decrypt old recorded conversations between Alice and Bob
- *Sit on the net between Alice and Bob (e.g. as a router) and examine and/or modify messages in transit between them*. Trudy can clearly prevent Alice and Bob from communicating, but she shouldn't be able to
    - learn information that would permit her to do an off-line password-guessing attack against either Alice's or Bob's secret information
    - learn the contents of Alice's and Bob's messages
    - hijack a conversation (continue a conversation started up by a legitimate party without the other side noticing the change)
    - modify messages or rearrange/replay/reverse the direction of messages, causing Alice and/or Bob to misinterpret their messages to one another
- *Some combination of the above*. There are clearly too many possibilities to enumerate, but some examples would be
    - Even after reading both Alice's and Bob's databases, it should not be possible to decrypt old recorded conversations between them.
    - Even after reading Bob's database and eavesdropping on an authentication exchange, it should not be possible to impersonate Alice to Bob.

It isn't necessarily the right engineering trade-off to devise a protocol that passes all the criteria we mention above. For instance, in some cases eavesdropping or address impersonation might be a sufficiently unlikely threat that a much simpler protocol will suffice. Also, sometimes secrets are chosen from a large enough space that password guessing is not feasible.

11.9 HOMEWORK

1. Suppose Trudy hijacks a conversation between Alice and Bob. This means that after the initial handshake, Trudy sends messages with source address equal to Alice's source address. Suppose the network allows Trudy to insert a fake source address (Alice's source address), but does not deliver packets destined for Alice's address to Trudy. What are the problems involved in having Trudy transmit a file to Bob as if she were Alice? Consider potential problems with flow control and file transfer protocols when Trudy cannot see return traffic from Bob.

2. In §11.2 *Mutual Authentication*, we discuss the reflection attack and note that Protocol 11-8 is susceptible, but Protocol 11-7 is not. How about Protocol 11-11?

3. In §11.3.1 *Shared Secret* we discuss various possibilities for forming a session key. Remember that R is the challenge sent by Bob to Alice, and A is Alice's secret, which Bob also knows. Which of the following are secure for a session key?

   $A \oplus R$ $\{R+A\}_A$ $\{A\}_A$ $\{R\}_{R+A}$

4. Design a variant of Otway-Rees (page 279) that only has one nonce generated by Alice and one nonce generated by Bob. Explain why it is still as secure.

5. Suppose we are using a three-message mutual authentication protocol, and Alice initiates contact with Bob. Suppose we wish Bob to be a stateless server, and therefore it is inconvenient to require him to remember the challenge he sent to Alice. Let's modify the exchange so that Alice sends the challenge back to Bob, along with the encrypted challenge. So the protocol is:

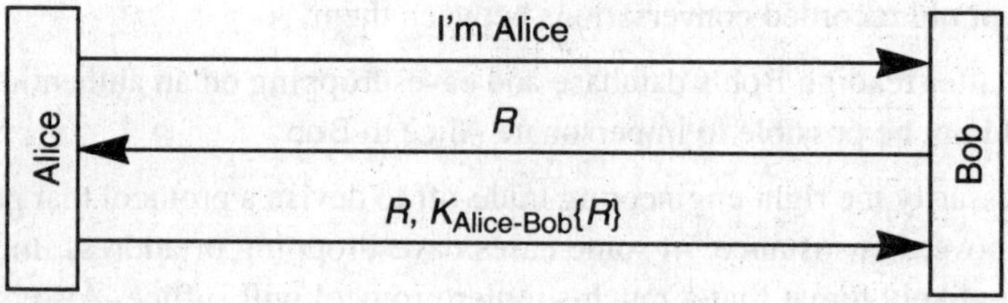

Is this protocol secure?

6. Let's modify the protocol from the previous problem so that Bob sends both a challenge, and a challenge encrypted with a key that only he knows, to Alice:

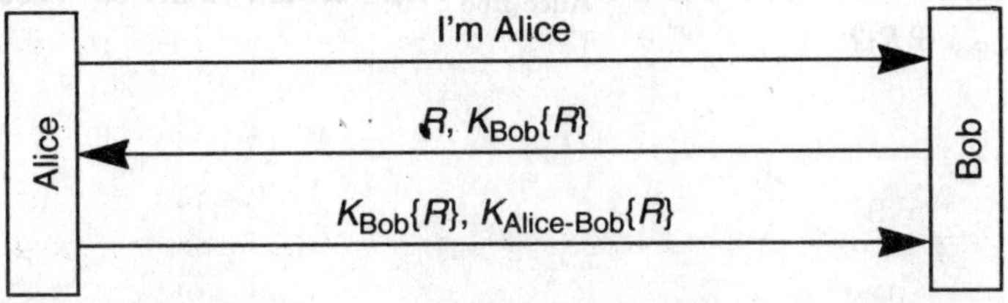

Is this protocol secure?

7. In the discussion of Protocol 11-3 on page 261, Bob remembers all the timestamps he's seen within the last 10 minutes. Why is it sufficient for him to remember only 10 minutes worth of timestamps?

8. Design a two-message authentication protocol, assuming that Alice and Bob know each other's public keys, which accomplishes both mutual authentication and establishment of a session key.

9. The Expanded Needham-Schroeder Protocol (page 278) can be shortened to a 6-message protocol without loss of security by merely removing the 7th message. Why is this true? (Hint: the purpose of the 7th message is to prove to Bob that he is talking to Alice, but he already knows that. Why?)

10. §11.4 *Mediated Authentication (with KDC)* describes several protocols. For each of those protocols, describe which nonces have to be unpredictable (i.e., sequence numbers would not be good).

11. As we pointed out in §9.1 *Password-Based Authentication*, cellular phones are vulnerable to a fraud known as "cloning". The protocol cellular phones use is that a phone transmits its telephone number followed by a cleartext password. The phone company checks its database of phone number/password to make sure the phone is legitimate before allowing the call to go through. The phone number is the one billed. Suggest a design based on public key, and one based on secret key, technology. Can you guard against the phone company database being stolen?

12. There is a product which consists of a fancy telephone that, when talking to a compatible fancy telephone, does a Diffie-Hellman key exchange in order to establish a secret key, and the remainder of the conversation is encrypted. Suppose you are a wiretapper. How can you listen to a conversation between two such telephones?

13. In §11.1.1 *Shared Secret*, we discussed using MD5($K_{\text{Alice-Bob}}|R$) as the method of encrypting R with $K_{\text{Alice-Bob}}$. (When we say $K_{\text{Alice-Bob}}|R$ we mean $K_{\text{Alice-Bob}}$ concatenated with R.) Suppose instead we used MD5($K_{\text{Alice-Bob}} \vee R$). Would that be secure? How about MD5($K_{\text{Alice-Bob}} \oplus R$)?

12 *Strong Password Protocols*

12.1 Introduction

Suppose a user, Alice, wants to use any workstation to log into a server, Bob. Assume she has nothing but a password with which to authenticate herself. Assume the workstation has no user-specific configuration, such as the user's trusted CAs, or the user's private key. Also assume that the software on the workstation is trustworthy. There are various ways Alice might use a password to authenticate herself to server Bob:

- Transmit it over the wire, in the clear. This leaves Alice's password vulnerable to discovery by an eavesdropper, or someone impersonating Bob.
- Do an anonymous Diffie-Hellman exchange to establish a secret key and an encrypted tunnel, and send the password over that encrypted tunnel. This protects Alice's password from a passive attacker, but not from someone impersonating Bob.
- Create an SSL connection, using the trust anchors configured into the client machine and a server certificate issued by one of those trust anchors, so that Alice's machine can authenticate Bob, and then send the password SSL-encrypted to Bob. This relies on the trust anchors at Alice's machine being configured properly, and none of the trust anchor organizations having inadvertently (or maliciously) certified a bogus public key as being Bob's.
- Compute a hash of Alice's password, and use that as a secret key in a challenge/response authentication handshake—Bob sends challenge R, Alice responds with f(password, R). This leaves Alice's password vulnerable to a dictionary attack, either by an eavesdropper or someone impersonating Bob.
- Use a one time password scheme like Lamport's hash or S/KEY (see §12.2 *Lamport's Hash*).
- Use a strong password protocol (see §12.3 *Strong Password Protocols*). Strong password protocols are secure even if the shared secret, typically a password, could be broken by an off-

line dictionary attack. The exchange is carefully designed to prevent the opportunity for either a passive attacker or someone impersonating either side to obtain data with which to do a dictionary attack.

12.2 LAMPORT'S HASH

It's a poor sort of memory that only works backwards.
—The White Queen (in *Through the Looking Glass*)

Leslie Lamport invented an interesting one-time password scheme [LAMP81]. This scheme allows Bob to authenticate Alice in a way that neither eavesdropping on an authentication exchange nor reading Bob's database enables someone to impersonate Alice, and it does it without using public key cryptography. Alice (a human) remembers a password. Bob (the server that will authenticate Alice) has a database where it stores, for each user:

- username
- n, an integer which decrements each time Bob authenticates the user
- $\text{hash}^n(\textit{password})$, i.e., hash(hash(...(hash(*password*))...))

First, how is the password database entry associated with Alice configured? Alice chooses a password, and a reasonably large number n (like 1000) is chosen. The user registration software computes x_1=hash(*password*). Then it computes x_2=hash(x_1). It continues this process n times, resulting in $x_n=\text{hash}^n(\textit{password})$, which it sends to Bob, along with n.

When Alice wishes to prove her identity to Bob, she types her name and password to her workstation. The workstation then sends Alice's name to Bob, which sends back n. Then the workstation computes $\text{hash}^{n-1}(\textit{password})$ and sends the result to Bob. Bob takes the received quantity, hashes it once, and compares it with its database. If it matches, Bob considers the response valid, replaces the stored quantity with the received quantity, and replaces n by n–1.

If n ever gets to 1, then Alice needs to set her password again with Bob. There is no completely secure way of doing this over an insecure network, since this scheme does not allow encryption or integrity protection of messages between Alice and Bob. But in practice, in many situations, it suffices for Alice to choose a new password, compute $\text{hash}^n(\textit{new password})$, and transmit $\text{hash}^n(\textit{new password})$ and n to the server unencrypted across the network.

An enhancement is to add **salt**, a number chosen at password installation time to be unique for user Alice. The salt is stored at Bob and concatenated to the password before hashing. So rather than computing $\text{hash}^n(\textit{password})$, the enhanced Lamport hash computes $\text{hash}^n(\textit{password}|\textit{salt})$. To

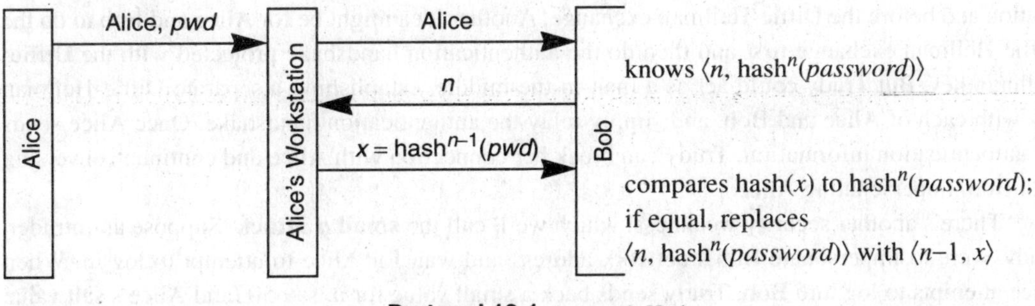

Protocol 12-1. Lamport's Hash

set the password, the workstation chooses a value for salt, and computes x_1=hash(*password*|*salt*), then x_2=hash(x_1), then continues this process n times, resulting in x_n=hash^n(*password*|*salt*), which it sends to Bob, along with n and *salt*.

What do we gain by adding salt? It allows Alice to securely use the same password on multiple servers as long as a different salt value is used when installing the password on each of the other servers. When she logs into Bob, she'll wind up decrementing the n stored at Bob, but this will not affect the n stored at other servers. In other words, when she logs into Bob, if Bob sends her workstation ⟨n=87, *salt*=69⟩, her workstation will compute hash^{86}(*password*|69). If when Bob hashes the received quantity the result matches hash^{87}(*password*|69) in his database, then Bob will decrement n and replace the stored hash with the received hash. When she logs into Fred, Fred might send her workstation ⟨n=127, *salt*=105⟩, in which case her workstation will compute hash^{126}(*password*|105) to send to Fred. A way of ensuring that the salt is different on different servers is to also hash in the server name, as in x_n=hash^n(*password*|*salt*|*servername*).

Another advantage of salt is that Alice does not need to change her password when n decrements to 1 at Bob. Instead the same password can be reinstalled with a different salt value.

There's an additional value to salt, which is the same as the original UNIX reason for adding salt to the password database (see §5.2.4.1 *UNIX Password Hash*). Adding salt prevents an intruder from precomputing hash^k for all passwords in a dictionary and all values of k from 1 through 1000, stealing the database at Bob, and then comparing the precomputed hashes with the stolen password hashes of all the users.

Lamport's hash has interesting properties. It is similar to public key schemes in that the database at Bob is not security sensitive (for reading), other than dictionary attacks to recover the user's password. It has several disadvantages relative to public key schemes. One problem is that you can only log in a finite number of times before having to reinstall password information at the server.

Another problem is there is no mutual authentication, i.e., Alice does not know she is definitely talking to Bob. This makes it difficult to establish a session key or prevent a man-in-the-middle attack. One might try to have Alice authenticate herself and then do a Diffie-Hellman exchange with Bob to establish a session key. But Trudy could hijack the conversation after the inital authentication and before the Diffie-Hellman exchange. Another idea might be for Alice and Bob to do the Diffie-Hellman exchange first and then do the authentication handshake protected with the Diffie-Hellman key. But Trudy could act as a man-in-the-middle, establishing a separate Diffie-Hellman key with each of Alice and Bob, and simply relay the authentication handshake. Once Alice sends the authentication information, Trudy can break her connection with Alice and continue conversing with Bob, impersonating Alice.

There's another security weakness, which we'll call the **small *n* attack**. Suppose an intruder, Trudy, were to impersonate Bob's network address and wait for Alice to attempt to log in. When Alice attempts to log into Bob, Trudy sends back a small value for n, say 50 (and Alice's salt value at Bob, which she can know from having eavesdropped on a previous authentication by Alice to Bob). When Alice responds with $\text{hash}^{50}(\textit{password})$, Trudy will have enough information to impersonate Alice for some time, assuming that the actual n at Bob is greater than 50. What can be done to protect against this? Alice's workstation could display n to the human Alice. If Alice remembers approximately what n should be, then Alice can do a rough sanity check on n.

Lamport's hash can also be used in environments where the workstation doesn't calculate the hash, for example when:

- Alice is logging in from a "dumb terminal"
- Alice is logging in from a workstation that does not have Lamport hash code, or
- Alice is logging in from a workstation that she doesn't trust enough to tell her password

We'll call this the **human and paper** environment, and call the other environment the **workstation** environment. The way Lamport's hash works in the human and paper environment is that when the information $\langle n, \text{hash}^n(\textit{password})\rangle$ is installed at the server, all the values of hash^i(password) for $i<n$ are computed, encoded into a typeable string, printed on a paper, and given to Alice. When she logs in, she uses the string at the top of the page, and then crosses that value out, using the next value the next time. This approach automatically protects against the small n attack. Of course, losing the piece of paper, especially if it falls into the wrong hands, is a problem.

How big a string does Alice have to type? Ordinarily, a hash function is 128 bits, which would mean a string of about 20 characters. This would be fairly annoying to type. But the scheme is sufficiently secure if a 64-bit hash is used, and then Alice only has to type about 10 characters. It's not necessary to invent a 64-bit hash function. Any hash function (such as MD5) can be used, and have all but 64 bits of the output discarded.

It is interesting that the human and paper environment is not vulnerable to the small n attack, since the human just always uses the next value on the list and can't be tricked into sending an item further down on the list.

There is a deployed version of Lamport's hash, known as S/Key, implemented by Phil Karn. It was standardized in RFC 1938 *A one-time password system*. It operates in both the workstation and human and paper environments. It makes no effort to address the small n attack, but it certainly is a vast improvement over cleartext passwords and is gaining popularity.

12.3 STRONG PASSWORD PROTOCOLS

Strong password protocols are designed so that someone who eavesdrops on an authentication exchange, or someone impersonating either end will not obtain enough information to do off-line verification of password guesses. An eavesdropper should not be able to gain any information from observing any number of legitimate exchanges. Someone impersonating either endpoint will be able to do a single on-line password guess. There's really no way to avoid that. If someone correctly guesses the password, they will be able to successfully authenticate. If they guess incorrectly, they will know that they have not successfully authenticated, and therefore their guess must not be the user's password. A false guess will result in an authentication failure, which should generate alarms if they occur in large numbers.

12.3.1 The Basic Form

Bellovin and Merritt created the first strong password protocol. They called it EKE for *encrypted key exchange*. There are other protocols, but they are all conceptually similar. The idea of EKE is that Alice and Bob share a weak secret W, which is a hash of Alice's password. Bob knows W because he stores W. Alice knows W because she computes it from the password.

They do a Diffie-Hellman exchange, encrypting the Diffie-Hellman numbers with W, and then do mutual authentication based on the agreed-upon Diffie-Hellman shared secret, which is a strong secret.

This protocol is quite subtle. The reason it is secure from an eavesdropper is that a Diffie-Hellman transmitted value looks like a random number. An eavesdropper doing a trial decryption of $W\{g^a \bmod p\}$ and $W\{g^b \bmod p\}$ cannot verify a password guess because decrypting with any password will still just look like random numbers. And someone impersonating one side or the other can verify a single password guess as incorrect or correct, but this is an on-line, auditable guess. There is no way to do an off-line dictionary attack. The Diffie-Hellman secret K is a strong secret because an attacker would both have to guess the password and break Diffie-Hellman.

The reason it is secure from someone, say Trudy, impersonating Alice or Bob is that Trudy only knows x for one value of $g^x \bmod p$. Once Trudy encrypts with W, she is committing to a single password guess. (See Homework Problem 14.)

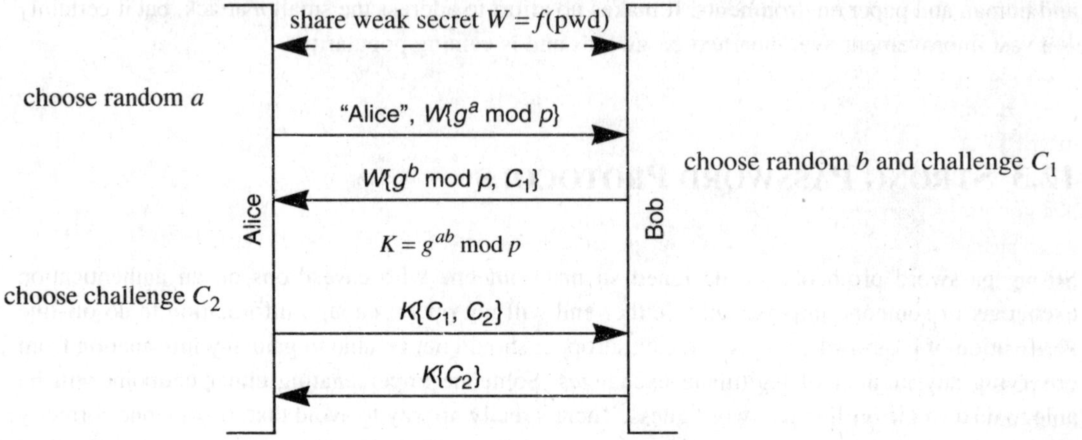

Protocol 12-2. Basic EKE Protocol

Several years later, more or less simultaneously, two other strong password protocols were invented. One was done by Jablon, and was called SPEKE (*simple password exponential key exchange*), and the other was done by Wu and known as SRP (*secure remote password*). We'll describe SRP in section §12.3.4 *SRP (Secure Remote Password)*. Several years after SRP and SPEKE, $\text{we}_{1,2}$ designed PDM (*password derived moduli*).

SPEKE uses W in place of g in the Diffie-Hellman exchange, so rather than transmitting $W\{g^a \bmod p\}$ and agreeing upon $K = g^{ab} \bmod p$ (as would be done in EKE), SPEKE transmits $W^a \bmod p$ and $W^b \bmod p$, and agrees upon the key $K = W^{ab} \bmod p$.

PDM chooses a modulus p which is a function of the password, and uses 2 as the base, so the Diffie-Hellman numbers transmitted are $2^a \bmod p$ and $2^b \bmod p$, and the agreed-upon Diffie-Hellman key is $2^{ab} \bmod p$.

12.3.2 Subtle Details

There is more to making these schemes secure than the basic idea. The original EKE paper proposed many variants of the protocol, many of which were later found to be flawed. The successor protocols have had similar difficulties. To be secure, a protocol must carefully specify some implementation details to avoid an eavesdropper being able to eliminate password guesses. Subsequent papers noted other potential implementation issues. For instance, assume a straightforward encryption of $g^a \bmod p$ with W. Since $g^a \bmod p$ will be less than p, an eavesdropper that does a trial decryption with a guessed password and obtains a value greater than p can eliminate that password. If p were just a little more than a power of 2, an incorrect password would have almost a 50% chance of being eliminated. Each time an eavesdropper saw a value $W\{g^a \bmod p\}$ (each time presumably with a different a), the eavesdropper could eliminate almost half of the passwords. With a dictionary of, say, 50000 potential passwords, the eavesdropper would only need to see about twenty exchanges before narrowing down the possibilities in the dictionary to a single choice.

If SPEKE were not designed carefully it would also have a flaw whereby an eavesdropper might be able to eliminate some password guesses based on seeing W^a mod p. The flaw can be eliminated by making sure that W is a perfect square mod p. Some numbers are generators mod p (g is a generator if $g^1, g^2, g^3, \ldots g^{p-1}$ mod p cycles through all the values from 1 through $p-1$). If g is a generator mod p, then its even powers are the perfect squares mod p (so half of all numbers mod p are perfect squares, and any power of a perfect square is also a perfect square). If some of the Ws generated from passwords for use in SPEKE were perfect squares and some not, then if an eavesdropper Trudy saw a value W^a mod p that was not a perfect square, she would know that none of the passwords that resulted in Ws that were perfect squares could have been Alice's password (since such a password could not have generated a value that was not a square). (To tell if a number is a perfect square mod p, raise it to the power $(p-1)/2$ and see if the result is 1 (mod p).) This is a less serious vulnerability than the EKE vulnerability in the previous paragraph, because in each EKE exchange a different half of the passwords could be eliminated. But in this SPEKE vulnerability, half the passwords (the ones for which W would be a square) would be eliminated if a value W^a mod p that was not a perfect square were seen by an eavesdropper, but there would be no further narrowing down the possibilities no matter how many exchanges were observed.

Both the vulnerabilities mentioned are easily avoided. The EKE vulnerability is avoided by choosing a p which is just a little less than a power of 2. The SPEKE vulnerability is avoided by ensuring that W is a perfect square—hash the password, then square it mod p to get W.

To build a workable protocol from the basic idea of PDM (generating the modulus deterministically from the password with reasonable performance) involves some math that we won't go into in detail because it's not that important for the purpose of this chapter. (For subtle reasons, using 2 for g, the modulus p has to be a safe prime, i.e. $(p-1)/2$ must also be prime, and p must be equal to 11 mod 24.) And there are other attacks that need to be avoided, including timing attacks and the attack in Homework Problem 6.

PDM has interesting performance characteristics. Generating an appropriate prime is very compute-intensive for the client machine (a few seconds). But since the modulus is secret, it is likely that the prime can be smaller than would be considered in traditional Diffie-Hellman, since Diffie-Hellman would have to be broken for each password guess, for each user. If this premise survives scrutiny, PDM can be much more efficient (a factor of about five) for the server. Server performance is more important than client performance because the compute-intensive step of generating the PDM modulus only has to be done once at the client, whereas a server has to process a large and unpredictable number of login attempts.

12.3.3 Augmented Strong Password Protocols

With the schemes in the previous section, if someone knew W, they could impersonate the user. A few years after publishing EKE, Bellovin and Merritt designed a strong password protocol with an additional security property which they called *augmented EKE*. The additional property was preventing someone who has stolen the server database from being able to impersonate the user. The information in the server database would allow an attacker, Trudy, to do a dictionary attack, and if Trudy found the user's password, then she could impersonate the user. But using an augmented form of a strong password protocol, if Trudy's dictionary attack on the stolen server database was unsuccessful, she would not be able to impersonate the user to the server.

All the basic schemes (EKE, SPEKE, and PDM) can be modified to have the augmented property. Another protocol which we'll describe (SRP) only has an augmented form. The idea is for the server to store a quantity derived from the password that can be used to verify the password, but the client machine is required to know the password (not the derived quantity stored at the server). The scheme in augmented EKE is overly complicated and takes too many messages, so we will instead show a simple scheme with the same properties. The strategy will work with any of the schemes (EKE, SPEKE, and PDM), but we'll show it with PDM.

The server will store p, the safe prime derived from the user's password. The server will also store 2^W mod p, where W is a hash of the user's password. The exchange is as follows:

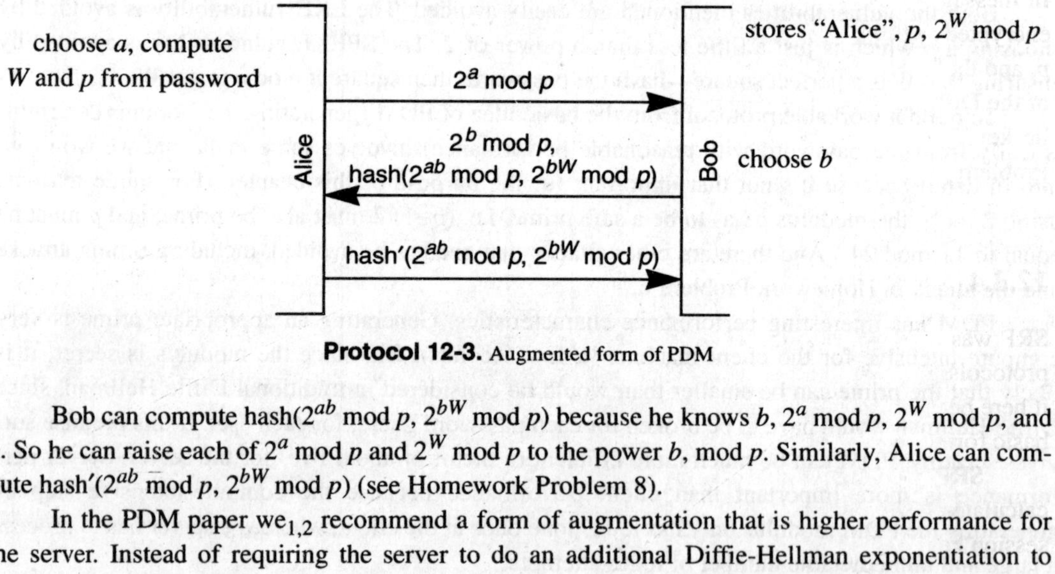

Protocol 12-3. Augmented form of PDM

Bob can compute hash(2^{ab} mod p, 2^{bW} mod p) because he knows b, 2^a mod p, 2^W mod p, and p. So he can raise each of 2^a mod p and 2^W mod p to the power b, mod p. Similarly, Alice can compute hash′(2^{ab} mod p, 2^{bW} mod p) (see Homework Problem 8).

In the PDM paper we$_{1,2}$ recommend a form of augmentation that is higher performance for the server. Instead of requiring the server to do an additional Diffie-Hellman exponentiation to achieve the augmented property, the server does an RSA verify operation, which is much less expensive. This is accomplished by having Bob store, for Alice, an RSA private key encrypted with

Alice's password, and the corresponding public key. Again, this can be done with any of the basic schemes (EKE, SPEKE, or PDM), but in Protocol 12-4 we'll show it using EKE:

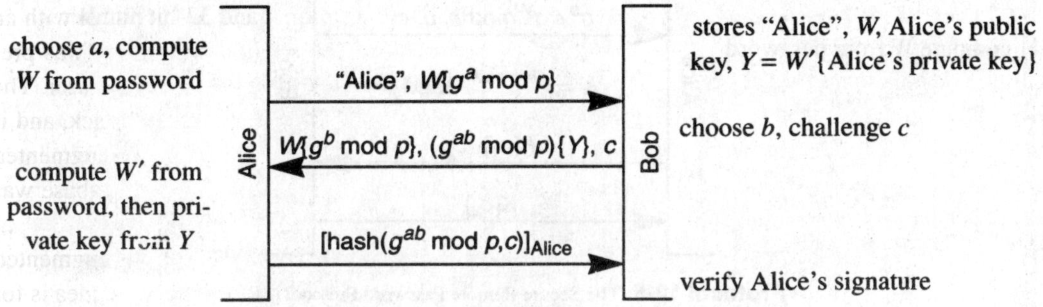

Protocol 12-4. Augmentation based on RSA public keys

In Protocol 12-4, Bob stores Y, which is Alice's private key encrypted with a function of her password. (Note that it has to be a different hash of the password than W, or else someone that stole the server database would be able to obtain her private key, which breaks the augmented property.) Bob also stores Alice's RSA public key corresponding to the encrypted private key. In message 1, Alice sends the usual first EKE message, consisting of her Diffie-Hellman value encrypted with W. In message 2, Bob sends his Diffie-Hellman value, along with Y (Alice's encrypted private key), encrypted with the agreed-upon Diffie-Hellman key. Alice extracts Y by decrypting with g^{ab} mod p, and then decrypts Y with her password to obtain her private key. In message 3, Alice signs a hash of the Diffie-Hellman key and the challenge c, and Bob verifies her signature using the stored public key. This achieves mutual authentication as well as the augmented property (see Homework Problem 9).

12.3.4 SRP (Secure Remote Password)

SRP was invented by Tom Wu [WU98] and is a popular choice by the IETF for strong password protocols. It is documented in RFC 2945. It is harder to understand than the others, but we describe it here because it does appear in many IETF protocols. Unlike EKE, SPEKE, and PDM, there is no basic form of SRP. The augmented property is an intrinsic part of the protocol.

SRP is Protocol 12-4. Bob stores g^W mod p, where W is a function of Alice's password. Alice calculates W from the password. The tricky part is how Alice and Bob each manage to compute the session key K (see Homework Problem 11).

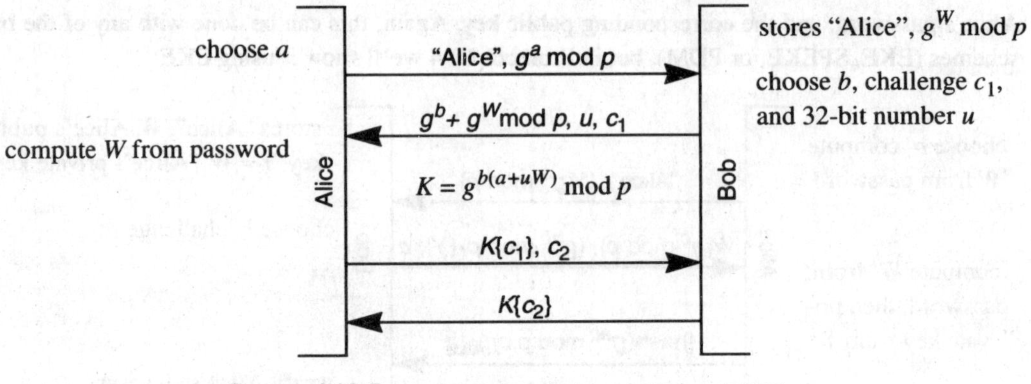

Protocol 12-5. The Secure Remote Password Protocol (SRP)

12.4 STRONG PASSWORD CREDENTIALS DOWNLOAD PROTOCOLS

A **credential** is something that can be used to prove who you are, or prove that you are authorized to do something. In this case, it is easiest to think of it as a private key. It might be nice to assume that Alice has a smart card, that she has remembered to bring her smart card to work, that it is still functional after she accidentally ran it through the washer, and that the workstation has a smart card reader.

But suppose Alice does not have a smart card. All she knows is her name and password. If Alice walks up to a workstation that has trusted software but no user-specific configuration such as her trust anchors, then if she can somehow obtain her private key, she can obtain all the other information necessary to recreate her environment by downloading it from a central place such as the directory. The stored information in the directory can be secure because information such as her trust anchors that need to be integrity-protected can be signed with her private key. Information such as her cookies or browser bookmarks that need to be kept private can be stored encrypted with her public key. So the only issue is obtaining her private key.

We can use strong password protocols to do this. The private key is kept in the directory, encrypted with the user's password. Call that quantity Y. You don't want to make Y world-readable, since someone that has Y can test passwords against it. And you can't use traditional access control since Alice can't prove she's Alice until she obtains Y (and decrypts it with her password). Strong password protocols are ideal for downloading credentials.

For credentials download, the augmented protocols provide no added security. The only purpose of a credentials download protocol is to download *Y*. If someone has stolen Bob's database, then they already know *Y*!

[PERL99A] includes an analysis of credential download protocols, along with a two-message version that can be built upon any basic strong password protocol. Other properties are explored, such as the ability for Bob to save computation by reusing his Diffie-Hellman exponent *b*. In Protocol 12-4 we show one built upon EKE.

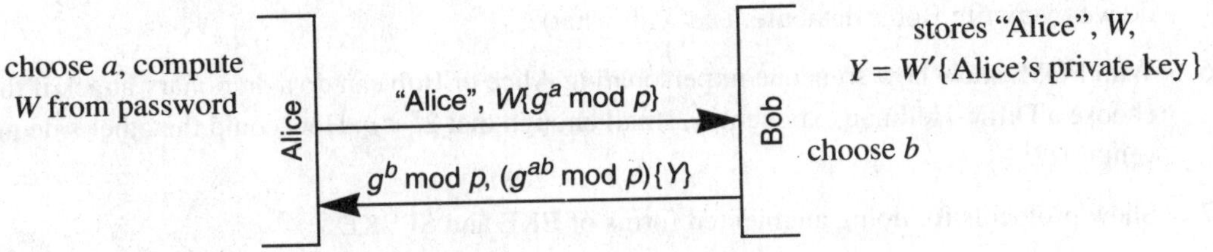

Protocol 12-6. Two-message credential download protocol

Bob cannot tell whether Alice really knew the password, but Alice can only guess one password in each on-line query, since once she encrypts by *W* she is committing to a single password. She only knows the *a* for the quantity she encrypted with the chosen *W*. So Bob can audit download requests and get suspicious if the credentials for the same user were requested too many times. Note that the key *W′* used to encrypt Alice's private key must be different from *W*, or else someone stealing Bob's database (not to mention Bob itself) would know Alice's private key.

12.5 HOMEWORK

1. Given that the Lamport hash (see §12.2 *Lamport's Hash*) value is sent in the clear over the network, why is it more secure than a password?
2. Is the Lamport hash protocol vulnerable to dictionary attack by an eavesdropper? Can someone impersonating the server do a dictionary attack?
3. In §12.2 *Lamport's Hash* we mentioned the notion of using only 64 bits of the hash. At each stage, 128 bits are computed, 64 bits are thrown away, and the hash of the retained 64 bits is used in the next stage. The purpose of only using 64 bits is so that a human does not need to type as long a string. Assuming the person will still only type 64 bits, does it work if hash^n does a hash of all 128 bits of hash^{n-1}, but what the person actually transmits is 64 bits of the result?

4. Design a variant of Lamport's hash using k times more storage at the server but needing only $1/k$ as much processing, on average, at the client.

5. Suppose we are using Lamport's hash, and Bob crashes before receiving Alice's reply. Suppose an intruder, Trudy, can eavesdrop and detect that Bob crashed (maybe Trudy can even cause Bob to crash). Then Trudy has a quantity (whatever Alice replied that Bob did not receive) which Trudy can use to impersonate Alice, if Trudy logs in before Alice attempts to log into Bob again. How can we modify Bob's behavior to prevent this threat? (Exactly when do we overwrite Bob's database, and with what)?

6. With PDM, show how someone impersonating Alice or Bob can do a dictionary attack if they choose a Diffie-Hellman exponent, x, small enough that $2^x < p$. How could the other side prevent this?

7. Show protocols for doing augmented forms of EKE and SPEKE.

8. Show how Alice computes hash(2^{ab} mod p, 2^{bW} mod p) in Protocol 12-3.

9. Show how in Protocol 12-3 Alice can be assured that it is Bob, i.e., that the other side has the information stored at Bob. Explain why someone who has stolen Bob's database cannot impersonate Alice to Bob.

10. (*) Suppose in message 3 in Protocol 12-4, Alice signs only c. What vulnerability would this have? (Hint: someone who has captured Bob's database can do a man-in-the-middle attack.)

11. Explain how each of Alice and Bob compute K in the SRP protocol (Protocol 12-4).

12. (*) In Protocol 12-4, Bob's Diffie-Hellman value g^b mod p is not encrypted with W. Argue why this is still secure. Note that it would not be secure for Bob to send g^b mod p without encrypting it with W in Protocol 12-2. Why is that? How could you modify Protocol 12-2 so that it would be secure for Bob not to encrypt g^b mod p with W?

13. Show credentials download protocols built upon SPEKE, PDM, and SRP.

14. Why is the EKE-based Protocol 12-7 insecure? (Hint: someone impersonating Bob can do a dictionary attack, but show how.) How can you make it secure while still having Bob transmit g^b mod p unencrypted?

15. (*) Consider Protocol 12-8. How would Alice compute K? How would Bob compute K. Why is it insecure? (Hint: someone impersonating Bob can do a dictionary attack, but show how.)

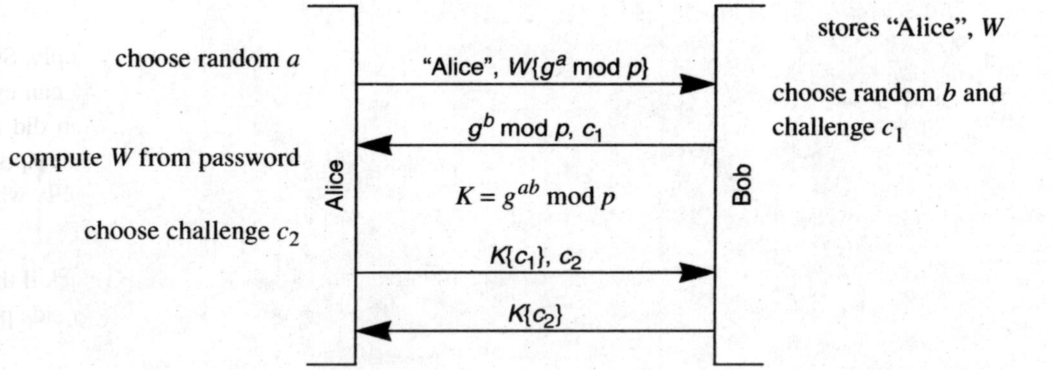

Protocol 12-7. For Homework Problem 14

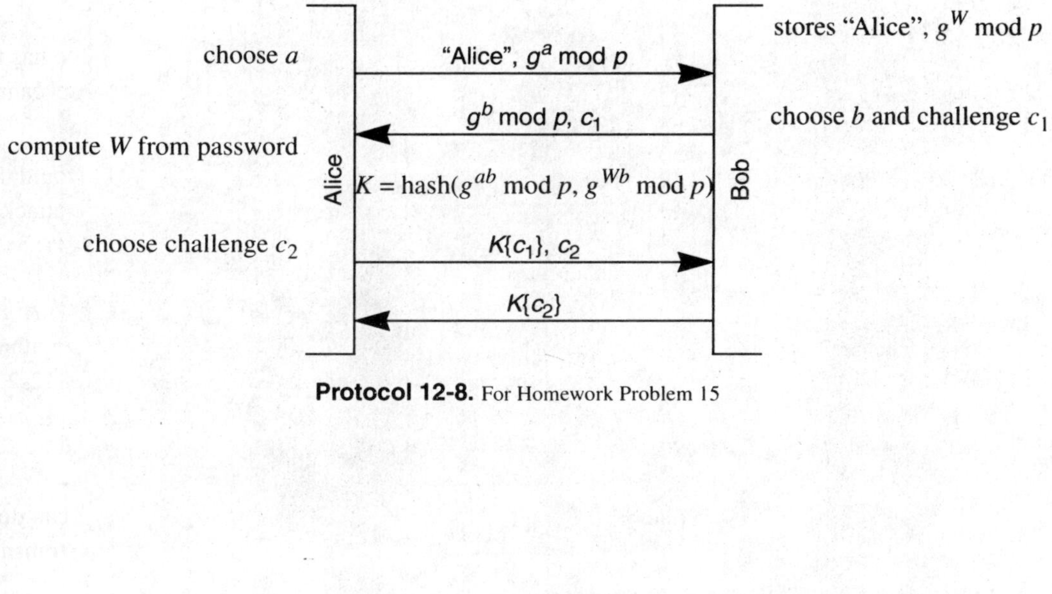

Protocol 12-8. For Homework Problem 15

PART 3

STANDARDS

13 KERBEROS V4

13.1 INTRODUCTION

Kerberos is a secret key based service for providing authentication in a network. When a user Alice first logs into a workstation, she'll type her account name and password. We'll call the period from when she logs in to when she logs out her **login session**. During her login session Alice will probably need to access remote resources (such as hosts on which Alice has accounts, or file servers on which Alice has files). These remote resources will need to authenticate her, but Alice's workstation performs the authentication protocol on Alice's behalf, and Alice need not be aware that it is happening. The network itself is assumed to be insecure. Bad guys might eavesdrop or modify messages.

Kerberos was originally designed at MIT. It is based on work by Needham and Schroeder (see §11.4 *Mediated Authentication (with KDC)*). The first three versions of Kerberos are no longer in use and hence are not of much interest. Version 4 and Version 5, although conceptually similar, are substantially different from one another and are competing for dominance in the marketplace. Version 4 has a greater installed base, is simpler, and has better performance, but works only with TCP/IP networks, while Version 5 has greater functionality. We'll describe Version 4 in detail in this chapter, and the differences between Version 4 and Version 5 in the next. For any inquiring minds out there, the name Kerberos is the name of the three-headed dog that guards the entrance to Hades. (Wouldn't it be more useful to guard the exit?)

An implementation of Kerberos consists of a Key Distribution Center (KDC) that runs on a physically secure node somewhere on the network, and a library of subroutines that are used by distributed applications which want to authenticate their users. While there are many possible modes of operation, Kerberos was designed for an environment where a user logs into a workstation by providing a user name and a password. These are used by the workstation to obtain information from the KDC that can be used by any process to access remote resources on behalf of the user. The basic ideas behind Kerberos should be familiar by now, since we've already discussed the concept of KDCs in §9.7 *Trusted Intermediaries* and §11.4 *Mediated Authentication (with KDC)*.

Some applications that have been modified to call subroutines in the Kerberos library as part of their startup include

- telnet (RFC 854)—a protocol for acting as a terminal on a remote system
- BSD rtools—a group of utilities included with BSD UNIX that support remote login (rlogin), remote file copying (rcp), and remote command execution (rsh)
- NFS (Network File System, RFC 1094)—a utility that permits files on a remote node on the network to be accessed as though they were local files

13.2 TICKETS AND TICKET-GRANTING TICKETS

The KDC shares a secret key, known as a **master key**, with each **principal** (each user and each resource that will be using Kerberos). When Alice informs the KDC that she wants to talk to Bob, the KDC invents a session key K_{AB} for Alice and Bob to share, encrypts K_{AB} with Alice's master key for Alice, encrypts K_{AB} with Bob's master key for Bob, and returns all this information to Alice. The message consisting of the session key K_{AB} (and other information such as Alice's name) encrypted with Bob's master key is known as a **ticket** to Bob. Alice can't read what's inside the ticket, because it's encrypted with Bob's master key. Bob can decrypt the ticket and discover K_{AB} and Alice's name. Bob knows, based on the ticket, that anyone else who knows K_{AB} is acting on Alice's behalf. So Alice and Bob can authenticate each other, and optionally encrypt or integrity-protect their entire conversation, based on the shared key K_{AB}. The session key K_{AB} together with the ticket to Bob are known as Alice's **credentials** to Bob.

Alice logs into a workstation by supplying her name and password. Alice's master key is derived from her password. The workstation, which performs the authentication protocol on behalf of Alice, could remember her password during the whole login session and use that when proof of her identity was required. But that is not good security practice for various reasons. One worry is that Alice might, during the login session, run untrustworthy software that might steal her password. To minimize harm, the first thing that happens is that the workstation asks the KDC for a session key S_A for Alice to use for just this one session. The session key S_A is then used on Alice's behalf when asking for tickets to resources on the network. The key S_A is only valid for some small amount of time, generally a few hours. If anyone steals S_A, then they can impersonate Alice, but only until S_A expires.

During the initial login, the workstation, on Alice's behalf, asks the KDC for a session key for Alice. The KDC generates a session key S_A, and transmits S_A (encrypted with Alice's master key) to the workstation. The KDC also sends a **ticket-granting ticket** (**TGT**), which is S_A (and other information such as Alice's name and the TGT's expiration time) encrypted with the KDC's master key.

The workstation uses Alice's master key (derived from her password) to decrypt the encrypted S_A. Then the workstation forgets Alice's password and only remembers S_A and the TGT. When Alice later needs to access a remote resource, her workstation transmits the TGT to the KDC, along with the name of the resource to which Alice needs a ticket (say Bob). The KDC decrypts the TGT to discover S_A, and uses S_A to encrypt the Alice-Bob session key for Alice. Essentially, the TGT informs the KDC to use S_A instead of Alice's master key.

Earlier versions of Kerberos did not have the notion of a TGT. The user's master key was always used when communicating with the KDC. Later, for enhanced security, the notion of obtaining a limited-lifetime session key at login time was added. The idea was that only TGTs were gotten from the KDC, and that other tickets were obtained from what was theoretically a different entity, which Kerberos calls a **Ticket-Granting Server** or **TGS**. However, the Ticket-Granting Server has to have the same database as the KDC (it needs to know Bob's secret key in order to give Alice a ticket for Bob). So in Kerberos, the Ticket-Granting Server and the KDC are really the same thing. It would be easier to understand Kerberos if the documentation didn't refer to two different entities (KDC and TGS) and two sets of protocol messages that basically do the same thing. The reason it is described that way in Kerberos documentation is solely due to how the protocol evolved.

The Kerberos documentation refers to an Authentication Server (AS) and a Ticket-Granting Server (TGS) which are collocated at the KDC, meaning they are really the same thing. We will use the terms KDC, AS, and TGS interchangeably, since we do not find the distinction to be useful for understanding Kerberos, and in reality there is no distinction.

13.3 CONFIGURATION

As we said before, each principal has its own secret key, known as the master key for that principal. The Kerberos server is called a KDC (Key Distribution Center). Sometimes the Kerberos documentation calls the KDC an Authentication Server, or a KDC/AS. The KDC has a database of names of principals and their corresponding master keys. To keep the KDC database reasonably secure, the stored master keys are stored encrypted by a key that is the personal secret of the KDC, known as the **KDC master key**. The master key for a human user is derived from the user's password. Resources other than human beings are configured with their own master keys.

Kerberos is based on secret key technology, and all current implementations use DES. Kerberos V5 has fields in packets for identifying the cryptographic algorithm, so theoretically an algorithm other than DES can be used in V5, but in reality we can assume the algorithm is DES because there are no implementations of Kerberos with the ability to use a different algorithm.

To summarize, human users need to remember a password. Other network devices need to remember a secret key. The KDC needs to have a database of names of all the principals for which it is responsible, together with a secret key for each of them. It also needs a secret key K_{KDC} for itself (in order to encrypt the database of user keys and in order to generate ticket-granting tickets).

13.4 LOGGING INTO THE NETWORK

By way of introduction, let's look at the steps that take place as Alice uses the network. She'll expect the login procedure to be pretty much the same as for logging into an operating system. First, the workstation prompts Alice for a name and a password.

13.4.1 Obtaining a Session Key and TGT

Alice types her account name and password at the workstation. The workstation sends a message to the KDC, in the clear (unencrypted), which gives Alice's account name. On receipt of the request, the KDC returns credentials to the KDC, encrypted with Alice's master key. The credentials consist of

- a session key S_A (a secret key to be used during the login session).
- a ticket-granting ticket (TGT). The TGT contains the session key, the user's name, and an expiration time, encrypted with K_{KDC}. Because it is encrypted with the KDC's master key, the TGT is an unintelligible bunch of bits to anyone other than the KDC.

These credentials are sent back to the workstation encrypted with Alice's master key, K_A. Note that the information in the TGT is therefore doubly encrypted when transmitted by the KDC—first with K_{KDC} and then with K_A. Kerberos V4 is sometimes criticized for this minor performance suboptimality, since encrypting the already-encrypted TGT offers no security benefit.

The workstation converts the password Alice types into a DES key. When the workstation receives the credentials, it attempts to decrypt them using this DES key. If this decryption succeeds (which it will if Alice typed her password correctly), then the workstation discards Alice's master key (the key derived from her password), retaining instead the TGT and the session key.

Kerberos documentation refers to the request sent by the workstation to the KDC as a **KRB_AS_REQ**, for **Kerberos Authentication Server Request**. We'll call it **AS_REQ**. The message in which the KDC returns the session key and TGT is known in the Kerberos documentation as a **KRB_AS_REP**, for **Kerberos Authentication Service Reply**. We'll call it **AS_REP**.

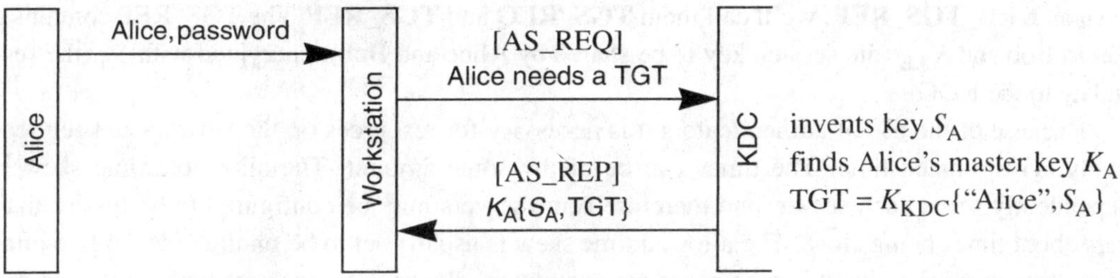

Figure 13-1. Obtaining a TGT

Actually, Kerberos V4 does not prompt the user for her password until after the workstation has received the credentials from the KDC. This is because Kerberos V4 was very serious in following the generally good security rule of having the workstation know the user's password for the minimum time possible. Waiting the few seconds to get the credentials before asking the user for the password really doesn't enhance security significantly, and in fact V5 has the user type the password before the workstation sends the AS_REQ. The reason V5 changed the order was that V5 requires the workstation to prove it knows the user's password before it sends the credentials, which makes it less easy to obtain a quantity with which to do off-line password guessing. An eavesdropper will still be able to do off-line password guessing with V5, but in V4 all you have to do is send the name Alice to the KDC and it will return a quantity with which you can do password guessing. This is likely to be easier than eavesdropping.

What is the purpose of the TGT? When Alice needs to access a remote resource, her workstation sends the TGT to the KDC along with a request for a ticket to the resource's node. The TGT contains the information the KDC needs about Alice's login session (session key, Alice's name, expiration time,...). This allows the KDC to operate without having any volatile data; it has a largely static database, and for each request it sends a response and then forgets that it happened. This offers a number of operational advantages, like making it easy to replicate the KDC and not having to maintain state across crashes.

An interesting variant might be to have the workstation generate the TGT (see Homework Problem 1).

13.4.2 Alice Asks to Talk to a Remote Node

Suppose that after logging in as described above, Alice types a command that requires access to a remote node (like rlogin Bob, which logs Alice into Bob). The workstation sends to the KDC the TGT, the name Bob, and an **authenticator** which proves that the workstation knows the session key. The authenticator consists of the time of day encrypted with the session key (in this case S_A). This request is known in the Kerberos documentation as a **KRB_TGS_REQ**, and the reply is known as **KRB_TGS_REP**; we'll call them **TGS_REQ** and **TGS_REP**. The TGS_REP contains a ticket to Bob and K_{AB} (the session key to be shared by Alice and Bob), encrypted with S_A (the session key to the KDC).

Because of the use of authenticators it is necessary for resources on the network to keep reasonably synchronized time. The times can be off by some amount. The allowable time skew is independently set at each server, and therefore some servers may be configured to be fussier than others about times being close. The allowed time skew is usually set to be on the order of five minutes on the assumption that it is possible to get computers' clocks to be accurate within five minutes without undue administrative burden. In practice, that assumption has turned out to be more problematic than expected. Distributed time services, once deployed, make much tighter synchronization straightforward.

It turns out that there is no security or functionality gained by having Kerberos require an authenticator when Alice's workstation requests a ticket to Bob. If someone who didn't know the session key transmitted the TGT and the name Bob to the KDC, the KDC would return information encrypted with S_A, which would be of no use to someone who didn't know Alice's session key. The reason the designers of Kerberos did it this way is to make the protocol for talking to the Ticket-Granting Service of the KDC be the same as for talking to other resources. When talking to most resources other than the KDC, the authenticator does provide security, because it prevents the replay of old requests and authenticates the sender (which is important if the reply is unencrypted).

The KDC decrypts the TGT (with K_{KDC}) and discovers the session key S_A. It also checks the expiration time in the TGT. If the TGT is valid, the KDC constructs a new key K_{AB}, for use in talking between Alice and Bob, and constructs a **ticket**, which consists of the newly generated key K_{AB}, the name Alice, and an expiration time, all encrypted with Bob's master key, K_B. The KDC sends the ticket, along with the name Bob and K_{AB}, to the workstation. Again this information must be encrypted, and it is encrypted with S_A. On receipt, the workstation decrypts the information using S_A.

Now the workstation sends a request to Bob. In the Kerberos documentation this request is called a **KRB_AP_REQ**, for *application request*, which we'll call **AP_REQ.** It consists of the ticket and an authenticator (in this case the time encrypted with the session key K_{AB}). The reply from Bob is known in Kerberos as **KRB_AP_REP**, and we'll call it **AP_REP**. Bob decrypts the ticket and discovers the key K_{AB} and the name Alice. Bob now assumes that anyone with knowledge of K_{AB} is acting on Alice's behalf. Then Bob decrypts the authenticator to know that the party to which he is speaking does indeed know the session key K_{AB}. He checks that the time in the decrypted authenticator is close to current (within five minutes) to ensure that this is not a replay of some earlier request.

To make sure it is not a replay of a request recent enough to look current given the time skew, Bob should keep all timestamps he has received recently, say in the last five minutes (a parameter set appropriately for the maximum allowable time skew) and check that each received timestamp from a given source is different from any of the stored values. Any authenticator older than five

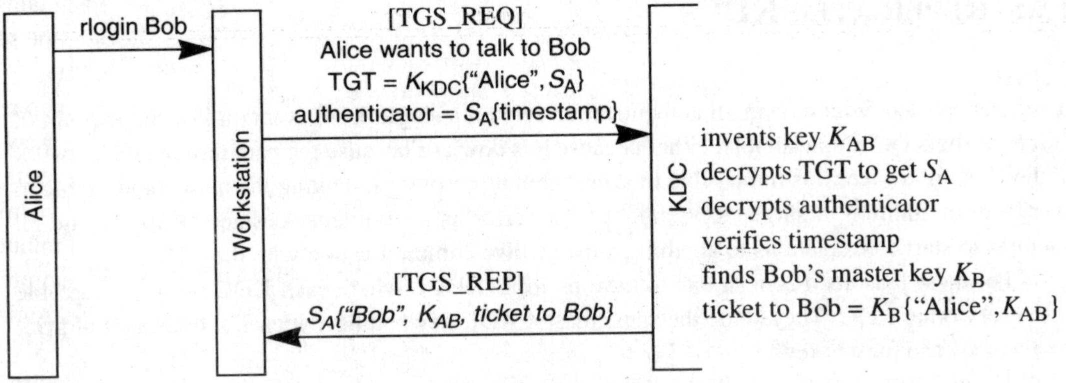

Figure 13-2. Getting a ticket to Bob for Alice

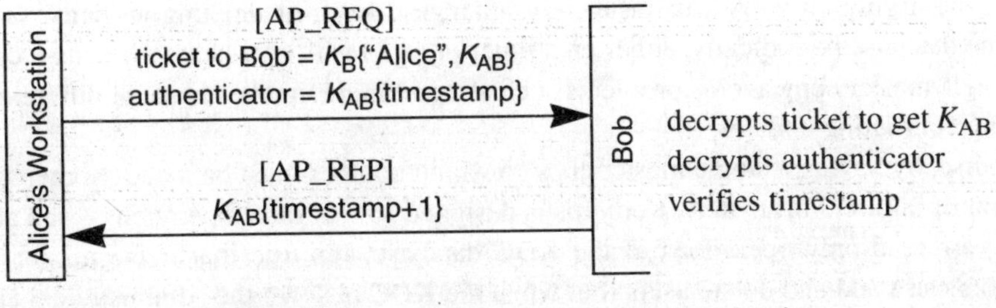

Figure 13-3. Logging into Bob from Alice's workstation

minutes (or whatever the value of the maximum allowable time skew) would be rejected anyway, so Bob need not remember values older than 5 minutes. Kerberos V4 doesn't bother saving timestamps. Saving timestamps doesn't help anyway if Bob is a replicated service in which all the instances of Bob use the same master key. The threat of an eavesdropper replaying the authenticator Alice sent to one instance of Bob to a different instance of Bob could have been avoided if Kerberos had done something like put the network layer address of the instance of Bob in the authenticator.

To provide mutual authentication, Bob adds one to the time he decrypted from the authenticator, reencrypts that with K_{AB} and sends it back. Alice's workstation is now reassured that it is talking to Bob, since the party at the other side was able to decrypt the ticket, which meant he knew K_{AB}, which was encrypted with K_B.

Thereafter, depending on the application, messages between Alice and Bob may be unprotected, integrity-protected, or encrypted and integrity-protected. Some applications always use the same Kerberos protection (authentication only, data integrity protection, or data encryption plus integrity protection). Others make it optional (a switch setting when calling the application). The decision is a security vs. performance trade-off when using Kerberos.

13.5 REPLICATED KDCS

A serious problem with having all authentication rely on a single KDC is that it is a single point of failure. If the KDC is unavailable, either because it is down or because the path through the network to the KDC is broken, it is impossible to access remote resources, making the network unusable to everyone. In addition, a single KDC might be a performance bottleneck, since all logins and all attempts to start conversations to anything must involve communication with the KDC.

For these reasons it is desirable to have multiple KDCs, where each KDC is interchangeable with every other KDC. They share the same master KDC key and have identical databases of principal names and master keys.

Keeping the databases at all the KDCs the same is done by having one site hold the **master copy** to which any updates must be made. An update consists of adding an entry for ⟨principal name, key⟩, modifying an entry (for instance to change a key), or deleting an entry. Other sites download the database periodically, either on a timer or as a result of a human issuing a command. Having a single master copy avoids problems such as combining updates made at different replicas and resolving conflicting updates.

Of course, by having a single master copy to which updates must be made, Kerberos still has a single point of failure. Fortunately, Kerberos is designed so that most operations—and all critical operations—are read-only operations of the KDC database. It's true that if the master is down, administrators can't add and delete users (but when the KDC is down the administrators are probably too busy to bother with adding and deleting users since they're trying to fix the KDC), and users can't change their passwords (which may be inconvenient but is not life-threatening). These operations can wait for a few hours until the master copy is repaired. In contrast, the read-only KDC operations are required for any use of the network. If there were only a single KDC, and it was unavailable, none of the network users would be able to get any (computer-related) work done.

Another reason for replication is to avoid a performance bottleneck at the KDC. Updates are sufficiently rare that the master copy will be easily capable of keeping up with all updates. Most of the operations will be read-only, and these operations will be spread among the read-only replicas. Another reason that replication may improve performance is so that a KDC replica is usually nearby.

When downloading the KDC database from the master replica to a read-only slave, it is important to protect the data from disclosure and modification. Disclosure would permit an attacker to learn the master keys of all principals; modification would permit an attacker to create new accounts or change the properties of existing ones. This protection could have been provided by encrypting the KDC database as a unit when it was being transferred. The Kerberos designers chose not to do that.

Because the principals' master keys are stored in the database encrypted under the KDC master key, there is no serious disclosure threat. An attacker could learn the names of all principals and their properties, but not their master keys. The threat remains that an attacker could rearrange data in transit so that, for example, some privileged user was given the attacker's master key (by simply copying the encrypted key field). This second threat is avoided by transferring the KDC database as a file in the clear but then sending a cryptographic hash of the file in a Kerberos protected exchange. By using the integrity protection of Kerberos, which includes a timestamp, the protocol prevents the attacker from substituting an old version of the KDC database, for instance one from before the attacker was fired.

13.6 REALMS

Having a single KDC for an entire network is a problem for many reasons. With replicated KDCs, you can alleviate bottleneck problems and eliminate the single-point-of-failure problem. However, there is a serious problem which creation of redundant KDCs does not solve.

Imagine a big network consisting of several organizations such as companies in competition with each other, various universities, banks, and government agencies. It would be hard to find an organization that everyone would trust to manage the KDC. Whoever manages the KDC can access every user's master key, and therefore access everything that every user can access. Furthermore, that highly trusted entity would also be a busy one, having to process all instances of users and services joining and leaving the network.

Even if there were an organization everyone was willing to trust, this is not enough. Everyone must also trust the physical controls around every replica of the KDC, and there would have to be widely dispersed replicas to ensure availability and convenience. Compromise of any replica, no matter how obscurely placed it was, would yield everyone's keys.

For this reason the principals in the network are divided into **realms**. Each realm has its own KDC database. There can be multiple KDCs in a realm, but they would be equivalent, have the same KDC master key, and have the same database of principals' master keys. Two KDCs in different realms, however, would have different KDC master keys and totally different principals' master key databases, since they would be responsible for a different set of principals.

In V4, a name of a principal has three components, each of which is a null-terminated case-sensitive text string of up to 40 characters: NAME, INSTANCE, and REALM. The Kerberos protocol does not particularly care how the NAME and INSTANCE fields are used. They are merely text strings. However, in practice, services have a name, and the INSTANCE field is used to indicate the particular machine on which the service is running. For example the file service might be called **fileserv** and a particular instance might be **jailbreak**, for the name of one of the fileserver machines.

The INSTANCE field is not as useful for human principals, and usually the null string would be used for the instance part of the name. But as long as there is that component to a name, the convention for humans is that it is used to denote something about the role of the human for that particular login session. For example, someone can have the name Alice and the instance systemmanager, or the name Alice and the instance gameplayer. Presumably Alice.systemmanager would have access to many more network resources than Alice.gameplayer. In effect, a name is really a concatentation of the two strings NAME and INSTANCE. Kerberos could certainly have done without the concept of instance, and by convention principals could just use different names in their various roles. As a matter of fact, if "." were a legal character in the text string for a name, the names could be identical to what they are currently, without having to separate them officially into two fields (NAME and INSTANCE).

13.7 INTERREALM AUTHENTICATION

Suppose the world is partitioned into *n* different Kerberos realms. It might be the case that principals in one realm need to authenticate principals in another realm. This is supported by Kerberos. The way it works is that the KDC in realm *B* can be registered as a principal in realm *A*. This allows users in realm *A* to access realm *B*'s KDC as if it were any other resource in realm *A*.

Suppose Alice, in realm Wonderland, wishes to communicate securely to Dorothy in realm Oz. Alice (or rather her workstation, on her behalf) notices that Dorothy is in a different realm. She asks her KDC for a ticket to the KDC in realm Oz (see Figure 13-4). If the managers of Wonderland and Oz have decided to allow this, the KDC in Oz will be registered as a principal in Wonderland, and the Wonderland KDC will have assigned a master key to Oz's KDC. Wonderland's KDC will give Alice a ticket (encrypted with that master key) to the KDC in Oz. Then Alice sends a TGS_REQ to Oz's KDC. The message lists Wonderland as the source realm, which tells Oz's KDC what key to use to decrypt the ticket. The Oz KDC then issues a ticket for Alice to talk to Dorothy.

After Alice sends this ticket to Dorothy, Alice and Dorothy will know they are talking to each other, and they will have a key $K_{\text{A-D}}$ they can use to protect data they send back and forth, exactly as if they were in the same realm.

It doesn't work in Kerberos V4 to start in realm *A*, get a ticket to realm *B*, and from there get a ticket to realm *C*. In order for a principal in realm *A* to talk to a principal in realm *C*, *C*'s KDC has to be registered as a principal in realm *A*. What prevents going from realm *A* to *C* through *B*? Suppose realms *A* and *B* share a key, and realms *B* and *C* share a key, but *A* and *C* do not share a key. Suppose Alice@*A* would like to talk to Carol@*C*. Alice can indeed get a ticket to *B*, since *B* is registered as a principal in realm *A*. Then, with a ticket to *B*, Alice can request, from *B*, a ticket to *C*. *B*

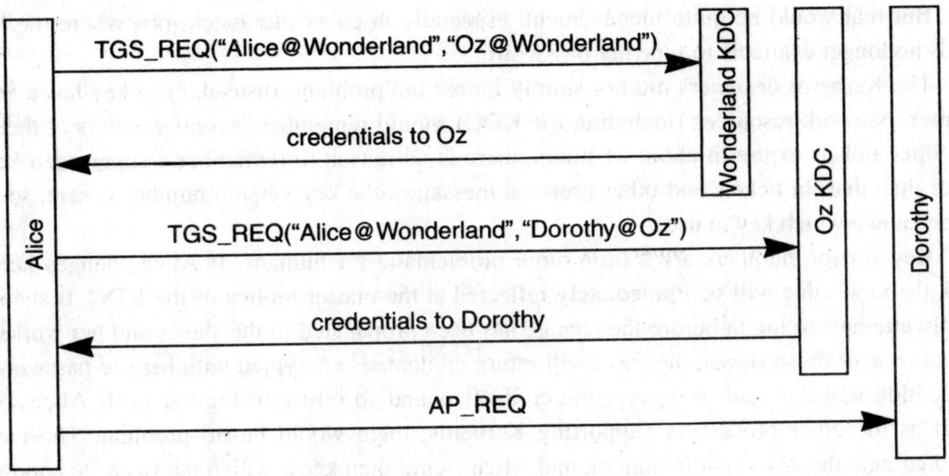

Figure 13-4. Interrealm authentication

will comply, since *B* thinks of *C* as just another principal in realm *B*. But then when *A* attempts to ask *C* for a ticket to Carol, the TGS_REQ she sends *C* will have the REALM field as *B* (so that *C* will know what key to use to decrypt the ticket), and in the ticket, Alice's realm will be *A*. *C* will refuse to issue a ticket for Carol since the two realms don't match. (See §13.12.5 *TGS_REQ* for a description of the fields in the TGS_REQ.)

Kerberos V4 deliberately prevents access through a chain of KDCs. If it didn't, then a rogue KDC could impersonate not only its own users, but those of any other realm, by claiming to be the penultimate KDC in a chain.

13.8 KEY VERSION NUMBERS

In most operating systems, Alice can change her password without inconveniencing anyone else. The Kerberos designers wanted the same to be true when using Kerberos. However, with Kerberos, a change in a principal's master DES key or a change in the KDC's master DES key would affect tickets held by other users. For instance, if Alice has a ticket to Bob, and Bob changes his master DES key, Alice's ticket will still be encrypted with Bob's old master DES key. Similarly, if Alice has a TGT with a session key for her login session, and the KDC's master key is changed, then Alice's TGT will still be encrypted with the old KDC master key.

The Kerberos designers could simply have ignored the problem, and then communication would fail. Presumably principals would at that point ask for a new ticket and things would proceed. But that would be quite inconvenient, especially in cases like batch jobs where the human user is no longer available to type her password.

The Kerberos designers did not simply ignore the problem. Instead, each key has a **version number**. Network resources (including the KDC) should remember several versions of their own key. Since tickets expire in about 21 hours, there is no reason to remember a superseded key any longer than that. In tickets and other protocol messages, the key version number is sent, so that it can be known which key to use.

Key version numbers are a little more problematic for humans. If Alice changes her password, the new value will be immediately reflected at the master replica of the KDC. If she subsequently attempts to log in before the change has been propagated to the slaves and her workstation contacts one of those slaves, the slave will return credentials encrypted with her old password. Her workstation will then fail to decrypt the credentials and so refuse to log her in. If Alice were as robust as the other processors supporting Kerberos, there would be no problem. The message would contain the key version number, and Alice would then know which password to supply. The Kerberos designers decided wisely not to introduce this piece of complexity into the user interface, but it does have the downside that for some period after a password change, the new password may fail. If the user tries the old password in such a situation, it may work, and the user may be a little confused.

13.9 ENCRYPTION FOR PRIVACY AND INTEGRITY

Many of the data structures that Kerberos encrypts need to be protected from both disclosure and modification. In a ticket, for example, the KEY field needs to be protected from both disclosure and modification, and the NAME and EXPIRATION fields need to be protected from modification.

Unfortunately, there is no standard mechanism for protecting both the confidentiality and integrity of a message with a single cryptographic pass. Generally the most useful way to protect the confidentiality of a message is to encrypt it in CBC mode (see §4.2.2 *Cipher Block Chaining (CBC)*). The most standard way to protect its integrity is with a CBC residue. But securely applying both of these techniques would require double the encryption effort and two separate keys (see §4.3.1 *Ensuring Privacy and Integrity Together*).

Intuitively, it seems like it should be possible to make do with a single cryptographic pass by including some redundant information in the message to be encrypted and then to have the integrity of the message protected by having the recipient check that the redundancy is correctly done. A number of schemes have been proposed for doing this. Many have been found to have cryptographic weaknesses. None has gained general acceptance. The designers of Kerberos came up with their own variation on this theme, and subsequently cryptographic flaws were found with it. The flaws were not so egregious as to justify recalling Kerberos V4; however, a different approach is followed in Kerberos V5.

One method for using DES on a long message is CBC. CBC does a good job on privacy. An intruder will not gain any information from analysis of the encrypted blocks. However, there is no integrity check that Kerberos can do to assure an application that the data was not tampered with. If an intruder were to modify block c_n, then m_n would be garbage, as would m_{n+1}, but starting from m_{n+2} everything would decrypt properly. Kerberos would not be able to detect that m_n and m_{n+1} had been garbled. Some applications might be able to tell, but Kerberos would like to provide the integrity assurance without depending on the application.

Therefore, Kerberos did a modified version of CBC which they called **Plaintext Cipher Block Chaining (PCBC)**. It is similar to CBC except that in addition to ⊕ing c_n with m_{n+1}, m_n is also ⊕'d. In other words, in CBC, $m_{n+1} \oplus c_n$ is encrypted to yield c_{n+1}. In PCBC, $m_{n+1} \oplus c_n \oplus m_n$ is encrypted to yield c_{n+1}.

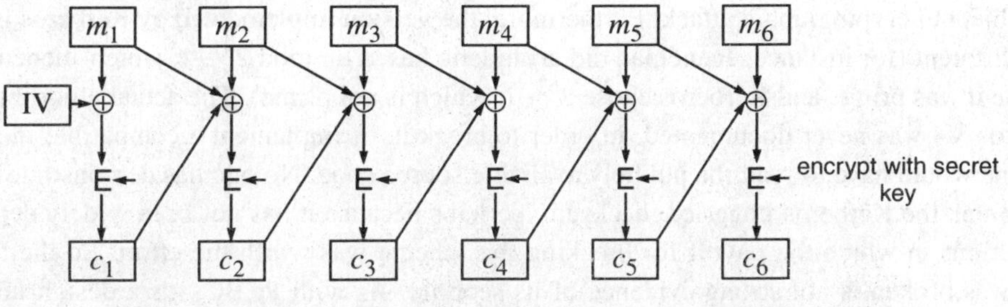

Figure 13-5. Plaintext Cipher Block Chaining (PCBC)

PCBC has the property that modifying any c_i will result in garbling of all decrypted plaintext blocks starting with m_i all the way to the end. Kerberos puts some recognizable data at the end of a message that it will encrypt so that it can recognize whether the final block decrypts properly. It makes the assumption that if the final block decrypts properly, then the data has not been tampered with between the time it was transmitted by the source and received by the destination.

However, using PCBC and checking the contents of the final decrypted block does not guarantee that Kerberos will be able to detect message corruption. For instance, if an intruder were to swap two adjacent blocks, PCBC will "get back in sync" after those two blocks, and the final block will decrypt properly (see Homework Problem 5).

13.10 ENCRYPTION FOR INTEGRITY ONLY

Kerberos is often used by applications just for authentication. Kerberos also provides integrity protection and combined privacy and integrity protection for those applications that desire this facility. Combined privacy and integrity protection is provided by PCBC as described above. Integrity protection without privacy is described in this section.

Kerberos V4 was designed with the expectation that DES encryption would be done in software, and that the processing cost of doing so would be a limiting factor in its acceptance. The designers were willing to use new or even cryptographically weak techniques in order to improve the performance. When integrity-protecting messages, the most straightforward and standard technique would have been to compute a DES CBC residue. Instead, they invented their own. It was based on a checksum algorithm designed by Jueneman [JUEN85]. Jueneman intended for his checksum to be used as a piece of redundant information inside an encrypted message, where it was less subject to cryptographic attack. Furthermore, the version implemented by Kerberos is substantially different (for instance, Jueneman did arithmetic based on mod $2^{31}-1$, which Jueneman chose because it was prime, and Kerberos chose $2^{63}-1$, which is not prime). The actual algorithm used by Kerberos V4 was never documented. In order to break it, or implement a compatible implementation, one would have to read the publicly available source code. No one has demonstrated the ability to break the Kerberos integrity checksum, perhaps because it has not been widely deployed for applications in which the payoff for breaking the scheme was worth the effort. So the fact that it never was broken is not strong evidence of its security. As with PCBC, it's a design upon which cryptographers would frown, but in practice it appears to have been good enough.

The V4 checksum is computed on the session key concatenated with the message. Only the message and the checksum are transmitted—the session key is not sent. An intruder would not be able to compute a valid checksum on a modified message, since that would require knowledge of the session key.

There are two possible problems with the use of the V4 checksum as a message digest function. One is that it might not be as cryptographically strong as a real message digest, and therefore it might be relatively easy to find a different message that yielded the same checksum, even without knowing the session key, since it might be possible to know how to modify a message in a way that would not change the value of the checksum. The second, and potentially more serious, problem is that it might be reversible. An intruder can see the entire plaintext message and the checksum. If it's possible to calculate the previous block, then perhaps it's possible to work backwards from the end and calculate the session key.

Because of these possible weaknesses, this approach was abandoned in Kerberos V5. Instead, a choice of checksum algorithms is given, and in cases such as integrity-only, one of the standard message digest functions is used (see §14.8.1 *Integrity-Only Algorithms*).

13.11 NETWORK LAYER ADDRESSES IN TICKETS

When Alice requests a TGT or a ticket to Bob, the KDC puts her 4-octet IPv4 address inside the ticket. Bob, when presented with a ticket, will check to make sure that the network layer source address on the connect request is the same as the one specified inside the ticket. Likewise, when the KDC receives a ticket request, it checks that the request is coming from the network layer address specified in the TGT. There are two reasons for putting Alice's network layer address in the ticket. The first reason is to prevent Alice from giving the ticket and session key to some third party, Ted, so that he can impersonate Alice. This restriction makes it more difficult for an intruder to walk up to the workstation Alice is using (when Alice steps out of her office), steal her session key and TGT, and use them from a safe location. But the restriction also prevents delegation, where Alice legitimately wants to allow something to act on her behalf. Indeed in Kerberos V5 delegation is specifically allowed (see §14.3 *Delegation of Rights*). The second reason is to prevent some third party Trudy from intercepting the ticket and authenticator on the wire and using it from Trudy's network layer address. Without Alice's network layer in the ticket, Trudy merely has to eavesdrop to obtain the ticket and an authenticator, use them within five minutes (or whatever the allowable clock skew is), and arrange for the authenticator as transmitted by Alice not to arrive. With Alice's network layer address in the ticket, Trudy has to additionally impersonate Alice's network layer address. This isn't necessarily difficult, but it adds one more hurdle for the attacker.

It might be better to have Alice's network layer address be in the authenticator rather than the ticket. This allows the person using the ticket to pick the network layer address, which makes it easier to support a principal with multiple network layer addresses (Alice can choose which one to put into the authenticator), and it allows delegation. If Alice is willing for Ted to act on her behalf, and has therefore given him the session key and ticket, he can put his own network layer address into the authenticator. But Fred, who has not been given permission by Alice to act on her behalf, cannot generate an authenticator with his network layer address, so any security against eavesdroppers gained by having the network address in the ticket is equally applicable to having the network layer address in the authenticator.

Putting the network layer address in the ticket instead of the authenticator is done to specifically disallow delegation. Kerberos V5 does allow delegation, but only with the mediation of the KDC and only if the originally acquired ticket explicitly permits it.

We feel that since it is usually easy to forge a network layer source address, all the effort Kerberos has put into checking network layer source addresses is more trouble than it's worth. As with any higher-layer protocol that embeds layer 3 addresses as data, there are potential problems with NATs (see§17.2.1 *NAT (Network Address Translation)*) and migration to different address formats (e.g., IPv6).

13.12 MESSAGE FORMATS

In this section we'll go through the Kerberos V4 message formats. In all of the messages, we assume that Alice wants to talk to Bob. In Kerberos documentation Alice is sometimes referred to as the *client* and Bob as the *server.* We find that terminology confusing since both Alice and Bob are clients of the Kerberos system, and principals like file servers can indeed act in the role of client in terms of a Kerberos authentication. Therefore we will not use that terminology and will instead use *Alice* for the initiator of an authentication and *Bob* for the entity with which Alice would like to communicate, and the pronouns *she* for *Alice* and *he* for *Bob.*

Fields that appear in packets:

- NAME/INSTANCE/REALM of Alice or Bob—variable-length null-terminated character strings.
- TIMESTAMP—a four-octet value representing the number of seconds since 00:00:00 GMT, 1 January, 1970. This is a common representation of time in UNIX-based systems. If treated as a signed integer, it can represent times between 1902 and 2038. If treated as an unsigned integer, it can represent times between 1970 and 2106. In Kerberos, some of the messages in which timestamps appear use the most significant bit as the D BIT (see below); in other messages, the most significant bit is set to zero. Therefore, Kerberos V4 effectively expires in 2038. (It's hoped that most people will have converted to V5 by then—or is that V19?). Kerberos V5 will not expire until December 31, 9999 (at least the timestamps will last till then).
- D BIT, DIRECTION BIT—The purpose of this flag is to prevent an intruder from mirroring a message back to the sender (called a reflection attack) and having the sender accept it as a response. An asymmetry is created between the two ends of a conversation based on IP address. When the packet is traveling from the higher IP address to the lower IP address, the D BIT is set to 1. When the packet is traveling between two processes in a single node (so that both ends of the conversation have the same IP address), the TCP port number is used as a tie-breaker. By checking the D BIT, the receiver of a message can be assured that the message was generated by the other end of the connection. In the actual layout of the data, the D BIT is stolen from the high-order bit of the TIMESTAMP. Note that this is a dependency on IP, though one that could be adapted to most communication protocols.
- LIFETIME—a one octet field, specified in units of 5 minutes. Therefore the maximum lifetime that can be expressed is a little over 21 hours. This limit has been seen as a major shortcoming of Kerberos V4, since it prevents giving tickets to long-running batch jobs.
- 5-MILLISECOND TIMESTAMP—This field extends the TIMESTAMP field to give time granularity down to 5 milliseconds instead of 1 second. Its purpose is to allow more than one authenticator to the same service to be generated in a single second without having it rejected as a dupli-

cate. Actual time accuracy at that granularity is never needed. An acceptable implementation of this field would be a sequence number within the second.

- PADDING—a field containing between zero and seven octets added to the end of any message that will be encrypted to ensure that the value to be encrypted is a multiple of eight octets.
- NETWORK LAYER ADDRESS—a four-octet quantity which is an IPv4 address.
- SESSION KEY—an eight-octet quantity which is used as a DES key.
- KEY VERSION NUMBER—a one-octet quantity (see §13.8 *Key Version Numbers*).
- KERBEROS VERSION NUMBER—a one-octet quantity equal to the constant 4.
- MESSAGE TYPE—a one-octet quantity, with the low-order bit stolen for the B BIT (see next item). The high-order seven bits indicate one of the following message types:
  - AS_REQ—Used when asking for the initial TGT.
  - AS_REPLY (also TGS_REP)—Used to return a ticket, either a TGT or a ticket to some other principal.
  - AP_REQ (also TGS_REQ)—Used to talk to another principal (or the TGS) using a ticket (or a TGT).
  - AP_REQ_MUTUAL—This was intended to be used to talk to another principal and request mutual authentication. In fact, it is never used; instead, applications know whether mutual authentication is expected.
  - AS_ERR—Used for the KDC to report why it can't return a ticket or TGT in response to AS_REQ or TGS_REQ.
  - PRIV—This is a message that carries encrypted integrity-protected application data.
  - SAFE—This is a message that carries integrity-protected application data.
  - AP_ERR—Used by an application to report why authentication failed.

Note: the names of the message types above do not match the names used in either the Kerberos V4 documentation or code. Because there was no consistent pattern, we used the names for the equivalent functions from Kerberos V5.

- B BIT, BYTE-ORDER FLAG—This bit indicates whether fields holding four-octet integers have them in **big-endian** (most significant octet first) or **little-endian** (least significant octet first) order. Different machines have different native internal formats. Most protocols define a **network byte order** and force machines with a different native format to byte-swap whenever they send or receive integers. By use of this flag, Kerberos allows either order in transmitted packets, so in the common case where the native formats on the communicating machines are the same, no byte-swapping is necessary. This approach trades complexity for performance. If B BIT = 1, it means the least significant octet is in the lowest address in a multi-octet field. This is convenient for little-endian machines; big-endian machines like to put the most significant octet in the lowest address and are most happy with B BIT = 0.

The following three data structures are never actually free-standing messages, but are instead pieces of information included in other messages. They are tickets, authenticators, and credentials.

13.12.1 Tickets

A ticket for Bob is an encrypted piece of information that is given to principal Alice by the KDC and stored by Alice. It is encrypted by the KDC with Bob's master key. Alice cannot read what is inside, but she sends it to Bob who can decrypt it and thereby authenticate her.

# octets		
1	B	
≤40	Alice's name	null-terminated
≤40	Alice's instance	null-terminated
≤40	Alice's realm	null-terminated
4	Alice's Network Layer address	
8	session key for Alice↔Bob	
1	ticket lifetime, units of 5 minutes	
4	KDC's timestamp when ticket made	
≤40	Bob's name	null-terminated
≤40	Bob's instance	null-terminated
≤ 7	pad of 0s to make ticket length multiple of eight octets	

Now some comments about the fields which are not self-explanatory.

- B BIT, BYTE-ORDER FLAG—LSB in a one-octet field, with the other bits unused.
- ALICE'S NETWORK LAYER ADDRESS—four octets. Note that the field is fixed-length and four octets. Kerberos was designed to run in the network using the TCP/IP protocol suite. This fixed-length field means that this version of Kerberos cannot be used in a network with longer addresses.
- TICKET LIFETIME. The units are 5 minutes, so the maximum ticket lifetime is a little over 21 hours.
- TIMESTAMP—four octets. Time when ticket was created (the number of seconds since 00:00:00 GMT, 1 January, 1970).

- BOB'S NAME and INSTANCE. Including Bob's name and instance is of dubious value. There are two possible reasons for inclusion of this field in the ticket. One reason is that the field supports a node where several services share a key. If someone were to get a ticket to the gameplaying service on node DoD, and that service used the same key as the nuclear-missile-launching service on the same node (it happened in *War Games*, right?), then having the name of the service in the ticket makes it impossible to use the ticket for the wrong service. For instance, suppose only once in a while (hopefully) does anyone ever use the nuclear-missile-launching service, but people often use the gameplaying service. Good guy *A* has rights to both services, and often uses the gameplaying service. One day bad guy *C* intercepts the ticket and authenticator that *A* was attempting to use to get to the gameplaying service, and then *C* quickly (within the clock skew) impersonates *A*'s network layer address, substitutes as the destination socket number the nuclear-missile-launching service, and starts World War III. You wouldn't want *that* to happen now, would you?

  The other dubious purpose for this field is so that Kerberos can tell that the ticket decrypts properly. Kerberos V4 uses PCBC (see §13.9 *Encryption for Privacy and Integrity*), and therefore assumes that any tampering with the data would result in the final block not decrypting properly. Since the final blocks include Bob's name and instance, Bob will be able to recognize if they are correct. (This is not a strong reason for the field because, even if PCBC worked as hoped, there is no value to be gained from tampering with a ticket and turning the information inside to garbage. User data is a different matter, however, and the PCBC check is more valuable there.)

13.12.2 Authenticators

The authenticator is a piece of information included in a message at the start of a communication attempt between Alice and Bob which enables Alice and Bob to prove to each other that they are who they claim to be. It is encrypted with the session key Alice requested from the KDC for conversing with Bob. We will assume in the following that Alice is sending the authenticator to Bob.

# octets		
≤40	Alice's name	null-terminated
≤40	Alice's instance	null-terminated
≤40	Alice's realm	null-terminated
4	checksum	
1	5-millisecond timestamp	
4	timestamp	
≤ 7	pad of 0s to make authenticator multiple of eight octets	

- ALICE'S NAME/INSTANCE/REALM. The presence of these fields avoids an extremely obscure threat. Without these fields, if two principals have the same master key, then an attacker who could intercept messages between one of them and the KDC could change the AS_REQ to have the other principal's name. The returned ticket would then be for the other principal, so that when this principal used the ticket to Bob, Bob would believe it to be the other principal. Now you know.

- CHECKSUM—four octets. This field can be used in an application-specific way. None of the applications that have been Kerberized use this field in a way in which the name *checksum* makes sense. Many applications set this field to Alice's process id. The application that copies the KDC database to KDC replicas sets this field to the size of the KDC database. The sample application provided to help implementers build a Kerberized application suggests having the user type in a value for that field.

- 5-MILLISECOND TIMESTAMP. This field extends the TIMESTAMP field to give time granularity down to 5 milliseconds instead of 1 second. Its purpose is to allow more than one authenticator to the same service to be generated in a single second without having it rejected as a duplicate. The simplest implementation of this field would actually be a sequence number within the second (in which case the name is misleading, since it has nothing to do with the unit of time of 5 milliseconds).

- TIMESTAMP—four octets, time in seconds. This is really the main information in the authenticator. Bob decrypts the authenticator, verifies that the time is acceptably close to current, and, if mutual authentication is used, increments this field, encrypts the result, and sends it back to Alice. Because only Bob (or Alice) is able to encrypt the incremented value, when Alice verifies the response she knows that the authenticator arrived at Bob.

13.12.3 Credentials

The CREDENTIALS field in a message is encrypted. When returned in an AS_REP (the message that returns a ticket-granting ticket), it is encrypted in Alice's master key. When returned in a TGS_REP (the message which requests a ticket to another principal, from the Ticket-Granting Server), it is encrypted with Alice's session key.

Again, we're assuming Alice has requested to talk to Bob.

# octets		
8	session key for Alice↔Bob	
≤40	Bob's name	null-terminated
≤40	Bob's instance	null-terminated
≤40	Bob's realm	null-terminated
1	ticket lifetime	
1	Bob's key version number	
1	length of ticket	
variable	ticket	
4	timestamp	
≤ 7	pad of 0s	

- SESSION KEY—eight octets. In an AS_REP, this gives the login session key for Alice. In a TGS_REP, this gives the key to be used when Alice communicates with Bob.

- BOB'S NAME/INSTANCE/REALM. These fields identify the ticket target. Since Alice sends the ticket request unprotected, the presence of these fields assures Alice that the ticket is for whom she thinks it is for.

- TICKET LIFETIME—one octet. Number of 5-minute intervals from the time in TIMESTAMP during which the ticket should be valid.

- KEY VERSION NUMBER. This field allows Bob to change his key in a way that won't disrupt principals that are currently talking to Bob or holding tickets for Bob. Bob must keep track of his old keys for 21 hours after he reports the new key to the KDC (or somewhat longer to allow for propagation to slave KDCs). All such **active** keys for Bob should have unique key version numbers. When a ticket arrives, Bob can use the key version number in the unencrypted header to decide which key to use to decrypt it. 21 hours after Bob reports a new key, any issued tickets encrypted under older keys will have expired and Bob can safely forget the older keys.

- TIMESTAMP—four octets. Time when ticket generated.

13.12.4 AS_REQ

This message is used to ask for a ticket (when one doesn't already have a TGT). It is almost always used to ask for a TGT, which is a ticket to the Ticket-Granting Service. Theoretically it could be used to ask for a ticket to any service, using the requester's master key.

# octets		
1	version of Kerberos (4)	
1	message type (1) | B	
≤40	Alice's name	null-terminated
≤40	Alice's instance	null-terminated
≤40	Alice's realm	null-terminated
4	Alice's timestamp	
1	desired ticket lifetime	
≤40	service's name	null-terminated
≤40	service's instance	null-terminated

- MESSAGE TYPE. AS_REQ (1).
- B BIT, BYTE-ORDER FLAG.
- ALICE'S TIMESTAMP. This field is here in order to help Alice match up requests with replies.
- DESIRED TICKET LIFETIME—one octet. In units of 5 minutes, how long the requester would like the issued ticket to be good for. This was a mistake in the design—the upper bound (about 21 hours) is not long enough for some applications.
- SERVICE'S NAME. For the normal case of a request for a ticket to the Ticket-Granting Service, the name will be the constant krbtgt.
- SERVICE'S INSTANCE. For the normal case of a request for a ticket to the Ticket-Granting Service, the instance will be the realm name.

13.12.5 TGS_REQ

The TGS_REQ is used by Alice to request a ticket to Bob from the TGS. In order to do this, Alice needs to send the TGS the TGT (so that the TGS can know the proper session key for Alice), and an authenticator. It turns out sending an authenticator in a TGS_REQ has no security value, but it is necessary in an AP_REQ, and therefore it is in the TGS_REQ to make the two protocols similar.

# octets			
1	version of Kerberos (4)		
1	message type (3)	B	
1	KDC's key version number		
≤40	KDC's realm		null-terminated
1	length of ticket-granting ticket		
1	length of authenticator		
variable	ticket-granting ticket (TGT)		
variable	authenticator		
4	Alice's timestamp		
1	desired ticket lifetime		
≤40	Bob's name		null-terminated
≤40	Bob's instance		null-terminated

- MESSAGE TYPE. AP_REQ (3).
- KDC'S KEY VERSION NUMBER. Copied from BOB'S KEY VERSION NUMBER in the credentials which Alice obtained in the KRB_TGS_REP she received when she asked for a TGT.
- KDC'S REALM. This field is here so that the KDC, in interrealm authentication, will know which key to use to decrypt the ticket. Suppose the KDC in realm *B* is registered in many different realms. The KDC in *B* will have a different key for each realm in which it is registered. For example, if realm *B* can talk to realm *A*, then *B* will have a master key stored at realm *A*'s KDC. If *B* can also talk to realm *C*, then *B* will have a different master key stored at realm *C*'s KDC. When Alice, in realm *A*, gets a ticket to the KDC in *B*, and then asks *B* for a ticket to a principal in *B*'s realm, it is necessary to inform *B* which key it should use to decrypt the ticket (in this case, the one it shares with the KDC in realm *A*).

13.12.6 AS_REP and TGS_REP

This message is the reply to an AS_REQ or a TGS_REQ. It's really a single message type (2), but it can occur in response to two different sorts of request.

In the following fields, we'll assume the reply is in response to a request from Alice to get a ticket for Bob.

# octets	field	
1	version of Kerberos (4)	
1	message type (2) — B	
≤40	Alice's name	null-terminated
≤40	Alice's instance	null-terminated
≤40	Alice's realm	null-terminated
4	Alice's timestamp	
1	number of tickets (1)	
4	ticket expiration time	
1	Alice's key version number	
2	credentials length	
variable	credentials	

- MESSAGE TYPE. AS_REP (2).
- ALICE'S NAME/INSTANCE/REALM. Useful in case there are multiple principals on the same node. If a response comes back, the service might not be able to know to which principal the credentials belongs without that field there. Given that the field is not encrypted, it has no security value. It is just there to prevent nonmalicious confusion. The MIT implementation ignores these fields.
- ALICE'S TIMESTAMP. As sent in request (this is to match requests and replies).
- NUMBER OF TICKETS—one octet. Ignored by Kerberos Version 4. In earlier versions of Kerberos, it was possible to request multiple tickets in a single request. Because this feature was never used and complicated the message formats, it was simplified out of V4. This field remains for backwards compatibility.
- TICKET EXPIRATION TIME—four octets.
- ALICE'S KEY VERSION—one octet. Unused if this message is in response to a TGS_REQ.
- CREDENTIALS LENGTH—two octets.
- CREDENTIALS.

13.12.7 Error Reply from KDC

This message is in response to an AS_REQ or a TGS_REQ, if the KDC fails to reply with a ticket. Again, assume this is in response to principal Alice requesting a ticket for principal Bob.

# octets		
1	version of Kerberos (4)	
1	message type (32) | B	
≤40	Alice's name	null-terminated
≤40	Alice's instance	null-terminated
≤40	Alice's realm	null-terminated
4	Alice's timestamp	
4	error code	
≤40	error text / additional explanation of error	null-terminated

The defined values for error code are:

1—Alice's database entry at the KDC expired. (Note: Kerberos allows database entries to expire. There is an expiration date on each entry.)

2—Bob's database entry expired.

3—authenticator on the request expired.

4—wrong protocol version number.

7—byte order unknown. (C'mon—it's a bit! How can you not know the two values of a bit?!—and we left out errors 5 and 6 because they were even sillier, and they also were never invoked in the code, so they are irrelevant.)

8—Alice or Bob not found in database.

9—Alice or Bob found in multiple places in the database (though it seems like it would be more sensible to generate an error when adding a duplicate rather than checking for it on every read).

10—Alice or Bob found, but no key is in the database.

20—Generic error from KDC.

13.12.8 AP_REQ

This message is sent from Alice to Bob early in their conversation in order to authenticate. Exactly how this message is passed within the application protocol is not defined by Kerberos. The receiving end must be able to figure out that this is a Kerberos message and pass it to its own Kerberos subroutines.

# octets			
1	version of Kerberos (4)		
1	message type (8)	B	
1	Bob's key version number		
≤40	Bob's realm		null-terminated
1	length of ticket		
1	length of authenticator		
variable	ticket		
variable	authenticator		

- BOB'S REALM. This is in case Bob is registered in different realms, with different keys in each one. This field enables Bob to choose the proper key to use to decrypt the ticket.

13.12.9 AP_REP

The Kerberos documentation does not define an explicit reply from Bob when Alice sends an AP_REQ. However, the library routines include subroutine krb_sendauth, used by Alice, and krb_recvauth, used by Bob, which most applications use. If all that is necessary is for Bob to authenticate Alice, then there is no necessity for a Kerberos reply from Bob. The application just starts conversing.

If mutual authentication is desired, then Bob needs to send information to Alice that will prove that Bob has decrypted the ticket and therefore knows the session key. The Kerberos routine krb_recvauth accomplishes this by having Bob extract the value of the CHECKSUM field and increment it.

The message format of the message sent by krb_recvauth is the same as KRB_PRV (described in following section), but the data part of the ENCRYPTED STUFF field is the four-octet incremented checksum.

13.12.10 Encrypted Data (KRB_PRV)

Some applications want privacy as well as authentication, i.e., they want their data encrypted. They call a Kerberos subroutine that encrypts the application-supplied data and packages it into a message of the following form:

# octets	field	
1	version of Kerberos (4)	
1	message type (6)	B
4	length of encrypted stuff	
variable	encrypted stuff	

The ENCRYPTED STUFF is encrypted using DES in the PCBC mode using the session key. Once decrypted, its format is:

# octets		field
4		length of data
variable		data
1		5-millisecond timestamp
4		sender's IP address
4	D	timestamp
variable		padding

By the nature of PCBC, the sender's IP address and the timestamp serve as an integrity check on the data. The timestamp serves a second function of providing some protection against replay.

Because encryption for privacy is an export-controlled technology, certain versions of Kerberos exclude the capacity to encrypt application-supplied data. This message type will still occur, however, in the context of a mutual authentication message.

13.12.11 Integrity-Checked Data (SAFE)

For some applications, privacy of the data is not a concern, but protection of the integrity of the data in transit is. Others may be willing to give up privacy in order to get better performance or in order to satisfy government regulations, but are still willing to pay a price for integrity protection.

The SAFE message is basically application data to which Kerberos appends a checksum and timestamp. The format for integrity-protected data is

# octets		
1	version of Kerberos (4)	
1	message type (7)	B
4	length of data	
variable	data	
1	5-millisecond timestamp	
4	sender's IP address	
4	D	timestamp
16	(pseudo-Jueneman) checksum	

- SENDER'S IP ADDRESS. It does not appear that having this field in every message adds anything to security, but the Kerberos code checks that it matches the address from which the packet came.
- TIMESTAMP. The purpose of this field is to prevent delayed and replayed messages. An application could save all timestamps that were used within the allowable clock skew and refuse additional messages with the same timestamp. It could also require that messages encrypted under a given key be processed in strictly ascending order by timestamp (if using a connection type that prevents reordering). All the Kerberos-V4-provided subroutine does is make sure the timestamp is within the allowable clock skew.
- 5-MILLISECOND TIMESTAMP. This field allows more than one message within a second. Theoretically it is in units of 5 milliseconds, but in practice can be a sequence number of messages sent within a particular value of the four-octet TIMESTAMP field. If this format survives long enough, a limit of one message every 5 milliseconds may someday be a problem.
- CHECKSUM. The modified Jueneman checksum is seeded with the session key as described in §13.10 *Encryption for Integrity Only* so that only someone with knowledge of the session key can compute a new valid checksum for a modified message.

13.12.12 AP_ERR

This is returned if the authentication failed.

# octets		
1	version of Kerberos (4)	
1	message type (8) | B	
4	error code	
≤40	error text / additional explanation of error	null-terminated

The possible errors are

31—can't decode authenticator.

32—ticket expired.

33—ticket not yet valid.

34—repeated request. Receiver of message remembers receiving the same timestamp and 5-millisecond timestamp before.

35—ticket isn't for us. Well, we're not sure what they intended by this error message, but it's never used anywhere. The intention was most likely for Bob to check Bob's name and instance inside the ticket, but none of the applications implemented actually check this.

36—request is inconsistent. The name, instance, and realm of Bob as listed in the ticket does not match the name, instance, and realm in the authenticator.

37—delta_t too big. There is too much skew in the clocks. This is determined based on comparison of the timestamp in the authenticator and the local time at Bob. This skew can be set independently at each node, but a common time is five minutes.

38—incorrect net address. The address in the ticket does not match the source address in the Network Layer header of the received message.

39—protocol version number mismatch.

40—invalid message type.

41—message stream modified. Either the checksum failed or some other piece of bad formatting was detected in an encrypted or integrity-protected message.

42—message out of order. Timestamps are not in ascending order. This assumes the application is running over a reliable transport protocol (in this case, TCP), so that reordering is not due to the network.

43—unauthorized request. This is an application-specific complaint, i.e., it is not generated by Kerberos. It might be used by Bob to tell Alice that Alice is not authorized to use Bob.

13.13 HOMEWORK

1. Design a variant of Kerberos in which the workstation generates a TGT. The TGT will be encrypted with the user's master key rather than the KDC's master key. How does this compare with standard Kerberos in terms of efficiency, security, etc.? What happens in each scheme if the user changes her password during a login session?
2. §13.5 *Replicated KDCs* explains that the KDC database isn't encrypted as a unit. Rather each user's master key is independently encrypted with the KDC master key. Suppose replication were done with a simple download (i.e., no cryptographic integrity check is performed). How could a bad guy who is a principal registered with a KDC impersonate Alice, another principal registered with that KDC? Assume he can see and modify the KDC database in transit, but that he does not know the KDC master key.
3. Why is the authenticator field not of security benefit when asking the KDC for a ticket for Bob, but useful when logging into Bob?
4. Specify the Kerberos messages involved from the time a user first walks up to a workstation to the time the user is successfully talking to something in another realm.
5. With CBC, if one ciphertext block is lost, how many plaintext blocks are lost? With PCBC, why do things get back in sync if c_n and c_{n+1} are switched? How about if a ciphertext block is lost? How about if ciphertext block n is switched with ciphertext block $n+2$? How about any permutation of the first n blocks?

14 KERBEROS V5

This chapter describes Kerberos Version 5, but it assumes you already understand Kerberos V4. So even if you think you're only interested in V5, it's a good idea to read the previous chapter first.

Kerberos V5 represents a major overhaul of Version 4. While the basic philosophy remains the same, there are major changes to the encodings and major extensions to the functionality. The motivation behind the changes in Kerberos V5 is to allow greater flexibility in the environments in which Kerberos can be used.

14.1 ASN.1

ASN.1 [ISO87, PISC93] is a data representation language standardized by ISO. It looks very similar to data structure definitions in programming languages. ASN.1 is popular among spec writers and standards bodies because it gives people a way to precisely define data structures without worrying about different data representations, such as bit and octet order, on different machines.

Where Kerberos V4 messages had a largely fixed layout with variable-length fields marked in an ad hoc way, Kerberos V5 uses ASN.1 syntax with the Basic Encoding Rules (BER), which makes it easy for fields to be optional, of varying length, and tagged with type information to allow future versions to include additional encodings.

This flexibility comes with a price. ASN.1 has a lot of overhead. It adds octets of overhead in databases and octets on the wire, and increases the complexity of the code. Often when people define things in ASN.1, they don't realize what the actual format will be. It is possible to use ASN.1 in a way that would create less overhead, but that takes expertise in ASN.1, and there are very few security protocol designers who have any interest in the specifics of ASN.1.

To illustrate the point, in Kerberos V4 an address is four octets. Admittedly this is not sufficiently flexible, since it assumes IP addresses. Had the Kerberos designers custom-designed a more flexible address format, they'd probably have designed something like

- a one-octet address type (defining type codes for IP and perhaps DECnet, CLNP, IPX, and Appletalk)

- a one-octet length, specifying the length in octets of the address (this is needed because some address types, for instance CLNP, are variable-length)
- and then the address.

With this format it would have taken six octets to encode an IP address, rather than four in Kerberos V4. However, Kerberos V5 defines an address using the ASN.1 definition:

```
HostAddress ::= SEQUENCE {
                addr-type[0]      INTEGER,
                address[1]        OCTET STRING }
```

What does this mean? It means that an address has two components: **addr-type** and **address**. That sounds reasonable. But what does the Kerberos V5 definition of an address actually expand into? Somehow it adds 11 octets of overhead to each address, meaning that encoding an IP address in V5 requires 15 octets instead of V4's four octets.

Where does this 11 octet overhead come from? The construct **SEQUENCE** requires an octet to specify that it's a sequence, and an octet to specify the length of the entire sequence. The first component, **addr-type[0] INTEGER**, requires four octets of overhead in addition to the single-octet integer that specifies the type of address:

- **addr-type[0]** requires an octet to specify that it's type 0, then an octet to specify the length of what follows.
- **INTEGER** requires a minimum of three octets: an octet to specify that it's an integer (TYPE), an octet to specify how many octets (LENGTH) of integer, and at least one octet giving the value of the integer.

Similarly, the next component, **address[1] OCTET STRING**, requires four octets of overhead in addition to the actual address.

With clever use of ASN.1, it would have been possible to reduce the overhead substantially. For instance, by defining things with **IMPLICIT**, the representations are more compact, because then the TYPE and LENGTH fields do not appear. For example, four octets of overhead are avoided by defining an address as follows:

```
HostAddress ::= SEQUENCE {
                addr-type[0]      IMPLICIT INTEGER,
                address[1]        IMPLICIT OCTET STRING }
```

The above definition would reduce the overhead from 11 octets to 7 octets. An ASN.1 guru might define an address as follows:

```
HostAddress ::= CHOICE {
      ip_address[0]     IMPLICIT OCTET STRING,
      clnp_address[1]   IMPLICIT OCTET STRING,
```

```
ipx_address[2]    IMPLICIT OCTET STRING,
...}
```

That definition produces only two octets of overhead for an address (provided that the world doesn't invent more than 64 types of address), since it expands into a type (the number in square brackets), followed by a length, followed by the address.

Because ASN.1 is ugly to look at, and since the actual octet-expansion is pretty much irrelevant to any reader of this book, when we describe message formats and data structures in Kerberos V5 we'll just list the contents without being specific about the exact encoding.

In Kerberos V4, the B BIT in all the messages specifies the octet order of multi-octet fields. In V5, fields are described using ASN.1 syntax, which defines a canonical format for integers. This is an example where use of ASN.1 hides the complexity of the protocol, since ASN.1 ensures a canonical format.

14.2 NAMES

In Kerberos V4, a principal is named by the three fields NAME, INSTANCE, and REALM, which must each be a null-terminated text string up to 40 characters long (including the null). The size of these fields is too short for some environments, and certain characters (like ".") are illegal inside Kerberos strings but required for account names on some systems. In V5, there are two components: the REALM and the NAME. The NAME component contains a type and a varying number of arbitrary strings, so the purpose served by the V4 INSTANCE field is accomplished by using an extra string in the NAME component. In V4, REALMs are DNS standard names, whereas in V5 they can be DNS standard names or X.500 names, and the syntax allows for other name types as well.

14.3 DELEGATION OF RIGHTS

Delegation of rights is the ability to give someone else access to things you are authorized to access. Usually delegation is limited in time (Alice allows Bob to access her resources only for a specified amount of time), or limited in scope (Alice only allows Bob to access a specified subset of her resources). Why would Alice want to let Bob use her resources? Alice might want to start up a batch job on some remote node Bob that will run in the middle of the night and need to access many of her files located around the network. Or Alice might be logged into host Bob but then want to log into host Earnest from Bob.

One way delegation could be provided is for Alice to send Bob her master key (in an encrypted message to Bob), allowing him to obtain tickets to whatever resources he might need on Alice's behalf. That is clearly not desirable, since it would allow Bob to forever be able to impersonate Alice. You might think that if Alice knew what resources Bob would need to access on her behalf, she could obtain tickets for those resources in advance and send Bob the tickets and keys (in an encrypted message to Bob). Or if she didn't know all the resources in advance, she could give Bob her TGT and session key, which he could use to obtain specific tickets on Alice's behalf as necessary. Not only are these mechanisms inconvenient and/or insecure and therefore undesirable, but they wouldn't work with Kerberos (either V4 or V5) because the ticket contains a network layer address, and Kerberos insists that a ticket must be used from the specified network layer address. In V4, the network layer address in the ticket is the address from which the ticket was requested.

Kerberos V5 explicitly allows delegation by allowing Alice to ask for a TGT with a network layer address different from hers. As a matter of fact it allows Alice to specify multiple addresses to include (in which case the ticket can be used from any of the specified addresses), or allows Alice to request that no address be included (in which case the ticket can be used from any address). Alice logs in as in Kerberos V4, getting a session key and a TGT with her own network layer address. When she later decides that she needs to allow Bob to act on her behalf, she requests a new TGT from the KDC, but this time specifically says that she'd like the network layer address in the TGT to be Bob's address. The new TGT so obtained is not usable by Alice directly, but can be passed to node Bob (along with the corresponding session key). It is a policy decision by the KDC as to whether to issue tickets with no specified address. It's also a policy decision by services on the network as to whether to accept such tickets.

Kerberos could have provided delegation by removing the network layer address from tickets and TGTs and instead having the network layer address in the authenticator. The Kerberos method has the disadvantage and advantage that Alice has to do an extra interaction with the KDC. It's a disadvantage for performance reasons. But it's an advantage because requiring Alice to do something that lets the KDC know she's delegating to Bob enables the KDC to audit delegation events. In the event of a security compromise, the audit trail will tell which nodes had access to which resources.

Sometimes Alice might know enough and be sufficiently security-conscious to specify the range of rights she wishes to delegate to Bob. Kerberos V5 supports two forms of limited delegation:

- Alice can give Bob tickets to the specific services he will need to access on her behalf (rather than giving him a TGT, which would allow him to request tickets to any services).
- When requesting a ticket or TGT that she intends to give to Bob, Alice can request that a field AUTHORIZATION-DATA be added to the ticket or TGT. The field is not interpreted by Ker-

beros, but is instead application-specific, which means it is left up to the application to define and use the field. The intention is that the field specifies to the application restrictions on what Bob is allowed to do with the ticket. If the field is in a TGT Alice gives to Bob, the field will be copied by the KDC into any ticket Bob gets using that TGT. OSF/DCE security (see §24.6 *DCE Security*) and Windows 2000 (see §24.7.2 *Windows 2000 Kerberos*) make extensive use of this field.

Because there is not universal agreement that allowing delegation is always a good idea, Kerberos V5 makes it optional. A flag inside a TGT indicates whether a request for a TGT or ticket with a different network layer address should be allowed. The Kerberos protocol itself does not specify how the KDC should know how to set the various permission flags when creating an initial TGT. One method is the method the MIT implementation chose, which is to configure instructions for setting the permissions into the user's entry in the KDC database. Another possible way of deciding how to set various flags inside the TGT would be to ask the user Alice when she logs in, but that leaves the potential for a horrible user interface: Name________ Password________ Proxiable? (Y/N)__ Allow postdated? (Y/N)__ Forwardable? (Y/N)__ Renewable? (Y/N)__ Aisle/Window__ Smoking/Nonsmoking__ ....

There are two flags in a TGT involving delegation permission. One indicates that the TGT is **forwardable**, which means that it can be exchanged for a TGT with a different network layer address. This gives Alice permission to give Bob a TGT, with which Bob can request tickets to any resources on Alice's behalf. When Alice uses a forwardable TGT to request a TGT to be used from Bob's network layer address, she also specifies how the FORWARDABLE flag should be set in the requested TGT. If she requests that the TGT have the FORWARDABLE flag set, then Bob will be able to use that TGT to obtain a TGT for some other entity Carol, allowing Carol to act on Alice's behalf.

The other flag indicates that the TGT is **proxiable**, meaning that it can be used to request tickets for use with a different network layer address than the one in the TGT. This gives Alice permission to get tickets that she can give to Bob, but not a TGT for use by Bob. The Kerberos documentation refers to tickets Alice gives to Bob for use on her behalf as **proxy tickets**.

TGTs have a FORWARDED flag. Tickets have a FORWARDED flag and a PROXY flag. A TGT given to Bob by Alice is marked forwarded. The FORWARDED flag will also be set in any ticket Bob obtains using a TGT marked forwarded. A ticket given to Bob by Alice is marked proxy. The reason for marking tickets in this way is that some applications may want to refuse to honor delegated tickets, and need to recognize them as such. Note that allowing both the KDC and applications to make decisions on whether delegation is allowed makes for a flexible but confusing access control model.

14.4 TICKET LIFETIMES

In V4, the maximum lifetime of a ticket was about 21 hours, since the time in a ticket was encoded as a four-octet start time and a one-octet lifetime (in units of 5 minutes). This was too short for some applications. In Kerberos V5, tickets can be issued with virtually unlimited lifetimes (the farthest in the future that can be specified with a V5 timestamp is Dec 31, 9999). The timestamp format is an ASN.1-defined quantity that is 17 octets long. Although it has a virtually unlimited lifetime (unlike the V4 timestamp), it is only in seconds, and Kerberos V5, in some cases, would have preferred time expressed down to microseconds. As a result, much of the time when Kerberos V5 passes around a timestamp it also passes around a microsecond time, which is an ASN.1 integer whose representation requires sufficiently many octets to express the value (in this case one to three octets, since 999999 is the biggest value), plus a type and length.

Long-lived tickets pose serious security risks, because once created they cannot be revoked (except perhaps by invalidating the master key of the service to which the ticket was granted). So V5 has a number of mechanisms for implementing revocable long-lived tickets.

These mechanisms involve use of several timestamp fields in tickets (and TGTs). Each timestamp is encoded, using glorious ASN.1 format, in 17 octets of information. First we'll give the names of the timestamps, and then we'll explain how they're used:

- START-TIME--time the ticket becomes valid.
- END-TIME—time the ticket expires.
- AUTHTIME—time at which Alice first logged in, i.e., when she was granted an initial TGT (one based on her password). AUTHTIME is copied from her initial TGT into each ticket she requests based on that TGT.
- RENEW-TILL—latest legal end-time (relevant for renewable tickets, see below).

14.4.1 Renewable Tickets

Rather than creating a ticket valid for say, 100 years, the KDC can give Alice a ticket that will be valid for 100 years, but only if she keeps renewing it, say once a day. Renewing a ticket involves giving the ticket to the KDC and having the KDC reissue it. If there is some reason to want to revoke Alice's privileges, this can be done by telling the KDC not to renew any of Alice's tickets.

The KDC is configured with a maximum validity time for a ticket, say a day. If there is a reason for Alice's ticket to be valid for longer than that time, then when Alice requests the ticket, the KDC sets the RENEWABLE flag inside the ticket. The RENEW-TILL time specifies the time beyond which the ticket cannot be renewed.

In order to keep using the ticket, Alice will have to keep renewing it before it expires. If she is ever late renewing it, the KDC will refuse to renew it. Why did Kerberos choose to do it that way? It seems somewhat inconvenient. Node Alice has to keep a demon running checking for tickets that will expire soon, and renew them. If Kerberos allowed renewal of expired tickets, then Alice could wait until she attempts to use a ticket and gets an error message indicating the ticket expired, and then renew it. This would be more convenient. The reasoning in Kerberos is that if Alice could present a ticket a long time after it expired, then if the KDC has been told to revoke the ticket it would have to remember the revoked ticket until that ticket's RENEW-TILL time. As it is, it just has to remember the revoked ticket for a maximum validity time.

The END-TIME specifies the time at which the ticket will expire (unless renewed). When Alice gives the KDC a renewable ticket and requests that it be renewed, the KDC does this by changing END-TIME to be the maximum ticket lifetime as configured into the user's entry in the KDC database, added to the current time (but not greater than RENEW-TILL).

14.4.2 Postdated Tickets

Postdated tickets are used to run a batch job at some time in the future. Suppose you want to issue a ticket starting a week from now and good for two hours. One possible method is to issue a ticket with an expiration time of one week plus two hours from the present time, but that would mean the ticket would be valid from the time it was issued until it expired. Kerberos instead allows a ticket to become valid at some point in the future. Kerberos does this by using the START-TIME timestamp, indicating when the ticket should first become valid. Such a ticket is known as a **postdated ticket**.

In order to allow revocation of the postdated ticket between the time it was issued and the time it becomes valid, there's an INVALID flag inside the ticket that Kerberos sets in the initially issued postdated ticket. When the time specified in START-TIME occurs, Alice can present the ticket to the KDC and the KDC will clear the INVALID flag. This additional step gives the opportunity to revoke the postdated ticket by warning the KDC. If the KDC is configured to revoke the postdated ticket, the validation request will fail.

There's an additional flag inside the ticket, the POSTDATED flag, which indicates that the ticket was originally issued as a postdated ticket. An application could in theory refuse to accept such a ticket, but none currently do and we can't imagine why any applications would care.

A flag, MAY-POSTDATE, which appears in a TGT, indicates whether the KDC is allowed to issue postdated tickets using this TGT.

14.5 KEY VERSIONS

If Alice holds a ticket to Bob and then Bob changes his key, Kerberos enables Alice's ticket to work until it expires by maintaining multiple versions of Bob's key, and tagging Bob's key with a version number where necessary for the KDC or for Bob to know which key to use.

In the KDC database, each version of Bob's key is stored as a triple: ⟨*key*, *p_kvno*, *k_kvno*⟩. *key* is Bob's key encrypted according to the KDC's key. *p_kvno* is the version number of this key of Bob's (*p_* stands for *principal*). *k_kvno* is the version number of the KDC's key that was used to encrypt *key*, since the KDC might also have changed its key recently (*k_* stands for *KDC*).

If Alice asks for a ticket to Bob, the KDC encrypts the ticket with the key for Bob with the highest *p_kvno*. In V4, the KDC did not keep track of more than one key for Bob. It was up to Bob to keep track of all his keys for a ticket expiration interval, in order for Bob to honor unexpired tickets issued with his old key. So why does the KDC need to keep track of multiple keys for Bob in V5? It is because of renewable tickets and postdated tickets. If Alice has a renewable ticket to Bob, and Bob changed his key since the ticket was originally issued, the KDC needs to be able to decrypt the ticket, so it needs to have stored the key with which that ticket was encrypted. When the KDC renews the ticket, it will issue the renewed ticket with the most recent key for Bob. That way the KDC and Bob can forget old key version numbers after a predictable, reasonably small time (like a day) (except for postdated tickets, which is somewhat of a design flaw in Kerberos).

14.6 MAKING MASTER KEYS IN DIFFERENT REALMS DIFFERENT

Suppose Alice is registered in different realms, and suppose Alice is human. Given that humans have a limited capacity for remembering passwords, Alice might wish to have a single password in all the realms in which she is registered. This means that if an intruder discovers her master key in one realm, he can impersonate her in the other realms as well.

In Kerberos V5, the password-to-key conversion hash function uses the realm name. This means that the function, given the same password, will come up with a different master key if the name of the realm is different. The function is such that it is not possible to derive the master key in realm FOO even if the master key derived from the same password in realm BAR is known.

This does not protect against an intruder who manages to obtain Alice's password. This just helps in the case where Alice has chosen a good password and an intruder manages to steal a KDC database from some realm. Stealing that database will allow the intruder to impersonate Alice in that realm, but not to impersonate Alice in any other realms for which she is using the same password. Note that stealing the database will also allow an intruder to mount an off-line password-guessing attack, and if the password-guessing attack succeeds, then the intruder *can* impersonate Alice in other realms for which she is using the same password.

14.7 OPTIMIZATIONS

There were certain fields in Kerberos V4 that were not necessary and were taken out in V5. In particular, encryption is expensive (especially when done in software), so it is undesirable to unnecessarily encrypt information. In Kerberos V4, a ticket is included in the CREDENTIALS portion of an AS_REP, and the entire CREDENTIALS field, including the ticket, is encrypted. A ticket is already an encrypted message. There is no reason to encrypt the ticket an additional time. (It had better not be necessary—tickets are later sent across the network unencrypted.)

An example of a field that was removed in Kerberos V5 because it was only slightly useful (if at all) was the name of the ticket target inside a ticket; that is, if Alice gets a ticket to Bob, then Bob's name is in the V4 ticket to Bob, but not in the V5 ticket.

14.8 CRYPTOGRAPHIC ALGORITHMS

Kerberos V4 assumes DES is the encryption algorithm. There are two problems with DES. One is that it is not secure enough for high-security environments. The other is that it is considered by the U.S. government to be too secure to export. Kerberos V5 is designed in a modular way which allows insertion of different encryption algorithms. When encryption is used, there is a type field allowing the receiver to know which decryption algorithm to use.

Since different encryption systems use different-length keys, and since some encryption systems allow variable-length keys, in V5 keys are tagged with a type and length.

DES continues to be used in all actual implementations of Kerberos (to our knowledge). Two cryptographic weaknesses in Kerberos V4 (modified Jueneman checksum, which was used for integrity protection without encryption, and PCBC, which was used for encryption and integrity protection) were repaired.

14.8.1 Integrity-Only Algorithms

The modified Jueneman checksum used in Kerberos V4, while never (publicly) broken, was not considered sufficiently secure (see §13.10 *Encryption for Integrity Only*). So in V5 it was replaced by a choice of algorithms.

Why did V5 not simply choose one known-to-be-secure integrity protection algorithm? No algorithm is ever known to be secure. It's just not known to be broken. So V5 selected a few algorithms, with the intent that if a serious cryptographic flaw was found in one of the algorithms being used, a different one could be substituted without changing the rest of the implementation. Unfortunately, if a recipient does not accept all defined algorithms, there is a possibility of non-interoperability (acceptable algorithms are not negotiated). Another problem with having a choice of algorithms is that Kerberos is really only as secure as the weakest algorithm the recipient will accept rather than the strongest. The reason for this is that if one algorithm is weak, then even if your implementation does not transmit it, a forger could use the weak algorithm to impersonate you to any implementation which accepts it.

If Kerberos V5 were designed today, the algorithms of choice would probably be AES-CBC and HMAC-SHA-1. Kerberos V5 does something probably equivalent in terms of security, but harder to explain. Much harder to explain, as a matter of fact. We agonized as to whether to bother you with the details. The algorithms are baroque and technically uninteresting. There never would be a reason to implement them except to be compatible with a Kerberos V5 implementation. But in the interest of completeness, we'll explain them here.

Kerberos V5 documentation refers to an integrity check as a *checksum*. We prefer the term *MAC* (message authentication code). The MACs specified in V5 are as follows, using the names in the Kerberos documentation. Three of them are required to be supported by implementations. The other two are optional.

- rsa-md5-des (required)
- des-mac (required)
- des-mac-k (required)
- rsa-md4-des (optional)
- rsa-md4-des-k (optional)

14.8.1.1 rsa-md5-des

This MAC is one of the required ones. The name is not particularly helpful, except that it's a combination of md5 and des. It has nothing to do with RSA other than that RSADSI (the company) owns rights to MD5, which is freely distributable provided that RSADSI is credited with every mention of it (or some such legalism).

The way the MAC is calculated is as follows:

1. Choose a 64-bit random number, known as a **confounder.**
2. Prepend it to the message:

confounder	*message*

3. Calculate the MD5 message digest of the result, getting a 128-bit quantity.
4. Prepend the confounder chosen in Step 1 to the message digest:

64 bits	128 bits
confounder	*message digest*

5. Calculate a modified key by taking the KDC-supplied shared secret key and ⊕ing it with $F0F0F0F0F0F0F0F0_{16}$. Call the result K'.
6. Encrypt the result, using DES in CBC mode, using K' and an IV (initialization vector) of 0, resulting in a 192-bit encrypted quantity. That 192-bit quantity is the MAC.

How is this MAC verified? It's actually quite straightforward. You just reverse all the steps.

1. Calculate the modified key, by performing Step 5 above (⊕ing the KDC-supplied shared secret key with $F0F0F0F0F0F0F0F0_{16}$ to get K').
2. Decrypt the MAC, using K' in CBC mode, resulting in a 192-bit quantity. Let's call the first 64 bits of the decrypted quantity X, and the remainder Y:

64 bits	128 bits
X	Y

3. The first 64 bits of the result (X) should be the confounder. To verify that, append X to the message, and calculate the MD5 message digest of the result.

X	*message*

4. If the 128-bit result matches Y, then the MAC is verified as valid.

14.8.1.2 des-mac

This is another of the required MACs. To calculate it do the following:

1. Choose a 64-bit random number, known as a **confounder**.

2. Prepend it to the message:

confounder	message

3. Calculate the DES CBC residue of the result (confounder prepended to the message) using the unmodified KDC-supplied shared secret key K, and using an IV of 0. The result is a 64-bit quantity we'll call R, for the *Residue*.
4. Calculate the modified key $K' = K \oplus \text{F0F0F0F0F0F0F0F0}_{16}$.
5. Prepend the 64-bit confounder C to the 64-bit residue R, getting a 128-bit value.
6. Perform DES encryption in CBC mode on the 128-bit $C|R$ from the previous step, using K' as the key, and an IV of 0.
7. The result is the 128-bit MAC.

Verifying this MAC is straightforward (see Homework Problem 9).

14.8.1.3 des-mac-k

This is another of the MACs which are required. The MACs that end with "-k" in their name are the old-style ones, before it occurred to the Kerberos designers that using a modified key would be a good idea. These are no longer recommended, but need to be implemented for backward compatibility.

This MAC is calculated by doing a CBC-residue over the message using the original key K, and using K also as the IV. The MAC is verified the same way.

14.8.1.4 rsa-md4-des

This MAC is the same as rsa-md5-des, except that MD4 is used instead of MD5.

14.8.1.5 rsa-md4-des-k

This MAC is no longer recommended, and is only there for backward compatibility. Again, the "-k" in the name indicates that it was designed before the Kerberos designers realized it would be a good idea to use a modified version of the key for calculating the MAC.

This MAC is calculated as follows. First calculate MD4 of the message, yielding 128 bits (16 octets). Take the result and encrypt it using DES in CBC mode, with the unmodified session key K used as both the encryption key and the IV. The 128-bit result of the encryption is the MAC.

14.8.2 Encryption for Privacy and Integrity

The algorithms in this section provide encryption and integrity protection. The idea is to have an algorithm that not only encrypts the data, but allows Kerberos, when decrypting it, to detect if the message has been altered since being transmitted by the source.

The three algorithms are known in the Kerberos documentation as des-cbc-crc, des-cbc-md4, and des-cbc-md5. The basic idea is that a checksum is combined with the message, and then the message is encrypted with DES in CBC mode. The algorithms use the checksums CRC-32, MD4, and MD5, respectively. All the algorithms do the following:

1. Choose a 64-bit random number known in the Kerberos documentation as a **confounder**.
2. Create the following data structure, where the field CHECKSUM is filled with zeroes and is of the right length for the checksum algorithm of choice (32 bits for des-cbc-crc and 128 bits for the others):

confounder	*checksum*	*message*

3. Calculate the appropriate checksum over the above data structure.
4. Fill in the result in the CHECKSUM field
5. Add enough padding to make the data structure an integral number of 64-bit chunks:

confounder	*checksum*	*message*	*padding*

6. Encrypt the result using DES in CBC mode with an IV of 0.

14.9 HIERARCHY OF REALMS

In Kerberos V4, in order for principals in realm *A* to be authenticated by principals in realm *B* it was necessary for *B*'s KDC to be registered as a principal in *A*'s KDC. For full connectivity, this means that if there are *n* realms, the KDC in each realm has to be registered as a principal in each of the other *n*–1 realms. This is increasingly nightmarish as *n* gets large (see §9.7.4.1 *Multiple KDC Domains*).

In Kerberos V5, it is allowable to go through a series of realms in order to authenticate. For instance, a principal in realm *A* might wish to be authenticated by a principal in realm *C*. However, realm *C* might not be registered in *A*. But perhaps realm *B* is registered in *A*, and realm *C* is registered in *B*. A principal in *A* can get a ticket for something in *C* by first getting a ticket for *B*, and then asking *B* for a ticket to the KDC in *C*.

By allowing realm *B* to act as intermediary between realm *C* and other realms, we give the KDC at *B* the power to impersonate anyone in the world. Kerberos fixes this vulnerability somewhat by including in tickets a TRANSITED field which lists the names of all the realms that have been transited to obtain the ticket.

Why is the TRANSITED field useful? Suppose Woodward@Washington-Post.Com is contacted with a ticket that indicates the ticket was issued to the principal named Deep-Throat@WhiteHouse.gov, with the TRANSITED field indicating KGB.Russia. It is possible that Woodward should not assume the party using the ticket is really Mr. or Ms. Throat, since it would be in the interest of and the ability of the owner of the KGB realm's KDC to create a ticket that claims the source is anything. The KGB KDC can give such a ticket, along with the corresponding session key, to a confederate. Or the KDC can use the ticket and session key to impersonate the named source directly.

The only thing the KGB KDC cannot do is avoid being named inside the ticket, since a KDC will reject a ticket if the final entry in the TRANSITED field doesn't match the key with which the ticket is encrypted. If Alice gives Bob a ticket, Bob knows which KDC issued the ticket (it's the one with which he shares the key used to encrypt the ticket). But for all the other information in the ticket (like Alice's name and the other realms mentioned in the TRANSITED field), Bob has to trust the KDC which issued the ticket. And although the KDC which issued the ticket to Bob might be trustworthy, if there's any KDC in the path that isn't, all the earlier realms mentioned in the TRANSITED field and the original principal's name (Alice) are suspect.

The TRANSITED field in the ticket gives enough information for Bob (the service being accessed with the ticket) to know whether there are any realms on the path that Bob considers untrustworthy. A realm might be considered completely untrustworthy as a transit realm, but trustworthy when it claims to be acting on behalf of principals in its own realm. Each principal will have its own policy for which realms to trust.

You could say that by doing this, Kerberos is permitting maximum flexibility in possible policies. Or you could say that Kerberos is abdicating responsibility for this crucial decision by throwing it to the whim of application developers who will almost certainly get it wrong.

Either way, some sort of policy is necessary. One such policy—and a likely one at that—is to arrange realms into a tree such that each realm shares a key with each of its children and with its parent. The set of realms trusted for any authentication is the shortest path through the tree, i.e., the

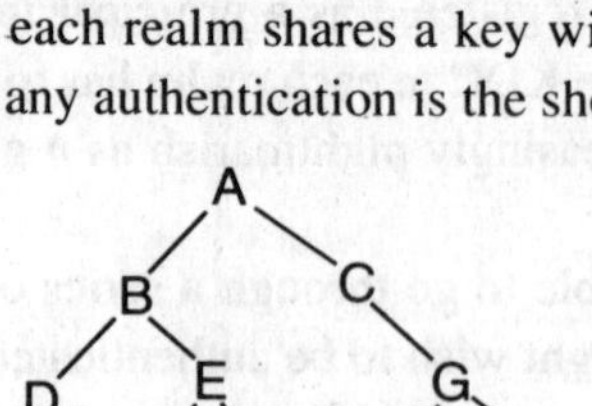

path that gets no closer to the root than the common ancestor lowest in the tree.

For example, in the above diagram, realm G shares a key with its parent realm (C) and each of its children (H and I). To get from realm I to realm H, you'd go through G. To get from realm F to realm D, you'd go through the lowest common ancestor (B), and to get there you'd have to go through E, so the path would be F–E–B–D.

It's especially convenient if the path of realms can be identified solely on the basis of the syntax of names. If realm names were just unstructured strings, it would be difficult to find a path. Luckily realm names in all current implementations of Kerberos are hierarchical, since they follow either Internet or X.500 naming. For instance, assume Cat@Hat.Com wishes to access Dennis@Menace.Com. Cat@Hat.Com resides in realm Hat.Com. Dennis@Menace.Com resides in Menace.Com. The next level of hierarchy is simply called Com. If we create a realm named Com that shares a key with all realms with names of the form *x*.Com, it can then serve as an authentication intermediary. In general, to get from one realm to another, one travels upward to a common ancestor, and then downward to the destination realm.

It is likely that some administrative entity exists which would be a likely CA operator for the Com realm, because some such entity must ensure that there are no name collisions in the .Com space.

Sometimes it might be desirable to shortcut the hierarchy. This might be for efficiency reasons (so authentication between two realms distant in the naming hierarchy does not need to be done via a long sequence of KDCs), or for trust reasons (there might be KDCs along the naming hierarchy path that the two realms would prefer not to have to trust).

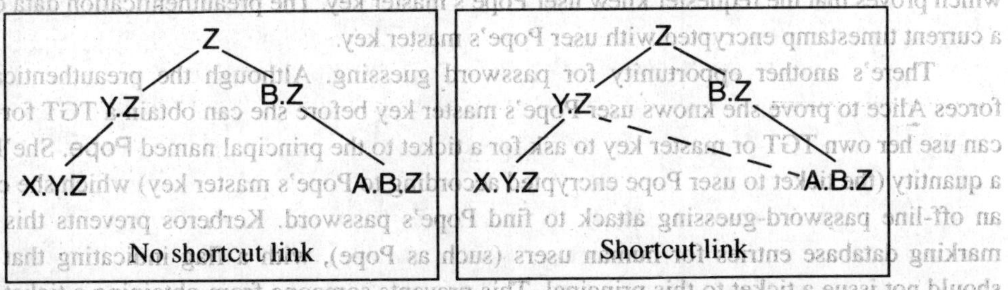

It is possible to have links between KDCs that wouldn't ordinarily be linked based on the naming hierarchy. Such links are usually called **cross-links**. A safe rule with cross-links is that when traversing the naming hierarchy to get to the target, cross-links should always be used if they make the path shorter, because it means fewer KDCs need to be trusted.

There are two issues with realm paths. One is how the initiator finds a realm path to the target. As we've shown, if names are hierarchical and the path of realms follows the same hierarchy, with the possible addition of cross-links, it is easy to find a path. The other issue is how the target decides whether the realm path used was acceptable. As we said, Kerberos leaves it up to the application.

The TRANSITED field lists the sequence of transited realms, omitting the source and destination realms. Realm names are listed separated by commas. Since the list of realms might get large, Kerberos permits various abbreviations. If the realm list is empty, no realms were transited. But if the realm list consists of a single comma, it means that the hierarchy of realms was transited in the normal way (parent to parent from the source up to the first common ancestor, then child to child down to the destination). Two consecutive commas in a list (or a leading or trailing comma) indicate that the hierarchy was transited in the normal way between the two realms surrounding the comma pair (or between source realm and first-listed realm, or between last-listed realm and destination realm). There are other abbreviation rules as well.

14.10 EVADING PASSWORD-GUESSING ATTACKS

With Kerberos V4, there is no authentication of the request to the KDC for a TGT. Anyone can send a cleartext message to the KDC requesting a TGT for user Pope@Vatican.Com, and the KDC will send back a ticket, encrypted according to Pope's master key. Since the function that maps a password string to a DES key is publicly known, an intruder can use the encrypted credentials for an off-line password-guessing attack to find Pope's password.

To avoid this attack, a mechanism has been added to Kerberos V5 in which information known as PREAUTHENTICATION-DATA can be sent along with the request for a TGT for user Pope which proves that the requester knew user Pope's master key. The preauthentication data consists of a current timestamp encrypted with user Pope's master key.

There's another opportunity for password guessing. Although the preauthentication data forces Alice to prove she knows user Pope's master key before she can obtain a TGT for Pope, she can use her own TGT or master key to ask for a ticket to the principal named Pope. She'll get back a quantity (the ticket to user Pope encrypted according to Pope's master key) which she can use for an off-line password-guessing attack to find Pope's password. Kerberos prevents this attack by marking database entries for human users (such as Pope), with a flag indicating that the KDC should not issue a ticket to this principal. This prevents someone from obtaining a ticket for something whose master key is derived from a password (and therefore vulnerable to password guessing). If, in the future, Kerberos is used for an application where it might make sense to create a ticket to a human user (for instance, electronic mail), then some other mechanism would need to be devised to prevent Alice from guessing passwords based on tickets she requests (see Homework Problem 5).

This does not avoid password-guessing attacks completely. Someone can still guess passwords by constructing a request to the KDC for each password guess, and eventually one will be accepted. If passwords are even moderately well chosen, however, this is likely to be a very time-consuming task. Furthermore, a KDC could include code to record the frequency of wrong password guesses and lock the target account and/or alert an administrator should a threshold be exceeded. A more important attack is that an eavesdropper who sees the initial Kerberos login exchange can perform an off-line password guessing attack using either the preauthentication data provided by the user or the TGT sent in response.

14.11 KEY INSIDE AUTHENTICATOR

Suppose Alice wants to have two separate conversations with Bob. If she uses the same key (the Alice-Bob session key chosen by the KDC) for both conversations, then theoretically an intruder could swap the data from one conversation with the other, and confuse Alice and Bob. Alice could get two tickets for Bob, but instead, Kerberos allows Alice to choose a different key for a particular conversation and put that into the authenticator. If the authenticator has a session key that Alice inserted, Bob will use the Alice-Bob session key to decrypt the authenticator, but will use the session key Alice put into the authenticator in that conversation with Alice.

14.12 DOUBLE TGT AUTHENTICATION

Suppose Alice needs to access service Bob, but Bob does not know his master key. We'll assume Bob used his master key to obtain a TGT and session key, and then forgot his master key. Usually, if Alice asks for a ticket to Bob, the KDC will give her a ticket encrypted with Bob's master key. But Bob will not be able to decrypt the ticket, since Bob no longer knows his master key. If Bob is a user at a workstation, the workstation could at this point prompt Bob to type in his password again, but this would be inconvenient for the user.

Kerberos assumes Alice knows that Bob is the type of thing who is unlikely to know his own master key. In a method unspecified in Kerberos, Alice is supposed to ask Bob for his TGT. Alice then sends Bob's TGT as well as her own TGT to the KDC. (Hence the name **double TGT authentication**). Since Bob's TGT is encrypted under a key that is private to the KDC, the KDC can decrypt it. It then issues a ticket to Bob for Alice which is encrypted with Bob's session key rather than Bob's master key.

The application which inspired this bit of the design was XWINDOWS. XWINDOWS clients and servers are backwards from what one might have guessed. The XWINDOWS server is the process that controls the user's screen. XWINDOWS clients are applications that make requests to the server to open windows and display information. While the user of an XWINDOWS terminal may need to authenticate himself to some remote application in order to start it, that application must authenticate itself to the XWINDOWS server to get permission to display its output. The human, Bob, logs into a workstation. The workstation then gets a TGT and session key on behalf of Bob and then promptly forgets Bob's master key. The application which is writing onto Bob's workstation must authenticate itself to the workstation. Since the workstation has no credentials other than Bob's TGT and session key, only a double TGT authentication as described above can work.

14.13 PKINIT—PUBLIC KEYS FOR USERS

The design center for Kerberos is users with passwords and servers with high-quality secret keys shared with the KDC. There have been various efforts since at least 1990 to allow use of a public key infrastructure as an alternative to passwords for authenticating users. The dream of every user having a public/private key pair—preferably stored on a smart card—has been no more than a few years off for all of that time, but it continues to elude us. PKINIT would provide the bridge between public key enabled users and legacy servers that know only secret key technology.

Servers don't know or care how a user authenticated to a KDC. They only see the resulting ticket, which vouches for the user's name. If a user had a private key and a certificate and obtained a TGT or Ticket from a KDC using a public key authentication protocol, this could be transparent and backwards compatible with existing servers. This is the exchange PKINIT defines.

The simplest form of PKI integration that Kerberos could have defined would be for the KDC to list the user's public key in its database instead of the user's password. The TGS_REP message could then have been sent to the user encrypted under that public key. It would also have to be signed by the KDC with some public key the user could verify—otherwise the user could be tricked by someone impersonating the KDC and subsequently impersonating other servers. This simple construction was one of the early proposals, but it did not survive ten years of committee deliberations.

Recall that there was a period from April 29, 1997 and September 20, 2000 when the patent on Diffie-Hellman had expired but the patent on RSA had not. During that period, there was an effort in the IETF to mandate use of unencumbered algorithms even if they were not technically appropriate. The suite pushed during that period was using DSS for signatures and Ephemeral Diffie-Hellman for encryption. So PKINIT was transformed to mandate that the ticket request be signed and the reply be encrypted because that is what those algorithms required. Use of RSA is still allowed, but the optimization of allowing only a single private key operation on the client and being independent of PKI was not reinstated.

There is a structural similarity between using a series of KDCs to authenticate and having a chain of certificates in a PKI. In each case, a set of intermediaries is being trusted. In each case, the decision of which intermediaries should be trusted to authenticate which identities to one another could be configured either into the infrastructure itself (possibly using name constraint rules) or into each endpoint. Kerberos chose to leave that decision to the endpoints. To be consistent with that decision, a Kerberos KDC makes no judgement as to whether a particular chain of certificates is acceptable. Instead, it confirms that it knows (has configured) the name and public key of the first CA in the chain, and lists that and all subsequent CAs as transited realms in the issued ticket. While this leaves maximum flexibility to the configuration of the server, it means that it is unlikely that PKINIT meet its original goal of connecting public key enabled clients to existing Kerberos enabled servers without requiring reconfiguration of the server. PKINIT does allow (but does not require) a translation table in a KDC so that the client name sent to the server can be a familiar Kerberos name rather than the X.500 name taken from the client's certificate.

14.14 KDC DATABASE

Each entry in the V5 KDC database contains the following information. The structure of the database is somewhat implementation-specific, but since all current implementations are derived from the MIT implementation, we describe the MIT implementation.

- *name*—name of principal
- *key*—principal's master key
- *p_kvno*—principal's key version number. If this principal has *k* different valid keys, there will be *k* database entries for this principal. This could have been done more compactly by allowing multiple ⟨*key*, *p_kvno*, *k_kvno*⟩ entries per database.
- *max_life*—maximum lifetime for tickets issued to this principal
- *max_renewable_life*—maximum total lifetime for renewable tickets to this principal
- *k_kvno*—KDC key version under which *key* is encrypted
- *expiration*—time when this database entry expires
- *mod_date*—time of last modification to this entry

- *mod_name*—name of the principal who made the last modification to this entry
- flags indicating the KDC's policy on various things; for instance, whether to require pre-authentication data, whether to allow certain types of tickets such as forwardable, renewable, proxiable, postdated, and so on
- *password expiration*—time when password expires. This is used to force the user to change passwords occasionally.
- *last_pwd_change*—time when user last changed password
- *last_success*—time of last successful user login (i.e., last AS_REQ with correct preauthentication data)

14.15 KERBEROS V5 MESSAGES

Given that the Kerberos V5 messages are defined in ASN.1 notation, it isn't useful to show exact message formats. We will instead just list the information in each of the messages.

14.15.1 Authenticator

The authenticator is not a free-standing message, but rather is contained in a TGS_REQ or an AP_REQ. The entire thing is encrypted, using the key in the ticket that always accompanies an authenticator. Assume the authenticator is being sent in a message transmitted by Alice. When decrypted, the authenticator contains the following fields:

AUTHENTICATOR-VNO	version number (5)
CNAME, CREALM	Alice's name and realm
CKSUM	(optional) checksum of application data that might have been sent along with the AP_REQ
CTIME, CUSEC	time at Alice (in seconds, microseconds)
SUBKEY	(optional) key Alice would like to use instead of the key in the ticket, for the conversation with Bob
SEQ-NUMBER	initial sequence number that Alice will use in her KRB_SAFE and KRB_PROT messages to Bob
AUTHORIZATION-DATA	application-specific data limiting Alice's rights

14.15.2 Ticket

A ticket is not a free-standing message, but is rather carried in messages such as TGS_REQ, AS_REP, TGS_REP, AP_REQ, and KRB_CRED. A ticket given to Alice for use with Bob looks like this:

MSG-TYPE	message type (1)
TKT-VNO	protocol version number (5)
REALM, SNAME	Bob's name and realm
The remainder of the fields are encrypted with Bob's master key (unless this ticket was obtained using Bob's TGT as in §14.12 *Double TGT Authentication*):	
FLAGS	FORWARDABLE, FORWARDED, PROXIABLE, PROXY, MAY-POST-DATE, POSTDATED, INVALID, RENEWABLE, INITIAL (ticket was issued using AS_REQ rather than TGS_REQ) PRE-AUTHENT (user authenticated himself to the KDC before the ticket was issued) HW-AUTHENT (user was authenticated before ticket issued, using something like a smart card)
KEY	key to be used when communicating with Alice
CNAME, CREALM	Alice's name and realm
TRANSITED	names of realms transited between Alice's realm and Bob's realm
AUTH-TIME, START-TIME, END-TIME, RENEW-TILL	timestamps. START-TIME and RENEW-TILL are optional. Described in §14.4 *Ticket Lifetimes*.
CADDR	(optional) the set of addresses from which this ticket will be valid
AUTHORIZATION-DATA	application-specific data limiting Alice's rights

14.15.3 AS_REQ

An AS_REQ is used to request a TGT. It can also be used to ask for regular tickets, but tickets requested with an AS_REQ (as opposed to a TGS_REQ) will return credentials encrypted with the requester's master key. The TGS_REQ contains a TGT, and the credentials returned in response to a TGS_REQ are encrypted according to the session key in the TGT. Let's assume that the request is on behalf of Alice in Wonderland. Let's assume she's asking for either a TGT or a ticket to Bob.

MSG-TYPE	message type (10)
PVNO	protocol version number (5)
PADATA	(optional) preauthentication data—timestamp encrypted with Alice's master key
KDC-OPTIONS	flags—each flag indicates a request to set the corresponding flag in the ticket the KDC will return (see below)
CNAME	Alice's name (the "c" comes from "client")
SNAME	Bob's name (or the name krbtgt if the request is for a TGT)
REALM	realm in which both Alice and Bob reside
FROM	(postdated ticket) desired start-time
TILL	desired end-time, which is the expiration time in the ticket
RTIME	desired renew-till time (only in request for renewable ticket)
NONCE	number to be returned in the reply to prevent replay attacks (MIT implementation uses current timestamp as the nonce)
ETYPE	type of encryption Alice would like KDC to use when encrypting the credentials
ADDRESSES	network layer addresses to include in ticket—used in proxy or forwardable tickets, or when Alice has multiple network layer addresses

The flags that make sense in an AS_REQ are:

- FORWARDABLE—Please set the FORWARDABLE flag in the returned TGT (so that the TGT can later be sent back to the KDC to request a TGT with a different network layer address inside).
- PROXIABLE—Please set the PROXIABLE flag in the returned TGT (so that the TGT can be used to request a ticket with a different network layer address inside).
- ALLOW-POSTDATE—Please set the ALLOW-POSTDATE flag in the returned TGT (so that this TGT can be used to request postdated tickets).
- POSTDATED—Make the returned ticket or TGT postdated, using the START-TIME in the request. Note that the START-TIME is an optional field, and it probably would have been more elegant to merely assume, if the requester included a START-TIME, that the requester wanted the ticket to be a postdated ticket. But the way Kerberos is defined, if the requester includes a START-TIME and does not set the POSTDATED flag, then the START-TIME is ignored and an ordinary, non-postdated ticket is returned.
- RENEWABLE—Please set the RENEWABLE flag in the returned ticket or TGT.
- RENEWABLE-OK—The requester wants a ticket with a long lifetime. If the KDC is not willing to issue a ticket with that long a lifetime, the requester is willing to settle for a renewable ticket with an initial expiration time as far in the future as the KDC is willing to issue and renewable until the requested expiration time.

14.15.4 TGS_REQ

A TGS_REQ is used to request either a TGT or a ticket.

MSG-TYPE	message type (12)
PVNO	protocol version number (5)
PADATA	ticket and authenticator
KDC-OPTIONS	flags from AS_REQ, plus a few more explained above
SNAME	(or the name krbtgt if the request is for a TGT)
REALM	realm in which Bob resides (Alice might reside in a differerent realm in the case of a TGS_REQ)
FROM	(postdated ticket) desired start-time
TILL	desired end-time, which is the expiration time in the ticket
RTIME	desired renew-till time (only in request for renewable ticket)
NONCE	number to be returned in the reply to prevent replay attacks (MIT implementation uses current timestamp as the nonce)
ETYPE	type of encryption Alice would like KDC to use when encrypting the credentials
ADDRESSES	network layer addresses to include in ticket—used in proxy or forwardable tickets, or when Alice has multiple network layer addresses
AUTHORIZATION-DATA	application specific data to be copied into TGT and tickets requested using that TGT, intended to convey restrictions on use. Note that this field is encrypted and integrity-protected.
ADDITIONAL-TICKETS	Bob's TGT in the case where Bob does not know his master key (see §14.12 *Double TGT Authentication*)

The differences between a TGS_REQ and an AS_REQ are:

- The TGS_REQ contains a TGT or a renewable or postdated ticket (the AS_REQ does not).
- The TGS_REQ includes an authenticator in its PADATA field, proving the requester knows the key contained in the TGT or ticket in the request. The AS_REQ contains an encrypted timestamp in its optional PADATA field, proving the requester knows Alice's master key.
- The reply to a TGS_REQ is usually encrypted with the key inside the TGT or ticket enclosed with the request. However, if the authenticator contains a different key (called a subkey), the reply is encrypted with the subkey inside the authenticator. In contrast, the reply to an AS_REQ is always encrypted with the requester's master key.

- There are more flags that might be relevant in a TGS_REQ. All the flags applicable to an AS_REQ are applicable to a TGS_REQ. In addition, the following flags are applicable in a TGS_REQ:
  - FORWARDED—A list of addresses appears in the request which is different than the list of addresses (if any) that appears in the ticket. The list in the request should be included in the returned ticket, and the FORWARDED flag should be set in the returned ticket.
  - PROXY—Same as FORWARDED, except this flag is used when requesting a TGT.
  - ENC-TKT-IN-SKEY—Included in this request is Bob's TGT (see §14.12 *Double TGT Authentication*).
  - RENEW—Please renew the enclosed ticket.
  - VALIDATE—Please validate the enclosed postdated ticket.
- The AS_REQ contains the field CNAME, which does not appear in a TGS_REQ. It is not needed in the TGS_REQ because the KDC obtains the name of the requester from inside the ticket or TGT enclosed with the TGS_REQ.
- The TGS_REQ contains the field AUTHORIZATION-DATA, and the AS_REQ does not. This field is supposed to be copied from the request into the ticket or TGT returned with the reply. It's actually somewhat of a nuisance that Kerberos does not allow this field in an AS_REQ. If you want a TGT or ticket with AUTHORIZATION-DATA, then you have to first obtain a TGT without that field, and then use that TGT in a TGS_REQ to request a TGT with AUTHORIZATION-DATA. Note that in order to prevent an intruder from modifying AUTHORIZATION-DATA in the request on its way to the KDC, the field is encrypted and integrity-protected with the key in the enclosed ticket or TGT, or if a subkey is present in the authenticator, then it's encrypted with that subkey. Note that AUTHORIZATION-DATA is treated differently than the other fields in the request, such as Bob's name, which are sent unencrypted and without integrity protection. Alice knows those other fields arrived intact because they are encrypted and integrity-protected when the KDC returns the credentials to Alice.
- The TGS_REQ also contains the field ADDITIONAL-TICKETS, which if ENC-TKT-IN-SKEY is set in the KDC-OPTIONS field in the TGS_REQ, contains Bob's TGT.

14.15.5 AS_REP

An AS_REP is the reply from the KDC to an AS_REQ. It returns a TGT or ticket.

In practice, PADATA is absent, indicating that the salt to be used is the user's name and realm. If a different salt is specified, it is not possible to transmit PADATA in the AS_REQ, because the user's master key would not be known.

MSG-TYPE	message type (11)
PVNO	protocol version number (5)
PADATA	(optional) salt to combine with the user's password in order to compute the master key derived from the user's password (see below)
CREALM	Alice's realm
CNAME	Alice's name. The purpose of Alice's name and realm is to help Alice's workstation figure out what key to use to decrypt the encrypted data.
TICKET	the ticket to Bob that Alice requested
ENC-PART	encrypted portion (see below)

Kerberos does provide mechanisms for recovery in case Alice's workstation does not know the proper value of salt. One plausible reason why Alice's workstation would not know the salt is that the realm name has changed since Alice last set her password. If the workstation has the wrong salt value, it will supply an incorrect value for PADATA in the request, and the KDC will return an error message. The error message returned by the KDC contains the proper salt value, and then Alice's workstation can try again, this time knowing the proper salt value.

The ENC-PART is encrypted with Alice's master key. When decrypted, it contains the following fields:

KEY	encryption key associated with the ticket enclosed in the AS_REP
LAST-REQ	a sequence of from 0 to 5 timestamps specifying such information as when Alice last requested a TGT, or last requested any ticket. The specification is vague about how these times are supposed to be synchronized across KDC replicas. Indeed, the MIT implementation (as of the writing of this book) does not implement any of these, and always returns no timestamps in this field.
NONCE	the nonce copied from the AS_REQ
KEY-EXPIRATION	(optional) time when user's master key will expire for the purpose of warning Alice to change her password
FLAGS	a copy of the flags that appear inside the ticket (so that Alice can check if the KDC granted all she requested in the request, and also allows her to detect malicious modification that might have been done to the AS_REQ)
AUTH-TIME, START-TIME, END-TIME, RENEW-TILL	timestamps; START-TIME and RENEW-TILL are optional (see §14.4 *Ticket Lifetimes*)
SREALM, SNAME	Bob's name and realm
CADDR	(optional) the set of addresses from which this ticket will be valid

14.15.6 TGS_REP

A TGS_REP is the reply from the KDC to a TGS_REQ. It is virtually identical to an AS_REP. The differences are

- There is never a PADATA field in a TGS_REP, whereas it is optional in an AS_REP. (The PADATA field in an AS_REP contains the salt.)
- There is no KEY-EXPIRATION field in a TGS_REP, whereas it is optional in an AS_REP.
- The ENC-PART field is encrypted with the key in the TGT or ticket sent in the TGS_REQ; or if a subkey is included in the authenticator sent in the TGS_REQ, then the ENC-PART is encrypted with that subkey.

14.15.7 AP_REQ

An AP_REQ is the first message when Alice, who has obtained a ticket to Bob, actually attempts to communicate with Bob.

MSG-TYPE	message type (14)
PVNO	protocol version number (5)
AP-OPTIONS	flags, of which two are defined: USE-SESSION-KEY, which means the ticket is encrypted under the session key in Bob's TGT (rather than Bob's master key—see §14.12 *Double TGT Authentication*) MUTUAL-REQUIRED, which tells Bob mutual authentication is requested
TICKET	the ticket to Bob
AUTHENTICATOR	an authenticator, proving Alice knows the key inside the ticket

14.15.8 AP_REP

An AP_REP is Bob's reply to an AP_REQ from Alice.

MSG-TYPE	message type (15)
PVNO	protocol version number (5)
The rest is encrypted:	
CTIME	the time copied from the CTIME field of the authenticator in the AP_REQ
CUSEC	the low order bits of CTIME, since CTIME is expressed in seconds; this field specifies microseconds
SUBKEY	an optional field intended for Bob to be able to influence the Alice-Bob session key in an application-specific way
SEQ-NUMBER	starting sequence number for messages sent from Bob to Alice

The encrypted section (CTIME through SEQ-NUMBER) is encrypted with the key inside the ticket from the AP_REQ, unless a SUBKEY field is included in the AUTHENTICATOR from the AP_REQ, in which case it is encrypted with the subkey.

14.15.9 KRB_SAFE

A KRB_SAFE message transfers data between Alice and Bob with integrity protection.

MSG-TYPE	message type (20)
PVNO	protocol version number (5)
USER-DATA	whatever the application wants to send
TIMESTAMP	(optional) current time in seconds at the originator of the message, so the recipient can put messages in order, and can make sure the timestamp is within acceptable clock skew
USEC	(optional) the low-order bits (the microsecond portion) of the time, since TIMESTAMP is in seconds
SEQ-NUMBER	(optional) sequence number of this message, so the recipient can detect lost messages and put messages in order
S-ADDRESS	the network address of the sender of the message (the same address is presumably in the network layer header, but here it is cryptographically protected)
R-ADDRESS	the recipient's network address. Again, presumably it is equal to the destination address in the network layer header, but here it is cryptographically protected.
CKSUM	checksum on the fields USER-DATA through R-ADDRESS, using one of the checksum types defined in §14.8.1 *Integrity-Only Algorithms*

14.15.10 KRB_PRIV

A KRB_PRIV message is encrypted (and integrity-protected) data sent between Alice and Bob. It is encrypted with the key arranged for this conversation.

MSG-TYPE	message type (21)
PVNO	protocol version number (5)
The rest is encrypted:	
USER-DATA	whatever the applications wants to send
TIMESTAMP	(optional) current time in seconds at the originator of the message, so the recipient can put messages in order, and make sure the timestamp is within acceptable clock skew
USEC	(optional) the low order bits (the microsecond portion) of the time, since TIMESTAMP is in seconds
SEQ-NUMBER	(optional) sequence number of this message, so the recipient can detect lost messages and put messages in order
S-ADDRESS	the network address of the sender of the message (the same address is presumably in the network layer header, but here it is cryptographically protected)
R-ADDRESS	the recipient's network address. Again, presumably it is equal to the destination address in the network layer header, but here it is cryptographically protected.

14.15.11 KRB_CRED

A KRB_CRED message is used for passing credentials (a ticket and session key) for the purpose of delegation (see §14.3 *Delegation of Rights*). Assume Alice would like to delegate to Ted her right to access Bob. Alice would send Ted a KRB_CRED message containing a ticket to Bob, along with the session key corresponding to Bob's ticket. The encrypted portion of the KRB_CRED message is encrypted using a key that has been established between Alice and Ted, so the assumption is that Alice has already initiated a Kerberos protected conversation to Ted, and they now share a key.

MSG-TYPE	message type (22)
PVNO	protocol version number (5)
TICKETS	a sequence of tickets
The rest is encrypted with the Alice-Ted conversation key:	
TICKET-INFO	information corresponding to each ticket in TICKETS field, see below
NONCE	(optional) a number supplied by Carol to Alice, which Alice puts into the KRB_CRED message when delegating to Carol, to reassure Carol that the KRB_CRED is not a replay transmitted by an intruder, and is indeed recently transmitted by Alice
TIMESTAMP	(optional) current time in seconds at the originator of the message, so the recipient can put messages in order, and make sure the timestamp is within acceptable clock skew
USEC	(optional) the low order bits (the microsecond portion) of the time, since TIMESTAMP is in seconds
S-ADDRESS	the network address of the sender of the message (the same address is presumably in the network layer header, but here it is cryptographically protected)
R-ADDRESS	the recipient's network address. Again, presumably it is equal to the destination address in the network layer header, but here it is cryptographically protected.

The TICKET-INFO field is a sequence of one or more repetitions of the following information:

KEY	encryption key associated with the corresponding ticket enclosed in the KRB_CRED
PREALM, PNAME	(optional) Alice's name and realm
FLAGS	(optional) a copy of the flags that appear inside the ticket
AUTH-TIME, START-TIME, END-TIME, RENEW-TILL	(optional) timestamps
SREALM, SNAME	(optional) Bob's name and realm
CADDR	(optional) the set of addresses from which this ticket will be valid

14.15.12 KRB_ERROR

In Kerberos V4 there were two types of error messages, one that would be returned by the KDC, the other returned by an application when authentication failed. In Kerberos V5 there is only one error message defined, and it is used for both purposes. None of the information in the error message is encrypted or integrity-protected. Let's assume that Alice has sent a message to Bob, and that Bob is returning the error message to Alice because of some problem with Alice's message.

MSG-TYPE	message type (30)
PVNO	protocol version number (5)
CTIME, CUSEC	(optional) CTIME and CUSEC fields copied from the message generated by Alice that caused the error
STIME, SUSEC	time at Bob when he generated the KRB_ERROR message
ERROR-CODE	the error code, indicating the type of error
CNAME, CREALM	(optional) Alice's name and realm
REALM, SNAME	Bob's realm and name
E-TEXT	additional information to help explain the error, in printable text
E-DATA	additional information to help explain the error. Not guaranteed to be printable text.

Here are all the error codes. Error codes 1–30 come only from the KDC, in response to a AS_REQ or TGS_REQ. The others can come from either the KDC or an application, in response to an AP_REQ, KRB_PRIV, KRB_SAFE, or KRB_CRED.

code	reason
0	No error. (Really, it's in the documentation! I'm sure it's annoying to get an error message telling you that you *didn't* make an error but it's not going to do what you asked it to do anyway. In reality, this would never appear, and is probably listed in the documentation just to ensure nobody assigns error code 0 to a real error.)
1	Alice's entry in the KDC database has expired.
2	Bob's entry in the KDC database has expired.
3	The requested Kerberos version number is not supported.
4	The KDC has forgotten the key with which Alice's entry in its database was encrypted. (It was an old version number, and the KDC didn't save that key.)
5	The KDC has forgotten the key with which Bob's entry in its database was encrypted.
6	The KDC never heard of Alice.
7	The KDC never heard of Bob.
8	Either Bob or Alice appears in the KDC database multiple times. (Really, it would make more sense to check this when modifying the KDC database, or have a utility that checks this every once in awhile rather than checking this when requests are made.)
9	Either Bob or Alice's entry in the KDC does not contain a master key (see parenthetical remark for error 8).
10	Alice asked for a postdated ticket, but her TGT does not allow this.
11	The requested start time is later than the end time (maybe the KDC should just give Alice the useless ticket that she requested).

code	reason
12	KDC policy does not allow the request.
13	KDC cannot grant the requested option.
14	KDC doesn't support this encryption type.
15	KDC doesn't support this checksum type.
16	KDC does not support this type of PADATA.
17	KDC does not support the transited type. (The TRANSITED field has a type and a value. The type is one that the KDC does not understand.)
18	Alice's credentials have been revoked—the account is marked invalid in KDC, or Alice's TGT has been revoked.
19	Bob's credentials have been revoked.
20	TGT has been revoked.
21	Alice's entry is not yet valid—try again later.
22	Bob's entry is not yet valid—try again later.
23	Alice's password has expired.
24	Pre-authentication information invalid.
25	Pre-authentication required.
26	Ticket doesn't match server name in double-TGT authentication.
27	Double-TGT authentication is required by KDC.
28	Set of transited KDCs is not acceptable to KDC.
29	Bob does not have the requested service.
31	Integrity check on decrypted field failed.
32	The ticket has expired.
33	The ticket is not yet valid.
34	The request is a replay.
35	This ticket isn't for us.
36	The ticket and authenticator don't match.
37	The clock skew is too great.
38	The network address in the network layer header doesn't match the network layer address inside the ticket.
39	The protocol version number doesn't match.
40	The message type is unsupported.
41	The checksum didn't check. (The documentation describes this error as *message stream modified*, but we prefer not to place blame—there might be a perfectly innocent explanation.)

code	reason
42	The message is out of order. In both encrypted and integrity-checked data, there is a sequence number. The network can certainly reorder messages, and such innocent reordering of messages should not generate an error. If the messages are being delivered with a reliable transport layer protocol, then this error would be generated because of some deliberate tampering with the message stream, which can be detected by Kerberos. If the messages are being delivered with a datagram service (like UDP), then since the sequence number is optional, it should not be used.
44	The specified version of the key is not available.
45	Bob doesn't know his key.
46	Mutual authentication failed.
47	The message direction is incorrect. In V4 this was determined based on the D BIT. The D BIT no longer exists in V5, but instead, in integrity-protected and encrypted data, there is a SENDER'S ADDRESS and a RECEIVER'S ADDRESS field. If Bob receives a message from Alice and these fields are swapped, it indicates that an intruder is trying to trick them by mirroring messages back.
48	*Alternative authentication method required.* For instance, Bob does not know his master key, but does have a TGT (see §14.12 *Double TGT Authentication*).
49	The sequence number in the message is incorrect.
50	*Inappropriate type of checksum in message.* Presumably, this is because Bob doesn't support that checksum type. The wording in the documentation implies that Bob is making a value judgement on Alice's choice of checksum. For instance, if Alice were to choose CRC-32 as an integrity check instead of a message digest, Bob might sneeringly send this error message.
60	Generic error. The description is in E-TEXT.
61	Some field is too long for this implementation.
62	Alice's certificate is unacceptable to the KDC (PKINIT).
63	The KDC doesn't have a certificate from an acceptable CA (PKINIT).
64	Alice's signature is invalid (PKINIT).
65	Alice's key isn't big enough to suit the KDC.
66	Alice's name doesn't match the name in her certificate.
70	The KDC can't verify Alice's certificate.
71	One of Alice's certificates is invalid.
72	One of Alice's certificates is revoked.
73	The KDC can't figure out whether one of Alice's certificates is revoked.
74	The KDC can't reach Alice's certificate revocation service.
75	Alice's name doesn't match the name in her certificate.
76	The KDC is not who Alice thinks it is.

14.16 HOMEWORK

1. Suppose the Kerberos V5 password to key conversion function is identical to V4, but then takes the output that V4 would compute and ⊕s it with the realm name. This would produce a different key in each realm, as desired. What is wrong with this algorithm? (Hint: the reason it is good for your key to be different in different realms is so that if your key in one realm is known, it does not divulge your key in other realms.)
2. Consider the following variant of Kerberos. Instead of having postdated or renewable tickets, a server which notes that the start-time is older than some limit presents the ticket to the TGS and asks if it should believe the ticket. What are the trade-offs of this approach relative to the Kerberos V5 approach?
3. The philosophy behind requiring renewable tickets to be renewed before they expire is that a KDC should not need to remember blacklist information indefinitely. But does that work for postdated tickets, given that a postdated ticket can be requested with a start-time arbitrarily far into the future?
4. Design a different method of Bob authenticating Alice when Bob does not remember his own master key, which places the work on Bob instead of Alice. In other words, Alice will act as if Bob was an ordinary civilized thing that does remember its own master key, and Bob interacts appropriately with the KDC so that Alice will be unaware that Bob didn't know his own master key.
5. Suppose it was desired to use Kerberos for securing electronic mail. The obvious way of accomplishing this is for Alice, when sending a message to Bob, to obtain a ticket for Bob and include that in the email message, and encrypt and/or integrity-protect the email message using the key in the ticket. The problem with this is that then the KDC would give Alice a quantity encrypted with Bob's password-derived master key, and then Alice could do off-line password guessing. How might Kerberos be extended to email without allowing off-line password guessing? (Hint: issue human users an extra, unguessable master key for use with mail, and extend the Kerberos protocol to allow Bob to safely obtain his unguessable master key from the KDC.)
6. In the mutual authentication in the Needham/Schroeder protocol upon which Kerberos is based, the authenticator contained only an encrypted timestamp. The protocol is that Alice sends Bob the authenticator, and then Bob must decrypt the authenticator, add one to the value inside, re-encrypt it, and send it back to Alice. Why was it necessary for Bob to increment the value before re-encrypting it and sending it to Alice? Why isn't it necessary in Kerberos V5, in the AP_REP message? In Kerberos V4, it is the checksum field (which isn't

really a checksum—see §13.10 *Encryption for Integrity Only*) that is extracted and incremented. Would it have been just as secure in V4 for Bob to send back the contents of the checksum field encrypted and not incremented?

7. In the KRB_SAFE message, there is both a timestamp and a sequence number. Presuming that both timestamp fields (TIMESTAMP and USEC) are sent, and that the application makes sure the timestamp increases on every message, does the sequence number provide any additional protection?

8. Prove that if there is a 64-bit value that works as a DES checksum, the value ⊕'d with $F0F0F0F0F0F0F0F0_{16}$ will also have a correct DES checksum.

9. Give the algorithm for verifying the MAC described in §14.8.1.2 *des-mac*.

15 PKI (PUBLIC KEY INFRASTRUCTURE)

15.1 INTRODUCTION

In the early days of the Indian Territory, there were no such things as birth certificates. You being there was certificate enough. —Will Rogers

A **public key infrastructure (PKI)** consists of the components necessary to securely distribute public keys. Ideally, it consists of certificates (see §9.7.2 *Certification Authorities (CAs)*), a repository for retrieving certificates, a method of revoking certificates, and a method of evaluating a chain of certificates from public keys that are known and trusted in advance (**trust anchors**) to the target name. There have been some public-key-based systems deployed that leave out components such as revocation, or even certificates. Whether such systems are worthy of being called PKIs is a matter for debate (and a fairly dull debate at that). In practice, many people do use public key technology for protecting communication and don't use a PKI. Instead, they exchange public keys in email, or download the public key from the IP address at which they assume their target is located. In theory, if an active attacker were watching when the initial exchange occurred, the attacker could change the public key in the message and act as a man-in-the-middle. But in practice, this mechanism is reasonably secure.

In this chapter we assume certificate-based PKIs, and focus on the generic issues as well as the details of the standards. In subsequent chapters we discuss choices made in deployed systems, such as S/MIME, PGP, SSL, and Lotus Notes. This chapter assumes each entity knows its own private key. We address the particular problem of getting the private key to a human in §12.4 *Strong Password Credentials Download Protocols*.

A certificate is a signed message vouching that a particular name goes with a particular public key, as in [Alice's public key is 829348]$_{\text{Carol}}$. If Bob does not know Carol or Carol's key, then such a certificate will not help him gain confidence that 829348 is Alice's key. But if Bob knows Ted's key, then the chain

[Carol's key is 348203]$_{\text{Ted}}$ → [Alice's public key is 829348]$_{\text{Carol}}$

would mathematically allow Bob to verify Alice's key. However, there are several potential problems. Although Bob might trust Ted for vouching for Carol's key, should he trust Carol for vouching for Alice's key? Maybe Carol is careless and can be tricked into signing a certificate for a bogus key. Maybe she can be bribed. Maybe she is simply one of the bad guys trying to disrupt operations on the Internet by feeding in bad data. Furthermore, how does Bob know Ted's key?

In this chapter we'll discuss issues such as these, as well the details of the certificate formats as designed by committee.

15.2 SOME TERMINOLOGY

If Alice signs a certificate vouching for Bob's name and key, then Alice is the **issuer** and Bob is the **subject**. If Alice wants to find a path to Bob's key, then Bob's name is the **target**. If Alice is evaluating a chain of certificates, she is the **verifier**, sometimes called the **relying party**. Anything that has a public key is known as a **principal**. A **trust anchor** is a public key that the verifier has decided through some means is trusted to sign certificates. In a verifiable chain of certificates, the first certificate will have been signed by a trust anchor.

15.3 PKI TRUST MODELS

Suppose Alice wants to send an encrypted email message to Bob. She needs to securely find out Bob's public key. The PKI trust model defines where Alice gets her trust anchors, and what paths would create a legal chain from a trust anchor to the target name ("Bob" in this example).

15.3.1 Monopoly Model

In this model, the world chooses one organization, universally trusted by all companies, countries, universities, and other organizations to be the single CA for the world. The key of that one organization is embedded in all software and hardware as the PKI trust anchor. Everyone must get certificates from it. This is a wonderfully simple model, mathematically. This is the model favored by organizations hoping to be the monopolist. However, there are problems with it:

- There is no one universally trusted organization.

- Given that all software and hardware would come preconfigured with the monopoly organization's key, it would be infeasible to ever change that key in case it were compromised, since that would involve reconfiguration of every piece of equipment and software.
- It would be expensive and insecure to have a remote organization certify your key. How would they know it was you? How would you be able to securely send them your public key? Although transmission of the public key does not require secrecy, it requires integrity. Otherwise the CA could be tricked into certifying the public key as yours.
- Once enough software and hardware was deployed so that it would be difficult for the world to switch organizations, the organization would have monopoly control, and could charge whatever it wanted for granting certificates.
- The entire security of the world rests on that one organization never having an incompetent or corrupt employee who might be bribed or tricked into issuing bogus certificates or divulging the CA's private key.

15.3.2 Monopoly plus Registration Authorities (RAs)

This model is just like §15.3.1 *Monopoly Model* except that the single CA chooses other organizations (known as RAs) to securely check identities and obtain and vouch for public keys. The RA then securely communicates with the CA, perhaps by sending signed email with the information that would go into the certificate, and the CA can then issue a certificate because it trusts the RA.

This model's advantage over the §15.3.1 *Monopoly Model* is that it is more convenient and secure to obtain certificates, since there are more places to go to get certified. However, all the other disadvantages of the monopoly model apply.

RAs can be added to any of the models we'll talk about. Some people believe that it is better for their organization to run an RA and leave the operation of the CA to an organization more expert at what it takes to be a CA. However, in practice, the CA just rubber-stamps whatever information is verified by the RAs. It is the RA that has to do the security-sensitive operations of ensuring the proper mapping of name to key. The CA might be better able to provide a tamper-proof audit trail of certificates it has signed.

15.3.3 Delegated CAs

In this model the trust anchor CA can issue certificates to other CAs, vouching for their keys and vouching for their trustworthiness as CAs. Users can then obtain certificates from one of the delegated CAs instead of having to go to the trust anchor CA.

The difference between a delegated CA and an RA is whether Alice sees a chain of certificates from a trust anchor to Bob's name, or sees a single certificate. Assuming a monopoly trust anchor, this model has security and operational properties similar to §15.3.2 *Monopoly plus Registration Authorities (RAs)*. Chains of certificates through delegated CAs can be incorporated into any of the models we'll discuss.

15.3.4 Oligarchy

This is the model commonly used in browsers. In this model, instead of having products preconfigured with a single key, the products come configured with many trust anchors, and a certificate issued by any one of them is accepted. Usually in such a model it is possible for the user to examine and edit the list of trust anchors, adding or deleting trust anchors. It has the advantage over the monopoly models that the organizations chosen as trust anchors will be in competition with each other, so the world might be spared monopoly pricing. However it is likely to be even *less* secure than the monopoly model:

- In the monopoly model, if the single organization ever has a corrupt or incompetent employee, the entire security of the world is at risk. In the oligarchy model, though, *any* of the trust anchor organizations getting compromised will put the security of the world at risk. It is of course far more likely that at least one of n organizations will wind up with a misused key when n is bigger than 1.
- The trust anchor organizations are trusted by the product vendor, not by the user. Why should the vendor decide whom the user should trust? Also, how does the vendor choose which organizations to trust? You'd like to assume that there is some elaborate procedure by which the vendor evaluates the trustworthiness of the organization before adding its key to the trust anchor set. The policy is at the discretion of the vendor, and some vendors have chosen to include any organization willing to pay for the privilege of being included in the preconfigured trust anchor set.
- It might be easy to trick a naive user into adding a bogus trust anchor into the set. This depends on the implementation. One could imagine an implementation that, upon seeing a certificate signed by an organization that wasn't in the set, would show the user a pop-up box saying, *Warning. This was signed by an unknown CA. Would you like to accept the certificate anyway?* (The user will almost certainly say *OK*.) *Would you like to always accept this certificate without being asked in the future?* (*OK*.) *Would you like to always accept certificates from the CA that issued that certificate?* (*OK*.) *Would you like to always accept certificates from any CA?* (*OK*.) *Since you're willing to trust anyone for anything, would you like me to make random edits to the files on your hard drive without bothering you with a pop-up box?*

(*OK*.) (You might want to see how many of these questions your browser asks, and it would be an interesting psychology exercise to see how outrageous you can be before a user stops clicking *OK*.) Note that if a user is sufficiently sophisticated and careful, she can ask for information about the certificate before clicking *OK* to accept it. She will be informed of the name of the signer, say Mother Teresa (the most trustworthy imaginable signer). But this does not necessarily mean it was really signed by Mother Teresa. It just means that whoever signed it (say *SleazeInc*) put the string Mother Teresa into the ISSUER NAME field.

- Users will not understand the concept of trust anchors. If they have been assured that the application they are using does encryption, they will assume that it will be secure even if they're using a public workstation, perhaps in a hotel room or at an airport. Although it will always be an issue if a user can be tricked into using a public workstation with malicious code, it would be easier for the previous user of the workstation to modify the set of trust anchors and the proxy to be used (probably not a privileged operation) than to change the software.

- There is no practical way for even a knowledgeable user to be able to examine the set of trust anchors and tell if someone has modified the set. Browsers today come shipped with about 80 trust anchors. You can examine them by name, but someone could delete the key of *TrustworthyInc*, and put in a new key claiming that it belongs to *TrustworthyInc*. You might even be able to look at digests of the keys, but what user will be sufficiently paranoid to have printed out all the message digests of the 80 or so trust anchors that get shipped with the application and compare them with the configured set?

15.3.5 Anarchy Model

This is the model used by PGP. Each user is responsible for configuring some trust anchors, for instance, public keys of people he has met and who have handed him a business card with a PGP **fingerprint** (the message digest of the public key), and sent him email containing a public key with that digest. Then anyone can sign certificates for anyone else. Some organizations (for instance, MIT does this today) volunteer to keep a certificate database into which anyone can deposit certificates. To get the key of someone whose key is not in your set of trust anchors, you can search through the public database to see if you can find a path from one of your trust anchors to the name you want. This absolutely eliminates the monopoly pricing, but it is really unworkable on a large scale:

- The database would get unworkably large if it were deployed on Internet scale. If every user donated, say, ten certificates, the database would consist of billions of certificates. It would be impractical to search through the database and construct paths.

- Assuming somehow Alice could piece together a chain from one of her trust anchors to the name Bob, how would she know whether to trust the chain? So, Carol (her trust anchor) vouches for Ted's key. Ted vouches for Gail's key. Gail vouches for Ken's key. Ken vouches for Bob's key. Are all these individuals trustworthy?

As long as this model is used within a small community where all the users are trustworthy, it will work, but on the Internet scale, when there are individuals who will purposely add bogus certificates, it would be impossible to know whether to trust a path. Some people have suggested that if you can build multiple chains to the name that you can be more assured of the trustworthiness. But once someone decides to add bogus certificates, he can create arbitrary numbers of fictitious identities and arbitrary numbers of certificates signed by those entities. So sheer numbers will not be any assurance of trustworthiness.

15.3.6 Name Constraints

The concept of name constraints is that the trustworthiness of a CA is not a binary value where a CA would either be completely untrusted or trusted for everything. Instead, a CA should only be trusted for certifying some subset of the users. For instance, MIT's CA, most likely managed by playful undergraduates, should be trusted for certifying name/key binding of MIT students, but not for certifying the key of, say, president@whitehouse.gov.

Assuming users have hierarchical names, such as radia@alum.mit.edu, it is easy to specify a policy for trusting the MIT CA. The MIT CA should be trusted for certifying names in the namespace under mit.edu, but not names of the form foo@harvard.edu. Although I_2 might be a Sun employee, you would not trust the Sun CA to certify the name radia@alum.mit.edu. But you would trust the Sun CA to certify the name radia.perlman@sun.com. The name by which you know someone determines whom you trust to certify that name. Users might have multiple names. The PKI doesn't care. Each name is a separate PKI entity. They might use the same public key, in which case someone might happen to notice that radia@alum.mit.edu and radia.perlman@sun.com are most likely the same individual because the two entities have the same public key. Or I_2 might use different keys for my$_2$ different identities.

15.3.7 Top-Down with Name Constraints

This model is similar to the monopoly model in that everyone must be configured with a pre-ordained, never changing root key, and that root CA delegates to other CAs. However, the delegated CAs are only allowed to issue certificates for their portions of the namespace. In this model it is easy to find the path to a name (just follow the namespace from the root down). But it has the other problems of the monopoly model, in that everyone has to agree upon a root organization, and that organization and its key would be prohibitively expensive to ever replace.

15.3.8 Bottom-Up with Name Constraints

This model is not deployed, although the design of Lotus Notes is close (see §24.5 *Lotus Notes Security*). It was originally proposed for Digital's security architecture in the late 1980s (see §24.4 *DASS/SPX*). We believe this model, or something close to it, will better serve the Internet because of the reasons we give at the end of this section. The philosophy of this model is that each organization can create its own PKI and then link to others. The model assumes a hierarchical namespace in which each node is represented by a CA. Not only does the parent certify the child's name, but the child certifies the parent's name. In other words, .edu would certify mit.edu, and mit.edu would certify .edu. In addition to up-links (where the child certifies the parent) and down-links (where the parent certifies the child), cross-links are allowed, where a **cross-link** is a link from any node to any other node where neither is an ancestor of the other. (See Figure 15-1.) The certificate by which one node creates a cross-link to another node is known as a **cross-certificate**.

Note that with links in both directions (from child to parent and from parent to child), it is possible to navigate the namespace starting from any node. Instead of using the root as your trust anchor, you can start anywhere—the uppermost key within your own organization, or even your own key! If the trust anchor is your own key, the only thing you need to know a priori is your own key pair. If the trust anchor is something other than your key, you also need to know the trust anchor's public key.

We define an **ancestor** of a name to be any prefix of that name (where the strings delimited by slashes are considered atomic), including the name itself. To find a path to a target, start at your trust anchor. If it is an ancestor of the target name, go down from there to the name. If not, look for a cross-certificate to an ancestor of the target. If you don't find a suitable cross-certificate, go up to the parent, look for cross-certificates to an ancestor of the target, and so forth, until you either find a suitable cross-certificate or get to the least common ancestor of the trust anchor and the target. (The least common ancestor is the node with the longest name which is a prefix of both names.) Once at an ancestor of the target, just follow down-links to the target.

The rule is you follow up-links as far as necessary (until you encounter a cross-link to an ancestor of the target at or below the least common ancestor, or until you reach the least common ancestor), then you follow at most one cross-link, and then you follow down-links from there. Without cross-links, the set of CAs you must trust are all your ancestors and all the target's ancestors up to the least common ancestor. With cross-links, the set of CAs that you must trust is a subset of that.

So for instance, imagine user A/B/X in Figure 15-1 wishes to find the key of user A/C/Y, and user A/B/X uses her own key as her trust anchor. So she looks in the directory under her own record (A/B/X) for cross-certificates. Since there are none, she goes up to her parent (A/B) and looks for

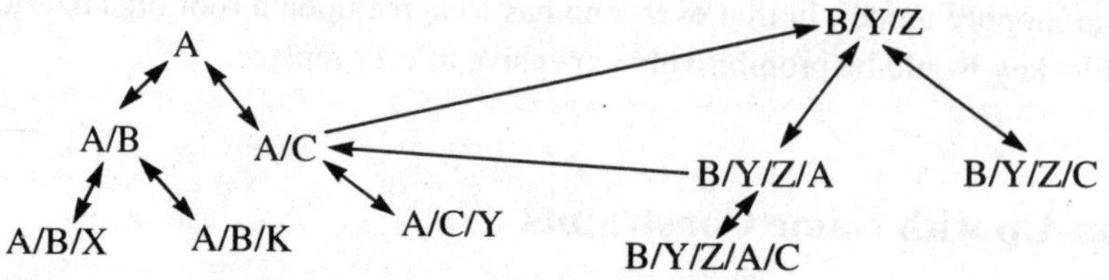

Figure 15-1. Bottom-Up PKI Model

cross-certificates. Since there are none, she goes to its parent (A), and at that point she has reached the least common ancestor, so she can go down to the target name.

Now suppose A/C/Y wants to find the key of B/Y/Z/C. She'd go up to her parent (A/C), and then follow the cross link to B/Y/Z, and then go down to B/Y/Z/C.

But there is no path back from B/Y/Z/C to A/C/Y since the PKI does not go up to a common ancestor of those two names, and there is no cross link from an ancestor of B/Y/Z/C to an ancestor of A/C/Y. It might look as though B/Y/Z/C could go up one level to B/Y/Z, and then down to B/Y/Z/A from which there is a cross link to A/C. In order to be able to find such a path, the search rules would be very complex, since each link would have to be followed in case it led to a cross link to the target name. But a thornier issue is whether to trust any intermediary other than the CAs up to a common ancestor. If the trust rules are clear, e.g., only CAs along the name path are trusted, then it's easy to find and blame the compromised CA, and it's also easy to know what damage can be caused by a given CA's being compromised. If you trust any CA for anything it won't be secure. If you have any rule between those two extremes, the security becomes very complicated to configure.

If it were important for there to be a path from B/Y/Z/C to A/C/Y, then B/Y/Z/C or one of its parents would create a cross link to A, A/C, or A/C/Y. Eventually organizations would tire of maintaining many cross-links. At that point there arises a business opportunity to provide inter-organization connectivity (which we'll call **root service**), but in competition with other organizations providing root service. An organization that offers root service would advertise its rates, how much liability it is willing to assume, would explain its policies and procedures for how carefully it checks information before issuing a certificate, and so forth.

We like this model. It was originally proposed for Digital's security architecture in the late 1980s. With the trust anchor being the uppermost key in one's own organization, it is similar to the PKI for Lotus Notes, and the bridge CA model used for the Federal PKI. The **bridge CA** is simply a CA that certifies and is certified by the uppermost CA in each organization. The advantages of this model are:

- It is easy to find out if a path exists.

- The policy of assuming that the name by which something is known implies whom you'd trust to certify the name is something people can understand, and is sufficiently flexible and simple that it might actually work.
- PKI can be deployed in any organization independently of the rest of the world. There is no reason to pay a commercial CA for certificates. There is no reason to wait for the entire world-encompassing PKI to get put into place before you can use PKI in your own organization, or between a few organizations.
- Since authentication paths between users in your own organization never go outside of your own organization, security of what is presumably the most security-sensitive operation—authenticating users in your own organization—is entirely in your own hands. Compromise of any CA outside of your own organization will not allow anyone to impersonate one of your own users to your own services.
- Replacing any key is reasonably easy. For instance, assume that a few companies offering root service successfully manage to acquire a large customer base. If a root service's key gets compromised, then it only affects the top CA of each of the root service's customers. Each such CA has to revoke the old certificate it issued to the root service and issue a new certificate containing the new key, and automatically all the users in the CA's subtree are using the new key in place of the old key.
- No organization gets so entrenched that it can start charging monopolistic prices. Competition is always possible.
- Configuration is very easy. At the very least you need to know your own key pair. With this PKI model, that is *all* you need to know, since all the other CAs can be reached by paths starting with your own key. Your private key might be carried on a smart card; for other methods of obtaining your private key, see §12.4 *Strong Password Credentials Download Protocols*. To use a key other than your own as the trust anchor, for instance the uppermost key in your organization, you will need to also know the public key of that trust anchor.

How would this be deployed? Suppose an organization, say finance.east.bigorg.com, deploys PKI-based security using this model. When someone, say Joe, is hired into that organization, he visits the CA operator. This is just another step in the process of getting hired, like visiting the badge-making office. Joe obtains a public key pair, perhaps by generating it on his own machine or obtaining a smart card. Given that the CA (like the badge facility) is probably on site, it is easy for him to physically meet the CA operator and be introduced by someone the CA operator knows. It is therefore secure and convenient for him and the CA to certify each other's public keys. Then the up-link certificate can be stored in a directory so that Joe can plug his smart card into any workstation and search the directory for all the other certificates he will need.

Joe may have a life other than as an employee. He might get another certificate (and name and virtual identity) from his ISP for email and from his credit card company for securely ordering things. He could decide which identity to use for any particular activity. These identities might or might not use the same public key. There may be no way of knowing when two different entities in the PKI namespace happen to map to the same carbon-based life form.

15.3.9 Relative Names

Relative names is another useful concept found in DASS/SPX, useful because if an entire subtree of the namespace moves, most of the certificates do not need to be reissued. This is done by having certificates carry **relative names** rather than absolute names. That means that instead of putting in the entire name joe.finance.east.bigorg.com, the down-link certificate (the one from parent to child) would carry the name joe. Now, in case the company reorganizes, so that finance is moved up under bigorg.com (so it is now finance.bigorg.com), only the new certificates between bigorg.com and finance.bigorg.com need to be issued. All the certificates for the subtree under finance would remain the same.

With relative names, a child certificate would carry only the component which is the extension of the parent's name. A parent certificate would not carry a name at all, but instead say *this is my parent*. There is an interesting issue with what to put into a cross-certificate. There are two possibilities. One possibility is to put an absolute name into a cross-certificate. That way if the issuer's portion of the namespace gets moved, but the subject's portion hasn't changed, then the certificate will still be valid. The other possibility is to put in a relative name (like ../../B/C), in which case the certificate would remain valid if a branch of the namespace containing both names were moved as a whole (see Homework Problem 2).

Although relative names have some attractive properties, there are some very complex issues, such as what name to put into a cross-link and how an entity learns its own name. Since nothing with relative names has been deployed, it would be an interesting area to study. SDSI and SPKI (RFC 2693 *SPKI Certificate Theory*) present a design that uses a form of relative names.

15.3.10 Name Constraints in Certificates

The certificate format adopted by PKIX (see §15.6 *PKIX and X.509*) has a field called NAME CONSTRAINTS, which allows the issuer to specify what names the subject is trusted to certify. The field can contain allowed names and disallowed names. PKIX certificates can be used to build any of the models we've mentioned. To build the bottom-up model, a child or cross-certificate would specify that the subject was only allowed to certify names in the subtree below the subject's name. A parent certificate would contain the constraint *any names except myself and below.*

We'd still recommend mostly building the bottom-up model, but there is some amount of flexibility that the strict *up* – cross once – down** algorithm might not give. For instance, an organization might have a cross-link to other-org.com, but realizing that other-org.com also keeps cross-certificates to yet-another.com and still-another.com, the name constraint in the cross-certificate might say that the subject would be trusted to certify names in the namespaces of any of other-org.com, yet-another.com, and still-another.com. Or there might be several root organizations that all cross-certify each other, with each having certified some subset of the organizations. Since two organizations might not have been certified by the same root, it might be necessary to go up to the root, then find a path across the roots to the target's root, and then go down. This could be accomplished by having roots cross-certify each other using the name constraint *trusted for all names*. The further one gets from the bottom-up model, and the closer one gets to the anarchy model, the more complex it will be to search all valid paths.

15.3.11 Policies in Certificates

The PKI in PEM (see Chapter 21 *PEM & S/MIME*) had built-in policies. The PEM PKI consisted of a single root CA which certified multiple hierarchies, each with its own policy. Some hierarchies had pre-defined (by the standards body) policies. PEM allowed future hierarchies with different published policies. If you wanted to get certified in a particular hierarchy you had to follow the policies of that hierarchy, and you could only get certified in one hierarchy—the one whose policies you followed. Policies were intended to be things like how carefully you checked identity before issuing a certificate and how often you administered drug tests to the CA operators (see §21.5 *PEM Certificate Hierarchy*). The PEM PKI was a failure and was never substantially deployed, in part because of its rigidity.

PKIX provides certificate extensions for policies, intended to support something along the lines of what the PEM hierarchy designers envisioned. Instead of defining what the policies are, PKIX allows for putting in OIDs, which are hierarchically assigned globally unique identifiers. The meaning of these is not standardized. Anyone can obtain an OID and define it to mean anything.

Policies don't have values associated with them. So, for instance, if what you want is a policy for security level, you couldn't say *policy = security level, value = confidential*. Instead, you'd have to choose separate OIDs for each level of security, for example an OID for *top secret*, a different OID for *secret*, and yet another for *confidential*. If you want a certificate chain where every link in the chain is at least secret, then the top secret links would have to specify they meet confidential, secret, and top secret policies. It is not possible for the application to say that each link in the chain can be either secret or top secret. Instead there has to be a chain that has the same OID in each certificate.

To further complicate things, it is possible, assuming two organizations are using OIDs for similar enough policies that they are willing to consider them equivalent, the cross-certificate from one organization to the other can contain mapping rules such as *OID1=OID2*. That means that if a chain which must contain OID1 in the first organization crosses into the other organization's PKI, all subsequent certificates in the chain must contain OID2.

The way policies are processed in a chain is that the application specifies what policy OIDs, if any, it wants to see in certificates. For example, the application might specify *OID1 or OID2 or OID3*. A chain must have the same OID in every link. So for instance, even if the application doesn't care whether it's OID1 or 2 or 3, if the first certificate in the chain contains only OID2 and the next certificate in the chain contains only OID3, then the chain is not valid. If the first certificate contains OID1 and OID2 and the next one contains OID2 and OID3, then the chain so far is valid, but every subsequent certificate in the chain must now contain OID2, since that was the only acceptable OID that was contained in both of the first two certificates.

If policy mapping happens in the middle of the chain, and OID2 is declared equivalent to OID5, then (assuming OID2 needed to be in all the remaining certificates in the chain) OID5 must appear in all the remaining certificates in the chain.

These rules are somewhat arbitrary, and whether people wind up using the PKIX policies in any useful way remains to be seen.

15.4 REVOCATION

If someone realizes their key has been stolen, or if someone gets fired from an organization, it is important to be able to revoke their certificate. Certificates typically have expiration dates in them, but since it is a lot of trouble to issue a certificate (especially if the CA is off-line), the validity time is typically months, too long to wait if it needs to be revoked.

This is similar to what happens with credit cards. They, too, have an expiration date. They are usually issued to be good for a year or more. However, if one is stolen, it is important to be able to revoke its validity quickly. Originally, the credit card companies published books of bad credit card numbers, and distributed these books to all the merchants. Before accepting the card, the merchant would check to make sure the credit card number wasn't in the book. This mechanism is similar to a CRL (certificate revocation list) mechanism.

Today the usual mechanism for credit cards is that for each transaction the merchant calls someplace that has access to a database of invalid credit card numbers (or valid credit card numbers), and the merchant is told whether the credit card is valid (and if there is sufficient credit limit for the purchase). This is similar to an OLRS (on-line revocation service) mechanism. The PKIX standard protocol for requesting revocation status of a certificate is called OCSP (on-line certificate status protocol), and is documented in RFC 2560.

Why do certificates have expiration times at all? Assuming there is a method of revoking them, the only security reason to have them expire is to make the revocation mechanism more efficient, for instance by keeping the CRL of manageable size. There are two additional real-world reasons for designing certificates with expiration times:

- many deployed systems don't bother with revocation at all, and depend on expiration instead
- companies that want to collect revenue from issuing certificates want to be able to collect multiple times for the same certificate.

True story: At one time most browsers, by default, did not check expiration date, and even today all of them allow you to choose to ignore the expiration date in a certificate. To get PKI deployed, Verisign initially issued certificates with reasonable terms (e.g., low issuing fee) and lifetimes of two years. But once safely entrenched, the terms they demanded for renewing these certificates were far less favorable. Many server administrators noticed that most browsers didn't check the expiration date, and so didn't bother getting new certificates. In order to be compatible with the many servers with expired certificates, browsers are very casual about expiration date (e.g., having the default be not to check it, or making it very easy for the user to agree to ignore it).

15.4.1 Revocation Mechanisms

The basic idea of a CRL is that the CA periodically issues a signed list of all the revoked certificates. This list must be issued periodically, even if no certificates have been revoked since the last CRL, since otherwise an attacker could post an old CRL (from before his certificate was revoked). If a timestamped CRL is issued periodically, then the verifier can refuse to honor any certificates if it cannot find a sufficiently recent CRL. Each CRL contains a complete list of all the unexpired, revoked certificates.

15.4.1.1 Delta CRLs

Delta CRLs are intended to make CRL distribution more efficient. Let's say you want to have revocation take effect within one hour. With a CRL, that would mean that every hour the CA would have to post a new CRL, and every verifier would have to download the latest CRL. Suppose the CRL was very large, perhaps because the company just laid off 10000 people. Every hour, every verifier would have to download a huge CRL, even though very few certificates had been revoked after that layoff.

A delta CRL lists changes from the last complete CRL. The latest full CRL would have to be posted (and downloaded to each verifier) along with the periodic delta CRLs. The delta CRL would say *these are all the certificates that have been revoked since February 7, 10 AM, which is the most recent full CRL*. The delta CRL would be very short, often containing no certificates. Issuing delta

CRLs periodically obviates the need to issue full CRLs periodically. Instead one can issue a full CRL in place of a delta CRL when the delta CRL gets sufficiently large.

15.4.1.2 First Valid Certificate

This is an idea $\text{we}_{1,2}$ designed for making the CRL small again after it has become too large. This scheme also allows certificates to not have a predetermined expiration time when issued. Instead, they are only marked with a serial number, which increases every time a certificate is issued (or the issue time could be used instead of a serial number). Our version of a CRL would have one additional field that is not included in X.509. The CRL would contain a FIRST VALID CERTIFICATE field. Any certificates with lower serial numbers (or issue times) are invalid.

Certificates in our scheme would have no predetermined expiration time. As long as the CRL is of manageable size there is no reason to reissue any certificates. If it looks like the CRL is getting too large, the company issues a memo warning everyone with certificate serial numbers less than some number n that they'll need new certificates by, say, a week from the date of the memo. The number n might be the next-to-be-issued certificate serial number, or it could be some earlier one. The number n is chosen so that few of the serial numbers in the current CRL are less than n. Revoked certificates with serial numbers greater than n must continue to appear in the new CRL, while valid certificates with numbers greater than n do not have to be reissued. Some time later, say two weeks after the memo is sent, the CA issues a new CRL with n in the FIRST VALID CERTIFICATE field. Affected users (those with serial numbers less than n) who ignored the memo will thenceforth not be able to access the network until they get new certificates, since their certificates are now invalid.

There are cases when even with this scheme it might be reasonable to have expiration times in certificates. For example, at a university, students might be given certificates for use of the system on a per-semester basis, with a certificate that expires after the semester. Upon paying tuition for the next semester, the student is given a new certificate. But even in those cases, it may still be reasonable to combine expiration times in some certificates with our scheme, since our scheme would allow an emergency mass-revocation of certificates.

15.4.2 OLRS Schemes

An OLRS (on-line revocation server) is a system that can be queried over the net about the revocation status of individual certificates. If Alice is using service Bob, then Bob is the verifier (the one making sure Alice's certificate is valid). The design most people envision is that the server Bob queries the OLRS through some authenticated communication.

You might think that introducing an on-line server into a PKI eliminates an important security advantage of public keys, because you now have an on-line trusted service. But the OLRS is not as security sensitive as a CA (or KDC). The worst the OLRS can do is claim that revoked certificates are still valid, but at least the damage is limited. It does not have a vulnerable database of user secrets (like a KDC does). Its key should be different from the CA's key, so if its key is stolen, the CA's key would not be compromised.

An OLRS variant is to have Alice obtain a certificate from the OLRS declaring that *as of 8 AM on June 3 Alice's certificate was not revoked*. Assuming Alice will be visiting many resources, this saves the OLRS the work of talking to multiple verifiers, saves the verifier the work of querying the OLRS, and saves the network from the bandwidth used by having multiple verifiers query the OLRS. Alice would present two certificates to Bob: her long-lived certificate obtained from the CA, and the certificate of non-revocation from the OLRS.

Bob can decide how quickly revocation should take effect. If he wants revocation to take place within, say, one hour, then he can insist that Alice's non-revocation certificate be time-stamped within the last hour. If he complains it isn't sufficiently recent, then Alice can obtain a new one.

Alice can proactively refresh her certificate, knowing that most servers would want one that is, say, less than an hour old. Then the round-trip querying of the OLRS does not need to be done at the time of a transaction.

Even with Bob (instead of Alice) querying the OLRS, it is possible to do caching and refreshing. Bob can keep track of the users that tend to use his resource and proactively check with the OLRS to see if any of them have been revoked.

15.4.3 Good-lists vs. Bad-lists

The standards assume that the CRL will contain all the serial numbers of bad certificates, or that the OLRS would have a database of revoked certificates. This sort of scheme is known as a **bad-list** scheme, since it keeps track of the bad certificates.

A scheme which keeps track of the good certificates is more secure, however. Suppose the CA operator is bribed to issue a certificate, using a serial number from a valid certificate, and that no audit log indicates that this bogus certificate has been issued. Nobody will know this certificate needs to be revoked, since no legitimate person knows it was ever issued. It will not be contained in the CRL.

Suppose instead that the CRL contains a list of all the valid certificates (and not just serial numbers, but hashes of the certificate for each serial number). Then the bogus certificate would not be honored, because it would not appear in the list of good certificates.

There are two interesting issues with good-lists:

- The good-list is likely to be much larger than the bad-list, and might change more frequently, so performance might be worse than with a bad-list.

- An organization might not want to make the list of its valid certificates public. This is easily answered by having the published good-list contain *only* hashes of valid certificates, rather than any other identifying information.

Note that usually the good-list or bad-list, especially if publicly readable, will contain only serial numbers and hashes of the certificates rather than any other identifiable information. Then the only information divulged is the number of valid certificates (in the good-list case) or invalid certificates (in the bad-list case). There is no reason to believe that the count of good certificates is more security sensitive than the count of bad certificates.

The X.509 standard says it is not permitted to issue two certificates with the same serial number, and that all certificates issued must be logged. But we can't assume that a bad guy would be hindered from issuing bogus, unaudited certificates just because it would violate the specification!

15.5 DIRECTORIES AND PKI

A PKI can be facilitated by a distributed hierarchical database indexed by a hierarchical name, where associated with each name is a repository of information for that name. We call this system a **directory**. Each name (e.g., radia.east.sun.com) represents a node in the tree which is a record that stores information about that name, such as its IP address, or the certificates it has signed, or the certificates other principals have signed certifying its key. Each record could in theory be stored on a different machine or set of machines. To go up or down (find the parent record or a child record), the directory should keep the information necessary to find the location of the parent or child record.

One widely deployed directory is DNS. It uses names such as radia.east.sun.com. The Internet works because DNS is pretty much universally deployed.

Another directory standard is X.500, along with languages for querying it such as LDAP (RFC 2251). The X.500 proponents tend to scoff at DNS as being merely a "lookup service" and not a directory, since they envision the main purpose of a directory to be to answer complex queries, such as *find all things that have the attribute 'hair=red'*. With DNS, you start with a specific name and look up stored attributes for that name. For many applications, especially automated ones, fast lookup based on a name is the most important thing. The Internet had gotten along just fine without an X.500-type directory, and it would not work at all today without DNS, because although there are some X.500 directories deployed, there is not a globally connected X.500 directory that you can navigate to look up information about all names, as there is with DNS.

DNS has captured the low end of functionality where efficiency is needed. It provides lookup by name and nothing else. For further functionality, there are web search engines that are much more flexible than X.500, and these are used extensively by people searching the web. It's not clear a directory like X.500 has a viable niche.

Today, most deployed PKIs do not use directories. Here are some ways to build a PKI without a directory:

- There could be a single CA for the world. Alice would keep her own certificate, and present it when she wants to authenticate herself, or present it on request when someone wants to, for instance, send her an encrypted message.
- Still with a single root CA for the world, Alice can present a chain of certificates from the root CA instead of a single certificate.
- With several root CAs, Alice might have a chain from one or more of the root CAs. Bob and Alice can negotiate to find a CA that Bob trusts as a root CA for which Alice has a chain of certificates.

But it's much more convenient and flexible if there is a directory. For instance, it allows Alice to encrypt a message for Bob without first communicating with Bob.

15.5.1 Store Certificates with Subject or Issuer?

Assuming there is a lookup service for retrieving information associated with each hierarchical name, under which name should certificates be stored? If Carol signs a certificate for Alice's name/key, the certificate could be stored in Carol's record, in Alice's record, or in both. PKIX specifies that it must be stored in the subject's record, but it is permissible to additionally store it in the issuer's record.

This decision by PKIX indicates a bias towards a top-down model, where parents sign certifidates for children and give the certificate to the child to store. But this decision makes it difficult to implement cross-certificates or up-certificates. Since the up-certificate or cross-certificate is for the benefit of the issuer and its descendents rather than the subject (it gives the nodes in the subtree under the issuer a path to the names in the subject's subtree), it would not always be the case that the issuer would have write access to the subject's record. Imagine a popular name, such as the IRS (popular in that a lot of principals will want to have a secure path to its public key). Millions of Americans might sign a cross-certificate to it. But they would not have the right to store this certificate in the IRS's record.

For a CA that offers root service, and that might have many children, it is more convenient for down-certificates from the CA to be stored in the subjects' records, because otherwise the data in the CA's record would get too large and difficult to search through.

If a principal knows its key has been compromised, it should notify everyone that has certified its key. If the certificates are stored in the subjects' records, then the subject knows everyone that has certified its key. It has to notify all the issuers of all the certificates stored in its record.

But if certificates are instead stored in the issuer's record, then the subject does not necessarily know who needs to be notified. Obviously its children and its parent would need to be notified. But it does not necessarily know which principals have signed cross-certificates. There are various solutions to this:

- Make it the responsibility of the issuer to check the validity of the key periodically. This might be done by checking a URL at which the subject promises to advertise key changes, or by finding in the PKI some other certificate chain to the subject, and checking with the subject if the key found is different from the one in the cross-certificate, or periodically querying the subject about its key.
- Have the ability for the issuer to request that the subject notify the issuer in the case of a key compromise. This would take less storage than having the issuer store the certificate in the subject's record. And there is no reason for this information to be stored in the subject's record; rather, it can just be kept in the subject's private storage until needed.

There is one other important reason for storing the certificate in the issuer's record rather than the subject's. Except for the top-down model, it makes more sense to create a path from a trust anchor to the target name, and this is difficult to do if the certificate is stored in the subject's record. This is discussed in the next section.

15.5.2 Finding Certificate Chains

To securely know Alice's public key, Bob will need to find a path from one of Bob's trust anchors to Alice. This can be done by starting with Alice and working towards the trust anchors, or vice versa. PKIX shows its bias by referring to starting with Alice as *building in the forward direction*, while building from a trust anchor is referred to as *building in reverse*.

Building "forward" does not work as well if name constraints or policies are used. Suppose there was a fairly rich mesh of cross-certificates, but with name constraints used as specified in §15.3.10 *Name Constraints in Certificates*. If chains are built from the trust anchor, the name constraint in the certificate can tell you whether it is worth following that link in the chain. If you are trying to build a chain to a/b/c/d, and the name constraint does not include that name, then there is no need to see where that certificate might lead. If, however, you attempt to build the chain from the target, the name constraint will not help you eliminate chains that don't originate with one of your trust anchors.

Likewise with policies. If creating a chain from the trust anchor, a certificate that doesn't have the correct policy can be immediately ruled out. However, if building in the other direction, even if the application insists that OID7 must appear, and the certificate contains OID9, the path must still be explored in case a certificate closer to the trust anchor maps OID7 into OID9.

15.6 PKIX AND X.509

PKIX is a profile of X.509, which means PKIX specifies which X.509 options should be supported. X.509 is a particularly awkward format for certificates, but it seems to be what the world is assuming PKIs will be based upon. Despite its awkwardness, it is not totally unusable. We$_{1,2}$ both manage to implement products with it, but we hope you'll forgive us poking a little fun at it in our description below.

15.6.1 Names

How easily and efficiently the PKI concepts can be implemented is influenced by the certificate formats. Somewhat astonishingly, the IETF chose to base the certificate formats on X.509. Given how simple the basic concept is—signing a name, issue date, expiration date, and public key—X.509 was a particularly inappropriate and unfortunate choice. The names were X.500 names. We are all familiar with Internet names (known as *DNS names*). They look like sun.com or mit.edu. We are also familiar with Internet email names, such as user@organization.com.

X.500 names, on the other hand, look like C=US, O=examplecompany name, OU=research, CN=Alice, where C means *country*, O means *organization*, OU means *organizational unit*, and CN is *common name*. There are rules about what types of name components are allowed to be under what others. And the example name C=US, O=examplecompany name, OU=research, CN=Alice is supposed to be human-friendly. That's not how it's actually encoded. The actually encoding consists of OIDs (see section §15.6.2 *OIDs*) for each of the name component types (C, OU, etc.). Compared to OIDs, the OU= syntax *is* human-friendly. There is no standard for display of X.500 names—different applications display them differently.

Few if any Internet applications use X.500 names. Choosing ASN.1 as the encoding dooms certificates to be inefficient in space and computationally expensive and memory intensive to parse.

What happens when you try to use a certificate format for binding names to public keys, but your applications use a different form of name than what appears in the certificate? You wind up either with security flaws or the invention of awkward work-arounds. For instance, an Internet email standard, S/MIME, uses X.509 certificates. How do you reconcile an email name such as radia@alum.mit.edu with an X.500 name? Older implementations mandated that the X.500 name contain a newly invented component email=radia@alum.mit.edu (displayed differently by different applications). All the X.500 name components other than email would be ignored, though they were available for the user to examine if she so chose. The standard later specified that you should put the email name into the SUBJECTALTNAME field in the certificate.

SSL had the same problem since it uses X.509 certificates. URLs contain DNS names, not X.500 names. When someone visits the site www.sun.com, and the server presents a certificate that contains an X.500 name, how can this be at all useful to reassure the user Alice that the site she is talking to is really what she expects it to be? Some browser implementations ignored the name entirely, but still made sure the certificate was properly signed. So if Alice mistakenly contacted snakeoil.com instead of her broker, the site would present a certificate with an X.500 name, Alice's browser would happily do the math and decide it was properly signed, and reassure Alice that everything was secure! It certainly isn't difficult to get a certificate.

A more common (and secure) work-around is to demand that the CN portion of the X.500 name be the DNS name.

Eventually X.509 added the ability to have alternate names. PKIX allows end entities (non-CAs) not to have X.500 names, but CAs still must have X.500 names even if they also have a DNS name in the SUBJECTALTNAME field in the certificate.

There is no widely deployed X.500 directory. There is a widely deployed directory for Internet names—DNS. DNS may be just a "lookup service" and not a "true directory" according to the X.500 proponents' definition. But frankly, when we want to be able to look up attributes of a name, such as its IP address, its certificate, cross-certificates it has signed, etc., the fancy X.500 system doesn't let us do that because there isn't a widely deployed set of X.500 directory servers with referrals for name resolution. To be fair, certificates are not posted in DNS today, either. Given that there is no way to look up certificates in directories today, strategies in deployed systems today include emailing certificates (as in S/MIME) or sending them as part of the exchange (as in SSL/TLS, and IPsec). One place where certificates are posted today is in LDAP directories serving closed user communities (e.g., within a company).

15.6.2 OIDs

An **OID (object identifier)** is a hierarchically assigned value consisting of a sequence of numbers separated by periods, used in ASN.1. It is a way of obtaining unique numbers for things without having any central administration hand out values. In IETF, the IANA (Internet Assigned Numbers Authority) assigns numbers, and they used to periodically publish an RFC titled *Assigned Numbers* which listed all the numbers that were assigned for parameter values in various protocols. For instance, in the PROTOCOL field in IP, the value 6 means TCP, 50 means ESP, and 51 means AH.

The final such RFC was 1700. Now the IANA publishes the numbers on their web site as http://www.iana.org/numbers.html.

With ASN.1, instead of having to send a request in to IANA for a value, you can obtain your own number by going to anyone who already has an OID. For example, if someone already has the value 1.2.840.113549.1.1.2, you can ask them to give you an OID, and they might give you 1.2.840.113549.1.1.2.79. Then you can assign all the values you want provided they all have the prefix 1.2.840.113549.1.1.2.79. As you see, OIDs can get quite large.

Furthermore, different organizations can give different OIDs to the same thing. In fact, even the same organization can give different OIDs to the same thing. For instance, in the PEM standard, there are two possible ways of specifying RSA. One uses the OID 2.5.8.1.1, which is defined as RSA with one parameter specifying the number of bits in the RSA modulus. The other uses OID 1.2.840.113549.1.1.1 and takes one parameter, which is null.

15.6.3 Specification of Time

UNIX time, defined a decade before ASN.1 defined a format for time, was in units of seconds, took four octets to specify, and lasted until 2038. ASN.1, a decade later, came up with a format that was also in units of seconds, but took fifteen octets to specify! Furthermore, it only had a two-digit year! The PKIX people decided that the two digits could be used for specifying years between 1950 and 2049, so at least it expired in 2049 rather than 1999. There is another name form in ASN.1 called GeneralizedTime, which has a four-digit year and uses seventeen octets. PKIX mandates use of the two-digit-year format (called UTCTime—universal coordinated time) for specifying all dates through 2049, and use of GeneralizedTime for dates after 2049.

15.7 X.509 AND PKIX CERTIFICATES

An X.509 certificate contains the following information:

- VERSION. There are currently three versions defined, version 1 for which the code is 0, version 2 for which the code is 1, and version 3 for which the code is 2.
- SERIALNUMBER. An integer that, together with the issuing CA's name, uniquely identifies this certificate. (Note it's illegal according to the spec to issue two certificates with the same serial number, but that doesn't mean someone can't misuse the CA's key and do just that, in which case it would not, of course, uniquely identify the certificate.)

- SIGNATURE. Deceptively named, this specifies the algorithm used to compute the signature on this certificate. It consists of a subfield identifying the algorithm followed by optional parameters for the algorithm.
- ISSUER. The X.500 name of the issuing CA.
- VALIDITY. This contains two subfields, the time the certificate becomes valid, and the last time for which it is valid.
- SUBJECT. The X.500 name of the entity whose key is being certified. This field is mandatory in X.509 but PKIX manages to make it optional, while still being conformant with X.509, by saying that it is allowed to be an empty sequence, which is kind of like a null string but in ASN.1 it takes two octets to specify. In PKIX it is permitted to utilize the optional SUBJECTALTNAME extension to name things according to the way that Internet applications would want to name things (such as using a DNS name).
- SUBJECTPUBLICKEYINFO. This contains two subfields, an algorithm identifer (itself containing two subfields, one identifying the algorithm and the other providing optional parameters for it), and the subject's public key.
- ISSUERUNIQUEIDENTIFIER. Optional (permitted only in version 2 and version 3, but deprecated (i.e., recommended against being used) in PKIX). Uniquely identifies the issuer of this certificate.
- SUBJECTUNIQUEIDENTIFIER. Optional (permitted only in version 2 and version 3, but deprecated (i.e., recommended against being used) in PKIX). Uniquely identifies the subject of this certificate.

The purpose of the optional UNIQUEIDENTIFIER fields is to eliminate the possibility of confusion when a name is reused. For example, John Smith might leave an organization and then the organization might hire another John Smith, assigning the new John Smith the same X.500 name.

> *The author of that poem is either Homer or, if not Homer, somebody else of the same name.*
> —Aldous Huxley

- ALGORITHMIDENTIFIER. This repeats the SIGNATURE field. This field is completely and utterly redundant and didn't need to be there. PKIX renamed this field SIGNATUREALGORITHM rather than removing it.
- ENCRYPTED. Perhaps it would have been better to call this field *signature*. But that name was already taken. Anyway, this field contains the signature on all but the last of the above fields. PKIX boldly renamed it to SIGNATUREVALUE.

- EXTENSIONS. These are only in X.509 version 3. X.509 allows arbitrary extensions, since they are defined by OID. PKIX recommends the following. Remember, these are extensions agreed upon by a large committee of people before products seriously used any of these features, so most likely a lot of them will prove not to be terribly useful:
  - AUTHORITYKEYIDENTIFIER. This identifies the key of the CA that signed this certificate. PKIX specifies that it should be a number that, together with the CA's name, uniquely identifies the key.
  - SUBJECTKEYIDENTIFIER. This is typically a hash of the subject's public key, but it can be anything that, together with the subject's name, uniquely identifies the key. So even a sequence number is OK. The purpose of this field is to match against the identifier that the subject will use in the AUTHORITYKEYIDENTIFIER field if the subject signs a certificate with this key.
  - KEYUSAGE. A bit string in which each bit specifies something for which the subject is allowed to use the key. There are nine defined, for uses such as signatures, key encipherment (the usual case of encryption with a public key, where you use the key to encrypt a secret key), data encipherment (if the data were short enough that you'd want to directly encrypt with the public key), signing X.509 certificates (which gives the subject permission to be a CA), and CRL signing (which is used to indicate the key is used for signing CRLs). CRLs are signed with the same issuer name as the CA, but usually with a different key. So the CA typically signs a certificate with its own name (and different key) as subject, without permission to sign certificates but with permission to sign CRLs.
  - PRIVATEKEYUSAGEPERIOD. This contains two timestamps (which are the four-digit-year variety since there was no backward compatibility issue). Note that the VALIDITY field already specifies when the key is supposed to be valid for. Apparently someone thought it would be useful to specify the interval when the subject is allowed to be using the key separately from the interval when the subject's certificate is valid. The conceivable use of this—and it's a stretch—is that the subject is allowed to use the key for a shorter time than verifiers might want to be able to verify the signature.
  - CERTIFICATEPOLICIES. This is a sequence of OIDs, and, optionally, qualifier fields. Each OID represents a policy, and the optional qualifier for a policy OID might be something like a text string explaining that policy. The idea the committee had in mind was that a policy in an *end entity* certificate (an **end entity** is something other than a CA) would be something like how carefully identity was checked before the certificate was issued, and a policy in a CA-to-CA certificate would be which policies the issuing CA trusts the subject CA to assert.

- POLICYMAPPINGS. This is a sequence of pairs of OIDs, mapping from a policy in the issuer's domain to a policy in the subject's domain, assuming that the policies are similar but just defined by different OIDs.
- SUBJECTALTNAME. This is a sequence of names. This is the way to actually use the names that Internet applications might use, such as DNS names.
- ISSUERALTNAME. This is encoded like SUBJECTALTNAME.
- SUBJECTDIRECTORYATTRIBUTES. This allows specifying attributes, such as date of birth or security clearance, of the subject.
- BASICCONSTRAINTS. This gives permission to the subject to issue more certificates. There are two constraints listed. One is a flag indicating whether the subject is allowed to be a CA (duplicating the KEYUSAGE flag that indicates the same thing), and the other indicates the length of chain allowed following the subject (where 0 means one more certificate is allowed in the chain).
- NAMECONSTRAINTS. This indicates the names for which the subject is trusted to issue certificates. Permitted as well as excluded subtrees can be specified.
- POLICYCONSTRAINTS. This extension allows the issuer to specify that, after *n* more certificates in the chain, policy mapping is no longer permitted. It also allows the issuer to specify that policy OIDs must appear in subsequent certificates, even if the application verifying the chain doesn't care. One defined policy is *any policy,* which means the CA doesn't care about policies. But if a previous CA wants all subsequent CAs to not only put in policies, but to not weasel out of it by using the special *any policy,* then it can use the INHIBITANYPOLICY extension (see below).
- EXTENDEDKEYUSAGE. These are additional key usages, defined by an OID, to make it easy to define new key usages. A few are defined in PKIX, with usages that are consistent with some of the usages in the regular KEYUSAGE field. For instance, one of the defined extended key usages is for timestamping, which PKIX says is consistent with KEYUSAGE of *digital signature* and/or *nonrepudiation*.
- CRLDISTRIBUTIONPOINTS. This describes how to find the CRL, and if the CRL issuer is not the CA, who the CRL issuer is.
- INHIBITANYPOLICY. This specifies that the subject (or a CA at a specified distance down the chain) is not allowed to use *any policy* in its POLICYCONSTRAINT field.
- FRESHESTCRL. Describes how to obtain delta CRLs.
- AUTHORITYINFOACCESS. Describes how to find information about the issuer of this certificate.

◆ SUBJECTINFOACCESS. Describes how to find information about the subject of this certificate. For instance, if the subject is a CA, it might specify how to find the certificates issued by that CA.

15.7.1 X.509 and PKIX CRLs

An X.509/PKIX CRL contains the following information:

- SIGNATURE. Identical to the SIGNATURE field in certificates, this specifies the algorithm used to compute the signature on this CRL.
- ISSUER. Identical to the ISSUER field in certificates, this is the X.500 name of the issuing CA.
- THISUPDATE. This contains the time the CRL was issued.
- NEXTUPDATE. Optional. This contains the time the next CRL is expected to be issued. A reasonable policy is to treat as suspect any certificate issued by a CA whose current CRL has a NEXTUPDATE time in the past.

The following three fields repeat together, once for each revoked certificate:

- USERCERTIFICATE. This contains the serial number of the revoked certificate.
- REVOCATIONDATE. This contains the time the certificate was revoked.
- CRLENTRYEXTENSIONS. This contains various optional information such as a reason code for why the certificate was revoked.
- CRLEXTENSIONS. This contains various optional information such as authority key identifier, issuer alternative name, the CRL number, the delta CRL indicator (used in delta CRLs to specify the base CRL number), and a flag indicating that the CRL only contains CA certificates or only contains end entity certificates.
- ALGORITHMIDENTIFIER. As for certificates, this repeats the SIGNATURE field.
- ENCRYPTED. This field contains the signature on all but the last of the above fields.

15.8 AUTHORIZATION FUTURES

The two most important problems in network security are *Who are you?* and *Should you be doing that?* Authorization is the *Should you be doing that?* part of network security. In the remainder of this chapter we discuss how authorization could be done using PKI, although no deployed PKIs today do authorization as described here.

15.8.1 ACL (Access Control List)

Typically the way a server decides whether a user should have access to a resource is by first authenticating the user, and then consulting a database associated with the resource that indicates who is allowed to do what with that resource. For instance, the database associated with a file might say that Alice can read it and Bob and Carol can both read and write it. This database is often referred to as an **ACL (access control list)**.

15.8.2 Central Administration/Capabilities

Another model of authorization is that instead of listing, with each resource, the set of authorized users and their rights (e.g., *read*, *write*, *execute*), you would have a database that listed, for each user, everything she was allowed to do. If everything were a single application, then the ACL model and the central administration model would be basically the same, since in both cases there would be a database that listed all the authorized users and what rights each had. But in a world in which there are many resources, not all under control of the same organization, it would be difficult to have a central database listing what each user was allowed to do, and it would have scaling problems if there were many resources each user was allowed to access, especially if resources were created and deleted at a high rate.

There might be a suite of applications all accessed through a single portal. For instance, you might log into the "human resources" suite of applications that would allow you to select whether you wanted to submit an expense report, record vacation time, or choose health care options. In this case you could consider the entire suite of applications as a single application with a common ACL, and even if rights for the suite are centrally administered, as long as the suite is considered as one application, it would be equivalent to the ACL model. However, it might become burdensome to have all the application-specific rights centrally administered. When the maintainer of the expense reporting application decided to add a new frill, say something that allows the user to preauthorize business class airfare, it might be easier to have an application-specific ACL that listed *preauthorize business class airfare* as one of the rights rather than adding it into the suite's ACL.

Some people worry that ACLs don't scale well if there are many users allowed access to each resource. But the concept of groups answers that concern.

15.8.3 Groups

If there is a file that should be accessible to, say, any Sun employee, it would be tedious to type in all the names of the authorized individuals, especially if there were more than one resource with the same authorizations. The concept of a **group** was invented to make ACLs more scalable. It is possible to include a group name on an ACL, which means that any member of the group is allowed access to the resource.

Traditionally a server that protected a resource with a group named on the ACL needed to know all the members of the group. But it is useful to allow more flexible group mechanisms in order to support cross-organizational groups where no one server is allowed to know all the members, or anonymous groups, where someone can prove membership in the group without having to divulge their identity.

Traditionally groups were centrally administered, so it was easy to know all the groups to which a user belonged, and the user would not belong to many groups. But in many situations it is useful for any user to be able to create a group (such as Alice's friends, or students who have already turned in their exams in my course), and have anyone else be able to name such a group on an ACL.

Scaling up this simple concept of users, groups, and ACLs to a distributed environment has not been solved in practice. This section describes how it might be done. There exist secret-key-based systems (DCE, Windows NT, and Windows 2000/Kerberos) that distribute group membership information from a central server.

15.8.3.1 Cross-Organizational and Nested Groups

An ACL should be able to contain any boolean combination of groups and individuals. Likewise, group membership should be any boolean combination of groups and individuals, e.g., the members of Alliance-executives might be CompanyA-execs, CompanyB-execs, and John Smith. Each of the groups Alliance-executives, CompanyA-execs, and CompanyB-execs is likely to be managed by a different organization and the membership is likely to be stored on different servers. How, then, can a server that protects a resource that has the group Alliance-executives on the ACL know whether to allow Alice access? If she's not explicitly listed on the ACL, she might be a member of one of the groups on the ACL. But the server does not necessarily know all the members of the group. Let's assume that the group name can be looked up in a directory to find out information such as its network address and its public key.

- The server could periodically find every group on any ACL on any resource it protects, and attempt to collect the complete membership. This means looking up all the members of all subgroups, and subgroups of subgroups. This has scaling problems (the group memberships might be very large), performance problems (there might be a lot of traffic with servers querying group membership servers for membership lists), and cache staleness problems. How often would this be done? Once a day is a lot of traffic, but also a lot of time to elapse for Alice's group membership to take effect, and for revocations to take effect.

- The server could ask the on-line group server whether Alice is a member of the group at the time Alice requests access to a resource on which a group appears. This could also be a performance nightmare with many queries, especially in the case of unauthorized users. At the least, once Alice is discovered to either belong or not belong, the server should cache this information. But again, if the cache is held for a long time it means that membership can take a long time to take effect, and revocation can also takes a long time to take effect.
- All groups to which Alice belongs could be added into her Kerberos ticket. This implies that the KDC or some central authorization service knows all the groups she is in. This makes it difficult to support cross-organizational groups, where no one entity knows all the groups a user is in, and it can have scaling problems as well if a user is in many groups.
- Groups to which Alice belongs could be listed in Alice's certificate. This also has scaling problems if she is in many groups. It also implies that the CA knows all the groups Alice belongs to, and requires reissuance of the certificate any time Alice joins or leaves a group.
- Alice might be given a set of group membership certificates for each group to which she belongs. She could present them all whenever attempting to access a resource, or the server could request certificates for relevant groups.
- The server could tell Alice in which groups she should prove membership to gain access to the resource. Then Alice, if she has membership certificates for those groups, could send the certificates to the server, or obtain group membership certificates as needed. This is an attractive solution for many reasons. In many situations it is better to have the clients do the work than the servers, because of denial-of-service attacks on the servers. Also, a single interaction with the group membership server would allow Alice to use that certificate on many servers. Further, Alice's workstation can keep track of which group memberships she has recently needed, and proactively refresh credentials. This frees servers from checking revocation status on certificates. Instead of checking for revocation, they can insist that the group membership certificate Alice presents is reasonably fresh (say less than three hours old). Each server can have its own policy for how fresh group membership certificates must be, and refuse group membership certificates staler than that.

15.8.4 Roles

The term **role** is used in many different ways. The most common concept is that Alice can be logged in as role *Alice–ordinary user* or *Alice–system administrator*, and she gets different privileges depending on which role she's in. Authorization based on roles is referred to as RBAC (role based access control), and as with the term *role*, the term *RBAC* means different things to different people. Some advocates of the roles concept claim that the purpose of roles is to allow central administration of rights, instead of having an ACL for each resource. They claim such a system (which lists all the privileges that go along with a role) will scale better than an ACL model, but if centralized administration really were easier, then wouldn't the same argument apply to individuals and groups?

Usually people think of a role as something that needs to be consciously invoked by a user, often requiring additional authentication such as typing a different password. In contrast, with groups it is assumed that all members are automatically given all rights of the group as long as they are members. Users may or may not be allowed to simultaneously act in multiple roles, and perhaps multiple users may or may not be allowed to simultaneously act in a particular role (like *President of the United States*).

Some things people would like to see roles solve:

- When a user is acting in a particular role, the application presents a different user interface. For instance, when a user is acting as *manager*, the expense reporting utility might present commands for approving expense reports, whereas when the user is acting as *employee*, the application might present commands for reporting expenses.
- Having roles enables a user to be granted a subset of all the permissions they might have. This makes it less likely that a typo will cause a user to inadvertently do an undesirable privileged operation, because they'd only invoke the privileged role briefly, and only when necessary to do a specific action.
- Allowing a user to be able to run with a subset of her rights (not invoking her most privileged role except when necessary) gives some protection from malicious code. While running untrusted code, the user would be careful to run in an unprivileged role.
- Sometimes there are complex policies, such as that you are allowed to read either file A or file B but not both. Somehow, proponents of roles claim roles will solve this problem. This sort of policy is called a **Chinese wall**.

On a single machine, some of these concepts of roles can be implemented straightforwardly. But what about in a distributed environment?

Most of the functionality that people envision for roles can be done with groups. But there are three concepts: individuals, groups, and roles. What might be the difference between a role and a group? A role has to be explicitly invoked, and perhaps with additional authentication. So in that case, what is the difference between a role and an individual? Why not just consider *administrator* and *user* as different entities? The reason is that for auditing purposes it is useful to know which user was acting in the *administrator* role when a particular action was taken.

Making fancy policies work in a distributed fashion is at best a subject of research today. If you want to ensure that only one user is acting in a particular role at any time, or that a user must not be allowed to see both files A and B, a conceivable method for implementing this is to have a central service (which might for robustness or performance be implemented on multiple machines, coordinating amongst themselves) which keeps track of who has done what and grants permissions for actions. This wouldn't be a central service for the entire inter-organizational internet, but rather a service for a suite of applications. The user logs into the central server, so it can keep track of what role(s) the user has at the moment and what actions the user has taken.

15.8.5 Anonymous Groups

If a user can prove she is a member of a group which is authorized access to the resource, it is not necessarily the case that she needs to divulge and prove her identity. In many cases it *will* be necessary, for auditing purposes. But in some cases, it might be desirable to anonymously prove group membership.

This can be accomplished by having Alice authenticate herself to the group membership server, provide it with a public key P (different from Alice's long-term key), and have the group membership server issue a certificate stating that the holder of the private key associated with P is a member of the group. In order to not allow someone to correlate uses of the public key to know that the same user did both actions, a user might want to have a lot of group membership certificates for the anonymous group, each with a different key.

If it is desired that even the group membership server should not know which key is associated with which member, then the group membership server could do a **blind signature**, a concept invented by David Chaum in which Bob signs something without knowing what he's signing!

It is rather surprising that such a protocol exists, that it would be useful for anything, and that anyone would have thought of it! But assuming you'd want to be able to use your privileges as a member of the group without anyone being able to know which individual you were, this feature would be useful. With blind signatures, Bob does not know which keys belong to which members, and so cannot divulge this information.

A blind signature is easy to understand. Assume the signature algorithm is RSA, and that Bob's public key is $\langle e,n \rangle$. If Alice wants a particular certificate c signed by Bob, then she picks a random number R, and raises R to e mod n, and multiplies c by the result. So she gets $c(R^e \bmod n)$. Bob can't distinguish this from a random number. He signs the result, meaning that he raises it to his private exponent d. So he computes $c^d(R^{ed}) \bmod n$. R^{ed} is just R. So Alice divides what she gets from Bob by R and her certificate is now validly signed by Bob. Note that this only obscures what Bob has signed if Bob signs lots of things with that key. And note that this is only secure if Bob has a different key for each kind of assertion he signs.

15.9 HOMEWORK

1. Referring to Figure 15-1, which CAs must B/Y/Z/A/C trust in order to find a path to A/C/Y?
2. In a relative names PKI as described in §15.3.9 *Relative Names*, suppose a cross-certificate from A/B/C to A/B/D/X indicates how many levels up from the issuer the least common ancestor is (in this case, one level up, since the parent is A/B and is also an ancestor of A/B/D/X), followed by the name down from there. So the cross-certificate from A/B/C to A/B/D/X would contain "../D/X" (go up from my name one level, and then go down to D/X). In what case of namespace reorganization would this scheme not require the cross-certificate to be reissued, whereas with an absolute name it would? In what case would the absolute name certificate remain valid whereas the scheme proposed in this problem would need to be reissued?
3. What name constraints would you put into PKIX certificates to build the anarchy model?
4. Compare the following schemes for obtaining Bob's public key, in terms of bandwidth and computation efficiency, security, flexibility, and any other criteria you can think of: downloading Bob's key from the node located at a particular IP address (via an unauthenticated interaction), looking up Bob's key in a directory via an unauthenticated interaction, having an authenticated conversation to the directory, having the directory sign the information you request, storing and retrieving certificates from the directory, having no directory but having each principal responsible for keeping its own certificate and sending it to someone who needs to talk to it.
5. Why must a CRL be reissued periodically, even when no new certificates have been revoked?
6. If there is a revocation mechanism, why do certificates need an expiration date?
7. Compare revocation schemes of verifiers downloading complete CRLs, clients obtaining non-revocation certificates, and verifiers checking individual validity status. Consider in overhead (on bandwidth, verifiers, clients, the OLRS) and revocation timeliness. Consider factors such as how many clients a verifier serves and how many services a client visits.
8. Why is it important in a good-list revocation scheme to keep hashes of the valid certificates, rather than just their serial numbers?
9. Show how (using policies and policy mapping as described in §15.3.11 *Policies in Certificates*), it is possible for the only legal path to contain a loop. Show a path that requires going around a loop twice in order to meet the policy requirements.

10. Discuss mechanisms for support of groups, and compare them for ability to support large numbers of groups and members, cross-organizational groups, dynamically changing groups, and quick revocation and group joining.

16 Real-time Communication Security

A real-time protocol is one in which the parties negotiate interactively to authenticate each other and establish a session key, in contrast to a protocol such as email in which one party prepares a message that can later be decrypted and authenticated by the intended recipient. Standards for real-time public-key-based security protocols include IPsec, SSL/TLS, and SSH. In this chapter we cover the problems and solutions generically, rather than diving into the idiosyncracies of particular protocols, because the actual protocols (especially the ones defined by committee) are gratuitously complex. The subsequent chapters deal with the specifics of IPsec and SSL/TLS.

At a minimum, the protocols provide mutual authentication between Alice and Bob and establish a session key for cryptographic protection of the subsequent conversation. The conversation protected with that session key is known as a **security association**. Other features such protocols might provide, and which are explained in this chapter, are perfect forward secrecy, clogging protection, escrow-foilage, and endpoint identifier hiding. This chapter also discusses the differences between protocols such as IPsec, which is said to be "implemented at layer 3", and protocols such as SSL/TLS and SSH, which are said to be "implemented at layer 4".

16.1 What Layer?

Definition of a layer n protocol: anything defined by a committee whose charter is to define a layer n protocol. —Radia Perlman (in *Interconnections: Bridges, Routers, Switches, and Internetworking Protocols*)

SSL/TLS and SSH are said to be "implemented at layer 4", whereas IPsec is said to be "implemented at layer 3". What does it mean that a real-time communication security protocol is implemented at layer 3 vs. layer 4, and what are the implications? (For a definition of the layers, see §1.5.1 *OSI Reference Model.*)

For brevity, since for the principles discussed in this chapter, SSL/TLS and SSH have the same properties, in this chapter we'll simply say SSL when we mean any of the protocols SSL, TLS, or SSH.

Many IP stacks are implemented so that layer 4 (e.g., TCP) and below are implemented in the operating system, and anything above is implemented in a user process. The philosophy of SSL is that it is easier to deploy something if you don't have to change the operating system, so these protocols act "above TCP". It requires the applications to interface to SSL instead of TCP. The name Secure Sockets Layer comes from the most popular API to TCP, which is called "sockets". The API to SSL is a superset of the API to TCP sockets. Modifying an application to work on top of SSL requires minimal changes. Of course, the security benefits are limited if the richer API is not used.

Although the applications have to be modified (albeit minimally), the operating system, which includes TCP and the layers below it, does not need to be modified. "Transport Layer Security" is somewhat of a misnomer because rather than being at layer 4, these protocols tend to act like a layer on top of layer 4.

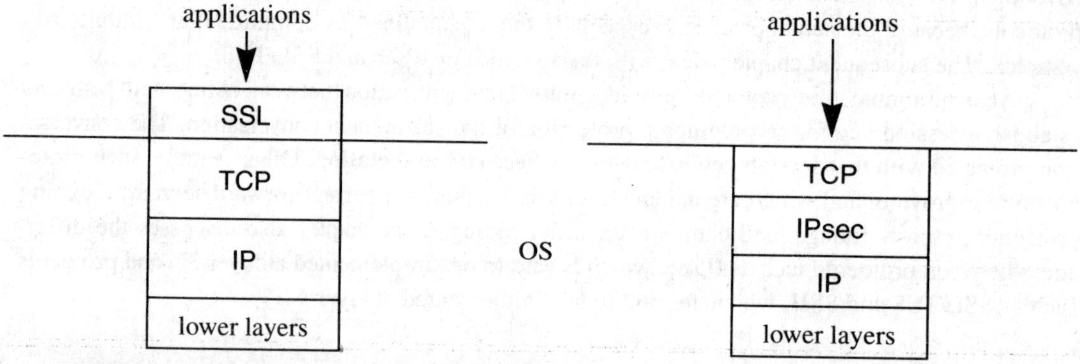

SSL/TLS or SSH operate above TCP. OS doesn't change. Applications do.

IPsec is within the OS. OS changes. Applications and API to TCP are unchanged.

Figure 16-1. Implementing at layer 3 vs. layer 4

In contrast, the philosophy behind IPsec is that implementing security within the operating system automatically causes all applications to be protected without the applications having to be modified.

There is a problem in operating above TCP. Since TCP will not be participating in the cryptography, it will have no way of noticing if malicious data is inserted into the packet stream, as long as the bogus data passes the (noncryptograpic) TCP checksum. TCP will acknowledge such data and send it up to SSL. SSL will discard it because the integrity check will indicate the data is bogus, but there is no way for SSL to tell TCP to accept the real data at this point. When the real data arrives, TCP will assume it is duplicate data and discard it, since it will have the same sequence numbers as the bogus data. SSL has no choice but to close the connection, since it can no longer provide the service that the API claims it offers, namely a lossless stream of data. An attacker can launch a successful denial-of-service attack by inserting a single packet into the data stream. IPsec's approach of cryptographically protecting each packet independently can better protect against such an attack.

In contrast, IPsec's constraint of not modifying the applications winds up with its own serious problem. With the current commonly used API, IP tells the application only what IP address it is talking to, not what user is on the other end. So IPsec, with the current API, cannot tell the application anything more than which IP address is on the other end, even though IPsec is capable of authenticating an individual user. Most applications need to distinguish between users. If IPsec has authenticated the user, it could in theory tell the application the user's name, but that would require changing the API and the application.

Implementing IPsec without changing the application has the same effect as putting firewalls between the two systems and implementing IPsec between the firewalls. It accomplishes the following:

- It causes the traffic on the path between the communicating parties to be encrypted, hiding it from eavesdroppers.
- As with firewalls, IPsec can access a policy database similar to what a firewall can access. For instance, it can specify which IP addresses are allowed to talk to which other IP addresses, or which TCP ports should be allowed or excluded. This is true whether the endpoint of the IPsec connection is a firewall or an endnode (see §23.1 *Packet Filters*).
- Some applications do authentication based on IP addresses (see §9.2 *Address-Based Authentication*). The API informs the application of the IP address from which information was received. Before IPsec, the source IP address was assumed based solely on the value of the SOURCE ADDRESS field in the IP header. With IPsec, address-based authentication becomes much more secure because one of the types of endpoint identifiers IPsec can authenticate is an IP address.

What IPsec (with the current API and an unmodified application) does *not* accomplish for the application is authentication of anything other than IP addresses. Most principals would have some identity such as a name, and be allowed to access the network from a variety of IP addresses. In these cases, the most likely scenario for using IPsec is that IPsec would do its highly secure and expensive authentication, authenticating based on the user's public key and establishing a security association to the user's name, but would have no way of telling the application who is on the other side. The application would have to depend on existing mechanisms, most likely a name and password, to determine which user it is talking to. IPsec is still of value in this scenario in which the (unmodified) application authenticates the user based on name and password, since the name and password will now be encrypted when transmitted.

To take full advantage of IPsec, applications will have to change. The API has to change in order to pass identities other than IP addresses, and the applications have to change to make use of this information. So the best solution is one where both the operating system *and* the applications are modified. This illustrates why security would best be done by being designed in from the start, rather than being added in with the least modification to an existing implementation.

One other advantage of the packet-by-packet cryptographic handling of IPsec is that it is easier to build an outboard device that does IPsec processing. To implement an SSL-type protocol that operates over TCP in an outboard device, the device would have to implement TCP, including buffering out-of-order packets.

16.2 SESSION KEY ESTABLISHMENT

In Chapter 11 *Security Handshake Pitfalls* we discuss various protocols and pitfalls for doing mutual authentication. Cryptographic mutual authentication is certainly an improvement over passwords in the clear, but it is also important to cryptographically protect the conversation after the initial handshake. Obviously it is desirable to protect the data from disclosure or modification. But another vulnerability if cryptographic protection ends after the initial handshake is **session hijacking**, in which someone takes over Alice's session to Bob by forging Alice's IP address as the source address on packets sent to Bob, and using TCP sequence numbers larger than what Alice would be using. Without cryptographic protection, Bob can't distinguish these packets from authentic packets from Alice. Once Bob accepts the attacker's larger TCP sequence numbers, Alice's data just gets ignored as duplicate data. It looks to Alice like the connection breaks, but the attacker is now logged in as Alice, and can do anything Alice is allowed to do. So, a session key is used after the initial mutual authentication to cryptographically protect the conversation from disclosure, modification, or hijacking.

A sequence number is typically used to prevent replay or reordering. A new session key should be established for each new session, and during a session, if the sequence number might be reused (i.e., wrap around).

The session key must be unpredictable to an attacker. (For instance, Goldberg and Wagner [GOLD96] reverse engineered an implementation of the SSL protocol and discovered that the session key was based on three quantities: the time of day in units of microseconds, the process id, and the parent process id. This meant that an attacker who knew the approximate time the session was created had a feasible search space to search for keys. Even though the key was 128 bits long, given a bit of cleverness to narrow down the potential process ids, the attacker would only have to search from an approximately 30-bit space to find the key.

Both communicating parties should contribute to the session key, for instance by having each side send a value to the other, encrypted with the other side's public key, and using a hash of the two values as the session key. This rule makes it less likely that the protocol will have flaws in which someone will be able to impersonate one side or the other in a replay attack. For instance, in a protocol in which Alice sends the session key to Bob, encrypted with his public key, someone impersonating Alice can simply replay all Alice's messages.

Another reason for having both sides contribute to the session key is that if *either* side has a good random number generator, then the session key will be sufficiently random.

16.3 PERFECT FORWARD SECRECY

A protocol is said to have **perfect forward secrecy** (PFS) if it is impossible for an eavesdropper (Sam) to decrypt a conversation between Alice and Bob even if Sam records the entire encrypted session, and then subsequently breaks into *both* Alice and Bob and steals their long-term secrets. The trick to achieving perfect forward secrecy is to generate a temporary session key, not derivable from information stored at the node after the session concludes, and then forget it after the session concludes. If the session will last for a long time, it is common to generate and forget keys periodically so that even if Sam seizes Alice's and Bob's computers while the conversation is still going on, he will not be able to decrypt messages received before the last key rollover. Protocol 16-2 is an example of a protocol with perfect forward secrecy. It uses Diffie-Hellman to agree on a session key, which achieves perfect forward secrecy assuming both sides generate an unpredictable Diffie-Hellman private number and forget both the private number and the agreed-upon session key after the session ends. Also, each side signs the Diffie-Hellman quantity to foil a man-in-the-middle attack (see §6.4.2 *Defenses Against Man-in-the-Middle Attack*).

In the first two messages, each side identifies itself, and supplies a Diffie-Hellman value signed by its private key. In the next two messages, each side proves knowledge of the agreed-upon Diffie-Hellman value g^{ab} mod p by sending a hash of it, with each side sending a different hash. If each side forgets g^{ab} mod p and its private Diffie-Hellman number (a or b) after the session, there is no way for anyone to reconstruct g^{ab} mod p from knowledge of both long-term private keys and the entire recorded conversation.

What kind of protocol would not have perfect forward secrecy? Examples include

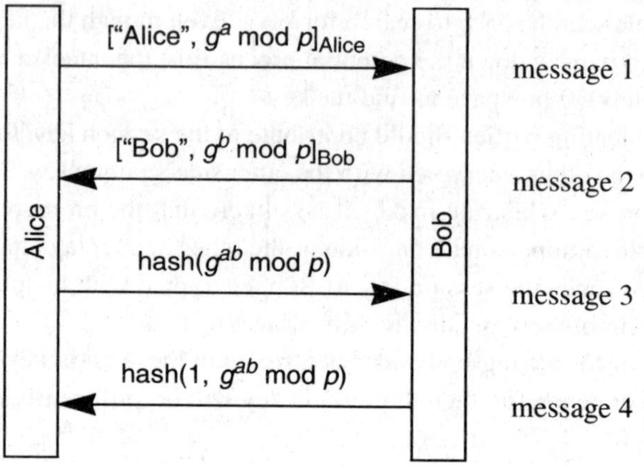

Protocol 16-2. Diffie-Hellman for perfect forward secrecy using signature keys

- Alice sends all messages for Bob encrypted with Bob's public key, and Bob sends all messages for Alice encrypted with Alice's public key.
- Kerberos (since the session key is inside the ticket to Bob, and is encrypted with Bob's long-term secret).
- Alice chooses the session key, and sends it to Bob, encrypted with Bob's public key.

Perfect forward secrecy might seem like it only protects against a fairly obscure threat. However, protocols designed with perfect forward secrecy usually have another property, which is particularly popular with the IETF crowd, which we'll call **escrow-foilage**. This means that even if the forces of darkness (and we make no value judgments here), have required Alice and Bob to give their long-term private keys to some benign, completely trustworthy organization, the conversation between Alice and Bob will still be secret between only Alice and Bob. In other words, even with prior knowledge of Alice and Bob's long-term keys, a passive eavesdropper cannot decrypt the conversation.

Of course if Sam has prior knowledge of all of Alice's and Bob's secrets, then he can impersonate Alice or Bob, and perhaps trick them into divulging what they would have divulged in the conversation. Maybe you'd think Alice and Bob could start off the conversation by asking each other a few personal questions like, "What café did we meet at in Paris?" but Sam could be acting as an active man-in-the-middle, decrypting and reencrypting the traffic, relaying the personal questions and answers, and this would be very difficult to detect.

Anything with perfect forward secrecy will also have escrow-foilage against a passive attack, since anything you can do by having recorded the conversation and learned the secret later you can also do knowing the secrets in advance and eavesdropping in real-time. But often with escrowed systems a user has two public key pairs, one for encryption and one for signatures. And in those cases, only the encryption key is escrowed, since law enforcement would like to decrypt data, but does not need the ability to forge signatures. It would be counterproductive for them to have a user's private signature key, because then the user can repudiate his signature since anyone else with access to the key might have signed the message. So assuming the signature keys are not escrowed, then Protocol 16-2 will have escrow-foilage even against active attacks.

16.4 PFS-FOILAGE

Even if the protocol is designed for perfect forward secrecy and escrow-foilage, an implementation can fail to achieve those properties. I_2 am familiar with a design proposed by someone who wanted to ensure, even in the presence of the types of protocols designed by "those anarchist IETFers," that the ability of Big Brother to monitor traffic would not be impeded. This was done by having the client machines generate all random numbers based on a seed provided by (and stored at) a server. The assumption was that the servers were managed by completely trustworthy individuals, all servers were physically protected at all times, and there were no security vulnerabilities in servers to be exploited, so it was okay that the servers would be able to decrypt all encrypted data. The thing that annoyed me_2 most about the design was the claim that forcing the client machine to generate all random numbers from a seed escrowed at the server would *enhance* security, because "the client machine was incapable of generating as high-quality a random seed as the server machine could generate." Some problems with this reasoning:

- The client machine is actually *more* capable of generating random numbers since it has access to a nice source of randomness, a human, providing all sorts of unpredictable inputs, e.g., keystrokes and mouse movements.
- If the server really wanted to "help out" by giving the client a really high quality seed, the client machine should merely use that as one more of the inputs to its random number generator, say by hashing the received seed with the random number the client would have generated without the server's help.
- The necessity for the server to securely send the seed to the client is another opportunity for vulnerabilities and design complexity.

But of course the real reason for this design was to provide PFS-foilage, not to enhance security.

16.5 DENIAL-OF-SERVICE/CLOGGING PROTECTION

Even if Trudy can't impersonate Alice without knowing her secret, in many protocols she can lock out legitimate users by forcing Bob to use up all his state or computation resources with authentication attempts. This sort of attack happens on the Internet, and the impostor often launches the attack packets with forged IP addresses. Using forged IP source addresses makes it difficult to catch the attacker, and it makes it difficult to allow firewalls to easily recognize and discard traffic from the impostor. It is easy to put any address into the source address field of an IP packet, but it is more difficult to be able to receive packets sent to a randomly chosen IP address.

16.5.1 Cookies

The designers of Photuris (an early key management protocol for IPsec which will be more fully described in §18.1 *Photuris*) provided for denial-of-service protection by adding a feature which the designers called *cookies*. Despite the name, this feature has nothing to do with web browser cookies [see §25.5 *Cookies*].

The Photuris cookie is a number chosen by Bob, and unpredictable to the side initiating communication with Bob. When Bob receives a connection initiation from IP source address *S*, Bob sends this number, in the clear, to the IP address *S*. Bob does no significant computation until he receives the same cookie back from that IP address. This assures that the initiator can receive packets sent to the IP address from which it claims to be transmitting.

This feature makes it somewhat harder to mount a certain narrow set of attacks. It doesn't hurt, other than making the protocol slightly more complex, and adding a round-trip delay (in the case of Photuris). In theory, cookies could be used only when a node is getting swamped, saving the round-trip delay in the usual case (see Homework Problem 2).

A server has a limited amount of memory for keeping track of connections. If an attacker were sending zillions of connect requests, and Bob had to remember what cookie he sent for each request, then even if the attacker couldn't return the correct cookie, he could still swamp Bob's memory so that Bob couldn't accept connections from legitimate users. This is similar to the attack known as the TCP SYN attack ("SYN" is the first packet that Alice sends to Bob to initiate a TCP connection to Bob), where TCP requires Bob to keep state after receiving the first connection request, and an attacker can fill up Bob's table.

So we'd like Bob not to have to remember which cookies he sent to which connection initiators. The Photuris protocol provided for **stateless cookies**. The idea is to have the cookie be a function of the IP address and a secret known to Bob, so that Bob can calculate what cookie he would have sent to a particular IP address. One possibility is hash(IP address, secret). So the cookie protocol might look like Protocol 16-2.

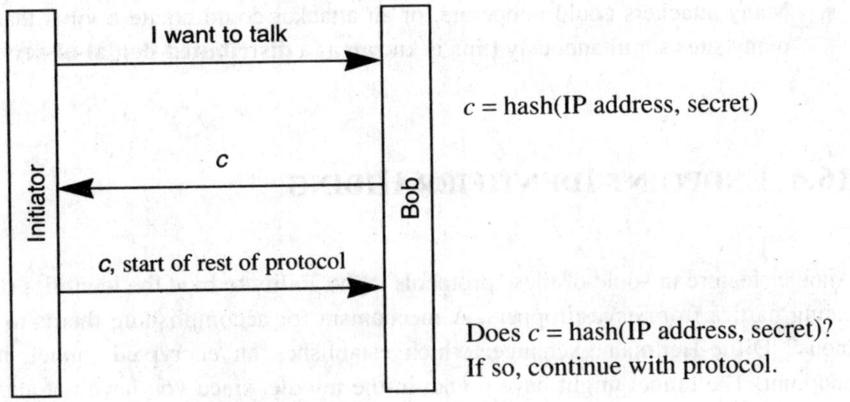

Protocol 16-3. Stateless cookie protocol

16.5.2 Puzzles

Juels and Brainard [JUEL99] came up with a clever alternative scheme for some amount of protection from a denial-of-service attack of this sort, where there are more initiators than Bob has computation or storage to handle. The idea is that if Bob is getting swamped, then Bob can require initiators to do more computation in order to connect. Bob can require each one to solve a puzzle, for instance making them compute a number whose message digest is a particular value. Bob can require arbitrary amounts of computation from an initiator by varying the size of the unknown number ("what 27-bit number has an MD of x?"). He can also make it stateless, in a similar way to stateless cookies (Homework Problem 3). This would not help very much if there are a lot more attackers than legitimate connection initiators, but it will slow down a single attacker making a lot of connection attempts.

Verifying a puzzle answer is fast, since it merely involves doing a message digest. However solving the problem is exponential in the number of the bits Bob chooses for the size of the puzzle.

The idea would be that non-hostile connection initiators might not mind having to do a few seconds worth of computation in order to connect, but it would slow down attackers, since any single attacker would not be able to get to the point of requiring storage and significant computation from Bob more than once every few seconds.

Some issues are:

- There are orders of magnitude of difference in the computational power of machines, and the amount of computation necessary to slow down a powerful machine would make it prohibitive to connect from a wimpy, ancient (e.g., two-year-old) machine.

- Many attackers could cooperate, or an attacker could create a virus that would attack from many sites simultaneously (this is known as a **distributed denial-of-service attack**).

16.6 ENDPOINT IDENTIFIER HIDING

Another feature in some of these protocols is the ability to hide the identities of the two communicating parties from eavesdroppers. A mechanism for accomplishing this is to first do an "anonymous" Diffie-Hellman exchange, which establishes an encrypted tunnel, but to an unknown endpoint. The tunnel might have a man-in-the-middle, since you have not authenticated the other side (indeed you don't even know who the other side is claiming to be). After the anonymous Diffie-Hellman exchange establishes a key, the two parties divulge their identities, encrypted with the anonymous Diffie-Hellman key. Then a passive attacker will not learn their identities, but an active attacker acting as a man-in-the-middle might (depending on the particular protocol) learn one or both of the identities. In addition to divulging their identities, they should also authenticate each other based on the keys associated with their identities. An active attacker doing a man-in-the middle attack would be detected at this point, after having discovered the endpoint identities.

Note that by carefully designing the protocol, you can arrange for the man-in-the-middle to only be able to learn one of the two identities before being discovered by the other side as an impostor. Which identity is better to hide from an active attacker? One argument says that it is better to hide the initiator's identity (Alice) than the responder's identity (Bob), because Bob's identity is probably already known. He has to be sitting at a fixed IP address waiting to be contacted, whereas Alice might be dialing in from anywhere, and her identity could not be guessed from her IP address.

But a different argument says that it is better to hide Bob's identity. If Bob divulges his identity first, then anyone can initiate a connection to Bob and get him to divulge his identity. Unless there is a strict client/server model in which clients never accept connections and only initiate them, having a protocol in which the responder divulges his identity first makes it trivial to find out who is at a given IP address. In contrast, for an active attacker to trick Alice into revealing her identity, it requires impersonating Bob's address and waiting for Alice to initiate a conversation.

An example protocol, assuming the two sides have public signature keys, might be Protocol 16-4.

In this protocol an active attacker will be able to discover Alice's identity, but not Bob's. It is easy to arrange instead to hide Alice's identity (see Homework Problem 4).

If Alice and Bob know in advance to whom they will be talking (perhaps they are two spies who will be contacting each other at a specific time), then a protocol based on a shared secret key

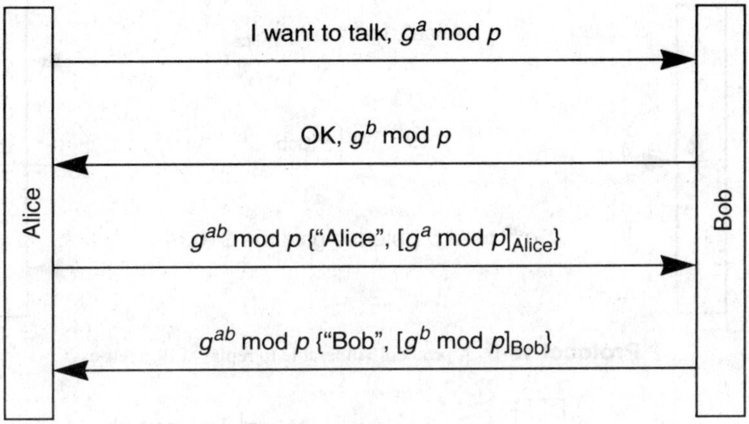

Protocol 16-4. Identity hiding

will hide both identities. This is accomplished by authenticating based on the secret key and not sending identities at all (see Homework Problem 6).

If Alice already knows Bob's public encryption key, it is possible to hide both identities from active attackers (see Homework Problem 5).

16.7 LIVE PARTNER REASSURANCE

If Trudy can replay messages from previous conversation negotiations, she might be able to get Bob to waste space on a connection, or worse yet, she might be able to replay the subsequent data messages and, even if she can't decrypt the conversation, she might be able to cause Bob to repeat actions. For instance, when Bob (an ATM machine) talked to Alice, she might have requested Bob to put $100 into the money tray, as in Protocol 16-5.

An hour later, if Trudy replays Alice's messages, it is important that Bob realize that this is not a conversation with the live Alice. If Bob chose a different b in each Diffie-Hellman exchange, then there wouldn't be a problem, but it is computation intensive to compute g^b, so it might be nice to be able to reuse b.

A way to allow Bob to reuse b and avoid replay attacks is for Bob to choose a nonce for each connection attempt, and have the session key be a function of the nonce as well as the Diffie-Hellman key. So the protocol might be modified to look like Protocol 16-6.

Here the session key is a function of the nonce N as well as the Diffie-Hellman value. This seems similar to a cookie, but it is desirable for a cookie to be stateless, so that Bob does not have to

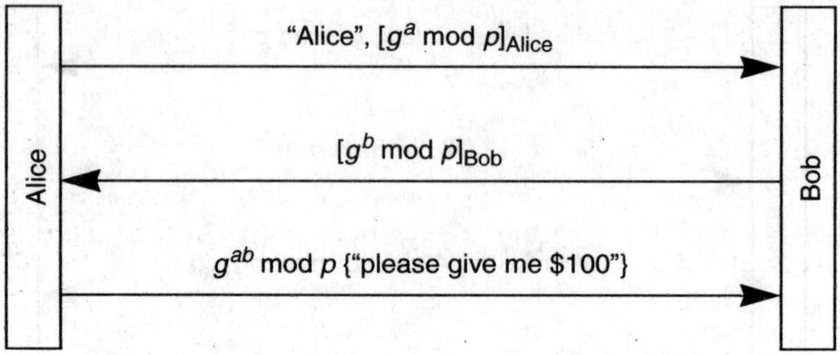

Protocol 16-5. A protocol vulnerable to replay if Bob reuses *b*

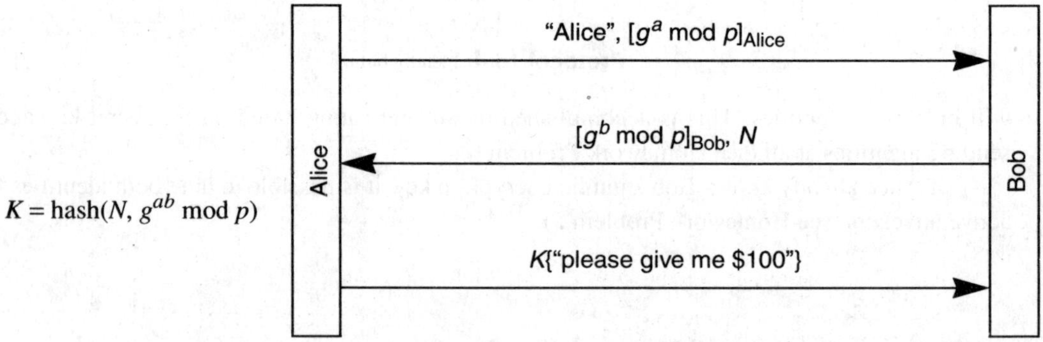

Protocol 16-6. Using a nonce so Bob knows it's not replayed messages from Alice

keep state until he's at least sure the other end can listen at the IP address it claims to be sending from. With the most straightforward implementation of a stateless cookie, the cookie will be reused, so wouldn't work as a nonce. It is possible to design a protocol that will allow something to work both as a nonce and as a stateless cookie (see Homework Problem 10).

Note that we've only ensured that Bob knows it's the live Alice (and not replayed messages). How would Alice know it's the real Bob? If Alice chooses a different *a* each time, and if Alice receives proof from the other side that it knows *K* (for instance, by acting on her request, which was encrypted with *K*), then she knows it's the real Bob. But suppose Alice, like Bob, would like to reuse *a* to save herself from computing $g^a \bmod p$ (see Homework Problem 11).

16.8 ARRANGING FOR PARALLEL COMPUTATION

A lot of protocols require both Alice and Bob to compute a shared Diffie-Hellman key. This might take a long time (seconds perhaps, on slow devices). It can speed up the total elapsed time for an exchange if Alice and Bob can be computing at the same time, as in Protocol 16-7.

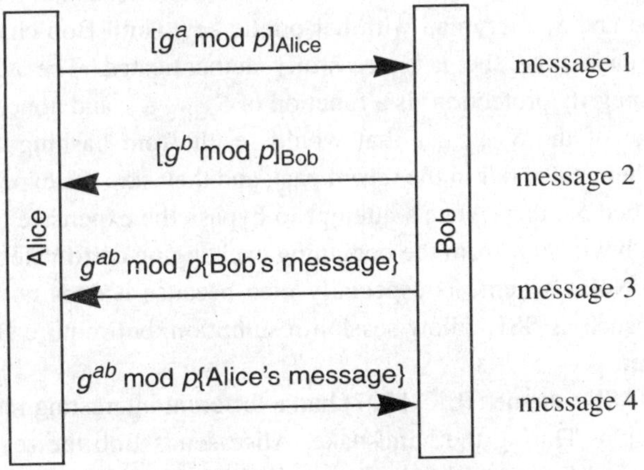

Protocol 16-7. Parallel computation

This exchange might seem silly. Why not combine message 2 with message 3? The reason is that telling Alice g^b mod p gives Alice a head-start on computing g^{ab}. She can be computing g^{ab} at the same time Bob is computing it. Al Eldridge probably was the first to invent this trick of sending an extra message in order to allow the computation-intensive calculations to be done in parallel. He implemented it in Lotus Notes. In Lotus Notes, Bob sends something encrypted with Alice's public key in msg k, and then later sends his signature on that message in msg k+1. This lets Alice do the expensive private key decryption while Bob is doing the expensive signature.

Notice that although this adds a message it doesn't add any round-trip times, so it can be faster even if Alice and Bob are very far apart, talking to each other via, say, carrier pigeons (see RFC 1149 or RFC 2549).

16.9 SESSION RESUMPTION

Another trick is the ability to bypass the initial expensive public key authentication if the server has recently authenticated the client and established a shared secret session key.

In Lotus Notes, Bob (the server) has a secret S that he shares with nobody, and changes periodically (once a month). After Bob authenticates Alice, he sends her a secret, $S_{\text{Alice-Bob}}$, which is a hash of her name and S, encrypted with her public key. Until Bob changes S, he'll give Alice the same $S_{\text{Alice-Bob}}$ each time she is successfully authenticated. The actual session key (used for encryption and integrity protection) is a function of $S_{\text{Alice-Bob}}$ and nonces sent by each side. If Alice shows knowledge of the $S_{\text{Alice-Bob}}$ that would result from hashing S and her name, then Bob assumes he's authenticated her in the recent past, and they skip the expensive public key operations. If Bob has switched Ss, then Alice's attempt to bypass the expensive authentication step will fail, and Alice and Bob will start from the beginning exchanging certificates, signing things, etc.

The Lotus Notes scheme is especially nice because it does not require Bob to keep state. Other protocols, such as SSL, allow session resumption, but require Bob to remember the Alice-Bob session secret.

Digital's DASS scheme (RFC 1507) had a different interesting method of bypassing the public key cryptography. During the handshake, Alice sends Bob the session key S, encrypted with Bob's public key and signed with Alice's private key. Call that quantity (the encrypted, signed S) $X_{\text{Alice-Bob}}$. If Bob remembers $X_{\text{Alice-Bob}}$ from a recent Alice-Bob session, then he merely compares the received value from Alice with the stored $X_{\text{Alice-Bob}}$. If they match, he doesn't have to bother decrypting it to extract S. But if he doesn't remember it, or it's different from the stored one (perhaps because Alice doesn't remember the previous session, or wants to change keys), then he verifies Alice's signature and decrypts with his private key to obtain the new S. If Bob doesn't remember the previous session, but Alice does, then Alice still saves time. If they both remember the previous session, then they both save time. What's interesting about this protocol is that the protocol messages look the same whether state has been kept or not.

16.10 PLAUSIBLE DENIABILITY

If a protocol involves having Alice sign something containing Bob's name, then it offers proof that Alice intentionally talked fo Bob (though it still gives no indication of what they talked about). In some cases Alice would like to assure Bob that it is her, but not provide proof that she talked to Bob. If Alice and Bob are authenticating each other based on a shared secret, then there is no way to prove to a third party that Alice and Bob communicated with each other, because the entire conversation could have been constructed by Alice or Bob. If Alice and Bob authenticate each other using public encryption keys, *anyone* could create an entire conversation that looks like a conversation between Alice and Bob (e.g., consider Protocol 16-7, and change the first two messages from being signed by the sender to being encrypted with the recipient's public key. No knowledge of either side's private key is required to create such messages). If Alice and Bob authenticate each other using public signature keys, then it is possible to create a protocol in which each signs information including the other's identity, in which case there is no plausible deniability. But it is also possible to avoid signing the other side's identity, and therefore preserving plausible deniability (see Protocol 16-7).

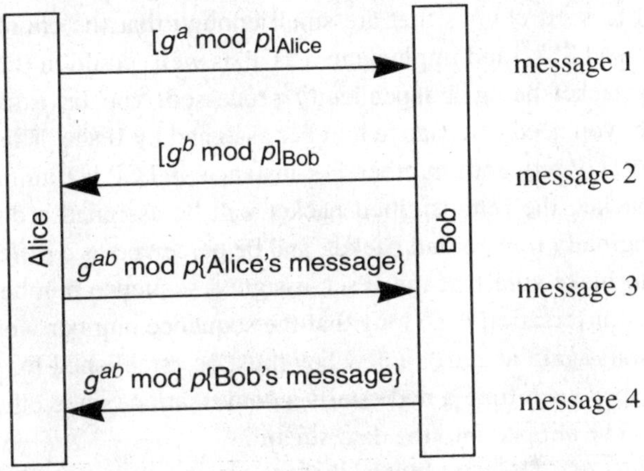

Protocol 16-8. Plausible deniability with signature keys

16.11 DATA STREAM PROTECTION

TCP's job is to accept a stream of data at the source and deliver that same stream to the process running on top of TCP at the destination. The mechanics of TCP doing its job—breaking the stream into packets, retransmitting lost packets, reordering packets—these are irrelevant to the process running on top of TCP. Protocols such as SSL that run on top of TCP break the data into whatever size chunks are convenient. For instance, SSL sends chunks that might be as large as 16K octets. The chunks will arrive in order (TCP does that), but they may have been broken into smaller pieces, which would certainly happen if the chunk was as large as 16K octets. A chunk cannot be integrity-checked by SSL until all its pieces arrive.

With IPsec, however, individual packets are self-contained so that they can be encrypted and integrity-protected independently of other packets in a conversation. This is a performance advantage, since if each packet can be processed individually, it is easier to off-load the cryptographic processing onto an outboard device. It requires no buffering since each packet can be processed immediately.

This is an argument which is often made (that IPsec can be implemented in an outboard device and SSL can't), but I_2'm not completely comfortable with that argument. If an IP packet as transmitted by the source is too large, it might get fragmented on some intermediate link. In that case IPsec has the same problem, and can't integrity check a received fragment. It has to wait until all the fragments of the originally transmitted packet are reassembled, just as in the SSL case. And if SSL is careful to send chunks that are small enough that the chunks arrive intact, an outboard device that processed SSL (and implemented TCP as well) could in theory be built.

With each packet being independently processed, you have to be careful to avoid replay attacks. Therefore you need a sequence number assigned by IPsec. This sequence number has nothing to do with the TCP sequence number. For instance, if TCP is running on top of IPsec, and needs to retransmit a packet, the retransmitted packet will be assigned a different sequence number by IPsec than the originally transmitted packet, and be perceived as a different packet by IPsec.

You have to make sure that the IPsec-assigned sequence number is not used twice with the same key. So if a conversation is so long that the sequence number would wrap (i.e., reach a maximum value and start again at zero), a new key must be established for that session. And a new key should be established each time a node starts a conversation, since otherwise a packet from a prior conversation could be slipped into the data stream.

To ensure that two plaintext blocks that are equal will not result in the same ciphertext when encrypted with the same session key, there are various tricks that can be used:

- Explicitly put an IV into each packet, and use that IV for encrypting that packet in, for instance, CBC mode. Note that although the final ciphertext block of packet $n-1$ is a reasonable choice for the IV for packet n, since you can't guarantee that packet $n-1$ is available to IPsec when it is decrypting packet n, the IV must appear explicitly in each packet.
- Have the IPsec-assigned sequence number be included in the first encryption block, so that the first block of data in each packet to be encrypted is guaranteed to be different for each packet that is encrypted with the same key.
- Use a mode such as counter mode (see §4.2.5 *Counter Mode (CTR)*), using the IPsec-assigned sequence number as the block number.

16.12 NEGOTIATING CRYPTO PARAMETERS

It's fashionable today for security protocols to negotiate cryptographic algorithms, rather than simply having the algorithms be part of the specification of the protocol. It certainly makes the protocols more complex. Examples of things to negotiate are an algorithm for encryption, including key size, or an algorithm for compression, or the prime to use in a Diffie-Hellman exchange.

One reason for allowing choice of cryptographic algorithms is so that over time systems can migrate to stronger but slower crypto as attackers' and defenders' machines get faster. Also, it allows migration from a cryptographic algorithm that gets broken. The cynic might observe that it also avoids the necessity for the committee to make a decision, and it allows them to pass the responsibility for a decision to a different committee (or worse yet, the user).

One potential security flaw, if the negotiation isn't done right, is that an active attacker Trudy might be able to trick Alice and Bob into using weaker cryptography by removing from Alice's suggestions the ones that Trudy can't break. Alice and Bob would like to agree on the strongest possible cryptography that they both support. If Alice is willing, if necessary, to use weak crypto, and a weak algorithm is among the choices, and Bob is willing, if necessary, to use weak crypto, removing the strong choices from Alice's list may cause them to agree on weak crypto, if the protocol is not carefully designed.

The reason this is a common vulnerability is that while Alice and Bob are negotiating about cryptographic algorithms, they probably do not yet have a shared secret with which to do integrity protection of the packets. The solution is to wait until they have established a shared secret, and then detect the tampering by having Alice reiterate (in a cryptographically protected way) what proposals she had made.

IKE (§18.5.5 *Negotiating Cryptographic Parameters*) separately negotiates algorithms for encryption, integrity, authentication, etc. One way of doing this would be to say "I can use any of these algorithms for encryption, any of these for integrity," and so forth. But the IKE designers were concerned that not every set of choices would interoperate. For instance, DSA is supposed to only use SHA-1 as the hash. So the choice for IKE was to separately specify each combination Alice was willing to support. This could lead to an exponential explosion of choices.

SSL/TLS's negotiation is much simpler. The specification predefines suites, with each suite specifying each of the algorithms. This is less flexible, unless every possible combination of cryptographic algorithms was a predefined suite. But in reality, there is no reason to support more than a few suites.

16.13 EASY HOMEWORK

- Why can an active attacker break an SSL connection, but not an IPsec connection?
- Why is it a good idea for the session key to be a function of random numbers chosen by both endpoints?
- What does a non-stateless cookie protect against? What is the advantage of making the cookie stateless?
- Remove the nonce from Protocol 16-6. What is the security vulnerability?
- Show a flawed protocol in which Alice and Bob negotiate what cryptographic algorithms to use, and an active attacker can trick them into using weaker cryptography. Show how to fix the protocol.

16.14 HOMEWORK

1. Talk about the properties of each of the following protocols, such as perfect forward secrecy, escrow foilage against passive attacks, escrow foilage against active attacks, identity hiding, perfect forward secrecy for identity hiding. Assume private encryption keys are escrowed and private signature keys are not escrowed.
   - Protocol 16-2.
   - A modified form of Protocol 16-2 in which the first two messages are encrypted with the other end's public key rather than signed by the transmitter's private signature key. So in message 1 Alice sends {"Alice", $g^a \bmod p$} encrypted with Bob's public key, and Bob in message 2 sends {"Bob", $g^b \bmod p$} encrypted with Alice's public key.
   - Protocol 16-4.
   - Protocol 16-9, where Alice and Bob share a secret key S.
   - Each side sends a nonce encrypted with other's public encryption key, resulting key is $\oplus$ of two nonces
   - Assume Alice and Bob share a secret S. Design a protocol in which they can do mutual authentication and establish a shared secret with PFS. Can it be done without Diffie-Hellman or any other form of public key cryptography?

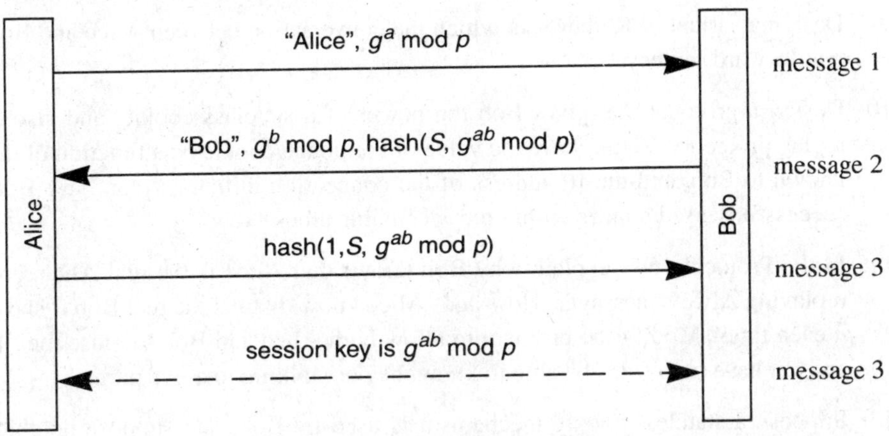

Protocol 16-9. Protocol for Homework Problem 1

- Protocol 16-2, but with each side deterministically generating the Diffie-Hellman private numbers as described in §16.4 *PFS-Foilage* from a seed given to the client machine and escrowed at the server machine.

2. Design a protocol in which Bob chooses whether to require Alice to send a cookie (see §16.5.1 *Cookies*).

3. Design a method of utilizing puzzles in a stateless manner similar to stateless cookies (see §16.5.2 *Puzzles*).

4. Referring to §16.6 *Endpoint Identifier Hiding*, modify Protocol 16-4 to hide the initiator's identity rather than the target's identity.

5. As mentioned in §16.6 *Endpoint Identifier Hiding*, it is possible to design a protocol that will hide both identifiers from an active attacker, assuming that Alice (the initiator) already knows Bob's public key. Show such a protocol.

6. Also as mentioned in §16.6 *Endpoint Identifier Hiding*, it is possible to hide both identities from active attackers if Alice and Bob share a secret key and there is a small set of entities that might initiate a connection to Bob. Show such a protocol.

7. Devise a protocol based on a pre-shared secret key that hides identities and gives PFS for identity hiding. Make two variants, one in which an active attacker can learn only the initiator's identity, and one in which an active attacker can learn only the target's identity.

8. Assuming private key operations are very slow, show a protocol that runs faster with an extra message. Suppose transmission delay is longer than the time it takes to do a private key operation. Would the protocol still complete faster with an extra message?

9. Design a variant of Kerberos in which the conversation between Alice and Bob can have perfect forward secrecy.

10. Design a protocol that gives Bob the power of a stateless cookie, and also ensures against replay protection. (Hint: have the value of the nonce/cookie be a function of the time, a secret known to Bob, and the IP address of the connection initiator. Also, have Bob remember all successfully used nonces within the acceptable clock skew.)

11. In the Protocol 16-6, explain why Bob knows that Alice is the real Alice, and not someone replaying Alice's messages. How does Alice know that it's the real Bob if she uses a different a each time? Modify the protocol to allow both Alice and Bob to reuse their a and b values, and yet have both sides be able to know they are talking to a live partner.

12. Suppose a stateless cookie mechanism is used by Bob, and suppose he changes his secret periodically. What can he do to assure a connection attempt will succeed even if he changed his secret between the time the initiator asked for the cookie and returned it (assuming the initiator doesn't wait too long before returning the cookie)?

13. Assume a stateless session resumption scheme as described in §16.9 *Session Resumption*. Suppose Bob changes his S every ten minutes, and yet you'd like to be able to resume sessions that have been idle for longer than that, say two hours. How might that work?

14. Explain how, and under what circumstances, in the DASS session resumption protocol described in §16.9 *Session Resumption*, only Alice saves computation, only Bob saves computation, and they both save computation.

15. Describe various methods of having Alice and/or Bob remember state from the last time they authenticated each other that allows them to resume a session and bypass the expensive public key cryptography. Describe a method in which Bob can save computation even if he hasn't kept state. Is there a clever way of having Bob remember state and not Alice?

17 IPSEC: AH AND ESP

IPsec is an IETF standard for real-time communication security. The concepts behind such a protocol were already covered in Chapter 16 *Real-time Communication Security*. The main pieces of IPsec are AH and ESP, which describe the IP header extensions for carrying cryptographically protected data, and IKE, which is a protocol for authenticating and establishing a session key. This chapter covers AH and ESP, and Chapter 18 *IPsec: IKE* will cover IKE.

17.1 OVERVIEW OF IPSEC

The part of IPsec that we cover in this chapter assumes that two nodes already have a shared session key, which might have been configured manually, or established through IKE.

Since Bob might be receiving IPsec-protected packets from many sources, maybe even different processes using the same source IP address, there has to be a way for Bob to know which cryptographic key and which algorithms to use to process the packet. This is done by inserting an IPsec header (AH and/or ESP) into the IP packet which tells Bob to which security association the packet belongs (see §17.1.1 *Security Associations*). IPsec works with IPv4 or with IPv6.

17.1.1 Security Associations

An IPsec security association (SA) is a cryptographically protected connection. Associated with each end of the SA is a cryptographic key and other information such as the identity of the other end, the sequence number currently being used, and the cryptographic services being used (e.g., integrity only, or encryption+integrity, and which cryptographic algorithms should be used). The SA is considered unidirectional, so a conversation between Alice and Bob will consist of two SAs, one in each direction.

The IPsec header includes a field known as the SPI (SECURITY PARAMETER INDEX) which identifies the security association, allowing Alice to look up the necessary information (such as the cryptographic key) in her SA database. The SPI value is chosen by the destination (Bob), so it would seem as though the SPI alone should allow Bob to know the SA, since Bob can ensure that the SPI is unique with respect to all the sources that Bob has SAs with. But it is possible for Bob to also be receiving multicast data, in which case Bob would not have chosen the SPI, and it might be equal to one that Bob already assigned. Therefore the SA is defined by both the SPI and the destination address. (The destination address of a packet received by Bob will be Bob for unicast, or a group address if it's multicast.) Furthermore, IPsec allows the same SPI values to be assigned to different SAs if one SA is using AH and one is using ESP, so the SA is defined by the triple ⟨SPI, destination address, flag for whether it's AH or ESP⟩.

17.1.2 Security Association Database

A system implementing IPsec keeps a security association database. When transmitting to IP destination *X*, the transmitter looks up *X* in the security association database, and that entry will tell it how to transmit to *X*, i.e., it will provide the SPI, the key, the algorithms, the sequence number, etc. When receiving an IP packet, the SPI of the received packet is used to find the entry in the security association database that will tell the receiver which key, sequence number, etc., to use to process the packet.

17.1.3 Security Policy Database

Just as firewalls are configured with tables telling them what type of traffic to allow based on information such as the IP header source and destination addresses and TCP ports, IPsec is assumed to have access to a similar database specifying which types of packets should be dropped completely, which should be forwarded or accepted without IPsec protection, and which should be protected by IPsec, and if protected, whether they should be encrypted and/or integrity-protected. Decisions could, in theory, be based on any fields in the packet, e.g., source IP address, destination IP address, protocol type in the IP header, and layer 4 (TCP or UDP) ports.

17.1.4 AH and ESP

AH (Authentication Header, defined in RFC 2402) and ESP (Encapsulating Security Payload, defined in RFC 2406) are the two types of IPsec headers. AH provides integrity protection only. ESP provides encryption and/or integrity protection.

Given that ESP optionally provides integrity protection (in addition to optional encryption), it's natural to wonder why AH is needed. In fact many people argue (and we concur) that AH is not necessary. The integrity protection provided by ESP and AH are not identical, however. Both provide integrity protection of everything beyond the IP header, but AH provides integrity protection for some of the fields inside the IP header as well. See §17.1.6 *Why Protect the IP Header?*. AH can't protect all of the fields, because some of them are intended to be modified by routers (see §17.3.1 *Mutable, Immutable*).

There is one feature that AH provides that ESP does not. Firewalls and routers sometimes look at fields such as layer 4 ports in order to do packet filtering, content screening, or differential queuing. If everything beyond the header is encrypted (as it would be with ESP, if ESP is encrypting), then firewalls and routers are not able to look at those fields. One could use ESP for integrity only, but it would be impossible for a firewall or router to know whether an ESP-protected packet was encrypted or not. The source and destination know—it's either manually configured into the SA or negotiated through IKE. But there's nothing in the packet header that tells a router or firewall whether a packet is encrypted.

This "feature" of having routers and firewalls look at the TCP ports can only be used with unencrypted IP traffic, and many security advocates argue that IPsec should always be encrypting the traffic. Fields such as TCP ports should perhaps be hidden to avoid divulging information such as which applications are running. Firewalls base decisions on the port fields, but a malicious user can disguise any traffic to fit the firewall's policy database (e.g., if the firewall allows HTTP, then run all protocols on top of HTTP).

17.1.5 Tunnel, Transport Mode

The IPsec specification talks about two "modes" of applying IPsec protection to a packet. **Transport mode** refers to adding the IPsec information between the IP header and the remainder of the packet. **Tunnel mode** refers to keeping the original IP packet intact and adding a new IP header and IPsec information (ESP or AH) outside.

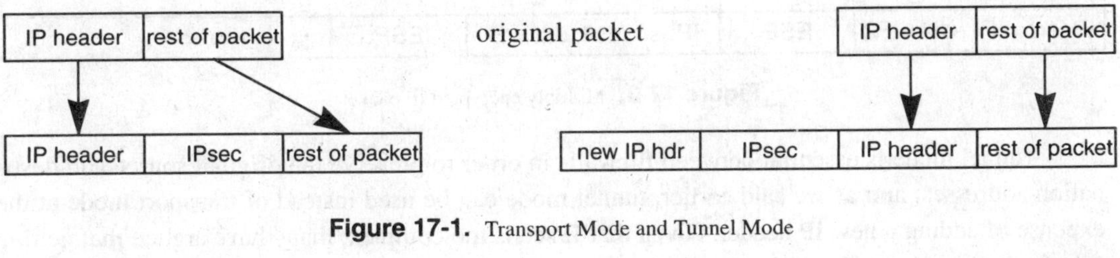

Figure 17-1. Transport Mode and Tunnel Mode

Transport mode is most logical when IPsec is being applied end-to-end. A common use of tunnel mode is firewall to firewall, or endnode to firewall, where the data is only protected along part of the path between the endpoints. Suppose two firewalls establish an encrypted tunnel to each other across the Internet (see Figure 17-2). They treat the tunnel as if it is an ordinary, trusted link. In order to forward packets across that link, F1 adds an IP header with destination=F2. When A launches an IP packet to destination B, it will have, in the IP header, source=A and destination=B.

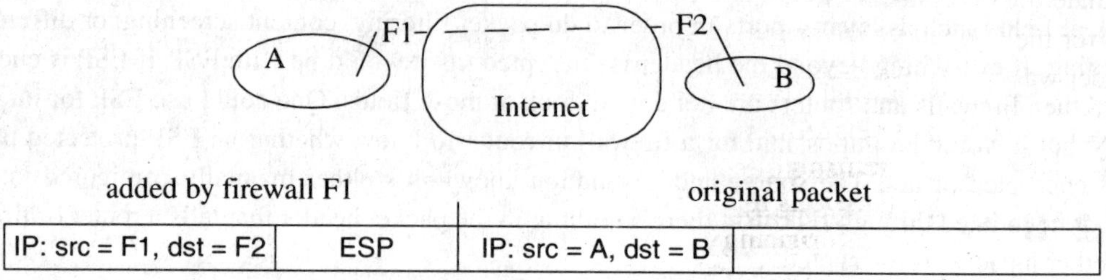

Figure 17-2. IPsec, tunnel mode, between firewalls

When F1 forwards the packet to F2 across the encrypted tunnel, it will use IPsec tunnel mode. F1 will not modify the inner header, other than doing what any router would do when forwarding a packet, such as decrementing the hop count. The outer IP header added by F1 will have source=F1 and destination=F2. The inner header will be unmodified by the routers along the path between F1 and F2. Those routers will only look at the outer IP header.

Transport mode is not strictly necessary, since tunnel mode could be used instead. Tunnel mode just uses more header space since there will be two IP headers.

The same packet might have multiple layers of IPsec (ESP and/or AH) headers, and might be multiply-encrypted (see Figure 17-3). Suppose A and B are talking with an encrypted end-to-end connection. Their packets will contain an ESP header. When F1 forwards it across the tunnel to F2, F1 takes the entire packet (including the IP+ESP header) and adds its own IP+ESP header. F1 encrypts the entire packet it received, including the IP header, with the key that F1 shares with F2.

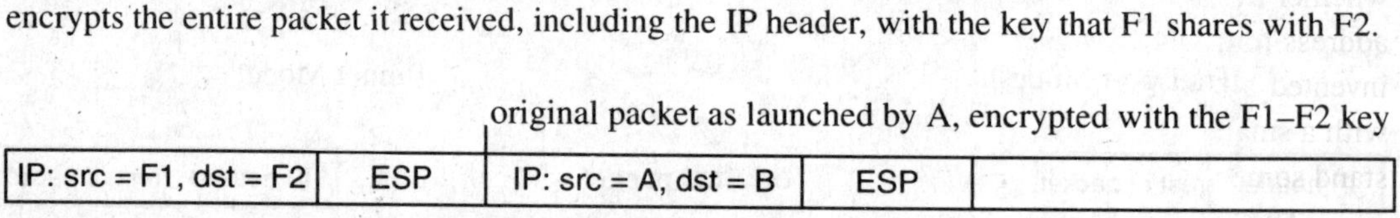

Figure 17-3. Multiply encrypted IP packet

Tunnel mode is essential between firewalls in order to preserve the original source and destination addresses; and as we said earlier, tunnel mode can be used instead of transport mode at the expense of adding a new IP header. Given that IPsec is too complex, many have argued that getting rid of transport mode would be one way of simplifying IPsec. But transport mode is such a small piece of the complexity of IPsec that we don't feel it's worth worrying about. Far more useful would be to get rid of AH and most of IKE.

17.1.6 Why Protect the IP Header?

AH advocates claim AH is needed because it protects the IP header. It is unclear why it is necessary to protect the IP header. If it were necessary, this could be provided by ESP in tunnel mode. Intermediate routers cannot enforce AH's integrity protection, because they would not know the session key for the Alice-Bob security association. So AH can at best be used by Bob to check that the IP header was received as launched by Alice.

17.2 IP AND IPV6

IP is what's known in ISO terminology as a *network layer*, or *layer 3* protocol. It puts a source address and destination address on data, much like addressing an envelope to be sent through snail mail. IP was designed with 32-bit addresses, and many people started to realize in the mid-1980s that 32 bits was too few. There were other layer 3 protocols deployed at the time with adequate address space, and the IETF could have adopted one of those. In fact, in 1992, the IAB (Internet Architecture Board) recommended replacing IP with the CLNP packet format, a format that was very similar to IP, but had larger addresses. CLNP had been standardized by ISO and implemented by most of the vendors.

If the IETF had adopted CLNP in 1992, most likely at this point the Internet would be using larger addresses and would certainly be better off than it is now, but certain very vocal IETF members wanted to invent their own header format. The new header format designed by IETF is known as **IPv6**, and because they've been designing it for so long, it is unfortunately not at all clear whether the world will ever migrate to IPv6. It would have been much easier to migrate to a larger address format in the early '90s, when the Internet was smaller and people hadn't out of necessity invented all sorts of kludges (like NAT, see §17.2.1 *NAT (Network Address Translation)*) to live with a smaller address space. The reason all this is relevant for this book is that you need to understand some of the politics in order to understand the design of IPsec.

The "v6" in the name "IPv6" comes from the first four bits of an IP header, which is the VERSION NUMBER field, which is set to 4 for the current version of IP, so IP is sometimes known as **IPv4**. I_2 bet you'd guess that 5 would be the next version number after 4, but 5 was already assigned for a little-known and little-used protocol, so the next version of IP needed to be 6. If you really care about all this, $we_{1,3}$ recommend my_2 book *Interconnections: Bridges, Routers, Switches, and Internetworking Protocols*. (I_2 modestly abstain.)

In order to understand IPsec, you need to understand both the IPv4 and IPv6 formats, and you need to understand some of the politics associated with the design of IPv6 in order to understand things like why there is an AH header and why it looks different than the ESP header.

The IPv6 designers were frustrated that the world didn't immediately deploy IPv6, after they spent 10 years (so far) designing it. Although bigger addresses are good for you, people don't get excited about learning something new and doing radical changes to all their software if things are working. "What would I get for converting to IPv6?" "Bigger addresses." "What's an address?" You see, it just doesn't motivate people to turn their environment inside out. Especially when you consider the other thing you get by converting to IPv6, which is noninteroperability with the 600 million current Internet nodes.

So the IPv6 proponents hoped that IPsec (among other features) would be the motivator for moving to IPv6. Some IPv6 advocates proposed making it illegal to make any improvements (including IPsec) to IPv4, so that if the world wanted any of the stuff IETF designed in the last 10 years it would have to move to IPv6. But the IPsec designers were more interested in security, and didn't care whether it was deployed with 4-octet or 16-octet addresses, so they designed it to work with either format. The IPv6 specification says that IPsec is a mandatory feature of IPv6, so sometimes people claim that "Security is built into IPv6, whereas it's an add-on to IPv4." In reality, the "mandatory-ness" of IPsec with IPv6 is just words on paper. There are implementations of IPv6 without IPsec, and there are implementations of IPv4 with IPsec. And IPsec works just as well with IPv4 as IPv6.

17.2.1 NAT (Network Address Translation)

Another thing you need to understand is one of the kludges that has allowed the Internet to survive and thrive with 32-bit addresses during the many years in which IPv6 was being designed. The kludge is known as **NAT, network address translation**. With a NAT box, the computers on your internal network do not need global IPv4 addresses in order to connect to the Internet. Instead the NAT box translates an internal node's IP address into a globally unique address when that node is talking to something on the Internet. NAT complicates everything, especially because many of the higher layer protocols violate layering and carry IP addresses inside their data.

An IPsec tunnel cannot go through a NAT box because the NAT box wants to update the IP addresses inside the encrypted data and it doesn't have the key. Even IPsec transport mode has problems because the IP address is included in the computation of the TCP or UDP checksum—the NAT box cannot correct the checksum because it is encrypted. NAT boxes sometimes make multiple computers appear at the same IP address by assigning each a subset of the TCP and UDP port ranges. This technique also fails with NAT boxes because IPsec encrypts the port information. There are carefully crafted configurations where IPsec can be used through NAT boxes by encapsulating IPsec packets inside UDP packets.

Absent encryption, NAT boxes are willing to go to extreme lengths to make protocols work. A particularly amusing and nasty example of this is the protocol FTP (File Transfer Protocol, RFC 959). FTP is an application layer protocol, so it is encapsulated within both layer 3 and layer 4. FTP not only carries IP addresses, but carries them in what is called **dotted decimal notation**, where each octet of the 4-octet IP address is represented in ASCII as decimal numbers and delimited by periods, e.g., 178.201.19.175. Each octet of the IP address might require between one and three ASCII characters (not counting the periods), since leading 0s are not transmitted. So the NAT box not only needs to change the IP address in the IP header, but has to know that the packet is FTP, and know to change the address carried inside the FTP data! Worse than that, it might have to replace a string such as 178.201.19.175 with a string of a different length, such as 22.51.111.9. The problem with changing the size of the data is that TCP numbers octets, not packets, so if the NAT box changes the length of one of the packets in a conversation, it has to compensate by changing the TCP sequence numbers for the entire duration of that conversation to compensate!

So everyone hates NAT, but NAT boxes are very popular because really what users want is for things to work and they don't care about architectural purity. NAT particularly infuriates the IPv6 proponents because it makes it possible for the world to delay migrating to IPv6. The longer the world delays, the harder it will be to get everyone to convert. So the IPv6 proponents actually go out of their way to design things that will not work with NAT, hoping that this will cause the world to abandon NAT (and then, they hope, move to IPv6). That is one reason they like AH, because the AH integrity check will fail if a NAT box modifies the IP header.

17.2.2 Firewalls

Another important issue is firewalls. Various network administrators like to have firewalls observe packets and discard (**filter**) packets based on characteristics, such as which protocol is being used. Many IETF people hate firewalls, since they tend to make it difficult to deploy new applications, and they break many existing applications. Security is strongest if done end-to-end. IPsec encrypts information on which firewalls like to base decisions, such as the PORT fields in the TCP header that can help them know whether the data is email or telnet. The people designing the protocols believe such information is nobody's business except the endpoints. Some firewall administrators feel they need that information in order to monitor and control traffic to and from their network.

Some people hope that IPsec will make firewalls go away, since IPsec encryption will prevent firewalls from being able to do a lot of what people use firewalls for. But more likely, many firewall administrators would rather forgo end-to-end security than give up their ability to monitor and control the traffic between their net and the Internet. If enough firewall administrators decide to throw away any packets that are encrypted because they can't inspect them, people will be highly discouraged from using IPsec. As much as people would like their traffic to be protected in transit, they're even more anxious for their traffic to be delivered at all.

Some would argue that firewalls exist to compensate for poorly protected, poorly managed end systems on the inside, and that the very existence of IPsec on a system means that that system is well-protected and well-managed. Therefore, they'd argue, it is safe for the firewall to forward encrypted traffic and assume that an end system smart enough to have IPsec must know what it is doing. That may well be how things initially roll out, but it's unlikely to last. Systems supporting IPsec are not necessarily any better managed than those without it, and sometimes the firewall administrators are trying to prevent anti-social actions like downloading pornography rather than just trying to protect against carelessness.

One of the most amusing consequences of firewalls is that people find ways of disguising the traffic that firewalls administrators would like to block so that it looks to the firewall like the kind of traffic the firewall is configured to allow. For instance, protocols are being defined to work on top of HTTP to make something like file transfer or system administration look like web browsing. This is extremely inefficient because there are extra layers of protocol. And as a final irony, the term for disguising traffic to look like something the firewall is configured to pass through, when the firewall administrator intends to keep that traffic out, is **firewall-friendly**.

17.2.3 IPv4 Header

The IPv4 header is defined in RFC 791. Its fields are

size		
4 bits	version	
4 bits	header length (in 4-octet units)	
1 octet	type of service	
2 octets	length of header plus data in this fragment	
2 octets	packet identification	
3 bits	flags (don't fragment, and last fragment)	
13 bits	fragment offset	
1 octet	hops remaining, known as TTL (time to live)	
1 octet	protocol	50=ESP, 51=AH
2 octets	header checksum	
4 octets	source address	
4 octets	destination address	
variable	options	

For the purposes of this chapter, the most important field is the PROTOCOL field, which indicates what follows the IP header. Common values are TCP (6), UDP (17), and IP (4). When PROTOCOL indicates IP, it is a tunneled packet, i.e., following the IP header is another IP header. Note that the PROTOCOL field value of 4 for IP has nothing to do with the version number for IPv4; if the next header is IPv6, the protocol field will still be 4.

IPsec defines two new values for the protocol field in the IP header: ESP=50 and AH=51. For example, if TCP is on top of IP without IPsec, the PROTOCOL field in the IP header will be 6. If TCP is used with IP using AH, for instance, then the PROTOCOL field in the IP header will equal 51, and the PROTOCOL field in the AH header will be 6 to indicate that TCP follows the AH header. If the packet is encrypted using ESP, then the PROTOCOL field in the IP header will be 50, but the actual PROTOCOL field, the one that would have appeared in the IP header if encryption with ESP was not being used, will be encrypted, and therefore not visible until the packet is decrypted.

17.2.4 IPv6 Header

The IPv6 header is defined in RFC 2460, and its fields are

# octets	
4	version (4 bits) |type of service|flow label
2	payload length
1	next header
1	hops remaining
16	source address
16	destination address

In IPv6, the equivalent field to IPv4's PROTOCOL is NEXT HEADER. It has the same values defined as the IPv4 PROTOCOL field, so ESP=50 and AH=51. IPv6-style extension headers (roughly equivalent to OPTIONS in the IPv4 header) are encoded as

# octets	
1	next header
1	length of this header
variable	data for this header

LENGTH OF THIS HEADER is in units of 8-octet chunks, not counting the first 8-octet chunk. AH looks like an IPv6 extension header, but its PAYLOAD LENGTH is in units of 4-octet chunks instead of 8-octet chunks (and like other IPv6 extension headers, doesn't count the first 8-octets). This violates one of the protocol folklore rules described in Chapter 26 *Folklore*, which is that the LENGTH field should always be defined the same way for all options, so that it is easy to skip over unknown options.

DATA FOR THIS HEADER is a sequence of options, each one **TLV-encoded**, which means a TYPE field, a LENGTH field, and a VALUE field. The TYPE field is one octet long, and one of the bits in the TYPE field for options that appear in some extension headers indicates whether the option is

mutable (might change along the path) or **immutable** (relevant for AH, see section §17.3 *AH (Authentication Header)*). The mutable flag is only useful for AH, and if AH ever goes away, the flag in IPv6 will be very mysterious.

17.3 AH (AUTHENTICATION HEADER)

The AH header provides authentication only (not encryption), and is defined in RFC 2402. It looks like

# octets	
1	next header
1	payload length
2	unused
4	SPI (Security Parameter Index)
4	sequence number
variable	authentication data

This is the same format as IPv6 extension headers, which all start with NEXT HEADER and PAYLOAD LENGTH (which gives the length of the AH header), except, as we said in the previous section, AH's PAYLOAD LENGTH is in different units than the equivalent field in an IPv6 extension header. AH is intended not only to protect the data, but the IP header as well. In IPv4, the AH header must be a multiple of 32 bits, and in IPv6 it must be a multiple of 64 bits. So the AUTHENTICATION DATA field must be an appropriate size to make the header size be the right length.

Some integrity checks require the data to be a multiple of some block size. If the data is not a multiple of the block size, then AH is computed as if the data were padded to the proper length with 0s, but the 0s are not transmitted.

The fields in AH are

- NEXT HEADER. Same as PROTOCOL field in IPv4. For example, if TCP follows the AH header, then NEXT HEADER is 6.
- PAYLOAD LENGTH. The size of the AH header in 32-bit chunks, not counting the first 8 octets.
- SPI. Discussed in §17.1.1 *Security Associations*.
- SEQUENCE NUMBER. The sequence number has nothing to do with TCP's sequence number. This sequence number is assigned by AH and used so that AH can recognize replayed packets and discard them. So, for example, if TCP retransmits a packet, AH will just treat it like a

new packet and give it the next sequence number. AH will not know (or care) that this is a retransmitted TCP packet.

- AUTHENTICATION DATA. This is the cryptographic integrity check on the data.

17.3.1 Mutable, Immutable

Some fields in the IP header get modified by routers, so they can't be included in AH's end-to-end integrity check. For example, the TTL field must be decremented by every router. The immutable fields are the ones that the AH designers do not believe should ever legitimately be modified in transit.

The IPv4 AH defines the mutable fields as TYPE OF SERVICE, FLAGS, FRAGMENT OFFSET, TIME TO LIVE, and HEADER CHECKSUM.

Some of the choices for which fields are considered mutable are surprising. As envisioned by the original IP designers, TYPE OF SERVICE would be an immutable quantity, and indeed worthy of protecting. It contained the desired routing metric and priority chosen by the source. But that use of the TYPE OF SERVICE field as originally defined in the IP header did not prove to be useful, and now network administrators are playing around with various uses of the field, such as categorizing the packet when it enters their domain. So routers today want to be free to modify that field.

Why is PAYLOAD LENGTH considered immutable? If a packet requires fragmentation, the PAYLOAD LENGTH must be modified (since PAYLOAD LENGTH is the length of the data in this fragment, not the original size of the packet as launched by the source), so it would seem like it should be considered mutable. However, the reason it can be considered immutable is that IP at the destination must reassemble the packet before AH can verify the integrity check, in which case although PAYLOAD LENGTH was modified en route, it has been restored to its original value before the AH header is processed. Theoretically the same logic would apply to FRAGMENT OFFSET, which should be set to 0 when launched by the source, and might be modified by routers along the path if the packet is fragmented, but will be restored to 0 again after the packet is reassembled at the destination, and before the AH header is processed. But AH has chosen to define FRAGMENT OFFSET as a mutable field, and therefore not covered by the AH integrity check. Not that it matters, since as we said earlier, there's no reason to bother protecting any of the IP header. Note that since FRAGMENT OFFSET is always 0 when the AH header is processed, whether it's immutable or not is irrelevant.

In IPv6 the mutable fields are TYPE OF SERVICE (because routers want to be able to modify it), FLOW LABEL (because the IPv6 designers still don't know what to do with the field, so maybe whatever they'll decide to use it for will require it to change en route), and HOP LIMIT (which is decremented by each router along the path).

17.3.2 Mutable but Predictable

The DESTINATION ADDRESS is not quite considered immutable, but it is included in the AH integrity check, since there is one situation in which it might be modified in a way considered legitimate by the AH designers (as opposed to being modified by a NAT box, which the AH designers do not consider legitimate). This case is when the source specifies source routing as an option. The way source routing works in IP is that the source chooses a path consisting of a sequence of intermediate destinations to be visited in order, say D1, D2, D3, D, where D is the ultimate destination. In IPv4

IP Source routing

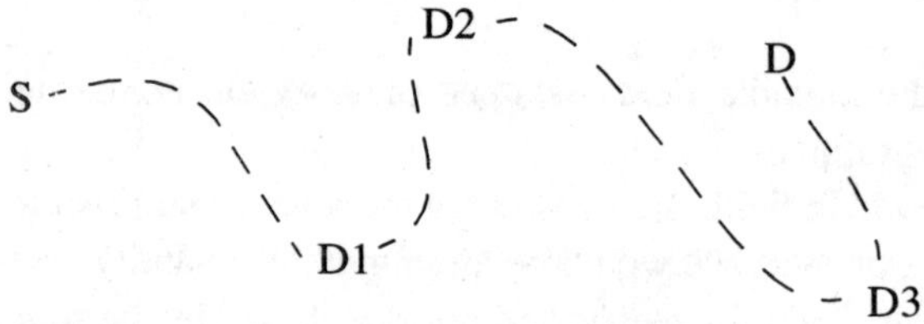

there is an option called "source routing" that would include these intermediate destinations. In IPv6 it's an extension header called the "route header", which is the same idea. When source routing is specified, the DESTINATION ADDRESS in the IP header (in both v4 and v6) specifies the next destination in the source route header, not the ultimate destination. So DESTINATION ADDRESS is clearly mutable, since in this example it would start out, when launched by S, as D1, get overwritten as D2 once it reached D1, get overwritten as D3 once it reached D2, and ultimately wind up at the destination as D.

But the source knows what the DESTINATION ADDRESS will look like when it arrives at D (the DESTINATION ADDRESS field will specify D). So even though S launches it with DESTINATION ADDRESS set to D1, S computes the AH integrity check as though DESTINATION ADDRESS were set to D. Then when D evaluates the AH, it will compute properly as received.

So fields that are **mutable but predictable** are included in the AH integrity check, but with the values they will have when received at the other end. The only one listed in the AH spec is the DESTINATION ADDRESS, but in theory the TOTAL LENGTH field in IPv4 should be listed as mutable but predictable rather than immutable, since if the packet were fragmented, that field would be modified en route, but would be restored by IP at the destination before IPsec at the destination saw the packet. But it isn't a problem since immutable and mutable-but-predictable fields are treated the same way at the destination.

17.4 ESP (ENCAPSULATING SECURITY PAYLOAD)

ESP allows for encryption and/or integrity protection. If you want encryption, you must use ESP. If you want integrity protection only, you could use ESP or AH. If you want both encryption and integrity protection, you could use both ESP and AH, or you could do both integrity protection and encryption with ESP. The security association database would tell you what to use when transmitting to a particular IP address. It's a little odd to call ESP a "header" because it puts information both before and after the encrypted data, but everyone seems to call it a header so we will too.

Technically, ESP always does encryption, but if you don't want encryption you use the special "null encryption" algorithm. The working group had a lot of fun writing the RFC specifying the null encryption algorithm, extolling its virtues like how fast it was and how it could take any size keys, and source and destination would even interoperate if they had different keys. For a bit of security-geek humor, read RFC 2410.

The presence of the ESP header is indicated by having the PROTOCOL field in IPv4 or the NEXT HEADER field in IPv6 equal to 50. The ESP envelope itself consists of

# octets	
4	SPI (Security Parameters Index)
4	sequence number
variable	IV (initialization vector)
variable	data
variable	padding
1	padding length (in units of octets)
1	next header/protocol type
variable	authentication data

The fields are

- SPI. Same as for AH, discussed in §17.1.1 *Security Associations*.
- SEQUENCE NUMBER. Same as for AH, explained in §17.3 *AH (Authentication Header)*.
- INITIALIZATION VECTOR. An IV is required by some cryptographic algorithms, such as encryption with CBC mode. Although the IV is variable length (it may even be zero length), it's fixed length for a particular cryptographic algorithm. Once the SA is established, the cryptographic algorithm is known, and therefore the length of the IV field is fixed for the duration of the SA. This is also true of the field AUTHENTICATION DATA.

- DATA. This is the protected data, probably encrypted. If it is a tunnel mode packet, then the beginning of the data would be an IP header. If it would have been TCP, and ESP is being used in Transport mode, then the beginning of the data would be the TCP header.
- PADDING. Padding is used for several reasons: to make the data be a multiple of a block size for cryptographic algorithms that require it; to make the encrypted data be a different size than the plaintext, so as to somewhat disguise the size of the data (limited because PADDING LENGTH is only one octet); and to ensure that the combination of the fields DATA, PADDING, PADDING LENGTH, and NEXT HEADER are a multiple of four octets.
- PADDING LENGTH. Number of octets of padding.
- NEXT HEADER. Same as PROTOCOL field in IPv4 or NEXT HEADER in IPv6, or NEXT HEADER in AH.
- AUTHENTICATION DATA. The cryptographic integrity check. Its length is determined by the authentication function selected for the SA; it is zero length if ESP is providing encryption only.

If encryption is used, the fields DATA, PADDING, PADDING LENGTH, and NEXT HEADER are encrypted. The AUTHENTICATION DATA appears only if the security association requests integrity protection with ESP. If ESP integrity protection is used, all fields in the ESP (starting with SPI and ending with NEXT HEADER) are included in the ESP integrity check.

17.5 So, Do We Need AH?

We clearly need ESP, since it's the only one that provides encryption. But since you can do integrity-only with ESP, as well as encryption+integrity with ESP, it might seem like AH is unnecessary. What reasons do people give for keeping AH?

- AH protects the IP header itself, whereas ESP only protects everything beyond the ESP header. We don't think protecting the IP header matters for security.
- An implementation of IPsec that only implemented AH might be more exportable. Indeed, at least one vendor reported that they were able to get export approval for their implementation of IPsec specifically because it only supported AH. But other vendors were able to get export approval for ESP. It's not unusual for different companies to get different answers for export, and the rules change with time. We think that even if an implementation of IPsec that only did AH were more exportable, it's not very important because who would buy it?

- As we discussed in §17.1.4 *AH and ESP*, with ESP, even when not using encryption, firewalls and routers cannot look beyond the layer 3 header at information such as TCP ports. This sounds like a reasonable argument, and indeed a proposal was made for TF-ESP (transport-friendly ESP), which allowed for copying all fields of interest into an unencrypted portion of the header. The arguments against TF-ESP which convinced people not to bother with it were
  - Routers and firewalls have no right to look at anything above layer 3.
  - Anything copied over in cleartext exposes some information that might be better hidden from eavesdroppers.
  - Since the IPsec key is end-to-end, it is impossible for intermediate devices to verify that the cleartext fields are accurate. It would be possible to sneak past a firewall, for instance, if you set the ports in cleartext to something the firewall would allow through. The destination could, in theory, check that the cleartext fields are the same as the fields inside the ESP-protected payload when they arrive. But someone colluding with the source could change them back after the packet gets through the firewall, or if the destination were colluding with the source, it could simply not do the check.

The arguments against TF-ESP are credible, but it is unfair to simultaneously claim that intermediate devices have no right or need to look at upper layer information, and to criticize ESP for not exposing layer 4 information. It seems very unlikely that anyone would bother with IPsec for integrity protection only, and so "fixing" ESP to give people (e.g., firewall administrators, and router vendors who want to claim that their routers do some fancy thing) what they want is probably the only way to provide those features. In other words, rather than seeing the feature of exposed layer 4 information as a reason to keep AH, we believe that IPsec should be considered as essentially always providing encryption, and therefore if the layer 4 information needs to be exposed, there will have to be a way of exposing it with ESP. Or (our preference) decide the world can and should do without this information, especially since there's no way, even with AH, to ensure that the information is accurate, except at the endpoints.

17.6 COMPARISON OF ENCODINGS

AH was designed by IPv6 fans, and looks similar to IPv6 extension headers. (The only difference is that its LENGTH field is expressed in different units.) The ESP designers didn't really care about IPv6 and designed ESP to be as technically good as it could be, unconstrained with having to look like something else. And there's no reason why, even if used with IPv6, that ESP has to look like the other IPv6 extension headers.

There are two wasted octets in AH (the "unused" octets) in order for all the fields to be on 4-octet boundaries. But AH can cleverly avoid padding the data, because the integrity check is calculated as if the data is padded to a multiple of a block size, but the padding is not transmitted. Therefore, if the data needed more than two octets of padding, AH winds up being smaller. Of course, this is assuming that IPsec is being used for integrity-only, which as we said, we think will be rare. If the data is encrypted, then it would be much more overhead to use AH and ESP simultaneously than just using ESP for both integrity protection and encryption.

Having the MAC appear before the data (as it is in AH) means that the data needs to be buffered and the integrity check computed before the packet can be transmitted. In contrast, in ESP, the MAC appears after the data.

IPv6 proponents hate NAT because it makes it possible for the world to continue to live with IPv4. This is another reason why they like AH, because having a NAT modify the IP addresses in the header will cause AH to reject the packet, and so they hope that AH will cause NAT to go away. But as we said, AH isn't intrinsically useful enough to kill NAT. More likely NAT would kill AH.

Attempting to protect the IP header, and needing to classify every field and every option according to whether it's mutable or immutable, makes AH very complicated.

At one of the final IETF meetings before AH and ESP were finalized, someone from Microsoft got up and gave an impassioned speech about how AH was useless given the existence of ESP, cluttered up the spec, and couldn't be implemented efficiently (because of the MAC in front of the data). $\text{Our}_{1,2}$ impression of what happened next was that everyone in the room looked around at each other and said, "Hmm. He's right, and we hate AH also, but if it annoys Microsoft let's leave it in, since we hate Microsoft more than we hate AH."

17.7 EASY HOMEWORK

1. Why isn't the SPI value sufficient for the receiver to know which SA the packet belongs to?
2. Why is the integrity check processing more convenient with ESP than with AH?

17.8 HOMEWORK

1. Suppose Alice is sending packets to Bob using IPsec. Suppose Bob's TCP acknowledgment gets lost, and Alice's TCP, assuming the packet was lost, retransmits the packet. Will Bob's IPsec implementation notice that the packet is a duplicate and discard it?

2. Suppose a company's network is attached to the Internet via two NAT boxes, and packets might exit via either one. How might a protocol such as FTP complicate implementation of multiple NAT boxes? Suggest methods of making this work.

3. Suppose you wanted the transmitter to assign the SPI rather than the receiver. What problems might this cause? Can it be made to work?

4. Would it be possible for the SA to be defined only by the destination address and the SPI (i.e., leave out whether it's ESP or AH)? Would this require any changes to the IPsec protocol? Would an implementation of a receiver that defined the SA based solely on destination address and SPI interwork with one that did what the IPsec specification says?

5. When sending encrypted traffic from firewall to firewall, why does there need to be an extra IP header? Why can't the firewall simply encrypt the packet, leaving the source and destination as the original source and destination?

6. Referring to Figure 17-2, suppose A and B already have an IPsec SA between them and are using ESP. What would be the advantages/disadvantages of having F1, in the case where there's already an ESP header, merely forwarding the packet to F2 without doing a second encryption?

7. Referring to Figure 17-2, assume that A and B are using IPsec in transport mode, and F1 and F2 have established an encrypted tunnel using IPsec. Assume A sends a TCP packet to B. Show the relevant fields of the IP header(s) as given to A's IPsec layer, as transmitted by A, as transmitted by F1, and as received by B.

18 IPSEC: IKE

Progress might have been all right once, but it has gone on too long.
—Ogden Nash

The previous chapter covered how IPsec works once the security association (SA) is set up, the session key established, and so on. This chapter covers IKE (Internet Key Exchange). IKE is a protocol for doing mutual authentication and establishing a shared secret key to create an IPsec SA. IKE took many years to come out of IETF. The original contenders were Photuris (RFC 2522) and SKIP (http://skip.incog.com/inet-95.ps). Either of these protocols would have been just fine in practice. But due to committee politics, neither one was chosen and instead IKE/ISAKMP emerged, almost a decade after work began, with a protocol so complex and specification so incomprehensible that nobody had the patience to understand what was being decided upon, and so nobody had objections. The result had lots of ambiguities and flaws, though the world did manage to have interoperable implementations and a fair amount of deployment because of the power of public domain reference implementations and interoperability testing workshops.

There are two ways to design a system. One is to make it so simple there are obviously no deficiencies. The other is to make it so complex there are no obvious deficiencies.
—C. A. R. Hoare

The specification of IKE is in three pieces; ISAKMP (Internet Security Association and Key Management Protocol, RFC 2408), IKE (RFC 2409) and the DOI (Domain of Interpretation, RFC 2407). As of the writing of this book, the IETF WG realizes the problems with IKE, especially the documentation of IKE, and will almost certainly replace it. In this chapter we describe the current IKE in detail because there is no other place in which it is described in a readable way (especially no place that also critiques it). Even if the IETF makes a decision to replace it with something else, it is likely that implementations will persist for quite some time. And, there is a lot to learn from analyzing its idiosyncracies.

The intention of IKE is to do mutual authentication using some sort of long term key (pre-shared secret key, public signature-only key, or public encryption key), and establish a session key. In addition to variants necessitated by having different types of keys, there are variants depending on what features you want (e.g., hiding endpoint identifiers, or the ability to negotiate cryptographic algorithms rather than having them chosen by the initiator), trading off those features against extra messages. Each of the variants has subtle differences in security properties, which we explain. We also describe some of the alternatives/precursors to IKE.

18.1 PHOTURIS

Photuris was one of the two main candidates for this piece of IPsec (the other being SKIP). Photuris was basically a signed Diffie-Hellman exchange, with identity hiding by first doing an anonymous Diffie-Hellman, and using an initial stateless cookie (see §16.5.1 *Cookies*). Alice transmits C_A,

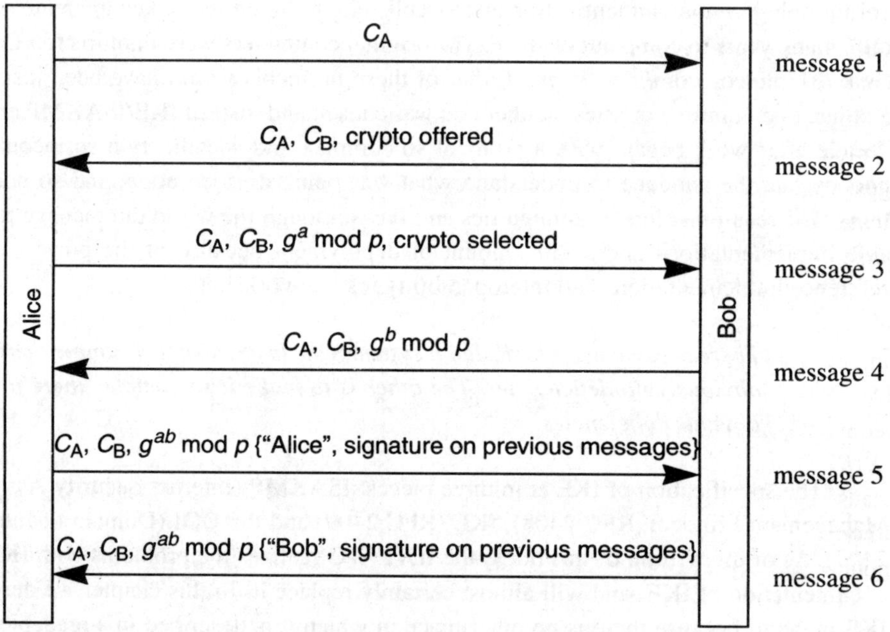

Protocol 18-1. Photuris

which Photuris calls a cookie, but it's not for the same purpose as Bob's stateless cookie C_B. C_A is just a way for Alice to keep connection attempts separate, in case she is initiating multiple simultaneous connections to Bob. Messages 3 and 4 consist of the Diffie-Hellman exchange, and the resulting Diffie-Hellman key is used to encrypt the identities in messages 5 and 6. In addition to the identities, the signatures on the previous messages are sent in message 5 and 6.

This is somewhat simplified. There's also crypto parameter negotiation, and choosing of SPI values for each direction. (SPI identifies the SA; see §17.1.1 *Security Associations*).

C_B is for denial of service protection. It is desirable for Bob to be stateless until message 3 (when he knows that Alice can return a valid cookie). The only way he can do this is to reuse his Diffie-Hellman secret number b for many connections. But if he *always* uses the same b, perfect forward secrecy will be lost. Therefore he should change his b periodically.

18.2 SKIP

SKIP (Simple Key-Management for Internet Protocols) has some interesting ideas, and was at one point widely deployed. SKIP uses long term Diffie-Hellman public keys (e.g., $g^a \bmod p$). Assuming Alice knows Bob's public key ($g^b \bmod p$), and her own private key (a), then she can compute $g^{ab} \bmod p$, the shared secret between herself and Bob, thus establishing a session key in zero messages! If they don't already know each other's public keys, they would have to send each other certificates, or retrieve certificates from a directory, in which case it wouldn't be zero messages, of course.

It's bad cryptographic practice to use a key for encrypting a lot of data. So SKIP doesn't use the shared key $X = g^{ab} \bmod p$ for encrypting the data. It only uses it for encrypting the data encryption key. Each packet of data is encrypted with some key S, and has a SKIP header that contains $X\{S\}$. You could use the same S for many packets, and would be able to tell efficiently (without needing to decrypt $X\{S\}$) that the key was still S because the header would start with the same value of $X\{S\}$. Or you could change the key on every packet. The SKIP designers really liked this feature because it somewhat got around the 40-bit key limit imposed at that time by the U.S. government. Although S was only 40 bits, if a conversation involves breaking 1000 Ss, then an attacker had 2^{50} amount of work to do to decrypt an entire conversation.

Later SKIP was modified in order to meet some of the objections of the IPsec working group. Perfect forward secrecy was added, which meant periodically doing more Diffie-Hellman exchanges, and the data packet format used AH and ESP, which added more complexity since SKIP's idea of including $X\{S\}$ in each packet was not all that well-suited to being encoded with AH and ESP. Although widely deployed before IKE, once IKE was standardized most deployments migrated to IPsec.

18.3 HISTORY OF IKE

While SKIP and Photuris proponents were fighting with each other, ISAKMP (Internet Security Association and Key Management Protocol, RFC 2408) emerged, a gift to the IETF from the NSA. ISAKMP wasn't a protocol but was a framework in which fields could be exchanged to create a protocol. It is specified as running over UDP rather than TCP, and is woefully underspecified on issues such as what happens when messages get lost. Given how thrilled IETF usually is at anything having to do with the NSA, and given how ISAKMP didn't actually *do* anything, it was astonishing that the IETF embraced it and decided that IPsec would somehow have to operate within the ISAKMP framework. Adopting ISAKMP gave an excuse not to adopt either SKIP or Photuris, because once the requirement of working with ISAKMP was assumed, neither protocol met that requirement.

Another document was written, supposedly as a protocol that would work within the ISAKMP framework, and that was called OAKLEY (RFC 2412). Another proposal was SKEME [KRAW96]. Then IKE (RFC 2409) was written, crediting ideas from OAKLEY and SKEME, and using ISAKMP syntax. But even at that it was incomplete, and there's another document, *The Internet IP Security Domain of Interpretation for ISAKMP* (RFC 2407) that defines a lot of the fields. ISAKMP's idea of a **domain of interpretation** (**DOI**) is that a DOI specifies a particular use of ISAKMP, and the intention is that for each DOI value there would be a specification that would define what all the parameters mean for that DOI value. So you need RFCs 2407, 2408, and 2409 in order to know how to implement IKE.

The distinction between IKE and ISAKMP is very confusing. Probably the best way to think of it is that IKE is a profiling (i.e., defining fields, choosing options) of ISAKMP, but it isn't that straightforward. The impression is that the IKE authors attempted to make their document self-contained but ran out of energy and deferred to the ISAKMP spec for encodings. The terms tend to be used inconsistently, adding to the confusion. For instance, a direct quote from the IKE spec (RFC 2409):

> *While Oakley defines "modes", ISAKMP defines "phases". The relationship between the two is very straightforward and IKE presents different exchanges as modes which operate in one of two phases.* —RFC 2409

Imagine trying to read 150 pages of this (80 for ISAKMP, 30 for DOI document, and 40 for IKE), and you'll see why ISAKMP/IKE never got much scrutiny, though miraculously, people were able to implement it and even interoperate. In the next sections we'll describe the protocols conceptually, together with an analysis of them and suggestions for improvement.

18.4 IKE PHASES

IKE defines two phases. Phase 1 does mutual authentication and establishes session keys. It is based on identities such as names, and secrets such as public key pairs, or pre-shared secrets between the two entities. Then using the keys established in phase 1, multiple phase-2 SAs between the same pair of entities can be established. The phase-1 exchange is known as the ISAKMP SA, or sometimes it is referred to as the IKE SA. An ESP or AH SA would be established through phase 2.

Why not just establish an ESP or AH SA in a single exchange and not bother with a separate phase 2? It would certainly be simpler and cheaper to just set up an SA in a single exchange, and do away with the phases, but the theory is that although the phase-1 exchange is necessarily expensive (if based on public keys), the phase-2 exchanges can then be simpler and less expensive because they can use the session key created out of the phase-1 exchange. This reasoning only makes sense if there *will* be multiple phase-2 setups inside the same phase-1 exchange. Here are some arguments people give for the two phases:

- The ISAKMP designers assumed ISAKMP would be used by more than just IPsec, and in addition to setting up IPsec (e.g., AH, ESP) SAs, it might be used to establish SAs for other protocols. The IETF even assigned values for DOI for some routing protocols such as RIP and OSPF, but never wound up designing exchanges for them. And indeed since those protocols run on top of IP, they didn't need their own protocol. They could use IPsec.

- Some people advocate setting up different SAs for different traffic **flows** (conversations). In that case, a firewall-to-firewall link might require many SAs, one perhaps for each source/destination/port pair. Even if the SA is end-to-end, there might be multiple processes on one machine talking to processes on the other.

  The concern is that there might be security weaknesses if different flows used the same key. Indeed such a weakness was discovered if the SA used encryption only (no integrity protection). Imagine two machines M_1 and M_2 with an SA over which traffic for many source/destination pairs flows. The source/destination pairs might be applications on M_1 and M_2, or M_1 and M_2 might be firewalls forwarding traffic from one portion of the net to machines on another portion of the net. Suppose there are conversations between *A* and *B*, and between *C* and *D* that go through the M_1-M_2 SA. If *C* wants to decrypt a packet sent by *A* to *B*, then it can record an encrypted packet between *A* and *B*, and between *C* and *D*, and splice the first encrypted part (the part that contains the source and destination) from the *C-D* packet onto the *A-B* encrypted packet, and forward the packet to M_2. M_2 will decrypt the spliced packet, deliver the decrypted data from the *A-B* packet to *D* (because the initial portion of the packet was spliced from a packet that indicated M_2 should forward the packet to *D*).

This is not an issue if integrity protection is used, because the spliced packet would not pass the integrity check, and there is no excuse for ever using encryption without integrity protection. But because of this bug with multiplexing flows over an encryption-only SA, some people think it is safer not to multiplex flows over an SA. Without multiplexing flows, there might then be many SAs between the same pair of machines.

- Key rollover is cheaper using phase 2 rather than restarting the phase-1 connection setup.
- You can set up multiple connections with different security properties, such as integrity-only, encryption with a short (insecure, snooper-friendly) key, or encryption with a long key. We disagree with this since it would seem logical to use the strongest protection needed by any of the traffic for *all* the traffic rather than having separate SAs in order to give weaker protection to some traffic. There might be some legal or performance reasons to want to use different protection for different forms of traffic, but this should be a relatively rare case not worth optimizing for. A cleaner method of doing this would be to have completely different SAs rather than multiple SAs loosely linked together with the same phase-1 SA.

18.5 PHASE 1 IKE

18.5.1 Aggressive Mode and Main Mode

There are two types of phase-1 exchanges, called **modes. Aggressive mode** accomplishes mutual authentication and session key establishment in three messages. **Main mode** uses six messages, and has additional functionality, such as the ability to hide endpoint identifiers from eavesdroppers and additional flexibility in negotiating cryptographic algorithms.

In main mode there are six messages. In the first pair of messages, Alice sends a cookie and requested cryptographic algorithms, and Bob responds with his cookie and the cryptographic algorithms he will agree to. Messages 3 and 4 are a Diffie-Hellman exchange. Messages 5 and 6 are encrypted with the Diffie-Hellman value agreed upon in messages 3 and 4. In messages 5 and 6, each side reveals its identity and proves it knows the relevant secret (e.g., private signature key, or pre-shared secret key).

In aggressive mode (Protocol 18-2), there are only three messages. The first two messages include a Diffie-Hellman exchange to establish a session key, and in the second and third messages each side proves they know both the Diffie-Hellman value and their secret.

In main mode (Protocol 18-3), Alice starts by giving all the cryptographic algorithms she supports, in order of preference, and Bob responds by making a choice. In aggressive mode, Alice can also propose cryptographic algorithms, but since she has to send a Diffie-Hellman number she

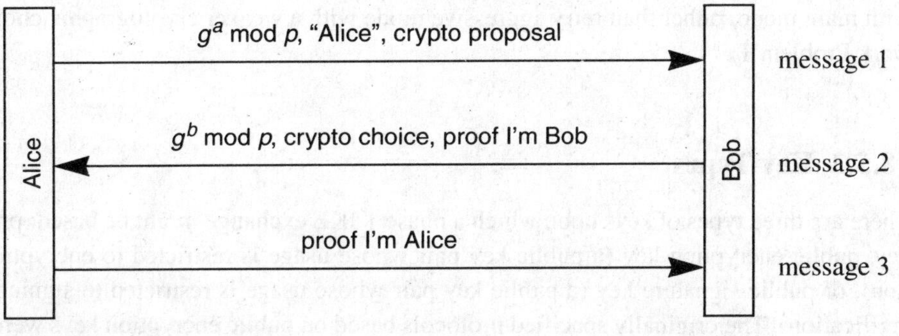

Protocol 18-2. General idea for all IKE phase-1 protocols, Aggressive Mode

has to specify a unique flavor of Diffie-Hellman (e.g. g and p) and hope Bob supports it. Otherwise, Bob will refuse the connection, and not even tell her what he would have supported.

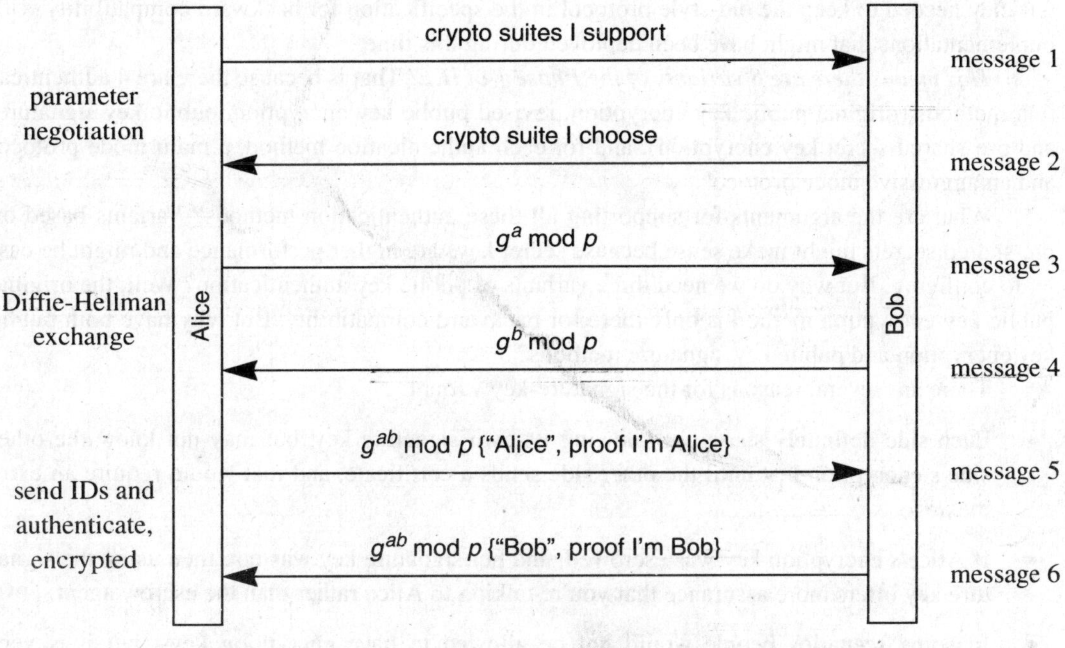

Protocol 18-3. General idea for all IKE phase-1 protocols, Main Mode

Note that there is no way for Bob to cryptographically protect a message complaining about Alice's cryptographic choices, since Alice and Bob haven't established a session key yet, so Alice can't be sure a refusal message is coming from Bob. Although the specification doesn't say what Alice should do if Alice's aggressive mode message is refused, Alice should attempt to reconnect with main mode, rather than retry aggressive mode with a weaker cryptographic choice (see Homework Problem 1).

18.5.2 Key Types

There are three types of keys upon which a phase 1 IKE exchange might be based: pre-shared secret key, public encryption key (a public key pair whose usage is restricted to encryption and decryption), or public signature key (a public key pair whose usage is restricted to signing and signature verification). The originally specified protocols based on public encryption keys were replaced with more efficient protocols. The original public key encryption variants separately encrypted each field with the other side's public key, instead of using the well-known technique of encrypting a randomly chosen secret key with the other side's public key and encrypting all the rest of the fields with that secret key. Apparently a sufficiently long time elapsed before anyone noticed this that they felt they needed to keep the old-style protocol in the specification for backward compatibility with implementations that might have been deployed during this time.

This means there are 8 variants of the Phase 1 of IKE! That is because there are 4 authentication methods (original public key encryption, revised public key encryption, public key signature, and pre-shared secret key encryption), and for each authentication method, a main mode protocol and an aggressive mode protocol.

What are the arguments for supporting all these authentication methods? Variants based on pre-shared secrets might make sense because secret keys are higher performance and might be easier to configure. But why do we need three variants of public key authentication? Well, the original public key encryption method is only there for backward compatibility. But why have both public key encryption and public key signature methods?

There are several reasons for the signature-key variant:

- Each side definitely starts out knowing its own signature key, but may not know the other side's encryption key until the other side sends a certificate, and that would require an extra message.
- If Alice's encryption key was escrowed, and her signature key was not, then using the signature key offers more assurance that you're talking to Alice rather than the escrow agent.
- In some scenarios people would not be allowed to have encryption keys, but it is very unlikely that anyone who would have an encryption key would not also have a signature key.

The IKE specification gives two properties that it claims the public key encryption variants have that the public key signature variants do not provide. One is plausible deniability that the conversation took place, since someone with knowledge of both public keys could construct a complete conversation (Homework Problem 3). The other is that the way the protocol is designed you'd have to break both Diffie-Hellman and RSA in order to break the protocol.

Both arguments are the kind of far-fetched properties that only a theorist could get excited about. In practice neither of them matters, certainly not enough to cause the world to implement twice as many protocols and force the user to make a choice of which exotic cryptographic properties she wants for a particular conversation. But the first argument (plausible deniability that Alice talked to Bob) isn't even true. With IKE's signature variant, Alice signs a hash before she even knows who she's talking to, so the record of her IKE session can't be used to prove she had a conversation with Bob. All it can possibly prove is that she tried to use the public signature key variant of IKE to talk to *somebody*.

As for the argument about needing to break both Diffie-Hellman and RSA, this is an extremely implausible advantage, especially when applied to a real-time communication standard (as opposed to a standard for encrypted stored data).

Another point in favor of the signature key variant is that the public key encryption variants are operationally unusable in many situations, since they require Alice to know Bob's public key before she begins the exchange.

There is one interesting property one might gain from using public key encryption rather than public key signatures. With public key signatures or pre-shared keys, one side has to reveal its identity to the other first. If it's the responder that reveals his identity first, then anyone can initiate an IPsec connection to Bob's IP address to find out who is there. If it's the initiator that reveals her identity first, then an active attacker might be impersonating Bob's IP address to see who might be connecting. But with public key encryption, it is possible to have both sides reveal their identity only to whom they intend to authenticate themselves, by encrypting their identity and any other identifying information (such as their certificate) with the other side's public key. But this can only be done if at least one side already knows the public encryption key of the other side.

One can come up with arguments for all the key types, but is it worth specifying, implementing, and presumably asking users to decide between all these variants? I_1 once explained to me_2 how to make my_2 house less cluttered. Pick up each item, one at a time, and ask my_2self, "Would I_2 pay $1.00 for this if I_2 saw it at a garage sale?" This is the question the world needs to ask, for each of the variants.

18.5.3 Proof of Identity

The proof of identity (transmitted in messages 2 and 3 of aggressive mode, and 5 and 6 of main mode), proves the sender knows the key associated with the identity (the pre-shared secret key, the private encryption key, or the private signature key), and it also serves as integrity protection on the previous messages. In IKE the proof of identity is different for each key type, and each consists of some hash of the key associated with the identity, the Diffie-Hellman values, the nonces, the cryptographic choices Alice offered, and the cookies. It would have been much more straightforward to just use a hash of the previous messages in their entirety, and as it turns out, at least one of the fields left out of IKE's hash (vendor ID payload, and Bob's accepted cipher suite) could possibly be exploited by an attacker. This was pointed out by Tero Kivinen and is something that will be most likely be fixed in a later version of IKE.

One example of a field that should have been protected is the cryptographic suite Bob chooses. Theoretically, if one of the choices Alice is willing to accept is so weak that it can be broken in real time, then a man-in-the-middle, Trudy, could replace Bob's choice of a good crypto suite with that weak suite. Then, before Alice times out the connection, Trudy could break the cryptography and impersonate Bob for the remainder of the session. This is admittedly far-fetched, but given that a more straightforward protocol is more secure, there's really no excuse.

Leaving fields such as the private use fields out of the integrity check might be more of an issue. By definition, we have no idea what they might be used for and whether Trudy can cause some problem by modifying them.

18.5.4 Cookie Issues

Photuris had the ability for Bob to remain stateless until he knew that the initiator was able to return his cookie. Like Photuris, IKE has Alice and Bob each transmit a cookie in messages 1 and 2. However, amidst all the complexity and over-engineering of the cryptographic functions, apparently nobody noticed until too late that IKE no longer had the ability for Bob to remain stateless. For instance, he has to remember the set of cryptographic proposals Alice requests in message 1 because they are included in the hashes used in the proof of identity. If Alice were to repeat the necessary information from message 1 in message 3, Bob could be stateless until receipt of message 3.

With stateless cookies, Bob would send the same cookie to the same IP address for some time (until Bob changes his secret), because Bob needs to be able to reconstruct, from the IP address alone, what cookie value he would have sent. ISAKMP requires the cookies to be unique for each connection, so even if IKE took our suggestion from the previous paragraph and had Alice repeat the information from message 1 in message 3, the ISAKMP specification would forbid Bob from choosing stateless cookies.

Another problem with the design of the ISAKMP/IKE cookies is duplicate connection identifiers. The IKE exchange is identified by the pair of cookies ⟨initiator cookie, responder cookie⟩. There is nothing to prevent Alice from being the initiator in one exchange and the responder in another and having the same cookie pair established. If the order in which events happens is that Alice initiates a connection, choosing *X* as the initiator cookie, and then someone initiates a connection to Alice, and chooses *X*, to which Alice chooses *Y* for the responder cookie, then if the responder in the exchange that Alice initiated also happened to choose *Y* there would be two connections with the same connection identifier, and no way for Alice to have prevented it. This is unlikely to happen (unless attackers are observing Alice's packets and doing it on purpose) since cookies are large (8 octets) and ISAKMP requires they be randomly chosen. But the randomness requirement which is needed to prevent duplicate connection identifiers is another reason why Bob can't choose cookies designed for stateless operation.

A more straightforward design, which also eliminates this flaw, would be to have each side choose an SPI for identifying traffic going towards it, as is done in ESP and AH.

18.5.5 Negotiating Cryptographic Parameters

IKE allows the two sides to negotiate which encryption, hash, authentication method, and Diffie-Hellman parameters they will use. Alice proposes acceptable suites of algorithms and Bob chooses. Bob does not get to choose 1 from column A, 1 from column B, 1 from column C, and 1 from column D, so to speak. Instead Alice transmits a set of complete proposals. While this is more powerful in the sense that it can express the case where Alice can only support certain combinations of algorithms, it greatly expands the encoding in the common case where Alice is capable of using some of the algorithms in any combination. For instance, if Alice can support 3 of each of 4 types of algorithm, and would be happy with any combination, she'd have to specify 81 (3^4) suite choices to Bob in order to tell Bob all the combinations she can support! Each choice must specify each of encryption, hash, authentication, and Diffie-Hellman group.

A much simpler scheme is to predefine a few suites, and only allow a choice of one of the suites. This is what is done in SSL/TLS.

But if the flexibility is really desired for independently mixing-and-matching cryptographic algorithms, it would be better if IKE had allowed Alice to make a set of proposals, where each set is independent, but within a set there are allowed to be choices. For instance, proposal 1 might be to use any of three algorithms for encryption, either of 2 algorithms for hash, a specific authentication method, and any of 6 Diffie-Hellman groups. Proposal 2 might be to use any of some other (possibly overlapping) set of encryption algorithms, any of a set of hash algorithms, etc.

But back to IKE as specified. In the first message of phase 1 IKE, Alice makes a set of proposals for cryptographic algorithms, and Bob chooses. Main mode vs. aggressive mode is not negotiated. Alice just decides which to do, and specifies which she chose. If she chose aggressive mode, then all proposed suites have to have the same Diffie-Hellman group, and it has to be the one that she uses in message 1. Examples of algorithms to be negotiated are:

- encryption algorithm (e.g., DES, 3DES, IDEA)
- hash algorithm (e.g., MD5, SHA)

- authentication method (e.g., pre-shared keys, RSA public key signature, DSS, RSA public key encryption with the old protocol, RSA public key encryption with the new improved protocol)
- Diffie-Hellman group (e.g., modular exponentiation with a particular g and p, elliptic curve with a particular set of parameters)

In all of the main mode exchanges, all cryptographic algorithms can be negotiated (encryption algorithm, hash algorithm, authentication method, Diffie-Hellman group). Alice makes a proposal and Bob chooses. IKE specifies at least one algorithm of each category as MUST implement. The MUST-implements in IKE are encryption method=DES, hash=MD5 and hash=SHA, authentication method=pre-shared key, Diffie-Hellman group=modular exponentiation with a canned g and p).

Optionally within a choice Alice can specify a lifetime beyond which the SA should not be used. IKE suggests that, when the lifetime is close to being exceeded, the SA should be closed and, if needed, a new SA established. The lifetime is specified as a quantity of data and/or a duration, and is considered exceeded when either limit is exceeded. If only one type of lifetime (duration or data quantity) is specified, the default for the other is assumed (duration=8 hours, data quantity=infinite).

In aggressive mode, there is no way to negotiate the group for the Diffie-Hellman exchange since Alice has already chosen one and included the Diffie-Hellman value in the message. However, the Diffie-Hellman choice still has to appear in the menu and is necessary information to Bob so that he can interpret what kind of Diffie-Hellman value Alice has sent to him.

Although none of the aggressive mode variants allow negotiation of the Diffie-Hellman group, some of the other cryptographic algorithms can be negotiated. The only ones that cannot be negotiated are those that Alice has to use in message 1. For instance, in both public key encryption variants, Alice may send a hash of Bob's certificate (allowing Bob to identify which of his keys is needed to decrypt the information Alice is sending him), so Alice must choose the hash algorithm. And in the aggressive mode using the revised public key encryption algorithm, Alice additionally uses secret key encryption, so she must choose the secret key encryption algorithm. She's not allowed to propose anything different once she's used something.

18.5.6 Session Keys

IKE Phase 1 establishes 2 session keys: an integrity key and an encryption key for the purpose of integrity-protecting and encrypting the last of the phase 1 IKE messages and all phase 2 IKE messages. The keys are hashes of the Diffie-Hellman values used in the exchange, the nonces, the cookies, and in the case of a pre-shared secret, that secret. It also creates a keying material seed to be used to mix into the information in the phase 2 exchanges to create unique keys for the phase 2

SAs. It's a little surprising that IKE doesn't establish 4 session keys (integrity and encryption for each direction), since cryptographers generally recommend using different keys in the two directions to avoid reflection attacks. And indeed IKE is vulnerable to reflection attacks, though most likely the reflection attacks can only cause denial of service, e.g., closing SAs.

IKE uses the term "prf" (for "pseudo random function") for the kind of function you'd use as an integrity check that takes two arguments, a key and the data, and outputs a hash. Examples of such a function are DES CBC residue (see §4.3 *Generating MACs*), or HMAC (see §5.7 *HMAC*). When there are several items that are essentially hashed together, in order to fit the form factor for a prf function, the items are concatenated together in order to make it look like exactly two inputs to the prf function.

IKE needs to calculate various types of keys (integrity, encryption for the IKE SA, and keys for IPsec SAs established with phase 2). First IKE hashes the information from the IKE exchange (e.g., the nonces, the cookies, the Diffie-Hellman values) to get a quantity mysteriously known as SKEYID. It is a bad name because it isn't an ID of anything. A better name would be something like KEYSEED. Equally baffling, SKEYID is produced by hashing together different information depending on which key type was used. This was mostly due to taking the functions from the SKEME paper, which had different protocols, and sometimes had reasons for not being able to use the same SKEYID (such as to allow SKEYID to be computed before the Diffie-Hellman shared value). But these reasons, for the most part, were no longer valid for the IKE protocols. IKE could therefore have been much simpler. For readability, we'll leave out "mod p" and assume the reader assumes exponentiation, such as g^{xy} is intended to mean mod p. IKE defines SKEYID as:

- in the case of signature public keys, prf(nonces, g^{xy})
- in the case encryption public keys, prf(hash(nonces), cookies)
- in the case of pre-shared secret key, prf(pre-shared secret key, nonces)

The double hash in the case of encryption public keys probably looks strange to you. Again, there was no reason for it, nor was there any reason why the cookies had to be there, other than copying it from the SKEME paper (where they weren't necessary either).

Next, the IKE paper defines what it calls SKEYID_d, which is the secret bits used to create the other keys. It is defined as prf(SKEYID, (g^{xy}, cookies, 0)). (Remember, IKE wants the hash to take two arguments so the last three arguments are considered to be concatenated to form one argument.)

The integrity protection key is called SKEYID_a, (where "a" is for "authentication"). SKEYID_a is defined as prf(SKEYID, (SKEYID_d, (g^{xy}, cookies, 1)).

The encryption key is called SKEYID_e, and is defined as prf(SKEYID, (SKEYID_a, g^{xy}, cookies, 2)).

The proof of identity for Alice is prf(SKEYID, (g^x, g^y, cookies, Alice's initial crypto-parameters proposal, Alice's identity)).

The proof of identity for Bob is prf(SKEYID, (g^y, g^x, cookies, Alice's initial crypto-parameters proposal, Bob's identity)).

18.5.7 Message IDs

IKE messages contain a 32-bit "message ID" which ISAKMP specifies should be randomly chosen. The IKE message ID serves the purpose that would be served with sequence numbers in most protocols, and does it less well, since in order to recognize a replay, you would have to remember all message IDs you've ever seen. With a sequence number, it's much easier to recognize messages you've seen already. For instance, if your window size is one and the last one you processed had message n, then anything other than n+1 will be rejected as a replay or out of window. Given that the header is the same in both directions (initiator cookie, responder cookie), and the session keys are the same in both directions, not only can an attacker replay messages to the same recipient, but the attacker can also reflect messages back to the sender. The reflection problem could have been solved by using different keys in the different directions, or by reversing the order of the cookies, so that the recipient's cookie value appears first in the message (thus treating it like IPsec's SPIs). And using sequence numbers for the message IDs is simpler and solves the replay problem.

18.5.8 Phase 2/Quick Mode

Once an IKE SA is set up between Alice and Bob, either Alice or Bob can initiate an IPsec SA through the phase 2 "quick mode" exchange (i.e., the initiator of a phase 2 SA does not have to be the same party that initiated the phase 1 SA). The quick mode exchange establishes an ESP and/or AH SA, which involves negotiating crypto parameters, optionally doing a Diffie-Hellman exchange (if perfect forward secrecy is desired), and negotiating what traffic will be sent on the SA.

18.5.9 Traffic Selectors

IPsec allows each side of a phase 2 SA to restrict the traffic sent on that SA, by IP address, protocol type (the field in the IP header that indicates UDP, TCP, etc.), and/or TCP/UDP port. This is done by having the phase 2 initiator give a proposal for what IPsec calls a "traffic selector", which is an IP address or (address, mask) pair, a port or all ports allowed, a protocol or all protocols allowed. The other side can either accept it exactly as specified, or refuse.

Note that there is an asymmetry here. If the initiator of a phase 2 SA requests a larger set of addresses than the other side is configured to want, the connection will be refused, with no hint as to what traffic selector would have been acceptable. But if the other side (the one with the more restrictive configuration) initiated the SA, then it would work.

Why does IKE include this feature of specifying the type of traffic that will go over the SA? Perhaps a firewall is configured to only allow certain types of traffic, in which case telling the other side your policy might detect misconfiguration and give some clue as to why traffic is not getting through. In the case where people would want many different SAs between the same pair of nodes, so that traffic from different flows are not multiplexed over a single SA, it is necessary for the two sides to agree on what traffic each SA should be used for.

18.5.10 The IKE Phase 1 Protocols

We now describe all 8 Phase 1 IKE protocols. In the first message, Alice transmits her "cookie" value. After that, all messages start with the cookie pair (initiator cookie, responder cookie), and that pair serves as the IKE connection identifier. Note that in an IKE exchange between Alice and Bob, all messages start with the same cookie pair, in the same order. If Alice initiated the IKE connection, her cookie value always appears in the "initiator cookie" field. To reduce clutter, we won't write "(initiator cookie, responder cookie)" in the figures for the messages.

Fields that are optional are indicated with square brackets ("[" and "]"). When the message is encrypted is it indicated by being enclosed in curly brackets. "{ }". To reduce clutter, CP indicates crypto proposal, and CPA indicates crypto proposal accepted.

18.5.10.1 Public Signature Keys, Main Mode

In this mode, the two parties have public keys capable of doing signatures. Both endpoint identifiers are hidden from an eavesdropper, but an active attacker can figure out the initiator's identity.

The reason for including nonces in messages 3 and 4 is so that Alice and/or Bob can save themselves computation by using the same Diffie-Hellman private value for many exchanges. If they *always* use the same value, then there will not be perfect forward secrecy, so it's a good idea to change it periodically. Mysteriously (and for no good reason), in the public signature key variants, K is also a function of the cookies.

If Bob instead appended the information from message 6 onto message 4 then the exchange would complete in 5 messages instead of 6. However, there is a disadvantage of doing that, since Alice and Bob can't be computing the Diffie-Hellman key in parallel. (See §16.8 *Arranging for Parallel Computation* and Homework Problem 4.)

The proof of identity consists of a signature on the hash of all the information discussed in §18.5.3 *Proof of Identity*.

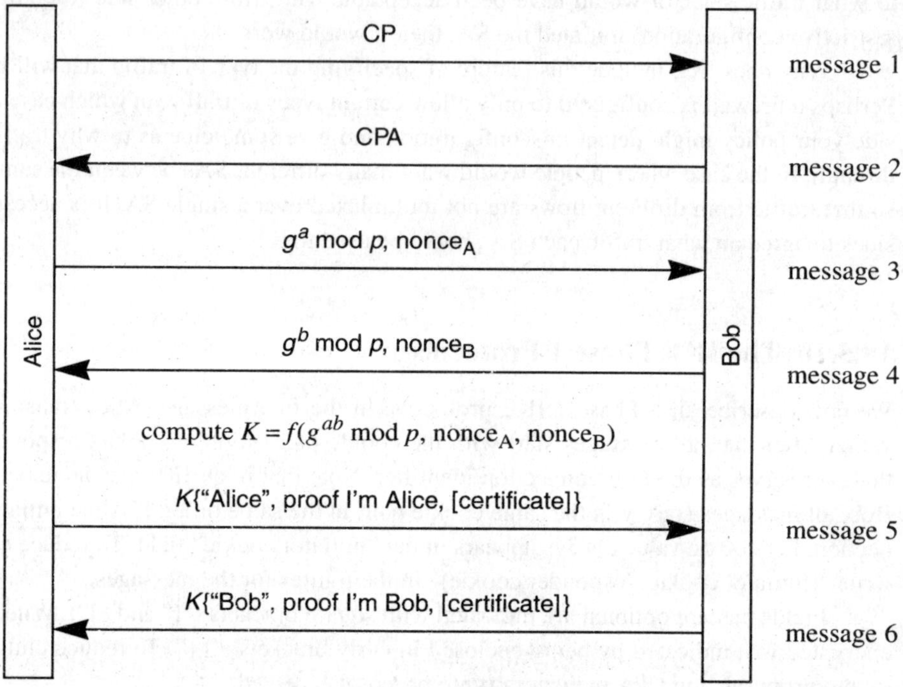

Protocol 18-4. Public signature keys, main mode

18.5.10.2 Public Signature Keys, Aggressive Mode

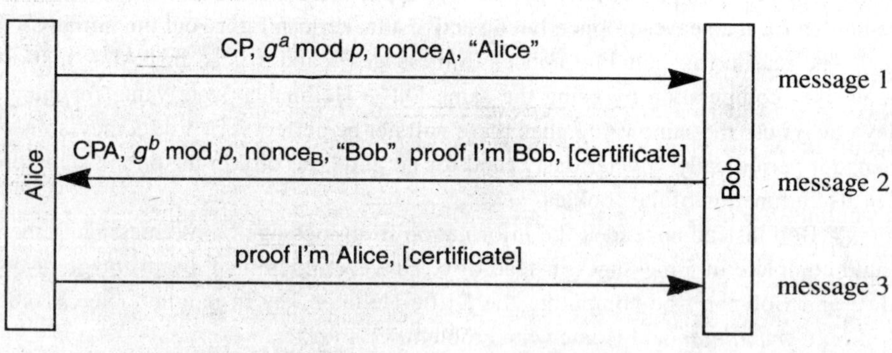

Protocol 18-5. Public signature keys, aggressive mode

Note that messages 2 and 3 are not encrypted, even though the same information is encrypted in the main mode public signature key variant. The identities could have been encrypted and have the exchange still be 3 messages (see Homework Problem 5).

18.5.10.3 Public Encryption Key, Main Mode, Original

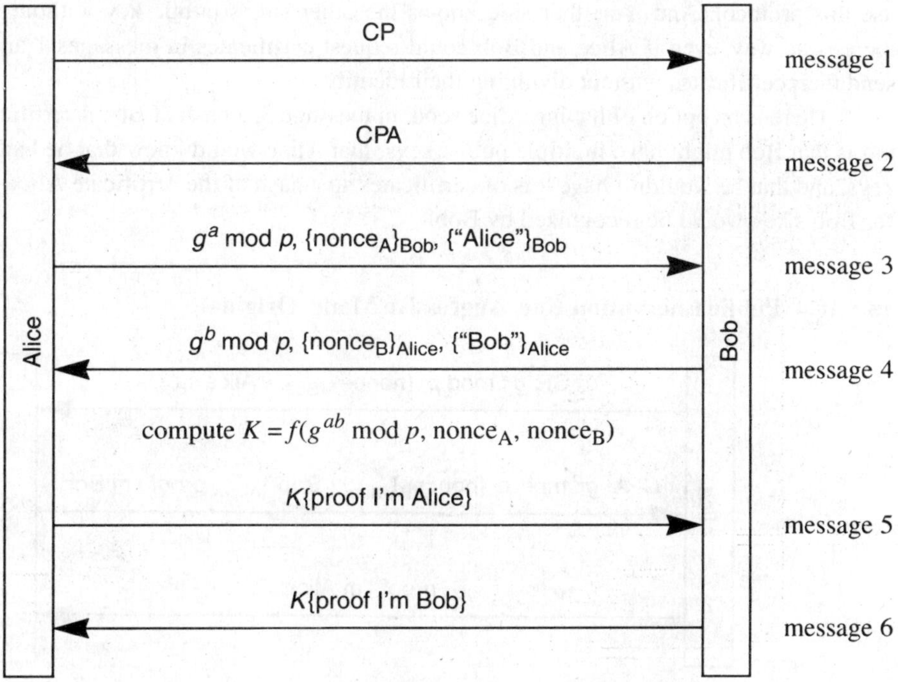

Protocol 18-6. Public Encryption Keys, main mode, original protocol

IKE specifies 4 different phase-1 protocols for public encryption keys, because the original protocols (main mode and aggressive mode) were inefficient (separately encrypted multiple fields with public keys, requiring multiple private key operations). It's astonishing that they left the original protocols in the spec once they redesigned them.

A problem with this variant is that in message 3 there are two fields separately encrypted with Bob's public key, so he needs to do two private key operations to decrypt it. Likewise Alice needs to do two private key operations to decrypt message 4.

Another problem would occur if a nonce or a name were larger than the public key with which it is being encrypted. The spec could have defined some sort of CBC mode for encrypting something larger than a key, but it didn't. Note that with X.500 names it would not be far-fetched for a name to be very long.

Alice and Bob prove they know their private keys because they are able to decrypt the nonce from the other side. They prove this both by knowing K and the hashes used in the proofs in messages 5 and 6, since they are all functions of (among other things) the nonces.

As we discussed in §18.5.2 *Key Types*, there's no way for either Alice or Bob to ask the other side to send them their certificate! If you don't already know the other side's public key, you can't use this protocol. And if neither side knows the other side's public key without their certificate, there is no way, even if Alice and Bob could request certificates in messages 1 and 2, for them to send their certificates without divulging their identity.

There is an option of having Alice send, in message 3, a hash of Bob's certificate. The reasoning is that Bob might have multiple public keys, that Alice would know that he had multiple public keys, and that he wouldn't have lots of certificates so a hash of the certificate Alice happens to have for Bob's key would be recognized by Bob.

18.5.10.4 Public Encryption Key, Aggressive Mode, Original

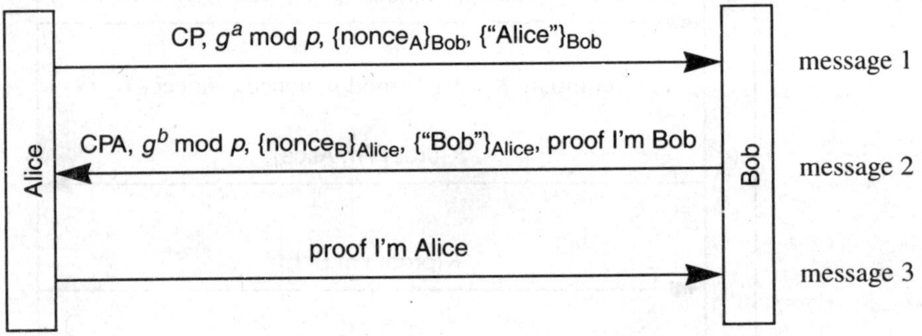

Protocol 18-7. Public Encryption Keys, aggressive mode, original protocol

This protocol is almost the same as the main mode version except that messages 1 and 2 are removed (and crypto suites other than Diffie-Hellman group are negotiated in parallel with the other information in messages 1 and 2) and Bob provides his proof in message 2 rather than, as in main mode, doing it after Alice presents her proof. The proof consists of a hash of the nonce presented by the other side (which requires knowledge of the private key to decrypt), along with the Diffie-Hellman values and the cookie values.

18.5.10.5 Public Encryption Key, Main Mode, Revised

The public encryption protocol was revised to require only a single private key operation on each side (rather than two in the original). This is done by encrypting with a secret key which is a function of the nonce, and the nonce is encrypted with the other side's public key. Thus the other side uses its private key to retrieve the nonce, but then decrypts the other fields with a secret key.

The revised protocol allows Alice to optionally send Bob her certificate. It still has the problem that Alice needs to know Bob's public key.

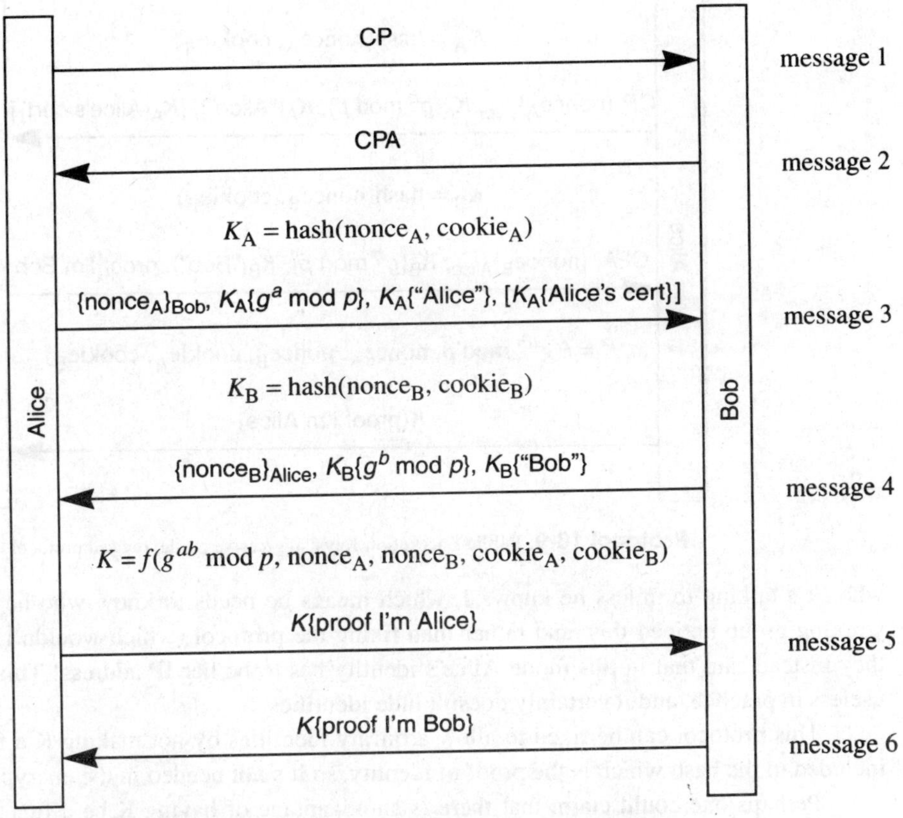

Protocol 18-8. Public Encryption Keys, main mode, revised protocol

18.5.10.6 Public Encryption Key, Aggressive Mode, Revised

18.5.10.7 Shared Secret Key, Main Mode

This is the one required protocol. And it is the most broken. One situation in which this protocol might be useful is in the "road warrior" case, where an employee's laptop is configured with a shared secret with the company's firewall. This would allow the employee to authenticate to the firewall and establish an encrypted tunnel. But the way this mode is designed requires the identities to be the IP addresses. This makes it useless in the road warrior case, because a road warrior's IP address is dependent on where she is that day. And if the identity has to be the IP address, why go to all the work of hiding it by using the 6-message main mode protocol?

The problem with this protocol is that Alice sends her identity in message 5 encrypted with a key K which is a function of the shared secret J. Bob can't decrypt message 5 in order to find out

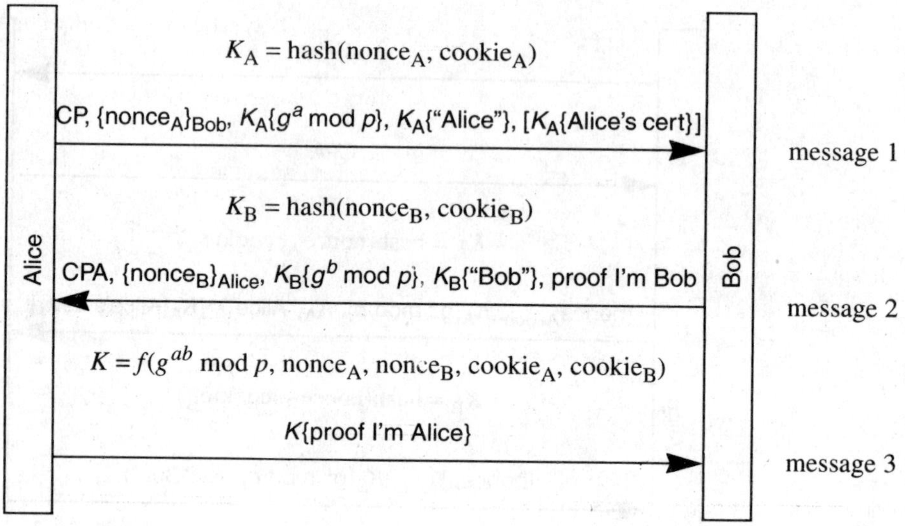

Protocol 18-9. Public Encryption Keys, aggressive mode, revised protocol

who he's talking to unless he knows J, which means he needs to know who he's talking to. The working group noticed this, and rather than fixing the protocol (which wouldn't have been hard), they instead said that in this mode Alice's identity has to be her IP address! This makes it almost useless in practice, and it certainly doesn't hide identities.

This protocol can be fixed to allow arbitrary identities by not making K a function of J. J is included in the hash which is the proof of identity, so it's not needed in the encryption key.

Perhaps one could claim that there is an advantage of having K be a function of J, since it hides both identities from active attackers. But if Bob doesn't know in advance who will be connecting, or at least have a very small set of candidates, then you're stuck with using the IP address as the identity, which as we said, makes it almost useless, and certainly doesn't hide identities from anyone. And if Bob *does* know in advance who will be connecting, then there's no reason for Alice to send her identity at all. And certainly Alice knows who she's talking to, since she knows what J to use. So Bob doesn't need to tell Alice his identity, either.

18.5.10.8 Shared Secret Key, Aggressive Mode

This protocol doesn't have the problem that the main mode shared secret protocol has, because the identities are not sent encrypted.

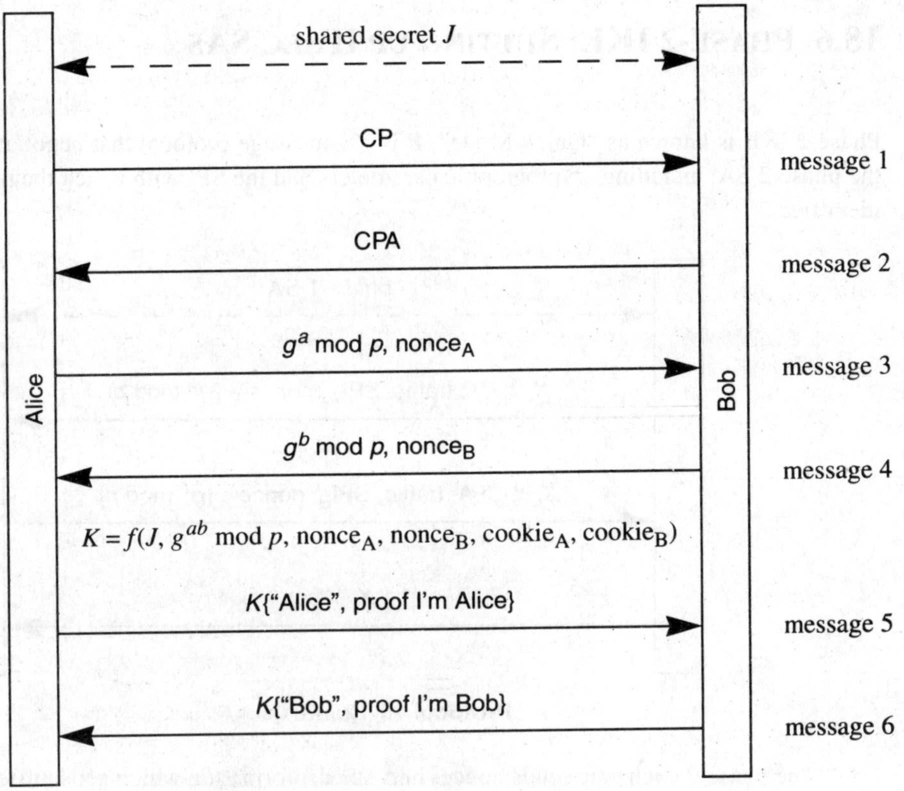

Protocol 18-10. Pre-shared secret, main mode

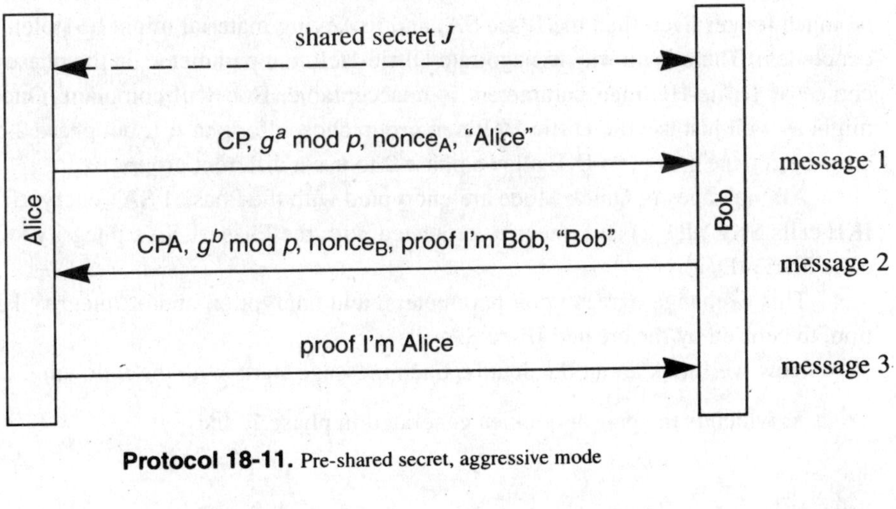

Protocol 18-11. Pre-shared secret, aggressive mode

18.6 PHASE-2 IKE: SETTING UP IPSEC SAS

Phase-2 IKE is known as "Quick Mode". It is a 3-message protocol that negotiates parameters for the phase-2 SA, including cryptographic parameters and the SPI with which the phase-2 SA will be identified.

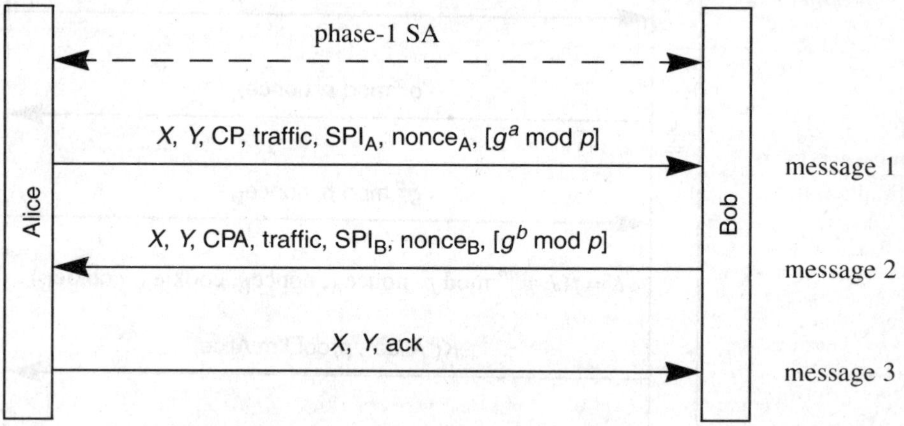

Protocol 18-12. IKE Quick Mode

The phase-2 exchange sends nonces and other information which get shuffled into the SKEYSEED computed in the IKE SA to compute integrity and encryption keys for the IPsec SA, It can optionally do a Diffie-Hellman exchange if it would like PFS for the IPsec SA (the IKE SA might be much longer lived than the IPsec SA, and its keying material might be stolen after the IPsec SA concludes). There is no way to negotiate Diffie-Hellman parameters in the phase-2 exchange. If her choice of Diffie-Hellman parameters is unacceptable, Bob will complain. One would think they might as well just use the Diffie-Hellman group chosen for phase 1, but phase 2 does have the initiator specify the group, so IKE allows phase 2 to use a different group.

All messages in Quick Mode are encrypted with the Phase 1 SA's encryption key K_{enc} (which IKE calls SKEYID_e) and integrity protected with the Phase 1 SA's integrity key K_{int} (which IKE calls SKEYID_a).

This exchange agrees upon parameters, and encryption and/or integrity keys for each direction, to be used by the created IPsec SA.

Now we'll talk about the details. Each message starts with the following, unencrypted:

- X, which is the pair of cookies generated in phase 1, and

- Y, a 32-bit number chosen by the phase-2 initiator to distinguish this phase-2 session setup from perhaps many phase-2 sessions simultaneously being set up within the same phase-1 session. There are two problems with this design. One is the replay problem (see §18.5.7 *Message IDs*). The other is that it is possible for Bob and Alice to each initiate a phase-2 exchange, and choose the same value for Y, which would create confusion. The IKE specification notes this possibility but remarks that it's "unlikely". But they could easily have reduced the probability of Y-value collisions from "unlikely" to zero by having a convention whereby the initiator of the phase 1 exchange chooses odd Y's and the responder of the phase 1 exchange chooses even Y's.

The rest of each message (following X and Y) is encrypted, using SKEYID_e, and integrity protected using SKEYID_a. The IV for the first message is the final ciphertext block of the last message of phase 1 hashed with Y. The IVs for the other messages in the exchange consist of the final ciphertext block of the previous phase 2 message. The other fields in the phase 2 exchange are:

- authenticator (an integrity check on the message using SKEYID_a)
- proposed crypto parameters (message 1), and accepted crypto parameters (message 2)
- nonces in messages 1 and 2
- optionally Diffie-Hellman values in messages 1 and 2
- optionally a description of the traffic to be sent (see §18.5.9 *Traffic Selectors*)

18.7 ISAKMP/IKE ENCODING

In this section we describe the formats, together with our rants about the idiosyncracies. The distinction between ISAKMP and IKE is fuzzy, and definitions are spread among all three documents (RFCs 2407, 2408, and 2409).

Messages have a fixed header, and then a sequence of what ISAKMP refers to as *payloads*. Similar in spirit to IPv6 extension headers, each payload starts with TYPE OF NEXT PAYLOAD and LENGTH OF THIS PAYLOAD.

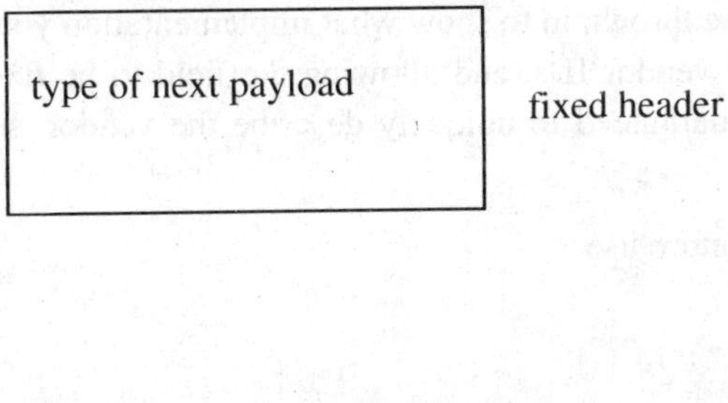

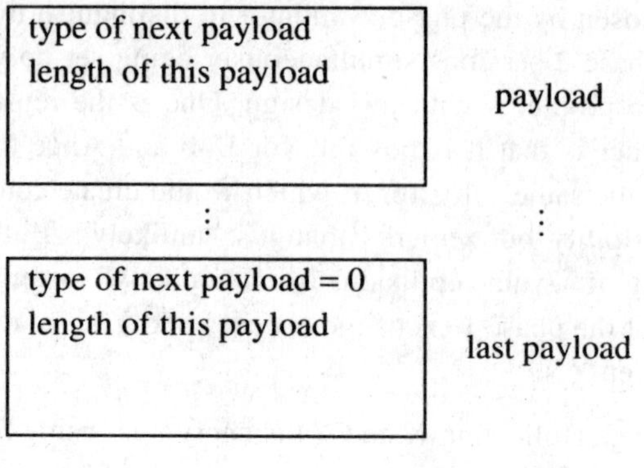

The payload types are:

- 0 = end (i.e., no next payload)
- 1 = SA (security association): contains DOI and "situation", a modifier of DOI, and must include payloads 2 and 3
- 2 = P (proposal): proposed SPI, or SPI in reverse direction
- 3 = T (transform): cryptographic choices
- 4 = KE (key exchange):, the Diffie-Hellman value
- 5 = ID (endpoint identifier in phase 1, traffic selector in phase 2)
- 6 = CERT (certificate)
- 7 = CR (certificate request) (can include the name of the certifier from whom you'd like a certificate)
- 8 = hash (some sort of checksum)
- 9 = signature
- 10 = nonce
- 11 = notification
- 12 = delete (subtype of notification, meaning you are closing this SPI)
- 13 = vendor ID (can be thrown in to show what implementation you're using). To avoid dealing with a registry of vendor IDs, and allowing the field to be fixed size, this is an MD of some sort of string guaranteed to uniquely describe the vendor, such as its name and telephone number.
- 14–127 reserved for future use

- 128–255 = private use (i.e., so NSA can use it and not publish what they're using it for)

18.7.1 Fixed Header

All messages start with a 28-octet fixed length header.

# octets		
8	initiator's cookie	
8	responder's cookie	
1	next payload	
1	version number (major/minor)	
1	exchange type	
1	flags	
4	message ID	
4	message length (in units of octets)	(after encryption)

The fields are:

- initiator's cookie (8 octets)
- responder's cookie (8 octets). Note this will =0 in the first message, since it is unknown at that point
- next payload type
- version (1 octet). This is worth ranting about. The version number field is divided into two 4-bit fields. The intention is that the top nibble is the major version number and the bottom nibble is the minor version number. We think the concept of split version number fields of this sort originated in the early 1980's with DECnet routing, and the intention of the split version number was that the major version would be incremented for incompatible changes, and the minor version would be incremented for compatible changes. A compatible change, at least for routing, might be something like the ability to treat high priority traffic preferentially. Since differences in the minor version wouldn't create incompatibilities, the minor version field served more as information to the higher version node than as anything to worry about if the versions were different. So two nodes would talk if they both supported the same major version number.

  But ISAKMP has all the complexity of a split version field without any actual advantages over a simple, single version number field. In ISAKMP you are required to reject the connection if the other guy's version field is larger than yours. (Actually, it says you must reject it if the major version is larger than yours, or if the major version is the same as yours, if the minor version is larger...which works out to the same thing as "reject if the other guy's 8-bit number is larger than yours.") So the result is exactly the same as if it was just an 8-bit field, but it's more complicated to understand and will run out of numbers more quickly than an 8-bit field since there are only 16 major version numbers. Unless someone worries about numbers getting used up and mandates that you must use up all the minor version numbers before you're allowed to bump the major version number. Anyway, ISAKMP gives no insight into what the designers were trying to accomplish by splitting the field into major and minor. The first version of ISAKMP was major=0, minor=1. The current version (as of writing this book) is major=1, minor=0.

Also, ISAKMP doesn't exactly say you reject it if the version is larger than yours. It says you SHOULD reject it. So implementations are free to ignore the version number, but perhaps feel a little guilty about it.

- exchange type (1 octet). The values defined are:
    - ◆ 1 = base. An exchange type defined by ISAKMP but not used by IKE. This adds an extra message to aggressive mode, so that Alice (the initiator) can send her proposed parameters before sending her Diffie-Hellman value, so that the Diffie-Hellman group could also be negotiated.
    - ◆ 2 = identity protection. This is what is called "main mode" in IKE.
    - ◆ 3 = authentication only. Not used by IKE.
    - ◆ 4 = aggressive. Same as what's called "aggressive mode" in IKE.
    - ◆ 5 = informational. Not really an "exchange", since it's a single message without an acknowledgment, used to tell the other side something such as that you are refusing the connection because you don't like the version number.
    - ◆ 6–31 = reserved values by ISAKMP for assignment by IANA as new ISAKMP exchange types
    - ◆ 32–239 = to be defined within a particular DOI
    - ◆ 240–255 = for private use
- flags:
  bit 0 (LSB): encrypted—whether the fields after the header are encrypted
  bit 1: commit—A flag so badly named, and so confusingly defined in ISAKMP, that IKE wound up using the same bit and the same name for almost the opposite purpose. In ISAKMP the intention seems to be that the sender, say Bob, is saying he's not yet ready to accept messages on this SA, so Alice should wait for Bob to send an "I'm ready" message. IKE inter-

preted it as a request by Bob for Alice to acknowledge this message. So ISAKMP uses it for Bob to tell Alice to wait for Bob's ack, and IKE uses it for Bob to tell Alice to send an ack.

bit 2: authentication only—this means that the fields after the header are not encrypted. This bit gives no additional information over merely not setting the "encrypted" flag. And you'd probably think that this bit would always be set to the opposite of the encrypted flag, but if it had been defined that way surely someone would have noticed this flag as being useless. Instead, this flag is only set during phase 2, when the assumption is all messages are encrypted, to note a message that isn't encrypted. The only such message would be an informational message.

- message ID: this is used in phase 2 in order to tie together related packets. In other words, if lots of phase 2 SAs are being negotiated simultaneously within the same phase 1 SA, this field differentiates the messages for the different SAs. The specification says that these values must be chosen randomly so that there probably won't accidentally be two phase 2 exchanges with the same message ID (see §18.5.7 *Message IDs*).
- message length: Length of entire message, in units of octets.

18.7.2 Payload Portion of ISAKMP Messages

After the fixed header comes a set of ISAKMP "payloads", reminiscent of IPv6 "next headers". Each one starts with four octets consisting of:.

# octets	
1	type of next payload
1	reserved (unused, set to zero)
2	length of this payload

The encoding would be more intuitive to have each payload indicate the type of that payload rather than the following one, but this way works too. It's this way because it looks more like IPv6.

18.7.3 SA Payload

Assembly of SA payload requires great peace of mind.

—Paraphrase of Robert Pirsig, from *Zen and the Art of Motorcycle Maintenance*

The SA payload for IKE includes the P (proposal) and T (transform) payloads. The encoding is extremely confusing for no good reason. The SA, P and T each look like independent payloads, but ISAKMP defines Ts as being carried inside a P, and Ps carried inside an SA payload. For example, if you have an SA payload that includes 2 proposals, the first of which includes 4 transforms, and the second of which includes 2 transforms, you'd have the payloads SA, P, T, T, T, T, P, T, T.

18.7.3.1 Ps and Ts within the SA Payload

The P payload indicates what "protocol" you're trying to negotiate, e.g., phase 1 IKE, ESP, AH, or IP compression. For phase 1 IKE, there would only be a single P within an SA, because you're only trying to negotiate phase 1 IKE. For phase 2 IKE, there might be several Ps within an SA, because you might be making a proposal for AH only, ESP only, AH+ESP, or any of those plus IP compression.

Within a P there are a set of T payloads. Each T payload indicates a complete suite of cryptographic algorithms needed by that P. For instance, for Phase 1 IKE, you need 4 (authentication (integrity protection), hash, encryption, and Diffie-Hellman group), and optionally a lifetime. There is a default lifetime of 8 hours, so if no lifetime appears within a T, it is the same as including it explicitly with 8 hours. For an AH proposal, there's only an authentication (integrity protection) algorithm, and optionally a lifetime.

Each P payload is assigned a number by the initiator. If there are two P payloads with the same number, it implies both payloads constitute a single proposal. For instance, if Alice would like to have the SA do both ESP and AH, she would include two P payloads, both with the same proposal number, and if Bob accepts that proposal number, he is accepting an SA that will do both ESP and AH. Of the P numbers offered by Alice, Bob chooses one or refuses them all.

Each T payload also includes a number. For instance, suppose a P payload has been assigned the number 3, and has associated T payloads for that P numbered 1, 2, 3. The other side might accept proposal #3, transform suite #2.

18.7.3.2 Payload Length in SA, P, and T Payloads

The PAYLOAD LENGTH in the SA payload is the length of the entire set of the payloads consisting of the SA and all Ps and Ts associated with that SA. The payload length of each P is the length of that P payload plus the T payloads that follow. The payload length of each T payload is actually the length of that T payload.

18.7.3.3 Type of Next Payload

The TYPE OF NEXT PAYLOAD field in the SA payload is set to whatever follows the SA and all proposals, usually 0 (nothing) for main mode phase 1 IKE, or 4 (KE payload) for aggressive mode phase 1 IKE, or 10 (nonce) for phase 2 IKE. The TYPE OF NEXT PAYLOAD field in the P payload is either P or 0 (if it is the last proposal within an SA group). The NEXT PAYLOAD in a T payload is either T or 0 (if it's the last transform within a P group).

SA payload containing 2 proposals, first proposal has four T payloads, second proposal has two T payloads:

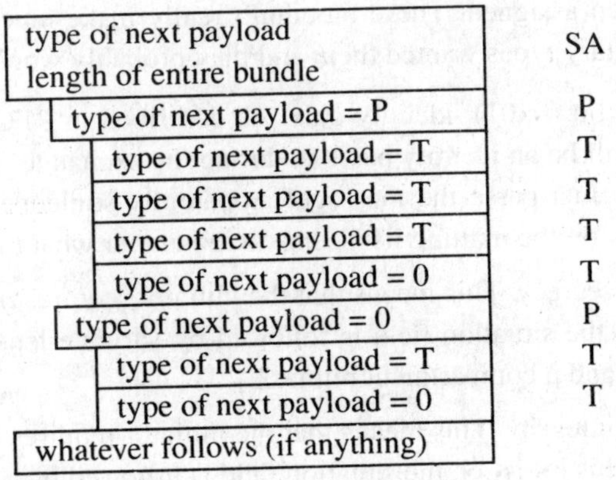

18.7.3.4 SA Payload Fields

# octets		
1	type of next payload	
1	reserved (unused, set to zero)	
2	length of this payload	
4	DOI	1 for IPsec
	situation	
	P payload	
	T payload	
	T payload	
	T payload	
	P payload	
	T payload	

In the diagram we assume the SA payload contains two proposals, with the first containing three transforms and the second containing one transform.

- type of next payload, length of this payload (explained in §18.7.3 *SA Payload*)

- DOI (domain of interpretation). The idea of this field is so that all parameters do not need to be centrally defined and given numbers. Instead, if someone wants to define their own protocols with ISAKMP, they only need a single number assigned, a DOI value, and then all other parameters are interpreted according to that DOI. If you don't know about that DOI value you can't interpret the SA payload. In IKE the DOI=1.
- situation: In ISAKMP the situation field is variable length, and its length and definition depend on the DOI. In IKE the situation field is defined in RFC 2407 as a 4 octet bit mask, of which 3 bits have been assigned. These bits don't really make much sense. They were put there because the military types wanted them and they probably won't be used for anything.
  - least significant bit (0x01): identity only. As described in RFC 2407 this bit indicates whether there will be an identity payload during the exchange. But you don't need a bit to tell you that. Just parse the message! Apparently someone thought it was a good idea, but nobody on the mailing list seems to remember what they wanted it for.
  - next bit (0x02): secrecy. This means that the initiator requires military-style labels, and if this bit is set, the situation field is followed by variable-length data that specifies a sensitivity level and a compartment bitmask.
  - next bit (0x04): integrity. This means that the initiator requires military-style labels for integrity, and if this bit is set, the situation field is followed by a military-style (sensitivity level, compartment) bitmask. If both the secrecy and integrity bits are set, then the integrity label follows the secrecy label.
- P and T payloads (nested as described in §18.7.3.1 *Ps and Ts within the SA Payload*)

18.7.4 P Payload

As explained before, this is not a free-standing payload, but is always nested inside the SA payload.

# octets	
1	type of next payload
1	reserved (unused, set to zero)
2	payload length (length includes nested Ts)
1	proposal number
1	protocol ID
1	SPI size
1	# of T payloads nested within this P
variable	SPI

- proposal number: the nickname given to this proposal so that the responder can accept this proposal by using that assigned number
- protocol ID: the protocol being proposed (e.g., phase 1 IKE=0, ESP=3, AH=2, IPcomp=4)
- SPI size: the size of the SPI that will be the ID of the SA this protocol is attempting to negotiate. In the case of phase 1 IKE, the SPI is the (initiator cookie, responder cookie) pair. The ISAKMP spec says in that case the SPI size can be anything, and the initiator is welcome to put whatever it wants into there, but the responder must ignore it. In the case of phase 2 IKE, the SPI is 4 octets, so the SPI size field is set to 4.
- # of T payloads nested within this P: self-explanatory
- SPI: The actual value of the SPI

18.7.5 T Payload

As explained before, this is not a free-standing payload, but is always nested inside a P, nested inside the SA payload..

# octets	
1	type of next payload
1	reserved (unused, set to zero)
2	length of this payload
1	transform number
1	transform ID
2	reserved
variable	attributes

- transform number: the nickname given to this transform so that the responder can accept this transform by using that assigned number
- transform ID: defined within the DOI and within the protocol (and the values are in RFC 2407). For instance, AH has values defined for MD5, SHA, and DES (CBC residue). ESP has a bunch of values defined for various encryption algorithms such as DES, 3DES, RC5, IDEA, and of course null.

- attributes: a sequence of variable-length fields. Each one consists of:.

# octets	
2	AFflag I attribute type
2	attribute length (if AF=0), attribute value (if AF=1)
variable	attribute value (if AF=1)

  - ♦ AF flag (attribute format flag)=0 means the value of this attribute fits within 2 octets. AF=1 means the value of this attribute takes more than 2 octets, so instead of putting the attribute value into the following 2 octets, the length is put there instead, and the variable length value follows.

18.7.6 KE Payload

# octets	
1	type of next payload
1	reserved (unused, set to zero)
2	length of this payload
variable	key data

- the first 3 fields are the same as in all the other payloads
- key data can be thought of as the transmitter's Diffie-Hellman number, though in theory some exchange other than Diffie-Hellman might have been negotiated. Its length depends on the chosen crypto suite.

18.7.7 ID Payload

The ID payload has different purposes in phase 1 and phase 2. In Phase 1 it is the name by which each side is known to the other, so that that identity can be authenticated. In phase 2 it is a description of the traffic to be transmitted on the SA (such as IP address ranges). Also, in phase 1, there is only one ID payload, which is the name of the transmitter. In phase 2 there are two ID payloads, one specifying a description of the sources of packets to be forwarded across the SA, and one specifying a description of the destinations of packets to be forwarded across the SA.

# octets	
1	type of next payload
1	reserved (unused, set to zero)
2	length of this payload
1	ID type
1	protocol ID
2	port
variable	Identification Data

- the first 3 fields are the same as in all the other payloads
- ID type: several are defined in RFC 2407, such as IPv4 address, IPv4 address range (IPv4 address, mask), IPv6 address, IPv6 address range (IPv6 address, mask), domain name (e.g., prenhall.com), user name (e.g., radia@alum.mit.edu), X.500 name.

18.7.8 Cert Payload

# octets	
1	type of next payload
1	reserved (unused, set to zero)
2	length of this payload
1	certificate encoding
variable	certificate

- first 3 fields, same as other payloads
- certificate encoding: a few are defined in ISAKMP, such as X.509 certificate for a signature key, X.509 certificate for a public key with usage key exchange, PGP certificate, Kerberos token
- certificate, the certificate, variable length

18.7.9 Certificate Request Payload

The certificate request payload contains:.

# octets	
1	type of next payload
1	reserved (unused, set to zero)
2	length of this payload
1	certificate type
variable	certificate authority

- first 3 fields, same as other payloads
- certificate type: same as "certificate encoding" defined in Certificate Payload
- certificate authority: depends on certificate type, but for X.509 it would be the name of the issuer or trust anchor. This is intended to help the other side know which certificate to send.

18.7.10 Hash/Signature/Nonce Payloads

These are all so straightforward and similar that to save space we're putting them in the same section. They all consist of the standard first 3 payload fields, followed by the hash or signature or nonce (depending on the payload type).

# octets	
1	type of next payload
1	reserved (unused, set to zero)
2	length of this payload
variable	hash or signature or nonce

18.7.11 Notify Payload

This can be used to inform the other side of error conditions, or anything else that someone might think of in the future. ISAKMP defines a lot of the notify messages, and leaves some values reserved "for private use" or "DOI specific". You might think that ISAKMP would not need to reserve values for DOI-specific. If the DOI in the notify payload indicates 0 (meaning ISAKMP), you'd go to the ISAKMP document to find the definition of that notify type. If the DOI is something else, you'd go to the spec defining those DOI-specific values.

However, ISAKMP's assumption is that if ISAKMP defines a value, the ISAKMP definition applies, regardless of the DOI. But for all DOIs other than ISAKMP, they would assign values from the same space as all non-ISAKMP DOIs and the definitions in their specification would apply.

# octets	
1	type of next payload
1	reserved (unused, set to zero)
2	length of this payload
4	DOI
1	protocol ID
1	SPI size
2	notify message type
variable	SPI
variable	notification data

- first 3 fields, as in other payloads
- DOI, the DOI under which the rest of the payload should be interpreted
- protocol ID, (e.g., AH, ESP)
- SPI size: size of the SPI.
- notify message type: something like "error: authentication failed"
- SPI
- notification data: whatever extra data might be associated with that notify message type.

18.7.12 Vendor ID Payload

This is defined in ISAKMP. It's intended to allow you to announce what vendor-proprietary extensions you support. The vendor ID is supposed to be a hash of a string such as "Example Company IPsec version 97.1", so that it is highly likely to be unique. It is OK to include multiple vendor ID payloads, to alert the other side that you support the proprietary extensions of all those vendors.

# octets	
1	type of next payload
1	reserved (unused, set to zero)
2	length of this payload
variable	vendor ID

18.8 HOMEWORK

1. Suppose if Alice's aggressive-mode IKE connection initiate is refused, Alice starts up another aggressive-mode connection initiate with her next (and weaker) choice of Diffie-Hellman group, rather than starting a main-mode exchange telling Bob all her supported Diffie-Hellman groups. What is the vulnerability, given an active attacker? (See §18.5.1 *Aggressive Mode and Main Mode*.)

2. What are the relative advantages of the various key types (pre-shared secret keys, public signature keys, public encryption keys) as a basis for an authentication exchange?

3. Show how someone who knows both Alice's and Bob's public encryption keys (and neither side's private key) can construct an entire IKE exchange based on public encryption keys that appears to be between Alice and Bob.

4. Write out the shortened version of main-mode public signature keys that hides Alice's ID from an active attacker. Explain why the 6-message version described in §18.5.10.1 *Public Signature Keys, Main Mode* allows parallel computation of g^{ab} mod p, whereas the shortened version does not.

5. How can you modify aggressive mode with public signature keys (see §18.5.10.2 *Public Signature Keys, Aggressive Mode*) to hide the endpoint identifiers from eavesdroppers? Which identity will be hidden from an active attacker? Give a disadvantage of this. (Hint: see §16.8 *Arranging for Parallel Computation*.)

6. For Photuris, and for each of the Phase 1 IKE variants, say how it performs on hiding endpoint identifiers. Does it hide the initiator's and/or the responder's IDs from eavesdroppers? How about active attackers? (Hint for one tricky case: what are the implications if Alice sends the hash of Bob's certificate as she can optionally do in the public encryption variants?)

7. Design a protocol in which one side has a public signature key and the other side has a public encryption key.

8. Design a protocol in which authentication is one-way since only one side has a public key. Do the protocol with a public signature key. Now do it with a public encryption key.

9. In the public encryption key case, SKEYID is defined as hash(nonces, cookies). SKEYID is supposed to be something that is not computable except by Alice and Bob. Why can't an eavesdropper or active attacker calculate SKEYID?

19 SSL/TLS

19.1 Introduction

In this chapter we cover the SSL family of protocols, which includes SSL versions 2 and 3 and TLS. SSL version 2 is rapidly being replaced by version 3, so we will focus on SSL v3 and TLS, and only discuss v2 when its difference from v3 is interesting (such as the exportability tricks). SSL/TLS allows two parties to authenticate and establish a session key that is used to cryptographically protect the remainder of the session.

19.2 Using TCP

SSL/TLS is designed to run in a user-level process, and runs on top of TCP. As discussed in §16.1 *What Layer?*, running on top of layer 4 allows deployment of SSL/TLS in a user-level process rather than requiring OS changes. Using TCP (the reliable layer 4 protocol) rather than UDP (the datagram layer 4 protocol) makes SSL/TLS a little simpler, because it doesn't have to worry about timing out and retransmitting lost data (TCP does that for it). SSL/TLS could have retained the advantage of being easily deployable as a user-level process and still avoided the rogue packet problem discussed in section §16.1 *What Layer?* by running on top of UDP, and doing all the time-out/retransmission work of TCP within SSL/TLS, but the decision was made to live with the rogue packet problem and keep SSL/TLS simpler.

19.3 Quick History

SSL (Secure Sockets Layer) version 2 (version 1 was never deployed) was originally deployed in Netscape Navigator 1.1 by Netscape in 1995. Microsoft improved upon SSLv2, fixing some security problems, and introduced a similar protocol known as PCT (Private Communications Technology). Then Netscape substantially overhauled the protocol as SSLv3. The IETF, realizing it was bad for the industry to have three similar but incompatible protocols for the same purpose, introduced a fourth similar but incompatible protocol—TLS (Transport Layer Security).

As of the writing of this book, SSLv3 is the most commonly deployed. TLS tweaked the cryptographic algorithms for key expansion and authentication to make cryptographers happier with it. This made TLS noninteroperable with SSLv3. TLS also mandated unencumbered crypto (DH and DSS) rather than RSA. But there was only a window of 2 years in which DH/DSS was unencumbered before the RSA patent expired, which was not a sufficient lure to migrate many implementations away from the widely deployed SSLv3. It remains to be seen whether the world will ever migrate to TLS.

19.4 SSL/TLS Basic Protocol

Using the reliable octet stream service provided by TCP, SSL/TLS partitions this octet stream into records, with headers and cryptographic protection, to provide a reliable, encrypted, and integrity-protected stream of octets to the application. There are four types of records: user data, handshake messages, alerts (error messages or notification of connection closure), and change cipher spec (which should be a handshake message, but they chose to make it a separate record type).

In the basic protocol the client (Alice) initiates contact with the server (Bob). Then Bob sends Alice his certificate. Alice verifies the certificate, extracts Bob's public key, picks a random number *S* from which the session keys will be computed, and sends *S* to Bob, encrypted with Bob's public key. Then the remainder of the session is encrypted and integrity-protected with those session keys. (There are actually six secrets computed when encryption algorithms that require IVs are used—for each direction: integrity protection key, encryption key, and IV.) First we'll present a simplified form of the protocol, then discuss various issues in the full protocol, and finally discuss the details.

- Message 1. Alice says she would like to talk (but doesn't identify herself), and gives a list of cryptographic algorithms she supports, along with a random number R_{Alice}, that will be combined with the *S* in message 3 to form the various keys.

- Message 2. Bob sends Alice his certificate, a random number R_{Bob} that will also contribute to the keys, and responds with one of the ciphers Alice listed in message 1 that Bob also supports.

- Message 3. Alice chooses a random number *S* (known as the **pre-master secret**) and sends it, encrypted with Bob's public key. She also sends a hash of the **master secret** *K* and the hand-

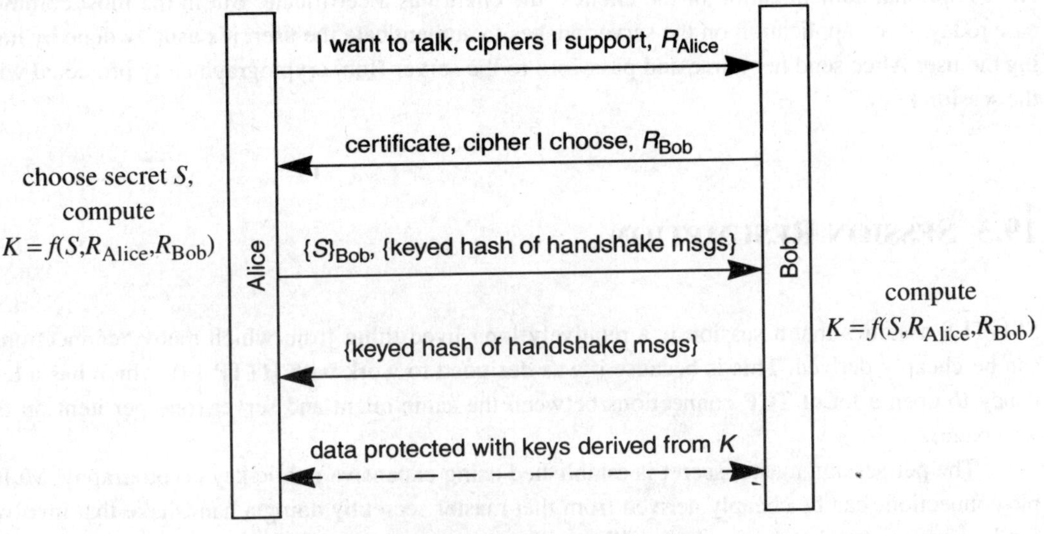

Protocol 19-1. (simplified) SSLv3/TLS

shake messages, both to prove she knows the key and to ensure that tampering of the handshake messages would be detected. The hash is an (unnecessarily) complex function based on one of the early versions of HMAC. To ensure that the keyed hash Alice sends is different from the keyed hash Bob sends, each side includes a constant ASCII string in the hash. The initiator constant is CLNT in SSLv3 and client finished in TLS. The constant Bob will hash into the stew is SRVR in SSLv3 and server finished in TLS. Surprisingly (and unnecessarily), the keyed hash is sent encrypted and integrity-protected. The keys used for encrypting the keyed hash, like the rest of the data in the session will be, are derived from hashing K, R_{Alice}, and R_{Bob}. The keys used for transmission are known as *write* keys, and the keys used for receipt are known as *read* keys. So, for instance, Bob's write-encryption key is Alice's read-encryption key. The keys are encryption, integrity, and IV in each direction, so there are six keys derived. (In SSLv2 there are only two session keys, one in each direction, each used both for integrity protection and encryption.)

- Message 4. Bob proves he knows the session keys, and ensures that the early messages arrived intact, by sending a keyed hash of all the handshake messages, encrypted with his write-encryption key, and integrity-protected with his write-integrity key. Since the session keys are derived from S this proves he knows Bob's private key, because he needed it in order to extract S.

At this point, Alice has authenticated Bob, but Bob has no idea to whom he's talking. As deployed today, authentication is seldom mutual—the client authenticates the server but the server does not authenticate the client. In theory SSL/TLS could be used for mutual authentication and the protocol allows optional authentication of the client if the client has a certificate. But in the most common case today, if the application on the server wishes to authenticate the user, it's usually done by having the user Alice send her name and password to the server Bob, cryptographically protected with the session keys.

19.5 Session Resumption

SSL/TLS assumes that a session is a relatively long-lived thing from which many "connections" can be cheaply derived. This is because it was designed to work with HTTP 1.0, which has a tendency to open a lot of TCP connections between the same client and server (one per item on the web page).

The per-session master secret is established using expensive public key cryptography. Multiple connections can be cheaply derived from that master secret by doing a handshake that involves sending nonces (so that session keys will be unique), but avoids public key operations.

SSL/TLS allows session resumption, but it is not stateless at Bob as in Lotus Notes (see §16.9 *Session Resumption*). If Bob wants to allow a session to resume, i.e., wants to be able to have multiple connections based on that session, he sends the client (in message 2) a session_id (which is not secret), and stores (session_id, master secret). If Alice presents (in message 1) a session_id that Bob remembers, they can skip the public key portion of the handshake. The shortened handshake will only succeed if Alice and Bob remember the same master secret. If Bob does not recognize the session_id, he returns a different session_id in message 2 (or leaves it out entirely if he wants to make the session non-resumable).

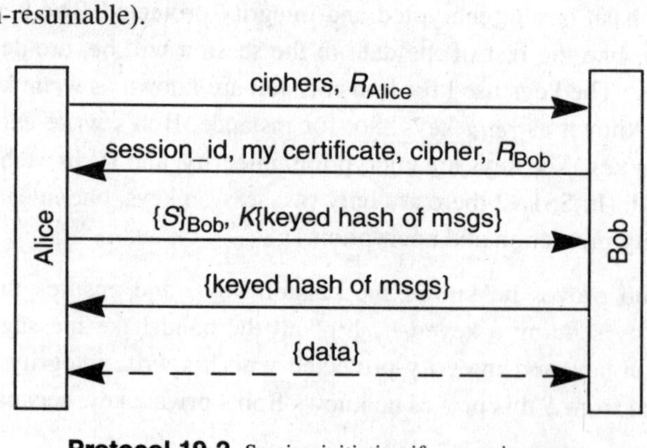

Protocol 19-2. Session initiation if no previous state

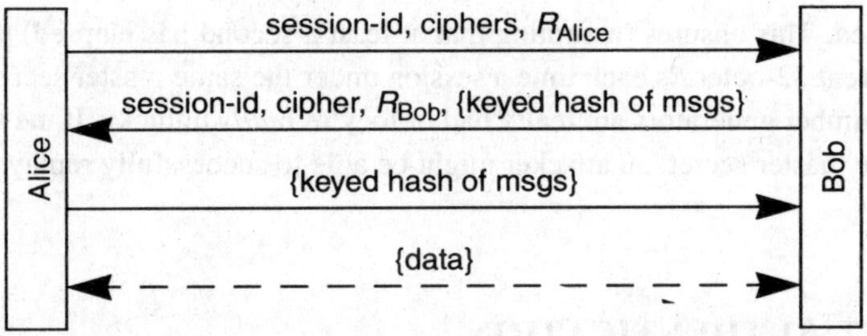

Protocol 19-3. Session resumption if both sides remember session-id

It might seem odd for Alice, when resuming the session, to send a set of ciphers rather than just the cipher used in the session. Even if Bob has lost state about the session, wouldn't he make the same choice of cipher, given the same choices, as he made when the session was created? Not necessarily, because perhaps his policy has changed. So Alice is allowed, when resuming a session, to send a set of choices, but the set must at least contain the cipher that had been chosen previously for that session.

19.6 COMPUTING THE KEYS

The secret S sent in the first exchange is the pre-master secret. It is shuffled with the two Rs to produce the master secret K. In other words $K = f(S,R_{\text{Alice}},R_{\text{Bob}})$. For each connection (including the first) the master secret is shuffled with the two Rs to produce the six keys used for that connection (for each side: encryption, integrity, and IV), i.e., each of the keys is $g_i(K,R_{\text{Alice}},R_{\text{Bob}})$.

Note that this is unnecessarily complex in the case of using RSA, since on the first connection, the Rs get shuffled in twice. It would have been fine with RSA to just use S the way K is used; for each connection, combine S with that connection's Rs to produce the six keys used for that connection. However, there are other authentication methods that would wind up always computing the same pre-master secret S. For instance, with Diffie-Hellman using a fixed Diffie-Hellman number as your public key, the same two parties (Alice and Bob) will always compute the same S. If S were kept around in memory, it's possible that malicious software might steal it. So it's safer to hash it with some nonces to produce K (the master secret), since if K is stolen, it will only affect communication between Alice and Bob during the single session.

The keyed hashes are keyed with K, and are sent protected with the data keys (i.e., encrypted using the encryption key and IV, and integrity-protected with the integrity key).

The Rs are 32 octets long, and it is recommended (but not enforced) that the first 4 octets not be randomly chosen, but instead be the Unix time (seconds since January 1, 1970) when the message was generated. This ensures (assuming that at least a second has elapsed) that Alice and Bob will choose different 32-octet *R*s each time a session under the same master secret is resumed, even if their random number generators are really bad or they're *really* unlucky. If the same *R*s were chosen with the same master secret, an attacker might be able to successfully replay packets.

19.7 Client Authentication

As deployed today it is unusual for clients to have certificates. However, it is possible in SSL/TLS for the server (Bob) to request that the client (Alice) authenticate herself. This is done by having Bob send a "certificate request" in message 2. Alice, upon seeing the request, sends her certificate, and her signature on a hash of the handshake messages, proving she knows the private key associated with the public key in the certificate.

19.8 PKI as Deployed by SSL

As deployed today, the client typically comes configured with public keys of various "trusted" organizations (trusted by the browser vendor, not necessarily by the user). The user at the client machine can modify this list, adding or deleting keys. The server sends a certificate to the client, and if it's signed by one of the CAs on the client's list, the client will accept the certificate. If the server presents a certificate signed by someone not on the list (such as a self-signed certificate), the user is typically presented with a pop-up box informing him that the certificate couldn't be verified because it was signed by an unknown authority, and would the user like to look at the certificate and/or import the signer onto the list of trusted root CAs? We discuss this model of PKI along with others in Chapter 15 *PKI (Public Key Infrastructure)*.

If the server wishes to authenticate the client, it sends a certificate request in which it specifies the X.500 names of the CAs it trusts, and the types of keys it can handle (e.g., RSA vs. DSS). This is a strange piece of asymmetry, since the client does not get to specify to the server what sort of certificate chain or key type it wants. And SSL/TLS insists on X.500 names, even though X.500 names are rarely if ever used on the Internet, and DNS names are now supported by the PKIX standard. The convention that browsers commonly use for equating a DNS name with an X.500 name is that the common name portion of the X.500 name holds the DNS name of the server and all the other name components in the X.500 name are ignored.

Another issue with the certificate request is that the name of a CA may not be sufficient description, since there might be several keys associated with a name, even possibly incorrectly associated with the name. It would have been better to have sent hashes of public keys.

In SSLv3 and TLS, a chain of certificates can be sent instead of a single certificate.

19.9 VERSION NUMBERS

The SSL/TLS designers had a strange idea about how to use a version number field. SSLv2 has a 2-octet field known as VERSION NUMBER which is set to 0.2 (0 in the high-order octet, 2 in the low-order octet). SSLv3 has a field known as VERSION NUMBER which is set 3.0 (3 in the high-order octet, 0 in the low-order octet). TLS has a field known as VERSION NUMBER which is set to 3.1 (3 in the high-order octet, 1 in the low-order octet). SSLv3 moved the VERSION NUMBER field! So you can't distinguish v2 and v3 messages by looking at the VERSION NUMBER field. An SSLv3 client cannot send an SSLv3 *client-hello* message, unless it knows somehow that the server it is contacting speaks SSLv3, since an SSLv2 server will misparse the packet and get confused. So it sends a v2 client-hello message, but fills in the VERSION NUMBER field as 3.0.

SSLv2 didn't specify what you do if you see a higher version number. Many implementations simply ignore the version number (that means they parse the message, not worrying if the VERSION NUMBER field indicates a higher version of the protocol than they support). SSLv3 and TLS implementations depend on this behavior. This implies of course that everything the client needs to say can be expressed in v2 format, which is true, and which makes you wonder why they needed to change the format for v3.

So an SSLv2 server that receives a message with a higher version number than it supports happily parses the message, assuming that nobody would have changed the message format in a later version of the protocol (even though the designers did just that for version 3!).

The designers of the higher versions were lucky that it is possible to distinguish a v2 message from a v3 or TLS message (if they hadn't moved the VERSION NUMBER field it would have been easy). For instance, it happens that the first octet of the v2 *client-hello* will be greater than 128, and the first octet of the v3 *client-hello* will be something between 20 and 23. There might indeed be other octets in the message that would distinguish v2 and v3. The spec doesn't say how to differentiate the two, which is dangerous, since it's conceivable someone might, in a future version, change the format again, and assume that implementations are differentiating versions based on the first octet when in fact they're looking elsewhere.

So SSLv3 clients send an SSLv2 *client-hello* message, as long as there might be a server out there still speaking SSLv2. Which means that in reality the SSLv3 *client-hello* never gets used, (except when resuming a session with a server that the client discovered was SSLv3). In the SSLv2 *client-hello* message, the v3 client puts the value 3.0. If the server speaks v3, it will respond with a v3 message. However, if the server is v2, it thinks its own version number is 0.2, and will interpret version 3.0 as 3×256+0, or 768. Wow! It never occurs to the SSLv2 server that the message might have gotten redesigned in between version 2 and version 768!

Suppose a v3 client somehow knew it was talking to a v3 server. Then it would be able to send a v3 *client-hello*. But that means that the server had better be able to tell the difference between a v2 *client-hello* and a v3 *client-hello*, since v3 clients that know that the server speaks v3 will send v3 *client-hello*s, while v2 clients or v3 clients that don't know what version the server speaks will send v2 *client-hello*s.

How does an SSLv3 client encode what it would like in an SSLv2 *client-hello*? Luckily there's nothing in the SSLv3 *client-hello* that can't easily be encoded in an SSLv2 *client-hello*. One interesting field is CIPHER SUITE, which had a 3-octet encoding in SSLv2 and a 2-octet encoding in SSLv3. It's easy to fit a 2-octet value into a 3-octet field. The reverse would have been more challenging. (See section §19.10 *Negotiating Cipher Suites*.)

It would be nice if the SSLv3 designers learned their lesson about version numbers based on the kludginess of v2/v3 interoperability, and had a fixed place in the packet for version number, and specified that a node that didn't support the higher version number should not attempt to parse the packet further but instead send back a message specifying the largest version it supported. But SSLv3 (and TLS) do the same thing SSLv2 did. If they see a higher version number, they happily parse the packet as if all future messages will be compatible with their version.

SSLv2 does not integrity-protect the *client-hello*. Therefore it's possible for an active attacker to modify a v3 client's v2 *client-hello* by changing the version number from 768 (SSLv3) or 769 (TLS) to 2. SSLv3 and TLS have a cute method of detecting this tampering despite the fact that the SSLv2 handshake doesn't explicitly protect against it. SSLv3 and TLS specify 3s as the least significant eight octets of the PKCS #1 padding (see §6.3.6.1 *Encryption*) when the client sends the pre-master secret (*S*) to the server.

So, if a v3 or TLS server receives a *client-hello* with version 2 and with the *S* value padding having 3s in the least significant eight octets, it breaks the connection and should issue an error. There is a 1 in 2^{64} chance that a v2 client might just happen to choose padding with the least significant eight octets being 3s, in which case its connection will get mysteriously rejected.

19.10 NEGOTIATING CIPHER SUITES

A cipher suite is a complete package (encryption algorithm, key length, integrity checksum algorithm—whatever needs to be defined in order to completely specify all the crypto SSL/TLS will need). Cipher suites are predefined and each is assigned a numeric value. In SSLv2 the value is 3 octets long, but in SSLv3 and TLS, it's 2 octets. This mercifully limits the number of suites that could potentially be defined in SSLv3/TLS to about 65000.

There are about 30 defined cipher suites, and there are 256 values reserved for private use (the ones with the most significant octet = ff_{16}. Private use values that have no way of coordinating their use are dangerous. You can define your own suite and choose any number out of the 256 reserved numbers for describing it. But there's no guarantee someone else won't define their own private suite and choose the same number. If two such systems attempt to talk, they'll think they are agreeing on the same suite, but in fact they will not interoperate.

In v2, each cipher suite had a 3-octet value. In v3, each is 2 octets. The way to specify a v3 cipher suite in the 3-octet v2 field is to set the most significant octet to 0, and have the v3 cipher suite value in the remaining 2 octets. Luckily, no v2 cipher suites had been defined with the most significant octet=0, so there was a convenient block of 2^{16} unused cipher suite values.

19.10.1 Who Makes the Decision?

In SSLv2, Bob returns the subset of Alice's suggested cipher suites that he is willing to support, but lets Alice make the final choice and announce it in message 3. (This is kind of silly, since Alice already said she'd support everything in her list. Bob should just pick one. Indeed one of the enhancements in SSLv3 is that Bob does make the choice, from the list Alice sent. If there's more than one that both he and Alice find acceptable, he makes the decision. And he could in theory make the decision in v2 by only returning one cipher suite rather than many.)

Not all supportable crypto suites are equal. The side choosing the suite will choose the most desirable (perhaps the strongest, or the fastest) one it can from the set of crypto suites that both sides support. An exportable suite is chosen only as a last resort (since the exportable suites are purposely weak).

19.10.2 Cipher Suite Names

Although cipher suites have 2-octet (or 3-octet in SSLv2) identifiers, they are referred to in the spec by names such as SSL_RSA_EXPORT_WITH_DES40_CBC_SHA:

- SSL means SSLv3, (the SSLv2 cipher suites have names starting with SSL2, e.g., SSL2_RC4_128_WITH_MD5),
- RSA means RSA,
- EXPORT means it's exportable (i.e., weak crypto, exportable before the rules were relaxed),
- WITH means the names weren't long enough,

- DES40 means DES with 40 bit keys,
- CBC means CBC-mode encryption, and
- SHA means HMAC-SHA is used for the MAC.

19.11 Negotiating Compression Method

Due to patent issues, only one compression method has been defined, which is NULL (type=0), the compression method that does not change the data. It is the belief of the TLS committee that implementing the NULL compression method will not infringe on any patents.

19.12 Attacks Fixed in V3

19.12.1 Downgrade Attack

In SSLv2, there is no integrity protection for the initial handshake, so an active attacker can remove the cipher suites with strong encryption from the list of requested cipher suites, causing Alice and Bob to agree upon a weaker cipher. In SSLv3 this was fixed by adding a *finished* message to the end of the initial handshake in which each side sends a digest of the messages in the handshake.

19.12.2 Truncation Attack

SSLv3 added a *finished* message to indicate that there is no more data to send. V2 depended on the TCP connection closing. But the TCP connection close is not cryptographically protected, so an attacker could close the connection by sending a TCP close message, and the other side would not be able to know that the session was abnormally terminated. Some applications have a way of specifying when the data is finished, but applications that don't might be fooled into incorrect behavior.

19.13 EXPORTABILITY

The acrobatics we had to go through back in the dark ages of export control! Even if export controls have been permanently relaxed, we have to understand the mechanisms they engendered, since that is what is deployed and what must be implemented in order to be compatible with what was deployed. The simplest thing to have done with export controls was to always use weak crypto, even domestically. But it was legal to deploy strong crypto domestically, so complex mechanisms were built in order to make something that could be as secure as possible within the political constraints, and have the domestic and exportable versions interoperate.

19.13.1 Exportability in SSLv2

SSLv2 domestic clients supported 128-bit encryption. But the U.S. government limited exportable cryptographic keys to 40 bits. Some "exportable" suites were defined for SSLv2 which effectively used a 40-bit encryption key even though the actual cryptographic algorithm used a 128-bit key. In these exportable suites, instead of sending a 128-bit secret encrypted with the server's public key, the client sends a 40-bit secret encrypted with the server's public key, and sends an additional 88 bits in the clear. So in a non-exportable suite, there will be 128 secret bits. In an exportable suite, there will be 40 secret bits and 88 non-secret bits. So in either case there are 128 bits, which are known in SSLv2 as the **client master key** (not a terrific name for a quantity in which most of the bits are not secret). This key is used to produce the session keys.

Interestingly, the export laws were that encryption was limited to 40-bit secret keys and 512-bit RSA encryption keys, the latter normally used to encrypt secret keys. This is kind of weird, because if the encryption key is 40 bits, why should they care if it's sent encrypted in a really long RSA key? Or likewise, if they felt they could break 512-bit RSA, why couldn't you use a long encryption key as long as it had been sent across the wire encrypted with a short (512-bit) RSA key? But non-weird was never an important consideration in export rules.

So exportable servers had 512-bit RSA keys. Domestic servers had large RSA keys (e.g., 1024 bits). If a domestic server were talking to an exportable client, the client would wind up sending its 40-bit secret in the domestic server's large RSA key, which was technically illegal but apparently nobody noticed until after the protocol was approved and shipped. At that point, they agreed to let SSLv2 continue to be exported, with clients that would encrypt a 40-bit key in a 1024-bit RSA key, though they warned the designers they would not approve the same approach in SSLv3.

19.13.2 Exportability in SSLv3

In SSLv3 the pre-master secret sent by the client (and encrypted with the server's public key) is always a 48-octet number, but only 46 octets are random. The other two octets are used for version number. In the domestic version the pre-master secret is hashed with the *R*s to produce the master secret, and the master secret is hashed with the *R*s to produce the stream from which the six data protection keys are extracted.

If the cipher suite negotiated is exportable, then the integrity keys are computed as before, because export rules did not preclude strong integrity, but only 40 bits are extracted for each of the two encryption keys. And (due to someone's misunderstanding of the export rules), the IVs are computed solely from the two *R*s, so for the exportable cipher suites, the IVs are not secret. The export rules would have allowed strong IVs, but non-secret IVs are not a security vulnerability anyway.

But the 40 bits are only seeds for the encryption keys. These 40-bit seeds are hashed with the two *R*s to produce 128-bit keys. The reason for this step is similar to the reason for using salt: although there is still only a work factor of 2^{40} for breaking any individual encrypted session, you couldn't build up a table of 2^{40} keys for all sessions, since although there are only 2^{40} possible keys in any one session, the total number of possible keys is 2^{128} (for encryption algorithms with 128-bit keys).

But wait! 40-bit encryption keys wasn't sufficient to meet export restrictions. It was also a crime to send the 40-bit secret encrypted with an RSA key larger than 512 bits. A domestic server would have a 1024-bit RSA key, and might be speaking to an exportable client. It wouldn't be legal for the client to send its pre-master secret encrypted with a 1024-bit RSA key.

SSLv3 solves this problem by having the server (Bob) generate at random a 512-bit RSA key. This key can be changed periodically and is signed by Bob using his long-term key. The 512-bit key is known as the **ephemeral key**. In SSLv2 the client chose the cipher suite, but in SSLv3, since the server chooses the cipher suite, Bob figures out from the client's list of cipher suites in message 1 (and his own cipher suite capabilities) if he needs to be speaking exportable crypto. So in message 2, if Bob chooses an exportable cipher suite, then, in addition to sending his regular certificate (the one certifying his long-term key), Bob sends his 512-bit ephemeral key, signed using his long-term key. The client then sends the pre-master secret encrypted with Bob's ephemeral key.

This could have been implemented in a way that improved performance by having Bob sign the 512-bit ephemeral key once and use it for many connections. He would then only have to do a 512-bit private key operation for each connection instead of having to use the longer key. But doing so would have introduced a security vulnerability since someone who learned or broke a single 512-bit key could impersonate Bob indefinitely. Rather than putting an expiration time under the signature and risking clock synchronization problems, the protocol requires that Bob sign a combination of the ephemeral public key and the two nonces.

Aside from the performance penalty, in a perverse way, this hack, created for exportability, enhances security, because it allows weak-key perfect forward secrecy. Once Bob forgets the ephemeral private key, it would require breaking the 512-bit ephemeral public key or the 40-bit encryption key in order to decrypt the conversation, whereas with the non-exportable cipher suites, someone obtaining Bob's long-term private key would be able to directly decrypt previous conversations. So ironically, the NSA would have been better off with the SSLv2 solution. Although this perfect forward secrecy solution would have been useful in the non-exportable case, it is not supported in any server.

19.13.3 Server Gated Cryptography/Step-Up

The U.S. allowed an exported client to use strong cryptography when talking to some servers doing financial transactions. This meant that the client had to have all the code necessary for doing strong cryptography. But it would only use strong cryptography if the server's certificate specified that the server was one with which the client was allowed to speak strong crypto. This concept was implemented by both Netscape and Microsoft, but called **SGC** (**Server Gated Cryptography**) by Microsoft and **Step-Up** by Netscape. The protocols are slightly different, and the certificate extensions are different, since they were independently developed.

Whereas the usual certificates would be honored if signed with a chain starting with any of the trust anchors, the SGC certificate had to be signed by Verisign or Thawte (but Verisign bought Thawte so it was just Verisign), since this wasn't a matter of whom the client trusted, but whom the U.S. government trusted. Whereas the set of trust anchors for regular certificates could be modified by the user, the trusted SGC-certificate issuer(s) were wired into the implementation.

In the Step-Up exchange between an exportable client (Alice) with Step-Up capability and a server (Bob) with the Step-Up extension in its Verisign-signed certificate, there is the usual initial exchange (see Protocol 19-1) in which Alice offers only weak (exportable) crypto suites, Bob selects one of the weak suites, and they complete an exchange with a 40-bit key K_1. But Alice notices the Step-Up extension in Bob's certificate, so she continues with another handshake, with the handshake protected with K_1. (Once an SSL connection is established, handshake messages are allowed as well as data messages, so it is possible to conduct a new handshake protected by the keys established by the previous handshake.) In the new exchange, Alice proposes strong crypto and Bob accepts a strong cipher, and the new handshake completes, this time agreeing upon a strong key K_2. Then Alice sends a ChangeCipherSpec message, indicating a change from the weak crypto suite and key K_1 to the strong crypto suite and key K_2.

This might seem like a lot of messages, but this protocol would allow a server without special Step-Up code to speak strong crypto as long as it is given a certificate with the Step-Up option. Microsoft's SGC protocol is more efficient, but requires the server to have code that supports a new SGC exchange in addition to a certificate with the SGC extension.

In SGC, Alice's message 1 offers weak crypto, and Bob's message 2 sends his certificate, and has him choose one of Alice's weak crypto suite offers. Alice notices the SGC extension in Bob's Verisign-signed certificate, and Alice then sends a new *client-hello*, this time offering strong crypto suites. This would confuse a server that did not have special SGC code, because it wouldn't expect a second *client-hello* within the same TCP connection.

19.14 ENCODING

The packet encodings in the SSL/TLS specifications are expressed in a pseudo-ASN.1 syntax that is very unpleasant to read and makes it difficult to imagine what the packets actually look like. Hopefully you will appreciate our translating them into pictures here. The problem with the ugly syntax in the spec is that not only does it give the reader a headache, but it resulted in weird formats, for instance redundant fields, and implementation bugs (e.g., see §19.14.2.4 *ClientKeyExchange*).

Since SSL/TLS runs on top of TCP, SSL/TLS can send an arbitrary-length chunk. TCP will handle breaking it up into packets and reassembling it. SSL/TLS has two layers of chunking itself, which operate somewhat independently. The unit of cryptographic protection is the **record**, which contains a header and a body, where the body is cryptographically protected if the protocol is far enough along. Records are limited to 2^{14} octets by the specification, but there are buggy implementations that send records of up to $2^{16}-1$ octets so a conservative implementation should be prepared to accept records up to that size. The parts of the handshake are divided into **messages**, which also contain a header and a body. In principle, a single message could be packaged in multiple records or multiple messages could be placed in a single record. In practice, most implementations combine the two layers and put one message in each record.

It would have been simpler (and more efficient) for each message to be its own record type, and to have only a single header on each handshake message. But instead the designers chose to have four record types, with most of the handshake messages being enclosed in records of type handshake. A handshake record can contain multiple messages in it, whereas the other records are really free-standing messages. If the server is going to send a *ServerHello*, a *Certificate*, and a *ServerHelloDone* (all of which are handshake messages), these could be sent as three records, or lumped together into a single record, or two of them could be in one record and the third in another record.

The four record types are:

- 20=ChangeCipherSpec. This is really part of the handshake, and it's rather strange to have it be its own record type. The reason they did this is that after the *ChangeCipherSpec* message the data is encrypted and integrity-protected with the key just agreed upon. It would not be possible for only part of a record to be encrypted, so *ChangeCipherSpec* had to be the last thing in a record. They could have had this be a handshake message, mandating that it be the final message in the record. But instead they said that it would be its own record type.

- 21=alert (any sort of notification)
- 22=handshake (any of many messages which is part of the handshake)
- 23=application_data (encrypted and integrity-protected data sent after the handshake is complete)

The record header, which is never encrypted, is:

# octets	
1	record type
2	version number
2	length

Following the record header is the contents of that record, which might be encrypted and integrity-protected. In the case of the handshake record, the record contains handshake messages, each message starting with a 1-octet type and a 3-octet length. It's somewhat mysterious why they would choose a 3-octet length field for the messages and a 2-octet length field for the record, but in theory if there were a message that was bigger than 2^{14} octets, it could be split into several records. So the 2-octet length of the record length field does not constrain messages to be smaller than 2^{16} octets. All multi-octet integers are sent in big-endian order (also known as network byte order).

19.14.1 Encrypted Records

Records sent after a *ChangeCipherSpec* record are cryptographically protected with the negotiated cipher suite. Integrity protection is provided using HMAC based on MD5 or SHA-1. Encryption uses any of a variety of encryption algorithms, all of which are block ciphers in CBC mode except RC4, which is a stream cipher.

HMAC takes two arguments, a key and data. The key used is the session integrity key for that direction. The data on which the HMAC is based consists of a 64-bit sequence number followed by the record header followed by the data. The sequence number is not actually transmitted. It only is used in the calculation of the HMAC. It protects against ordering and replay, but does not need to be explicitly transmitted because SSL runs over a reliable protocol (TCP). If TCP failed somehow and lost, reordered, or duplicated data, the two sides would disagree about the sequence number, the integrity check would fail, and this would result in a connection failure.

If a block cipher is to be used for encryption, the DATA | HMAC is padded to a multiple of the block size. Then DATA | HMAC | padding is encrypted. If a block cipher is used, the initial IV is computed along with the key and the final block of each record is used as the IV for the next.

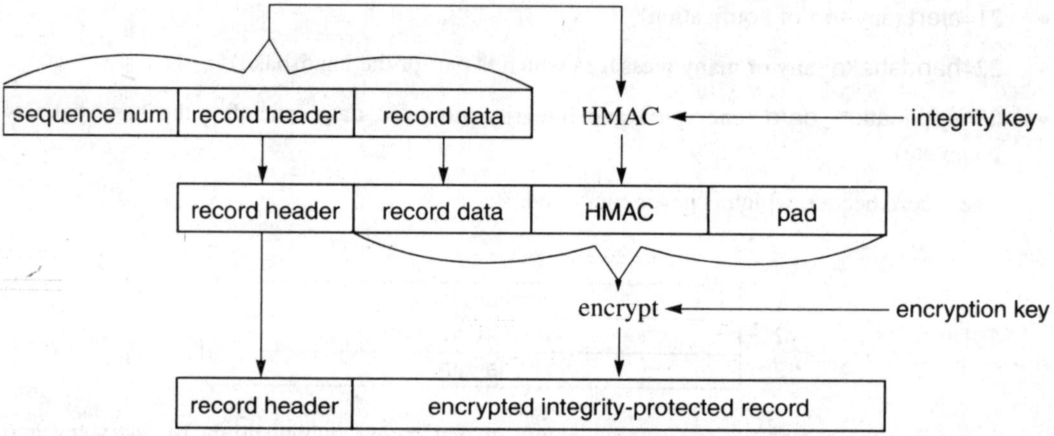

Figure 19-4. Cryptographically protected record format

For TLS, HMAC is computed as specified in RFC 2104. For SSLv3, the MAC is computed in a similar fashion, but is different both because the HMAC design was still evolving and they got an early draft and because a typographical error resulted in 40 octets of padding in a spot where there should have been 44. Neither of these differences is likely to affect the security, but they do complicate the documentation.

To summarize, what is transmitted is the record header, followed by an encrypted blob which, when decrypted, consists of the data followed by the HMAC, followed by padding including the padding length.

19.14.2 Handshake Messages

A handshake record (type 22) contains handshake messages. The specification allows someone to break a handshake message into pieces, and send each piece in a separate handshake record. It is also permissible for the handshake record to contain multiple handshake messages. For instance, the server might send a *ServerHello*, a *Certificate*, a *CertificateRequest*, and a *ServerHelloDone*, all within the same handshake record. The handshake messages are *ClientHello*, *ServerHello*, *ClientKeyExchange*, *Certificate*, *ServerHelloDone*, *HandshakeFinished*, *CertificateRequest*, *CertificateVerify*, and *ServerKeyExchange*.

19.14.2.1 ClientHello

# octets	
1	type=1
3	length
2	version number
32	random (R_{Alice})
1	length of session_id (or 0 if field absent)
variable	session_id
2	length of cipher suite list (in octets)
variable	sequence of cipher suites, each a 2-octet type
1	length of compression list (in octets)
variable	sequence of compression methods, each a single octet

This message contains the optional session_id (to allow a session to be resumed; see §19.5 *Session Resumption*), R_{Alice}, and Alice's list of cipher suites and compression methods.

19.14.2.2 ServerHello

# octets	
1	type=2
3	length
2	version number
32	random (R_{Bob})
1	length of session_id (or 0 if field absent)
variable	session_id
2	chosen cipher
1	chosen compression method

This message contains R_{Bob}, an optional session_id (to allow the session to be resumable), and Bob's choice of cipher and compression method.

19.14.2.3 ServerHelloDone

# octets	
1	type=14
3	length=0

This indicates that the server is finished sending its handshake messages. It is the final piece of message 2 in Protocol 19-1. It just has a type octet (=14) and a length field (3 octets of 0).

19.14.2.4 ClientKeyExchange

# octets	
1	type=16
3	length
2	length (missing in SSLv3, present in TLS)
variable	encrypted pre-master secret

This is the message in which Alice sends the pre-master secret encrypted with the server's public key. Note the extra length field. It serves no purpose with RSA or Diffie-Hellman. It was in the SSLv3 specification, but not in any implementations. TLS copied the SSLv3 spec, so left the extra length field in. As we said earlier, it is an artifact of the packet specification language they invented, and so difficult to read and visualize that it resulted not only in extra fields but implementation bugs.

Redundant length fields are a problem. At best it's extra work to set and look at them, and extra octets on the wire. And what are you supposed to do if they disagree? Also, note that the second length field is only 2 octets long and the first one is 3 octets long. If the length never needs to be larger than can be expressed in two octets, why is the other length field 3 octets?

Although the second length field is redundant in RSA and Diffie-Hellman, there are key exchange algorithms such as FORTEZZA that require multiple variable length fields to express the encrypted pre-master secret. Also, future algorithms might require more than 2^{16} octets of information. The information following the 3-octet length field is algorithm dependent, so they could have left out the 2nd length field for RSA and Diffie-Hellman, but had the data for FORTEZZA consist of (length, value) pairs.

19.14.2.5 ServerKeyExchange

# octets	
1	type=12
3	length
2	length of modulus
variable	modulus
2	length of exponent
variable	exponent
2	length of signature
variable	signature

This message is used in SSLv3 and TLS for export approval, in which the server signs a (short) ephemeral public key, signed with its long-term key. Instead of sending an X.509 certificate, it is just a signature on the new key. It is also used when the server's long-term public key can only be used for signing, for instance when the server's key is a DSS key.

19.14.2.6 CertificateRequest

# octets	
1	type=13
3	length
1	length of key type list
variable	list of types of keys (each one octet long)
2	length of CA name list
2	length of 1st CA name
variable	1st CA name
2	length of 2nd CA name
variable	2nd CA name
2	length of 3rd CA name
variable	3rd CA name
	...
2	length of last CA name
variable	last CA name

This message is sent by the server to request that the client send a certificate and authenticate. See §19.8 *PKI as Deployed by SSL*. There are several defined "key types", which not only specify the kind of key, but the kind of authentication method the user will use to authenticate. The most commonly used is type 1=RSA signing.

19.14.2.7 Certificate

# octets	
1	type=11
3	length
3	length (unnecessary field)
3	length of first certificate
variable	first certificate
variable	more (3-octet length, certificate) pairs, if more than one certificate is being sent

This message contains one or more certificates. Note this also contains a redundant length field. The second length field will always be 3 less than the first length field (since the first length field includes the second length field in the number of octets it is counting).

19.14.2.8 CertificateVerify

# octets	
1	type=15
3	length
2	length of signature
variable	signature

This message is sent by the client to prove it knows its private key. The signature (in the case of RSA, which is really all that's deployed), is a modified PKCS #1 RSA-signed quantity consisting of both the MD5 of the handshake messages and the SHA of the handshake messages. The modification to PKCS #1 is that the ASN.1 encoded digest type is omitted and the MD5 and the SHA digests are concatenated.

19.14.2.9 HandshakeFinished

# octets	
1	type=20
3	length=36 or 12
36 or 12	digest

This message ensures integrity of the exchange as well as proving knowledge of the key. In SSLv3 the digest, strangely, is a 36-octet quantity consisting of a concatenation of a 16-octet keyed MD5 hash and 20-octet keyed SHA hash of information including the handshake messages. In TLS the digest is 12 octets computed with a complex combination of MD5 and SHA.

19.14.3 ChangeCipherSpec

# octets	
1	record type=20
2	version number
2	length (set to 1)
1	ChangeCipherSpecType (set to 1)

This isn't a handshake message, but is instead its own record type. It indicates that all records following this will be protected with the ciphers agreed upon as of this message. The final field (CHANGECIPHERSPECTYPE) is mysterious. Only one value (1) has been defined, which means *change to the cipher suite we've agreed to now.* It's unclear when you would want to say anything other than that. But, if someone thinks of a new thing to say, they can define a new value for that field.

19.14.4 Alerts

An alert is sent to advise the other side of some condition. Most alerts are error messages, with a severity level of either 1=warning, or 2=fatal. The one defined alert which is not an error indication is the *closure* alert, in which one side notifies the other that it has no more data to send. This was added in SSLv3 because of a security vulnerability in SSLv2 known as the truncation attack. SSLv2 assumed the other side was finished sending data if the TCP connection closed. However, because TCP commands are not cryptographically protected, there is no way to know whether the TCP connection closed because the other side closed the TCP connection when it finished sending all its data, or an attacker sent the TCP command to close the connection.

19.15 FURTHER READING

Aside from the RFCs (RFC 2246 for TLS, www.netscape.com/eng/security/SSL_2.html for SSLv2, and home.netscape.com/eng/security/ssl3/index.html for SSLv3), we recommend the book *SSL and TLS: Designing and Building Secure Systems* by Eric Rescorla, published by Addison Wesley, 2000. The book goes beyond the specs in offering implementation tips and showing packet traces.

19.16 EASY HOMEWORK

1. What are the implications of SSL being implemented at layer 4, contrasted with IPsec's being implemented at layer 3?
2. If there is no integrity protection on Alice's initial message, how can an active attacker force Alice and Bob to agree on weaker crypto?
3. Compare the session resumption mechanisms in SSL and Lotus Notes.

19.17 HOMEWORK

1. As explained in §19.9 *Version Numbers*, the VERSION NUMBER field in v2 messages is in a different place from the VERSION NUMBER in v3 messages. Therefore, if a v3 client is not sure what version number the server is, it will send a v2-formatted *ClientHello* with the VERSION NUMBER field marked as 3.0, and hope that a v2 server will ignore the VERSION NUMBER and otherwise process the message. If the v3 client *does* know the server is v3, it will send a v3-formatted *ClientHello*. This explains why a v3 server must be able to receive either v2 or v3 messages, and distinguish them. Under what scenario would a v3 client not be able to predict whether it will receive a v2 message or a v3 message from a particular server?
2. Compare the performance of doing PFS as implemented in SSLv3, vs. the recommended modification in §19.13.2 *Exportability in SSLv3* vs. doing a Diffie-Hellman exchange for each connection. Assume the ephemeral key pair is of adequate length, rather than done to meet export rules. Assume also that PFS doesn't need to be "perfect", but rather the ephemeral key can change, say, every hour, and the cost of generating the key pair can be amortized over all the connection requests that occur during that hour.
3. What is the advantage, in the exportable SSLv3 case, of hashing the 40-bit secret with two non-secret values to produce a 128-bit key? How many keys would have to be tested to brute-force break a single session?

PART 4

ELECTRONIC MAIL

20 Electronic Mail Security

This chapter gives an overview of the issues involved in making electronic mail secure. First we discuss non-security-related issues such as distribution lists and mail forwarders. Then we list various security features, and in the remainder of the chapter we describe how each of these features might be implemented. A lot of the techniques are equally applicable to encrypting or integrity-protecting any sort of data, such as files kept on a file server or data stored on backup media. In the following chapters we discuss particular secure mail standards—S/MIME, PEM, and PGP. Another standard, X.400, was a collaboration between CCITT and ISO. The security aspects of it were never fully specified and never caught on, though some of the terminology has caught on, and some of the concepts (such as proof of delivery) are interesting to mention, since these concepts are not in S/MIME, PEM, or PGP. We won't discuss X.400 in detail, but we will mention some of the functionality the designers envisioned.

20.1 Distribution Lists

Electronic mail allows a user to send a message to one or more recipients. The simplest form of electronic mail message is where Alice sends a message to Bob.

```
To: Bob
From: Alice

Care to meet me in my apartment tonight?
```

Usually, a mail system allows a message to be sent to multiple recipients, for example:

```
To: Bob, Carol, Ted
From: Alice

Care to meet me in my apartment tonight?
```

Sometimes it is impossible or inconvenient to list all recipients. For this reason, mail is often sent to a **distribution list**, a name that stands for a set of recipients. For instance, a message might be sent to Taxpayers. There are two ways of implementing distribution lists.

The first way involves sending the message to a site at which the list is maintained, and that site then sends a copy of the message to each recipient on the list. We'll call that the **remote exploder method**.

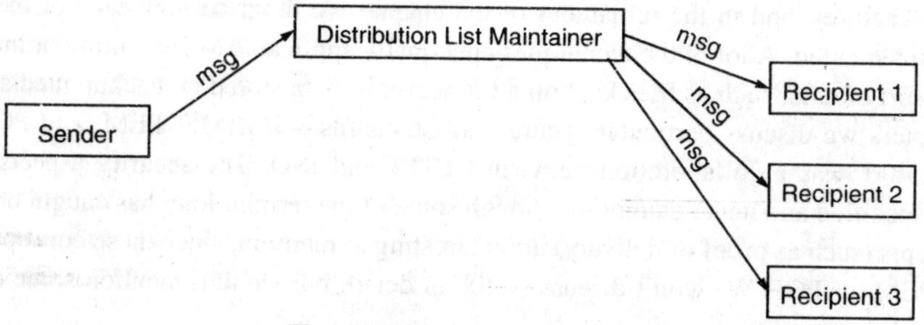

Figure 20-1. Remote Exploder

The second method is for the sender to retrieve the list from the site where it is kept, and then send a copy of the message to each recipient on the list. We'll call that the **local exploder method**.

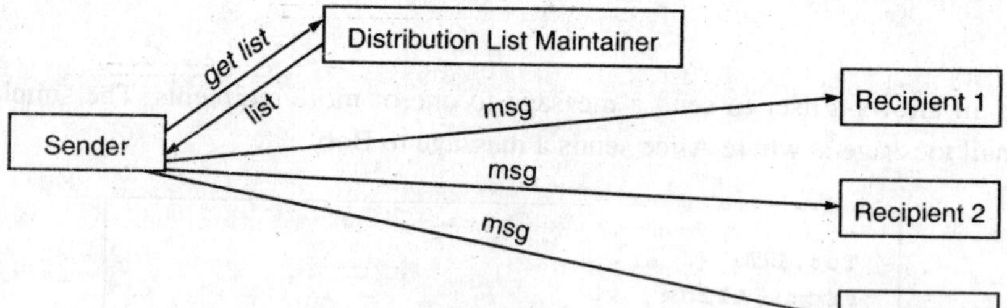

Figure 20-2. Local Exploder

Sometimes a member of a distribution list can be another distribution list. For instance, the mailing list Security Customers, used to advertise security products, might include law enforcers, bankers, Democratic National Committee, locksmiths, and members of organized crime. It is possible to construct a distribution list with an infinite loop. Suppose someone is maintaining a mailing list for cryptographers. Someone else is maintaining one for cryptanalysts. The cryptanalysts point out that they also want to hear the information sent to the cryptographers mailing list, so the distribution list Cryptanalysts is added to the Cryptographers mailing list. And for similar reasons Cryptographers is added to Cryptanalysts. The mail system must handle infinite loops in distribution lists in a reasonable manner, i.e., it must send each recipient at least one copy of each message but not an unreasonable number of copies of any. Loops like this effectively merge the mailing lists. (See Homework Problem 1.)

As we described above, there are two methods of implementing distribution lists. The advantages of the local exploder method are:

- It is easier to prevent mail forwarding loops.
- If there are multiple distribution lists, it is possible for the sender to prevent duplicate copies being sent to individuals on multiple lists.
- If the network billing is usage-based as opposed to flat-fee, it is easier for the sender to know in advance just how much bandwidth will be consumed to transmit the message.

There are several advantages to the remote exploder method:

- It allows you to send to a list whose membership you are not allowed to know. (*To U.S. spies living abroad from the IRS: friendly reminder—the tax deadline is April 15. Being caught or killed is not one of the grounds for automatic extension.*)
- If distribution lists are organized geographically, you need only send one copy of a message over an expensive link to a remote area. (*To Citizens of France from the U.S. government: Thanks for the big statue.*)
- When the distribution list is longer than the message, it is more efficient to send the message from the sender to the distribution list site than to send the distribution list to the sender. (*To people of planet earth: Greeting. Unless you stop transmitting reruns of the I Love Lucy show to us we will be forced to destroy your planet.*)
- When distribution lists are included on distribution lists, it would be time-consuming to track down the whole tree to get to all the individuals. Instead, the message can be making progress as it is sent to the various exploders. Parallelism is exploited.

20.2 STORE AND FORWARD

The simplest implementation of electronic mail consists of sending a message directly from the source machine to the destination machine. In order for a message to be successfully delivered under that scenario, it is necessary for both the source and destination machines to be running, and reachable from each other on the network. This might be especially inconvenient if the user machines are only occasionally connected to the network, for example a portable PC that dials into the network periodically. Thus came the concept of electronic post office boxes. Instead of sending mail directly to the user's workstation, the mail is instead sent to a machine which is more or less permanently on the network. When the user's workstation attaches to the network, it reads the mail from the appropriate mail storage machine.

In general, the **mail infrastructure** consists of a whole mesh of mail forwarders. X.400 calls them **Message Transfer Agents**, or **MTAs**. The mail processing at the source and destination machines is done by a program known by X.400 as the **User Agent** or **UA**. Mail is not simply sent from the source machine to a mailbox machine for the destination. Instead, it gets forwarded from UA to MTA to ... to MTA to UA.

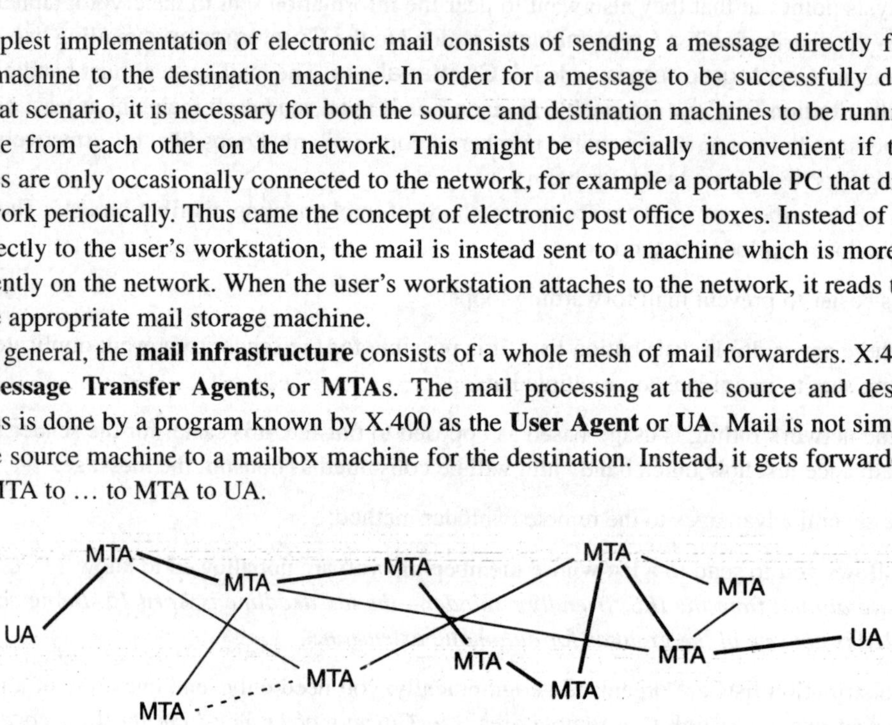

Figure 20-3. Mail Infrastructure Operation

Some reasons for needing multiple MTAs along a path from source to destination are:

- The path from source to destination might be intermittent. For instance, there might be portions of the network that are only occasionally connected, via some dial-up link.
- For security reasons, the MTAs might need to authenticate other MTAs as well as user machines. It might then be necessary to have a chain of MTAs to find a path from source to destination where each link is between a pair of MTAs that trust one another.
- For security reasons, a company might want a **security gateway**, a place through which all mail has to be forwarded. Usually the purpose of such a gateway is to prevent any access to the company's network except for mail. For instance, it would prevent people from logging in from a site external to the company's network.

- Different parts of the network might be using different protocol suites, for instance TCP/IP in some places and OSI in others.

There are interesting issues with how one supports routing with MTAs.

- How do MTAs find out about "neighbor" MTAs? This is usually done with manual configuration, though potentially they might be able to find each other in a directory service.
- How do MTAs compute a path to a destination, or at least find the next "closer" MTA? Again, this is usually done with manual configuration.

20.3 SECURITY SERVICES FOR ELECTRONIC MAIL

This section describes the kinds of security services one might desire for electronic mail. In following sections we describe how these features might be implemented. Most electronic mail systems do not provide most of these features. Even those designed specifically for security often only provide for some of these features.

- **privacy**—the ability to keep anyone but the intended recipient from reading the message. (see §20.5 *Privacy*)
- **authentication**—reassurance to the recipient of the identity of the sender. (see §20.6 *Authentication of the Source*)
- **integrity**—reassurance to the recipient that the message has not been altered since it was transmitted by the sender. (see §20.7 *Message Integrity*)
- **non-repudiation**—the ability of the recipient to prove to a third party that the sender really did send the message. This feature is also sometimes called **third party authentication**. The term *non-repudiation* means that the sender cannot later deny sending the message. (see §20.8 *Non-Repudiation*)
- **proof of submission**—verification given to the sender that the message was handed to the mail delivery system (the same basic idea as sending certified mail through the U.S. postal service). With certified postal mail you just receive proof that you sent something to a particular address on a particular date, but with electronic mail it is possible to have the mail system verify acceptance of the contents of a particular message, perhaps by signing the message digest of the contents of the message. (see §20.9 *Proof of Submission*)
- **proof of delivery**—verification that the recipient received the message. Postal mail has a similar feature (return receipt requested), but again it only verifies that something was deliv-

ered on a particular date to the recipient. With electronic mail it is possible to verify the contents, as we mentioned under proof of submission. (see §20.10 *Proof of Delivery*)

- **message flow confidentiality**—an extension of privacy such that Carol not only cannot know the content of the message Alice sent Bob, but cannot even determine whether Alice sent Bob a message. (see §20.11 *Message Flow Confidentiality*)
- **anonymity**—the ability to send a message so that the recipient can't find out the identity of the sender. (see §20.12 *Anonymity*)
- **containment**—the ability of the network to keep certain security levels of information from leaking out of a particular region. Methods for implementing this are in §20.13 *Containment*.
- **audit**—the ability of the network to record events that might have some security relevance, such as that Alice sent a message to Bob on a particular date. This would be fairly straightforward to implement, but is not mentioned in any of the secure mail standards, so we don't have a section on it.
- **accounting**—the ability of the mail system to maintain system usage statistics. In addition to providing clues for system resource management, this information allows the mail system to charge its clients according to their usage. For example, the system might charge by number of messages sent, as long as the system itself authenticates the source of each message to ensure that the proper party is billed. Again, there's not much to say about this, so we don't have a separate section on it.
- **self destruct**—an option allowing a sender to specify that a message should be destroyed after delivery to the recipient. This allows Alice to send a message to Bob that Bob cannot forward or store. The mail system will decrypt and display the message, but then delete it. (*Good morning Mr. Phelps...*). This can be implemented by marking the message as a *self-destruct* message, and having the mail program at the destination cooperate by deleting the message immediately after displaying it.
- **message sequence integrity**—reassurance that an entire sequence of messages arrived in the order transmitted, without any loss.

20.4 ESTABLISHING KEYS

Most security services are best provided by cryptographic means. But cryptography requires keys. If Alice wants to send a message to Bob, what keys does she have to know? How does she reliably and efficiently learn these keys? Who is involved in sending mail between Alice and Bob? Well,

Alice and Bob, of course. But there's also the mail infrastructure. And there might be distribution list exploders. In some cases keys are shared between Alice and Bob. In other cases keys are shared between Alice and the mail infrastructure. In still others, it might be between Alice and the distribution list exploder, and between the distribution list exploder and Bob.

For now, we'll explain how Alice and Bob establish the proper keys between each other. The mechanisms depend on whether public keys or secret keys are being used. When we discuss specific services, we'll explain who needs keys.

20.4.1 Establishing Public Keys

If Alice wants to send a signed message to Bob, she can just sign the message and send it, either hoping Bob will already have her certificate, can obtain it if necessary, or she can include her certificate in the email message. However, if she wants to send an encrypted message to Bob, she needs to know his public key before she can construct the message. There are various methods by which she may discover Bob's public key:

- she might have received Bob's public key through some secure out-of-band mechanism, and installed it on her workstation
- she might obtain it through a PKI (e.g., looking it up in a directory) (see Chapter 15 *PKI (Public Key Infrastructure)*)
- the email system could allow piggybacking of certificates (and perhaps CRLs) on email messages. Alice can send her certificates by sending Bob a signed message. If she doesn't already know Bob's public key, she can request that he send her a signed email message with his certificates (and perhaps relevant CRLs) attached.

20.4.2 Establishing Secret Keys

How can Alice and Bob establish a shared secret key for email? The simplest way is with some other means of private communication, for instance by meeting in person in a private place, or by talking on the phone (if they aren't paranoid about the phone being tapped). This strategy is OK for a few scattered private parties, but doesn't scale well at all.

A more scalable strategy would be for Alice to obtain a ticket for Bob from a KDC (see §11.4 *Mediated Authentication (with KDC)*), and include that ticket with her first message to Bob.

20.5 PRIVACY

Most people think that electronic mail is private. But there are many ways in which inquiring minds can read your messages:

- An eavesdropper can listen to the message while it is being transmitted on the wire. Perhaps the network provides link encryption, in which case this one threat is avoided.
- Relay nodes (routers or mail forwarders) might have software to store messages and divulge them to people other than the intended recipients. The relay node might be doing that because it has been compromised by a bad guy, or it might be the intended function of the node. For instance the relay node might be a security gateway, and the owners of the network may want the ability to monitor mail to and from the outside.

There are often conflicting security needs. Alice wants to keep the contents of her message to Bob private. But Alice's employer might want the capability of monitoring her mail to ensure she isn't revealing company secrets. Another example is that citizens might want to be able to carry on private conversations, but their government might want to be able, under appropriate circumstances (of course), to monitor all communications.

20.5.1 End-to-End Privacy

Alice might want to send a message to Bob in such a way that only Bob can read it. She can't depend on the network keeping the message secret, but she can ensure that nobody but Bob can read the message by using cryptography to encrypt the message.

The natural assumption is that if Alice wants to send Bob an encrypted message, she encrypts it using Bob's public key (if public key technology is being used for keys) or by using the key she shares with Bob (if secret key technology is being used). However, this is not how mail encryption is generally done, for several reasons:

- If Alice has a long message to send to multiple recipients, the long message would have to be encrypted once for each recipient, producing a different version to be sent to each recipient.
- Public key encryption is far less efficient than secret key encryption. So it is desirable to encrypt the message with secret key encryption even if Bob's key is a public key.
- As described in §9.8 *Session Key Establishment*, it's not desirable to use a long-term key more than necessary. So to preserve the useful lifetime of the long-term key Alice and Bob share, it is preferable to encrypt as little as possible with a key that is expensive to replace.

So the way it is done is that Alice chooses a random secret key S to be used only for encrypting that one message. She encrypts the message with S, encrypts S with Bob's key, and transmits both quantities to Bob. Even if the message is being sent to multiple recipients, she only encrypts the message once, with key S. But she encrypts S once for each recipient, with the appropriate key, and includes each encrypted S with the encrypted message.

Let's assume Bob's key is K_{Bob}, Carol's key is K_{Carol}, and Ted's key is K_{Ted}. If public key technology is being used, then K_{Bob} is Bob's public key. If secret key technology is being used, then K_{Bob} is the key that Alice shares with Bob. The message Alice would like to send to Bob, Carol, and Ted is m. S is the secret key Alice chose specifically for encrypting m. (We'll write $K\{x\}$ to indicate x encrypted with key K.) The mail message Alice will send includes:

- Bob's name; $K_{\text{Bob}}\{S\}$
- Carol's name; $K_{\text{Carol}}\{S\}$
- Ted's name; $K_{\text{Ted}}\{S\}$
- $S\{m\}$

So, for example, the message Alice sends might look like this:

```
To: Bob, Carol, Ted
From: Alice
Key-info: Bob-4280234208034
Key-info: Carol-48235235344848488
Key-info: Ted-99349248
Msg-info: RJekcr283hkjsdf8ghn327&3489724&#$*92
```

In that way, each recipient can decrypt the appropriate encrypted version of the secret key, and each will use the same secret key to decrypt the message.

20.5.2 Privacy with Distribution List Exploders

Suppose Alice is sending a message to a distribution list which will be remotely exploded, and Bob is only one of the recipients. Assume the distribution list is stored at some node remote from Alice, and that Alice does not even know the individuals on the distribution list. We can't assume she has keys for all the members of the distribution list. Instead, she has a key only for the distribution list exploder. Alice does not need to treat the distribution list exploder any differently than any other recipient of a message. It is merely someone she shares a key with and sends messages to. The distribution list exploder will need keys for all the individuals on the list.

As described in the end-to-end case, Alice will choose a random per-message secret key S, and encrypt the message with S. The distribution list exploder will decrypt S (but it does not need to decrypt the message!), and re-encrypt S with the key for each recipient to whom it is forwarding the message.

Local exploding requires different mechanisms. Alice still has to trust the maintainer of the mailing list, since a bad guy could insert extra names into the distribution list. The distribution list is most likely just a list of names. Alice will not be able to send a secure message to a name without establishing a key for that individual.

20.6 AUTHENTICATION OF THE SOURCE

With traditional (unsecured) mail systems, it is possible for Carol to send a message to Bob where the FROM: field says Alice. Obviously this can cause great harm if Bob takes the message seriously. For instance, Alice might be Bob's manager, and the message Carol sends might say Urgent meeting with a customer in Juneau, Alaska; I've left; meet me there tomorrow.

It would be desirable for the message system to assure Bob that the message did indeed come from Alice.

20.6.1 Source Authentication Based on Public Key Technology

Assuming Bob knows Alice's public key, Alice can digitally sign the message, using her private key, which will assure Bob that Alice wrote the message. The method usually chosen to sign a message is for Alice to first compute a hash of the message (for instance using MD5), and then to sign the message digest, since computing a message digest is faster than public key operations, and the message digest is usually a smaller quantity to sign than the message.

This method extends easily to multiple recipients and distribution lists. If Alice is sending a message to multiple recipients, the same signature will work for all recipients.

If Alice does not know that Bob knows her public key, she could send the message anyway and let Bob fetch the public key (together with finding a chain of certificates to certify Alice's key) if he needs to. Or she could include the public key in the header of the message, together with a chain of certificates. Or she might guess that he already has a lot of the certificates in the chain, and she might just furnish what she thinks is likely to be the remainder.

Note that Alice doesn't even have to know whether Bob is crypto-capable to send a signed message. Sometimes users send signed messages just to advertise the fact that they can. If the signature is formatted innocuously, it just looks like cybercrud in the mail header to non-crypto-capable recipients. Of course, added cybercrud sometimes annoys humans, even if it doesn't prevent them from deciphering the message. For example, the message

```
From: Alice
To: Bob
Subject: I got PEM working
... and I'm sending this message with PEM.
```

would look something like this when received by Bob:

```
To: Bob
Subject: I got PEM working
Date: Fri, 01 Apr 94 10:12:37 -0400
From: Alice

-----BEGIN PRIVACY-ENHANCED MESSAGE-----
Proc-Type: 4,MIC-CLEAR
Content-Domain: RFC822
DEK-Info: DES-CBC,31747476B4831B1D
Originator-ID-Asymmetric: MEMxCzAJBgNVBAYTAlVTMSYwJAYDVQQKEx1EaWd
 pdGFsIEVxdWlwbWVudCBDb3Jwb3JhdGlvbjEMMAoGA1UECxMDTEtH,02
MIC-Info: RSA-MD5,RSA,u1OHP1RwLqePAoaN5nPk9W7Q2EfjaP+yDBSaLyMcSgc
 MK2YicGSAqLz47O1+TUR4YmMD/JnHMtsCJerV2QFtFQ==

... and I'm sending this message with PEM.
-----END PRIVACY-ENHANCED MESSAGE-----
```

20.6.2 Source Authentication Based on Secret Keys

If Alice has a shared key with Bob, then she can reassure Bob that she is Alice by proving she knows the shared secret key. She does this by performing some cryptographic computation on the message using the shared secret key. This quantity also serves as an integrity check, and is called a **MIC** (message integrity code) by some and a MAC (message authentication code) by others (i.e., MIC and MAC are synonyms). The PEM standard calls it a MIC, but the term MAC is more commonly used today. Various possibilities for computing a MAC include:

1. The MAC is the CBC residue of the message computed with the shared secret key.

2. The MAC is the message digest of the shared secret appended to the message.

3. The MAC is the encrypted message digest, where the 128-bit message digest is encrypted with the shared secret key, for instance in ECB or CBC mode.

What if there are multiple recipients? Alice's shared secret with Bob will be different from Alice's shared secret with Ted. If the MAC method is 1 or 2 above, then Alice would have to do a computation-intensive cryptographic pass over the long message for each recipient. The third method is therefore preferable. Alice computes the message digest once, and computes the MAC on the message digest independently for each recipient.

20.6.3 Source Authentication with Distribution Lists

With public keys, source authentication is easy, even with distribution lists. Basically, the distribution list will merely forward the message without changing the authentication information. Alice's public key will authenticate the message. The distribution list exploder plays no part in the source authentication.

With secret keys it is more complicated. We can't assume Alice will share a secret key with every recipient, or even that Alice will know who the recipients are. The only choice is for Alice to share a key with the distribution list exploder. The distribution list exploder will be able to verify that the message came from Alice, but whatever authentication information Alice puts into the message will become meaningless after the distribution list exploder forwards the message. It must remove Alice's authentication information, and replace it with its own authentication information for each recipient. The recipients will know the message came from the distribution list exploder, but they will have to take the exploder's word that the message really did originate from Alice. When using mail exploders and secret key technology, it is vital that the mail exploder verify the source before forwarding the message, and include the name of the sender in the body of the message that the mail exploder cryptographically protects. PEM does not define a field to accomplish this, which would make it problematic to use secret key PEM with mail exploders. However, this was never a problem because:

- Nobody deployed PEM-aware mail exploders.
- Nobody used secret key PEM.

20.7 MESSAGE INTEGRITY

When Bob receives a message from Alice, how does he know that Carol did not intercept the message and modify it? For instance, she might have changed the message Fire Carol immediately to Promote Carol immediately.

It makes little sense to provide for authentication of the source without also guaranteeing integrity of the contents of the message. Who would care that the message originated with Alice, if the contents might have been modified en route? Indeed, all of the mail standards provide message integrity and source authentication together. They either provide both or neither. The mechanisms discussed in the previous section for source authentication provide message integrity as well.

20.7.1 Message Integrity without Source Authentication

Might someone want to provide message integrity protection without source authentication? The only vaguely plausible example we could come up with for when this might be useful was a ransom note. The kidnappers would want to prove that they were the kidnappers, perhaps by extracting some secret information from the victim. The note would give the proof that they were the kidnappers, and include directions for dropping off the ransom money. They'd want to keep the message private, since they wouldn't want someone else to get that secret, convince the family they were the kidnappers, and collect the ransom. Nor would they want some third party to see the directions for dropping off the ransom money, since someone else might try to pick up the money. (Kidnappers are such suspicious people.) The message would be anonymous, so there would be no source verification.

Integrity protection would be somewhat important, to prevent someone from guessing that the first part of the message was the proof that they were the kidnappers, and substitute a different second part of the message, with different directions for dropping off ransom money.

In some sense in this example there is source authentication—it's just not done with cryptography by the mail system. Instead the contents of the message provide source authentication by humans. We know of no systems that provide this odd combination (message integrity without source authentication), and kidnappers represent such a small market that none is likely to be developed.

It's meaningless to provide integrity protection without source authentication if the message is unencrypted, because anyone can remove the message from the wire and construct a different message. It isn't possible to do message integrity without source authentication with secret key technology, since the sender must share a secret with the recipient, so the recipient will know who the message came from based on which secret key is used.

If the message is encrypted (where the sender knows the public key of the recipient), it is possible to do something that could be considered integrity protection without source authentication. It is still possible for someone to remove the entire message from the wire and substitute a different message. But what can be ensured with an encrypted message is that the entire message came from one source, although the source is anonymous.

20.8 NON-REPUDIATION

Repudiation is the act of denying that you sent a message. If the message system provides for **non-repudiation**, it means that if Alice sends a message to Bob, Alice cannot later deny that she sent the message. Bob can prove to a third party that Alice did indeed send the message. For instance, if Alice sends a message to the bank that she wishes to transfer a million dollars to Bob's account, the bank might not honor the transaction unless it is sent in such a way that not only can the bank know the message was from Alice, but they can prove it to a court if necessary.

It is not always desirable to have non-repudiation. For instance, Alice might be the head of some large organization and want to give the go-ahead to her underlings for some scheme like, say, selling arms to Iran to raise money to fund the Contras. The underlings must be absolutely certain the orders came from Alice, so it is necessary to have source authentication of the message, but Alice wants plausible deniability (what a great phrase!), so that if any of her underlings are caught or killed, she can disavow any knowledge of their actions.

With public keys, it is very natural to provide non-repudiable source authentication, and more difficult to provide repudiable source authentication. With secret keys, it is very natural to provide repudiable source authentication and very difficult to provide non-repudiable messages.

20.8.1 Non-Repudiation Based on Public Key Technology

The usual method Alice uses to prove the authenticity of her message to Bob is to include her public key signature on the message digest of the message, using her private key. This method of source authentication not only reassures Bob that Alice sent the message, but Bob can prove to anyone else that Alice sent the message. Only someone with knowledge of Alice's private key could have signed the message digest with it. But anyone knowing her public key can verify her signature.

20.8.2 Plausible Deniability Based on Public Key Technology

How can Alice send a message to Bob in such a way that Bob knows it came from Alice, but Bob can't prove to anyone else that it came from Alice? Alice can send a public key based repudiable message *m* to Bob by doing the following.

First we'll review our notation. We use curly braces { } for encrypting something with a public key, with a subscript specifying the name of the individual whose public key we are using. We use square brackets [] for signing something with a private key, with a subscript specifying the name of the individual whose private key is being used.

1. Alice picks a secret key S, which she will use just for m.
2. She encrypts S with Bob's public key, getting $\{S\}_{\text{Bob}}$.
3. She signs $\{S\}_{\text{Bob}}$ with her private key, getting $[\{S\}_{\text{Bob}}]_{\text{Alice}}$.
4. She uses S to compute a MAC for m (for example, by using DES to compute the CBC residue of the message).
5. She sends the MAC, $[\{S\}_{\text{Bob}}]_{\text{Alice}}$, and m to Bob.

Bob will know that the message came from Alice, because Alice signed the encrypted S. But Bob can't prove to anyone else that Alice sent him m. He can prove that at some point Alice sent some message using key S, but it might not have been m. Once Bob has the quantity $[\{S\}_{\text{Bob}}]_{\text{Alice}}$ he can construct any message he likes and construct an integrity code using S.

20.8.3 Non-Repudiation with Secret Keys

It is surprising that it is possible to provide non-repudiation with secret keys. Let's say Alice is sending a message to Bob, and it has to be possible for Bob to prove later, to "the judge", that Alice sent the message. We'll need a notary N who must be trusted by Bob and the judge. (A **notary** is a trusted service that vouches for certain information.) Alice sends the message to N, and does source authentication with N so that N knows the message came from Alice. N does some computation on the message and Alice's name using a secret quantity S_N that N shares with nobody. We'll call the result of this computation N's **seal** on the message. (For instance N's seal might be the message digest of the concatenation of Alice, the message, and S_N.) Then the message together with the seal is sent to Bob. Bob can't tell whether N's seal is genuine, because that would require knowing S_N (which N shares with nobody). If Alice were dishonest and wanted to send a message to Bob that Bob would only accept if it were non-repudiable, then Alice could put in any cybercrud and pretend that it is authentication information from N.

There are two things we can do to assure Bob that the message was vouched for by N, and that therefore he can later prove to the judge that N vouched for the message.

- Bob and N could establish a shared key, and N could use it to generate a MAC for the concatenation of Alice, the message, and the seal. Bob can verify this MAC (since he knows the shared key) and thus verify the validity of the seal.
- Bob could, after receiving the message, send a request to N asking N if N's seal is genuine. This request would of course have to include Alice, the message, and the alleged seal.

Now let's assume at some later time Bob needs to prove to the judge that Alice sent the message. Bob sends Alice, the message, and the seal to the judge, who sends it to *N* in an integrity-protected conversation. *N* verifies the validity of the seal and reports that to the judge.

Note that *N* does not actually have to see the message, in case Alice and Bob want to keep the message private. Alice could instead just send the message digest to *N*, and *N* could compute the seal of the message digest.

20.9 PROOF OF SUBMISSION

When we send paper mail, the postal service allows us to send it *certified*, which means we pay extra money and get a piece of paper that verifies we submitted something on a particular date to a particular address. Some electronic mail systems offer a similar service, but by using cryptography on the contents of the message, it turns out to be more powerful than the postal service certified mail concept.

The mail system can implement this by computing a message digest of the message concatenated with any other information that might be useful, like the time of submission, and then sign the message digest. The user could later use the receipt to prove that the message was sent (though not that it was delivered).

20.10 PROOF OF DELIVERY

This feature corresponds to the paper mail postal service *return receipt requested*. It can be implemented in electronic mail by having either the destination or the mail delivery service sign a message digest of the message concatenated with any other information that might be useful (like the time of receipt). If the mail service gives the proof of delivery, it would be done after transmitting the message to the destination. If the destination gives the proof of delivery, it would be done after the destination receives the message. In either case this requires the cooperation of the recipient. It obviously requires the cooperation of the recipient if the recipient returns the proof of delivery. But it also requires the cooperation of the recipient if the mail system returns the proof of delivery, since the recipient might refuse to acknowledge the last packet of the message (once the recipient realizes the message is an eviction notice, for instance).

Note that it is impossible to provide a receipt if and only if the recipient got the message. The problem is, if the recipient signs before the message is delivered, then the message can get lost, but the mail system has the signature. If the recipient signs after receiving the message, the recipient might not furnish a signature at that point, but yet have the message.

20.11 MESSAGE FLOW CONFIDENTIALITY

This feature allows Alice to send Bob a message in such a way that no eavesdropper can find out that Alice sent Bob a message. This would be useful when the mere fact that Alice sent Bob a message is useful information, even if the contents were encrypted so that only Bob could read the contents. (For instance, Bob might be a headhunter. Or Bob might be a reporter and Alice might be a member of a secret congressional committee who is leaking information to the press.) The X.402 standard hints that such a service might be provided and hints at mechanisms for providing it.

If Alice knows that intruder Carol is monitoring her outgoing mail to look to see if she is sending messages to Bob, she can utilize a friend as an intermediary. She can send an encrypted message to Fred, with the message she wants to send to Bob embedded in the contents of the message to Fred. So the message Fred would read is This is Alice. Please forward the following message to Bob. Thanks a lot. followed by Alice's message to Bob. If Alice were sufficiently paranoid, she might prefer a service that is constantly sending encrypted dummy messages to random recipients. If Fred forwards Alice's message after a random delay, then even if Carol knows Fred provides this service, she cannot know to which recipient Alice was asking Fred to forward a message.

To be even more paranoid, a path through several intermediaries could be used. Alice does this by taking the (encrypted) message she'd like to send to Bob, enclosing that in an encrypted message to the last intermediary, enclosing that in an encrypted message to the penultimate intermediary, encloses that—you get the idea. Using the multiple intermediary technique, even if someone bribed one of the intermediaries to remember the directions from which it received and sent mail, Alice could not be paired with Bob. To discover that Alice had sent a message to Bob would require the cooperation of all the intermediaries.

20.12 ANONYMITY

There are times when Alice might want to send Bob a message, but not have Bob be able to tell who sent the message. One might think that would be easy. Alice could merely not sign the message. However, most mail systems automatically include the sender's name in the mail message. One could imagine modifying one's mailer to leave out that information, but a clever recipient can get clues. For instance, the network layer address of the node from which it was sent might be sent with the message. Often the node from which the recipient receives the message is not the actual source, but instead is an intermediate node that stores and forwards mail. However, most mail transports include a record of the path the message took, and this information might be available to the recipient.

If Alice really wants to ensure anonymity, she can use the same technique as for message flow confidentiality. She can give the message to a third party, Fred, and have Fred send the unsigned message on to Bob.

If Fred does not have enough clients, he can't really provide anonymity. For instance, if Alice is the only one who has sent a message to Fred, then Bob can guess the message came from her, even if Fred is sending out lots of messages to random people. Fred can have lots of clients by providing other, innocuous services, such as weather reports, bookmaking, or pornographic screen savers (where you are required to transmit a fixed-length, encrypted message in order to get a response), or by having the user community cooperate by sending dummy messages to Fred at random intervals to provide cover for someone who might really require the service. (We specified fixed-length messages to Fred so that people could not correlate the lengths of messages into and out of Fred—someone wanting to send a longer message would have to break it into multiple messages, and pad short messages.)

There's an amusing anecdote about anonymous mail. Someone does provide an anonymous mail service. The way it works is you send an ordinary mail message to the service, telling it to whom you'd like to send an anonymous message. It strips off your real address and substitutes a pseudonym for you. The first time you send a message it assigns you a pseudonym, but on subsequent messages it fills in the same pseudonym. So people won't know from whom the message came, but they'll know that different messages came from the same person. Mail sent to any of the pseudonyms assigned by the anonymity service will be directed to that service, which will substitute the real address instead of the destination's pseudonym (and incidentally, assign a pseudonym to the source and substitute that—this particular service didn't allow for non-anonymous mail to be sent to a pseudonym).

Anyway, one December day in 1993, someone decided to add him/herself to the IETF mailing list as the pseudonym assigned by the service. Then someone sent a message to the IETF mailing list (it happens). When the message was distributed by the mailing list, it was sent to all the members, including the pseudonym. When this pseudonym-addressed copy was received by the anonymous mail service, it assigned a pseudonym to the source (the mailing list) and sent an assignment message back to the mailing list, which of course got distributed to all the mailing list members:

```
To: ietf@nat-flnt{MHS:ietf@CNRI.Reston.VA.US}
From: 00000000 {MHS:"<@ns.novell.com:ietf-request@
```

```
ietf.nri.reston.va.us>"@sjf-domain-hub.Novell}
Subject: Anonymous code name allocated.
Date: 12/28/93    Time:  9:08a

You have sent a message using the anonymous contact service.
You have been allocated the code name an60254.
You can be reached anonymously using the address
an60254@anon.penet.fi.

If you want to use a nickname, please send a message to
nick@anon.penet.fi, with a Subject: field containing your nickname.

For instructions, send a message to help@anon.penet.fi.
```

This strange behavior was caused by the anonymity service's assumption that both parties using its service would want anonymity, which is not a reasonable assumption. It should be possible for two anonymous parties to communicate, but it is also reasonable for a non-anonymous party to communicate with an anonymous party. A pseudonym should not be assigned unless requested.

20.13 CONTAINMENT

This feature is modeled after nondiscretionary access controls (see §1.13.1 *Mandatory (Nondiscretionary) Access Controls*). The idea is that the network would be partitioned into pieces that are capable of handling certain security classes. Each message would be marked with its security classification, and the message routers would refuse to forward a message to a portion of the network that didn't handle its security class.

20.14 ANNOYING TEXT FORMAT ISSUES

There is unfortunately no single standard for text representation. Some systems have <LF> (line feed, ASCII 10) as the line delimiter. Others have <CR> (carriage return, ASCII 13). Others have <CR><LF> (<CR> followed by <LF>). Some systems have line-length limitations. Others happily wrap lines. Some systems expect parity on the high-order bit of each octet. Others get upset if the high-order bit is on. Still others don't get upset, but calmly clear the bit. Some systems don't even use ASCII, but use some other encoding for characters, such as EBCDIC.

When sending a text message to someone on another system, we'd like the message to appear to the human on the other end about the way it looked to the human who sent it. This is a messy, boring problem. Your system can't really know what the conventions are at the remote site, and the destination might have difficulties translating appropriately because it would not know what the conventions were at the source. The usual method of solving problems like these is to define a canonical format. The data is translated at the source into canonical format, and at the destination out of canonical format into local format. This way, each system only needs to know how to convert its local format to and from canonical format (as opposed to needing to know how to convert its local format to and from each other possible format).

Unfortunately, there is no single standard canonical format. SMTP (Simple Mail Transport Protocol, RFC 821) is a standard for Internet mail. The companion RFC 822 defines a canonical format that uses <CR><LF> as the line delimiter. But there are non-SMTP mail systems, and messages can get modified in non-reversible ways as messages pass through various sorts of gateways. For instance, some mail gateways remove white space at the ends of lines (spaces immediately preceding the end of the line), add line breaks to lines that seem too long to fit on a screen, or turn the tab character into five spaces.

These sorts of transformations are mostly harmless when trying to send simple text messages from one user to another across diverse systems, but it causes problems when trying to send arbitrary data between systems. Certainly if you're trying to send arbitrary binary data, having all your high-order bits cleared or having <CR><LF> inserted periodically will hopelessly mangle the data. But even if you are sending text, security features can get broken by mail gateways diddling with the data. For instance, a digital signature will no longer verify if any of the message is modified. It's difficult to predict exactly what kinds of modifications an arbitrary mail gateway will make to your file in its attempt to be helpful.

Mail is not the only application which has this problem. File transfer also has the problem. It would be easy just to send the bits in a file and have them appear at the destination machine exactly as they were at the source machine, but that is often not what is wanted. Because of the different representations for text, a text file might not display intelligibly on a different system. (And of course there are other problems besides displaying text. A floating point number is represented differently on different machines. Maybe you'd even like your executable code to run on a different machine!) Most file transfer protocols give you the choice of whether you are sending binary data (in which case it won't muck with your data) or text (in which case it will attempt to do transformations on the data so that it will display properly).

SMTP made the assumption that the only thing anyone would ever want to mail was text, so there is no capability of sending arbitrary data. The mail infrastructure is always allowed to play around with your data in an attempt to be helpful.

20.14.1 Disguising Data as Text

People have long wanted to mail types of data other than simple text (for instance, diagrams, voice, pictures, or even text in languages with large character sets), and they have done so by coming up with an encoding that will pass through all known maulers ;-). The classic way UNIX systems did this was to run a program called *uuencode* on the data, mail the result, and have the recipient *uudecode* it. The encoding process accepts arbitrary octet strings and produces strings containing only "safe" characters with an occasional end-of-line delimiter to keep the mailers happy. There are obviously fewer than 256 safe values for an octet (otherwise, arbitrary binary data would work just fine). It turns out there are at least 64 safe characters, but not much more than that, so the encoding packs 6 bits of information into each character, by translating each of the possible values of the 6 bits into one of the safe characters, and adding <CR><LF> sufficiently often. This encoding expands the information by about 33%.

S/MIME, PEM, and PGP make the assumption that they have to work with a mail system such as SMTP that will assume their data is text, so they both have a convention similar to uuencode/uudecode for packing and unpacking 6 bits into a character. We will use the term **encode** to mean any similar mechanism, even if it isn't exactly the transformation that the UNIX utility provides. X.400 has a method of transmitting data unmodified, so it does not need to do this.

So there are two transformations of data. One is canonicalization, which is minor diddling such as changing the end-of-line character into <CR><LF>. The other is encoding, which is packing 6 bits per character, thereby making the data completely unintelligible to humans and expanding it by about 33%.

There is a troublesome consequence of encoding, in that you can't always assume that the recipient of the mail message has S/MIME, PEM or PGP. The recipient might have to read the message with an ordinary mail program. Obviously they would not be able to read an encrypted message with an ordinary mail program, but you'd want them to be able to read a message that is unencrypted but integrity-protected.

Suppose Alice sends the message Bob, your terminal is about to explode. You'd better quickly run out of your office. She decides to use PEM so that it will add an integrity check to the message, since she *really cares* that Bob gets the message without it getting garbled. PEM helpfully reformats the message so that it now looks like:

```
-----BEGIN PRIVACY-ENHANCED MESSAGE-----
Proc-Type: 4,MIC-ONLY
Originator-ID-Asymmetric: MEMxCzAJBgNVBAYTAlVTMSYwJAYDVQQKEx1EaWd
 pdGFsIEVxdWlwbWVudCBDb3Jwb3JhdGlvbjEMMAoGA1UECxMDTEtH,05
MIC-Info: RSA-MD5,RSA,ZHiLe5DJdd4fE1/w++csvPbpFG9K9PWkPwU3fSLh9I+
 ZNyFdZ7pBklzPvXrya5+14XQcwIcb3Dcqk2RbnyzWzQ==

Qm9iLCB5b3VyIHRlcm1pbmFsIGlzIGFib3V0IHRvDQpleHBsb2RlLiAgWW91J2Qg
```

YmV0dGVyIHF1aWNrbHkgcnVuIG91dCBvZiB5b3VyIG9mZmljZS4NCg==
-----END PRIVACY-ENHANCED MESSAGE-----

The first five lines of cybercrud include information like the integrity check. The actual message is the bottom two lines:

Qm9iLCB5b3VyIHR1cm1pbmFsIGlzIGFib3V0IHRvDQpleHBsb2R1LiAgWW91J2Qg
YmV0dGVyIHF1aWNrbHkgcnVuIG91dCBvZiB5b3VyIG9mZmljZS4NCg==

Suppose Bob's mail program has not yet implemented PEM. It is reasonable to expect him to have problems understanding an encrypted message, but Alice did not encrypt the message. She merely requested an integrity check be added to the message. But PEM had to reformat the data, because the integrity check would fail if the text was modified in any way. The human Bob will have trouble processing

Qm9iLCB5b3VyIHR1cm1pbmFsIGlzIGFib3V0IHRvDQpleHBsb2R1LiAgWW91J2Qg
YmV0dGVyIHF1aWNrbHkgcnVuIG91dCBvZiB5b3VyIG9mZmljZS4NCg==

It's not encrypted—it is easy to turn it back into human-readable text, if there is a utility at Bob's node to do this. Without such a utility, Bob will probably take longer than is prudent (given the contents of Alice's message) to read the message.

Because of this problem, S/MIME, PEM, and PGP have the capability of sending something without modification. When you use that mode, they will not modify the message. It's your problem if mail gateways modify the message and the integrity check no longer matches. The programs add an integrity check without encoding the message. The message would then look like this:

```
-----BEGIN PRIVACY-ENHANCED MESSAGE-----
Proc-Type: 4,MIC-CLEAR
Originator-ID-Asymmetric: MEMxCzAJBgNVBAYTAlVTMSYwJAYDVQQKEx1EaWd
 pdGFsIEVxdWlwbWVudCBDb3Jwb3JhdGlvbjEMMAoGA1UECxMDTEtH,05
MIC-Info: RSA-MD5,RSA,ZHiLe5DJdd4fE1/w++csvPbpFG9K9PWkPwU3fSLh9I+
 ZNyFdZ7pBk1zPvXrya5+14XQcwIcb3Dcqk2RbnyzWzQ==

Bob, your terminal is about to explode. You'd better quickly run out of
your office
-----END PRIVACY-ENHANCED MESSAGE-----
```

If Alice sends her message to Bob in this mode using something like PEM, then it is possible that she'll be lucky and one of the following will be true:

- The message happens to be encoded in a way which no mail utility en route will feel obliged to modify. Bob's mailer has PEM and the integrity check will succeed.

- Bob's mailer does not have PEM, and the message does not get maliciously corrupted en route by some third party Carol. What Bob sees is the actual text of the message, plus some cybercrud for the signature and so on, which he ignores.

It is possible that she'll be unlucky (or rather, Bob will be unlucky in this case) and one of the following will happen:

- Bob's mail has PEM, and the message gets modified by a helpful mail utility in a "harmless" sort of way. The integrity check fails and Bob ignores the message.
- Bob's mailer does not have PEM, and bad-guy Carol modifies the message en route into something like, Are you still free for tennis today after work?

In either case, Bob gets blown to bits.

20.15 NAMES AND ADDRESSES

The designers of PEM (and S/MIME) chose X.509 for the certificate format. This was an unfortunate choice, since the email applications did not use X.500 names, which is what appeared in X.509 certificates (at the time when these standards were developed). What good is a certificate that certifies the public key of an X.500 name such as /C=US/O=CIA/OU=drugs/PN='Manuel Noriega' when the human specified the recipient with an Internet email address such as Alice@Wonderland.Edu?

The designers were assuming that the user would specify the X.500 name of the recipient, and some service would translate that into an email address by looking it up in some sort of directory. There was no need to have a certificate stating the recipient's email address because at worst the encrypted message to the name would get delivered to the wrong mailbox, but encrypted with a key that the reader of the wrong mailbox would not have. But a user interface of specifying an X.500 name of a recipient rather than an email address of the recipient did not catch on (and the directories for mapping X.500 name to email address didn't get deployed).

So to solve the problem that the user identified the recipient by a name that was not in the X.509 certificate, the S/MIME standard specifies that the email address should appear as an alternate name in the certificate. Hopefully the issuer of the certificate would be at least as careful about checking the mapping of the key with the alternate name containing the email address, as they would be with the subject name (the X.500 name) in the certificate. Especially since, if used with email, the subject name would be ignored by the application, according to the standard.

But since support of certificates with the alternate name field (X.509 version 3) was slower than the rollout of S/MIME, what implementations did was to invent a new component of the X.500

name which would contain the email address, e.g., /C=US/O=CIA/OU=drugs/PN='Manuel Noriega'/E=Alice@Wonderland.Edu. The other components of the X.500 name are ignored (except that the user could display them through some optional UI).

20.16 VERIFYING WHEN A MESSAGE WAS REALLY SENT

You can't depend on the date in a signed message being accurate. Someone who steals your private key can put an old date in a signed message. Someone with use of a key can sign a message with a date in the future as well. Keys get revoked. Keys get changed. How can one look at a five-year-old message and know whether the mail message was valid at the time it was sent? We'll discuss several scenarios and ways for coping with these circumstances, based on use of a notary (see §20.8.3 *Non-Repudiation with Secret Keys*). People have suggested all sorts of digital notary services, but we claim that all services can be accomplished with a notary that simply, given a pile of bits, will date and sign the pile of bits.

20.16.1 Preventing Backdating

An example problem that this protects against is a dishonest buyer. Suppose there is a company that allows electronic purchase orders. The deal is that you are responsible for any purchase orders signed with your key, unless you had reported your key stolen. From the time you declare the key stolen, all purchase orders signed with the key are invalid, but all purchase orders signed before that time are valid. Suppose Alice signed a purchase order with her private key a week ago. Then she decides she wants to renege on the deal, so she reports her key stolen. The company knows they received the purchase order a week ago, but how can they prove it? We can assume the purchase order has a date in it, which is integrity-protected with the signature, but anyone who has the private key can backdate a message.

One way the company can protect itself is to send each purchase order, when received, to a notary. Our version of the notary simply dates and signs the message, so the company can prove they received the message before the timestamp added by the notary. It will also be convenient for the company to store, with the purchase order, the certificates and certificate revocation lists (CRLs) it used originally to verify Alice's signature. Now if Alice denies having sent the message, the company can give a judge Alice's notarized message along with the certificates and CRLs, and the judge can determine that Alice's message was legally binding at the time it was received.

If the company is worried about Alice controlling a certification authority (CA), and therefore being able to fake dates on certificates or CRLs, then the company can have the notary also sign and date the certificates and CRLs. See Homework Problem 10.

20.16.2 Preventing Postdating

The notary, as described above, can only prove that a message was generated before the date on which the notary signed it. Someone could hold a message for years, and then have the notary sign it.

Suppose you want to prove that a message was generated after a certain date. This can be accomplished by including in the message something that you could not have known until that date, for instance the winning lottery number in some daily lottery drawing with sufficiently large numbers, or a signed timestamp from a notary for that day.

Kidnappers often use something like this to prove their victim is still alive (a photo of the victim holding the latest newspaper). In the cryptography world, this technique might be useful to ensure that someone that has temporary use of the CRL signing key does not postdate a CRL (without his certificate on it), to substitute for the real CRL generated in the future that *would* have his certificate on it.

20.17 HOMEWORK

1. Outline a scheme for sending a message to a distribution list, where distribution lists can be nested. Attempt to avoid duplicate copies to recipients that are members of multiple lists. Discuss both the local exploder and remote exploder methods of distribution list expansion.

2. If using secret keys for user keys, and sending a multi-recipient message, why is encrypting the MD of the message with the secret key associated with the recipient a more efficient MAC than doing a keyed MD of the message (again, using the secret key associated with the recipient)?

3. Using tickets as in §20.4.2 *Establishing Secret Keys*, suppose Alice's KDC is different from Bob's KDC. Alice will have to use a chain of KDCs to get a ticket for Bob (see §9.7.4.1 *Multiple KDC Domains*). Does Alice need to include the entire chain of tickets or merely the final ticket to Bob? How is this different from use of certificates?

4. Suppose Alice sends an encrypted, signed message to Bob via the mechanism suggested in §20.8.2 *Plausible Deniability Based on Public Key Technology*. Why can't Bob prove to third

party Charlie that Alice sent the message? Why are both cryptographic operations on S necessary? (Alice both encrypts it with Bob's public key and signs it with her private key.)

5. Assume we are using secret key technology. What is wrong with the following source authentication scheme? Alice chooses a per-message secret key K, and puts an encrypted version of K in the header for each recipient, say Bob and Ted. Then she uses K to compute a MAC on the message, say a DES-CBC residue, or by computing a message digest of K appended to the message. (Hint: it works fine for a single recipient, but there is a security problem if Alice sends a multiple-recipient message.)

6. Using the authentication without non-repudiation described in §20.8.2 *Plausible Deniability Based on Public Key Technology*, Bob can forge Alice's signature on a message to himself. Why can't he forge Alice's signature on a message to someone else using the same technique?

7. Suppose you changed the protocol in §20.8.2 *Plausible Deniability Based on Public Key Technology* so that Alice first signs S, and then encrypts with Bob's public key. So instead of sending $[\{S\}_{\text{Bob}}]_{\text{Alice}}$ to Bob, she sends $\{[S]_{\text{Alice}}\}_{\text{Bob}}$. Does this work? (i.e., can Bob be sure that the message came from Alice, but not be able to prove it to a third party)

8. Which security features can be provided without changing the mail delivery infrastructure, i.e., by only running special software at the source and destination?

9. Which security features (privacy, integrity protection, repudiability, non-repudiability, source authentication) would be desired, and which ones would definitely not be used, in the following cases:

   - submitting an expense report
   - inviting a friend to lunch
   - selling illegal pornography over the network
   - running an (illegal) gambling operation on the network
   - sending a mission description to the Mission Impossible team
   - sending a purchase order
   - sending a tip to the IRS to audit a neighbor you don't like but are afraid of
   - sending a love letter
   - sending an (unwanted) obscene note
   - sending a blackmail letter
   - sending a ransom note

- sending a resume to a headhunter

10. Suppose you are a judge trying to decide a dispute between a buyer and a supplier. The buyer claims not to have produced a particular email purchase order, while the supplier shows you the purchase order, and certificates and CRLs demonstrating that the purchase order was signed by the buyer, all signed by a notary. How would the dates on the various pieces of evidence influence your decision? What if only the purchase order was signed by the notary? Note that the security community continues to debate issues such as whether the CRL should be required to have a later date than the notary's signature.

11. Consider the following format for Alice sending signed, encrypted email to Bob. Alice invents a secret key S and sends $\{S\}_{\text{Bob}}$, the message encrypted with S, and the message digest of the message signed by Alice. Is this secure? (hint: the signed message digest is not encrypted)

21 PEM & S/MIME

21.1 Introduction

PEM (Privacy Enhanced Mail) was developed by the Internet community in the late '80s and early '90s as a means of adding encryption, source authentication, and integrity protection to ordinary text messages—the dominant form of email at the time. It is documented in four pieces. RFC 1421 describes the message formats. RFC 1422 describes the CA hierarchy. RFC 1423 describes a base set of cryptographic algorithms that can be used with PEM. RFC 1424 describes mail message formats for requesting certificates and for requesting or posting certificate revocation lists.

At about the same time, email was evolving to be more than just text. MIME (Multipurpose Internet Mail Extensions, RFC 2045) specified a standard way of encoding arbitrary data in email: pictures, rich text, video clips, binary files, etc. And it specified a way to indicate what the format of the data was so that a recipient could figure out how to process the data. S/MIME (RFC 2633) took many of the design principles of PEM, and incorporated them into the MIME structure, adding signed data and encrypted data as new types of data.

Even though PEM has pretty much died out, we'll discuss it since its text based encoding makes it possible to show examples. S/MIME has a format that is similar if you are a computer, but which is much harder to read if you're a human. Once you understand the concepts in PEM, it's simple to translate the ideas into S/MIME.

PEM and S/MIME were designed to work by having smart software only at the source and destination (as opposed to in the mail infrastructure, for instance in the mail gateways). They assume that the message they want to send will be carried by a mail infrastructure which might be based on some simple-minded mail transport protocol that might only be able to send ordinary text. A lot of PEM's, MIME's, and S/MIME's complexity involves encoding information in such a way that it will pass unmodified through all the mailers known at the time (there's no guarantee that someone won't invent a mail gateway which will mangle data in new and innovative ways, though).

The design of PEM lets you base user keys on secret key or public key technology, but basing user email keys on secret keys never caught on, for reasons that are pointed out in Chapter 20 *Electronic Mail Security*. (Message encryption is always done with secret key technology, even when user keys are based on public key technology—see §20.5.1 *End-to-End Privacy*.) Even though secret key PEM never caught on, it's interesting to see how the PEM designers envisioned their use. S/MIME only defines how to use public key technology for user keys. PEM and S/MIME were both designed to be used with a variety of cryptographic algorithms, and over time the set of specified algorithms has grown to include RSA, DSS, DES, RC2, 3DES, AES, and others.

First we'll describe PEM, and then we'll describe how to translate the ideas into S/MIME.

21.2 Structure of a PEM Message

A mail message can contain pieces that have been processed in different ways by PEM. For instance, part of a message might be encrypted, and another part might be integrity-protected. PEM puts markers before and after such blocks so that the PEM at the destination will know which pieces need what processing. PEM marks a piece that it has processed in some way (for instance encrypted) with a text string before and after the piece. PEM will insert

`-----BEGIN PRIVACY-ENHANCED MESSAGE-----`

before and insert

`-----END PRIVACY-ENHANCED MESSAGE-----`

at the end of the piece of the message that PEM has processed.

Extra information needs to be sent along with the PEM-processed message, for instance the (encrypted) key used to encrypt the data, or the message integrity code (MIC)[1]. S/MIME encodes this information as pure cybercrud, but PEM inserts a label for each piece of information attached to the message it has processed (apparently to make books like this one more readable). There are labels for each piece of PEM information, for instance Proc-Type, Originator-ID-Asymmetric, and MIC-Info. The intention is that most humans will ignore that stuff. The delimiting strings are indeed helpful to alert a human that might not have a PEM-capable mail reader as to why the message seems like junk. In §21.15 *Message Formats* we will walk through the PEM message syntax in its full glory, explaining exactly what each field means and which variations are allowed.

The different types of pieces PEM can combine into a message are

- ordinary, unsecured data
- integrity-protected unmodified data—An integrity check is added to the message, but the original message is included unmodified as part of the PEM message. The PEM terminology for this kind of data is MIC-CLEAR. The assumption is that the text will not be garbled in annoying ways along the route by meddling mail utilities. Otherwise the integrity check will

1. PEM refers to the cryptographic message integrity code as a MIC, which is a synonym for MAC, the term that has become more widely used.

not work. See §21.7 *Reformatting Data to Get Through Mailers*. (Note that, as with the types below, the integrity check also provides source authentication.)

- integrity-protected encoded data—PEM first encodes the message so that it will pass through all mailers unmodified. Then PEM adds an integrity check. PEM calls this MIC-ONLY. Since the encoded message is not readable by normal humans, the mail program at the destination must be able to convert the text back into human readable format.
- encoded encrypted integrity-protected data—PEM computes an integrity check on the message. PEM then encrypts the message and the integrity check with a randomly selected per-message secret key. The encrypted message, the encrypted integrity check, and the per-message key (encrypted by the interchange key—see §21.3 *Establishing Keys*) are each then encoded to pass through mailers as ordinary text. PEM calls this ENCRYPTED. Clearly in this case the mail program at the destination must be PEM-aware so that it can decrypt the message.

For example, let's assume the simple message

```
From: Alice
To: Bob
Subject: Keep this proposition private!
Date: Fri, 01 Apr 94 10:12:37 -0400
Care to meet me at my apartment tonight?
```

The MIC-CLEAR version would look like this:

```
From: Alice
To: Bob
Subject: Keep this proposition private!
Date: Fri, 01 Apr 94 10:12:37 -0400

-----BEGIN PRIVACY-ENHANCED MESSAGE-----
Proc-Type: 4,MIC-CLEAR
Content-Domain: RFC822
Originator-ID-Asymmetric: MEMxCzAJBgNVBAYTAlVTMSYwJAYDVQQKEx1EaWd
 pdGFsIEVxdWlwbWVudCBDb3Jwb3JhdGlvbjEMMAoGA1UECxMDTEtH,02
MIC-Info: RSA-MD5,RSA,u1OHP1RwLqePAoaN5nPk9W7Q2EfjaP+yDBSaLyMcSgc
 MK2YicGSAqLz47Ol+TUR4YmMD/JnHMtsCJerV2QFtFQ==

Care to meet me at my apartment tonight?
-----END PRIVACY-ENHANCED MESSAGE-----
```

The MIC-ONLY version would look like this:

```
From: Alice
To: Bob
Subject: Keep this proposition private!
Date: Fri, 01 Apr 94 10:15:02 -0400

-----BEGIN PRIVACY-ENHANCED MESSAGE-----
Proc-Type: 4,MIC-ONLY
Content-Domain: RFC822
Originator-ID-Asymmetric: MEMxCzAJBgNVBAYTAlVTMSYwJAYDVQQKEx1EaWd
 pdGFsIEVxdWlwbWVudCBDb3Jwb3JhdGlvbjEMMAoGA1UECxMDTEtH,02
MIC-Info: RSA-MD5,RSA,u1OHP1RwLqePAoaN5nPk9W7Q2EfjaP+yDBSaLyMcSgc
 MK2YicGSAqLz47Ol+TUR4YmMD/JnHMtsCJerV2QFtFQ==

G9yYXRpb24xDDAKBgNVBAsTA0xLRzESMBAGA1UEAxMJSm9obiBMaW5uMFcwCgYE
-----END PRIVACY-ENHANCED MESSAGE-----
```

The ENCRYPTED version would look like this:

```
From: Alice
To: Bob
Subject: Keep this proposition private!
Date: Fri, 01 Apr 94 10:10:31 -0400

-----BEGIN PRIVACY-ENHANCED MESSAGE-----
Proc-Type: 4,ENCRYPTED
Content-Domain: RFC822
DEK-Info: DES-CBC,31747476B4831B1D
Originator-ID-Asymmetric: MEMxCzAJBgNVBAYTAlVTMSYwJAYDVQQKEx1EaWd
 pdGFsIEVxdWlwbWVudCBDb3Jwb3JhdGlvbjEMMAoGA1UECxMDTEtH,02
Key-Info: RSA,Pv3W7Ds86/fQBnvB5DsvUXgpK7+6h5aSVcNeYf9uWtly9m2VHzC
 v2t7A6qgbXtIcf4kaMj1FL2yl9/N9mWpm4w==
MIC-Info: RSA-MD5,RSA,FUiVRM3x5Ku0aZveGIJ1hv/hi3Iowpmliypd9VP7MGw
 PPQra+42TkbR/2jhnqXyVEXLaJ7BSyNhBh/9znIUj5uk0N7IXeBxX
Recipient-ID-Asymmetric: MEMxCzAJBgNVBAYTAlVTMSYwJAYDVQQKEx1EaWdp
 dGFsIEVxdWlwbWVudCBDb3Jwb3JhdGlvbjEMMAoGA1UECxMDTEtH,05
Key-Info: RSA,dpUp7/QoY9YOZzZCVcIwxIDMN0WbGCFAGN3T+xlV/0pBu2n5+x8
 PmBvMUN0NcBi5vtqBS4cfmgShiK0I4zu05Q==

21OHDuHTP5BABnlsqENz1WVerZxxWo2AsPHhm2SIz9qpLMvxT/x0+8UEf8dDsTDr
wbQo9/x+
-----END PRIVACY-ENHANCED MESSAGE-----
```

Not only can these types of data be combined in a message, but they can be nested inside one another. For instance, assuming public key based user keys, Alice might enclose an integrity-protected message from Fred in an encrypted message to Bob. (Bob, I received the following message from Fred. Should I alert the authorities?)

21.3 ESTABLISHING KEYS

Suppose Alice is sending a message to Bob. For an integrity check, or for encryption, PEM has to find appropriate cryptographic keys. The per-message key used to encrypt a message is just a randomly selected number. But there is also a long-term key which PEM refers to as an **interchange key**. When public keys are used, the interchange key is Bob's public key. When secret keys are used, the interchange key is a key Alice and Bob share.

The interchange key is used to encrypt the per-message key:

PEM gives no hint as to how to establish secret key based interchange keys. The assumption is that there is some out-of-band mechanism for doing it, for instance calling someone on the phone and agreeing on a number. The PEM designers could have allowed fields for Kerberos-style tickets to be carried in the message, but interest in secret key based interchange keys for PEM is low, so there hasn't been a lot of thought on how to deploy secret key based PEM.

In the case of PEM based on public key technology, PEM defines a certification hierarchy based on the X.500 naming hierarchy. A hierarchical naming scheme means that names contain multiple components, like A/B/C/D, reflecting a tree structure where each successive component gives the next branch downwards. Having the certification hierarchy follow the naming hierarchy means that there is a CA named A/B/C that issues certificates for all the names of the form A/B/C/*, and there's a CA named A/B that certifies all the names of the form A/B/* (including CA A/B/C).

While it is hoped that eventually there will exist a global directory service in which all certificates can be stored to make them universally available, the PEM designers considered it important to be able to operate before such a directory service was deployed. For that reason, they specified how the header of a PEM message could contain certificates relevant to authenticating the sender of the message. This not only permits the receiver to verify the signature of a message without access to a directory service, it provides a convenient method for Bob to deliver certificates to someone who needs to know Bob's public key in order to send him an encrypted message.

Thus a convenient way for Bob to send Alice the necessary certificates is for Bob to use PEM to send Alice a message including all necessary certificates in the header. Note that even if Alice and Bob intend that all of their conversations be encrypted, the first message one of them sends the other must be unencrypted (since neither yet knows the other's public key). This will not be necessary if Alice can look up Bob's certificates in some directory service.

Note that certificates take up a lot of room, and they may not be necessary. Indeed, Alice may have cached Bob's certificates. In that case, there is no reason for Bob to send the certificates. Some PEM implementations allow the user to tell PEM to leave out the certificates for a particular message. If Bob sends a message without the certificates, but Alice really doesn't have them, then Alice can send Bob a message (or call him on the phone) and ask him to send a message with the certificates. Or perhaps she can retrieve them from the directory service.

21.4 Some PEM History

The PEM Certificate Hierarchy is somewhat baroque, and to understand why it is the way it is, it helps to know some history. It got to where it is by a series of compromises, each one of which made sense in context. Although it never got deployed and at this point never will be, it is instructive to understand it as an example PKI design.

The original vision for the PEM Certificate Hierarchy was to have a large number of independently operated CAs, each having responsibility for a subtree of the global namespace. Most X.500 names would list individuals as members of an organization, and it seemed natural for the organization to operate the CA for its own members. For instance, the organization CIA might have a CA called /C=US/O=CIA, and all the names of people in CIA start out with the string /C=US/O=CIA, for example /C=US/O=CIA/CN=Noriega. If an organization was large, it might create subsidiary CAs and delegate to them control of sub-parts of the organization's name space. For instance, there might be /C=US/O=CIA/OU=plumbers. Someone who worked in that organization would then have a name like /C=US/O=CIA/OU=plumbers/CN=Liddy. A single global root CA would certify the names and public keys of all the independent organizations. To be considered valid by the recipient, a certificate would have to follow the rule that the **issuer name** (the name of the CA that signs the certificate) be a prefix of the **subject name** (the name of the owner of the public key being certified). This would guarantee that a CA in one organization could not issue a valid certificate for a user in another. So for instance, with the certificate for Liddy, the issuer name would be /C=US/O=CIA/OU=plumbers and the subject name would be /C=US/O=CIA/OU=plumbers/CN=Liddy. (Note that PEM allows a CA to certify anything in its subtree, so the CA for /C=US/O=CIA would be allowed to issue a certificate for /C=US/O=CIA/OU=plumbers/CN=Liddy.)

PEM was intended to be deployed in the free-wheeling internet community where it would replace a system with virtually no security at all. The vision was for PEM to open up new applications by offering a single uniformly high standard of authentication. It might, for example, be possible to sign purchase orders as PEM messages and consider them legally binding. And it should be possible to send an encrypted message to someone around the world with complete confidence that only the intended recipient would be able to read it. Such confidence requires faith in both the cryptographic mechanisms used and the operational procedures of the people who create certificates. If there are "sloppy" CAs around who will issue certificates to anyone with an honest face, how can you know who is really sending and reading your messages?

The original vision for PEM, therefore, set a uniformly high standard for the operational procedures of CAs. Since the compromise of a CA's key would be particularly disastrous, it would be required that CAs be implemented in specially packaged hardware that made it nearly impossible to extract the CA's private key from the hardware. Strict administrative rules would be followed in qualifying the people who could operate the CAs and in the procedures they would follow in ensuring that they issued certificates only to people who had adequately proven their identities.

The root CA would be particularly sensitive, since its compromise would render the entire PEM infrastructure useless. The PEM designers assumed the root CA would be operated by an organization that would use draconian procedures to protect the integrity of its private key and its signing procedures. Since there would be no way to change the root key, whichever organization was chosen to be the root would have an eternal monopoly. RSADSI (the organization that licensed the RSA patent) was positioning itself to be that organization.

This structure had a side effect that it made possible a licensing structure and mechanism for RSADSI to collect fees for issuing certificates, and once this mechanism was sufficiently entrenched, it would allow them to continue to collect fees for certificates even after the RSA patent expired. The same CA hardware that protects the CA's private key could also act as a "postage meter" which keeps track of the number of certificates it issues and can require payment of a per-certificate fee to RSADSI. Collection of royalties is therefore distributed. RSADSI could enforce the use of metering hardware (or some alternative royalty arrangement) by refusing to certify an organizational CA until some accommodation was reached. Without such an organizational certificate, the certificates issued by a CA would not be accepted by "standard" PEM implementations.

This vision of the PEM certificate hierarchy was ultimately rejected by the IETF standards community for a number of reasons.

- Universities were not amenable to enforcing the same administrative procedures for authenticating their students as defense contractors were in authenticating their employees. No "one size fits all" compromise could be reached. It may have been discussions of mandatory drug testing for CA operators that pushed this over the edge.

- There were concerns about the availability and cost of the CA hardware. For several years, organizational certificates and the hardware remained "a few months" away.
- There was reluctance to trust RSADSI—or any single party—with the security of the entire system.
- There was a reluctance to expand the RSADSI monopoly. RSADSI was the sole licensing authority for the RSA algorithm, so it might seem that it was necessary to make peace with them in order to use PEM, but this was simplistic. The U.S. Government had rights to use the algorithm without payment of royalties. Several companies had already reached agreements with RSADSI and were afraid of having to "pay again". RSA was only patented within the U.S., and foreign concerns were afraid of having to pay for what they currently used for free. And since the RSA patent would expire on September 20, 2000, people were not happy about the possibility of having to continue to pay RSADSI after that date in order to obtain certificates.

In any case, it was decided that this relatively straightforward solution to the certificate hierarchy was unacceptable, and the designers embellished it in the minimal fashion that worked—they added another layer to the hierarchy and explicitly allowed people to go into competition with RSADSI. The result is the hierarchy we're about to describe.

21.5 PEM CERTIFICATE HIERARCHY

RFC 1422 recommends an organization of CAs. It recommends a single root CA, called the **IPRA**, which stands for **Internet Policy Registration Authority** and is managed by the Internet Society. Certified by the IPRA are CAs called **PCAs** (for **Policy Certification Authorities**), so named because each one has a written policy it will enforce in its issuance of certificates. The design envisions at least three kinds of policies that will be enforced. The names have not been standardized, so we'll arbitrarily name them for ease of explanation.

- High Assurance (HA)

A HA CA is meant to be super-secure. The rules aren't standardized, but some of the ideas are as follows.

A HA CA is supposed to be implemented on special hardware designed so that it is tamper-resistant (impossible to extract its private key even if you were to steal the whole box), and managed by people who have passed security checks and perhaps periodic drug tests or other procedures. Also, the people who run a HA CA have to have wonderfully paranoid criteria for authenticating you before issuing you a certificate. Furthermore, a HA CA will refuse to grant a certificate to any organization that doesn't have the same strict rules about how its CA is managed and how its CA grants certificates.

- Discretionary Assurance (DA)

  A DA CA is intended to be well managed at the top level, but it doesn't impose any rules on the organizations to which it grants CA certificates (other than that they actually "own" the name listed in their certificate). The managers of a DA CA will make sure that when an organization, say the Chaos Computer Club, asks for a certificate for their CA, that they really are the Chaos Computer Club. However, the DA CA managers will not make any constraints on how the Chaos Computer Club manages its CA.

  Note that technically the IPRA is of the DA type. It can't be of the HA type, because it will issue certificates to a DA CA and a NA CA (see below)

- No Assurance (NA)

  A NA CA has no constraints except that it is not allowed to issue two certificates with the same name. It is expected that users certified by a NA CA will not in general use their real names and may in fact operate under **personas** (pseudonyms) like Rabid Dog. Even the issuing NA CA might not know the true identity of the users it certifies.

The rule in RFC 1422 is that there can only be a single path through the CA hierarchy to any individual. What that means is that if an organization, say MIT, decides it wants to be certified with a DA CA, then it cannot also be certified with a HA CA. It also means that cross certificates (see §14.9 *Hierarchy of Realms*) are not allowed. The CA hierarchy is a tree.

This rule makes it easy to know the proper chain of certificates to give to someone. The maximal set of certificates they can need is the chain of certificates beginning with the IPRA. There are disadvantages to the restrictions, however. Cross certificates are often useful, so that the chain of certificates can be shorter between two organizations with a lot of mail traffic. And sometimes the two organizations would trust each other's CAs more than they'd trust the entire chain of CAs to and from the IPRA.

Also the rule prevents an organization that would like to get certificates from a HA CA (or made that decision at some point in the past) from granting a certificate to some suborganization's CA that will be less strict than the HA rules demand. An organization can accomplish this by operating two CAs, one which will follow the HA rules, and another which is not constrained by those rules.

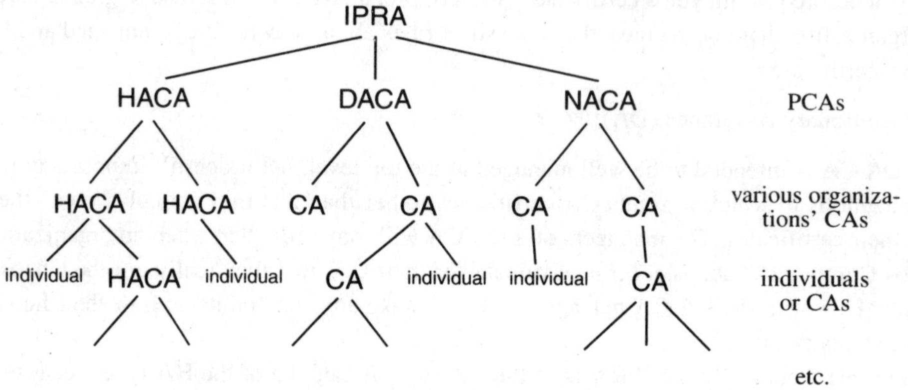

Figure 21-1. RFC 1422 Certification Authority Hierarchy

21.6 Certificate Revocation Lists (CRLs)

It is possible for PEM users to obtain both certificates and CRLs without the aid of PEM, assuming some sufficiently sophisticated (and as yet undeployed) directory service. PEM wants to be usable even if such a directory service is for some reason unavailable, so it allows Bob to send Alice the relevant certificates for him by including them in the header of a PEM message he sends to her. PEM doesn't include a field in the header for CRLs, though. Instead PEM defines a CRL service that sends the latest CRLs as a mail message in response to receipt of a request in a mail message.

PEM defines two message types for the CRL service—CRL-RETRIEVAL-REQUEST and CRL. You send a CRL-RETRIEVAL-REQUEST message to the CRL service. The request is unencrypted and unsigned, and consists of a sequence of encoded X.500 names of CAs whose CRLs you want. The service responds with a CRL message containing (as text) the requested CRLs encoded, unencrypted, and unsigned, though each included CRL is signed by the CA that issued it. For each CA, the CRL service sends only the CA's most recently issued CRL that it knows about.

Note that you don't always want the latest CRLs. You really want the ones that were valid at the time a message was received. You might be checking the signatures (on every relevant certificate) for a message that had been forwarded to you months after it was originally received. PEM doesn't provide such a service. The original recipient would have had to obtain the relevant CRLs immediately upon receiving the message, and then kept them with the message. Alternatively, some sort of library service could be set up to archive all CRLs.

21.7 REFORMATTING DATA TO GET THROUGH MAILERS

As discussed in §20.14 *Annoying Text Format Issues*, the mail infrastructure on which PEM depends for delivering messages might modify messages. PEM needs a reversible encoding of a message that will transit through all known kinds of mail gateways (and even those the PEM designers don't know about, hopefully) without having the gateways feel compelled to mess with the data. The theory is, if no "funny" characters are used, lines are a reasonable length, you don't care about the value of the high-order bit (the parity bit), and all lines are terminated with <CR><LF>, your data will be safe from helpful mail forwarders.

PEM packs 6 bits of information into each 8-bit character. It takes 24 bits of input and converts that into 32 bits (4 characters, each of which will be transmitted as 8 bits). If the data does not consist of an integral number of 24-bit chunks, it is padded with 0 bits to the next multiple of 24 bits, and each octet of pad bits is encoded by =. Actually, PEM packs 65 values into the 8 bits, since the padding gets converted to the = character, which is not one of the 64 characters used for encoding information. The encoding characters consist of the 26 upper-case (A–Z) and 26 lower-case (a–z) letters, the ten digits (0–9), +, and /. PEM uses the character = for the one or two possible padding characters necessary at the end of the data. For those who care, the table of encodings is as follows:

value	character	ASCII representation
0	A	101 octal
⋮	⋮	⋮
25	Z	132 octal
26	a	141 octal
⋮	⋮	⋮
51	z	172 octal
52	0	60 octal
⋮	⋮	⋮
61	9	71 octal
62	+	53 octal
63	/	57 octal
padding	=	75 octal

Figure 21-2. PEM 6-Bit Encoding

21.8 GENERAL STRUCTURE OF A PEM MESSAGE

A PEM message is sent like an ordinary mail message. As a matter of fact, the PEM portion might only be a small piece inside an ordinary mail message. If public key interchange keys are being used and Alice is sending a message to Bob, the PEM portion has the following structure:

marker indicating PEM-processed portion of the message follows: `-----BEGIN PRIVACY-ENHANCED MESSAGE-----`	
header, including information such as which of the three modes is being used (MIC-CLEAR, MIC-ONLY, ENCRYPTED)	
Initialization Vector (IV) for DES-CBC [field present only for ENCRYPTED message]	
certificate for Alice, signed by Alice's CA	optional (see below)
certificate for Alice's CA, signed by CA_2	
⋮	
certificate signed by IPRA	
Message Integrity Code (MIC), which is encrypted if the message is encrypted	
secret key used to encrypt the message, encrypted with Bob's public key [field present only for ENCRYPTED message]	
blank line	
message, either encrypted [if ENCRYPTED], merely mangled to fit into 6-bit canonical get-through-any-mailer format [if MIC-ONLY], or actually human-intelligible [if MIC-CLEAR]	
marker indicating PEM-processed portion of the message is finished: `------END PRIVACY-ENHANCED MESSAGE------`	

It is optional how many certificates in the chain to include. If Alice is pretty sure Bob has the remaining certificates, she can stop at some point before the IPRA. It is possible that no certificates appear explicitly, in which case what appears in their place is the serial number and issuer name of Alice's certificate.

If secret key interchange keys are being used, the structure is:

marker indicating PEM-processed portion of the message follows: `-----BEGIN PRIVACY-ENHANCED MESSAGE-----`
header, including information such as which of the three modes is being used (MIC-CLEAR, MIC-ONLY, ENCRYPTED)
Initialization Vector (IV) for DES-CBC [field present only for ENCRYPTED message]
secret key used to encrypt the message, encrypted with the interchange key shared by Alice and Bob [field present only for ENCRYPTED message]
Message Integrity Code (MIC), encrypted using the interchange key shared by Alice and Bob.
blank line
message, either encrypted [if ENCRYPTED], merely mangled to fit into 6-bit canonical get-through-any-mailer format [if MIC-ONLY], or actually human intelligible [if MIC-CLEAR]
marker indicating PEM-processed portion of the message is finished: `-----END PRIVACY-ENHANCED MESSAGE-----`

21.9 ENCRYPTION

A message is encrypted using a randomly chosen per-message secret key, in CBC mode with a randomly chosen 64-bit initialization vector (IV). The per-message key is different from the interchange key, even when secret key interchange keys are used. Given that each message will be encrypted with a different per-message key, the reason for needing an IV is very subtle. Ordinarily, the purposes of an IV are:

- to ensure that if two messages begin with the same text and are transmitted using the same key, a bad guy seeing the encrypted version will not be able to tell that the messages begin the same
- to prevent a bad guy who can supply messages to be encrypted, from mounting a chosen plaintext attack against the key

With PEM, however, every message is sent with a different key, so these concerns do not arise. The reason PEM uses an IV is to make exhaustive attacks against per-message keys more difficult in the case where several messages are sent and the attacker happens to know they all begin with the same text and knows that text (e.g., "Dear sir:"). Assume 56-bit keys. In that case, an attacker with a fast crypto engine could start encrypting that text with all 2^{56} keys and check whether the resulting block matched the first block of any of the captured messages. In 2^{56} encryptions, the attacker can crack all of the messages. With PEM's IV, however, the attacker has to try 2^{56} keys for each message, since the first blocks of text will be different after the IVs are ⊕ed.

Each message to be CBC-encrypted is padded with 1 to 8 bytes to make it a multiple of 8 bytes (even if it started out as a multiple of 8 bytes). The content of each of the pad bytes is the number of pad bytes. So a message that was already a multiple of 8 bytes would be padded with eight 8s. A message that was 2 more than a multiple of 8 would have 6 bytes of 6s.

21.10 Source Authentication and Integrity Protection

Integrity protection is provided by calculating a MIC (Message Integrity Code) for the message. The defined types of MIC are MD2 and MD5, though originally the DES CBC residue was also defined. That mode of MIC was removed after $we_{1,2}$ showed that it was completely insecure (see §21.16 *DES-CBC as MIC Doesn't Work*). But a message digest by itself is not a MIC since anyone can modify the message and compute the message digest of the modified message. So the message digest has to be cryptographically protected. In the public key case, this is done by signing the message digest; in the secret key case, it is done by encrypting the message digest with the interchange key.

In the public key case, why must the MIC be encrypted when the message is encrypted? The reason is that the message digest can be computed from the MIC by using Alice's public key. Someone can guess the contents of the message, and then be able to verify it by checking the message digest of the guess against that of the message. For instance, if they guess the message will say either attack or retreat, they can compute the message digest on both guessed messages, and see whether either guess is correct. It's nice that the MIC doesn't need to be encrypted when the message is not encrypted. In that case a per-message key can be dispensed with entirely and the sender need not learn the public key of the recipient in order to send a signed message.

21.11 MULTIPLE RECIPIENTS

A signed but unencrypted message can be sent to any number of recipients without modification. PEM merely signs the message with the sender's private key:

`-----BEGIN PRIVACY-ENHANCED MESSAGE-----`
header, saying `MIC-CLEAR` or `MIC-ONLY`
MIC (message digest signed with Alice's private key)
unencrypted message
`-----END PRIVACY-ENHANCED MESSAGE-----`

To transmit an encrypted message to multiple recipients, PEM encrypts the message once (with, as usual, a randomly chosen key), and then separately encrypts the per-message key for each recipient:

`-----BEGIN PRIVACY-ENHANCED MESSAGE-----`
header, saying `ENCRYPTED`
MIC (message digest signed with Alice's private key and encrypted with message key)
Message key encrypted with Bob's public key
Message key encrypted with Ted's public key
encrypted message
`-----END PRIVACY-ENHANCED MESSAGE-----`

Note that the message is encrypted only once, but the per-message key must be encrypted once for each recipient.

It is possible to mix usage of public and secret keys. For instance, suppose Alice is sending a message to Bob and Carol, where Bob has a public key, but Carol has a secret key shared with Alice, and Carol's node cannot execute public key cryptographic algorithms (perhaps because Carol hasn't made the proper licensing arrangement). Alice picks a per-message secret key, encrypts the message with that secret key, and then encrypts the per-message key with Bob's public key (for Bob), and encrypts it with the key she shares with Carol (for Carol). The integrity check need only appear once to take care of all recipients capable of dealing with public keys. Alice merely signs the message digest with her private key. However, just because Alice has a public key does not mean that all the recipients can make use of it. For instance, those U.S. recipients who haven't licensed RSA cannot legally verify the signature. Alice needs to include a separate MIC for each recipient who cannot deal with her public key. For instance, for Carol, Alice will include the message digest encrypted with the secret key that Alice and Carol share.

`-----BEGIN PRIVACY-ENHANCED MESSAGE-----`
header, saying `ENCRYPTED`
MIC (message digest signed with Alice's private key and encrypted with message key)
Message key encrypted with Bob's public key
MIC (message digest encrypted with the key Alice and Carol share)
Message key encrypted with the key Alice and Carol share
encrypted message
`-----END PRIVACY-ENHANCED MESSAGE-----`

21.12 Bracketing PEM Messages

Bob has just received a message. How does his PEM processor know whether the message is a PEM message, or just an ordinary message? Even if PEM knows (somehow) that the message is a PEM message, it's not always obvious where PEM should start processing, and where to end processing. For instance, Alice might have sent a signed message to Bob, so that the entire message as transmitted by Alice should be processed by PEM, but mail gateways en route might add cybercrud to the beginning and/or end of the message. (Luckily most mail gateways are sufficiently well-behaved so that they don't add things to the middle of a message—if they did, PEM would not be able to cope.) By the time Bob receives the message his PEM processor might need to skip the first few lines, start processing at some point, and end at some other point in the message. As a matter of fact, it isn't strictly necessary for an entire message from Alice to be PEM-processed. She might just want to encrypt a small portion of the message. For example:

```
Hello Bob
This is to inform you that your raise has gone through and your new salary is
-----BEGIN PRIVACY-ENHANCED MESSAGE-----
```
header saying `encrypted`
```
afdsjklasdfjklas;f
```
```
-----END PRIVACY-ENHANCED MESSAGE-----
Once again congratulations on the good work.
Sincerely, Alice
```

That is why PEM marks the beginning of the PEM-processed portion of the message with the string

`-----BEGIN PRIVACY-ENHANCED MESSAGE-----`

and the end of the message with the string

`-----END PRIVACY-ENHANCED MESSAGE-----`

This might sound straightforward, but there are problems. A human being is perfectly capable of typing the above strings (we did, for instance). Suppose

`-----END PRIVACY-ENHANCED MESSAGE-----`

appears in the middle of a message. For instance, Alice might be transmitting a portion of this book (after getting written permission from the publisher, of course!).

Note that if the message is encoded (as a MIC-ONLY or ENCRYPTED message will be), then the string

`-----END PRIVACY-ENHANCED MESSAGE-----`

can't possibly appear inside the (encoded) body of the message (even if it was in the original message) because "-" is not one of the encode characters. But PEM does have to worry about disguising the PEM end marker in MIC-CLEAR messages.

Although the end marker is the only string that could confuse PEM, instead of only searching for

`-----END PRIVACY-ENHANCED MESSAGE-----`

PEM always modifies every line of the text of a MIC-CLEAR message that begins with a dash, just because RFC 934 did it that way for forwarded mail markers. When PEM sees a line that begins with a dash, it adds the two characters "- " (dash space) to the beginning of the line. So the string

`-----END PRIVACY-ENHANCED MESSAGE-----`

would appear as

`- -----END PRIVACY-ENHANCED MESSAGE-----`

if it appeared in the middle of a MIC-CLEAR message. Any other line that started with a dash would also appear that way. For example,

```
--Sincerely, Alice--
```

would appear as:

```
- --Sincerely, Alice--
```

Bob's PEM processor will most likely remove the extra characters before displaying the text of the message to Bob. However, if Bob does not have PEM, Bob will see the PEM cybercrud, and see the mysterious "- " added to the beginning of some of the lines of the text of the message.

PEM really can't defend itself from being confused in all cases. For instance, Alice might have typed the following message and sent it with a non-PEM mailer.

```
To: Bob
     Have you heard about this new PEM standard? I don't
completely understand it, but it seems to imply that I can make my
message to you secret by adding the string
-----BEGIN PRIVACY-ENHANCED MESSAGE-----
and some other stuff like MIC-INFO and RFC-1822 at the beginning
of the message and putting the string
-----END PRIVACY-ENHANCED MESSAGE-----
at the end. I don't understand how this could prevent anyone from
reading the message, although maybe enough cybercrud on the
beginning of the message would convince them the message must be
hopelessly garbled and they might not even attempt to read it.
--Alice
```

If Bob's machine has PEM, it will see those markers and attempt to parse the message as a PEM message. It will probably notice that the message is ill-formed, though Alice could have typed something that happened to have all the text looking like correct fields. At that point it would probably notice that signatures would not verify or that it was lacking the proper certificates. If Alice did indeed manage to type in a completely correct PEM message, then PEM at Bob's node will not notice (Alice will have passed a warped form of the Turing test).

Another issue is nested messages. It is permissible to have, for instance, an encrypted message inside a signed message, or Alice might be forwarding a signed message from Fred as an enclosure in a signed message to Bob (see §21.13.1 *Forwarding a Message*). The PEM processor at Bob's node presumably has to process the outer message, which might involve decrypting and/or decoding. Once the outer message is processed, the string

```
-----BEGIN PRIVACY-ENHANCED MESSAGE-----
```

might be uncovered, and PEM has the same problem as we mentioned before, which is to somehow determine whether that is really the beginning of a PEM message, or whether Alice just happened to have included that particular string in her message.

The PEM protocol was designed so that it is conceptually possible to nest PEM processing, but it would require PEM processors far more sophisticated than anyone is likely to ever implement to deal with all possible cases, and furthermore the user interface would be horrible to contemplate. (See Homework Problem 8.)

21.13 FORWARDING AND ENCLOSURES

Alice might want to forward to Bob a message she received from someone else, inside a message of her own:

`-----BEGIN PRIVACY-ENHANCED MESSAGE-----`
header, saying `MIC-CLEAR`
MIC (message digest signed with Bob's private key)

`Bob–`
`Get a load of the outrageous stuff Fred is sending me!`
`- --Alice`
`- ----BEGIN PRIVACY-ENHANCED MESSAGE-----`

header, saying `MIC-CLEAR`
MIC (message digest signed with Fred's private key)

`Alice–`
`The rhythm of your typing at the terminal is driving me insane.`
`Either type completely rhythmically or completely unrhythmically.`
`I will complain to upper level management if you don't adjust your`
`typing.`
`- - --Fred`
`- ----END PRIVACY-ENHANCED MESSAGE-----`
`-----END PRIVACY-ENHANCED MESSAGE-----`

21.13.1 Forwarding a Message

What should you do to a message from Fred before forwarding it to Bob so that Bob can verify Fred's signature? With non-PEM mailers, one often extracts text from one message and includes it in another. PEM certainly doesn't stop you from doing that, but if you don't send a message with the PEM information intact, there's no way for Bob to cryptographically verify that the original text was really from Fred. With public keys, it is possible to usefully forward PEM signatures. But secret key based source authentication information cannot be usefully forwarded because such information cannot be verified by a third party. Therefore, in this section, we'll assume user keys are based on public key technology.

Suppose Alice is just forwarding a message from Fred to Bob without adding any annotations of her own, and in the same format as she received it (ENCRYPTED, MIC-CLEAR, or MIC-ONLY). In that case she processes the message like a distribution list exploder:

- In the case of a MIC-CLEAR or MIC-ONLY message, she just forwards it, without having to do any processing on it.
- In the case of an ENCRYPTED message, she decrypts the per-message key, reencrypts it with Bob's key, and adds the encrypted key and Bob's name to the header.

It could be that Alice wants to change the format of the message. The term **upgrading** means that she turns an unencrypted message into an encrypted message. The term **downgrading** means she turns an encrypted message into an unencrypted message. The PEM designers were careful to have the signature on a message apply to the unencrypted message, so that a message can be downgraded or upgraded without changing the signature.

For example, let's assume Alice has a MIC-ONLY message from Fred. It contains

- header, saying MIC-ONLY
- MIC (message digest signed with Fred's private key)
- message (encoded but unencrypted)

In order to encrypt it to send it to Bob, Alice picks a per-message key *K* in order to encrypt the message. Now, she can't simply encrypt the encoded message, since PEM mandates that encryption is based on an unencoded message. So she has to decode the message, encrypt the result, and encode the result of the encryption. So what she sends is

- header, saying ENCRYPTED
- *K* encrypted with Bob's public key
- encrypted MIC, consisting of the message digest signed with Fred's private key and encrypted with *K*. Note that Alice can't sign the MIC with Fred's private key, so she has to use the MIC she received. Since the MIC she received from Fred is encoded (to pass through mailers), she has to decode the MIC to obtain the actual message digest signed with Fred's public key. That is the quantity she encrypts and then encodes.
- message encrypted with *K*

Downgrading a message is just reversing the process. If Alice wants to annotate Fred's message before forwarding it, then she can enclose the complete message inside the text of her message, and then sign or encrypt her own message as she desires.

21.14 UNPROTECTED INFORMATION

PEM only provides integrity protection or privacy on the *contents* of a message. There is other information in a message, however, and if people use PEM carelessly there are interesting security flaws that can be exploited. PEM does not protect the SUBJECT, TO, FROM, or TIMESTAMP field. How can a bad guy exploit the fact that PEM does not protect these fields?

Why would it be nice to cryptographically protect the subject line? A naive user might put private information into the subject line, and expose the information to an eavesdropper. Or suppose Alice sees a message from Fred, in which Fred suggests some outrageous idea. Alice forwards Fred's message, integrity-protected, with the subject line Fire this Bozo immediately, but someone modifies the unprotected subject line to Great idea! Implement this suggestion immediately. Since the subject line is not protected, the message will arrive signed by Alice, but having the subject line modified completely changes what she intended to say.

The TO and FROM fields cannot be encrypted because the mail infrastructure needs to see them. Theoretically they could be included in the integrity protection even though they couldn't be privacy-protected. PEM didn't do this because mailers tend to mangle these fields. PEM could have gotten around this by making a copy of that information and moving it inside the message.

It's unfortunate that PEM doesn't integrity-protect the TO field. For instance, Alice might send the signed message I agree to donate $1000 to your organization to organization Z, and the message might be copied and used by organization Y to fool Alice's underlings into sending them money also.

An example of where it is unfortunate that PEM didn't do something with the FROM field is where secret key based interchange keys are used and Alice sends a message to a distribution list located on a remote exploder. The remote exploder has to check Alice's MIC and then add its own per-recipient MIC. PEM does not provide any cryptographically protected method for the exploder to assert that it did indeed check and the message had come from Alice.

The other piece of header information that is not cryptographically protected is the timestamp. This doesn't seem too important. Even naive users would realize that if the time of sending a message were important, they should date the message in the text. Naive users would probably not even know that the mail infrastructure adds a time of posting.

Note that even if PEM protected all the header fields, it would be possible to misuse electronic mail. For instance, if Alice sends Bob the signed message I approve, Bob can't use the message later to prove that Alice okayed his action, since the message isn't explicit about what Alice was approving.

If Alice is careful, most of these PEM problems can be worked around. To protect the header information, Alice should include the header information in the text. The only problem we've described that has no PEM workaround is that a remote mail exploder cannot cryptographically assert that a message using secret interchange keys did originate with Alice.

21.15 MESSAGE FORMATS

The PEM message formats have fields that consist of text. Sometimes the fields are encrypted, and sometimes they are encoded (which looks encrypted to humans but isn't).

The types of messages are MIC-CLEAR, MIC-ONLY, and ENCRYPTED, and the format for each of these varies slightly depending on whether public or secret key cryptography is being used. We'll describe the public key and secret key variants separately. If some recipients use public key and some use secret key, then fields from both variants must be present.

Each field in the message has a label indicating what it contains. There are a few reasons for this label:

- To provide a visual clue to a human reader wondering what all the cybercrud is (but a civilized PEM mailer ought not show the cybercrud to the human)
- To identify the field—the position of the field in the message does not uniquely identify it because some fields are optional and/or repeated (e.g., CA CERTIFICATE)

21.15.1 ENCRYPTED, Public Key Variant

`----BEGIN PRIVACY-ENHANCED MESSAGE----`	pre-encapsulation boundary
`Proc-Type: 4,ENCRYPTED`	type of PEM message (version,type)
`Content-Domain: RFC822`	message form
`DEK-Info: DES-CBC,` *16 hex digits*	message encryption algorithm, IV
`Originator-Certificate:` *cybercrud*	sender's encoded certificate (optional)
`Originator-ID-Asymmetric:` *cybercrud,number*	sender ID (present only if sender's certificate not present)
`Key-Info: RSA,` *cybercrud*	key-info for CC'd sender (if needed)
`Issuer-Certificate:` *cybercrud* ⋮	sequence of zero or more CA certificates (possibly whole chain from the sender's certificate to the IPRA's)
`MIC-Info: RSA-MD`*x*`,RSA,` *cybercrud*	message digest algorithm, message digest encryption algorithm, encoded encrypted MIC
`Recipient-ID-Asymmetric:` *cybercrud,number* `Key-Info: RSA,` *cybercrud* ⋮	for each recipient: recipient ID (encoded X.500 name of CA that signed certificate, certificate serial number); key-info for recipient
	blank line
cybercrud	encoded encrypted message
`----END PRIVACY-ENHANCED MESSAGE-----`	post-encapsulation boundary

`-----BEGIN PRIVACY-ENHANCED MESSAGE-----`

PRE-ENCAPSULATION BOUNDARY. This is just to show that a PEM-processed portion of the mail message is about to begin.

`Proc-Type: 4,ENCRYPTED`

MESSAGE TYPE. The first subfield (4) specifies that this is version four of PEM. There are currently no other legal values for this field. The second subfield (ENCRYPTED) specifies that this is an encrypted message. The other legal values for this field are MIC-ONLY and MIC-CLEAR.

Content-Domain: RFC822

MESSAGE FORM. The intention is that there might eventually be lots of types of mail messages, such as PostScript, spreadsheet, bitmap, executable image for an XYZ processor, and so on. However, the only defined type is RFC822, which is an Internet standard for ordinary text messages.

DEK-Info: DES-CBC,0123456789ABCDEF

MESSAGE ENCRYPTION ALGORITHM, IV. The first subfield identifies the cryptographic algorithm used to encrypt the message. Currently the only "registered" algorithm is DES-CBC. The second subfield specifies the IV as 16 hex digits. So in the example above, the IV is $0123456789ABCDEF_{16}$.

Originator-Certificate: **MIIBfzCCASkCAQIwDQYJKoZIhvcNAQECBQAwQzELM
AkGA1UEBhMCVVMxJjAkBgNVBAoTHURpZ210YWwgRXF1aXBtZW50IENvcnBvcmF0a
W9uMQwwCgYDVQQLEwNMS0cwHhcNOTIwOTA4MjAxODMzWhcNOTQwOTA4MjAxODMzW
jBXMQswCQYDVQQGEwJVUzEmMCQGA1UEChMdRGlnaXRhbCBFcXVpcGllbnQgQ29yc
G9yYXRpb24xDDAKBgNVBAsTA0xLRzESMBAGA1UEAxMJSm9obiBMaW5uMFcwCgYEV
QgBAQICAgADSQAwRgJBAMEom520pxxpN7Y+0e8nWsI2yVK4YPu30+meJEwH9w0Xu
O3hmHTHowzrNwgdgFeic4SHlkFOwf1K7RrOgnTurQ0CAQMwDQYJKoZIhvcNAQECB
QADQQBq/+L5hKVZvN/jtgsjeUE5eQBrMpSf3ND4kqyP65xj29OhFk5Mbh4DpfJ+7
wOwJATwUjOERhzwVJm5WmI0oRs4**

SENDER'S CERTIFICATE. BIG pile of cybercrud as specified in X.509. Since a certificate is ASN.1-coded information (as opposed to nice printable text strings), the certificate is encoded as per §21.7 *Reformatting Data to Get Through Mailers*. Certificates are described in Chapter 15 *PKI (Public Key Infrastructure)*.

Originator-ID-Asymmetric: **MEMxCzAJBgNVBAYTAlVTMSYwJAYDVQQKEx1EaWd
pdGFsIEVxdWlwbWVudCBDb3Jwb3JhdGlvbjEMMAoGA1UECxMDTEtH,216**

SENDER ID. This field can replace the SENDER'S CERTIFICATE field to save space. It consists of the X.500 name of the CA that issued the sender her certificate, coded in ASN.1 and encoded 6 bits per character, followed by a comma, followed by the serial number of the sender's certificate in decimal using decimal digits. In the example above, the serial number is 216.

Key-Info: RSA,**Pv3W7Ds86/fQBnvB5DsvUXgpK7+6h5aSVcNeYf9uWtly9m2VHzC
v2t7A6qgbXtIcf4kaMj1FL2yl9/N9mWpm4w==**

KEY-INFO. This is strictly necessary only if the sender CC's herself on the message. It is also useful when the mail system returns the message to the sender due to some error condition. The purpose of this field is to enable the sender to decrypt the message. The first subfield specifies the cryptographic algorithm used for encrypting the per-message key. The only defined public key algorithm is RSA. The second subfield contains the per-message key encrypted with the sender's public key and then encoded.

```
Issuer-Certificate: MIIBXzCCAQkCAQowDQYJKoZIhvcNAQECBQAwNzELMAkGA
 1UEBhMCVVMxKDAmBgNVBAoTH1RydXN0ZWQgSW5mb3JtYXRpb24gU31zdGVtcyBQQ
 0EwHhcNOTIwOTA4MTk0NTQzWhcNOTQwOTA4MTk0NTQzWjBDMQswCQYDVQQGEwJVU
 zEmMCQGA1UEChMdRGlnaXRhbCBFcXVpcG11bnQgQ29ycG9yYXRpb24xDDAKBgNVB
 AsTA0xLRzBXMAoGBFUIAQECAgIAA0kAMEYCQQDkwhgRGX6ScwOHTVk48NK07tiih
 t9bBExsbxphdp7brUrypA4kZDYqZNVv9Ee5kHv5qn428Pc31bGH+z1S7bq/AgEDM
 A0GCSqGSIb3DQEBAgUAA0EARfI+2huFXK9jsROeK+CaohcB23cBFjzqhslhI50UU
 Y4rBx8QhcApY/g+mhXzBz1JPe/HANQMG567DHB3AJKaTQ==
```

CA CERTIFICATE. The certificate of one of the CAs in the chain from the sender to the IPRA. The first one certifies the sender's CA, the next one certifies the sender's CA's parent, …, the last one certifies the IPRA. However, it is permissible to include in the message only an initial subsequence of this certificate chain (even an empty subsequence!), as long as no certificates are skipped.

```
MIC-Info: RSA-MD5,RSA,FUiVRM3x5Ku0aZveGIJ1hv/hi3Iowpm1iypd9VP7MGw
 PPQra+42TkbR/2jhnqXyVEXLaJ7BSyNhBh/9znIUj5uk0N7IXeBxX
```

MESSAGE DIGEST ALGORITHM, MESSAGE DIGEST ENCRYPTION ALGORITHM, MIC. The choices for message digest algorithm are RSA-MD2 and RSA-MD5. RSA-MD2 is merely MD2. RSA-MD5 is MD5. In both cases, RSA is included in the name to acknowledge that MD2 and MD5 were donated for use in PEM by RSADSI. The choices for message digest encryption algorithm are RSA. (Luckily RSA is a good choice). The MIC (the message digest encrypted with the sender's private key, then encrypted with the per-message key) is an encoded 512-bit number.

```
Recipient-ID-Asymmetric: MEMxCzAJBgNVBAYTAlVTMSYwJAYDVQQKEx1EaWdp
 dGFsIEVxdWlwbWVudCBDb3Jwb3JhdGlvbjEMMAoGA1UECxMDTEtH,729
```

RECIPIENT ID. This is an identifier for a recipient's certificate. It consists of the X.500 name of the CA that issued this recipient's certificate, coded in ASN.1 and encoded 6 bits per character, followed by a comma, followed by the serial number of the certificate in decimal using decimal digits. In the above example, the serial number is 729. Note that identifying the recipient in this arcane manner, rather than simply by name, allows a recipient with multiple public keys to know which key to use to decrypt his KEY-INFO field:

```
Key-Info: RSA,dpUp7/QoY9YOZzZCVcIwxIDMN0WbGCFAGN3T+x1V/0pBu2n5+x8
 PmBvMUN0NcBi5vtqBS4cfmgShiK0I4zu05Q==
```

KEY-INFO. This field provides the recipient (identified by the immediately preceding RECIPIENT ID field) with the per-message key. The second subfield contains the per-message key encrypted with the recipient's public key and then encoded. The first subfield specifies the cryptographic algorithm used for encrypting the per-message key. The only defined public key algorithm is RSA. Note that even if there were more choices, there would be no reason to specify the algorithm since the algorithm is whatever algorithm is specified for the key in the recipient's certificate. However, bit-bumming the encoding of mail messages did not seem to be a priority with the PEM designers.

21OHDuHTP5BABnlsqENzlWVerZxxWo2AsPHhm2SIz9qpLMvxT/x0+8UEf8dDsTDr wbQo9/x+

ENCRYPTED MESSAGE. The message DES-CBC encrypted with the per-message key and then encoded.

-----END PRIVACY-ENHANCED MESSAGE-----

POST-ENCAPSULATION BOUNDARY. This is just to show that a PEM-processed portion of the mail message has ended.

21.15.2 ENCRYPTED, Secret Key Variant

-----BEGIN PRIVACY-ENHANCED MESSAGE-----	pre-encapsulation boundary
Proc-Type: 4,ENCRYPTED	type of PEM message (version,type)
Content-Domain: RFC822	message form
DEK-Info: DES-CBC, *16 hex digits*	message encryption algorithm, IV
Originator-ID-Symmetric: *entity identifier, issuing authority, version/expiration*	sender ID
Recipient-ID-Symmetric: *entity identifier, issuing authority, version/expiration* **Key-Info: DES-ECB,RSA-MDx,** *16 hex digits, 32 hex digits* ⋮	for each recipient: recipient ID; key-info for recipient
	blank line
cybercrud	encoded encrypted message
-----END PRIVACY-ENHANCED MESSAGE-----	post-encapsulation boundary

-----BEGIN PRIVACY-ENHANCED MESSAGE-----

PRE-ENCAPSULATION BOUNDARY. This is just to show that a PEM-processed portion of the mail message is about to begin.

Proc-Type: 4,ENCRYPTED

MESSAGE TYPE. The first subfield (4) specifies that this is version four of PEM. There are currently no other legal values for this field. The second subfield (ENCRYPTED) specifies that this is an encrypted message. The other legal values for this field are MIC-ONLY and MIC-CLEAR.

Content-Domain: RFC822

MESSAGE FORM. The intention is that there might eventually be lots of types of mail messages, such as PostScript, spreadsheet, bitmap, executable image for an XYZ processor, and so on. However, the only defined type is RFC822, which is an Internet standard for ordinary text messages.

DEK-Info: DES-CBC,0123456789ABCDEF

MESSAGE ENCRYPTION ALGORITHM, IV. The first subfield identifies the cryptographic algorithm used to encrypt the message. Currently the only "registered" algorithm is DES-CBC. The second subfield specifies the IV as 16 hex digits. So in the example above, the IV is $0123456789ABCDEF_{16}$.

Originator-ID-Symmetric: Alice@Wonderland.edu,,

SENDER ID. This field uniquely identifies the sender to the recipients. There are three subfields. The first subfield identifies the sender. The other two subfields are useless, but are there to make the sender ID have the same format as the recipient IDs. In practice, the two useless subfields are omitted (except for the delimiting commas). There is no standard for the format of any of the subfields, but RFC 1421 strongly recommends using an internet mail address for the first subfield.

Recipient-ID-Symmetric: WhiteRabbit@Wonderland.edu, MadHatter@Wonderland.edu,1

RECIPIENT ID. This field uniquely identifies the interchange key to be used by the recipient. There are three subfields. The first subfield identifies the recipient (so that the recipient knows this field and the immediately following KEY-INFO field are for him). The second subfield identifies the issuer of the shared key (in the event that multiple issuing authorities have assigned shared keys between the sender and recipient). The third subfield uniquely identifies the key (in the event that multiple keys have been issued between the sender and recipient by the same issuing authority). There is no standard for the format of any of the subfields, but RFC 1421 strongly recommends using an internet mail address for the first subfield.

Key-Info: DES-ECB,RSA-MD5,0123456789ABCDEF, FEDCBA98765432100123456789ABCDEF

KEY-INFO. This field provides the recipient (identified by the immediately preceding RECIPIENT ID field) with the per-message key and the MIC. The first subfield specifies the cryptographic algorithm used to encrypt the per-message key. The choices are DES-ECB (see §4.2.1 *Electronic Code Book (ECB)*) and DES-EDE (see §4.4 *Multiple Encryption DES*). DES-EDE is used when the shared interchange key is double length. The second subfield specifies the algorithm used to compute the message digest. The choices are RSA-MD2 (for MD2) and RSA-MD5 (for MD5). The third subfield is the per-message key encrypted with the interchange key, expressed as a 16-digit hexadecimal number. The fourth subfield is the MIC, which is the message digest encrypted with the per-message key in ECB mode, expressed as a 32-digit hexadecimal number.

21OHDuHTP5BABnlsqENz1WVerZxxWo2AsPHhm2SIz9qpLMvxT/x0+8UEf8dDsTDr wbQo9/x+

ENCRYPTED MESSAGE. The message DES-CBC encrypted with the per-message key and then encoded.

-----END PRIVACY-ENHANCED MESSAGE-----

POST-ENCAPSULATION BOUNDARY. This is just to show that a PEM-processed portion of the mail message has ended.

21.15.3 MIC-ONLY or MIC-CLEAR, Public Key Variant

----BEGIN PRIVACY-ENHANCED MESSAGE-----	pre-encapsulation boundary
Proc-Type: 4,MIC-ONLY *or* MIC-CLEAR	type of PEM message (version,type)
Content-Domain: RFC822	message form
Originator-Certificate: *cybercrud*	sender's encoded certificate (optional)
Originator-ID-Asymmetric: *cybercrud,number*	sender ID (present only if sender's certificate not present)
Issuer-Certificate: *cybercrud* ⋮	sequence of zero or more CA certificates (possibly whole chain from sender to the root)
MIC-Info: RSA-MD*x*, RSA, *cybercrud*	message digest algorithm, message digest encryption algorithm, encoded MIC
	blank line
message	message (encoded if MIC-ONLY)
----END PRIVACY-ENHANCED MESSAGE-----	post-encapsulation boundary

The only differences between an ENCRYPTED public key PEM message and a MIC-ONLY or MIC-CLEAR public key PEM message are the following:

- The TYPE OF MESSAGE field specifies MIC-ONLY or MIC-CLEAR.

- The MIC is not encrypted, though it is encoded 6 bits per character.
- The message is not encrypted; for MIC-ONLY it is encoded 6 bits per character, while for MIC-CLEAR it is included unmodified (except for the insertion of a "- " before each beginning-of-line "-").
- The MESSAGE ENCRYPTION ALGORITHM, IV field is omitted.
- All the fields giving per-recipient information are omitted.
- The KEY-INFO field for giving information about the sender's key is omitted.

21.15.4 MIC-ONLY and MIC-CLEAR, Secret Key Variant

`----BEGIN PRIVACY-ENHANCED MESSAGE-----`	pre-encapsulation boundary
`Proc-Type: 4,MIC-ONLY` *or* `MIC-CLEAR`	type of PEM message (version,type)
`Content-Domain: RFC822`	message form
`Originator-ID-Symmetric:` *entity identifier, issuing authority, version/expiration*	sender ID
`Recipient-ID-Symmetric:` *entity identifier, issuing authority, version/expiration* `Key-Info: DES-ECB,RSA-MDx`, *16 hex digits, 32 hex digits* ⋮	for each recipient: recipient ID; key-info for recipient
	blank line
message	message (encoded if MIC-ONLY)
`----END PRIVACY-ENHANCED MESSAGE-----`	post-encapsulation boundary

The only differences between an ENCRYPTED secret key PEM message and a MIC-ONLY or MIC-CLEAR secret key PEM message are the following:

- The TYPE OF MESSAGE field specifies MIC-ONLY or MIC-CLEAR.
- The message is not encrypted; for MIC-ONLY it is encoded 6 bits per character, while with MIC-CLEAR it is included unmodified (except for the insertion of a "- " before each beginning-of-line "-").
- The MESSAGE ENCRYPTION ALGORITHM, IV field is omitted.

21.15.5 CRL-RETRIEVAL-REQUEST

`----BEGIN PRIVACY-ENHANCED MESSAGE-----`	pre-encapsulation boundary
`Proc-Type: 4,CRL-RETRIEVAL-REQUEST`	type of PEM message (version,type)
`Issuer:` *cybercrud* ⋮	for each CRL requested: the encoded X.500 name of the issuing CA
`----END PRIVACY-ENHANCED MESSAGE-----`	post-encapsulation boundary

21.15.6 CRL

`----BEGIN PRIVACY-ENHANCED MESSAGE-----`	pre-encapsulation boundary
`Proc-Type: 4,CRL`	type of PEM message (version,type)
`CRL:` *cybercrud* `Originator-Certificate:` *cybercrud* ⋮	for each CRL retrieved: encoded X.509 format CRL; encoded X.509 certificate of the CA that issued the CRL
`----END PRIVACY-ENHANCED MESSAGE-----`	post-encapsulation boundary

21.16 DES-CBC AS MIC DOESN'T WORK

Originally, PEM had an additional method of obtaining a MIC on a message, which was the DES-CBC residue. The PEM documentation referred to this form of integrity check as DES-MAC. Ironically, they included this because the MD functions were new and therefore cryptographically suspect, whereas DES CBC residue was used in banking and therefore known to be secure. And it was in the banking context. But not for email. In banking it is used as an integrity check, and has the property that if someone doesn't know the secret key that Alice and Bob share, they cannot modify or forge a message between Alice and Bob. It is instructive to see how something as seemingly straightforward as an integrity check, especially one known to be secure in a highly sensitive application like banking, can have problems. The DES-MAC version of integrity checking has several interesting security problems:

- If Alice uses secret key interchange keys and ever sends a message to multiple recipients, say Bob and Ted, then Bob can thereafter send DES-MAC integrity check messages

(MIC-CLEAR, MIC-ONLY, or ENCRYPTED) to Ted, claiming to be Alice (and Ted can likewise send such messages to Bob claiming to be Alice). This is true regardless of the choice of integrity check (DES-MAC, MD2, or MD5) Alice chose when she sent the multi-recipient message.

- If Alice is using public key technology for interchange keys and uses DES-MAC as the integrity check when sending an ENCRYPTED message to Bob, Bob can thereafter send messages to anyone he wants, claiming to be Alice.
- With public key interchange keys, if Alice sends a MIC-CLEAR or MIC-ONLY (as opposed to ENCRYPTED) message to Bob, anyone who eavesdrops on the message can thereafter send messages to anyone she wants, claiming to be Alice.
- Suppose Alice, knowing that DES-MAC is not a secure integrity check, never uses it herself. But Ted is happy to accept DES-MAC messages. If Alice sends a message using either MD2 or MD5, someone can use her signature on that message to create a forged message that uses DES-MAC and would appear to come from Alice; Ted would accept such a message as genuine. (Vulnerabilities depend on whether interchange keys are secret or public, and whether the message was encrypted or not. See Homework Problem 12).

We'll have to describe how DES-MAC is specified in the earlier PEM specification. Suppose Alice is sending a message to Bob and Ted. The algorithm for using DES-MAC as the integrity check is as follows:

1. Choose a per-message key (this is the same key PEM would use if PEM was going to encrypt the message).
2. Modify the per-message key by ⊕ing it with $F0F0F0F0F0F0F0F0_{16}$ (to avoid the classic cryptographic flaw described in §4.3.1 *Ensuring Privacy and Integrity Together*).
3. Compute the 64-bit CBC residue with the modified per-message key.
4. Encrypt the residue. If secret key based interchange keys are used, encrypt the CBC residue with the interchange key associated with Ted, plus encrypt the CBC residue with the interchange key associated with Bob, and send both quantities along with the message. If public key based interchange keys are used, Alice signs the residue with her private RSA key.

The problem is that it is possible, given a 64-bit quantity x and a DES key k, to generate a message m such that the CBC residue of m with key k is x. (We'll demonstrate that later in this section.) Let's look at several cases:

- Alice sends a MIC-ONLY message to Bob, using public key interchange keys, using DES-MAC as the integrity check. Carol eavesdrops on the message. She can see that it came from Alice. She finds Alice's public key, extracts the signed DES-MAC from the message header, and reverses the signature on the DES-MAC, thereby retrieving the DES-MAC of the message. Carol now knows the quantity x (the DES-MAC) and the quantity y, which is Alice's signature on x. As we said, she can invent any key k and construct a message m with DES-MAC x (using key k). She can then send m to anyone she wants, say Ted, and claim that the message was from Alice, because she'll include y as the signed DES-MAC for m.

- Suppose instead that Alice sends an encrypted message to Bob. In this case only Bob knows the quantities x (the DES-MAC of the message) and y (Alice's signature on x) because PEM specifies that if the message is encrypted, the integrity check is encrypted with the key used to encrypt the per-message key. But that means that Bob can now send messages claiming to be Alice, just like any eavesdropper could have done in the previous example.

- Alice sends a message with DES-MAC integrity check to both Bob and Ted, using secret key interchange keys. So she shares a key K_{AB} with Bob, and shares a key K_{AT} with Ted. The DES-MAC is included twice, once encrypted with K_{AB} and once encrypted with K_{AT}. Furthermore the per-message key k is sent twice, once encrypted with K_{AB} and once encrypted with K_{AT}. An eavesdropper cannot discover the DES-MAC of the message even if the message isn't encrypted—she can't compute it because she doesn't know k, and she can't decrypt the encrypted DES-MAC because she doesn't know either K_{AB} or K_{AT}. However, Bob does know the DES-MAC x, and can see $K_{AT}\{x\}$. He also knows k and $K_{AT}\{k\}$. So after receiving this message from Alice, Bob can construct a message m with CBC residue x, send it to Ted using per-message key k, claim that Alice is sending it, and send $K_{AT}\{k\}$ as the encrypted per-message key and $K_{AT}\{x\}$ as the encrypted DES-MAC.

- Alice sends a message with MD5 integrity check to Bob and Ted, using secret key interchange keys. PEM specifies that each of the two 64-bit halves of the MD5 is encrypted with the interchange key of each recipient. Let's say that the halves are x_1 and x_2. So Alice will send $K_{AT}\{x_1\}$ and $K_{AB}\{x_1\}$ as well as $K_{AT}\{x_2\}$ and $K_{AB}\{x_2\}$. Now even though Alice wasn't using DES-MAC, Bob knows a 64-bit quantity (say x_2) and what that quantity looks like when encrypted with K_{AT}. He also knows the per-message key k and $K_{AT}\{k\}$. So Bob can construct a message m with CBC-residue x_2 and send it to Ted using per-message key k, claiming that it was from Alice and that DES-MAC was the integrity check used. Note that any of the quantities x_1, x_2, or k could have been chosen to be the per-message key and/or the DES-MAC of the forged message.

Now we'll show how, given a 64-bit value r and a key k, it is possible for Carol to construct a message m with r as the CBC residue (using key k) (see Figure 21-3). Carol can actually construct any message she wants. The only constraint on the message is that somewhere inside the message there has to be a 64-bit block (8 characters) that must be filled with a value determined only by the rest of the message and r and k.

Let's assume that there's one 8-byte block of the message, say m_4, that Carol can fill with "garbage" without suspicion. She constructs the message she wants in the remaining plaintext blocks. She will be sending a message to Ted, signed by Alice. Ted might think it strange to have 8 bytes of crud in the middle of the message, but maybe Carol can cleverly write the message so that somewhere inside the message she says something like, *Hey, did I tell you about how I fixed my porch this weekend? It went well until I hit my thumb with the hammer. Then I said, "@f#!Ruoe"! Now, back to business ...*

Alternatively, mailers are so wonderfully user-friendly that cybercrud appears in them all the time. PEM headers certainly are ugly and would be ignored by a human. Even non-PEM messages often contain obscure-looking headers and postmarks. If Carol were to embed arbitrary cybercrud there it probably would not create suspicion.

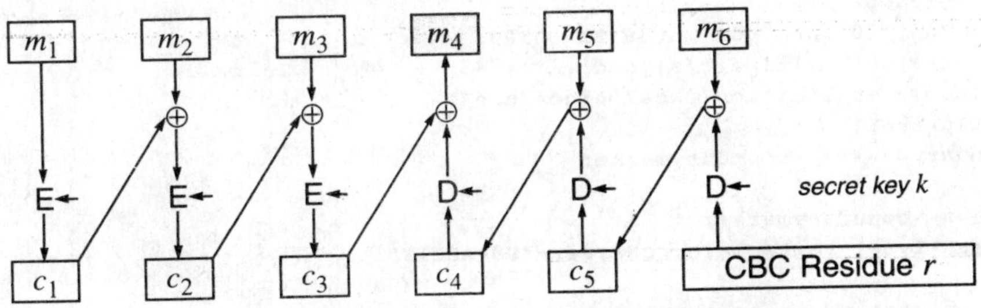

Figure 21-3. Generating a Message with a Given CBC Residue

Anyway, Carol works backwards from r. DES is reversible, so she can decrypt r and ⊕ that value with m_6 to discover what c_5 should be. She then decrypts c_5 and ⊕s it with m_5, to compute c_4.

Also, she works forward. She can encrypt m_1 to get c_1. Then she ⊕s c_1 with m_2 and encrypts the result to get c_2 and then ⊕s c_2 with m_3 and encrypts the result to get c_3. Now she has gotten to where the two ends of the computation meet. She ⊕s c_3 with the decryption of c_4 to get m_4.

Why don't the other types of MIC have the problems we've described in this section? The reason is that with message digests it is impossible for Carol to come up with another message with a particular message digest. So the PEM designers simply removed DES-MAC as a permissible integrity check.

21.17 DIFFERENCES IN S/MIME

MIME specifies how to encode non-text data and type labels into what will look like a text message to intermediate mailers. Like PEM, it had to deal with overly helpful mail transfer agents and defined its own 6-bits-per-byte encoding, so S/MIME doesn't have to. S/MIME says that its encrypted blobs are binary data and MIME takes care of encoding them. But S/MIME still has some encoding issues to deal with. As with PEM, signed messages can be in one of two forms: clear-signed and encoded. Clear signed messages can be read by mail readers that don't understand S/MIME (they notice the signature as a part of the message they don't know how to process and they ignore it). MIME itself was designed so that mailers that don't understand MIME will display text messages so that users will be able to find the message amid a substantial amount of cybercrud. That makes it possible for a user with an old mailer to make sense of an S/MIME signed message if they are sufficiently determined.

```
From: Alice
To: Bob
Subject: Keep this proposition private!
MIME-Version: 1.0
Date: Sun, 20 Jan 2002 15:38:21 -0500
Content-Type: multipart/signed;
 protocol="application/pkcs7-signature";
 micalg=sha1;
 boundary=-------boundarymarker

---------boundarymarker
Content-Type: text/plain; charset="US-ASCII"

Care to meet me at my apartment tonight?

---------boundarymarker
Content-Type: application/pkcs7-signature; name="smime.p7s"
Content-Transfer-Encoding: base64
Content-Disposition: attachment; filename="smime.p7s"
Content-Description: S/MIME Cryptographic Signature

MIAGCSqGSIb3DQEHAqCAMIIIlgIBATELMAkGBSsOAwIaBQAwCwYJKoZIhvcNAQcBoIIG7jCCAX4w
ggEooAMCAQICBDY+EqcwDQYJKoZIhvcNAQEEBQAwRjELMAkGA1UEBhMCVVMxDTALBgNVBAgTBE1B
U1MxDTALBgNVBAoTBElyaXMxGTAXBgNVBAMTEElyaXMgSW50ZXJuZXQgQ0EwHhcNOTgxMTAyMDgx
NDAwWhcNMDgxMDMwMDgxNDAwWjBGMQswCQYDVQQGEwJVUzENMAsGA1UECBMETUFTUzENMAsGA1UE
ChMESXJpczEZMBcGA1UEAxMQSXJpcyBJbnRlcm5ldCBDQTBcMA0GCSqGSIb3DQEBAQUAA0sAMEgC
        -----30 more lines like this deleted from this example-----
AQkFMQ8XDTAyMDEyMDIwMzgyMVowIwYJKoZIhvcNAQkEMRYEFMfSZKBY4a55CM7L1rg+sk3TR1M2
MEMGCSqGSIb3DQEJDzE2MDQwBwYFKw4DAh0wDgYIKoZIhvcNAwICAgCAMAoGCCqGSIb3DQMHMA0G
CCqGSIb3DQMCAgEoMA0GCSqGSIb3DQEBAQUABE8DVCKj7dYs0Uho2cY/o4VFDe6wUBdBC3R1bhK5
FnUKIrJLUC3QnBQgm70tWQvL5vK9IGyqvZfovPnDUI/2zd0nS9JHnyjqo2pEVvE0uzb0AAAAAA==
---------boundarymarker
```

MIME includes text canonicalization rules that increase the chances that the message will arrive unmodified, but it is still somewhat safer to send messages in an encoded format. The encoded format has an additional advantage. If the recipient has a mailer that does not understand

S/MIME, the encoded format will appear to it as an empty message with a file attachment with the name smime.p7m. If the mailer is configured to process file attachments with external utilities based on the file name suffix, it can be set up to hand off the smime.p7m file to an S/MIME program without any special configuration in the mailer.

S/MIME defines two new data formats for MIME to encode: application/pkcs7-signature, and application/pkcs7-mime. Type application/pkcs7-signature holds "detached" signatures within a multipart/signed structure. The format application/pkcs7-mime is used for both encrypted messages and encoded signed messages. Because MIME includes recursive encapsulation of messages as a natural thing to do, S/MIME does not have a concept of a message that is signed and encrypted as a single operation. Instead, S/MIME will sign a message yielding a signed message, and then encrypt the result. A minor security advantage gained with this approach is that the identity of the signer, and even the fact that the message is signed, is invisible to anyone who does not have a key to decrypt the message. This does make life difficult for mailers that would like to display message status (encrypted?, signed?, already read?, sender, ...) in a summary screen before opening individual messages. The S/MIME specification explicitly allows a sender to encrypt a message and then sign the result, or even sign the message, encrypt the result, and then sign the encrypted version again. Each variation has subtly different security properties, but none are actually used.

S/MIME defines a large set of header fields for both encrypted and signed messages. Since more years have passed since the time of the PEM design, ever larger numbers of options have been specified. Examples include being able to indicate in the header of a signed message what cryptographic algorithms the sender of the message supports, and which public key (possibly of many) she would like the recipient to use when responding. This evolved from the fact that such information is not encoded in certificates, and the common certificate distribution technique of sending out signed messages in order that the recipient can reply with an encrypted one.

Unlike PEM, which encoded its header fields individually with human readable text labels, S/MIME encodes its header information and data using ASN.1. Thus in the box on page 562, the signature field contains sender certificates and other such information, but it's not readily apparent. The encoding is specified in RFC2630: Cryptographic Message Syntax.

Issues around mailing list exploders for S/MIME messages are the same as those for PEM messages, except that examples are harder to look at. A remailer can simply forward signed messages. To forward encrypted messages, it would have to decrypt the message header and then reencrypt it for each recipient. The layering of encryption over signatures makes it even more straightforward to do this without invalidating the signature.

21.18 S/MIME Certificate Hierarchy

An important reason why S/MIME succeeded while PEM failed is that S/MIME did not try to prescribe a particular public key infrastructure. An important side effect was that the security gained from using it is limited (though that could improve if a workable PKI gets deployed). There are several hierarchies people use with S/MIME.

21.18.1 S/MIME with a Public Certifier

Several companies, most notably Verisign and Thawte, have tried to make a business of issuing certificates to S/MIME users related to their businesses creating SSL certificates for public web servers. They have different levels of assurance with which users can be authenticated, where that assurance level is indicated in the certificates issued. Presumably, the certificates with a greater degree of assurance cost more, since the higher levels of assurance involve more administrative overhead.

Both companies have been fairly successful with their free certificates with low assurance that they issue as a loss leader to get people into the system.

21.18.2 S/MIME with an Organizational Certifier

An alternative to getting certificates from a public certifier is to get them from an organization with which you have some affiliation—typically an employer. Several commercial mail products include CAs that allow certificate generation for their users. The challenge with non-public certifiers is getting the recipients' software to trust the issuer of the certificate. For mail sent within organizations, this can be done as a matter of configuration. Also within organizations, users' certificates can be listed in an organizational LDAP directory so that senders can look up recipients' public keys in order to send them encrypted mail.

21.18.3 S/MIME with Certificates from Any Old CA

The way S/MIME is most frequently used is without a directory for storing certificates and without a need for trusted certifiers. If I want to send you encrypted mail, I first get you to send me signed mail. Your signed mail contains your certificate, which I accept into my personal address book and tell my system to trust. (If you have a certificate from a certifier I already trust, this is a little easier, but if not I just say "OK" to one more security warning that I don't understand.)

This mechanism for securing mail has many theoretical flaws. An attacker could impersonate us to one another or read or forge mail. But in practice, attackers do not yet have the technical sophistication to do these things. S/MIME used in this manner is very effective against passive eavesdropping, which is the attack most people worry about. Even the most sophisticated PKI can't protect you from someone breaking into your machine, stealing your keys, and reading your email that way, which is probably the most common attack in practice.

21.19 HOMEWORK

1. Why doesn't the message portion of a PEM message need a label (such as KEY-INFO:?). In other words, how does a parser know which portion of the PEM message is the actual body of the message?
2. How does Bob, when receiving a signed PEM message from Alice using a public key interchange key, verify the signature on the message?
3. In the public key case of ENCRYPTED messages, there is a KEY-INFO field for each recipient (where the per-message encryption key is encrypted with that recipient's public key), plus a KEY-INFO field for the sender of the message, say Alice, where the per-message encryption key is encrypted with Alice's public key. The purpose of the KEY-INFO field for Alice is so that if she were later to see a copy of the encrypted message, she'd be able to decrypt it.) In the secret key case of ENCRYPTED messages, however, there is no such field for Alice (though there is still one for each recipient). Why was it considered necessary to include a KEY-INFO field for Alice in the public key case and not in the secret key case?
4. Design a mechanism to allow Alice and Bob to establish a secret key cryptographic interchange key, using something like Kerberos KDCs. Assume for simplicity that Alice and Bob are in the same realm. If Alice does not keep track of KDC-assigned interchange keys for people to whom she has previously sent messages, how can your design ensure Alice would be able to later decrypt an encrypted message she had sent to Bob?
5. Why are the KEY-INFO fields not necessary in public key MIC-CLEAR and MIC-ONLY messages, whereas they are necessary in public key ENCRYPTED messages and in all secret key messages?
6. If Alice is sending an ENCRYPTED message, she first signs the message digest with her private key (as she would have done for a MIC-CLEAR or MIC-ONLY message), and then encrypts the message digest with the per-message secret key. Why was this last encryption considered necessary for encrypted messages and not for MIC-CLEAR or MIC-ONLY?

Now assume Alice sends Bob a MIC-ONLY or MIC-CLEAR message with secret key based interchange keys. PEM requires her to encrypt the MIC with Bob's interchange key. Why is this necessary?

7. In §21.16 *DES-CBC as MIC Doesn't Work* we described how Carol, given a 64-bit value x and a key k, could construct a message m with DES-CBC x. Suppose Carol can't really send an arbitrary 8 bytes of garbage embedded in the message. For instance, suppose she wants to send the forged message MIC-CLEAR, so each byte is constrained to have one of only 64 valid values. Assume Carol is reasonably flexible about the message she'd like to send (for instance there might be two places in which crud could be embedded). Find a computationally feasible method for Carol to generate a message which will satisfy the constraint.

8. Describe a plausible algorithm and user interface for a PEM processor at a receiver that deals with nested PEM messages, embedded strings that look like begin and end PEM markers, and messages in which some of the PEM enclosures fail PEM processing due to signatures not verifying or certificates missing.

9. Given that each message will be encrypted with its own per-message key, why does PEM also provide an IV?

10. Suppose PEM signed an encrypted message (rather than signing the unencrypted message and encrypting the result)? Design a mechanism for allowing Bob, the recipient of such a message from Alice, to forward it to Carol, so that Carol can both verify Alice's signature and read the contents of the message.

11. Assume an encryption mechanism such as ⊕ with a one-time pad, where the one-time pad is the per-message key. Why would such an encryption scheme not work with the design in Homework Problem 10? (Hint: Carol should not believe Alice signed the message.)

12. As described in §21.16 *DES-CBC as MIC Doesn't Work*, there are many scenarios in which messages can be forged. Suppose Alice sends an ENCRYPTED message to Bob, using MD5 as the MIC, but Ted accepts DES-CBC. Can an eavesdropper now forge messages from Alice to Ted? How about Bob? If so, how? If not, why not? Suppose Alice's message was MIC-CLEAR or MIC-ONLY?

13. Why is DES CBC secure for banking, but not for email? (Hint: What cryptographic properties does banking depend on? What cryptographic properties does email depend on?)

14. Suppose DES-CBC was only used with secret interchange keys, and the CBC was always computed using the interchange keys (rather than the per-message key). Would this be secure?

22 PGP (PRETTY GOOD PRIVACY)

22.1 INTRODUCTION

PGP is another secure mail protocol. It started out as a single public-domain implementation that was, in the words of Phil Zimmermann, the original author, *guerrilla freeware*. It was the author's intention that it be distributed widely (anyone with a copy is invited to send copies to friends; copies can also be obtained from a bunch of Internet FTP sites). Unfortunately, both RSADSI, by enforcing the RSA patent, and government authorities, by enforcing export control of dangerous technologies like nuclear weapons and the ability to encrypt mail, caused PGP to start its life as contraband. Its history is colorful, serving as a test case in a number of legal challenges to U.S. export laws. We recommend GARF95 as an entertaining and informative telling of its early history and use. Ironically, PGP has been, from the start, legal and freely available in many other countries because the RSA patent is U.S.-only and other governments have different policies about the export, import, and use of privacy protection technology. For a while, the most popular site distributing PGP over the Internet was in Finland. Finland is very liberal about cryptography (but is still snitty about selling nuclear weapons, we presume).

The PGP documentation is delightfully conspiratorial and fun to read. Phil starts out by asserting that although we honest people don't really think we need to encrypt our email—we're not hiding anything—we should all start encrypting our mail so that in case someone needs privacy, the poor soul won't arouse suspicion by being the only one encrypting mail. Phil uses the analogy with paper mail. If the "standard" scheme were to write everything on postcards, and then only in unusual cases where you felt you didn't want the government or the next door neighbor reading your mail would you enclose it in an envelope, then a letter in an envelope would arouse suspicion and save the snooper time—every letter in an envelope would probably contain something interesting to the snooper. The questionable legality of PGP inspired a cult following, with people using it as a statement in support of personal freedoms and geek pride, independent of any need for secrecy.

If privacy is outlawed, only outlaws will have privacy.

—Phil Zimmermann

In trying to accommodate patents, export laws, a desire for commercialization, and committees of people trying to help, PGP has unfortunately evolved into a Tower of Babel. PGP Classic (Version 2.6.*) gained a large user community using the RSA and IDEA encryption algorithms. Through arduous negotiations, one version (2.6.2) became legal for non-commercial use within the U.S. and was freely downloadable from an MIT web site. And it was possible to buy a license making it legally usable for any purpose. Not satisfied with that, an incompatible PGP using patent-free algorithms (DSS, Diffie-Hellman, and Triple DES) was developed. It also avoided U.S. export law by a novel mechanism. U.S. export law covers software, but not books (books existed when the first amendment was drafted, but the Internet did not). The source code for PGP was published as a book, the book was legally exported from the U.S., and then someone outside the U.S. optically scanned the book and turned it back into software outside the U.S. In large part to publicly embarrass the export authorities, the book was published in an OCR font (a font designed for Optical Character Recognition before scanners became good enough to accurately scan almost any font) and digital checksums were included on each page. Surprisingly, the book also sold well to the public, who bought it either out of ignorance or to be able to display a great hack. This had the potential for getting PGP out from under patent and export restrictions, but it fragmented the user community (since the two versions could not interoperate).

In trying to harness the market buzz around "Open Software", the internal data representations of PGP were redesigned by an IETF committee and dubbed "Open PGP". Several independent (and not always interoperating) versions of Open PGP have been deployed including one called GPG (Gnu Privacy Guard). While all of this was going on, the RSA patent expired in September 2000 potentially making PGP Classic finally legal for all uses everywhere. Unfortunately, a patent on the IDEA algorithm that expires in 2007 has postponed that possibility. The formats described in the remainder of this chapter are for PGP Classic. The newer ones are more complex, but similar in spirit and goals.

22.2 OVERVIEW

PGP is not just for mail. It performs encryption and integrity protection on files. Mail is not treated any differently from ordinary files. Someone wishing to send a secure mail message could first transform the file to be mailed using PGP, and then mail the transformed file using a traditional mailer. Similarly, if one were to receive a PGP-encrypted mail message, one could treat the received message as a file and feed it to PGP to process. This is a bit inconvenient. So PGP source code comes with modifications for a number of common mail systems, enabling people to integrate PGP into their mail systems.

22.3 KEY DISTRIBUTION

PGP uses public key cryptography for personal keys. The most important differences between PGP, PEM, and S/MIME lie in how public keys are certified and how certificate chains are verified. PEM assumes a rigid hierarchy of CAs. PGP assumes anarchy. S/MIME is agnostic, but as deployed assumes a number of parallel independent hierarchies, a subset of which are trusted by each user. With PGP, each user decides which keys to trust. If Bob has talked in person to Alice, and Alice has written down her key for him, Bob can store Alice's public key and trust that it is hers. If he trusts Alice sufficiently, and Bob receives a certificate signed by Alice's key that says Carol's public key is *P*, then Bob can trust that *P* really does belong to Carol.

While with PEM the infrastructure decides whom you should trust to certify people, PGP leaves it up to you. This means PEM is potentially more convenient, while PGP is potentially more secure (if you're careful). It also means that PEM is unusable until you "hook into" an infrastructure. Deployment of PEM was held up for years trying to settle the details of how that infrastructure would work. PGP is easy to use "out of the box", but it's an open question whether it will be able to scale to large environments.

In the PEM model, finding a path of certificates is very simple. The certificate chain follows the naming hierarchy (approximately), and the path is simple—one simply goes down from the root (the Internet PCA Registration Authority).

Knowing whether to trust a path is simple in PEM. There is only one path and you are expected to trust it. S/MIME assumes there are multiple certificate hierarchies, and software will be configured with which ones to trust. You trust all certificates in a trusted hierarchy.

You can trust me. —used car salesman, Westboro, MA, April 4, 1993

PGP doesn't require certificates at all, though they can make life simpler. To send someone encrypted mail or to verify their signature, you need to know their public key. People publish their PGP fingerprints (cryptographic hashes of public keys) on their web sites, on their business cards, or even in their books. For example, my$_1$ PGP fingerprint is 29 6F 4B E2 56 FF 36 2F AB 49 DF DF B9 4C BE E1. They are also short enough to be read over the phone.

Certificates are an optional in PGP. Anyone can issue a certificate to anyone else. And users decide whose certificates they are willing to trust in authenticating someone. As a result, with PGP there might be several certificate paths to a particular person. For instance, you might have the following certificates:

Carol's key is P_1	signed with P_2
Alice's key is P_2	signed with P_4
Carol's key is P_1	signed with P_5

It might even be the case that the last certificate instead said

Carol's key is P_3	signed with P_5

There are several issues:

- You might have a disorganized mass of certificates. How can you find a chain that leads from a key you know to Carol's key?
- There might be multiple chains, and some might lead to different keys for Carol.
- If you do find a chain, how much do you trust that chain?

In order to trust a chain of certificates you have to believe that the first public key in the chain really belongs to whom you think it does, and that you trust every individual in the chain. Should you trust a certificate signed by what you believe is Ted's key? Even if you're sure that Ted's public key is P_5, can you trust Ted not to certify anything in sight for a $100 bribe? Even if Ted is honest, can you trust him not to be sloppy about checking that the key really belongs to the named person? In other words, are Ted's pre-certification policies and procedures for authenticating users adequate?

Suppose Ted is honest and usually very careful about checking a key before signing a certificate. Suppose Carol is Ted's ex-spouse, from whom he had a bitter divorce. Should you then trust Ted's signature to certify Carol's public key?

PGP cannot answer these questions, of course. Not even people can really answer these questions. But PGP asks you for advice, and stores with each key a quantity indicating how much the key should be trusted as being legitimate and how much the owner of the key should be trusted in certifying other keys. With a particular signature (as in the case where you'd trust Ted to certify just about any key except Carol's), PGP also asks its user for advice and stores information about how much that particular signature should be trusted.

It's worth noting that the commercial version of PGP tried to address these issues with a less anarchistic structure. That's because it was marketed to organizations where the users were not considered sufficiently motivated and competent to make the right decisions, but where the system administrators were.

22.4 EFFICIENT ENCODING

To appreciate how clever PGP is, let's review inefficiencies of encoding in PEM (S/MIME inherits most of its encodings from MIME, making it non-comparable).

Both PEM and PGP are designed to work in the environment where the contents of a message might be restricted by two problems. The first problem is that intermediate mail relays insist that the message contain only innocuous ASCII characters and limited-length lines. The second problem is that the representation of text at the destination machine may be different from the representation at the source machine. The solution to this problem is to turn the message into canonical format before encrypting or signing it. This includes converting the end-of-line indication, which might be linefeed only (<LF>) at the source, into <CR><LF> which is the SMTP standard. This may make the message a little bit bigger.

PEM expects to be handed ordinary text. If the message being sent with PEM is not in fact text consisting of innocuous ASCII characters, then in order to send it through PEM it must be encoded with a utility such as uuencode, which expands it by about 33%.

Then PEM does whatever processing it needs to do. For instance it might encrypt the (newly expanded) message. Once encrypted, the message has to get encoded by PEM so that it will consist of only innocuous ASCII characters with <CR><LF>s occurring sufficiently frequently. If the message started out as ordinary text, then only PEM will do the encoding and the message will expand by about 33%, but if the message needed to be encoded for submission to PEM, then the data will have been encoded twice, resulting in an expansion of about 78%. A message sent MIC-CLEAR will not need to be expanded even once. To summarize, there are four cases:

1. Text sent with PEM as MIC-CLEAR—the message does not get expanded at all.
2. Text sent with PEM as MIC-ONLY or ENCRYPTED—the message gets expanded once (33%).
3. Non-text sent with PEM as MIC-CLEAR—the message gets encoded before submittal to PEM, thus expanded once (33%).
4. Non-text sent with PEM as MIC-ONLY or ENCRYPTED—the message gets expanded twice (78%).

Since PEM is going to encode the message anyway, why do you need to encode the message before handing it to PEM? The reason is the canonicalization step that PEM insists on performing. If you have a file that would be damaged by the canonicalization, you have to encode it so that PEM won't damage it.

In contrast, PGP allows you to specify, when handing a file to PGP to process, whether the file is text or binary. (Though PGP checks up on you when you tell it you're giving it text—if it doesn't look like text, PGP will change the state of the flag associated with the file). If you tell PGP the file is binary, then PGP will not canonicalize it, and PGP will mark the PGP-processed message as binary so that the PGP at the receiver will know not to perform reverse canonicalization. By merely marking the file this way, PGP manages to avoid ever needing two encodings on a single message.

Furthermore, PGP does not always assume that the encrypted file needs to be encoded in order to get through mail relays. For instance, the file might be sent through a mail system (like X.400) that supports transparent transport of data. Or it might not be mailed at all, but merely transported via floppy disk. In some cases, PGP might know, based on the mail system into which it is integrated, whether the file needs to be encoded. In other cases, the user might explicitly tell PGP whether it should encode the output to prepare it for simple-minded mailers.

An additional trick that PGP does to conserve bits is to compress a file before sending it, whether it is binary or text. PGP uses the utility ZIP for compression. Typically, 50% compression is achieved, so even though PGP will need to do one expansion encoding after encrypting a file, what PGP actually has to transmit will often be smaller than the original file.

22.5 CERTIFICATE AND KEY REVOCATION

A certificate can be revoked by whoever signed the certificate. It does not necessarily mean that the key in the certificate is bad; it just means that whoever signed the certificate no longer wants to vouch for its authenticity. Given that anyone can issue a certificate for anyone, and then issue a revocation of the certificate, having a revoked certificate does not necessarily mean anything bad about the individual certified. Otherwise, an enemy of yours could issue a certificate for you and then immediately revoke it, making everyone suspicious of you. (The reasoning might be: Why was the certificate revoked? Must be because the person had lied or something...) If a certificate is revoked, then whoever was relying on that certificate to authenticate you will no longer be able to authenticate you.

Certificates can optionally have a validity period, in which case they expire after the specified time period. They can be renewed by being reissued. The current custom in PGP is to issue non-expiring certificates (by omitting the VALIDITY PERIOD field).

Keys can be revoked too. My key can only be revoked by me (or someone who stole my private key—but gee, if the bad guy is so obliging as to tell the world he stole my key, I'm not worried about him forging a key revocation for my key). The idea is that I will issue a key revocation only when I think someone has discovered my private key. I'll presumably generate a new key for myself, and distribute the key revocation for the old key as widely as possible (perhaps by publishing it in *The New York Times* as a legal notice).

Key and certificate revocations are distributed informally, just as are public keys and certificates. There are public servers where you can post and search for certificates. A ritual has developed for populating those servers. Frequently, at gatherings of nerds, there is a PGP key signing "party". People stand and state their name and public key fingerprint. People who know that person are encouraged to issue certificates for them. If you go to enough of these events, you're likely to get certificates from enough people that members of the community will be able to trust your key.

22.6 SIGNATURE TYPES

For each signed quantity, PGP indicates whether what is being signed is a message or a certificate. The reason for this is to guard against the remote possibility that you'd sign a message saying something like Let's do lunch, and the encoding of Let's do lunch could be parsed as a valid certificate. It's good practice whenever a key can be used for multiple things to explicitly say what kind of thing is being processed. This avoids any possibility of aliasing (in this case confusing messages and certificates).

One could argue that it's really ridiculously unlikely that a message could be parsed as a certificate, or vice versa, but PGP's SIGNATURE TYPE field is only one octet long, so why not?

22.7 YOUR PRIVATE KEY

If all you want to do is verify signatures on signed messages, you don't need a private key. However, if you want to sign your own messages, or if you want to receive encrypted PGP mail, you need a private key.

PGP will generate a private key for you. You can specify the size of the key. Then it asks you for a password, and it converts the string you type into an IDEA key by doing an MD5 message digest on it. Then it uses that IDEA key to encrypt the private key. Encryption is done with 64-bit CFB using a random IV which is stored with the encrypted private key.

22.8 KEY RINGS

A key ring is a data structure you keep that contains some public keys, some information about people, and some certificates. Usually this information is just stored locally, but some PGP users might share their key ring information, which would provide a quick method of building up your database of public keys.

PGP allows you to assert how much trust you place on different people. There are three levels of trust: none, partial, or complete. You might not trust Fred at all, so you would not trust a certificate signed by Fred, but you might want to keep Fred's public key around so that you can verify messages you receive from him, or be able to send encrypted messages to him.

PGP computes the trust that should be placed on certificates and public keys in your key ring based on the trust information you asserted on the people. A certificate signed by someone you indicated you don't trust at all will be ignored.

Whom or what you trust is a very private decision. You could have your own version of PGP that had arbitrarily complex trust rules. It does not have to be compatible with anyone else's. It could even always ask you to make the decision for each key and certificate, but give you the raw data (Carol and Ted both said this was Alice. You indicated before you have level 4 trust in Carol, level 6 trust in Carol's public key, level 5 trust in Ted, and level 2 trust in Ted's public key. How much trust would you like indicated for Alice's key?)

The public domain version of PGP gives you only three levels of trust (none, partial, or complete, as we said above). One completely trusted individual signing a certificate will yield a completely trusted certificate. Several partially trusted individuals signing certificates attesting to the same public key for Alice will yield a completely trusted public key for Alice. If you have a key for Alice that is not completely trusted, you can still verify messages from Alice, and send encrypted messages to Alice, but PGP will give you a warning.

22.9 ANOMALIES

22.9.1 File Name

PGP includes a FILE NAME field with any message (see §22.10 *Object Formats*). This field specifies the name of the file that was read to produce the PGP object so that the recipient can ask PGP to store the information using the same file name. We don't think this is very useful in the context of mail, although it can be helpful when PGP is used as a file encryption tool. But for mail, it means you have to be careful what you call the file on your machine (a name like TO-THE-DWEEB might offend the recipient, and you might have forgotten that PGP tells the recipient what you called the file on your machine).

Aside from being mostly useless, this feature is slightly dangerous. A careless user might be tricked into storing a received message that is actually a virus-containing executable with a file name (such as .login) that the system might understand and wind up executing. Admittedly, PGP warns you when it is about to overwrite an existing file, but the user might not have such a file, or might ignore the warning.

PGP also includes the time the file was last modified. As with FILE NAME, this can be useful for a file encryption tool, but its existence is probably a bad idea for mail, because again it's telling information that you may not realize it's divulging.

22.9.2 People Names

PGP allows you to choose any name you want. It does not enforce uniqueness or reasonableness. This causes an interesting problem. You can name yourself Richard Nixon (that might even be your name but you might not be *the* Richard Nixon). You might have lots of people willing to sign certificates as to your public key.

An unsuspecting person, say Julie, has a public key associated with the name Richard Nixon. She would completely trust the Richard Nixon she knows, but doesn't realize that the key she holds is yours, not his.

If I have two public keys, both indicating that the associated human is John Smith, I won't know which key to use when I send a message to one of the John Smiths. For this reason, it is helpful if the user identification string contains a little more information than just the name of the user, for instance, the user's email address. PGP recommends (but does not require) including Internet email addresses in the name.

22.10 OBJECT FORMATS

PGP reads and writes a variety of objects. Objects may contain a variety of fields, and some objects contain other objects. Each object can be represented in two formats—*compact* and *SMTP mailable*. The SMTP mailable format is computed from the compact format by performing the same encoding that PEM uses (see §21.7 *Reformatting Data to Get Through Mailers*) and adding a human-readable header and trailer so that a human (or a smart mail receiver) will know the cybercrud between the header and trailer needs to be processed by PGP. The human-readable header is

```
-----BEGIN PGP MESSAGE-----
Version 2.2
```

and the human readable trailer is

```
-----END PGP MESSAGE-----
```

22.10.1 Message Formats

PGP messages are composed of a sequence of primitive objects (see §22.10.2 *Primitive Object Formats*). We'll describe the message formats in this section.

Encrypted Message. PGP encrypts messages with the secret key algorithm IDEA using 64-bit CFB mode with a randomly chosen IV that is included with the message. The sending PGP chooses a random IDEA key for encrypting the message, and then encrypts that IDEA key with the public key of the recipient, placing the encrypted IDEA key in the header. If the message is being sent to multiple recipients, the IDEA key is individually encrypted with the key of each recipient, and all the encrypted keys are placed in the header.

IDEA key encrypted with recipient$_1$'s public key
IDEA key encrypted with recipient$_2$'s public key
⋮
IDEA key encrypted with recipient$_k$'s public key
message encrypted with IDEA key

When the final object is decrypted with the IDEA key, the result is either PLAINTEXT DATA or COMPRESSED DATA, depending on whether PGP decided the data was compressible. If PGP decided the data was compressible, then when the COMPRESSED DATA is uncompressed, the result is PLAINTEXT DATA.

Signed Message. This is likely to be COMPRESSED DATA. When uncompressed, the result is

signature
plaintext data

Encrypted Signed Message. This is just like an ENCRYPTED MESSAGE, but with the message replaced by a SIGNED MESSAGE.

IDEA key encrypted with recipient$_1$'s public key
IDEA key encrypted with recipient$_2$'s public key
⋮
IDEA key encrypted with recipient$_k$'s public key
signed message encrypted with IDEA key

When the final object is decrypted with the IDEA key, the result will probably be COMPRESSED DATA (unless PGP noticed that it was not compressible), which when uncompressed is a SIGNED MESSAGE.

Signed Human-Readable Message. Usually PGP modifies even an unencrypted message before mailing it, for two reasons. It compresses it for ecological reasons (saves bits), and it encodes it so it will have some hope of making it through mailers unmodified. This is nice but it means that if the recipient does not have PGP, the human at the other end will not be able to read the message (see §21.7 *Reformatting Data to Get Through Mailers*). So PGP allows you to tell it not to muck with the message. You will hold PGP harmless if the message gets modified by mailers and the signature then does not verify. This form of message is

`-----BEGIN PGP SIGNED MESSAGE-----`
cleartext message
`-----BEGIN PGP SIGNATURE-----` `Version: 2.2`
signature
`-----END PGP SIGNATURE-----`

Just like with PEM, we have to ensure that the string

`-----BEGIN PGP SIGNATURE-----`

does not appear in the text of the message. And just like PEM, PGP protects against such a mishap by prepending '- ' to any line that begins with '-'. The PGP at the receiver is smart enough to strip that off before attempting to verify the signature.

22.10.2 Primitive Object Formats

Primitive object formats are

CTB	*length*	*stuff*

where **CTB** stands for **cipher type byte** (aren't you glad you asked?) and specifies the PGP object type and the length of *length*. We'll describe the interpretation of *stuff* for the various object types in this section.

Certain object types contain one or more integers in their stuff field. Integers are encoded as a length in bits (two octets, most significant first) followed by the binary integer with leading 0 bits to pad to a multiple of 8 bits then packed into octets most significant first.

The CTB is interpreted bit by bit (most significant to least significant) as follows:

bit 7: 1

bit 6: reserved, i.e. set to 0 and ignored

bit 5–2: a 4-bit field indicating which type of object follows. The defined values are

0001—something encrypted using someone's public key (the only thing ever actually encrypted this way is an IDEA key)
0010—signature
0101—private key encrypted with a password
0110—public key
1000—compressed data
1001—something encrypted with a secret key
1011—plaintext data plus a file name and mode (binary or text)
1100—key ring trust information
1101—user identification
1110—comment

bits 1–0: a 2-bit field indicating the length of the length field. The defined values are:
00—1-octet length field follows CTB
01—2-octet length field follows CTB
10—4-octet length field follows CTB
11—there is no length field (this can only occur for the last object in a message—the length is to the externally determined end of data)

Key Encrypted under a Public Key (0001 in CTB).

	field description
1 octet	version number (2)
8 octet	key ID (low order 64 bits of RSA modulus)
1 octet	algorithm ID (1 for RSA, no others defined)
integer	IDEA key encrypted with RSA

IDEA key before RSA-encryption. PGP follows the PKCS #1 standard, which defines how to encrypt something with RSA, usually a key (see §6.3.6 *Public-Key Cryptography Standard (PKCS)*). PGP encrypts a little more than just the IDEA key. PGP encrypts a 19-octet quantity consisting of an octet = 1, the 16-octet IDEA key, and a 2-octet CRC-16 of the IDEA key. The purpose of the extra data is so that in case you accidentally decrypt with the wrong RSA key the contents will not look right. So PGP encrypts, using RSA,

0	2	*n* random non-zero octets	0	1	IDEA key	CRC

Signature (0010 in CTB).

	field description
1 octet	version number (2)
1 octet	# of octets before key ID field (5 if validity period missing, else 7)
1 octet	signature type (see below)
4 octet	time when signed
0 or 2 octet	validity period in days (0 means infinite)
8 octet	key ID (low order 64 bits of RSA key)
1 octet	public key algorithm (1 for RSA, no others defined)
1 octet	message digest algorithm (1 for MD5, no others defined)
2 octet	first two octets of message digest, to reassure us that we decrypted with the proper key
integer	message digest signed with RSA (see below)

The defined signature types (written in hex) are

- 00—signature on a binary message or document
- 01—signature on a text message with <CR><LF> indicating EOL
- 10—certificate with unspecified assurance
- 11—key certification with no assurance
- 12—key certification with casual assurance
- 13—key certification with heavy-duty assurance
- 20—key revocation (attempt to revoke key that signed this)
- 30—certificate revocation (revokes a certificate signed with the key that signed this)
- 40—signature of a signature (notary service)

The message digest is computed on

message to be signed	signature type	timestamp	validity period

The quantity signed using RSA is

0	1	*n* octets of FF_{16}	0	$3020300c06082a864886f70d020505000410_{16}$	message digest

The 18-octet constant is ASN.1 cybercrud meaning MD5.

Private key encrypted with password (0101 in CTB).

	field description
1 octet	version number (2)
4 octet	time when key created
2 octet	validity period in days (0 means infinite)
1 octet	public key algorithm (1 for RSA, no others defined)
integer	public modulus
integer	public exponent
1 octet	algorithm encrypting private key (1 for IDEA, no others defined)
8 octet	random if key encrypted, else 0
integer	encrypted quantity

The encrypted quantity, before encryption, looks like

	field description
integer	private exponent
integer	*p* (the first prime, in format of integer)
integer	*q* (the second prime, in format of integer)
integer	information for speeding up the RSA operations (see §6.3.4.4 *Optimizing RSA Private Key Operations*)
2 octet	CRC-16 of preceding fields

Encryption is done using IDEA in 64-bit CFB mode (see §3.4 *International Data Encryption Algorithm (IDEA)* and §4.2 *Encrypting a Large Message*)

Public key (0110 in CTB).

	field description
1 octet	version number (2)
4 octet	time when key created
2 octet	validity period in days (0 means infinite)
1 octet	public key algorithm (1 for RSA, no others defined)
integer	public modulus
integer	public exponent

Compressed Data (1000 in CTB). Any PGP object or sequence of objects can be compressed.

	field description
1 octet	compression algorithm (1 for ZIP, no others defined)
–	compressed data

Something Encrypted with a Secret Key (1001 in CTB).

	field description
–	encrypted data

Encryption is done using IDEA in 64-bit CFB mode with an IV of 0. The data being encrypted is

	field description
8 octet	random data
2 octet	last two octets of random data
–	unencrypted data

The purpose of the random data is so that successive encryptions of the same unencrypted data will result in different ciphertext. The purpose of repeating the last two octets of random data is to recognize that decryption worked properly.

Plaintext Data (1011 in CTB) .

	field description
1 octet	mode (ASCII b for binary, t for text)
1 octet	length of following field in octets
	file name (ASCII string)
4 octet	time file last modified, or 0
–	message

Key Ring. The key ring stores public keys and information about each key. The information about each key consists of the name of the human associated with the key (the user ID), the set of certificate signatures you've received vouching for the fact that that user has that public key, and trust information about each of the pieces of information. Key revocations and certificate revocations (see SIGNATURE object format) are also stored on the key ring.

So the key ring looks like

public key	trust	user ID	trust	signature	trust	...	signature	trust
public key	trust	user ID	trust	signature	trust	...	signature	trust
				⋮				
public key	trust	user ID	trust	signature	trust	...	signature	trust

The trust information following the public key indicates how much that public key is trusted to sign things, and is manually set. If the key has been revoked, the key revocation is inserted immediately before the user ID. The trust information following the user ID indicates how much confidence is placed on the public key belonging to the user, and is computed from the trust information following the signatures. The trust information following each signature is copied from the trust information of the public key that did the signing. Certificate revocations are included with the normal signatures.

PGP encourages people to share the information in their key rings. However, users should make their own trust decisions. So when key ring information is transmitted, the trust information is removed.

Key Ring Trust Information (1100 in CTB). Since this format is only used locally, we won't bother documenting its gory details, but we will say that it has two different interpretations depending on whether the previous item is a user ID or not.

	field description
1 octet	how much the preceding item should be trusted

User Identification (1101 in CTB).

	field description
–	ASCII string giving user's name, perhaps email address also

Comment (1110 in CTB).

	field description
–	ASCII string

PART 5
LEFTOVERS

23 *FIREWALLS*

A **firewall** (see Figure 23-1) is a computer that sits between your internal network and the rest of the network and attempts to prevent bad things from happening (such as internal users sending company secrets outside, or outside people breaking into systems inside) without preventing good things from happening (such as employees accessing information available externally). It is sometimes called other things, like a security gateway, or various more colorful names thought up by frustrated network users when it prevents them from doing what they want to do.

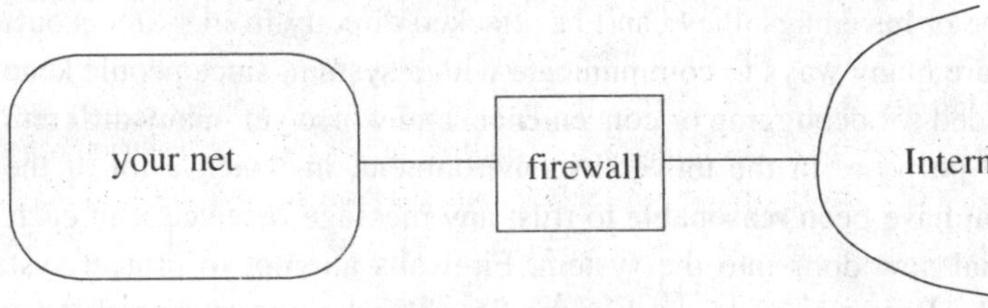

Figure 23-1. Firewall

Why is a firewall needed? It isn't if the systems on your internal network are properly secured, meaning that every system in the network has sophisticated authentication, the ability to do integrity-protected and encrypted communication whenever talking across the network, and is well-managed (when users rely on passwords, they choose good passwords; system accounts are not left with no password or a default password; all the latest security patches are installed; ...). Unfortunately many applications exist that were designed (and we use the term loosely) for an environment without bad guys, and most users view security (such as being forced to use long passwords) as an annoyance. Most corporate networks are not designed for security, and have survived because they have not been attacked. But now users want connectivity to the Internet. You want to be able to exchange mail with anyone. You want to occasionally share files. You want to communicate with publicly available services, and make some of your own services available to customers located outside your corporate network. But the Internet is a scary place. There are spies from unfriendly countries, users from competing companies, playful undergraduates, press people eager for a juicy scoop, criminals anxious to steal information for profit, disgruntled ex-employees, and vandals who attempt to compensate for their lack of a social life by annoying others.

One of the reasons systems are hard to secure is that they provide so many services, many by default. You might think that a user workstation would only initiate requests to servers on the user's behalf, but most user workstations provide services like remote access to their file systems and configuration databases. This makes workstations easier to centrally manage and makes it easier to share files, but every service is a point of attack. Even if the services are properly configured to only serve authorized users, they could be missing bounds checks in their input parsers so that a clever attacker can send an ill-formed request and sometimes get access to things the service was not designed to provide. It's common for a user who wants to share a file with another user to make his entire file system remotely mountable (because that's easier than limiting access to a single user and a single file). Often, he intends that things only be opened for a short time, but he forgets and leaves his system exposed indefinitely.

Firewalls centrally manage access to services in ways that individual systems should but don't. They can enforce policies such as *systems outside the firewall can't access file services on any systems inside the firewall.* With such a restriction, even if the internal systems are more open than they should be or have bugs, they can't be attacked directly from systems outside the firewall.

Also, there are many ways to communicate with a system, since people keep coming up with mechanisms intended for debugging or convenience, and worse yet, many different ways of accomplishing the same purpose. In the university environment, in which a lot of these utilities were developed, it might have been reasonable to trust any message received. But each of these mechanisms is a potential new door into the system. Firewalls attempt to protect systems inside from attack from outside. But in order to do this, the firewall administrator needs to understand all the mechanisms and come up with some way of disallowing the dangerous ones without disabling the necessary ones.

Some example mechanisms include:

- *finger* (port 79), which gives information such as who is logged in, or when a specific user last logged in.
- *telnet* (port 23), which allows someone to log into the system from across a network.
- *rlogin* (port 513), similar to *telnet*, but UNIX-specific. Also, whereas *telnet* requires explicit user authentication, *rlogin* (along with a few other UNIX utilities known as ***r* utilities**, such as *rsh*) avoids the inconvenience of explicit user authentication by trusting that the source address in the IP header is correct, and if that address is known to be the address of a host trusted by this system, then anything that the message asserts about the identity of the user is believed.
- *ftp* (port 21), which allows sharing of files. This protocol is tricky for firewalls because there are two connections made—one for control information and one for data. Although a host inside might initiate the transfer (in which case the firewall administrator would like to allow the transfer), the data connection is created by the other end. There is a modified version of

the ftp protocol (called **passive ftp**) in which both connections originate at the requester in order to make firewall logic easier; but until it is deployed everywhere, firewalls will need to deal with the original ftp.

- *X Windows* (port 177), which (like *telnet* and *rlogin*) allows you to interact with a remote machine, but the display assumes a real monitor that can handle colors and fonts, rather than a "dumb terminal".

- ICMP (Internet Control Message Protocol, RFC 792), is a protocol for sending messages to a node informing it of various conditions. There is no authentication of an ICMP message. ICMP packets can be recognized because the PROTOCOL field in the IP header is equal to 1. The other mechanisms run on top of TCP or UDP, and therefore can be distinguished based on the PORT field in the layer 4 header. Examples of ICMP messages a system Alice might receive include:
  - notification that some packet Alice had previously sent can't be delivered because the destination address, or an entire range of addresses including the destination's, is unreachable.
  - a *redirect*, telling Alice to use a particular router for forwarding to a particular address, presumably because the router Alice chose on a previous packet was not the best path to the destination.
  - a *ping*, which is supposed to be echoed back by the system that receives it. Ping is useful for seeing if a system is alive and reachable.

Notice that there are many ways of doing the same thing. To be logged into a remote machine, one might use *telnet*, *rlogin*, or the *X Windows* utility. None of these utilities were designed to be secure. *rlogin* is a particularly egregious example. Its primary "advantage" over *telnet* is that you often won't have to type your username or password. There is a file on a UNIX machine (called /etc/hosts.equiv) that lists IP addresses or host names (from which the IP address will be looked up in DNS). The hosts listed in that file are trusted to assert any user identity, and no password is required. The only authentication of the machine is that the IP header contains the trusted machine's IP address. Also, each user can have in his home directory a file named .rhosts which lists IP addresses or host names that are trusted to assert that user's identity without a password. This allows any user to open up access to his own account without administrative supervision. It also gives this right to any program the user runs.

If one machine is compromised inside your network, the firewall cannot help, since so many other machines, otherwise well-managed, will trust anything coming from the compromised machine.

A lot of the above utilities are dangerous. For instance, ICMP *ping* can be exploited to find machines to break into. Sending an ICMP message to Alice saying that some range of addresses is unreachable will cause Alice to hang up its connections to machines in the range specified by that ICMP message. Redirects can be used to cause a host to send traffic in a different direction, perhaps towards a compromised machine, making man-in-the-middle attacks easier. Finger can be used to find accounts to start attacking (searching the password space), or more ominously, to find personal information about users.

23.1 PACKET FILTERS

The simplest form of firewall selectively discards packets based on configurable criteria, such as addresses in the IP header. For example, it might be configured to only allow some systems on your network to communicate outside, or some addresses outside your network to communicate into your network. For each direction, the firewall might be configured with a set of legal source and destination addresses, and it drops any packets that don't conform. This is known as **address filtering**. Address filtering can protect internal nodes that have no business communicating with the outside world. Perhaps they are willing to let anyone log in with the administrator password that came preconfigured by the manufacturer, but if the firewall prevents any connections to them, the exposure is closed.

Packet filters usually look at more than the addresses. A typical security policy is that for certain types of traffic (e.g., email, web surfing), the rewards outweigh the risks, so those types of traffic should be allowed through the firewall, whereas other types of traffic (say *telnet*), should not be allowed through.

To allow certain types of traffic between host A and B while disallowing others, a firewall can look at the protocol type in the IP header and the ports in the layer 4 (TCP or UDP) header, as well as anything at any fixed offset in the packet. For web traffic, either the source or destination port will be 80, because *http* (see §25.3 *HTTP*) has been assigned port 80. For email, either the source or destination port will be 25.

Firewalls can be even fancier. Perhaps the policy is to allow connections initiated by machines inside the firewall, but disallow connections initiated by machines outside the firewall. Suppose machine A inside the firewall initiates a connection to machine B outside the firewall. During the conversation, the firewall will see packets from both directions (A to B as well as B to A), so it can't simply disallow packets from B to A. The way it manages to enforce only connections initiated by A is to look at the TCP header. TCP has a flag (called ACK) that is set on all but the first packet, the one that establishes the connection. So if the firewall disallows packets from B without ACK set in the TCP header, then it will have the desired effect, in general.

Unfortunately, there are protocols such as *ftp* and *X Windows* that require B to make a TCP connection to A, even though it was A that initiated the *ftp* or *X Windows* session. With intimate knowledge of the applications and implementations, the firewall can be configured to more or less do what you want. For instance, TCP has the client open a TCP connection for control traffic to the server, whereas the server then opens a TCP connection for data to the port from which the client initiated its TCP connection. The firewall can allow *ftp* sessions initiated from inside by allowing TCP connections initiated from outside as long as they are initiated to high numbered ports. (Dynamically assigned ports have high numbers, and a TCP client process will be assigned a dynamically assigned port.)

Another approach is a **stateful packet filter**, i.e., a packet filter that remembers what has happened in the recent past and changes its filtering rules dynamically as a result. A stateful packet filter could, for instance, note that a connection was initiated from inside using IP address *s*, to IP address *d*, and then allow (for some period of time) connections from IP address *d* to IP address *s*. In practice, the stateful packet filter would be much more cautious than that. For example, in the case of *ftp*, the stateful packet filter can notice when a connection is opened from *s* to the *ftp* control port (21) at *d*, and remember the incoming *ftp* data port (say *p*) requested by *s*. (The stateful packet filter has to parse *ftp* control packets to do this.) As long as the *ftp* control connection stays opened, the stateful packet filter will allow connections from the *ftp* data port (20) at *d* to port *p* at *s*.

Packet filters are frequently added as a feature to routers, allowing them to have minimal cost and impact on performance.

23.2 APPLICATION LEVEL GATEWAY

Another way to protect your vulnerable network is by use of an application level gateway. The gateway could have two network adaptors and act as a router, but more often it is placed between two packet filtering firewalls, using three boxes (see Figure 23-2). The two firewalls are routers that

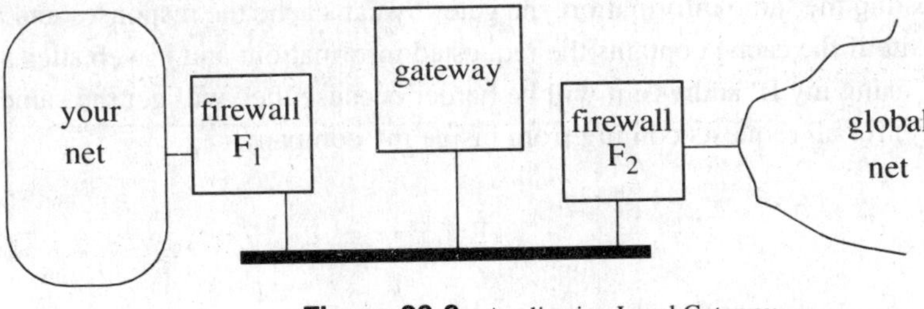

Figure 23-2. Application Level Gateway

refuse to forward anything unless it's to or from the gateway. Firewall F_2 refuses to forward anything from the global net unless the destination address is the gateway, and refuses to forward anything to the global net unless the source is the gateway. Firewall F_1 refuses to forward anything from your network unless the destination address is the gateway, and refuses to forward anything to your network unless the source address is the gateway. To transfer a file from your network to the global network, you need to have someone from inside transfer the file to the gateway machine, and then the file is accessible to be read by the outside world. Similarly, to read a file into your network a user has to arrange for it to first get copied to the gateway machine. To log into a machine in the global network you first log into the gateway machine, and from there you can access machines in the remote network. An application level gateway is sometimes known as a **bastion host**. It must be implemented and configured to be very secure. The portion of the network between the two firewalls (a single LAN in Figure 23-2), is known as the **DMZ** (demilitarized zone).

The gateway need not support every possible application. An example strategy is to allow only electronic mail to pass between your corporate network and the outside world. The intention is to specifically disallow file transfer and remote login. But electronic mail can certainly be used to transfer files. Sometimes a firewall might specifically disallow very large electronic mail messages, on the theory that this will limit the ability to transfer files. But often large electronic mail messages are perfectly legitimate, and any file can be broken down into small pieces. Because of such firewalls, many applications that post data for public retrieval on the Internet have automatic mail responders to which you can send an email message requesting the file, and the file will be sent back as an email message—several email messages, in fact, since such applications also realize that email messages have to be kept small in order to make it through the firewall. It is slow and painful for legitimate users to get files that way. Typically, the file arrives in several pieces. Each piece has to be extracted from the received email (to get rid of email headers). Then the pieces must be rearranged into proper order (since email tends to get out of order) and assembled into a file.

A common application to support on a gateway is *http*, the protocol used for web surfing. Web browsers were designed with the concept of a proxy. If my machine can't connect to the outside world, I can configure it to forward all *http* requests to a gateway that will make the requests for me and send me back the results. This has some additional advantages: if many people in my company are requesting the same information, the gateway can cache the responses and not go back to the remote web site if the cache contains the requested information; and if web sites are trying to track my browsing using my IP address, it will be harder because they will get the same IP address (that of the gateway) for all requests coming from inside my company.

23.3 ENCRYPTED TUNNELS

A tunnel is a point-to-point connection in which the actual communication occurs across a network.

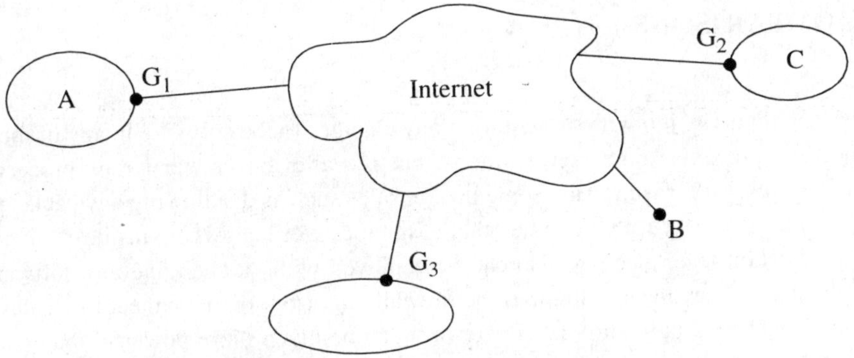

Figure 23-3. Connecting a Private Network over a Public Internet

Suppose the only reason you've hooked into the Internet is to connect disconnected pieces of your own network to each other. Instead of the example in Figure 23-3, you might have bought dedicated links between G_1, G_2, and G_3, and trusted those links as part of your corporate network because you owned them. But it's likely to be cheaper to have the Gs pass data across the Internet. How can you trust your corporate data crossing over the Internet? You do this by configuring G_1, G_2, and G_3 with security information about each other (such as cryptographic keys). All information between them is cryptographically protected. The most common protocol for encrypted tunnels is IPsec (see Chapter 17 *IPsec: AH and ESP*).

The mechanics of the tunnel, from the IP point of view, is that when A sends a packet to C, A will launch it with an IP header that has source=A, destination=C. When G_1 sends it across the tunnel, it puts it into another envelope, i.e., it adds an additional IP header, treating the inner header as data. The outer IP header will contain source=G_1 and destination=G_2. And all the contents (including the inner IP header) will be encrypted and integrity protected, so it is safe to traverse the Internet. G_1, G_2, and G_3 use the Internet like some sort of insecure wire. You might want your users to be able to access the corporate network from across the Internet as well. Suppose B is some sort of workstation that can attach to the Internet in any location. To do this, B would create a tunnel with one of the Gs. This configuration is often referred to as a **VPN** (virtual private network).

Another way to think about this is to consider your communication path to be a sequence of links, some of which are secure and some of which aren't. The right way to ensure secure communication is end-to-end, i.e., where the two communicating parties do all the security work and assume that the medium over which they are communicating is insecure. But the parties may not be capable of providing security, which is okay if all the links and routers in the path between them are secure. When some of the links are subject to eavesdropping, you can encrypt over those links. Only the endpoints of the tunnel need to do encryption and decryption.

23.4 COMPARISONS

A packet filter can do its job without requiring any changes to the software in any of the communicating nodes. It prevents some conversations, but the allowed conversations proceed normally (assuming the packet filter isn't using some bizarre rules such as disallowing any packet that has the ASCII pattern for pornography or some other suspicious word anywhere inside).

An application level gateway also can be deployed without changing any software, but it is visible to the users. They have to log into the firewall, and from there connect to whatever they are allowed to connect to. Application level gateways can be much more powerful than packet filters. For instance, because they are application-aware, they might be able to look at the data inside email messages to scan for viruses.

A VPN can also be deployed without changing any of the nodes inside your corporate network, but a node such as B in Figure 23-3 will need special software in order to create an encrypted tunnel to one of the Gs.

Packet filters and application level gateways are intended to allow limited communication between nodes inside your network and "outsiders". VPNs are intended to maintain an isolated private network that allows full access to "insiders", and no access to "outsiders".

23.5 WHY FIREWALLS DON'T WORK

Firewalls alone (without also doing end-to-end security) assume that all the bad guys are on the outside, and everyone inside can be completely trusted. This is, of course, an unwarranted assumption. Should employees have access (read and write) to the salary database, for instance?

Even if the company is so careful about hiring that no employee would ever do anything bad intentionally, firewalls can be defeated by somehow injecting malicious code into the corporate network. This can be done by tricking someone into downloading something from the Internet or launching an executable from an email message. It is quite common for an attacker to break into one system inside your firewall, and then use that system as a platform for attacking other systems. Someone once described firewall protected networks as "hard and crunchy on the outside; soft and chewy on the inside".

Firewalls often make it difficult for legitimate users to get their work done. The firewall might be configured incorrectly, or not recognize a new legitimate application. And if the firewall allows anything through (say email or *http*), people figure out how to do what they need to do by disguising it as traffic that the firewall is configured to allow. File transfer is common by sending the file in email. To prevent this, some firewalls are configured to not allow very large email messages, in which case the users circumvent the firewall by breaking the file into small enough chunks, each chunk sent as a different email message. It's clumsy and annoying, but it works.

The ironic term for disguising traffic in order to fool a firewall is to carry your traffic in a **firewall friendly** protocol. Since firewalls commonly allow *http* traffic (since it's the protocol used for browsing the web), there are many proposals for doing things over *http*, from network management to carrying IP over *http*, which would allow any traffic through! Firewall-friendly? The whole point is to defeat the best efforts of the firewall administrator to disallow what you are doing! It isn't somehow "easier" for the firewall to carry *http* traffic than any other. The easiest thing for the firewall would be to allow everything or nothing through!

Just as breaking a large file into lots of pieces to be individually carried in separate emails is inefficient, having protocols run on top of *http* rather than simply on top of IP is also inefficient in terms of bandwidth and computation.

23.6 DENIAL-OF-SERVICE ATTACKS

A **denial-of-service attack** is one in which an attacker prevents good guys from accessing a service, but does not enable unauthorized access to any services. In the naive old days, security people dismissed the prospect of denial-of-service attacks as unlikely, since the attacker had nothing to gain. Of course that turned out to be faulty reasoning. There are terrorists, disgruntled employees, and people who delight in causing mischief for no good reason.

In the earliest types of denial-of-service attacks, the attacker repeatedly sent messages to the victim machine. Most machines at the time were vulnerable to this sort of attack since they had resources that could easily be depleted. For instance, the storage area for keeping track of pending TCP connections tended to be very limited, on the order of, say, ten connections. The probability of ten legitimate users connecting during a single network round trip time was sufficiently small that ten was a reasonable number. But it was easy for the attacking machine to fill up this table, even if the attacking machine was attached to the Internet with a low-speed link.

To avoid being caught at this mischief, it was common for the attacker to send these malicious packets from forged source addresses. This made it difficult to find (and prosecute) the attacker, and it made it difficult to recognize packets from the malicious machine and filter them at a firewall.

In defense, people started deploying routers with the capability of doing sanity checks on the source address. These routers could be configured to drop packets with a source address that could not have legitimately come from the direction from which the packet was received. And end node storage areas were increased so that a single attacker, at the speeds at which such attackers were typically connected to the Internet, could not fill the pending TCP connection table.

Another level of escalation was to send a single packet that caused a lot of legitimate machines to send messages to the victim machine. An example of such a packet is a packet transmitted to the broadcast address on some LAN, with the packet's source address forged to the address of the victim's machine, asking for all receivers to respond. All the machines on that LAN will send a response to the victim's machine. Such a mechanism magnifies the effect the attacker can have from his single machine, since each packet he creates turns into n packets directed at the victim machine.

The next level of escalation is known as a **distributed denial-of-service attack**. In this form of attack the attacker breaks into a lot of innocent machines, and installs software on them to have them all attack the victim machine. These innocent machines are called **zombies** or **drones**. With enough zombies, any machine can be made inaccessible, since even if the machine itself can process packets as fast as they can possibly arrive (i.e., the speed of the wire attaching it to the Internet), the links or routers in front of that machine can be overwhelmed. Since the packets are coming from hundreds or thousands of innocent machines, it is hard to distinguish these packets from packets coming from legitimate users.

23.7 SHOULD FIREWALLS GO AWAY?

Even if the world deployed end-to-end security everywhere, firewalls still serve an important purpose. The can keep intruders from doing the equivalent of jiggling all the doors inside your building to see if someone accidentally left one unlocked. And they can help protect against denial-of-service attacks by keeping nuisance traffic off your net.

24 MORE SECURITY SYSTEMS

With every release, software gets more complex and less secure until the only security left is job security.

—Al Eldridge

A lot of systems have been deployed with security features, and it is rather surprising how different they can be from one another. In this chapter we give an overview of some of the systems we have found interesting. Some of them are quite old and have died out, but we describe them anyway because they have some interesting features, either positive or negative. Since these are not standards, we are not attempting to describe them in sufficient detail to implement them, but rather only enough to describe their interesting concepts.

Why haven't these systems been fully documented in the public literature? One reason is that lack of documentation makes it harder for a relatively unsophisticated cracker to exploit security flaws that might exist. Sometimes it is because a company considers the technology a trade secret. Often it is just because careful documentation of the security features is a lot of work and has little commercial benefit.

24.1 NETWARE V3

Novell's networking package is known as NetWare. This section describes the cryptographic security in Version 3. Version 4 security was enhanced to use public key cryptography. We describe Version 4 security in §24.2 *NetWare V4*.

Each server has a database consisting of information about each authorized client. The information includes the user's name, the salt, and the hash of the user's password with the salt. The salt is not actually a random number, but instead is a 32-bit user ID assigned by the server when the user is installed in the server database. The salt serves two purposes. It makes the hash of Alice's password server-dependent, so that if Alice uses the same password on multiple servers, the database at each server will, with high probability, store a different hash of her password. It also makes the hash of Ted's password different from the hash of Alice's password even if they have the same password. We'll use X to designate the hash of the password stored at the server.

username_1 $\text{userID}_1 = \text{salt}_1$ $\text{hash}(\text{salt}_1, \text{password}_1) = X_1$
username_2 $\text{userID}_2 = \text{salt}_2$ $\text{hash}(\text{salt}_2, \text{password}_2) = X_2$
⋮

Figure 24-1. Server Password Database

Alice tells her workstation her name, password, and the name of the server to which she'd like to log in. The workstation sends Alice's name to the server. The server sends the salt value and a random challenge R to the workstation. The workstation performs the hash of the password Alice typed with the salt, and now both the workstation and the server know the same secret value X (assuming Alice typed her password correctly).

Now the workstation and the server each computes hash(X,R) to get a value we'll call Y. The workstation transmits Y to the server, and if it matches hash(X,R), then the server considers Alice authenticated. At this point the workstation and the server each compute Z=hash(X,R,constant string). Z is what they'll use as a secret session key.

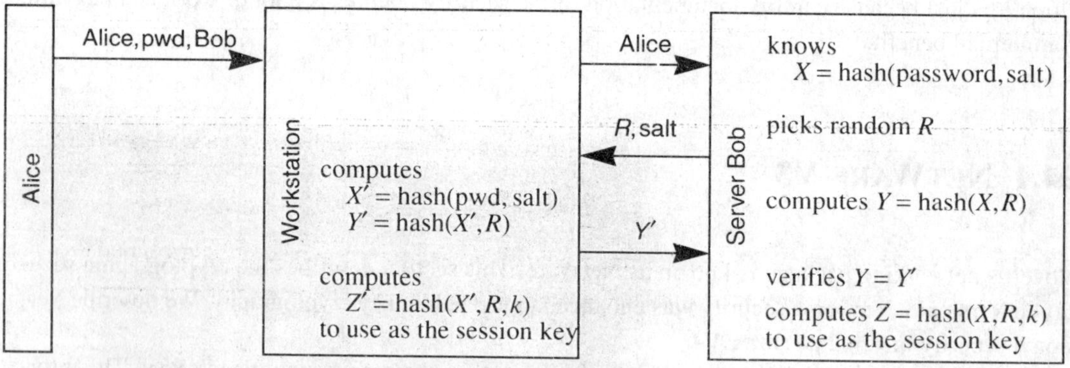

Figure 24-2. NetWare V3 Authentication

After the authentication exchange each packet is integrity-protected by performing a hash of the packet and Z. Once the workstation receives an integrity-protected packet from the server, mutual authentication has occurred, because the server has proven it knows Z.

Actually, for performance reasons, only the first 52 bytes of the packet are cryptographically checksummed. Checksumming the first 52 bytes of the packet is sufficient to answer the threats of eavesdroppers gaining information from the authentication exchange and intruders hijacking a session after the initial authentication exchange. It does not prevent an attacker from removing a packet in transit and substituting one with modified data after the first 52 bytes, but this is a far less realistic threat, particularly if the two communicating parties are on the same LAN.

Why did Novell choose 52 bytes rather than some nice power of 2? Because 52 bytes is long enough to protect all the information necessary to prevent hijacking, and there's additional information appended to those 52 bytes to form a single 64-byte message digest block. The extra information is the 4-byte packet length and the 8-byte secret.

Why does the server store the secret value *X* rather than simply the user's password? A workstation that knew the value *X* would be able to impersonate Alice without knowing Alice's password. But in terms of real-world threats, it is a lot more secure to store *X* than Alice's password. If Trudy were to steal the server's database and acquire *X*, she'd only be able to exploit *X* if she were able to acquire the client authentication code and modify it to use *X* rather than compute it from what the user types. In contrast, if the server stored the user's password directly, then if Trudy stole the server's database, she'd be able to impersonate Alice directly by typing her password at unmodified client code.

Storing *X* rather than the password will not prevent Trudy from doing an off-line password-guessing attack, but if Alice chose her password wisely, then an off-line password-guessing attack is unlikely to succeed.

Another reason it is more secure to store *X* than the user's password is because of the salt. Let's assume Trudy can modify the client code, and can therefore use *X* to impersonate Alice directly, and therefore *X* is as security-sensitive as Alice's actual password. Since *X* is very likely to be different at each server, even if Alice's password is the same, then Trudy will only be able to impersonate Alice at the server from which Trudy acquired the database.

24.2 NETWARE V4

There were two major reasons for modifying security in Version 4 of NetWare. The first was to utilize public key cryptography, which has the potential to make theft of the server database less of a security issue. The other was to simplify management. Instead of having a database entry for Alice separately managed at each server Alice is authorized to use, NetWare Directory Services (NDS) stores Alice's security information, and servers retrieve the information from NDS.

Each user has an RSA key, but of course the user does not remember that. The user remembers a password. NDS stores Alice's private key encrypted with her password. To prevent off-line password guessing, Alice's workstation must prove knowledge of her password before NDS will transmit her encrypted private key. The pre-authentication phase, where her workstation proves it knows her password, is similar to NetWare V3. NDS stores a hash of Alice's password and salt. In V3 we said the salt was useful because it made the hash of Alice's password different on different servers. That case does not apply for V4 since Alice's entry is only stored in one place—NetWare Directory Services. But the salt is still useful, since it means that an intruder who reads the directory service database has to conduct separate dictionary attacks against each account.

First Alice logs into the workstation by typing her name and password. The workstation then authenticates on Alice's behalf to NDS in order to obtain Alice's private key. For security as well as performance, once the workstation acquires Alice's private key from NDS, it converts it into a temporary Gillou-Quisquater (GQ) key (see §24.2.1 *NetWare's Guillou-Quisquater Authentication Scheme*) and then forgets her password and private RSA key.

Authentication with GQ is public key authentication, but there are two important differences from authenticating with RSA.

- A private RSA key lasts forever. A GQ key, as NetWare uses it, expires—the workstation determines when the GQ key should expire when it creates the GQ key from the RSA key. If some untrustworthy software steals Alice's password or private RSA key, it can impersonate her forever (or until she notices what has happened and changes her long-term private key). Conversion to a GQ key limits the amount of time in which damage can be done. Note that this is the same reasoning that led the Kerberos designers to introduce the concept of a TGT and session key for the user rather than using the user's master key throughout a session.
- GQ authentication is faster than RSA for the client (Alice, the thing proving her identity) but slower for the server (Bob, the thing authenticating Alice). The NetWare designers envisioned slow PCs for clients and fast PCs for servers.

NetWare could have implemented the conversion of the long-term secret into a short-term secret differently. Rather than generate a GQ key pair, the workstation could choose a new RSA key pair, generate a certificate for it by signing it with the user's long-term private RSA key, and then forget the user's long-term secret. That is what DASS does, as we'll see in §24.4 *DASS/SPX*. But generating a temporary GQ key is much faster than generating an RSA key, so the NetWare scheme has higher performance during login.

Once the workstation has acquired a GQ key for Alice, it stores it for the duration of her session and uses it to authenticate on her behalf to any servers she accesses during her session.

If Alice asks to log into server Bob, then Bob must retrieve Alice's public RSA key from NDS. Alice's temporary GQ key works with her permanent public RSA key, in the sense that a signature generated with her temporary GQ key is verified using her permanent public RSA key.

To summarize, the information stored for Alice in NDS includes

Alice's name	
hash(salt, password) = X	used to verify that Alice's workstation knows her password before NDS transmits her encrypted private RSA key
public RSA key	
encrypted private RSA key	encrypted using a hash of Alice's password

Figure 24-3. NetWare V4 NDS Database Entry for Alice

Here is the protocol in which Alice's workstation obtains her encrypted private RSA key from NDS:

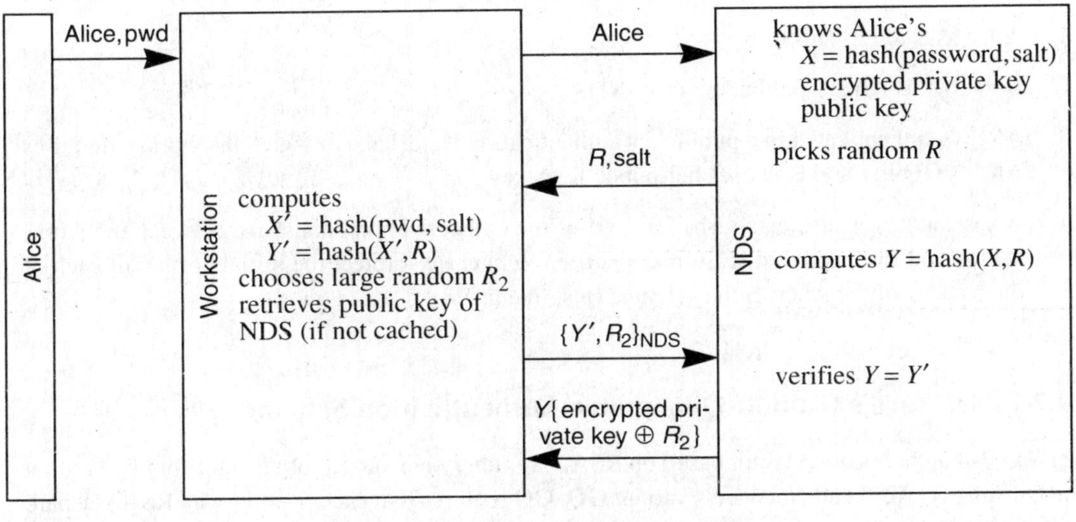

Figure 24-4. NetWare V4 Pre-authentication

First Alice logs in and her workstation communicates with NDS in order to obtain her private RSA key, which her workstation will use to generate a finite-lifetime GQ key for her:

1. Alice types her name and password to her workstation.
2. The workstation uses that information to authenticate Alice on her behalf to NDS, in an authentication exchange nearly identical to NetWare V3, except for the final message of the pre-authentication. The final message in V3 consists simply of Y, which is hash(X,R), where R is the challenge transmitted by the server. In V4, in addition to transmitting Y, the worksta-

tion transmits a large random number R_2 (chosen by the workstation), which will be used by NDS for concealing NDS's reply to the workstation from eavesdroppers. The entire message (Y and the random number R_2) is encrypted with the NDS's public key. Encrypting the message with NDS's public key means that an eavesdropper cannot use Y and R to verify password guesses off-line (as it could in V3).

3. Once NDS is assured that the workstation knows Alice's password, NDS transmits Alice's encrypted private RSA key to the workstation. To prevent off-line password guessing by eavesdroppers, the encrypted private RSA key is ⊕'d with the random number R_2 sent in the previous step, and then encrypted with Y.
4. The workstation decrypts Alice's private RSA key. It immediately turns it into a GQ key with an expiration time, and then forgets the password and private RSA key.

Here is what occurs when Alice accesses a network resource, say a server named Bob.

1. Alice asks to log into Bob.
2. Bob obtains Alice's public key from NDS.
3. Alice is authenticated in a public key authentication handshake in which the workstation uses Alice's GQ key and Bob uses her public RSA key.
4. A session key is also established as part of the authentication handshake between the workstation and Bob, and that session key is used to integrity-protect the initial portion of each of the packets of the Alice-Bob exchange (just like in V3).

24.2.1 NetWare's Guillou-Quisquater Authentication Scheme

NetWare V4 authentication is not based on RSA, but rather on a variant of an algorithm by Guillou and Quisquater. We'll call NetWare's variant **GQ**. GQ requires that each user have an RSA key pair. The user's private RSA key is used to generate a private GQ key with a temporary lifetime. Then the workstation forgets the user's private RSA key, and future authentication is done using only the GQ key and the user's public RSA key. The GQ key can only do signatures (it can't encrypt or decrypt). Signature verification uses the public RSA key.

This is how the workstation acquires a private GQ key for the user:

1. The workstation acquires the user's private RSA key.
2. The workstation generates a message, m_0, which includes the validity interval for the GQ key it is about to create.

3. The workstation signs m_0 with the user's private RSA key. This signature of m_0 is the user's private GQ key, Q. The workstation must not divulge this quantity.

4. The workstation forgets the user's private RSA key, but remembers m_0 (which is used, together with the user's public RSA key, to verify a GQ signature) and Q (the RSA signature on m_0).

This is how the GQ key is used to sign a message:

1. To sign a message, say m, the workstation needs to know Q, m, and the user's public RSA key. These quantities are all fed into a magic function that outputs a signature. As used by NetWare, m is the challenge supplied by the server.

2. The signature verification function requires as input m, the signature on m, m_0, and the user's public RSA key. With these inputs, the signature verification function decides whether or not the signature is valid.

The mathematics involved are ugly and unintuitive, but we'll document them here for completeness. We'll describe the mechanics, but to understand why it's secure, you should read [GUIL88].

- The user's RSA key pair is $\langle e,n \rangle$ for the public key, and $\langle d,n \rangle$ for the private key.
- $Q = {m_0}^d \bmod n$ is the RSA signature on m_0.

To sign a message m, do the following:

1. Generate eight random numbers $r_1, \ldots r_8$ in the range [2, n–2].
2. Compute eight quantities $x_1, \ldots x_8$, where $x_i = {r_i}^e \bmod n$.
3. Compute MD4($m|x_1|x_2|\ldots|x_8$).
4. Break the 128-bit message digest computed in the previous step into 8 16-bit quantities and call the pieces $c_1, \ldots c_8$.
5. Compute eight quantities $y_1, \ldots y_8$, where $y_i = r_i Q^{c_i} \bmod n$.
6. The GQ signature of m consists of $x_1, \ldots x_8$, and $y_1, \ldots y_8$.

To verify the GQ signature of m, do the following:

1. Receive m_0, m, $x_1, \ldots x_8$, and $y_1, \ldots y_8$.
2. Reliably find the user's public key $\langle e,n \rangle$.
3. Compute MD4($m|x_1|x_2|\ldots|x_8$).

4. Break the 128-bit message digest computed in the previous step into 8 16-bit quantities and call the pieces $c_1, \ldots c_8$.

5. Accept the signature if for each i, $y_i^e = x_i m_0^{c_i}$ mod n.

Why does this work?

$y_i = r_i Q^{c_i}$ mod n (this is how y_i got computed in the signing algorithm)

$y_i^e = (r_i Q^{c_i})^e = r_i^e (Q^e)^{c_i}$ mod n

$r_i^e = x_i$ mod n (this is how x_i got computed in the signing algorithm)

$Q = m_0^d$ mod n, so $Q^e = m_0$ mod n

$y_i^e = (r_i Q^{c_i})^e = r_i^e (Q^e)^{c_i} = x_i m_0^{c_i}$ mod n, which is what is being tested

24.3 KRYPTOKNIGHT

KryptoKnight was developed at IBM. Its product name is NetSP (Network Security Program). We really like the name KryptoKnight, so we'll use that rather than the probably more correct term NetSP. It is a secret key based authentication and key establishment system similar to Kerberos. There are several papers describing the concepts behind it [MOLV92, BIRD93, HAUS94, BIRD95, JANS95].

Ways in which KryptoKnight is similar to Kerberos:

- They both use KDCs, though KryptoKnight calls them **Authentication Servers**.
- There can be multiple realms, which KryptoKnight refers to as **domains**.
- There can be replicated KDCs within a single realm.
- Upon first login, the user's password is converted into a long-term key, which is used to obtain a TGT from the KDC, and then both the password and long-term key are forgotten by the workstation.
- Like Kerberos V5, to prevent an intruder from simply asking the KDC for a TGT for Alice and then using that TGT to mount an off-line password-guessing attack, Alice's workstation needs to prove to the KDC that it knows her password before the KDC will transmit a TGT.

KryptoKnight differs from Kerberos in the following ways:

- KryptoKnight uses message digest functions rather than DES for authentication and even for encryption of tickets. Using message digest functions rather than DES in authentication offers performance advantages and may make it easier to comply with export controls.
- With Kerberos, Alice must obtain a ticket to Bob before initiating a conversation. In KryptoKnight, there is the option for Alice to alert Bob directly that she would like to converse, and have Bob do the handshaking with the KDC(s). One example where this functionality is vital is where Bob is a firewall and prevents Alice from accessing anything inside the network, including the KDC, until Alice has been authenticated by Bob. Another example is where it is less expensive for Bob than Alice to communicate with the KDC, for instance if Alice has a very-low-bandwidth link into the network.
- Like Kerberos V4 but unlike Kerberos V5, interrealm authentication between Alice and Bob is only allowed when Alice's KDC and Bob's KDC have been administratively set up with a shared key; i.e., transit realms are not allowed.
- KryptoKnight does not rely on synchronized clocks, and can instead use random number challenges.
- The KryptoKnight designers were very careful to minimize the number of messages, lengths of messages, and amount of encryption (for example, Kerberos V4 unnecessarily encrypts an already-encrypted ticket). Ironically, in some cases KryptoKnight uses more messages than Kerberos, but this is because of not relying on synchronized clocks and therefore requiring an extra message to transmit a challenge.
- Other than pre-authentication, KryptoKnight does not bother with any of the features that got added to Kerberos V5, such as delegation, authorization data, postdated and renewable tickets, and hierarchical realms.

24.3.1 KryptoKnight Tickets

In Kerberos, when Alice asks for a ticket to Bob, she is given a quantity, encrypted with Bob's key, containing the session key Alice and Bob will share and other information such as Alice's name and the expiration time of the ticket.

In a ticket, the only information that requires encryption is the session key, but the rest of the information has to be protected from modification. KryptoKnight tickets are rather elegant. Indeed in a KryptoKnight ticket, the only thing that is encrypted is the session key. And it is encrypted using a message digest function, rather than by secret key encryption.

The most important fields in a ticket are Alice's name, the expiration time, and the encrypted session key. The session key is encrypted by ⊕ing it with a quantity that Bob and the KDC, but no one else, can compute. That quantity is the message digest of the concatenation of the secret Bob shares with the KDC, Alice's name, and the expiration time of the ticket. If someone were to modify the name or expiration time in the ticket, then when Bob computes the message digest of his secret|Alice|expiration time, he'll get a totally different value, and the ticket will decrypt to something totally unpredictable, and therefore useless to an intruder. So this encryption method for encrypting the session key also serves as integrity protection for the unencrypted fields in the ticket.

24.3.2 Authenticators

During the authentication handshake, Alice and Bob send each other something functionally equivalent to Kerberos authenticators. The Kerberos authenticator is a timestamp DES-encrypted with the shared secret. In KryptoKnight, it is instead a nonce, generated by the other side as a challenge. Alice "signs" Bob's challenge by prepending the secret she and Bob share and returning the message digest of the result. Similarly, Bob signs Alice's challenge. KryptoKnight provides all Kerberos V4 functionality (except encryption of user data) using message digest functions rather than secret key cryptography.

24.3.3 Nonces vs. Timestamps

We said before that KryptoKnight does not require synchronized time. Actually, the authentication protocols can use either timestamps or nonces. There is a trade-off between nonces and timestamps. Timestamps require somewhat-synchronized clocks. If time is only used to indicate expiration time, it doesn't need to be very accurate. But if an encrypted timestamp is sent as part of the authentication handshake, then time synchronization is more critical. Relying on timestamps also raises another security vulnerability, since the timekeeping mechanism has to be kept secure (or else an intruder can accomplish bad things by setting the clocks back a month or so). The disadvantages of using nonces instead of timestamps are that nonces require additional messages, and they do not allow Alice to hold onto a ticket to Bob and use it multiple times (see below).

Because sometimes one mechanism is preferable to the other, KryptoKnight tickets contain both a nonce and an expiration time, though usually only one of the fields will be security-relevant in any given exchange. Authenticators can also be based on time or nonces.

How does KryptoKnight work when it uses nonces instead of timestamps in the authentication handshake? The timestamp in a ticket to Bob assures Bob that Alice has obtained the ticket recently, because the expiration time has not yet occurred. In order to use a nonce instead of an expiration time, Alice needs to ask Bob for a nonce before she can request a ticket to Bob. She sends Bob's nonce to the KDC and it puts it into the ticket. Bob has to remember the nonce he gave to Alice, and make sure that the ticket is based on his nonce.

Actually the nonce does not need to be transmitted as part of the ticket. The nonce, instead of being explicitly in the ticket, is just one of the fields (along with Alice's name and the secret that Bob and the KDC share) which get input into the message digest that the KDC ⊕s with the session key.

With the nonce mechanism, once Alice is removed from the KDC database, she is unable to obtain more tickets. With the expiration time mechanism, once Alice obtains a ticket there is no way to revoke it until the expiration time occurs.

24.3.4 Data Encryption

Once a session is set up, if encryption is desired, the data is encrypted with a secret key cryptographic scheme. The prototype used DES. The product they shipped used a weakened secret key algorithm with a 40-bit key, which was the price IBM paid to make the product freely exportable from the U.S.

24.4 DASS/SPX

DASS stands for Distributed Authentication Security Service. It was deployed as SPX, pronounced Sphinx, and nobody has come up with an acronym expansion for SPX. It was developed at Digital Equipment Corporation and documented in RFC 1507 and [TARD91]. SPX is technically the product name, whereas DASS is the architecture, rather like NetSP and KryptoKnight. We'll use the term DASS because we think it is the more commonly used term for it in the security community, though we haven't done any official polls.

24.4.1 DASS Certification Hierarchy

DASS has a certificate hierarchy similar to what we describe in §15.3.8 *Bottom-Up with Name Constraints*. Conceptually there's a CA responsible for each node in the naming hierarchy. Each CA signs a certificate for its parent and for each of its children. These are known as up certificates and down certificates, respectively. DASS also allows cross certificates, where a CA can sign a certificate for any other CA, so that authentication can short-circuit the hierarchy for performance or security reasons. Also, there does not need to be a distinct CA for every node in the tree. One CA could be responsible for many parts of the naming tree.

DASS uses X.509 syntax for certificates and originally envisioned storing certificates in an X.500-style directory service, but since one was not deployed, the DASS designers invented their own certificate distribution service, which they called a CDC, for Certificate Distribution Center. It not only stores certificates, but also stores encrypted private keys. Certificates are publicly readable. To obtain the encrypted private key, the client machine must prove knowledge of the user's password, and must know the public key of the CDC in order for this exchange to be secure. DASS would benefit from one of the protocols described in §12.4 *Strong Password Credentials Download Protocols*, but they did not exist at the time of its design.

24.4.2 Login Key

Once the workstation retrieves the user's private key *P*, it immediately chooses what DASS refers to as a *login* RSA key pair and then generates a certificate, which we'll call the **login certificate**, signing it with *P*, stating the user's login public key and an expiration time. Then it forgets *P* and remembers only the login private key and the login certificate. This is similar to obtaining a TGT in Kerberos, or obtaining a GQ key in NetWare V4. The DASS method is lower-performance during login than the NetWare method because it takes more computation to generate an RSA key pair than a GQ key. During authentication the DASS method is lower-performance on the client side because RSA signature generation is slower than GQ signature generation. But the DASS method is higher-performance on the server side, because with small public exponents, RSA signature verification is faster than GQ signature verification. The DASS designers envisioned a world where workstations had cycles to burn while servers were overburdened. The NetWare designers envisioned the opposite.

24.4.3 DASS Authentication Handshake

Let's say user Alice accesses resource Bob. We won't distinguish between Alice's workstation and Alice. Obviously it's Alice's workstation that is performing the cryptographic operations, but we'll refer to the two ends of the conversation as Alice and Bob. The initial authentication handshake is a mutual authentication handshake based on public keys. Alice knows Bob's public key by looking up and verifying his certificate in the CDC. Bob knows Alice's long-term public key by looking up her certificate in the CDC (and verifying the certificate signature). But the key in Alice's certificate is not the key Alice will be using. Alice has to transmit her login certificate to Bob, and Bob, after following the certificate chain, now knows Alice's public key for this login session.

In the process of doing an authentication handshake, Alice and Bob establish a shared secret key. Future cryptographic operations, such as encryption of the conversation, are done using that shared secret key. For performance reasons, DASS is designed so that subsequent authentication exchanges between the same two parties can also be done without any public key operations, using only the shared secret key.

It is interesting how the secret key is established between Alice and Bob. Alice (her workstation of course) chooses a DES key $S_{\text{Alice-Bob}}$ at random, encrypts $S_{\text{Alice-Bob}}$ with Bob's public key, and signs the result using her login private key (for integrity protection). We'll use X to designate the encrypted signed $S_{\text{Alice-Bob}}$.

Alice sends her login certificate and X to Bob, along with an authenticator proving she knows the key $S_{\text{Alice-Bob}}$. Bob then does the following:

- gets Alice's long-term public key, by retrieving and verifying her certificate from the CDC
- verifies Alice's login certificate by using her long-term public key
- extracts Alice's login public key from her login certificate
- reverses Alice's signature on X by using her login public key
- reverses the encryption of X using his own private key, getting $S_{\text{Alice-Bob}}$
- verifies the authenticator by decrypting it using $S_{\text{Alice-Bob}}$ and checking whether the time is valid
- encrypts the timestamp using $S_{\text{Alice-Bob}}$ and returns it to provide mutual authentication

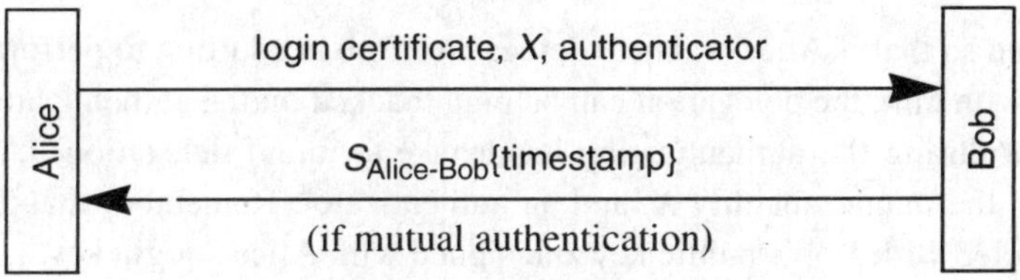

Figure 24-5. DASS Authentication

For performance reasons, both Bob and Alice cache both $S_{\text{Alice-Bob}}$ and X. If Alice accesses Bob again, Alice will transmit X again, with a new authenticator. So why does Bob need to remember X? The reason he does is to save himself the trouble of cryptographically unwrapping X again in order to obtain $S_{\text{Alice-Bob}}$. Alice might have forgotten $S_{\text{Alice-Bob}}$ and chosen a new secret. So Bob has to check if the X he receives is the same as the one he has cached, but if they match he can assume he's using the same key as before with Alice. If they don't match, or if Bob has forgotten the cached information, the authentication handshake works just fine. It just involves the extra computation of Bob cryptographically unwrapping X.

Why does Alice need to cache X? Since Alice does not know whether Bob has cached $S_{\text{Alice-Bob}}$, she has to send X again so that the authentication handshake can proceed whether or not

Bob has cached $S_{\text{Alice-Bob}}$. Since she has to perform cryptographic operations in order to regenerate X, it saves her time if she caches X.

An interesting feature of DASS is that the authentication handshake is designed to work in a single message in the case of one-way authentication, and two messages in the case of mutual authentication. The price it pays to reach this theoretical minimum number of messages is that it requires roughly synchronized clocks, like Kerberos.

24.4.4 DASS Authenticators

When Alice initiates a connection to Bob, she sends an authenticator. When mutual authentication is required, Bob sends an authenticator back to Alice. The authenticator is very different in the two directions. In the Alice→Bob direction, Alice sends Bob an unencrypted timestamp and a MAC. The MAC is computed by doing a DES CBC residue using the secret key $S_{\text{Alice-Bob}}$ and an IV of 0, computed over the timestamp and the network layer source and destination addresses extracted from the network layer header. The authenticator Bob sends back to Alice is the timestamp encrypted with $S_{\text{Alice-Bob}}$.

24.4.5 DASS Delegation

DASS is designed so that if Alice wants to delegate to Bob in addition to performing an authentication handshake with him, the delegation can be piggybacked on the authentication handshake.

Recall that during the authentication handshake (without delegation), Alice sends Bob her login certificate, the magic quantity X, and an authenticator. Remember that X is the session key $S_{\text{Alice-Bob}}$ encrypted with Bob's public key and signed with Alice's login key.

If delegation is being done as well as authentication, there's one less public key operation, because instead of sending X (which is the session key encrypted with Bob's public key and then signed with Alice's private key), Alice just sends the session key encrypted with Bob's public key. In order to delegate to Bob, she sends Bob her login private key encrypted with $S_{\text{Alice-Bob}}$. As in the non-delegation case, she also sends an authenticator proving she knows $S_{\text{Alice-Bob}}$. It takes some thought as to why, in the delegation case, it isn't necessary to sign the encrypted session key, whereas it is necessary in the non-delegation case. The DASS designers really enjoyed standing on their heads to minimize public key operations (see Homework Problem 1).

24.4.6 Saving Bits

While DASS was intended to work with a variety of protocols, and was only actually deployed with TCP/IP, the DASS designers wanted to integrate their protocols with DECnet Phase IV, which introduced some interesting constraints. They could only piggyback the security information on existing transport layer connection messages if the additional information did not make the transport layer connection messages longer than an Ethernet packet (approximately 1500 bytes). Alice initiates contact with Bob with a connect request message. Bob replies with a connect confirm message. There were only 16 spare bytes in a connect confirm, and DASS managed to only use 8 of them. DASS needed more space in a connect request, because Alice sends her login certificate, *X*, and an authenticator. Luckily, there was enough room. But there would not have been enough room if the DASS designers didn't spend a lot of time doing clever compression of the data they needed to send.

The exact packet formats are not important, but the most dramatic encoding trick they played was the encoding of Alice's login private key when she transmits it to Bob for delegation. Recall that an RSA public key consists of $\langle e,n \rangle$, where n is the modulus and e is the public exponent. An RSA private key consists of $\langle d,n \rangle$. Alice's login certificate contains $\langle e,n \rangle$. You'd expect Alice to send d in order to give Bob her login private key. But instead, she sends p, which is the smaller of the factors of n, and will be about half as big as d (so it will be about 256 bits instead of 512). Bob has to divide n by p to get q, and then use Euclid's algorithm to calculate d (given that he knows e and n from her login certificate). Actually, when doing delegation it's friendly to pass more than just d, since if Bob knows n's factorization he can do private key operations more efficiently. Given p, Bob can compute all the information that would have been good to send him. If instead, Alice were to pass all the information so that Bob didn't need to do any computation, it would take about 2½ times the size of the modulus (so about 1300 bits). The DASS method makes Bob do some work up front, but then he can sign efficiently on Alice's behalf.

DASS does use ASN.1 encoding, which might seem surprising since its designers were so worried about encoding efficiency. But they were very careful to avoid sending redundant information, and they were clever in their use of ASN.1 syntax. By using **`IMPLICIT`** and other tricks they avoided the size explosion found in Kerberos V5 and X.509.

24.5 LOTUS NOTES SECURITY

Lotus Notes has a security system without a cute name, or really any name at all. Lotus Notes was developed by a company called Iris Associates, which was acquired by Lotus (the name was changed to Lotus Notes after the acquisition, not due to some amazing coincidence). Later Lotus was assimilated by IBM, who changed the name of the server end of the product to Lotus Domino.

The first three versions had the clever names *version 1*, *version 2*, and *version 3*. In the first edition of this book, we boldly speculated that the version they were working on at the time would be called *version 4*. But we were wrong. The next two versions were called R4 and R5 (where R stands for "release"). Apparently there is some subtle marketing distinction between a version and a release. The next version about to be released as of the writing of this book is called "release 6", and the marketeers have sternly said that it is NOT to be called R6. While the security has evolved over the years—in particular the adding of S/MIME and SSL support for interoperation with other products—the Notes proprietary public key infrastructure (they prefer to call it pre-standard) has remained substantially the same.

Like the other systems we've discussed, Lotus Notes security provides for mutual authentication and establishment of a shared session key. It also provides for electronic mail security and for digitally signing active content. It is public key based, though just like all security systems, it uses public keys in conjunction with secret keys for encryption. The algorithms it uses are RSA, MD2, RC2, and RC4 (see glossary).

24.5.1 ID Files

An ID file contains the sort of user-specific security information that most other deployed schemes store in a directory service. Lotus Notes security assumes that a user Alice will carry her ID file on a floppy or smart card, or have it stored in nonvolatile memory on her workstation. Because an ID file might be stolen or lost, the ID file is encrypted with Alice's password.

There are interesting trade-offs between the ID file scheme and a directory service based scheme. The advantages of storing the user's security information in a directory service are:

- It is more convenient. If ID files are kept on floppies or smart cards, users have to carry something around, and if they lose it or forget it they can't log into the network. If ID files are kept on a workstation, then the user is restricted to using that workstation. It is possible to store a given user's ID file on more than one workstation, but it becomes infeasible in some environments to maintain a user's ID file on every possible workstation that that user might use. And operations like password changes become very awkward.
- It might be more secure. A directory service based scheme, if properly designed, can make it difficult for an intruder to capture a quantity with which to do password guessing. If an ID file is on a floppy, someone who steals the floppy can do an off-line password-guessing attack. If the ID file is stored on a workstation, anyone who can physically access the workstation can read out the information and do off-line guessing. In the case of a smart card, however, it is possible to design a smart card that will refuse to divulge its contents, and

which will limit the number of password guesses by disabling itself after too many incorrect guesses. In release 6, Lotus Notes offers the option of storing the ID file on a server and accessing it with a protocol similar to the ones in §12.4 *Strong Password Credentials Download Protocols*.

The advantages of the ID file scheme are:

- It might be more secure, because it provides "two-factor authentication", based on both *what you have* and *what you know*.
- It requires less of the network to be operational. Sometimes the environment is quite primitive, such as when the network itself is mostly broken and you need security for network management in order to fix the network, or when directory service replicas need to authenticate one another, or when a bunch of people with laptops show up at a meeting and want to form a private little network.
- It might be more secure because someone who had physical access to a directory service replica could read the directory service database and do off-line password guessing. With ID files, very careful users can keep their information out of the enemy's hands, whereas with a directory service solution, the users have to trust someone else to protect the directory service replicas.

Lotus Notes security does depend on the directory service for encrypting mail, finding cross certificates, and revoking certificates, but basic authentication and signature verification works even if the directory service is unavailable.

24.5.2 Coping with Export Controls

It is amusing to see what lengths Lotus had to go to in order to satisfy export criteria, and yet provide reasonable security where legal. Each user has two RSA key pairs, a long one and a short one. Bulk encryption, as you'd expect, is done using secret key cryptography. Again, to satisfy the export rules at the time Lotus asked for a license, there were two key lengths for secret keys, a short one (on the order of 40 bits) and a long one (on the order of 64 bits). The long keys were used within the U.S. and Canada. The short ones were used for encryption when (at least) one of the participants was outside the U.S. and Canada. As export controls changed, successively larger keys were permitted, but the need for backward compatibility forced negotiation among a large number of different sizes.

In R4, they introduced a particularly baroque mechanism for coping with export. At the time, the U.S. government was pushing Key Escrow (see §24.9 *Clipper*) as the solution that would allow people to be secure against anyone but them. But this idea was extremely unpopular. Lotus was faced with the difficult decision of continuing with 40 bit keys (which people had publicly broken and were not considered trustworthy) or developing a Key Escrow system (which everyone hated). They came up with a novel compromise. They used long secret keys both inside and outside the U.S., but when one of the parties of a communication was outside the U.S., they encrypted all but 40 bits of the key using a public key provided to them by the NSA, and included that encrypted blob in the message header. That way, customers outside the U.S. got 40 bits of protection from the NSA (the maximum allowed at the time) and good protection from everyone else (including the people who were demonstrating the weakness of 40 bit keys). They announced this compromise with great fanfare and press releases, but the feature went largely unnoticed. Ironically, years later the feature led to a scandal when a Swedish newspaper "discovered" (in the documentation) that the NSA had a secret back door in the product, and criticized Lotus for cooperating with Big Brother.

In R5, export controls were relaxed sufficiently that they could use the same encryption worldwide. But to this day, they have long and short RSA keys for interoperation with old versions.

In Lotus Notes electronic mail, as in PGP, PEM, and S/MIME, public keys are used for authentication and for encryption of per-session secret keys that are used for message encryption. To satisfy export criteria, if either participant is outside the U.S., a short secret per-message key is used. And it is encrypted with the short public key. But the signature on the message is computed using the sender's long public key, whether or not the participants are within the U.S. This means that the signature on the message is secure even against an adversary capable of breaking the shorter RSA keys and secret keys used for encrypting the message.

It isn't clear why the export control people insisted on requiring use of a short public key to encrypt a short secret key. If they can break short RSA keys, then they can extract the secret key, no matter how long, providing it is encrypted with a short RSA key. And if they can break short (40-bit) secret keys, they can decrypt any message encrypted with a short key even if that key is encrypted with a long RSA key.

24.5.3 Certificates for Hierarchical Names

The Lotus Notes public key infrastructure is fairly straightforward and resembles the model described in §15.3.8 *Bottom-Up with Name Constraints*. A user is given a certificate by the CA responsible for that portion of the naming hierarchy. (Actually, the user has two certificates, one for a long key and one for a short key, but we'll ignore that in our discussion.) There's a chain of certificates from the root of the organization down to the user, and every user and server stores that chain in its ID file. The user presents that chain when authenticating (see §24.5.5 *Lotus Notes Authentication*). In order to authenticate Alice, Bob needs the chain of certificates from a common ancestor of Alice and Bob down to Alice.

But there may not be a common ancestor. The name tree for Alice may be disjoint from the name tree for Bob. For instance, they might be in different companies, and there may be no common root level with a CA jointly managed by the two companies. In this case, the only way for Bob to authenticate Alice is through a cross certificate. Some ancestor of Bob has to have created a certificate for some ancestor of Alice.

Cross certificates are stored in the directory service. When Bob wants to authenticate Alice, he searches the directory service for a cross certificate from one of his ancestors to one of Alice's ancestors. If no such cross certificate exists, then Bob and Alice cannot authenticate. In any case in which Bob needs a cross certificate for Alice, Alice will likewise need to find a cross certificate for Bob in her directory service. If Alice is a human at a workstation when Lotus Notes discovers the need for a cross certificate, it will prompt with the name and public key of the organization and invite Alice to create a personal cross certificate to that organization. In practice, most users create the cross certificate without checking the public key or even understanding what the message means. The resultant security is still better than nothing, because the cross certificate can only be used to authenticate entities in the particular remote organization and Alice will be warned if she ever connects to a server from that organization that presents a different public key.

In other systems, like DASS, each CA in the naming hierarchy issues an up certificate for its parent CA, in addition to issuing down certificates for each of its child CAs. These certificates are stored in the corresponding directory. The DASS scheme is actually more convenient in the case where the key of a CA changes. With the DASS scheme, all that is necessary is for each child CA of the changed CA to reissue its up certificate, and the parent CA of the changed CA to issue a new down certificate. With the Lotus Notes scheme, if the key of a CA high up in the name space changes, a change has to be made to the ID file of each user. There is currently no automated method of doing this. On the other hand, the Lotus scheme has a lesser dependence on the directory service and can therefore be used when more network components are not functioning.

24.5.4 Certificates for Flat Names

In versions 1 and 2 of Lotus Notes, and maintained since for backward compatibility, they had a system of Flat Names (people's names were just their names, and could not be assumed unique between organizations and perhaps not even within organizations). We describe them here because they represent another interesting way to construct a PKI. With hierarchical names, it's fairly easy to choose a chain of certificates that authenticates Alice to Bob, assuming the CA hierarchy follows the naming hierarchy. Flat names, by definition, don't have any structure. With flat names we could assume (like PGP) that applications will somehow find an appropriate chain of certificates. The flat-name version of Lotus Notes does not use chains of certificates. Instead, Alice is responsible for obtaining certificates for herself from different CAs. If she has enough certificates from enough different CAs, then when she attempts to communicate with Bob, it is likely she'll have a certificate from a CA that Bob knows and trusts. Lotus certificates aren't X.509-encoded, but they contain basically the same information. In the flat name version, Alice starts out having one certificate, created by the administrator that created her account and ID file, and then she obtains other certificates as needed. In a small organization, there might only be a single CA.

The non-hierarchical version of Lotus Notes assumes there may be numerous CAs, and each has been configured to know some of the other CAs' public keys. If Alice has a certificate from CA_1, she can obtain a certificate from CA_2 if CA_2 has been configured with a public key for CA_1 and if Bob, the human who is managing CA_2, decides he wants to give Alice a certificate. The semi-automated method for Alice to get a certificate is to send a signed message to Bob asking him to give her a certificate. The signed message contains all of Alice's certificates. The mail program verifies Alice's signature and informs Bob of the list of CAs that have vouched for Alice's public key. Bob makes a policy decision based on Alice's name and the CA names. In particular, he must make sure that he has not already created a certificate for a different person whose name also happens to be Alice, and that no one is likely to confuse this Alice with some other one. If he thinks Alice's name is reasonable, and he trusts at least one of the CAs from which Alice has a certificate, he creates and mails back a certificate with Alice's name and public key signed by CA_2.

In this way Alice collects a bunch of certificates from some set of CAs. Lotus allows Alice to specify, for the CA corresponding to each of her certificates, whether Alice trusts that CA or not. If Alice marks a CA as being untrustworthy, then she will not necessarily believe a certificate signed by that CA. But even if she personally has nothing but contempt for some CA, say CA_d, she might need a certificate from CA_d in order to communicate with someone who does respect CA_d.

When two things, say Alice and Bob, authenticate, they each send the other a list of CAs they'll trust, and then each of them (hopefully) finds a certificate the other will believe and sends it to the other. For example, say Alice has certificates from CA_1, CA_2, and CA_3, and marks CA_2 and CA_3 as trusted. Suppose Bob has certificates from CA_1, CA_2, and CA_4, and marks CA_1 and CA_4 as trusted. Early in the authentication handshake, Alice sends the list of CAs she trusts, namely $\{CA_2, CA_3\}$ to Bob, and Bob sends $\{CA_1, CA_4\}$ to Alice. Alice has a certificate Bob will believe, namely the one signed by CA_1, so she sends that one to Bob. Bob also happens to have a certificate Alice will believe, the one from CA_2, and he sends that certificate to Alice.

It might have been nice to allow Alice to maintain a list of CAs she trusts rather than having the trust information be a flag on certificates, since then Alice could accept certificates from a CA that hasn't granted Alice a certificate.

24.5.5 Lotus Notes Authentication

The authentication handshake in Lotus Notes is similar to DASS, in that it allows caching of state from one connection to another. If both parties have cached the state, they can eliminate the step where they exchange and verify certificates.

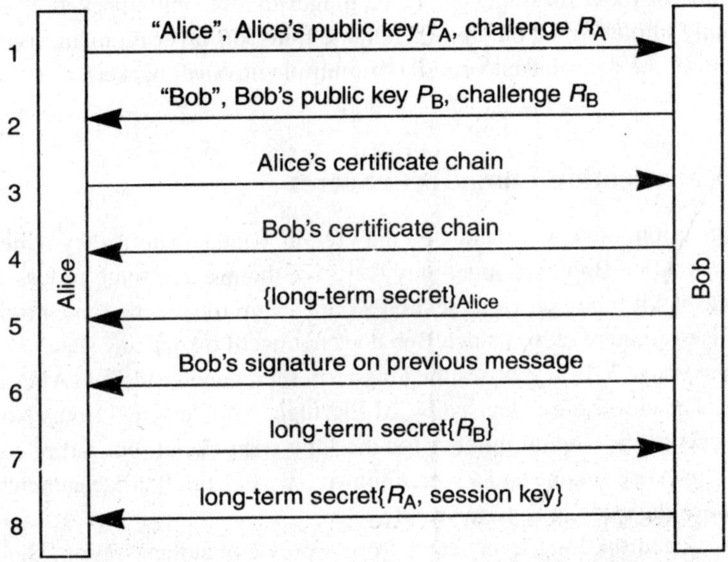

In the first two messages, Alice and Bob tell each other their public keys and give each other a challenge. In the next two messages, Alice and Bob send each other their certificate chains, starting from their organizational root (or, in the flat name case, there are an extra two messages where Alice and Bob exchange the names of CAs they trust). In messages 5 and 6, Bob sends Alice their long-term shared secret, encrypted with Alice's public key (to foil eavesdroppers) and signed with Bob's private key, to prove it's Bob sending the message (Alice takes Bob's word for it on their shared secret key).

There's a clever performance reason why messages 5 and 6 are sent as two messages rather than having Bob send the signed encrypted long-term secret as one quantity. The reason is to allow the computation-intensive private key operations, the one where Alice decrypts the long-term secret and the one in which Bob signs the encrypted long-term secret, to proceed in parallel. Remember that RSA public key operations can be made faster than private key operations by using a small public exponent (§6.3.4.3 *Having a Small Constant e*).

In message 7, Alice proves her identity. She needed to know her private key in order to extract the long-term secret, which she then uses to encrypt Bob's challenge.

In message 8, Bob proves his identity and securely sends Alice a session key they will share for this one conversation.

The reason Alice and Bob send the unsigned public keys in the beginning is for performance reasons. If the parties have, on a previous connection, exchanged and verified each other's certificates, then the step of exchanging and verifying the certificates can be skipped. In the case where they've maintained state, messages 3 through 6 are skipped.

Note that some of these messages might be longer than a single packet. The authentication handshake is actually implemented on top of a reliable transport layer protocol, so it is possible for any of the messages in the handshake to consist of multiple physical packets.

24.5.6 The Authentication Long-Term Secret

In a DASS authentication, both Alice and Bob may retain a cache, and if they remember information from a previous Alice-Bob exchange, they can save themselves some processing. The Lotus scheme as we described it in the previous section would seem to have the same property. However, the Lotus scheme is even more clever, since Bob does not need to keep any state!

Note that in message 5, Bob chooses the long-term secret and sends it to Alice encrypted with Alice's public key. The clever idea (devised by Al Eldridge, who designed Lotus Notes security) is that Bob does not choose a random number for the long-term secret, but rather computes it as a cryptographic hash of Alice's name and a secret known only to Bob. If Alice authenticates a second time, Bob will choose the same long-term secret.

If Alice has cached the long-term secret from a previous authentication, she can skip messages 3 through 6 and send message 7, which is Bob's challenge (from message 2) encrypted with the cached long-term secret. Bob computes the long-term secret based only on Alice's name and his own secret.

Why is this secure? Bob doesn't know what CA, if any, is vouching for Alice. But Bob does know that on some previous exchange he was impressed enough with Alice's certificates that he was willing to tell her a long-term secret.

Bob is allowed to change his own hashing secret and in fact does so periodically for security reasons. If Bob has changed his hashing secret since Alice's previous authentication, then Alice will have the wrong long-term secret. In that case her authentication will fail and she will revert to the unabridged authentication handshake, and this time (assuming Bob still likes her certificates) she'll get the new long-term secret.

Bob only changes his secret about once a month, which means that a server only needs to do one private key operation per user per month to support authentication. This gives it a substantial performance advantage over SSL, which does RSA operations much more frequently. A minor industry has grown up around building RSA accelerators to support SSL servers, but none is necessary with the Lotus Notes design.

24.5.7 Mail

The authentication handshake described in the previous section requires Alice and Bob to be actively communicating with each other. With electronic mail, however, Alice will compose a message to be transmitted to Bob, and Bob will eventually receive the message. He might be completely disconnected from the network at the time Alice composes and transmits the message, so Alice has to be able to accomplish message signing and message encryption without shaking hands with Bob.

Lotus Notes mail allows you to encrypt, sign, both encrypt and sign, or do no cryptographic protection of a message. Alice includes her certificates in any message she signs.

24.5.8 Certification Revocation

Since Alice sends Bob her certificates as part of authentication, certificate revocation is awkward in Lotus Notes security. There is no such thing as a certificate revocation list. Instead, a user's certificate is revoked by removing it from the directory service. The theory is, if Bob is paranoid he can check the directory service to ensure Alice's certificate is there when Alice logs in, or he can remember when he last looked up Alice's certificate so that he doesn't need to do it if he's done it recently. If Bob is not paranoid, he does not need to check the directory service, increasing availability and performance at the expense of security. For Lotus servers, this is a configuration option.

24.6 DCE SECURITY

I declare this thing open—whatever it is. —Prince Philip

DCE stands for *Distributed Computing Environment*. It is an OSF (Open Software Foundation) product. OSF is a multivendor consortium. DCE security has been incorporated into a number of products from a variety of vendors. DCE security is conceptually similar to Kerberos, and indeed uses Kerberos V5 as one of its components. DCE has a modular design. Kerberos V5 is used for authentication although alternative mechanisms can in principle be substituted. Authentication, authorization, and encryption mechanisms are architecturally separate.

Recall that Kerberos uses KDCs and Ticket Granting Servers, and in the Kerberos chapters we called both things the KDC, since they have to share the same database and same keys and therefore really are the same thing. DCE adds **Privilege Servers** and **Registration Servers**. In practice a Privilege Server and a Registration Server come packaged with a KDC. Privilege Servers and Registration Servers are on-line trusted entities, like KDCs. The purpose of a Privilege Server is to get the principal's UUID (universal unique ID), and the groups (see §15.8.3 *Groups*) to which that principal belongs, to be included in a Kerberos ticket in a secure way. The purpose of a Registration Server is to provide a combined database for a KDC and corresponding Privilege Server.

The KDC uses a master key for each principal, along with other stuff that's less interesting. The Privilege Server uses, for each principal, a UUID and the set of groups to which that principal belongs.

ACLs (access control lists) exist outside the context of DCE and in many of the operating systems that support DCE. ACLs could list principals by name, but names are long and subject to change. So in most implementations, ACLs list UIDs (user IDs) and GIDs (group IDs) instead. In Kerberos the principal's name is in a ticket, and Kerberos gives no help in translating from name to UID or in looking up the set of GIDs associated with a principal. Furthermore, Kerberos does not standardize UIDs and GIDs. Different platforms have different forms of UID and GID. For example, most UNIX systems have 32-bit UIDs and GIDs. Some really old UNIX systems have 16-bit UIDs and GIDs. Kerberos assumes systems will translate names to UIDs in some platform-specific way.

DCE standardizes group and user UUIDs at 128 bits long and standardizes DCE ACLs containing those UUIDs. Additionally, DCE does the translation from name to UUID, which is convenient for the applications but makes it difficult for them to use the native ACL format with DCE. The DCE designers, knowing that a UID field of 32 bits was really insufficient, hoped that they'd inspire the operating systems to migrate to their standard of 128 bits. In the meantime most DCE implementations use 32-bit UIDs and GIDs padded out with a constant to look like 128-bit UUIDs.

A UUID in an ACL can belong to either a principal or a group. A user Alice will in general not need to know her own UUID, but usually is capable of remembering her own name, so the login exchange is based on her name.

A user should be authorized to access something if the user's UUID is in the ACL or if a group to which the user belongs is listed in the ACL. DCE wanted an efficient method of knowing to which groups a user belongs, and this was done by including group information in the ticket.

It is interesting how the DCE designers managed to get this information to be included in Kerberos tickets without modifying Kerberos. It would have been a small change to Kerberos to have the KDC maintain UUID and group membership with each principal, and put that information into the ticket. But instead, they designed elaborate mechanisms so they could work with an architecturally pure Kerberos. They still can't use unmodified KDCs, however, because they access the KDC using DCE RPC instead of UDP datagrams, and because management depends on being able to modify data through the Registration Server.

Kerberos V5 has a field known as AUTHORIZATION DATA. Kerberos does not interpret the contents of this field. Rather it allows a user (say Alice), when requesting a TGT, to specify a value for that field. Kerberos just copies the requested value into the AUTHORIZATION DATA field of the TGT, and then copies that field into the AUTHORIZATION DATA field of any tickets issued based on that TGT. Alice's workstation requests TGTs and tickets on Alice's behalf, but does not maintain the database of Alice's UUID or group memberships. Even if it has that information, it can't be trusted to supply it. So Alice's Privilege Server supplies that information. The Privilege Server reads the database of user name/UUID/group membership from the Registration Server.

With DCE, Alice logs in just like in Kerberos (see Figure 24-6). Alice's workstation gets an ordinary Kerberos TGT with Alice's name inside. The workstation then requests a ticket to the Privilege Server, which to the KDC is just another principal in the realm. The workstation then contacts the Privilege Server. The Privilege Server extracts Alice's name from the ticket, looks up Alice's UUID and group membership, and requests a TGT from the KDC with the Privilege Server's name in the CLIENT NAME field, and Alice's UUID and group membership in the AUTHORIZATION DATA. This TGT is referred to in DCE as a **PTGT**, for **Privilege Ticket Granting Ticket**. The Privilege Server then, in an encrypted message, gives Alice's workstation the PTGT and the corresponding session key (the one encrypted inside the PTGT). Alice's workstation uses the PTGT and corresponding key instead of the original TGT. Note that the above description is architectural—since the Privilege Server and KDC are packaged together, the messages between them might not actually occur.

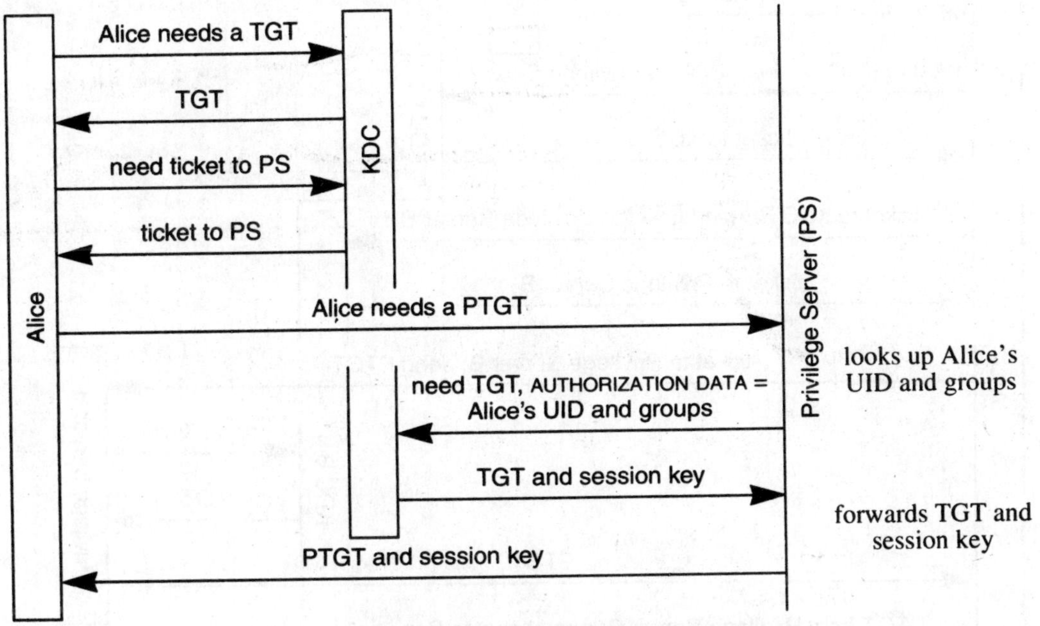

Figure 24-6. Obtaining a PTGT in DCE

Now let's say that Alice asks to talk to server Bob. The workstation sends the PTGT to the KDC, along with the request for a ticket to Bob. The KDC will return to Alice a ticket to Bob with the AUTHORIZATION DATA field copied from the PTGT (so that it will contain Alice's UUID and group membership), and with the CLIENT NAME field equal to the Privilege Server's name. The ticket does not contain Alice's name, but it is not needed, since ACLs list Alice's UUID or use group UUIDs.

A DCE application, Bob, refuses to honor Kerberos tickets unless the Privilege Server's name is in the CLIENT NAME field. Once Bob checks to make sure the Privilege Server's name is in the ticket, Bob uses the AUTHORIZATION DATA field to discover Alice's UUID and group membership. Since the only way for Alice's workstation to obtain such a ticket (and corresponding session key) is through following the proper procedure, Bob can be assured that the UUID and group information in the ticket is correct. Bob checks this against the ACL of the resource Alice is asking to use.

Multirealm DCE is similar to multirealm Kerberos. Suppose Alice is in realm A and Bob (the resource Alice would like to access) is in realm B. Furthermore, assume B is not a principal in A, so that it is necessary to go through transit realm C. (See Figure 24-7.)

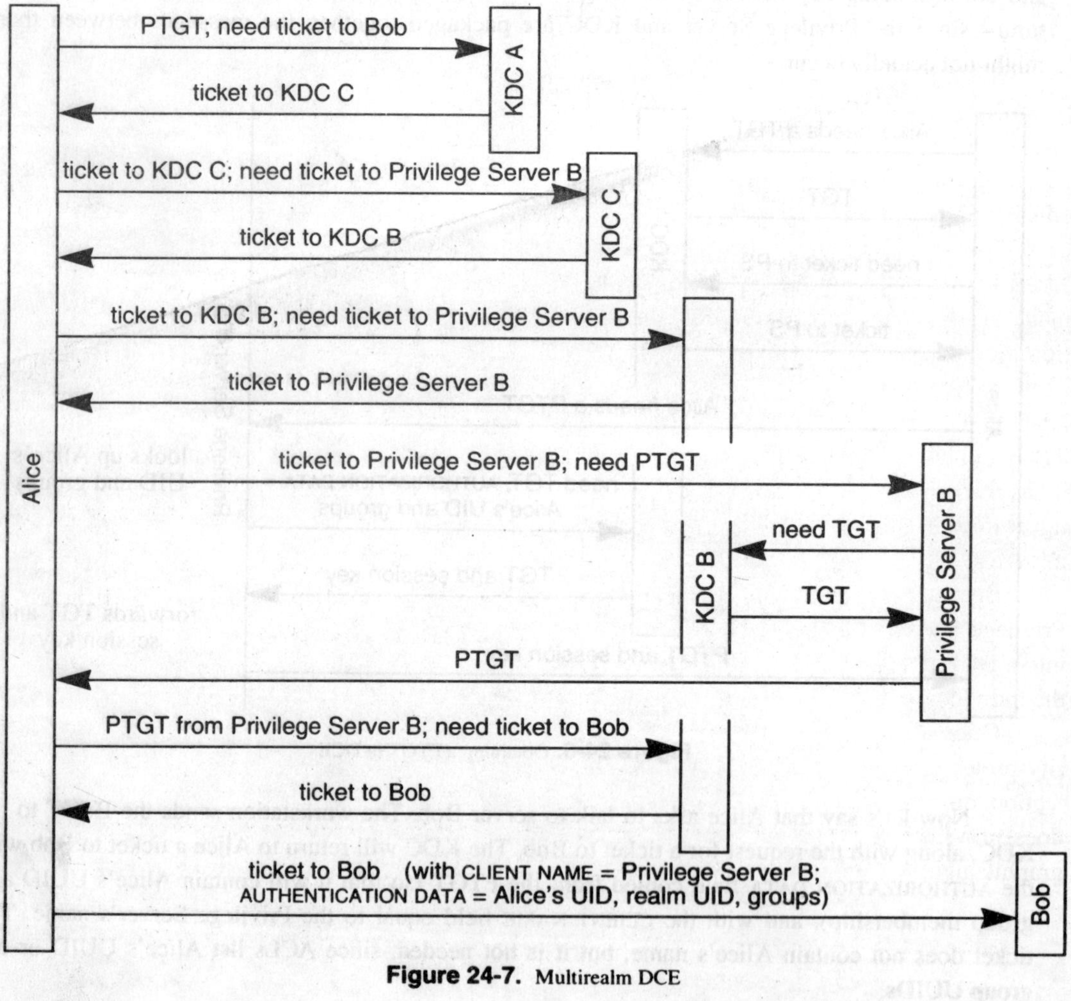

Figure 24-7. Multirealm DCE

Alice (her workstation) uses her PTGT to request from her KDC a ticket to Bob. Her KDC knows that Bob is not local, so instead gives her a ticket to the KDC in realm C. The AUTHORIZATION DATA and CLIENT NAME will get copied from the PTGT into the ticket to C, so the ticket to the KDC in realm C will still contain A's Privilege Server as CLIENT NAME, and Alice's UUID and groups in AUTHORIZATION DATA. Alice uses the ticket to the KDC in C to ask for a ticket to the Privilege Server in Bob's realm (B). C's KDC will return a ticket to the KDC in B. CLIENT NAME will still be A's Privilege Server. AUTHORIZATION DATA will still be Alice's UUID and groups. The TRANSITED field will contain C. Alice then uses the ticket to B's KDC to ask the KDC for a ticket to B's Privilege Server. The reason she needs to do this is to get a ticket with B's Privilege Server's name in the CLIENT NAME field, since Bob will not honor a ticket unless the CLIENT NAME is the name of the Privilege Server in Bob's realm. Alice then contacts B's Privilege Server.

B's Privilege Server checks the ticket for legality. Since the ticket is coming from outside the realm, B's Privilege Server will reject it if the CLIENT NAME is not the standard text string that denotes Privilege Server. B's Privilege Server also checks the TRANSITED field for acceptability. The recommended policy for an acceptable transit path is traversal of the tree implied by the hierarchical names, going up to the least common ancestor and then down, though with a single cross-link allowed on the path. With DCE security it is only Privilege Servers that check the TRANSITED field. In fact, once a Privilege Server returns a PTGT, the transit information is gone. DCE made the decision that it was more practical for the Privilege Server to check the transit information. Kerberos, remember, leaves it up to each application.

Assuming B's Privilege Server accepts the transit information, it requests a ticket from B's KDC that contains Privilege Server B as CLIENT NAME, and Alice's UUID, group information, and realm UUID as AUTHORIZATION DATA. That's a PTGT just like the original PTGT, except now it has B's Privilege Server's name instead of A's. Alice uses that PTGT to request, from B's KDC, a ticket to Bob. Finally she gets a ticket to Bob, with CLIENT NAME Privilege Server B and AUTHORIZATION DATA equal to her UUID, group membership, and realm UUID.

Because of the way that DCE did groups, a user can only be in groups maintained by the Privilege Server of the user's realm. It is possible to put groups and individuals from other realms into a DCE ACL, since each ACL entry effectively consists of a pair of UUIDs: the UUID of either the individual or the group, and the UUID of the realm in which the group or individual resides.

Once Alice and Bob have mutually authenticated, DCE does not use the Kerberos integrity-protected or encrypted data exchanges. Instead, DCE has its own mechanisms for integrity protection, or integrity plus privacy protection within its RPC protocol, using the session key Kerberos does provide. As with Kerberos, the protocols are designed to allow multiple different cryptographic algorithms, but today DCE uses MD5 and DES.

24.7 MICROSOFT WINDOWS SECURITY

24.7.1 LAN Manager and NTLM

LAN Manager comes equipped with a simple, straightforward cryptographic authentication protocol between client and server based on shared secrets. Each server that a user is entitled to access is configured with security information about that user, including a hash of the user's password. When a user Alice wishes to access a server, she types her name and password at her workstation, which contacts the server, sending Alice's name. The server sends a challenge, which the workstation encrypts using the hash of the user's password. Some applications (like RPC) continue cryptographic protection beyond the initial handshake using the user's hashed password to establish a session key.

This protocol is very similar to NetWare V3. In both protocols, the fact that the server stores a hash of the user's password rather than the actual password does not theoretically make the scheme more secure. A modified version of the client software could impersonate the user if it directly used the hash of the password rather than hashing the string the user types. But it would be a lot more convenient and practical for an intruder Trudy if she could capture the actual password rather than the hash of the password, since then Trudy could type the password at unmodified client code. One difference between the protocols is that the LAN Manager scheme does not use salt. That means that if the user uses the same password on multiple servers, and an intruder captures one server's database, the intruder can impersonate the user at other servers.

For NT, the scheme was extended in a way that was transparent to client machines. *Transparent* means that the new scheme works with the old client code and in fact a client machine cannot tell based on the protocol whether the server is using the old protocol or the new protocol. In the NT protocol, instead of keeping the security information at each server, security information is stored in a trusted on-line entity called a *domain controller*. The new scheme is called NTLM. It has the following advantages:

- Management is simplified, since user security information only needs to be configured into a single location, the domain controller.
- It is more user-friendly, since a user will have a single password that will work on all servers the user is entitled to use. In the old scheme, a user could certainly use the same password on all servers, but when the user Alice changed her password, she'd have to remember to change her password at all the servers.

The NT scheme works like the authentication facilitator node we discussed in §9.1.2 *Storing User Passwords*. The domain controller (which is what we called the authentication facilitator node), stores a secret for each server in the domain, which enables a server in the domain and the domain controller to communicate securely. The domain controller also stores security information for each human user in the domain, including a hash of the user's password, a list of groups to which the user belongs, when to prod the user to change her password, and the hours she's allowed to log in. When a user wishes to log into a server in the user's domain, that server sends a challenge to the user's workstation, which then generates a cryptographic response based on the user's password and the challenge (see Figure 24-8). Since the server does not store any security information for the user, it cannot evaluate the response. Instead, in an encrypted conversation to the domain controller, the server forwards its challenge and the workstation's response. The domain controller answers yes or no in the encrypted reply to the server. If the answer is yes, the domain controller also sends information about the user, such as to which groups the user belongs, and the user's hashed password. (This information, like all the sensitive information between the domain controller and the server, is encrypted.) The hashed password is transmitted so that the server can use it to compute a session key for protection of the remainder of the client-server conversation.

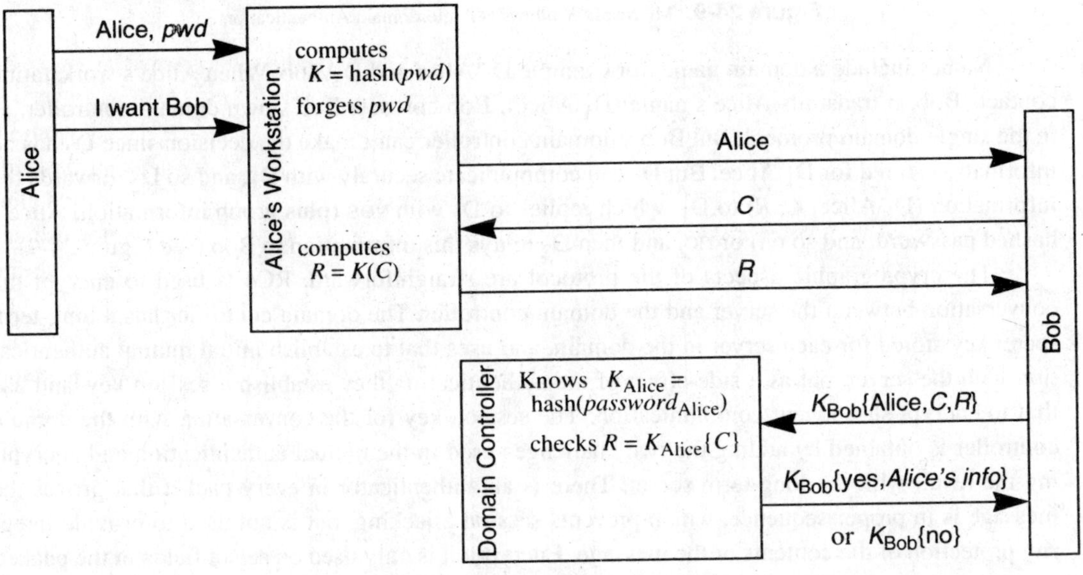

Figure 24-8. Microsoft Windows NT Authentication

It is possible for a client in one domain D_1 to be authenticated by a server in another domain D_2 provided that D_1 and D_2 have been preconfigured to trust each other. There is no transitivity, i.e., if Alice is in domain D_1 and Bob is in domain D_2, they can communicate if D_1 and D_2 have a trust relationship. It is not possible to transit through domain D_3 in the case where D_1 and D_3 trust each other and D_3 and D_2 trust each other but D_1 and D_2 do not trust each other. This is similar to Kerberos V4.

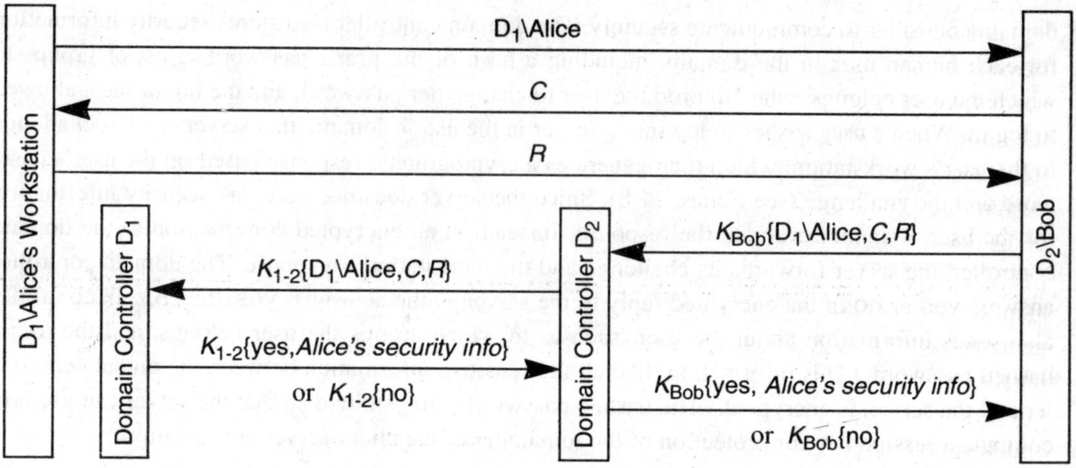

Figure 24-9. Microsoft Windows NT Interdomain Authentication

Names include a domain name, for example D_1\Alice and D_2\Bob. When Alice's workstation contacts Bob, it transmits Alice's name (D_1\Alice). Bob contacts Bob's own domain controller, as in the single domain protocol. But Bob's domain controller can't make the decision since D_2 has no information stored for D_1\Alice. But D_2 can communicate securely with D_1, and so D_2 forwards the information (D_1\Alice, C, R) to D_1, which replies to D_2 with yes (plus group information, Alice's hashed password, and so on) or no, and then D_2 relays this information to Bob (see Figure 24-9).

The cryptographic aspects of the protocol are straightforward. RC4 is used to encrypt the conversation between the server and the domain controller. The domain controller has a long-term secret key stored for each server in the domain, and uses that to establish initial mutual authentication with the server, but as a side-effect of the authentication they establish a session key, and use that to encrypt subsequent communication. The session key for the conversation with the domain controller is obtained by adding the two challenges used in the mutual authentication and encrypting the result with the long-term secret. There is an authenticator in every packet that proves the message is in proper sequence, which prevents session hijacking, but is not used to provide integrity protection of the contents of the message. Encryption is only used on select fields in the packet, i.e., only where necessary.

24.7.2 Windows 2000 Kerberos

With Windows 2000 came another step in the evolution of Windows authentication. User authentication information is moved from the Domain Controller to Active Directory, which serves as both KDC and directory service. The protocol is a modified version of Kerberos V5.

As with OSF DCE, the designers at Microsoft were faced with the challenge that while Kerberos is designed to provide authentication of the names of communicating principals, what the OS needs for users is not a name but rather a UID (user ID) and a list of GIDs (group IDs), since that is the information used to make access control decisions. Otherwise there would need to be a separate translation mechanism available to every server. The Microsoft design is similar to the OSF DCE design, but simpler and more controversial. Both use the AUTHORIZATION-DATA field in the Kerberos ticket to hold the additional information. But unlike OSF DCE, which stood on its head creating a virtual Privilege Server entity and had many additional round trips when logging in users, Win2K Kerberos simply had the KDC add the AUTHORIZATION-DATA field to the ticket when it was generated. Technically, this did not comply with the Kerberos specification (though there have been legalistic arguments over whether it does or does not) while the OSF DCE approach did. But only lawyers worry about compliance. Users and system administrators worry about interoperability, and both OSF DCE and Windows 2000 Kerberos offer only backward compatibility with "standard" Kerberos applications. They offer none with one another nor can their services authenticate users not registered with their own registries.

Another source of controversy is that the syntax of the authorization extensions is an "open secret". At the time of this writing, the design was posted at http://www.microsoft.com/technet/security/kerberos/ and was downloadable by anyone, but required readers to acknowledge that the information is a trade secret of Microsoft, that they may only read it for purposes of reviewing its security, and that they may not discuss it with anyone who had not agreed to the same terms. Whether a company can retain trade secret rights to published information is an interesting legal question. In the court of public opinion, most observers are unwilling to call such a design "open".

Another practical problem in Kerberos in the multi-realm case is that Kerberos doesn't specify how clients should find a sequence of realms that will allow them to authenticate to a remote server and doesn't specify how servers should decide whether a given sequence of realms is acceptable. This complex set of configuration issues is left to client and server implementations. In most cases, it would be more practical to configure this information in the KDCs. In the Windows 2000 Kerberos protocol, a client does not need to figure out the path to a remote service. It requests a service ticket from its local KDC, which instead returns a TGT to the next KDC in the chain. The client then repeats this process until it reaches the service's KDC, which gives it a service ticket. The KDCs should (and may) also check incoming requests to assure that the client has come through an acceptable sequence of KDCs on its way to the server and refuse to issue the next ticket if not. In this case, neither the client nor the server would need any knowledge of trust relationships. If authentication succeeds, it implies that the intermediate KDCs did all of the appropriate checks and it was OK. This extension has been proposed for standardization in the next revision of Kerberos.

24.8 NETWORK DENIAL OF SERVICE

The scheme in this section has not been commercially deployed, but it is being built on an experimental basis. It was devised by Radia Perlman and written up in [PERL88].

Routing in today's networks depends on the cooperation of all the routers. If a router were to generate confusing routing messages, or simply flood the network with enough garbage data to saturate the links, it can make a network inoperative. To some extent a network can be designed so that pieces are reasonably independent. For instance in a hierarchical network, although a rogue router in one piece can disable that piece of the network, if routing is properly designed the disruption will remain in that one section of the network. Some routing protocols are being enhanced with authentication information to ensure that only routing messages from authorized routers are accepted. However, such a network would still be disabled by a saboteur corrupting a legitimate router.

A fail-stop failure is one in which a computer is working perfectly one moment and then reverts instantaneously to halting. In real life, failures are not usually so civilized. Often a node starts acting erratically due to software failure, hardware failure, or misconfiguration. Without the help of saboteurs, many of today's networks have suffered collapse due to a sick node. It is only a matter of time before the vandals that have delighted in designing and deploying viruses expand their exploits into network sabotage.

But it is possible to design a network that will continue to function even when being attacked by saboteurs. Our scheme will guarantee that two nodes will be able to converse provided that some path of properly functioning routers and links connects the two nodes. (If no such path exists, then there is no scheme that could possibly work.) So with this scheme, a network can operate properly even with several corrupted routes.

The first part of the scheme involves robust broadcast, in which each message generated by a router is delivered to all the other routers. The robust broadcast mechanism will be used to distribute public key information for all the routers, so that routers need to start out knowing only a single public key. It will also be used to distribute routing information. The second part of the robust network design involves robust data packet delivery, in which a message generated by a node is delivered only to the specified destination.

24.8.1 Robust Broadcast

Flooding is a simple routing mechanism in which a router that receives a message forwards the message on each link except the one from which the message was received. Flooding has the basic property we want—a message is guaranteed to get delivered as long as at least one properly functioning path exists—but with one serious problem. Flooding will only work if we assume that the routers have infinite storage for buffered messages and the links have infinite bandwidth. Few networks have such characteristics, so simple flooding will not solve our problem.

The basic idea behind robust broadcast is that each router guarantees a fraction of its memory and bandwidth resources to each other router. Each router keeps a database of messages to be forwarded and reserves a portion of the database, say one buffer, for each other router. The messages are transmitted over each link, round robin, so each router's message will have a chance to be delivered over each link.

How do we ensure that the buffer reserved for a given router will be holding a message generated by that router? We do that with public key signatures. Each router signs each message it generates, and only a message with a valid signature can occupy a buffer.

How do we ensure that it is the most recently generated message from a router that occupies the buffer? We do that by using a sequence number. Let's say router R_1 receives a message with source R_2, a valid signature, and a higher sequence number than the message stored for R_2. Then R_1 overwrites the message it had for R_2.

How does R_1 know R_2's public key, so that R_1 can verify R_2's signature? We could use a standard off-line CA. Each router would know the public key of the CA. Each router could include its certificate in each message. But that would make revocation difficult. Another possibility is to have the CA on-line, and have the CA generate and broadcast a list of nodes and public keys whenever the list changes.

What happens if node R_2 is malfunctioning and generates a message with the highest possible sequence number (assuming the sequence number is a finite-sized field)? In that case, R_2 cannot generate any more messages until it gets a new public key and registers that new public key with the CA. At that point, R_2 can start over again with sequence number 1.

For efficiency, it would be nice to stop transmitting a particular message over a particular link once the neighbor on that link has received the message. This is done by marking each message in the database with an indication, for each neighbor, specifying whether that message needs to be transmitted to that neighbor or whether an acknowledgment for that message needs to be transmitted to that neighbor. When a message (with valid signature and new sequence number) with source R_2 is received by R_1 from neighbor N, R_1 stores the message in the database, marking it as needing to be acknowledged to N, and needing to be transmitted to all the other neighbors. If a duplicate message is received from neighbor N, then that message is marked as needing to be acknowledged to N (and not needing to be transmitted to N). If an acknowledgment for a message is received from neighbor N, that message is marked as not needing to be transmitted or acknowledged to N. When the link to N is available, the next marked message is transmitted, while the database is traversed in round-robin order. If the message is marked as needing to be transmitted, then the message is transmitted. If the message is marked as needing to be acknowledged, then an acknowledgment for that message is transmitted to N.

The following table shows a database with messages from four different sources: R_1, R_2, R_3, and R_4. The node keeping this database has four neighbors: N_1, N_2, N_3, and N_4. Each message is

message source	N_1	N_2	N_3	N_4
R_1	transmit	ack	ack	OK
R_2	OK	OK	OK	OK
R_3	transmit	transmit	transmit	ack
R_4	ack	ack	OK	OK

marked, for each neighbor, with transmit if the message needs to be transmitted to that neighbor, ack if an acknowledgment needs to be sent, or OK if neither needs to be sent. The database is scanned round robin per link, and messages are transmitted as marked.

24.8.2 Robust Packet Delivery

Now we know how to robustly broadcast messages. We could use broadcast for delivery of data messages, but it would be inefficient. Instead we will use the robust broadcast mechanism to reliably deliver routing information, and use the routing information to compute routes. Once a route is computed, it is set up with a special cryptographically protected route setup packet, but then data packets can be forwarded without any cryptographic overhead.

The type of routing protocol we will use is known as a **link state protocol**. In a link state protocol, each router is responsible for figuring out who its neighbors are and generating a packet known as a **link state packet (LSP)**, which gives the identity of the source router and the list of neighbors of that router. Each LSP is broadcast to all the other routers, and each router is responsible for maintaining a database of the most recently generated LSP from each other router. Given this database, it is possible to efficiently compute routes. For details on routing protocols, see [PERL99].

Now assume that source S computes a path to destination D. Assume S is lucky enough to compute a properly functioning path (all the routers and links along the path are working properly). S transmits a special route setup packet, cryptographically signed and with a sequence number, that causes all the routers along the path to remember, for source/destination pair S/D, from which link they should expect to receive packets and to which link they should forward packets. The route setup packet has a sequence number, and a router R is only required to remember the highest numbered route from S to D. With that rule, we bound the maximum number of routes a router will need to maintain to n^2, where n is the number of nodes. In practice, it would probably suffice to have a router remember some much smaller number of routes; if a router were asked to remember a route when it had run out of resources, it could complain and force the source to generate a route which did not include that router.

In conventional route setup, a router only needs to remember the outbound link for a particular source/destination pair. We are requiring the router to also remember the link from which it should expect to receive packets for that source/destination pair. If a router checks to make sure that a packet was received from the proper link, then as long as the source was lucky enough to choose a properly functioning path, there is nothing a node off the path can do to disrupt communication on that path. And data packets do not need to be cryptographically protected.

If S is not lucky enough to choose a correct path, it has a complete map of the network, and can therefore choose an alternate path. There isn't any completely satisfactory way of doing this, since there are an exponential number of possible paths between any pair of nodes. But in practice, since there are unlikely to be more than one or two corrupted routers, a source can start getting suspicious of routers that appear on paths that don't work, and avoid them. And in the worst case, if a source were to try a lot of paths, it could revert to broadcasting the packet, which would guarantee delivery provided any path exists.

We were vague about the difference between a *node* and a *router*. It is possible to only have the routers participate in the cryptographic protection, and have each router generate and sign route setup packets on behalf of the endnodes serviced by that router.

24.9 CLIPPER

Telephones are easy to tap, and cellular telephones make eavesdropping even easier. Because of this, people have developed encrypting telephones, which so far have been too expensive to catch on, but today it is technically feasible to make encrypting telephones inexpensively. This makes the government nervous because criminals are sometimes convicted using evidence gathered through wiretaps. To fill the need for encryption without the U.S. government giving up the ability to wiretap (with legitimate reason and through a court order), the U.S. government has proposed the Clipper chip. The Clipper proposal offers high-grade encryption while preserving the ability of the U.S. government to wiretap.

The politics of Clipper are at least as exciting as the technical aspects. We discuss the politics in §1.10 *Key Escrow for Law Enforcement*. Here we concentrate on the technical aspects.

Technically the concept of Clipper is reasonably simple. Each Clipper chip manufactured contains a unique 80-bit key and a unique 32-bit ID. For each key K, an 80-bit random number K_1 is selected, and then $K_2=K\oplus K_1$ is computed. Neither quantity K_1 nor K_2 gives any information about K, but if you know both K_1 and K_2, you can compute K easily, since it is $K_1\oplus K_2$. K_1 (and the unique ID) is given to one federal agency, and K_2 (and the unique ID) is given to a different federal agency. It hasn't been decided which agencies they'll be, but they should be agencies that everyone trusts, like the IRS, and that are independent of one another without likelihood of collusion, like the Army and the Navy.

Let's say that Alice, using a telephone containing a Clipper chip, wants to talk to Bob, who has a similar device. Alice's chip has been registered with the two agencies (as has Bob's). Let's say Alice's chip has unique ID ID_A and secret key K_A. With a court order, the government can obtain the two components of Alice's chip's key and then reconstruct K_A. Without a court order, K_A remains secret.

What key will Alice and Bob use for communicating? It can't be K_A or K_B (Bob's chip's secret key) because neither side wants to reveal its secret key. So Alice and Bob use some mechanism, unspecified in the Clipper standard, to produce a shared secret key S. A reasonable choice is Diffie-Hellman (see §6.4 *Diffie-Hellman*), which was what was implemented in the Clipper phones. Alice feeds S to her Clipper chip and Bob feeds S to his Clipper chip. The chips use S to encrypt and decrypt the data. So where does K_A come in, and how would the government, knowing K_A, be able to decrypt the conversation? Also, how does the government know the unique ID of Alice's chip in order to obtain (with court order) K_A? It would be an administrative nightmare for the U.S. government to try to keep track of who owns each Clipper chip.

The information the government needs is in a field known as the **LEAF**, for **Law Enforcement Access Field**, that Alice's and Bob's Clipper chips transmit along with the encrypted data. Although Bob's chip does not utilize any of the information in the LEAF it receives from Alice's chip, Bob's chip refuses to communicate unless it receives a valid-looking LEAF. The central challenge in the design of Clipper is preventing someone from building a device that uses a Clipper chip for secure communication but substitutes garbage for the LEAF before transmitting the data.

The Clipper design is very clever. The LEAF that Alice transmits to Bob contains ID_A, $K_A\{S\}$, and a checksum C. The field ID_A enables the government to retrieve K_A and then decrypt the field $K_A\{S\}$ to obtain S. Since the same key S is used in both directions, the government only needs one of the keys K_A or K_B in order to decrypt the entire conversation.

How does Bob's chip know whether the LEAF is valid? Bob's chip can't know whether ID_A is the correct value and it can't decrypt $K_A\{S\}$ to check if it's the correct encrypted key. Bob's chip makes its decision based on the value of the field C. C is basically some sort of message digest of the other fields in the LEAF (ID_A and $K_A\{S\}$) and the key S. Bob's chip computes the message digest of the values in the received LEAF for ID_A and $K_A\{S\}$, along with S (which Bob's chip knows). If the computed checksum matches the received C, then the entire LEAF is assumed to be valid.

The message digest algorithm used to compute C need not be secret, so what's to prevent someone from foiling the government's ability to wiretap by modifying the quantity $K_A\{S\}$ (or ID_A) and sending the matching C? To prevent modification of the LEAF, all Clipper chips share an 80-bit secret **family key**, F. The quantity $ID_A|K_A\{S\}|C$ is encrypted with F. Since Bob's chip knows F, it can decrypt the LEAF to extract ID_A, $K_A\{S\}$, and C. It can't verify that either ID_A or $K_A\{S\}$ is correct, but knowing S, it can compute C. If the C in the LEAF doesn't match the computed C, the chip will refuse to decrypt the conversation.

With the LEAF thus guaranteed, the government can (with a valid court order) tap Alice's line, read ID_A from the LEAF, and then retrieve K_A. Then it can read $K_A\{S\}$ from the LEAF and decrypt it to obtain S. At this point, it can decrypt the recorded conversation.

It is rather astonishing that all Clipper chips will know the value *F*, and yet the expectation is that the value will remain secret. Clipper chips are carefully manufactured so that it should not be possible, by taking one apart, to obtain *F*. The encryption algorithm (**SKIPJACK**) was originally intended to be kept secret, and the same technology that prevents someone from reverse-engineering the encryption algorithm would protect *F*. But eventually the government decided to declassify SKIPJACK.

How much of a disaster would it be if someone discovered *F*? It would not make Clipper-protected conversations less secure. However, it would mean someone could build a device that interoperated with Clipper devices and foiled wiretapping by generating garbage for $ID_A|K_A\{S\}$, computing the proper value for *C* based on the garbage and the session key *S*, and encrypting it all with *F*.

It has been pointed out that people could, with less effort, build a device that encrypted the data before transmitting it to the Clipper chip. Provided the receiver had a compatible device (Clipper plus the extra encryption device), the output stream would look like normal Clipper output, until someone, under court order, decrypted the conversation and realized they were obtaining ciphertext.

If you had a device capable of encrypting conversations, why would you bother going through the extra step of sending the encrypted stream through a Clipper chip? Perhaps you don't have complete faith in your cryptographic algorithm. Another reason surfaces if it becomes illegal or suspicious to use non-Clipper encryption. If you send your encrypted stream through a Clipper chip, the government would not know that you were using your own encryption, until after it obtained the court order and decrypted your conversation. One wonders what penalties could be associated with using non-Clipper encryption that would deter the sorts of people who are worried about being wiretapped.

Prosecutor: *Did you murder your wife?*
Defendant: *No.*
Prosecutor: *Do you know the penalty for perjury?*
Defendant: *No, but I bet it's less than the penalty for murder!*

—classic joke

If someone discovered *F* and built a Clipper-compatible device, then Alice, with that device, could foil wiretapping while talking to Bob, who had an ordinary Clipper device. If the government had Alice under suspicion, and therefore had obtained her Clipper key, it would still need to get a court order for Bob's Clipper key before it could decrypt the Alice-Bob conversation. If both Alice and Bob had one of these Clipper-compatible devices, then the government would discover, only after court order, that Alice and Bob were not using real Clipper devices, just as it would discover if Alice and Bob were using an extra encryption step before the Clipper chip.

Matt Blaze [BLAZ94] discovered an interesting property of the Clipper design that makes it possible for Alice, with a lot of effort, to forge a LEAF in a way that Bob will accept, but will prevent government wiretaps. The problem is that the quantity C is only 16 bits long. Remember that Bob's chip cannot verify that either of the quantities ID_A or $K_A\{S\}$ is correct. All the chip can do is verify that C is based on those quantities and the proper key S.

The LEAF is 128 bits long, consisting of 32 bits of ID, 80 bits of encrypted key, and 16 bits of checksum. Bob's chip will accept any sequence of bits for the ID and the encrypted key as long as those fields, plus the Alice-Bob session key, produce the correct 16-bit checksum. The implication of this is that if Alice were to send a 128-bit random number, it would have 1 chance in 2^{16} of having the correct checksum, when decrypted with the family key F.

Now we get to Matt Blaze's attack. Alice can use any Clipper chip as a tester. She tells it she wants to converse using the key she's agreed upon with Bob. Then she feeds it random 128-bit LEAF values. On average she'll only have to try 2^{15} random numbers before one will wind up with the correct checksum.

Now that she knows a LEAF value that will be accepted by Bob's chip for the key she's sharing with Bob, she needs a special piece of hardware that takes the output stream from her Clipper device, removes the LEAF values it transmits, and substitutes the one she found. Bob's device won't know there's a problem, and the problem will only be detected when the government attempts to wiretap.

Matt Blaze's attack is not important in practice, since it would either take a lot of parallel hardware or cause an unacceptable delay in conversation startup, but the discovery was useful in embarrassing the designers for having missed such an "obvious" flaw.

24.9.1 Key Escrow

The Clipper chip has become synonymous with key escrow in the public debate, and has given key escrow a bad name. But there are good reasons other than keeping Big Brother employed for wanting to back up keys.

It's certainly important to keep secret the key with which you encrypt your data. It's possible to be really careful about that. It could be that the only copy of your key is on your smart card, and the smart card is carefully engineered so that it is impossible to obtain the key from the smart card. Then one day your three-year-old finds it and flushes it down the toilet. Is it OK with you to accept that all your work is irretrievably gone? Maybe not.

A similar problem occurs with house keys. When you arrive home during a blizzard, and discover you've lost your key, you really don't want to sit outside until some other member of your family gets home. Typically you've hidden a key under the WELCOME mat (which is equivalent to having a key hung from a chain from the doorknob), or you've given a copy of the key to a neighbor, who hopefully won't break in but will be home when you need the key.

What can you do with your cryptographic key to ensure you can retrieve the key if you forget or lose the key? You could write it on a piece of paper and stick it in an obscure drawer at home, or you could lock it in your safe deposit box.

There are various mechanized approaches that don't involve obsolete technology like paper and safe deposit boxes. One possibility is to store your key on some sort of server. If you're paranoid someone will break into that server you could break your key into pieces, like the Clipper proposal does, where all the pieces need to be ⊕'d in order to recover the key. Then you could store each piece on an independent server.

Contacting all the servers to give them their pieces of your key might be some trouble. An elegant solution is to take each piece, encrypt it with the public key of the server to which you'd like to give that piece, and store it on your own machine. Then if you lose the key you can give the corresponding quantities to the corresponding servers and recover it.

24.10 HOMEWORK

1. In §24.4.5 *DASS Delegation* we describe how Alice manages to simultaneously establish a session key with Bob, pass along her login private key to Bob, and authenticate to Bob. Analyze the protocol as described. Why can't an eavesdropper discover Alice's login private key? Why can Bob discover Alice's login private key? How can Bob be sure that the authenticator came from Alice? In the non-delegation case, he knows that only Alice knows the session key (that encrypted the authenticator) because the session key, when passed to Bob, was signed with Alice's private key. But the signing step is omitted in the delegation case.

2. Propose an alternative design for Clipper where each chip knows only a public key and the government holds the corresponding private key, and where each party sends the session key encrypted under the public key as part of its transmission. How might Bob verify that the LEAF in your design is correct? What would the advantages and disadvantages of this scheme be over Clipper?

3. As described in §24.2.1 *NetWare's Guillou-Quisquater Authentication Scheme*, a GQ key, as NetWare uses it, expires. Describe how, using one of the strong credential download schemes in §12.4 *Strong Password Credentials Download Protocols*, and using only RSA keys, a workstation can create a temporary authentication key and forget the user's long-term key.

4. With the scheme described in §24.5.2 *Coping with Export Controls*, 24 bits of the 64-bit key are made accessible to the U.S. government. So is this scheme more secure than the traditional exportable scheme that uses 40-bit keys?

5. **Why aren't the escrowed keys for Clipper indexed by the name of the person whose phone will be tapped, or the telephone number to be tapped, rather than the ID of the device?**

25 WEB ISSUES

Until a few years ago, you could connect to the Internet and be in contact with hundreds of millions of other nodes, without giving even a thought to security. The Internet in the '90's was like sex in the '60's. It was great while it lasted, but it was inherently unhealthy and was destined to end badly. I'm just glad I didn't miss out this time. —Charlie Kaufman

25.1 INTRODUCTION

Web security issues are not as well defined as, say, cryptographic handshakes. "Web security" depends on details of standards that are likely to change, and details of implementation choices in browsers and servers, which also change, especially after problems are found. But it is instructive to see the kinds of security issues that can and have occurred.

The simplest concept of the web is that servers store static (i.e., constructed in advance) web pages, which consist of text, pictures, sound bites, etc., plus pointers to other pages. A user types a URL (universal resource locator) which connects him to a server and web page on that server. The content on the page might be a list of the U.S. presidents. Each president's name might actually be a link to another page that would give a biography of that president, with perhaps some of the information consisting of links for more information about items discussed in the biography, such as the Civil War. The basic idea of the web evolved for increased functionality and convenience for users, and the extra features brought about fascinating and perhaps frightening privacy and security concerns. As these are discovered, the standards and the implementations evolve.

The content of a web page is encoded in a language known as HTML (HyperText Markup Language), which the browser interprets and turns it into something fit for human consumption such as text and pictures on the screen. HTML consists of pieces of information preceded with a beginning tag and terminated with an ending tag, where the tags indicate what type of content is between the tags (text, picture, sound, URL, etc.).

The protocol for retrieving web pages is known as HTTP (HyperText Transfer Protocol). It is a stateless request/response protocol. The client machine makes a request (such as "give me the web page I'm specifying"), and the response is the contents of that page. (See §25.3 *HTTP*.)

It is common for HTTP interactions not to go directly from the client to the server which has the content. Instead the request might be relayed through one or more intermediaries known as **proxies**. Proxies save network bandwidth, since they can cache web pages, and send a cached web page directly back to the requester. The proxy might even be on the user's own machine. A proxy on the user's machine is not simply a cache. It is an extra piece of software that might have functionality not present in the user's browser, such as refusing to retrieve images suspected of being ads.

Another important web concept is of a **spider** or **robot**. This is an automated program used by search engines to search through the web and index the information, so that when someone does a search for specific information the search engine site can return the answer quickly. $I_{1,2,3}$ for one (three?) am incredibly impressed by the search engine sites that allow $me_{1,2,3}$ to search through the web as easily as searching through a single document.

25.2 URLs/URIs

URI (Uniform Resource Identifier) is a term that is used to mean either a URL (Uniform Resource Locator) or a URN (Uniform Resource Name). In reality the only UR things you'll trip over are URLs, so it's reasonable (though perhaps politically incorrect) to use the terms URI and URL interchangeably. The more familiar term is URL, so that's what we'll use, though some of the HTTP fields use the term URI.

A URL is what you type into your browser, and what appears in the HTML source on a link. It looks something like this:

http://www.domainname.com/info_that_the_server_will__use_however_it_wants

To the left of the initial "://" is the name of the protocol to be used, in this case HTTP (hyper text transfer protocol), which is the primary protocol for browsing the web. It could be something else, such as ftp. The next component (www.domainname.com) is the DNS name of the server. This is what will be looked up in DNS to find the IP address the client should contact. The fact that most URLs contain a server name that starts with "www." has nothing to do with the standards. It is just a convention that evolved. A particular site would own a domain name such as dec.com, and have perhaps lots of machines with names such as rabbit.dec.com, tiger.dec.com, panther.dec.com. (Often departments within companies choose "theme" names to come up with unique names for their machines within the company. So one department might name their machines after authors of great literature, and another after characters on Star Trek.) Another method of ensuring unique names for machines within the company is to add an extra level of hierarchy to the name, such as giving all machines in the U.S. names that end in us.dec.com. Then names of machines would look like happy.us.dec.com, grumpy.us.dec.com, etc., and the U.S. branches of the company would not have to coordinate with branches in other countries to ensure unique machine names, since there would be no ambiguity between the machines happy.us.dec.com and happy.oz.dec.com. The name www is conventionally the name of the machine that is accessible to the outside world for connecting to via HTTP and obtaining web content. Since companies that are posting content generally want it to be easy to find, the web content for dec.com is likely to be on the machine www.dec.com. If it were instead on a machine called arachnid.us.dec.com, users are unlikely to be able to guess or remember the URL.

In place of the server name, it is legal to put an IP address. The 32-bit IP address is represented with the traditional dotted decimal representation, such as 10.241.88.3, where each component is the decimal representation of one of the 4 octets of the IP address.

Some URLs allow embedding account names in front of the server name, in the format username@. For instance, the URL specification would consider http://radia@us.dec.com to be a perfectly valid URL. But the HTTP specification (RFC 2616) would not consider that URL as valid, because HTTP forbids user names embedded in its URLs. Most browsers, faced with a URL that contains a username field just throw away the username portion and use the rest of the URL when making an HTTP request, rather than complaining to the user that the URL is illegal. This is relevant because users can be tricked with complex-looking URLs (see §25.6.1 *Spoofing a Site to a User*).

URLs also allow specification of the user's password in the URL. The user's password, if present, appears after the username and before the @, separated from the user name with a colon as in radia:AsIfI'dPrintMyPasswordInABook. Although HTTP doesn't allow the username and password information, FTP does use it. A URL such as

ftp://radia:AsIfI'dPrintMyPasswordInABook@happy.us.dec.com/int/bookfile.ps

would indicate that the protocol to be used is FTP, and the login information to FTP would consist of radia as the username, and AsIfI'dPrintMyPasswordInABook as the password. After the first single slash appears int/bookfile.ps, which indicates the file bookfile.ps on the directory int/ on machine happy.us.dec.com.

Another thing that can appear in a URL is the layer 4 (TCP) port number. If present, it follows the server name and a colon separator, as in http://happy.us.dec.com:626/int/bookfile.ps, which would indicate port 626. In the case of HTTP, if no port is specified, the default is port 80.

25.3 HTTP

In order to focus on security implications, we will not delve into all the details of HTTP and instead give a conceptual overview with emphasis on features that have security implications. If you want the details of HTTP, you should read RFC 2616. RESC01 gives a brief tutorial, and there are several books available such as GARF95 and STEI98.

The two main HTTP request types are GET and POST. The best way to think of them is that GET is for reading a web page and POST is for sending information to a web server. The response contains information such as the content requested and status information (such as OK or not found or unauthorized). One status that might be included in a response is a redirect. This informs the browser that it should go to a different URL. The browser will then go to the new URL, as if the user had clicked on a link.

A request header can contain other information, such as the language requested (e.g., English) or IF-MODIFIED-SINCE (which indicates the time the cached copy was obtained, so that there would be no necessity of sending it again if it hadn't changed since then). Some of the information has security implications:

- FROM. The user's email address, which the browser can only know if the user has configured the browser to know this. This makes it very easy for a server to know which requests are coming from the same user, and which user it is (assuming the user has configured the email address as her real one). If you tell every web site what your email address is, you will wind up with lots of **spam** (nuisance email), since the email addresses a site collects can be sold. There are also privacy concerns with automatically sending your email address, since you might want to browse information (such as medical information) anonymously. Browsers today do not fill in this field. However, there is a good use for this field. Spiders are supposed to put the email address of someone to contact in case the spider program misbehaves in some way.
- AUTHORIZATION. This field contains information that allows the server to know who the user is. It is sent by a browser to a server which in the past has replied to a request with a status indicating authentication is required. There are two types of authorization information: basic, which consists of the username and password base64-encoded, and digest (see §25.4 *HTTP Digest Authentication*). In either case, the browser needs to prompt the user for her name and password in order to fill in this field. Once she's done so, though, the browser caches the information and it won't be necessary for her to do so again. The name and password are server-specific, since the user might certainly have different names and passwords on different servers, so the browser must prompt the user for name and password each time a different server returns a status code indicating authentication is required.

Note that the name of this field should really be called AUTHENTICATION rather than AUTHORIZATION. The HTTP specification seems to use the two terms interchangeably, for variety perhaps. The field for specifying the method of authentication is known as WWW-AUTHENTICATE, but the field for carrying the information is known as AUTHORIZATION [see §25.4 *HTTP Digest Authentication*].

- COOKIE. This is a piece of data given to the client by the server, and returned by the client to the server in subsequent requests (see §25.5 *Cookies*).
- REFERER.* The URL of the page from which the client came, either because the user explicitly clicked on a link, or because there was an embedded image pointing to this server.

25.4 HTTP DIGEST AUTHENTICATION

One could certainly use SSL in order to protect the client/server communication, but SSL is expensive, and doesn't in general provide authentication of the user. So HTTP has a "low budget" method of authenticating the user, which we describe in this section. The HTTP authentication can be used in combination with SSL, so for instance, if the authentication method involves sending the username and password in the clear, using that method in combination with SSL certainly improves security.

Because sending the username and password in the clear on every request to the server is not a particularly secure thing to do, methods of using cryptography, both for authenticating the user and for integrity protecting the data, were added. There are some challenges faced when designing cryptographic protection for HTTP:

- HTTP is stateless.
- What needs to be authenticated is the user, who might be connecting from a machine that has no user-specific configuration information, such as a cryptographic key for the user. So the exchange is based on passwords.
- A lot of requests might be made to the same server, and it would be nice to allow most of them to work without an extra round trip in order to receive a challenge.
- It would be nice to design it so that someone who steals the server database cannot use the information to impersonate the user on that server.

*The name of the field is not our typo. Someone in the early days of the web misspelled *referrer*, and because it is included in the wire protocol, it has never been fixed for reasons of backward compatibility. Though maybe it's not a typo and was done to save 8 bits of bandwidth.

- It would be nice to design it so that theft of one server's database would not allow someone to impersonate the user on a different server, even if she used the same password on that other server.

Assume a client Alice is going to make a request of a server Bob. Assume the user Alice is on a machine that currently has no state about her. She requests a resource on Bob that requires authentication. Her browser has no way of knowing this, so the request does not contain any authentication information (i.e., has no HTTP AUTHORIZATION field). Bob returns a response with a status code (401) indicating that the request failed because it was "unauthorized", and includes the WWW-AUTHENTICATE field that specifies what authentication method the server wants, such as

WWW-Authenticate: Digest

The response also has to contain additional information, such as a nonce to be folded into the hash. The browser now prompts the user for her name and password (for that server), uses it to form a new request, this time containing the AUTHORIZATION field containing the proper cryptographic combination of the user's password, the nonce, the URL, and other information, and caches the user's name and password for future interactions with that server. The next time a request is made to the same server, since the browser would have the user's name and password and other necessary information cached, the browser constructs information for the AUTHORIZATION field without bothering the user.

In order to prevent an eavesdropper from simply stealing the information from one request and including it with another request, the protocol could require the browser to obtain a new nonce for each request. But that would require an extra round trip. So instead, the browser reuses the nonce, but increments a counter known as the nonce count. If the server wants to protect against replays of requests, the server stores successfully used (nonce, nonce count) values and rejects a request with a previously used nonce count value. It can cut corners, though, without too much loss of security (see Homework Problem 3 through Homework Problem 6).

HTTP digest authentication is designed so that the server does not store the actual user password, but instead a hash of the user's password and the server name (or perhaps realm name, if there are a bunch of equivalent servers that can be grouped together for security purposes.) This way the server stores a password-equivalent for that server, but it would only work on that server (or in that realm). Therefore theft of the server database would allow someone to impersonate someone in that realm, but not in a different realm, even if the user used the same password.

The browser stores, for each server that requires authentication, the server name, the user's name and password, the nonce received from the server, the authentication method desired, and the nonce count. When a request goes to that server, the browser constructs the data for the AUTHORIZATION field, incrementing the nonce count.

One extra wrinkle is the ability not only to authenticate the user, but to integrity protect the data. In addition to sending a nonce, the server can specify whether it would like integrity protection, by including a field QOP="auth", or QOP="auth-int", or QOP="auth,auth-int". QOP means *quality of protection*, and auth means *authentication only*, auth-int means *authentication and integrity*, and auth,auth-int means *do integrity if you can, but authentication only would be acceptable*. These names are misleading. auth sounds like it's only doing authentication, but in fact at least part of the URL is also protected, and in a GET request, auth-int wouldn't protect any more than that. And auth-int sounds like it's protecting everything, when in fact the only extra thing protected is the body of the message. Left out of the integrity protection are cookies and fields such as REFERER.

25.5 COOKIES

If the client is browsing content that requires authentication and access control, or is accumulating information such as items in a virtual shopping basket to be purchased when the user is finished browsing the on-line catalog, the information for that session really needs to be kept somewhere. But HTTP is stateless. Each request/response interaction is allowed to take place over a fresh TCP connection. The **cookie** mechanism enables the server to maintain context across many request/response interactions. A cookie is a data structure created by the server and stored at the client.

25.5.1 Alternatives to Cookies

If the server wants to maintain context for the user's "session", there are several approaches one might think of that the HTTP designers could have adopted:

- The server could attempt somehow to recognize a new TCP connection as belonging to some existing client-server "session". It might be tempting to assume it could associate different TCP connections with the same session based on the IP address from which the request comes, but there might be many users on the same machine, all coming from the same IP address. Multiple users coming from the same IP address also results from requests going through the same proxy. If the server ever incorrectly assumed a request was part of a previous session, it would be similar to session hijacking; the new user would have the context of the previous user.

- Perhaps the server could refine the algorithm for mapping TCP connections to sessions based on using both the IP address and TCP port from which the request comes. This would not work for many reasons. It is common for the user's browser to open multiple TCP connections, and each one would be assigned a different port. Also, a proxy might open a single connection to a server and interleave requests from multiple users on that same connection.

Therefore, different users might appear to the server as coming from the same IP address and port, and the same user might appear to the server as coming from different ports.

- The server could dynamically generate the URLs on a page so that when you "click" from one page to the next, the target URL contains a session identifier and the page returned likewise has the session identifier in all of its embedded URLs. This approach would hurt performance, both because the server would have to generate all of those dynamic URLs and because web caches would not be able to share pages between different users' sessions.
- The browser could include the user's name (or email address) in every request. This is even legal according to the HTTP specification (e.g., the from field). But users might want to browse anonymously.
- The browser could generate a large random number each time a web surfing session was started. Call that number *X*. *X* could be sent in every request during a user's web surfing session. *X* would not identify the user, but would be used solely so that the server can associate multiple requests with the same web surfing session. This is a clever idea, but has security problems. If you typed your name and password at your stock broker's web site, and then *X* was used so that the server could recognize future requests as coming from you, then an eavesdropper could steal *X* and use it and be considered by your broker as authenticated as you.
- People could have redesigned HTTP to keep state, so that interaction with a particular site would consist of an explicit connection similar to a TCP connection. But they didn't.

Instead of these approaches, Netscape, in 1994, came up with the cookie design, a clever approach that solved the problem and sounded delicious.

25.5.2 Cookie Rules

The idea of a cookie is relatively simple. A server may, in any response, include a cookie. The client's browser is supposed to cache it and include it in future requests to the same site. The cookie might contain all the state necessary for maintaining the client's interaction with the server. For instance, it might contain all the items in the user's shopping basket. This form of cookie is useful when there are multiple related servers and no shared database, for instance, when there is a secure server that does checkout and takes credit cards and a less-protected one on which the user can browse the catalog. However, in order to prevent servers from taking up too much memory at the client, cookies are limited to 4K octets. So another solution is for the server to keep a database of all the information it needs about each of its current clients, and have the cookie value be an index into that database. Since there is no way to force users to "log out", database entries must time out and might then be reused for a new user. That presents an opportunity for confusion if two users wind up with the same cookie.

When the server sends the cookie, it also specifies restrictions on who should receive the cookie. If it specifies a domain name (e.g., dec.com), then the cookie will be sent to any machine in that domain (happy.dec.com, grumpy.dec.com). The cookie designers were concerned about sites sharing information through cookies. If a cookie were allowed to be sent to any site, then it is trivial to track everything someone does during a web surfing session; the first site gives it a cookie with a unique ID, specifying that the cookie should be sent to every site the user visits. Then every site the user visits sees that unique ID. They could have specified that a cookie only go to the machine which sent it, but there are cases where a session involves a group of machines; e.g., one for browsing the catalog, another for ordering. There might even be multiple machines with the same information on it for load sharing. So the compromise is to allow the server to specify a "domain" in which the cookie would be returned. To prevent the domain over which the cookie could be shared from being too large, under some top level domains (.com, .edu, .net, .org, .gov, .mil, .int) there must be at least 2 dots, as in foo.dec.com. Under any of the other top level domains there must be at least three dots.

If no domain name is specified, then it only goes to the machine which sent it. It can also specify a path name (e.g., /foo), in which case the cookie will only be sent if the portion of the URL following the first single slash starts with the specified path name.

Cookies have lifetimes. Along with sending the cookie the server can specify when the cookie should be deleted, and whether it should be discarded when the browser terminates. Browsers might have the ability for users to specify restrictions on cookies, such as that all of them should be discarded when the browser terminates, or cookies from any site other than xyz.com should be discarded.

Cookies have received severe criticism from privacy advocates, but in theory they could be used as a privacy *enhancement*. Instead of storing state about the user on the server, the state would be given to the client to hold. If the server were broken into, there would be no client information to steal. But cookies are mostly not used that way. Information *is* stored at the server, and the cookie is just to index into that database.

25.5.3 Tracking Users

It may be possible to track everything that was done during a web surfing session—which sites were visited, for instance—but not to identify the actual individual. Just that someone did x, y, and z on Tuesday, November 4. Or it might be possible to track him through many sessions, so that the site knows this is user 78394, the same user who visited a month ago. Or it may be possible in some cases to figure out who the actual user is—what his name is, where he lives, how old he is.

Correlating that the same entity visited multiple sites can be done by having those sites collude with each other, and share log information, or put information into the REFERER field or into URLs. This only tells these sites that *someone* did all those things. But that someone turns into a specific identifiable person if he authenticates to any of the colluding sites, perhaps by ordering something at an on-line merchant.

Why would anyone want to keep track of which sites a user visits? And why would anyone care if they did? Information is valuable, and can be sold. Even if it's not obvious what the information might be used for, there are sites that would like to collect it, just in case it proves valuable, e.g., for targeted advertising. Even if the profile of interests can't be traced to an individual, creating a profile for a class of individuals might be useful. For instance, ads for mail ordering live bait would probably not be particularly effective when displayed on a Martha Stewart web page devoted to hosting an elegant dinner party. It's possible that advertisers might figure this one out on their own, but by doing automated tracking of viewing history, they might find unexpected correlations.

A more frightening example is that insurance companies might want to know which individuals are browsing sites with medical information about serious diseases and on that basis deny coverage. Or information might be collected in order to embarrass an individual. A prominent American was once embarrassed by having someone publicize his history of video rentals.

Cookies take most of the heat for violating privacy. Legislation has even been proposed to outlaw cookies! But a lot of information is available even without cookies, and the design of cookies has attempted to prevent some of the more straightforward "evil" uses.

Cookies only go to the domain they are sent from. So how is it possible to correlate that the user who visited site A is the same user who visited site B? There are many ways of correlating information:

- Server logs. Servers can (and do) keep track of requests they receive; when they occurred, what the request consisted of, and what IP address it came from. This doesn't necessarily track an individual user. Since the user might browse from different machines on different days, or even have the IP address of his machine dynamically assigned, a given user might be using different IP addresses at different times. With multi-user machines and proxies, many users might be coming in from the same IP address. With proxies, many requests can be satisfied from the cache, and the server will never see the request and therefore it cannot appear in the log. But the server log will still contain some information.

- Eavesdropping. It might be possible to collect information by observing traffic. Even with encryption, the packet headers give some information, such as which sites are talking to each other. But there is no single wire through which all Internet traffic flows, so eavesdropping will only collect a small sample of the traffic.

- Proxy logs. A proxy can keep track of requests. It is common for an employer to log requests, as well as refuse connection to certain sites known to be non-business related. ISPs might also monitor web browsing patterns.
- Redirects or embedded images. Suppose two sites A and B have each given the user a cookie, so A knows the user as userxyz, and B knows him as userqvj. They would like to correlate that userxyz=userqvj. This can be done by having site A embed a redirect or an embedded image to B, tacking onto the end of the URL userxyz. When the user's browser visits site B, the URL will tell B that A knows the user by userxyz and the cookie that the user will return to B will tell B that this is the user B knows as userqvj. In particular, if there were a consortium of sites, one site, say C, could coordinate all the information, by having all consortium sites embed a redirect or embedded image to C on their web pages. The content to be fetched could be an invisible (1 pixel × 1 pixel) image known as a **web bug.** A user would never notice a web bug except by examining the HTML source of the web page.
- Software at the client. Browsers keep some information about sites visited. If someone could install software at user Alice's machine, perhaps without her knowledge, everything she does can be logged, even if she is careful to use encryption.

25.6 OTHER WEB SECURITY PROBLEMS

25.6.1 Spoofing a Site to a User

Suppose you want to trick a user into thinking he is visiting, say, his stock broker site, (say respectablestockbroker.com), but instead he is visiting EmbezzlersInc. Let's say that EmbezzlersInc manages to convince the manager of the domains under country code tv to give it an innocuous sounding name like gg.tv. If EmbezzlersInc can trick you into thinking they are your stock broker, they can connect to the site you want to talk to and act as a man-in-the-middle, learning your password, and then being able to make stock trades with your money. One would hope that using SSL would make this impossible. However, using SSL you can be assured you are talking to the correct site if:

- *None* of the CAs you trust ever accidentally or maliciously issued a certificate certifying EmbezzlersInc's public key as belonging to the name respectablestockbroker.com.
- Nobody maliciously or accidentally modified your configured list of trusted CA public keys to include the key of a disreputable organization.

- You carefully check the URL at the top of your browser page to make sure that you are indeed connected to respectablestockbroker.com. You also check the little lock at the bottom of your browser page to make sure the connection is using SSL. But URLs can be very confusing. Where does the URL
  http://www.respectablestockbroker.com!rated_AAA_by_US-Treasury-Dept@gg.tv/
  go to? SSL will check that the name in the certificate is really gg.tv, and will raise no warnings, but most users will assume that this URL really is to www.respectablestocker.com.

25.6.2 Merchants Unclear on the Concept

Suppose the user is very careful, so the user is talking to the correct server, and the user session is cryptographically protected. After the user does his SSL-protected transaction, where the credit card is cryptographically protected while on the wire, it is not uncommon for the merchant to subsequently email a confirmation to the user, in the clear, with all details of the transaction, including the credit card number!

25.6.3 Getting Impersonated by a Subsequent User

The authorization feature of HTTP lets a web server signal the browser that it should prompt the user for a username and password, and then the browser can calculate the proper authorization information for that server. It is natural for the browser to store the user's name and password so that on subsequent visits to that same site, the browser will not need to prompt the user for name and password again. The browser can complete the authentication on the user's behalf. This is similar to the behavior that would occur if the user typed her name and password at a login page at the server's site, and the server sent the client a cookie to be used with subsequent requests (so as to bypass the login page). If a user is surfing the web from a public workstation, say at a library, and then walks away from the machine without logging out of the browser, the next user who walks up to that machine will be assumed to be the authenticated previous user. For this reason, it is important for cookies and authorization information to only be cached for a short time, and certainly deleted when the user exits from the browser.

However, some cookies are retained in stable storage, and the next user to use the machine will have the use of those cookies. Few users have the expertise to make sure all cookies are deleted when they finish their session.

But it gets worse! Some browser vendors have thought up a really "helpful" feature that gives us the chills. When a server requests authorization information, causing the client machine to prompt the user for username and password, the browser asks the user Alice whether she'd like the browser to remember this information (in stable storage even after the user exits the browser) so that she won't be bothered in the future. How nice. That means that every subsequent user will be automatically authorized as Alice on any site that Alice authenticated at (assuming she answered "yes" to the browser's "would you like me to store your name and password so that you won't be bothered in the future and so that any person who walks up to the machine you are currently using can steal all your money?"). If Alice realizes her horrible error after answering "yes", and wants to take it back, there is no easy way. You might think that she can cause the prompt to appear and this time overwrite her real information with bogus information in order to erase the dangerous information from being stored for the next user. But the browser will never prompt again!

This is such a bad feature that it should certainly be removed from browsers. But until it is, servers should not use the authorization feature of HTTP and instead accomplish the same thing by presenting the user with a login page at the server site, and giving the client machine a cookie proving the user is authorized. And the server should specify that the cookie be deleted after the user exits the browser.

Browser vendors are finding new ways of making life convenient for the users, as well as creating more security issues. When a user fills in a form, such as her telephone number or address, the browser remembers the responses that have been filled into such a form recently, and shows the choices so the user can select one of those rather than going through the tedium of typing in the information. Again, if the browser is used by more than one user, the other user can see the information filled into the form by the other user. It is possible to configure such browsers not to store such information, but it takes sophistication, and someone at a public workstation might change those preference settings.

25.6.4 Cross-Site Scripting

One of the types of content that can be embedded in a web page is **active content**, i.e., a program, e.g., <SCRIPT>*script commands*</SCRIPT>. Types of active content are Java, Javascript, and ActiveX. Javascript is designed for commands such as "click on this button", to simulate what a user might do to a page (to save the user the work of doing it herself). Java runs in a limited sandbox on the client, so what it can do at the client is very limited, but it can send arbitrary commands to the server. ActiveX runs arbitrary executables on your desktop, but the safeguard is that these executables must have been signed.

It is theoretically possible for someone to post a message on a bulletin board with embedded active content, and anyone who displayed the message would inadvertently run his script. The script commands run in a sandbox on the client machine, but the client machine would allow the script to transmit anything it wants to the server. So the program can do anything on the server that the user duped into running the script is allowed to do. For instance, if the server stores the user's email, the script might send a command to delete all the user's email, or send email viruses to everyone he knows. The way this vulnerability was "fixed" was that servers that display such things check to make sure they aren't displaying anything dangerous. Figuring out whether something is dangerous is tricky, and if they don't get it right, there will be a loophole to exploit.

Cross-site scripting is a security vulnerability in which one site, A, can create a program (a "script") that they can trick you into running on another site B. It has been published as a theoretical vulnerability, but never been exploited (to our knowledge) for several reasons:

- It requires B to have a strange and not very good design, though the design would be legal within HTTP.
- It requires A to have reverse engineered B's design.
- It requires A to embed an incriminating piece of content in its page. There are paranoid people who have their browsers alert them to such things, and if it were ever found it would be widely publicized. Unlike a virus, in which it is difficult to trace the source, A would be to blame for its own web site. It could claim that someone had broken in and replaced their innocent content with the malicious content, but it is still A's fault for having lax security.

Even though it's probably not a real vulnerability, it is somewhat interesting to understand. Assume that the design of site B's web page is such that a client can issue commands by doing a GET of a URL, where the instructions for what to do (delete all your email, transfer money to an account number) are included in the portion of the URL to the right of the single slash. For instance,

http://www.respectablestockbroker.com/transfer&$50000.&mainacount&account#14567.

Assume the user has visited respectablestockbroker recently, so has a cookie from them identifying her. When she visits site A's web page and hits the embedded URL above, this will cause her to visit site B with that URL and her cookie. The cookie will identify her to B, so B will know what her account number is.

That example doesn't involve code. Here's an example, again convoluted and unlikely, that does involve code. Suppose site B's web site allows you to specify a greeting that it will display when you enter the web site, and the greeting is passed to it in the URL. So, if you entered B using

http://www.respectablestockbroker.com/hello there!

it would display hello there. But suppose instead of a text string, A puts an HTML file that specifies active content, e.g., <SCRIPT>*script commands*</SCRIPT>. When the user's browser does a GET of that URL, site B repeats the string back to the user's browser. Since site B is trusted, the browser will be willing to run the program.

This is far-fetched for many reasons. It's unlikely site B would use the information in the right-hand portion of the URL that way. If they did, they should ensure that it was just text, and not send it back if it contained active content.

25.6.5 Poisoning Cookies

Some servers used cookies without any cryptographic protection*. It was easy to look at their contents and modify them. For instance:

- if the cookie contained a user ID (an index into a database), user A could modify the user ID in the cookie so that the web site would assume user A was really user B (and had authenticated as B sometime in the recent past). This would enable A to impersonate B and have access, say, to his bank account.
- (this example actually occurred) An on-line merchant stored the contents of the user's shopping cart, including the prices of items, in the cookie. When the user checked out, the prices charged were those stored in the cookie. So it was easy to modify the prices in the cookie so that instead of paying $60 for an item, the user would pay 35 cents.

25.6.6 Other Misuse of Cookies

In the wonderful paper FORD94, four students describe their investigation of client authentication as actually implemented by various sites. By examining cookies received, modifying them, and testing which modified cookies the site accepted, they were able to gain unauthorized access to several sites, and even find out the secret key used to create the cryptographic authentication information used in one site's cookies!

The paper gives several examples of bad security practice. The most spectacular bad example, though, was one site that was intending their cookie to be a hash of the concatenation of the username and a server secret. Their mistake was in not understanding the property of the particular hash function they were using. By examing the cookies received with various user names, the authors were able to figure out that the site was concatenating the username with some sort of cryptographic MAC to create the client authenticator used in the cookie. By experimentation, the authors were able to determine that the MAC was the output of the UNIX function used for hashing passwords (see §5.2.4.1 *UNIX Password Hash*), with input consisting of a concatenation of the username and a server secret.

The problem is that function ignores all but the first 8 characters of the input string. So if the username was longer than 8 characters, the server secret would not affect the output of the hash. This enabled the authors to construct authenticators that would allow them to gain access to the site. All they needed to do was run the hash on a username of at least 8 characters to produce a cookie the site would accept (the username concatenated with the output of the hash on that username).

*We are using past tense because we are assuming that after the incident in the second bullet was publicized, servers used cryptographic protection on cookies to prevent modification. This is perhaps optimistic.

But it gets worse! They were also able to easily find out the server secret. They'd guessed that the site was using that particular hash function, because authenticators for all usernames with the same 8-character prefix were identical. If the username was 8 characters or more, the server secret was ignored. However, if the username was 7 characters, then the hash function would do its calculations on the username and the first octet of the server secret. That function uses the input string as a DES key, ignoring the high-order bit, so there were 128 possibilities for each octet of the server secret.

So the authors used a 7-character username, and tried each of the 128 possible values of the first octet of the server secret until they found an authenticator value that the server would accept. This told them the first character of the server secret. Next they tried a 6-character username, concatenated with the first character of the server secret, and tried each of the possible values of the second octet of the server secret (again, at most 128 values needed to be tried), until they found one that worked. They did this until they discovered the entire server secret, which turned out to be the ASCII string MARCH20. Even if the site had chosen a high quality 8-octet secret, at most 128×8 attempts would have been required to determine the secret. If, instead, a proper keyed hash had been done, it would have required 128^8 attempts.

25.7 HOMEWORK

1. How are search engines able to so quickly tell you all the web pages that contain a particular phrase?
2. What other design choices might there have been to allow a web surfing session through many pages on a site to appear to a person as a single connected experience (as in browsing a catalog, accumulating a shopping cart, and checking out)?
3. In digest authentication, if the server did not remember the nonce count, what would the effect be?
4. In digest authentication, if the server did not remember what nonces it has given, what would the effect be?
5. In digest authentication, if the server always gave the same nonce, what would the effect be?
6. In digest authentication, if the server only remembers the largest nonce count successfully used by a given client, what would the effect be? (Hint: it is legal for the client to send multiple requests in parallel.)

7. If HTTP basic authentication is used, what might the server database contain so as to avoid someone who steals the database from impersonating the user at that server?

8. What machine does the URL http://www.respectablestockbroker.com!rated_AAA_by_US-Treasury-Dept@gg.tv/ go to?

9. Compare the performance and security properties of: no authentication, HTTP basic authentication, HTTP digest authentication, SSL-only with server-side-authentication only, SSL with client authentication, and SSL (with and without client authentication) with HTTP authentication (with HTTP basic and with HTTP digest authentication).

26 FOLKLORE

Whenever I made a roast, I always started off by cutting off the ends, just like I'd seen my grandmother do. Someone once asked me why I did it, and I realized I had no idea. It had never occurred to me to wonder. It was just the way it was done. Eventually I remembered to ask my grandmother. "Why do you always cut off the ends of a roast?" She answered "Because my pan is small, and otherwise the roasts would not fit." —anonymous

Many things have become accepted security practice. Most of these are to avoid problems that could be avoided other ways if you really knew what you were doing. It's fine to get in the habit of doing these things, but it would be nice to know at least *why* you're doing them. A lot of these issues have been discussed throughout the book, but we summarize them here.

26.1 PERFECT FORWARD SECRECY

Perfect forward secrecy (PFS) (see also §16.3 *Perfect Forward Secrecy*) is a protocol property that prevents someone who records an encrypted conversation from being able to later decrypt the conversation, even if they have since learned the long-term cryptographic secrets of each side. A protocol designed with PFS cannot be deciphered by a passive attacker, even one with knowledge of the long-term keys, though an active attacker with knowledge of the long-term key can impersonate one of the parties or act as a man-in-the-middle. PFS is considered an important protocol property to keep the conversation secret from:

- an escrow agent who knows the long-term key
- a thief who has stolen the long-term key of one of the parties without this compromise being detected
- someone who records the conversation and later manages to steal the long-term key

- **law enforcement that has recorded the conversation and subsequently, through a court order, obtains the long-term key**

PFS isn't free. There are two ways to do it. One is what is done in IKE, which is to do a Diffie-Hellman exchange, and have both sides forget the Diffie-Hellman information after the conversation concludes. Diffie-Hellman is computationally more expensive than would be necessary for setting up a session key without worrying about PFS.

The other method is what is done in SSL/TLS, which is to have one side, say Bob, generate an ephemeral public/private key pair, and have the other side, say Alice, send a random number encrypted with the ephemeral public key. This is less expensive than Diffie-Hellman for Alice, but much more expensive for Bob. To get "perfect" PFS, Bob would have to forget the ephemeral private key after the first session created with that ephemeral key concludes. Generating a new ephemeral key pair is much more expensive than doing a Diffie-Hellman exchange. But to get "pretty good" forward secrecy, it would be fine for Bob to only generate a new ephemeral key pair every few hours or so. Therefore, the cost of creating the key pair would be amortized over many sessions. But even if Bob doesn't need to generate a new ephemeral public key pair for each session, he does have to do a private key operation (decryption).

In addition to the performance costs of providing for PFS, PFS makes getting export approval more difficult.

26.2 CHANGE KEYS PERIODICALLY

With many encryption schemes, the more examples of ciphertext you can see, the more likely it is you will be able to break the encryption and find the key. With an adequately strong encryption scheme, this shouldn't be a problem. But to be on the safe side, people like to change keys (do **key rollover**) before any key has been used on more than some amount of data.

For instance, when encrypting in CBC mode, it is desirable to change keys before it is likely that two cipherblocks will be equal. For example, with 64-bit blocks, by the birthday problem (see §5.1 *Introduction*) it is likely that after 2^{32} blocks, two ciphertext blocks will be equal. (What information would this leak? See Homework Problem 1.)

Another reason to do key rollover (with perfect forward secrecy) is in case the data encryption key were stolen without your knowledge in the middle of the conversation.

Yet another reason to rollover keys is when export rules require use of a key which is too small to really be secure. For instance, the SKIP protocol allowed changing the key on every packet by sending with each packet the data encryption key (of inadequate strength) encrypted with a key which was of adequate strength. With this approach, even if 40-bit data encryption keys were being used, if 2^{20} packets were sent during a conversation, it would take up to 2^{60} operations to break all the keys for the entire conversation.

26.3 MULTIPLEXING FLOWS OVER A SINGLE SA

Folklore says that different conversations should not be multiplexed over the same security association. For instance, suppose two machines, F1 and F2, are talking with an IPsec SA, and forwarding traffic between A and B and between C and D (where A and C are behind F1 and B and D are behind F2). F1 and F2 might be firewalls, with A, B, C, and D machines behind those firewalls. Or A and C might be processes on F1 and B and D might be processes on F2. Some people would advocate creating two SAs between F1 and F2, one for the A-B traffic, and one for the C-D traffic.

Creating multiple SAs is obviously more expensive in terms of state and computation. What are the reasons people advocate F1 and F2 creating multiple SAs rather than sending all the traffic they are forwarding to each other over a single SA?

26.3.1 The Splicing Attack

This attack is only relevant if F1 and F2 are doing encryption-only (no integrity protection). Suppose different conversations are multiplexed over this tunnel. Suppose C (or an accomplice) is capable of eavesdropping on the F1-F2 link, as well as injecting packets. It is possible for C to do a splicing attack and see the decrypted data for the A-B conversation. Assume that the beginning of the plaintext, say the first 16 octets, identifies the conversation to F2, most likely by specifying the source and destination. The splicing attack involves the following steps:

- record an encrypted packet from the C-D conversation
- record an encrypted packet from the A-B conversation
- overwrite the first 16 octets of ciphertext from the C-D packet onto the first 16 octets of the encrypted A-B packet
- inject the spliced packet into the ciphertext stream

When F2 decrypts the packet, it will observe from the first 16 octets that the packet should be delivered to D. The remainder of the packet is the data from the A-B conversation. If it were encrypted in ECB mode, all of the data from the A-B plaintext packet will be delivered to D. But if it were encrypted in, say, CBC mode, the first block of data will be garbled, but the remainder will be the plaintext from the A-B conversation. (See Homework Problem 4.)

Note that this flaw is only relevant if the F1-F2 link does encryption-only. If it has cryptographic integrity protection, this attack is not possible. However, since people found the flaw with encryption-only, some people think it would be safer to use separate SAs, just in case a similar flaw is found when integrity is also used.

Even if there is no security flaw due to multiplexing traffic from different conversations over an encrypted and integrity protected tunnel, if F1 is a machine at an ISP (Internet Service Provider) serving multiple customers, the customers often feel safer if their traffic is carried over its own SA. Since the ISP needs the customers, it is advantageous for it to make the customers feel safer.

26.3.2 Service Classes

Suppose some types of traffic being forwarded between F1 and F2 get expedited service, or some different routing that would make it likely for packets transmitted by F1 to get widely out of order. If F2 is protecting against replays based on a sequence number in the packet, a common implementation of this is for F2 to remember the highest sequence number seen so far, say n, and remember which sequence numbers in the range n-k to n-1 have already been seen. If F1 marks the packets with different classes of service, then packets with a lower priority might take a lot longer to arrive at F2. If more than k high priority packets launched by F1 can arrive before a lower priority packet launched earlier by F1, then the low priority packet will be discarded by F2 as out of the window.

For this reason, some people advocate creating a different SA for each class of service, so that each service class has sequence numbers from a different space.

26.3.3 Different Cryptographic Algorithms

Some people advocate different SAs for different flows because each flow might require a different level of security. Some flows might require integrity-only. Some encrypted traffic might require more security, and thus a longer key, than other traffic. One might think this could be solved by using the highest level of security for all traffic. But the higher security encryption might be a performance problem if it was used for all the traffic.

Another reason to use different cryptographic algorithms is if some of the flows are for customers who would, for their own reasons, like to use particular cryptographic algorithms. It might be vanity crypto developed by their own company or country, they might feel safer using different algorithms than what others use because they might have heard (different) rumors about potential weaknesses, or there might be legal reasons why particular algorithms might only be usable for traffic of certain customers.

26.4 USE DIFFERENT KEYS IN THE TWO DIRECTIONS

This avoids reflection attacks such as in §11.2.1 *Reflection Attack*. There are other ways of avoiding reflection attacks, for instance:

- have the initiator generate odd challenges, and the responder even challenges
- have the response to the challenge consist of a function of the challenged side's name in addition to the key and the challenge, e.g., *h(name, key, challenge)* or *key{name | challenge}*

If it's inconvenient to obtain large random numbers, a unique nonce such as a sequence number can be turned into an unpredictable nonce by hashing it with a secret known only by the sender.

26.5 USE DIFFERENT SECRET KEYS FOR ENCRYPTION VS. INTEGRITY PROTECTION

With CBC residue as an integrity check there are problems when the same key is used for encryption as well as integrity protection, as described in section §4.3.1 *Ensuring Privacy and Integrity Together*. But if the integrity protection were, say, keyed MD, then there are no known weaknesses of using the same key. However, people are worried that since there was a problem with using the same key for both purposes with CBC residue, perhaps someone will later find a weakness with other schemes, and using two different keys avoids the issue.

Another reason using two keys became popular in protocols was because of U.S. export laws. The allowed key-length for exportable encryption was 40 bits, which was definitely very weak. But the U.S. government did allow stronger integrity checks. They only wanted to read the data, not tamper with it, so it was okay with them if the integrity check were reasonably strong. As a result, protocols often wound up with two keys: a 40-bit one for encryption, and one of adequate size for integrity protection.

PEM, when calculating a CBC residue as an integrity check, used a variant of the encryption key for calculating the CBC residue (the encryption key ⊕'d with $F0F0F0F0F0F0F0F0_{16}$). Unfortunately, CBC residue is completely insecure as an integrity check for email (see §21.16 *DES-CBC as MIC Doesn't Work*). The problem isn't a subtle interaction when using a variant of the same key for encryption as integrity protection. The problem is that CBC residue does not have the property that a cryptographic hash has; it is easy to create an arbitrary message with a given CBC residue.

Using different keys for integrity and encryption has the disadvantage that it requires two cryptographic passes over the data (twice the computation). For many years people yearned for an algorithm that would be able to do a single cryptographic pass, simultaneously encrypting and calculating an integrity check on the data. There were several proposed, and then later found to be broken. There are a few that have been proposed recently, and not (yet?) found to be broken.

26.6 USE DIFFERENT KEYS FOR DIFFERENT PURPOSES

If the same key is used for, say, decrypting a challenge, and for decrypting data encryption keys in headers of encrypted messages, it is possible that someone could get tricked into decrypting or signing something. An extreme example is of a blind signature (see §15.8.5 *Anonymous Groups*). By definition, with a blind signature the signer has no idea what he's signing. So that key had better not be used for any other purposes, such as signing purchase orders.

But even when the application isn't purposefully designed to prevent the key owner from knowing what he's doing, it is very likely that one application might not recognize an action that would have meaning in another application. For example, if the private decryption key is used to decrypt a challenge in a challenge/response protocol, the "challenge" given could be an encrypted data encryption key extracted from an email header.

One method of preventing such cross-application confusion is to encode something application-specific in the padding of the information to be signed or encrypted using public key cryptography. So in a challenge/response protocol in which someone would be asked to sign the challenge, the challenge could be a 128-bit number, and the signer would pad the challenge, before signing, with an application-specific constant such as a hash of the string "authentication protocol QXV challenge-response". Likewise, a signature on, say, a PGP message could be defined as containing the hash of the string "PGP message signature". If all applications using that same key were carefully coordinated, no confusion would arise. However, if any application didn't insist on those rules, there could be vulnerabilities. Therefore it would be safest, in theory, to certify a key as only applicable for a given application. The downside of this is that maintenance of so many different keys could present its own vulnerabilities as well as performance issues.

26.7 USE DIFFERENT KEYS FOR SIGNING VS. ENCRYPTION

If a signature private key is forgotten, it's not a big deal. You can just generate a new one. But if an encryption private key is lost, you'd lose all the data encrypted with it. Therefore, it is common to err on the side of making it hard to lose the encryption key, by keeping extra copies of the private key, perhaps in lots of different places. But this makes the key easier to steal, a trade-off considered acceptable in some cases for an encryption key, given the high cost of losing all the encrypted data. But in most cases there's no advantage in keeping copies of a signature private key. It's better to make it less vulnerable to theft by not keeping copies.

Another reason for separate keys is for law enforcement or for a company that wants to be able to decrypt anything encrypted for any of its employees on any of its equipment. They would like the private encryption key readily accessible to people other than the person associated with that key. But they have no need to be able to forge something, so they do not need to have a copy of the person's signature private key. In fact, it's to their advantage not to have access to the signature key. Then the person cannot repudiate his signature on something, for instance, claiming that the death threat signed by his key was an attempt by law enforcement to frame him.

Yet another reason is that you'd like to treat old expired encryption keys differently than old signature keys. There's no reason to archive old private signature keys. Once the key is changed, just throw away the old one. Irretrievably discarding a private signature key once it isn't supposed to be used anymore safeguards against someone stealing the old key and backdating a document. But old encryption keys are likely to still be needed in order to decrypt data encrypted with them.

26.8 HAVE BOTH SIDES CONTRIBUTE TO THE MASTER KEY

It is considered good cryptographic form for both sides of a communication to contribute to a key. For instance, consider the protocol in which Alice and Bob each choose a random number, send it to the other side encrypted with the other side's public key, and use a hash of the two values as the shared secret. Although this protocol does not have PFS, it has "better" forward secrecy than something like SSL/TLS, because only by learning *both* side's private keys can you decrypt the recorded conversation. Another reason for having both sides contribute to the master key is that if *either* side has a good random number, the result will be a good random number.

26.9 DON'T LET ONE SIDE DETERMINE THE KEY

In addition to ensuring that each side contributes to the key, folklore says it is a good idea to ensure that neither side can force the key to be any particular value. For instance, if each side sends a random number encrypted with the other side's public key, if the shared key were the $\oplus$ of the two values, then it would be easy for whichever side sent the last value to ensure that the result would be a particular value. If instead the shared key were a cryptographic hash of the two values, this would be impossible.

Why is this an important property? In most cases it wouldn't matter. However, here is a subtle example where it would matter. Suppose the world were to do IPsec, but without any per-machine secrets. The purpose of IPsec would be to efficiently get encryption and integrity protection without the hassle of distributing keys. Unfortunately, without per-machine keys, there is no way to detect men-in-the-middle. But we'll assume that applications have keys, and can authenticate each other. We want to be able to authenticate and detect men-in-the-middle using the application keys, but once the applications know to whom they are talking, and are assured that there are no men-in-the-middle, we have the applications depend on the cryptographic protection provided by IPsec, since that will be more efficient than providing cryptographic protection at the application layer.

So suppose application Bob is on machine B which is supposed to be at IP address *x*. Machine C (owned by, say, Chaos Computer Club), impersonates IP address *x* and waits for someone to connect. Application Alice is on machine A and attempts to communicate with IP address *x*. IPsec establishes a tunnel to IP address *x*, which will be machine C. Machine C establishes a tunnel to machine B. This is a classic man-in-the-middle scenario of C interposing itself between A and B.

A way of detecting C is for the applications Alice and Bob to authenticate each other over the tunnel, using their secrets for a true end-to-end handshake. Since C can simply relay the handshake messages, the handshake would not automatically detect C. However, if machine A gave Alice a hash of the shared key (call it *H*), and machine B gave Bob a hash of the shared key, then they could use *H* in the handshake. For instance, if they have public signature keys, they could each sign *H*.

If C were able to force the key to be the same between itself and A and between itself and B, then this protocol would fail to detect C, since C could just forward the signed *H*.

26.10 HASH IN A CONSTANT WHEN HASHING A PASSWORD

Users tend to use the same password in multiple places. Suppose there is a protocol in which a secret key is derived from the user's password and used in a challenge-response protocol. (W=h(pwd), Bob sends challenge R, Alice sends response f(W,R)). W is a *password-equivalent*, because if someone knows W they can directly impersonate the user, even though W is not the string that the user types.

In such a protocol, the server will contain a database of each user's password-equivalent value. This database might be specific to a server, to one application, or to a machine that stores password-equivalents for all users in a domain. To prevent theft of one database from allowing someone to impersonate users using the same password on a different server (or different application, or different domain), have the server hash a constant into the password hash, such as the server name. In that way, a user with the password "albacruft" on server 1 would have a different hashed password on server 2, even if she used the same password on both. If someone were to steal server 1's database, they could impersonate her on server 1. But since the hash would be different on server 2, someone would not be able to impersonate her on server 2, unless they did a dictionary attack and discovered her actual password.

26.11 HMAC RATHER THAN SIMPLE MD

Folklore today says that in order to do a keyed cryptographic hash, you should use HMAC (see §5.7 *HMAC*). It is computationally slower than, say, doing hash(*message*|*key*). But it is possible, as we explain in §5.2.2 *Computing a MAC with a Hash*, to do the keyed hash incorrectly. If you do hash(*key*|*message*) and divulge the entire hash, then it is possible for someone who sees the message and the entire keyed hash to append to the message and generate a new keyed hash, even without knowing the key with which the hash is produced. With HMAC this attack is impossible. There are other ways of avoiding that attack that are simpler and faster and likely to be as secure, for instance only divulging half the hash (see §5.2.2 *Computing a MAC with a Hash*). But as described in §5.7 *HMAC*, HMAC comes with a proof, so it is gaining popularity despite its performance disadvantage.

26.12 KEY EXPANSION

Key expansion is the technique of using a small number of random bits as a seed and from it deriving lots of bits of keys. For instance, from a 128-bit random seed, you might want to derive 128-bit encryption keys and 128-bit integrity keys in each direction. Or you might want to periodically do key rollover (without PFS) lots of times, using the same seed.

The alternative to key expansion is obtaining independent random numbers for each key. It might be expensive to obtain that many random bits. For instance, if the random number is sent encrypted with the other side's public key, it is convenient to limit the size of the random number to fit within an RSA block. And if an unpredictably many future keys also need to be derived from the same keying material, you wouldn't know how large a random number you'd need.

If the random number is sufficiently large (say 80 bits or more), then it can be used as the seed for an unlimited number of keys. It is important to do this in such a way that divulging one key does not compromise other keys. So each key is usually derived from the random number seed and some other information (such as a key version number or timestamp), using a one-way function.

The random number from which all other keys are derived is often known as the **master key** or **key seed**.

In many protocols, creating and/or communicating the initial secret is expensive. For instance, in SSL/TLS it involves sending something encrypted with the other side's public key, and decrypting it will therefore be expensive. Another example is IPsec, in which creating the initial secret involves a Diffie-Hellman exchange, which is expensive for both sides. Reusing the original secret for generating new keys will be less expensive than creating and sending a new random seed.

In the cryptography community, companies with outrageous claims and bogus security products are known as "snake-oil" companies. A common claim made by the snake-oil marketeers is that the company's algorithm uses keys of some huge size, perhaps millions of bits, and that that makes them much more secure than, say, the 128-bit keys used by other companies. (And they usually have a "patented", proprietary encryption scheme.) There are many aspects of such a statement that should raise the suspicion that the claims are snake-oil. Often the million-bit key is generated from a very small seed, perhaps 32 bits, which through key expansion turns into many bits. So even though the key used might be a million bits, if the seed from which it is computed is 32 bits, then the key itself is equivalent to a 32-bit key.

26.13 Randomly Chosen IVs

Folklore says that the IV should not be something like a sequence number in which there would be a very small hamming distance (the number of bit positions in which one IV differs from the other) between IVs. The reason is that the IV gets ⊕'d with the first block of plaintext, and then encrypted. It is common for the first block of plaintext to be highly non-random, for instance being the length of the message. Therefore, if the IVs only differ in a few bit positions, it becomes very likely that an IV ⊕ 'd with its first plaintext block will equal a different IV ⊕ 'd with its corresponding first plaintext block. This will be readily observable, since the first ciphertext block of the two messages will be equal. Especially if the IVs are known, this leaks information about what the two plaintext blocks are (one is, say, the same as the other except for the low-order bit).

If the IVs are randomly chosen, then it is highly unlikely that the ⊕ of any IV with its plaintext will equal the ⊕ of a different IV with its plaintext.

Although folklore says that the IVs should be randomly chosen, they don't really need to be random or unpredictable. They just need to be very different from each other. A strategy such as using a hash of a sequence number will work.

26.14 USE OF NONCES IN PROTOCOLS

Nonces are values that should be unique to a particular running of the protocol. Protocols use nonces as challenges (Bob gives Alice a challenge, and she proves she knows her secret by returning a function of the challenge and her secret), or perhaps as one of the inputs into the session key derived from the exchange. Some protocols would be insecure if the nonces were predictable, whereas other protocols only require that the nonce be unique, and a sequence number would be perfectly secure. If you don't want to bother analyzing whether your protocol requires unpredictable nonces, it is usually safest to generate them randomly.

See §11.5 *Nonce Types* for examples of both types of protocol (those that require unpredictable nonces and those that do not). It has become fashionable to put lots of nonces into protocols, and furthermore, to require them all to be randomly chosen. For instance, IKE has nonces (which it says must be randomly chosen) as well as session identifiers (which it calls cookies and also requires to be randomly chosen), as well as message IDs (which should be sequence numbers, but IKE also requires them to be randomly chosen because randomly chosen has to be more secure, right?). All these values get thrown into the hash for the key, along with the Diffie-Hellman parameters which the spec says should also be unique for each session and of course must be randomly chosen.

In fact, if the Diffie-Hellman values are unique for each exchange there is no need for the nonces in IKE at all. And the message IDs are *more* secure if they are a sequence number rather than a randomly chosen value. The message IDs are used to recognize replays, so therefore sequence numbers work much better. With randomly chosen message IDs, you'd have to remember every message ID you'd ever seen or generated. IKE uses the same cryptographic keys in both directions, so if you don't remember a message ID you received, you will not recognize a replay of that message as a replay, and if you don't remember a message ID you generated, you will be vulnerable to a reflection attack.

26.15 DON'T LET ENCRYPTED DATA BEGIN WITH A CONSTANT

Folklore says you shouldn't let encrypted data begin with a constant. This worry is due to the fact that if there is no IV *and* the first block of data is a constant, *and* the key is short (perhaps 56 bits), then it would be possible to build a table mapping that known constant plaintext to its ciphertext with all possible keys. This is not a problem if there is an IV, or the key is of adequate length.

26.16 DON'T LET ENCRYPTED DATA BEGIN WITH A PREDICTABLE VALUE

Folklore also says to avoid having the beginning of your data being a predictable value such as a sequence number. The worry here is that if you were doing a brute-force attack, you'd be able to easily recognize the plaintext. Sometimes data is sufficiently recognizable that avoiding starting with a predictable value will not help, for instance, if the data is 7-bit ASCII with parity.

26.17 COMPRESS DATA BEFORE ENCRYPTING IT

Obviously, compressing data saves bandwidth, though this advantage might be offset by the disadvantage of additional computation to compress at the source and decompress at the destination. On the other hand, compression might provide a computation benefit because there are fewer octets to encrypt/decrypt after the data has been compressed. On the third hand ($we_{1,2,3}$ have 6 hands between us), there might be hardware support for the encryption algorithm, but no hardware support for the compression algorithm.

If encryption is used, then compression must occur before the data is encrypted. This is because compression algorithms depend on the data being somewhat predictable. Encrypted data looks random and therefore would not compress.

Another reason cryptographers think compression is a good idea is that they assume a brute-force attacker would have a harder time recognizing correct compressed data after a trial decryption. One would think that a perfect compression algorithm would yield data that was harder to recognize because it would have less redundancy than the uncompressed data. However, in practice, most compression algorithms make compressed data *easier* to recognize than the original plaintext. Some compression algorithms start with a fixed header. For others there are sequences that are detectably illegal by the decompression algorithm. If the compression algorithm is known, doing the extra decompression step should add negligible computation load on the attacker, because a good compression algorithm can be decompressed quickly.

26.18 DON'T DO ENCRYPTION ONLY

It is common for people to assume that if something is encrypted, it's also integrity protected. But there are many attacks that can occur if encryption is used without integrity protection.

For instance, a common form of encryption is RC4, which generates a pseudorandom stream of bits that is ⊕'d with the plaintext. Imagine a secret-key-based network security system in which a magic box, let's call it MB, is configured with user secrets, and shares a secret key with each server that a user might log into. Alice connects to server Bob, claiming to be Alice. Bob sends Alice a challenge and gets her response, and then sends to MB, over the encrypted tunnel, "Alice sent Z to challenge X." MB responds either "authentication success" or "authentication failure".

The problem with this protocol is that if Trudy would like to impersonate Alice, and can act as a man-in-the-middle between MB and Bob, she can fool Bob by doing the following:

- Connect to Bob, claiming to be Alice.
- Bob will send her challenge X.
- Trudy responds with anything, say Y. She knows this is almost certainly the wrong answer.
- Bob sends to MB "Alice sent Y to challenge X."
- MB will almost certainly respond "authentication failure".
- Trudy captures the ciphertext stream from MB to Bob, ⊕s it with the string "authentication failure", and then ⊕s the result with "authentication success", and transmits that to Bob.
- Bob will ⊕ what he receives with the RC4 stream to obtain the string "authentication success" and believe Trudy is Alice.

26.19 AVOIDING WEAK KEYS

As described in §3.3.6 *Weak and Semi-Weak Keys*, some algorithms (like DES) have some keys that are weak, in the sense that ciphertext encrypted with those keys would be easier to cryptanalyze. Folklore says that when choosing an encryption key, care should be taken to avoid choosing one of the weak keys. Having any weak keys was considered a disadvantage of a cryptographic algorithm for the purpose of finding reasons for choosing among the AES contenders.

In practice, as long as the probability of choosing a weak key is vanishingly small (16 out of 2^{56} in the case of DES), weak keys are really not a problem. In fact, even if a cryptographic algorithm had no weak keys in the sense that the cryptographic community defines weak keys, in practice any key which happens to be one of the first searched by a brute-force attacker would be dangerous to use. For instance, if brute force attackers tend to search the key space sequentially from the bottom, then it would be inadvisable to choose a numerically small key.

26.20 Minimal vs. Redundant Designs

Some protocols are designed so minimally that everything in them is essential. If you cut corners anywhere and don't follow the spec carefully, you will wind up with vulnerabilities. In contrast, it has become fashionable to over-engineer protocols, in the sense of accomplishing what is needed for security several different ways, when in fact $n-1$ of those ways are unnecessary as long as any one of them are done. An example is throwing in lots of nonces and other variables, each required to be random, whereas for security only one of them would be required to be random. We believe this fashion of redundancy is a dangerous trend, since the protocols become much more difficult to understand. And as the person writing the code for choosing the nonce notices that there is no reason for the nonce to be random, and therefore doesn't bother, and the person writing the code for a different variable notices that it doesn't need to be random (because the nonce will be), you wind up likely to have a protocol with flaws. It's OK to cut n-1 corners, but not n corners. IKE is an excellent example of something that is so redundant and complex that the protocol design, as well as implementations based on it, wound up with security flaws.

26.21 Overestimate the Size of Key

U.S. law enforcement was always trying to find the "right" key size, big enough to be "secure enough" but small enough that it would be breakable, if necessary, by law enforcement. Of course, such a key size couldn't be really secure, because "secure" means nobody, including them, would be able to break it. Anyway, the assumption was that they were smarter, or had more computation power, than the bad guys from whom you were trying to protect yourself. Even if that were true (e.g., that law enforcement had ten times as much computation power as organized crime), given that computers keep getting faster and encrypted data often needs to be protected for many years, something breakable by law enforcement today would be breakable by organized crime in a few years. But it's also absurd to assume that the bad guys (whoever they are) would have significantly less computation power at their disposal than law enforcement. So it's dangerous to try to pick the smallest "sufficiently secure" key size. It's better to pick the largest you are willing to live with in terms of performance, or pick the size that you think is definitely going to be secure for ten years and double it just to be safe. This practice also makes it less likely that in a few years you'll have to go through the annoyance of reconfiguring everything to use larger keys.

26.22 HARDWARE RANDOM NUMBER GENERATORS

Generating random numbers is tricky and there have been many examples of implementations that were insecure because of faulty random number generators. As a result, many people wish that computers would include a source of true randomness, which can be done at the hardware level by measuring noise of some sort. Indeed, it would be convenient and enhance security to have a hardware source of random numbers, but instead of depending on it as the sole source of randomness, it should be used to enhance other forms. However, suppose an organization was designing a hardware random number generator that was likely to become widely deployed. It would be very tempting to purposely (and secretly) design it so that it generated predictable numbers, but only predictable to the organization that designed the chip. It would be difficult or impossible for anyone to detect that this was done. For instance, each chip could be initialized with a true random 128-bit number as the first 128 bits of output, and each subsequent 128 bits of output could be computed as the previous 128 bits of output hashed with a large secret known only to the organization that designed and built the chips. Assuming the hash was good, the output would be indistinguishable from truly random. It would be more difficult to embed such a trap in software, since it is more easily reverse engineered.

Even if a hardware random number generator might have such a trap, it is still useful, and can be used in such a way that would foil even the organization that embedded the trap. The way it should be used is to enhance any other scheme for generating random numbers. So random numbers should be generated as they would be without the chip (for instance, using mouse and keyboard inputs and low-order bits of a fine-granularity clock). But the output of the hardware random number generator should also be hashed into the random number calculation.

26.23 TIMING ATTACKS

People want smart cards to be tamper proof, with no way of being able to obtain the private key from the card. An interesting attack that has been found on smart cards to gain information about the key is to observe how long it takes to do various operations on various types of input. This yields information such as how many 1 bits are in the exponent, because exponentiation takes longer when the exponent has a lot of 1's. Similarly, the smart card might use a different amount of power when it is exponentiating than when it is reducing mod *n*, so by measuring the power used, and knowing, for various inputs, when that input would need to be reduced given different sized exponents, more information about that smart card's private key can be obtained.

To defend against such attacks, it is possible to do things that make it harder for the system using the smart card to control what operations the smart card is doing. Instead of just exponentiating the supplied number, for example, the smart card could multiply the supplied number by a randomly chosen number, do the exponentiation, and then divide by the exponentiated random number. Techniques like this either add noise to the information returned by the timing attack or pad things out to a fixed value. The techniques usually come with some performance cost.

Some people misapply this smart card protection to servers speaking across a network, and attempt to yield no timing information about the exponent by introducing a random amount of delay when the server performs private key operations. This is usually unnecessary since any timing differences based on computation with a particular exponent would be dwarfed by network delays and delays due to server loading. There are some operations for which computation might be significant compared to the other delays. One example is the computation delays in PDM (see §12.3 *Strong Password Protocols*) of computing a safe prime from the user's password. This can be avoided by having the workstation compute the prime before it connects to the server, so an observer on the network cannot tell how long the workstation took to compute the prime.

A related problem in the network case is traffic analysis. For instance, as shown in SONG01, information can be gleaned by observing the pattern of packets. One example is being able to see how many characters are in a user's password, since some implementations would send a separate packet for each character typed. (To a computer, the delays between character strokes are really long: "Geesh. That human is sure a slow input device. I'm certainly not waiting around for it to type another character!")

26.24 PUT CHECKSUMS AT THE END OF DATA

Some protocols use a format for integrity-protected data where the integrity check is before the data, or possibly even in the middle of the data. It is better instead to have the integrity check at the end (as is done in ESP). If the integrity check is at the end, then it is possible to be computing it while transmitting the data; and then just append the computed integrity check at the end. The alternative, where the integrity check comes before the data (as is done in AH), requires the data to be buffered on output until the integrity check is computed and tacked onto the beginning. This adds delay and complexity. This rule is mainly for transmitted data. For received data, most likely it would be undesirable to act on the data before the integrity check is verified, so the data would need to be buffered no matter where the integrity check was stored.

Having the integrity check in the middle of the data (as is done in IKE) complicates both the specification and the implementation. Space for the integrity check must be provided, with the field set to zero, and then the integrity check calculated and stored into the field. On receipt, the integrity check must be copied to some other location, and then zeroed in its location in the message, so that the integrity check can be verified.

Especially complex is when an integrity check is computed based on selected fields, especially when some are optional and ordering is not strictly specified. The integrity check must be computed identically by the generator and verifier of the check.

26.25 FORWARD COMPATIBILITY

History shows that protocols evolve. It is important to design a protocol in such a way that new capabilities can be added. This is a desirable property of any sort of protocol, not just security protocols. There are some special security considerations in evolving protocols, such as preventing an active attacker from tricking two parties into using an older, possibly less secure version of the protocol.

26.25.1 Options

It is useful to allow new fields to be added to messages in future versions of the protocol. Sometimes these fields can be ignored by implementations that don't support them. Sometimes a packet with an unsupported option should be dropped. In order to make it possible for an implementation that does not recognize an option to skip over it and parse the rest of the message, it is essential that there be some way to know where the option ends. There are two techniques:

- Having a special marker at the end of the option. This tends to be computation-intensive, since the implementation must read all the option data as it searches for the end marker.

- TLV encoding, which means each option starts with a TYPE field indicating the type of option, a LENGTH field indicating the length of the data in this option, and a VALUE field, which gives option-specific information.

TLV encoding is more common because it is more efficient. However, the "L" must always be present, and in the same units, in order for implementations to be able to skip unknown options. Sometimes protocol designers who don't quite understand the concept of TLV encoding do clever things like notice that the option they are defining is fixed length, so they don't need the LENGTH field. Or that one option might be expressed in different units. For instance, although AH (see §17.3 *AH (Authentication Header)* is designed to look like an IPv6 extension header, its length is expressed in units of 32-bit words, when all the other IPv6 options are expressed in units of 64-bit words.

It is also useful to be able to add some options which should simply be skipped over by an implementation that does not support it, and to add other options which must be understood or else the packet must be dropped. But if an implementation does not recognize the option, how would it know whether it could be safely ignored or not? There are several possible solutions. One is to have a flag in the option header known as the **critical bit**, which if not set on an unknown option, indicates the option can simply be skipped over and ignored. Another possibility is to reserve some of the type numbers for critical options, and some of them for noncritical options (those that can be safely skipped if unrecognized).

26.25.2 Version Numbers

A lot of protocols have a field for version number, but don't specify what to do with it. IKE and SSL are typical culprits. The purpose of a version number field is to allow the protocol to change in the future without confusing old implementations. One way of doing this without a version number is to declare the modified protocol to be a "new protocol", which would then need a different multiplexor value (a different TCP port for instance). With a version number, you can keep the same multiplexor value, but there have to be rules about handling version numbers so that an old implementation won't be confused by a redesigned packet format.

26.25.2.1 Version Number Field Must Not Move

If versions are to be differentiated based on a version number field, then *the version number field must always be in the same place in the message*. Although this might seem obvious, when SSL was redesigned to be version 3, the version number field was moved! Luckily, there is a way to recognize which version an SSL message is (in version 2's client hello message, the first octet will be 128, and in version 3's client hello message, the first octet will be something between 20 and 23).

26.25.2.2 Negotiating Highest Version Supported

Typically, when there is a new version of a protocol, the new implementations support both versions for some time. If you support both versions, how do you know what version to speak when talking to another node? Presumably the newer version is superior for some reason. So you typically first attempt to talk with the newer version, and if that fails, you attempt again with the older version.

With this strategy it is important to make sure that two nodes that are both capable of speaking the new version wind up speaking the new version, and not getting fooled into speaking the older version because of lost messages or active attackers sending, deleting, or modifying messages. Why would an active attacker care enough to trick two nodes into speaking an earlier version of the protocol? Perhaps the newer version is more secure, or has features that the attacker would prefer the nodes not be able to use. (We'd hope there was *some* benefit to be gained by having designed a new version of the protocol!)

The right thing to do if you see a message with a higher version number than you support is to drop the message and send an error report to the other side indicating you don't support that version. But there will be no way for that error message to be cryptographically integrity-protected since the protocol has not been able to negotiate a key. So unless care is taken, nodes could be tricked into speaking the older version if an active attacker or network flakiness deleted the message of the initial attempt, or an attacker sent an error: unsupported version number message.

One method of ensuring that two nodes don't get tricked into talking an older version is to have two version numbers in the packet. One would be the version number of the packet. The other would be the highest version the sender supports. But a single bit suffices, indicating that the sender can support a higher version number than the message indicates. If you establish a connection with someone, using version *n*, and you support something higher than *n*, and you receive authenticated messages with the HIGHER VERSION NUMBER SUPPORTED flag, then you can attempt to reconnect with a higher version number.

26.25.2.3 Minor Version Number Field

Another area in which protocol designers get confused is the proper use of a MINOR VERSION NUMBER field. Why should there be both MAJOR VERSION NUMBER and MINOR VERSION NUMBER fields? The proper use of a minor version number is to indicate new capabilities that are backward compatible. The major version number should change if the protocol is incompatible. The minor version number is informational only. If the node you are talking to indicates it is version 4.7 (where 4 is the major version number and 7 is the minor version), and you are version 4.3, then you ignore the minor version number. But the version 4.7 node might use it to know that there are certain fields you wouldn't support, so it won't send them.

For instance, ISAKMP handles minor version numbers incorrectly. It has an 8-bit VERSION NUMBER field, split into 4 bits for MAJOR VERSION, and 4 bits for MINOR VERSION. The specification says you should reject a message if the major version is higher, or if the major versions are the same and the minor version is higher than yours. So the result is exactly the same as if it was just an 8-bit field, but it's more complicated to understand and will run out of numbers more quickly than an 8-bit field since there are only 16 major version numbers. (Unless someone worries about numbers getting used up and mandates that you must use up all the minor version numbers before you're allowed to bump the major version number.)

Most likely the confusion about the proper use of the minor version number is because software releases have major and minor version numbers, and the choice as to which to increment is a marketing decision.

26.25.3 Vendor Options

Another type of option is a vendor-defined option. The only difference between a vendor-defined option and the type of option we described in §26.25.1 *Options* is that a vendor-defined option might not be able to obtain one of the compact T values for specifying that option in TLV encoding. The organization that assigns T values might require that the option be publicly documented in order to obtain a number, and the vendor might want to keep their use proprietary. Or the vendor might want to experiment with the option before bothering to request a number. Or the vendor might fail to convince a standards organization to adopt the option, and T values might only be given to options that have been standardized.

If an option does not have one of the compact assigned T values, there must be a way for it to be assigned a unique number. ASN.1 defines a way to obtain OIDs, but OIDs are variable length. This complicates encoding of a vendor option. IKE encodes each vendor option in an explicit envelope with a type and length. The type code in the envelope is simply "vendor option" (i.e., the same for all vendor options). Inside the envelope is the specific vendor option data, and it is up to the vendor to define an encoding. Ideally the encoding is such that there is no potential ambiguity between different vendors' vendor options. This could be done by using an OID, or defining the first 16 octets to be a hash of information guaranteed to be unique, such as the vendor name, location, name of the capability, etc.

26.26 NEGOTIATING PARAMETERS

It is common today for security protocols to start out by negotiating which cryptographic algorithms they will use. It would certainly be simpler if the protocol specified the algorithms. So why all the complexity of negotiating cryptographic algorithms?

- There might be reasons to support different algorithms and trade off performance versus strength. Perhaps the application, knowing that the data was particularly sensitive, might negotiate a particularly strong suite of crypto.

- In order for domestic implementations capable of strong crypto to interwork with exported implementations, it was necessary to negotiate crypto, in order to use strong crypto when legal and weak crypto otherwise.
- A crypto algorithm might get broken. Therefore, if implementations support several cryptographic algorithms, removing a broken algorithm requires only a configuration change (stop using that algorithm) rather than new code to support a new algorithm.
- Some countries, companies, or governments, might want to use their own cryptographic algorithms (this is sometimes known as **vanity crypto**), in addition to being able to interwork with standard implementations.

Negotiation of cryptographic algorithms can either be done by defining suites of algorithms (as is done in SSL/TLS), or by individually negotiating choices for each specific algorithm (encryption, integrity, signature,...). The individual algorithms are not necessarily mix-and-match. Some algorithms can only be used with specific other algorithms, for instance DSS requires SHA-1 as the hash. Proposing each combination individually can lead to an exponential explosion of suite proposals, as in ISAKMP/IKE (see §18.5.5 *Negotiating Cryptographic Parameters*).

Care must be taken that an active attacker cannot trick Alice and Bob into talking weaker crypto. This is usually done by having Alice and Bob sign or otherwise integrity-protect the negotiation messages in order to detect tampering.

26.27 HOMEWORK

1. Suppose you were able to observe ciphertext that you knew had been encrypted in CBC mode, and you saw that two ciphertext blocks, say c_2 and c_5, were equal. Why would this leak information? (Hint: look at Figure 4-5 and compare $c_1 \oplus c_4$ with $m_2 \oplus m_5$. What would happen if you knew one of the plaintexts, say m_2?)
2. Suppose Alice and Bob negotiate a 64-bit key, and use the low-order 40 bits of it for encryption (for export reasons), and use the entire 64 bits for integrity protection. How much work would it be to brute-force break the key and construct a forged encrypted message using that key?
3. Consider the following protocol. Must the challenge be unpredictable, or is it sufficient to ensure Bob never chooses the same challenge twice, for instance, by using a sequence number?

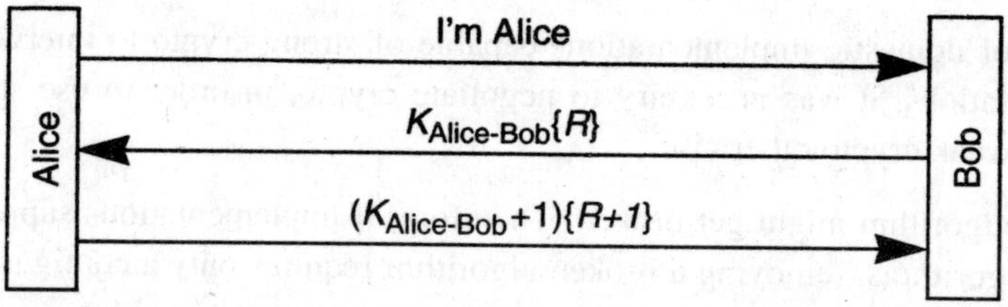

4. As described in §26.3.1 *The Splicing Attack*, if a C-D conversation is being multiplexed over the same encryption-only tunnel as an A-B conversation, C and D can collude with a splicing attack in order to decrypt the A-B traffic. Suppose encryption is CBC with 64-bit blocks. Assume that the first 16 octets of the plaintext packet consist of the source and destination address, and the remainder of the packet is data. The splicing attack will allow D to see all but the first block of data, which will be garbled because of the splice. Explain why the first block will be garbled, and why subsequent blocks will not be. How can C create the ciphertext so that D will receive all of the data? (Hint: assume that it is legal to create a larger ciphertext packet than the one recorded.)

BIBLIOGRAPHY

ALAG93 Alagappan, K., *Telnet Authentication: SPX*, RFC 1412, January 1993.

BALE85 Balenson, D., "Automated Distribution of Cryptographic Keys Using the Financial Institution Key Management Standard", *IEEE Communications*, Vol. 23 #9, September 1985, pp. 41–46.

BALE93 Balenson, D., *Privacy Enhancement for Internet Electronic Mail: Part III: Algorithms, Modes, and Identifiers*, RFC 1423, February 1993.

BELL74 Bell, D. E. and LaPadula, L. J., *Secure Computer Systems: Mathematical Foundations and Model*, M74-244, Mitre Corp., October 1974.

BELL90 Bellovin, S. M. and Merritt, M., "Limitations of the Kerberos Authentication System", *Computer Communications Review*, Vol. 20 #5, October 1990, pp. 119–132.

BELL92a Bellovin, S. M. and Merritt, M., "Encrypted Key Exchange: Password-Based Protocols Secure Against Dictionary Attacks", *Proceedings of the IEEE Computer Society Symposium on Research in Security and Privacy*, May 1992, pp. 72–84.

BELL92b Bellovin, S. M., "There Be Dragons", *UNIX Security Symposium III*, Baltimore, MD, September 1992, pp. 1–16.

BELL93 Bellovin, S. M. and Meritt, M., "Augmented Encrypted Key Exchange", *Proceedings of the First ACM Conference on Computer and Communications Security*, November 1993, pp. 244–250.

BELL94 Bellare, M. and Rogaway, P., "Optimal Asymmetric Encryption", *Advances in Cryptology—Eurocrypt '94*, 1994.

BIBA77 Biba, K. J., *Integrity Considerations for Secure Computer Systems*, ESD-TR-76-372, USAF Electronic Systems Division, April 1977.

BIHA91 Biham, E., and Shamir, A., "Differential Cryptanalysis of DES-like Cryptosystems", *Journal of Cryptology*, Vol. 4 #1, 1991, pp. 3–72.

BIHA92 Biham, E., and Shamir, A., "Differential Cryptanalysis of Snefru, Khafre, REDOC-II, LOCI, and Lucifer", *Advances in Cryptology—CRYPTO '91 Proceedings*, Springer-Verlag, 1992.

BIHA93 Biham, E., and Shamir, A., "Differential Cryptanalysis of the Full 16-Round DES", *Advances in Cryptology—CRYPTO '92 Proceedings*, Springer-Verlag, 1993.

BIRD93 Bird, R., Gopal, I., Herzberg, A., Janson, P., Kutten, S., Molva, R., and Yung, M., "Systematic Design of a Family of Attack-Resistant Authentication Protocols", *IEEE Journal on Selected Areas in Communications*, Vol. 11 #5, June 1993, pp. 679–693.

BIRD95 Bird, R., Gopal, I., Herzberg, A., Janson, P., Kutten, S., Molva, R., and Yung, M., "The KryptoKnight Family of Light-Weight Protocols for Authentication and Key Distribution", *IEEE Transactions on Networking*, 1995.

BIRR82 Birrell, A., Needham, R., and Schroeder, M., "Grapevine: An Exercise in Distributed Computing", *Communications of the ACM*, Vol. 25 #4, April 1982.

BIRR84 Birrell, A. D., *Secure Communication Using Remote Procedure Calls*, CSL-TR 84-2, Xerox Corporation, Palo Alto Research Center, September 1984.

BIRR86 Birrell, A. D., Lampson, B. W., Needham, R. M., and Schroeder, M. D., "A Global Authentication Service without Global Trust", *Proceedings of the 1986 IEEE Symposium on Security and Privacy*, IEEE Computer Society Press, April 1986, pp. 223–230.

BLAZ94 Blaze, M., "Protocol Failure in the Escrowed Encryption Standard", *Proceedings of the Second ACM Conference on Computer and Communications Security*, November 1994.

BLEI98 Bleichenbacher, D., "Chosen Ciphertext Attacks against Protocols Based on RSA Encryption Standard PKCS #1", *Advances in Cryptology—CRYPTO '98*, 1998.

BLUM86 Blum, L., Blum, M., and Shub, M., "A Simple Unpredictable Pseudo-Random Number Generator", *SIAM Journal on Computing*, Vol. 15 #2, 1986.

BORM93a Borman, D., *Telnet Authentication Option*, RFC 1416, February 1993.

BORM93b Borman, D., *Telnet Authentication: Kerberos Version 4*, RFC 1411, January 1993.

BRAD89 Braden, R., *Requirements for Internet Hosts—Communications Layers*, RFC 1122, October 1989.

BRAD94 Braden, R., Clark, D., Crocker, S., and Huitema, C., *Report of IAB Workshop on Security in the Internet Architecture*, RFC 1636, February 1994.

BURR90 Burrows, M., Abadi, M., and Needham, R. M., "A Logic of Authentication", *ACM Transactions on Computer Systems*, Vol. 8 #1, February 1990, pp. 18–36.

CHES94 Cheswick, W., and Bellovin, S., *Firewalls and Internet Security: Repelling the Wily Hacker*, Addison-Wesley, 1994.

COME00 Comer, D., *Internetworking with TCP/IP: Principles, Protocols, and Architecture*, Prentice Hall, 2000.

COOP89 Cooper, J. A., *Computer and Communications Security: Strategies for the 1990s*, McGraw-Hill, 1989.

CORM91 Corman, Leiserson, and Rivest, *Introduction to Algorithms*, MIT Press & McGraw-Hill, 1991.

CROC82 Crocker, D., *Standard for the Format of ARPA Internet Text Messages*, RFC 822, August 1982.

DAEM02 Daemen, J., and Rijmen, V., *The Design of Rijndael: AES—The Advanced Encryption Standard*, Springer-Verlag, 2002

DATA77 *Data Encryption Standard*, FIPS PUB 46, National Bureau of Standards, U.S. Department of Commerce, January 1977.

DAVI78 Davis, R. M., "The Data Encryption Standard in Perspective", *IEEE Communications Society Magazine*, Vol. 16 #6, 1978, pp. 5–9.

DAVI84a Davies, D. W. and Price, W. L., *Security for Computer Networks*, John Wiley and Sons, 1984.

DAVI84b Davis, D., Ihaka, R., and Fenstermacher, P., "Cryptographic Randomness from Air Turbulence in Disk Drives", *Advances in Cryptology—Crypto '94*, Springer-Verlag Lecture Notes in Computer Science #839, 1984.

DENB89 Den Boer, B., "Cryptanalysis of FEAL", *Advances in Cryptology—Eurocrypt 88*, Lecture Notes in Computer Science, Vol. 330, Springer-Verlag, 1989.

DENB92 Den Boer, B. and Bosselaers, A., "An Attack on the Last Two Rounds of MD4", *Advances in Cryptology—Crypto '91 Proceedings*, Springer-Verlag, 1992, pp. 194–203.

DENN76 Denning, Dorothy E. R., "A Lattice Model of Secure Information Flow", *Communications of the ACM*, Vol. 19 #5, May 1976, pp. 236–243.

DENN81 Denning, D. E., and Sacco, G. M., "Timestamps in Key Distribution Protocols", *Communications of the ACM*, Vol. 24 #8, August 1981, pp. 533–536.

DENN82 Denning, Dorothy E. R., *Cryptography and Data Security*, Addison-Wesley, 1982.

DENN90 Denning, P. (ed)., *Computers Under Attack: Intruders, Worms, and Viruses*, ACM Press/Addison-Wesley, 1990.

DEPA85 *Department of Defense (Dod) Trusted Computer System Evaluation Criteria (TCSEC)*, [Orange Book], DoD 5200.28-STD, December 1985.

DES81 *DES Modes of Operation*, FIPS PUB 81, National Bureau of Standards, U.S. Department of Commerce, 1981.

DESM86 Desmedt, Y. and Odlyzko, A. M., "A Chosen Text Attack on the RSA Cryptosystem and Some Discrete Logarithm Schemes", *Advances in Cryptology—CRYPTO '85 Proceedings*, Vol. 218 of Lecture Notes in Computer Science, Springer-Verlag, 1986, pp. 516–521.

DIFF76a Diffie, W. and Hellman, M. E., "A Critique of the Proposed Data Encryption Standard", *Communications of the ACM*, Vol. 19 #3, 1976, pp. 164–165.

DIFF76b Diffie, W. and Hellman, M. E., "New Directions in Cryptography", *IEEE Transactions on Information Theory*, Vol. 22 #6, 1976, pp. 644–654.

DIFF77 Diffie, W. and Hellman, M. E., "Exhaustive Cryptanalysis of the NBS Data Encryption Standard", *Computer*, Vol. 10 #6, 1977, pp. 74–84.

DIFF79 Diffie, W. and Hellman, M. E., "Privacy and Authentication: An Introduction to Cryptography", *Proceedings of the IEEE*, Vol. 67 #3, March 1979, pp. 397–427.

DIFF88 Diffie, W., "The First Ten Years of Public-Key Cryptography", *Proceedings of the IEEE*, Vol. 7 #5, May 1988, pp. 560–577.

DIRE88 *The Directory—Authentication Framework*, CCITT Recommendation X.509, 1988.

EAST94 Eastlake, D., Crocker, S., and Schiller, J., *Randomness Requirements for Security*, Internet RFC 1750, December 1994.

EBER92 Eberle, H., *A High-speed DES Implementation for Network Applications*, Digital Systems Research Center, Technical Report #90, September 1992.

EFF98 Electronic Frontier Foundation, *Cracking DES: Secrets of Encryption Research, Wiretap Politics & Chip Design*, Gilmore, J. editor, O'Reilly, 1998.

ELGA85 ElGamal, T., "A Public Key Cryptosystem and a Signature Scheme Based on Discrete Logarithms", *IEEE Transactions on Information Theory*, Vol. 31, 1985, pp. 469–472.

FARR91 Farrow, R., *UNIX System Security: How to Protect Your Data and Prevent Intruders*, Addison-Wesley, 1991.

FEIG87 Feige, U., Fiat, A., and Shamir, A., "Zero-Knowledge Proofs of Identity", *Proceedings of the ACM Symposium on the Theory of Computing*, ACM Press, 1987, pp. 210–217.

FEIS73 Feistel, H., "Cryptography and Computer Privacy", *Scientific American*, May 1973.

FELD89 Feldmeier, D. C., and Karn, P. R., "UNIX Password Security—Ten Years Later", *Advances in Cryptology—CRYPTO '89 Proceedings*, Springer-Verlag, 1989.

FINA82 *Financial Institution Message Authentication*, American National Standard X9.9, American National Standards Institute, 1982.

FINA85 *Financial Institution Key Management (Wholesale)*, American National Standard X9.17, American National Standards Institute, 1985.

FORD94 Ford, W., *Computer Communications Security: Principles, Standard Protocols, and Techniques*, Prentice Hall, 1994.

FU01 Fu, K., Sit, E., Smith, K., and Feamster, N., "Dos and Don'ts of Client Authentication on the Web", *Usenix Security Conference*, 2001.

GAIN56 Gaines, H. F., *Cryptanalysis*, Dover, New York, 1956.

GALV93 Galvin, J. and McCloghrie, K., *Security Protocols for version 2 of the Simple Network Management Protocol (SNMPv2)*, RFC 1446, April 1993.

GARF95 Garfinkel, S., *PGP: Pretty Good Privacy*, O'Reilly, 1995.

GARF02 Garfinkel, S., *Web Security, Privacy & Commerce*, O'Reilly, 2002.

GASS76 Gasser, M., *A Random Word Generator for Pronounceable Passwords*, Mitre Corp, Bedford, Mass., Report MTR-3006, November 1976.

GASS88 Gasser, M., *Building a Secure Computer System*, Van Nostrand Reinhold, 1988.

GASS89 Gasser, M., Goldstein, A., Kaufman, C., and Lampson, B., "The Digital Distributed System Security Architecture", *Proceedings of the 12th National Computer Security Conference*, NIST/NCSC, October 1989, pp. 305–319.

GASS90 Gasser, M., McDermott, E., "An Architecture for Practical Delegation in a Distributed System", *1990 Symposium on Security and Privacy.*

GOLD96 Goldberg, I., and Wagner, D., "Randomness and the Netscape Browser", *Dr. Dobb's Journal*, January 1996.

GUIL88 Guillou, L., and Quisquater, J., "A Practical Zero-Knowledge Protocol Fitted to Security Microprocessor Minimizing Both Transmission and Memory", *Advances in Cryptology—EUROCRYPT '88*, Springer-Verlag, 1988.

HAPG73 Hapgood, F., "The Computer Hackers", *Harvard Magazine*, October 1973, pp. 26–29 and 46.

HAUS94 Hauser, R., Janson, P., Molva, R., Tsudik, G., and Van Herreweghen, E., "Robust and Secure Password/Key Change Method", *Proc. of the Third European Symposium on Research in Computer Security (ESORICS)*, Lecture Notes in Computer Science, Springer-Verlag, November 1994, pp. 107–122..

HELL78 Hellman, M. E., "An Overview of Public-Key Cryptography", *IEEE Transactions on Communications*, Vol. 16 #6, November 1978, pp. 24–32.

HELL79 Hellman, M. E., "DES Will Be Totally Insecure within Ten Years", *IEEE Spectrum*, Vol. 16, 1979, pp. 32–39.

HELL81 Hellman, M. E., and Merkle, R. C., "On the Security of Multiple Encryption", *Communications of the ACM*, Vol. 24, 1981, pp. 465–467.

HOLB91 Holbrook, J. and Reynolds, J., *Site Security Handbook*, RFC 1244, July 1991.

ISO87 ISO/IEC 8825: *Information Technology—Open Systems Interconnection—Specification of ASN.1 Encoding Rules*, 1987. (Also ITU-T X.690 series Recommendations).

ISO97 ISO/IEC 9594-8:1997 *Information Technology—Open Systems Interconnection—The Directory—Authentication Framework*, 1997.

JABL96 Jablon, D., "Strong Password-Only Authenticated Key Exchange", *Computer Communication Review*, Vol. 26, no. 5, ACM SIGCOMM, October 1996, pp. 5–26.

JABL97 Jablon, D., "Extended Password Key Exchange Protocols Immune to Dictionary Attacks", *Proceedings of the Sixth Workshop on Enabling Technologies: Infrastructure for Collaborative Enterprises (WET–ICE '97)*, IEEE Computer Society, June 1997, pp. 248–255.

JANS95 Janson, P. and G. Tsudik, G., "Secure and Minimal Protocols for Authenticated Key Distribution", *Computer Communications Journal*, 1995.

JUEL99 Juels, A. and Brainard, J., "Client Puzzles: A Cryptographic Countermeasure against Connection Depletion Attacks", NDSS Conference, 1999.

JUEN84 Jueneman, R. R., Matyas, S. M., and Meyer, C. H., "Message Authentication with Manipulation Detection Codes", *Proceedings of the 1983 Symposium on Security and Privacy*, IEEE Computer Society Press, 1984, pp. 33–54.

JUEN85 Jueneman, R. R., Matyas, S. M., and Meyer, C. H., "Message Authentication", *IEEE Communications*, Vol. 23 #9, September 1985, pp. 29–40.

KAHN67 Kahn, D., *The Codebreakers: The Story of Secret Writing*, Macmillan, 1967.

KALI88 Kaliski, B. S., Rivest, R., and Sherman, A., "Is the Data Encryption Standard a Group? (Results of Cycling Experiments on DES)", *Journal of Cryptology*, Vol. 1, 1988, pp. 3–36.

KALI92 Kaliski, B., *The MD2 Message-Digest Algorithm*, RFC 1319, April 1992.

KALI93 Kaliski, B., *Privacy Enhancement for Internet Electronic Mail: Part IV: Key Certification and Related Services*, RFC 1424, February 1993.

KAUF93 Kaufman, C., *DASS—Distributed Authentication Security Service*, RFC 1507, September 1993.

KENT93 Kent, S., *Privacy Enhancement for Internet Electronic Mail: Part II: Certificate-Based Key Management*, RFC 1422, February 1993.

KNUT69 Knuth, D. E., *The Art of Computer Programming: Seminumerical Algorithms*, Volume 2, Addison-Wesley, 1969.

KOHL93 Kohl, J. and Neuman, C., *The Kerberos Network Authentication Service (V5)*, RFC 1510, September 1993.

KONH81 Konheim, A., *Cryptography: A Primer*, John Wiley & Sons, 1981.

KRAW96 Krawczyk, H., "SKEME: A Versatile Secure Key Exchange Mechanism for Internet", NDSS, 1996.

KURO00 Kurose, J., and Ross, K., *Computer Networking: A Top-Down Approach Featuring the Internet*, Addison-Wesley, 2000.

LAMP73 Lampson, B., "A Note on the Confinement Problem", *Communications of the ACM*, Vol. 16 #10, October 1973, pp. 613–615.

LAMP74 Lampson, B., "Protection", *ACM Operating Systems Review*, Vol. 8 #1, January 1974, pp. 18–24.

LAMP81 Lamport, L., "Password Authentication with Insecure Communication", *Communications of the ACM*, Vol. 24 #11, November 1981, pp. 770–772.

LAMP91 Lampson, B., Abadi, M., Burrows, M., and Wobber, E., "Authentication in Distributed Systems: Theory and Practice", *Proceedings of the 13th ACM Symposium on Operating System Principles*, October 1991.

LEE94 Lee, R. and Israel, J., "Understanding the Role of Identification and Authentication in NetWare 4", *Novell Application Notes*, Vol. 5 # 10, October 1994, pp. 27–51.

LEVY84 Levy, S., *Hackers—Heroes of the Computer Revolution*, Doubleday, New York, 1984.

LINN90 Linn, J., "Practical Authentication for Distributed Computing", *IEEE Symposium on Security and Privacy*, May 1990.

LINN93a Linn, J., *Privacy Enhancement for Internet Electronic Mail: Part I: Message Encryption and Authentication Procedures*, RFC 1421, February 1993.

LINN93b Linn, J., *Generic Security Service Application Program Interface*, RFC 1508, September 1993.

LINN93c Linn, J., *Common Authentication Technology Overview*, RFC 1511, September 1993.

MADR92 Madron, T., *Network Security in the '90s: Issues and Solutions for Managers*, John Wiley & Sons, 1992.

MATY85 Matyas, S. M., and Meyer, C. H., "Generating Strong One-Way Functions with Cryptographic Algorithm", IBM Technical Disclosure Bulletin, v. 27. March 1985, pp. 5658–5659.

MENE96 Menezes, A., Van Oorschot, P., and Vanstone, S., *Handbook of Applied Cryptography*, CRC Press, 1996.

MERK78 Merkle, R., "Secure Communication over Insecure Channels", *Communications of the ACM*, Vol. 21, April 1978, pp. 294–299.

MERK90 Merkle, R., "A Fast Software One-Way Hash Function", *Journal of Cryptology*, Vol. 3 #1, 1990, pp. 43–58.

MEYE82 Meyer, C. and Matyas, S., *Cryptography: A New Dimension in Computer Data Security*, Wiley, 1982.

MILL87 Miller, S., Neuman, C., Schiller, J., and Saltzer, J., *Kerberos Authentication and Authorization System*, MIT Project Athena Technical Plan, Section E.2.1, December 1987.

MIYA88 Miyaguchi, S., Shiraishi, A., and Shimizu, A., "Fast Data Encryption Algorithm Feal-8", *Review of Electrical Communications Laboratories*, Vol. 36 #4, 1988, pp. 433–437.

MOLV92 Molva, R., Tsudik, G., Van Herreweghen, E., and Zatti, S., "KryptoKnight Authentication and Key Distribution System", *European Symposium on Research in Computer Security*, 1992, pp. 155–174.

MORR79 Morris, R. and Thompson, K., "Password Security: A Case History", *Communications of the ACM*, Vol. 22, November 1979, pp. 594–597.

NATI91 National Research Council, System Security Study Committee, *Computers at Risk: Safe Computing in the Information Age*, National Academy Press, 1991.

NEED78 Needham, R. M., and Schroeder, M. D., "Using Encryption for Authentication in Large Networks of Computers", *Communications of the ACM*, Vol. 21, December 1978, pp. 993–999.

NEED87 Needham, R. M., and Schroeder, M. D., "Authentication Revisited", *Operating Systems Review*, Vol. 21 #1, January 1987, pp. 7.

OTWA87 Otway, D, and Rees, O., "Efficient and Timely Authentication", *Operating Systems Review*, Vol. 21 #1, January 1987, pp. 8–10.

PASS85 *Password Usage*, FIPS Pub 112, National Bureau of Standards, May 1985.

PATE97 Patel, S., "Number Theoretic Attacks On Secure Password Schemes", *1997 IEEE Symposium on Security and Privacy*, May 1997.

PERL88 Perlman, R., *Network Layer Protocols with Byzantine Robustness*, MIT Laboratory for Computer Science Technical Report #429, October 1988.

PERL99 Perlman, R., *Interconnections: Bridges, Routers, Switches, and Internetworking Protocols*, Addison-Wesley, 1999.

PERL99A Perlman, R. and Kaufman, C., "Secure Password-Based Protocol for Downloading a Private Key", *Proceedings of the 1999 Network and Distributed System Security*, February 1999.

PERL00 Perlman, R. and Kaufman, C., "Key Exchange in IPSec: Analysis of IKE", *Internet Computing Journal*, Special Issue on Security Solutions, November/December 2000.

PERL01 Perlman, R. and Kaufman, C., "Analysis of the IPsec Key Exchange Standard", *Proceedings of the IEEE 10th International Workshops on Enabling Technologies: Infrastructure for Collaborative Enterprises*, June 2001.

PERL01A Perlman, R. and Kaufman, C., "PDM: A New Strong Password-based Protocol", *10th USENIX Security Symposium*, August 2001.

PFLE89 Pfleeger, C. P., *Security in Computing*, Prentice Hall, 1989.

PISC93 Piscitello, D., and Chapin, A. L., *Open Systems Networking: TCP/IP and OSI*, Addison-Wesley, 1993.

PLAT91 Plattner, B., Lanz, C., Lubich, H., Muller, M., Walker, T., *X.400 Message Handling: Standardes, Interworking, Applications*, Addison-Wesley, 1991.

POME81 Pomerance, C., "On the Distribution of Pseudoprimes", *Mathematics of Computation*, Vol. 37 #156, 1981, pp. 587–593.

POST82 Postel, J., *Simple Mail Transfer Protocol*, RFC 821, August 1982.

RABI79 Rabin, M. O., *Digitized Signatures and Public Key Functions as Intractable as Factorization*, MIT Laboratory for Computer Science, Technical Report 212, January 1979.

RABI80 Rabin, M. O., "Probabilistic Algorithm for Primality Testing", *Journal of Number Theory*, Vol. 12, 1980, pp. 128–138.

RESC01 Rescorla, E., *SSL and TTS: Designing and Building Secure Systems*, Addison-Wesley, 2001.

RIVE78 Rivest, R. L., Shamir, A., and Adleman, L., "A Method for Obtaining Digital Signatures and Public-Key Cryptosystems", *Communications of the ACM*, Vol. 21 #2, February 1978, pp. 120–126.

RIVE91a Rivest, R. L., "The MD4 Message Digest Algorithm", *Advances in Cryptology—Crypto '90 Proceedings*, Lecture Notes in Computer Science 537, Springer-Verlag, 1991, pp. 303–311.

RIVE91b Rivest, R., letter to NIST dated 26 October 1991 circulated on the Internet.

RIVE92a Rivest, R., *The MD4 Message-Digest Algorithm*, RFC 1320, April 1992.

RIVE92b Rivest, R., *The MD5 Message-Digest Algorithm*, RFC 1321, April 1992.

ROBS95 Robshaw, M., *Security Estimates for 512-bit RSA*, RSA Data Security Inc., June 1995.

ROSI99 Rosing, M., *Implementing Elliptic Curve Cryptography*, Manning Publications, 1999.

RUSS91 Russell, D. and Gangemi, G. T., *Computer Security Basics*, O'Reilly & Associates, Inc., July 1991.

SAND91 Sandler, C., Badgett, T., and Lefkowitz, L., *VAX Security*, John Wiley & Sons, Inc., 1991.

SCHN96 Schneier, B., *Applied Cryptography: Protocols, Algorithms, and Source Code in C*, John Wiley & Sons, Inc., 1996.

SCHR84 Schroeder, M., Birrell, A., and Needham, R., "Experience with Grapevine: The Growth of a Distributed System", *ACM Transactions on Computer Systems*, Vol. 2 #1, February 1984.

SEBE89 Seberry, J. and Pieprzyk, J., *Cryptography: An Introduction to Computer Security*, Prentice Hall, 1989.

SECU93 *Secure Hash Standard*, National Institute of Science and Technology, Federal Information Processing Standard (FIPS) 180, April 1993.

SHAM81 Shamir, A., *On the Generation of Cryptographically Strong Pseudo-Random Sequences*, Department of Applied Mathemenatics, The Weizmann Institute of Science, 1981.

SHAN48 Shannon, C., "A Mathematical Theory of Communication", *Bell System Journal*, Vol. 27, 1948, pp. 379-423 and pp. 623-656.

SHIM88 Shimizu, A. and Miyaguchi, S., "Fast Data Encipherment Algorithm FEAL", *Advances in Cryptography—Eurocrypt 87*, Lecture Notes in Computer Science, Vol. 304, Springer-Verlag, 1988.

SKOU02 Skoudis, E., *Counter Hack: A Step-by-Step Guide to Computer Attacks and Effective Defenses*, Prentice Hall, 2002

SOLO77 Solovay, R., and Strassen, V., "A Fast Monte-Carlo Test for Primality", *SIAM Journal on Computing*, Vol. 6., March 1977, pp. 84–85.

SONG01 Song, D. X., Wagner, D., and Tian, X., "Timing Analysis of Keystrokes and Timing Attacks on SSH", *Usenix Security Conference*, 2001.

SPAF88 Spafford, E. H., *The Internet Work Program: An Analysis*, Purdue Technical Report CSD-TR-823, Purdue University, November 1988.

STEI88 Steiner, J. G., Neuman, C., and Schiller, J. I., "Kerberos: An Authentication Service for Open Network Systems", *Proceedings of the USENIX Winter Conference*, February 1988, pp. 191–202.

STEI98 Stein, L., *Web Security: A Step-by-Step Reference Guide*, Addison-Wesley, 1998.

STER92 Sterling, Bruce, *The Hacker Crackdown: Law and Disorder on the Electronic Frontier*, Bantam Books, 1992.

STEV94 Stevens, W., *The Protocols (TCP/IP Illustrated, Volume 1)*, Addison-Wesley, 1994.

STOL89 Stoll, C., *The Cuckoo's Egg: Tracing a Spy Through the Maze of Computer Espionage*, Doubleday, 1989.

STUB92 Stubblebine, S. G. and Gligor, V. D., "On Message Integrity in Cryptographic Protocols", *IEEE Symposium on Research on Security and Privacy*, May 1992, pp. 85–104.

STUB93 Stubblebine, S. G. and Gligor, V. D., "Protecting the Integrity of Privacy-Enhanced Electronic Mail with DES-Based Authentication Codes", *PSRG Workshop on Network and Distributed Systems Security*, February 1993.

TANE87 Tanenbaum, A., *Operating Systems—Design and Implementation*, Prentice Hall, 1987.

TANE96 Tanenbaum, A., *Computer Networks*, Prentice Hall, 1996.

TARD91 Tardo, J. J., and Alagappan, K., "SPX: Global Authentication Using Public Key Certificates", *Proceedings of the 1991 IEEE Symposium on Security and Privacy*, May 1991, pp. 232–244.

TRUS87 *Trusted Network Interpretation (TNI) of the Trusted Computer System Evaluation Criteria (TCSEC)*, [Red Book], NCSC-TG-005 Version 1, 1987.

WRAY93 Wray, J., *Generic Security Service API: C-bindings*, RFC 1509, September 1993.

WU98 Wu, T., "The Secure Remote Password Protocol", *Proceedings of the 1998 Internet Society Network and Distributed System Security Symposium*, March 1998, pp. 97-111.

ZWIC00 Zwicky, E. D., Cooper, S., Chapman, D. B., Russell, D., *Building Internet Firewalls (2nd Edition)*, O'Reilly, 1995.

GLOSSARY

access control—a mechanism for limiting use of some resource to authorized users.

access control set—a synonym for access control list; some people make the distinction that the order of entries in an access control set cannot be significant, while the order of entries in an access control list might be.

ACL (access control list)—a data structure associated with a resource that specifies the authorized users.

active attack—one in which an attacker does something other than simply eavesdropping, for instance, transmits data, modifies data, or subverts the system so that it can impersonate an address.

ANSI—one of several organizations that develop and publish standards for computer networking. It stands for American National Standards Institute.

API (Application Programming Interface)—a description of how one body of software uses another.

ASCII—a mapping between text characters and numbers. It stands for American Standard Code for Information Interchange.

ASN.1 (Abstract Syntax Notation 1)—an ISO standard for data representation and data structure definitions. We can hardly wait to see ASN.2.

asymmetric cryptography—public key cryptography.

Athena—a project conducted at the Massachusetts Institute of Technology that developed a number of interesting technologies including the Kerberos cryptographic authentication system.

ATM—automatic teller machine. (Though in a book on computer networking, you'd probably expect this to have something to do with Asynchronous Transfer Mode, a high performance networking technology.)

audit—keep a record of events that might have some security significance, such as when access to resources occurred.

authenticate—to determine that something is genuine. In the context of this book, to reliably determine the identity of a communicating party.

authentication—the process of reliably determining the identity of a communicating party.

authorization—permission to access a resource.

background authentication—authentication that takes place automatically when a user requests a service without the user having to do anything.

bad guy—someone who is trying to defeat a cryptographic or other security mechanism. (No moral implications here; some of our best friends are bad guys.)

batch job—a process run on behalf of a particular user while the user need not be physically present at any terminal and no terminal is associated with the process. The user will presumably return later and harvest the results.

big-endian—most significant to least significant, usually applied to the ordering of bits and/or bytes.

biometric device—a device that authenticates people by measuring some hard-to-forge physical property, like a fingerprint or the strokes and timing of a signature.

bit— a binary digit: 0 or 1; an element of $\mathbf{Z}_2$; the smallest unit of memory in a binary computer; the amount of information conveyed by the result of an experiment with two equally likely outcomes.

block encryption—scrambling, in a reversible manner, a fixed-size piece of data into a fixed-size piece of ciphertext.

bucket brigade attack—getting in between two legitimate users, relaying their messages to each other, and thereby spoofing each of them into thinking they are talking directly to the other.

byte—some number (usually 8) of contiguous bits (see *octet*).

byte-swap—conversion between big-endian and little-endian by reversing the order of bytes.

CA—certification authority. Something that signs certificates.

call back—a security mechanism for dial-in connections to a network whereby a user calls in, requests a connection, and hangs up. The computer system then calls him back and thus reliably knows the telephone number of the caller.

caller ID—a relatively new service offered by the telephone system whereby the recipient of a call is reliably informed of the number of the phone originating the call.

captive account—an account on a timesharing system that allows someone who uses that account to run only a single program which carefully controls access to system resources.

CBC (cipher block chaining)—a method of using a block encryption scheme for encrypting an arbitrary-sized message.

CBC residue—the last block of ciphertext when encrypting a message using cipher block chaining. Since it is difficult to find two messages with the same CBC residue without knowing the key, CBC residue is often used as an integrity-protecting checksum for a message.

CCITT—a standards organization dominated by European telephone companies known as PTTs, where PTT stands for Postal, Telephone, and Telegraph Authority, and CCITT stands for something or other in French. (If you insist, it's Comité Consultatif International de Télégraphique et Téléphonique.) CCITT publishes standards for computer networking, including the X.400 series of documents concerning electronic mail and the X.500 series of documents concerning directory services. Its name is now ITU.

CDC (certificate distribution center)—the name the DASS system gives to their on-line system that distributes certificates and user private keys.

certificate—a message signed with a public key digital signature stating that a specified public key belongs to someone or something with a specified name.

certificate revocation list (CRL)—a digitally signed data structure listing all the certificates created by a given CA that have not yet expired but are no longer valid.

certification authority (CA)—something trusted to sign certificates.

CFB (cipher feedback)—a method of using a block encryption scheme for encrypting an arbitrary-sized message.

challenge—a number given to something so that it can cryptographically process the number using a secret quantity it knows and return the result (called the response). The purpose of the exercise is to prove knowledge of the secret quantity without revealing it to an eavesdropper. This is known as challenge/response authentication.

Chaos Computer Club—a loosely knit organization centered in Germany that made the news by staging some high-profile break-ins to computer networks.

checksum—a small, fixed-length quantity computed as a function of an arbitrary length message. A checksum is computed by the sender of a message and recomputed and checked by the recipient of a message to detect data corruption. Originally, the term checksum meant the specific integrity check consisting of adding all the numbers together and throwing away carries. Usage has extended the definition to include more complex non-cryptographic functions such as CRCs, which detect hardware faults with high probability, and cryptographic functions such as message digests, which can withstand attacks from clever attackers.

Chinese wall—a policy that says that someone is authorized to access resource A or B, but not both. It is common in a brokerage or investment banking firm representing two different clients, to avoid conflict of interest.

CIA (Central Intelligence Agency)—the arm of the United States government responsible for spying, and hence a convenient target for our lame jokes.

classified—an adjective describing something the government does not want divulged for national security reasons. There are various categories of classified, including CONFIDENTIAL, SECRET, and TOP SECRET.

cleartext—a message that is not encrypted.

client—something that accesses a service by communicating with it over a computer network.

Clipper—the name by which the U.S. government's scheme for encrypting telephones is known. The scheme allows high-grade encryption while allowing wiretapping with a court order. (The name will change due to trademark violation, but that's the name it's known by now.)

CLNP (Connectionless Network Protocol)—an OSI standard network layer protocol for sending data through a computer network.

clogging protection—protection against denial-of-service attacks consisting of overwhelming a node with requests.

COCOM—a treaty among many leading Western nations that coordinated export control regulations on technologies of military significance, including cryptography. The treaty is no longer in force, but similar export regulations in many countries remain as its legacy.

compromise—in common English usage, to give up some things in order to reach agreement on something; this usage rarely arises in the security community. In the context of security, to invade something by getting around its security. A person who has been compromised might be someone who has accepted a bribe. A computer that has been compromised might be one that has had a Trojan horse installed.

confidentiality—the property of not being divulged to unauthorized parties.

confinement—not allowing information of a certain security classification to escape from the environment in which it is allowed to reside.

cookie—three meanings:

1. data given to a web browser that the web browser returns on subsequent calls in order to create the illusion of an ongoing session.
2. a term first used in Photuris; an anticlogging token.
3. a delicious concoction, preferably containing chocolate chips and no nuts.

cracker—a person who uses other people's computers for criminal purposes. It's not a very good word, but we hope people will use it instead of "hacker" so as not to sully the true spirit in which the word "hacker" was invented (see *hacker*).

CRC (cyclic redundancy code)—a form of noncryptographic integrity check popular as error detection.

CRC-32—a particular CRC that produces a 32-bit output.

credentials—secret information used to prove one's identity in an authentication exchange.

CRL (Certificate Revocation List)—a digitally signed message that lists all the unexpired but revoked certificates issued by a particular CA. It is similar to the book of stolen charge card numbers that stores receive frequently to enable them to reject bad credit cards.

cryptanalysis—the process of finding weaknesses or flaws in cryptographic algorithms.

cryptographic checksum—an integrity check with the property that it is infeasible to find a valid checksum for a message unless you know some secret.

cryptography—mathematical manipulation of data for the purpose of reversible or irreversible transformation.

CSMA/CD (Carrier Sense Multiple Access with Collision Detect)—a LAN technology using contention for sharing the wire. Examples are 802.3 and Ethernet.

cybercrud—mostly useless computer-generated gibberish that people either ignore or are intimidated and annoyed by.

dæmon process—a process that runs on a computer with no associated user, usually to carry out some administrative function.

DASS (Distributed Authentication Security Service)—a public key-based authentication protocol defined in RFC 1507.

DCE (Distributed Computing Environment)—a group of programs and protocols standardized by the Open Software Foundation built atop a cryptographically protected remote procedure call protocol.

decipher—to decrypt.

decrypt—to undo the encryption process.

delegation—giving some of your rights to another person or process.

DES (Data Encryption Standard)—a secret key cryptographic scheme standardized by NIST.

Diffie-Hellman key exchange—a method of establishing a shared key over an insecure medium, named after the inventors (Diffie and Hellman).

directory service—a service provided on a computer network that helps you locate things.

discrete logarithm—an integer x satisfying the equation $y = b^x \bmod n$ for given y, b, and n. More generally, an integer x satisfying the equation $y = b^x$ for given y and b in a given finite group.

discretionary access controls—a mechanism allowing the owner of a resource to decide who can access the resource. Outside the military environment, they are usually simply referred to as *access controls*.

DNS (Domain Name System)—the naming convention defined in RFC 1033. DNS names are often referred to as *internet addresses* or *internet names*.

download—to send a program over the network to be loaded and executed, typically by a special-purpose device like a printer or router.

DSS (Digital Signature Standard)—a public key cryptographic system for computing digital signatures (i.e., it does not do encryption).

eavesdrop—to listen in on a conversation without the knowledge or consent of the communicating parties.

EBCDIC—IBM's encoding of characters. It serves the same purpose as ASCII, but is incompatible with ASCII. Stands for Extended Binary Coded Decimal Interchange Code.

ECB (electronic code book)—a method of using a block encryption scheme to encrypt a large message. It's the most straightforward method, consisting of independently encrypting each plaintext block.

EDE (encrypt/decrypt/encrypt)—a method of making a secret key scheme more secure using multiple keys. The technique is to first encrypt the message with one key, then do a decryption with a different key on the resulting ciphertext, and finally encrypt the result with either the first key used, or a third key.

ElGamal—a public key cryptographic system whose security depends on the difficulty of computing discrete logarithms. It is best known for its method of computing digital signatures, though the specification includes a technique for encryption as well. Named after its inventor (ElGamal, in case you couldn't guess).

encipher—to encrypt. Used in international standards documents instead of *encrypt* because the French interpret *encrypt* to mean to put some body into a crypt; *decrypt* would presumably mean to retrieve them.

encrypt—to scramble information so that only someone knowing the appropriate secret can obtain the original information (through decryption).

encrypted tunnel—a means of achieving private communication in a public world by using a cryptographically protected connection across a public network instead of using a physically secure link.

escrow—in the context of cryptography, it means keeping a copy of a key at a third party so it can be restored if the owner loses it, or if law enforcement or some other party wishes to decrypt the key owner's data.

escrow-foilage—preventing a passive attacker from decrypting a conversation between Alice and Bob even if the attacker knows Alice's and Bob's long-term secrets at the time they are having the conversation.

Euclid's algorithm—an algorithm to find the greatest common divisor of two numbers. It can also be used to compute multiplicative inverses in modular arithmetic.

execute—in the case of a program, to run the program.

exploder—a component of an electronic mail system that takes a single message addressed to a distribution list and turns it into many mail messages to the individual recipients.

field—a mathematical structure comprising a set of elements (including 0 and 1) with addition and multiplication operators on those elements satisfying familiar properties.

FIPS (Federal Information Processing Standard)—one of a series of U.S. government documents specifying standards for various aspects of data processing, including the Data Encryption Standard (DES).

form factor—the outward appearance of a function, for instance the number and size of the inputs and the number and size of the outputs.

gcd—greatest common divisor.

GF(p^n)—the finite field (Galois field) with p^n elements, where p is a prime and n is a positive integer. If $n = 1$, we sometimes write $\mathbf{Z}_p$.

good guy—someone using a cryptographic or other security system in the manner in which its designers intended (see *bad guy*).

greatest common divisor—the largest integer that evenly divides each of a set of provided integers.

group—1. a named collection of users, created for convenience in stating authorization policy. 2. a mathematical structure comprising a set of elements (including an "identity" element) and a binary operator on those elements satisfying some familiar properties.

hacker—someone who plays with computers for the pure intellectual challenge. The proper use of the word is as applied to the kind of extraordinarily talented and dedicated people who, if given an opportunity to spend six weeks on the beach, would build a computer out of sand and write the operating system and all utilities. Unfortunately, the media has taken to using the term *hacker* to apply to people who use computers for criminal purposes. The most malicious thing a true hacker would ever do is sneak his or her own bicycle into the building after management has issued an anti-bicycle edict, or refuse to bathe.

hash—a cryptographic one-way function that takes an arbitrary-sized input and yields a fixed-size output.

hop—a direct communication channel between two computers. In a complex computer network, a message might take many hops between its source and destination.

HTTP (HyperText Transfer Protocol)—the protocol for retrieving web pages.

IANA (Internet Assigned Numbers Authority)—the authority for assigning and publishing numbers used in Internet protocols.

IDEA (International Data Encryption Algorithm)—a secret key cryptographic scheme gaining popularity.

IETF (Internet Engineering Task Force)—a standards body whose focus is protocols for use in the Internet. Its publications are called Internet RFCs (Requests For Comments).

integrity—correctness. A system protects the integrity of data if it prevents unauthorized modification (as opposed to protecting the confidentiality of data, which prevents unauthorized disclosure).

intermediary—something that facilitates communication between parties that wish to communicate.

Internet—when not capitalized, it means a connected collection of computer networks. I_2've always hated the term since I_2'd define a network as the collection of nodes that have connectivity between them. Once you interconnect a bunch of networks, the result is one big network! But the world uses the term. When capitalized, *the Internet* refers to the large and still growing network that started as the ARPANET, a research network funded by the U.S. Department of Defense.

IRS (Internal Revenue Service)—the universally beloved branch of the United States government that rightfully, equitably, and fairly collects taxes. And they have a wonderful sense of humor and won't mind when we occasionally poke fun at them in this book.

ISO (International Standards Organization)—an international organization tasked with developing and publishing standards for everything from wine glasses to computer network protocols. In this book, references to ISO are to its standards for computer networking known as Open Systems Interconnect (or OSI).

ISP (Internet Service Provider)—a company that sells connectivity to the Internet.

ITAR (International Trafficking in Arms Regulation)—the collection of laws in the United States that regulate the export of dangerous technologies like nuclear weapons and personal mail encryption.

IV (initialization vector)—a number used by the CBC, OFB, and CFB encryption techniques to initialize the first round. Subsequent rounds use the results of the earlier rounds.

KDC (key distribution center)—an on-line trusted intermediary that has master keys for all principals and which generates conversation keys between principals when requested.

Kerberize—(Don't you hate it when people verbify a noun?) to enhance an application to use Kerberos for authentication and/or encryption.

Kerberos—a DES-based authentication system developed at MIT as part of Project Athena and subsequently incorporated into a growing collection of commercial products.

key—a quantity used in cryptography to encrypt or decrypt information.

KGB—Russian equivalent of the CIA.

LAN (Local Area Network)—a method of interconnecting multiple systems in such a way that all transmissions over the LAN can be listened to by all systems on the LAN.

LEAF (law enforcement access field)—the field that must be transmitted by one Clipper chip to the Clipper chip at the other end of the conversation. Without it, the receiving Clipper will refuse to decrypt the conversation. The LEAF field enables law enforcement to decrypt the conversation, after a court order to obtain the sending Clipper's unique key.

little-endian—least significant to most significant, usually applied to the ordering of bits and/or bytes.

logarithm—the base b logarithm of x is the exponent to which b must be raised to get x, so $b^{\log_b x} = x$. The security of most public key cryptographic algorithms depends on the difficulty of computing discrete logarithms (see *discrete logarithm*).

logic bomb—a piece of code maliciously added to a program that specifically is designed to lay dormant until some event occurs, such as a specific date being reached or a user typing some command. The classic example of a logic bomb is a piece of code inserted into a critical program by a disgruntled employee in order to cause trouble long after the employee is gone.

MAC—see *message authentication code* or *mandatory access controls*. (And if that isn't enough, it also stands for *medium access control* in data link layer networking jargon, where it has nothing to do with the security sense of *access control*.)

man-in-the-middle attack—synonym for bucket brigade attack. An active attack which involves getting on the path between two legitimate users, relaying their messages to each other, and thereby spoofing each of them into thinking they are talking directly to the other.

mandatory access controls—an access control mechanism where the owner of data does not have full control over who may access the data. For example, a system may keep track of the fact that a file contains TOP SECRET data and deny access to that data to a user without the proper clearance even if the creator of the data wishes to grant access.

masquerade—to pretend to be X when you are not X, and without X's permission.

MD (message digest)—an irreversible function that takes an arbitrary-sized message and outputs a fixed length quantity. MD2, MD4, and MD5 are message digest algorithms documented in RFCs 1319, 1320, and 1321.

message authentication code (MAC)—a synonym of message integrity code (MIC).

MIC (message integrity code)—a fixed-length quantity generated cryptographically and associated with a message to reassure the recipient that the message is genuine. The term is most often used in connection with secret key cryptography, since a public key MIC is usually called a digital signature. This term was used as a synonym for MAC, but MAC is now more common.

Minesweeper—an addictive game bundled with Windows® in a ploy by Microsoft to reduce productivity in the rest of the industry. It would be more appropriately named *Mindsweeper*.

MS/DOS—a primitive operating system used by most personal computers.

mutual authentication—when each party in a conversation proves its identity to the other.

naming service—a place in which, knowing the name of something, you look up its attributes (much like looking up a telephone number in a phone book).

NAT (Network Address Translation)—a mechanism for attaching more nodes to the Internet than you have IP addresses for. It works by dynamically assigning IP addresses to those nodes inside your net that are currently communicating outside your net. An extension known as NAPT (network address and port translation) allows multiple of these nodes to use the same IP address outside, by using the layer 4 ports to distinguish between them.

NIS—Network Information Service, formerly known as YP, Sun Microsystem's Directory Service.

NIST (National Institute of Standards and Technology)—an agency of the U.S. government whose mission is to develop and promote measurements, standards, and technology. Formerly known as NBS (National Bureau of Standards).

nonce—a number used in a cryptographic protocol that must (with extremely high probability) be different each time the protocol is run with a given set of participants in order to ensure that an attacker can't usefully inject messages recorded from a previous running of the protocol. There are many ways of generating nonces, including suitably large random numbers, sequence numbers, and timestamps.

non-discretionary access controls—same as *mandatory access controls*.

non-repudiation—the property of a scheme in which there is proof of who sent a message that a recipient can show to a third party and the third party can independently verify the source.

nonvolatile memory—storage that maintains its state without external power, for example, magnetic disks and core memories.

OCSP (on-line certificate status protocol)—a protocol defined by IETF's PKIX working group, for finding out the revocation status of certificates.

octet—8 contiguous bits, i.e., an 8-bit byte (see *byte*).

OFB (output feedback mode)—a method of turning a secret key block cipher into a stream cipher. OFB effectively generates a pseudo-random one-time pad by iteratively encrypting the previous block, starting with an IV.

OID (object identifier)—a hierarchical identifier represented as a sequence of numeric fields used in ASN.1-encoded structures. Someone with the right to use a particular OID is allowed to assign OIDs with their own OID as a prefix.

OLRS (on-line revocation server)—an on-line service that answers queries about the revocation status of certificates.

on-line server—something that provides a service and is generally available on the network (i.e., it can run unattended).

one-time pad—an encryption method where a long string known to sender and receiver is ⊕'d with plaintext to get ciphertext and ⊕'d with ciphertext to recover plaintext. This extremely simple encryption method is provably secure for keeping a message confidential if the string used is truly random, known only to the communicating parties, and any given string is only used for encryption once.

one-to-one mapping—a function that assigns an output value to each input value in such a way that each input maps to exactly one output, and no two inputs map to the same output.

Open—1. Open is supposed to mean that the thing described was developed by a committee from which no interested party was excluded, the thing is documented in sufficient detail to enable independent interworking implementations based on documentation alone, and there are no patent, copyright, or trade secret impediments to its deployment. 2. A marketing term meaning *good*.

OSF (Open Software Foundation)—an organization founded as an industry consortium to develop and license open software (see *open*). It is best known for OSF/1, a UNIX variant, and DCE, a family of protocols centered around a secure RPC and distributed file system.

OSI (Open Systems Interconnect)—the name of the computer networking standards approved by ISO. In the networking community, the terms "OSI" and "ISO" tend to be used interchangeably, annoying the purists. We tend to use them interchangeably.

out of band—by some mechanism separate from the transmission of data. An out-of-band mechanism for key distribution would be something other than sending messages across the network, for example, by having people talk on the phone to each other or give each other pieces of paper or floppies.

Ovaltine—some combination of sugar and chemicals sold as a milk additive.

overrun—two meanings:

1. compromise, i.e., taken over by a bad guy.
2. in the phrase *buffer overrun*, a type of software bug in which the software does not check whether the input fits within its buffer.

pad—additional bits added to a message to make it a desired length, for instance an integral number of bytes. This meaning of pad has no relation to the word *pad* in the phrase *one-time pad*, or the word *pad* in the phrase *Post-it® Pad*.

passive attack—an attack in which an attacker only eavesdrops.

password—a supposedly secret string used to prove one's identity.

PC (personal computer)—we use the term interchangeably with *workstation*. In common usage, a PC is an inexpensive device with an inadequate operating system while a workstation has neither of these properties. Sometimes PC is intended to refer exclusively to Wintel personal computers, but that distinction is never intended in this book.

permutation—a method of encryption where parts of the message are rearranged. Encryption by permutation is not very secure by itself, but it can be used in combination with substitution to build powerful ciphers like DES.

PFS (perfect forward secrecy)—a property of a protocol in which someone who records an encrypted conversation cannot later decrypt the conversation, even if the attacker has since learned the long-term cryptographic secrets of each side.

Photuris—a protocol for providing mutual authentication and session key establishment. This protocol, along with SKIP, was one of the contenders for selection for the IETF IPsec protocol.

PIN (Personal Identification Number)—a short sequence of digits used as a password.

PKCS (Public-Key Cryptography Standard)—a series of documents produced and distributed by RSA Data Security, Inc., proposing techniques for using public key cryptographic algorithms in a safe and interoperable manner.

PKZIP™—a software package for data compression and backup from PKWare, Inc.

plausible deniability—a situation in which events are structured so that someone can claim not to have known or done something, and no proof exists to the contrary. Whenever this term comes up, the person in question is almost certainly guilty.

Post-it® Pad—the original brand of those yellow sticky things you write notes on and leave on people's doors, chairs, etc. In the context of security, it is a common means of attaching a written representation of your password to your workstation.

PostScript®—a write-only programming language created by Adobe Systems Inc. to describe printed pages.

preauthentication—a protocol for proving you know your password before you are allowed access to a high quality secret encrypted with that password. Preauthentication is there to prevent an intruder from easily obtaining a quantity with which to do off-line password guessing.

principal—a completely generic term used by the security community to include both people and computer systems. Coined because it is more dignified than *thingy* and because *object* and *entity* (which also mean thingy) were already overused.

privacy—when we use the term, it means protection from the unauthorized disclosure of data. Security purists use confidentiality for this because the word privacy has been co-opted by the lawyers to mean approximately the opposite: privacy legislation consists of laws requiring governments and businesses to tell people what information those organizations are storing about them.

private key—the quantity in public key cryptography that must be kept secret.

privileged user—a user of a computer who is authorized to bypass normal access control mechanisms, usually to be able to perform system management functions.

protected subsystem—a program that can run at a higher level of privilege than the user of the program is entitled to, because it has very structured interfaces that will not allow any but security-safe operations.

public key—the quantity in public key cryptography that is safely divulged to as large an extent as is necessary or convenient.

public key cryptography—also known as *asymmetric cryptography*, a cryptographic system where encryption and decryption are performed using different keys.

RC2—a proprietary secret key encryption scheme marketed by RSADSI. It's a block encryption scheme with 64-bit blocks and a varying length key. It reportedly stands for *Ron's Cipher #2*, and we believe you can guess who Ron is.

RC4—another proprietary secret key encryption scheme marketed by RSADSI. It's a stream encryption algorithm that effectively produces an unbounded length pseudorandom stream from a varying length key. The stream is ⊕'d with the data for encryption and decryption.

rcp—a UNIX command for copying a file across the network.

realm—a Kerberos term for all of the principals served by a particular KDC.

recursion—see *recursion*.

Reference Monitor—a piece of code in a computer system that oversees all security-related activity such as resource access.

reflection attack—an attack where messages received from something are replayed back to it.

replaying—storing and retransmitting messages. The word is usually used when implying that the entity doing the replay of messages is mounting some sort of security attack.

repudiation—denying that you did something or made some statement.

revocation—taking back privileges, either from a person who is no longer trusted (as when an employee quits) or from a secret (when its rightful owner believes it may have been divulged).

RFC (request for comments)—the document series published by the IETF, and available for free download from the IETF web site (www.ietf.org), that describes the protocols standardized by the IETF. Despite the name (RFC), comments are not particularly welcome at that stage in the process, but are more welcome in the preliminary stage, when the document is known as an "internet draft", also available from the IETF web site.

rlogin—a UNIX command for logging into a machine across the network.

rollover—changing keys during a conversation in order to limit the amount of data or time over which a key is used.

RPC—remote procedure call.

RSA—a public key cryptographic algorithm named for its inventors (Rivest, Shamir, and Adleman) that does encryption and digital signatures.

RSADSI—an abbreviation for RSA Data Security, Inc., the company that licences the RSA technology.

rsh—the UNIX remote shell command, which executes a specified command on a specified machine across the network.

safe prime—also known as a Sophie Germain prime, a prime p for which $(p-1)/2$ is also prime.

salt—a user-specific value cryptographically combined with that user's password to obtain the hash of that user's password. Salt serves several purposes. It makes the hash of two users' passwords different even if their passwords are the same. It also means that an intruder can't precompute hashes of a few thousand guessed passwords, and compare that list against a stolen database of hashed passwords. The salt can be a random number which is stored, in the clear, along with the hash of the user's password, or it could consist of the user's name or some other user-specific information.

secret key—the shared secret quantity in secret key cryptography that is used to encrypt and decrypt data.

secret key cryptography—also known as *symmetric cryptography*, a scheme in which the same key is used for encryption and decryption.

SA (security association)—the shared state such as cryptographic key, identity of the other side, sequence number, and cryptographic algorithms to be used, for carrying on a cryptographically protected conversation.

SDSI (simple distributed security infrastructure)—an experimental PKI design based on relative names.

security kernel—the part of an operating system responsible for enforcement of security. Usually used in the context of an operating system constructed with such functions partitioned from the rest of the O/S to minimize the chances of security-relevant bugs.

self-synchronizing—(as used in this book) an encryption scheme in which, if some of the ciphertext is garbled by the addition, deletion, or modification of information, some of the message will be garbled at the receiver, but at some point in the message stream following the ciphertext modification, the message will decrypt properly.

server—some resource available on the network to provide some service such as name lookup, file storage, or printing.

session hijacking—an attack possible when cryptographic protection of a conversation ends after the initial authentication. An intruder breaks into the conversation and impersonates one side to the other.

sign—to use your private key to generate a digital signature as a means of proving you generated, or approve of, some message.

signature—a quantity associated with a message which only someone with knowledge of your private key could have generated, but which can be verified through knowledge of your public key.

Simple—the first word in the name of many protocols in the Internet suite.

SKIPJACK—a secret key encryption algorithm using 64-bit blocks and 80-bit keys. It is embedded in Clipper chips, and is classified by the U.S. government (meaning they won't tell you what it is).

smart card—a credit-card-sized object used for authentication that contains nonvolatile storage and computational power. Some smart cards are capable of performing cryptographic operations on the card.

SMTP (Simple Mail Transport Protocol)—a protocol for sending electronic mail across a network, standardized by the IETF.

SNMP (Simple Network Management Protocol)—a protocol for controlling systems across a network, standardized by the IETF.

SPI (security parameter index)—the value in the AH or ESP header of IPsec that tells the destination which security association the packet belongs to.

SPKI (simple public key infrastructure)—a PKI presented as an alternative to PKIX, and described in RFC 2693.

spoof—to convince someone that you are some entity *X* when you are not *X*, without *X*'s permission. Synonyms are *impersonate* and *masquerade*.

stream encryption—an encryption algorithm that encrypts and decrypts arbitrarily sized messages.

strong—a cryptographic algorithm is said to be strong if it would take a large amount of computational power to defeat it.

strong authentication—authentication where someone eavesdropping on the authentication exchange does not gain sufficient information to impersonate the principal in a subsequent authentication.

substitution—an encryption algorithm where a one-to-one mapping is performed on a fixed-size block, for example where each letter of the alphabet has an enciphered equivalent. Substitution ciphers are not very secure unless the block size is large, but they can be combined with permutation ciphers in a series of rounds to build strong ciphers like DES.

superuser—an operating system concept in which an individual is allowed to circumvent ordinary security mechanisms. For instance, the system manager must be able to read everyone's files for the purpose of doing backups.

symmetric cryptography—secret key cryptography. Called *symmetric* because the same key is used for encryption and decryption.

TCP (Transmission Control Protocol)—the reliable connection-oriented transport layer protocol defined in the Internet suite of protocols.

telnet—the protocol for remote terminal connection service.

TGT (ticket-granting ticket)—a Kerberos data structure which is really a ticket to the KDC. The purpose is to allow a user's workstation to forget the user's long-term secret soon after the user logs in.

3DES (Triple DES)—an encryption standard based on three successive invocations of DES.

ticket—a data structure constructed by a trusted intermediary to enable two parties to authenticate each other.

tiger teams—groups of people hired by an organization to defeat its own security systems in order that the organization can learn weaknesses.

totient function—$\phi(n)$, the number of positive integers less than n which are relatively prime to n.

transparent—the illusion of not being there, as in, can be deployed without changing existing applications.

trap door function—a function that appears irreversible, but which has a secret method (a *trap door*) which, if known, allows someone to reverse the function.

Trojan horse—a piece of code embedded in a useful program for nefarious purposes, for instance to steal information. Usually the term *Trojan horse* is used rather than *virus* when the offending code does not attempt to replicate itself into other programs.

trusted intermediary—a third party such as a KDC or CA that permits two parties to authenticate without prior configuration of keys between those two parties.

trusted server—something that aids in network authentication.

trusted software—software that has been produced in a way that makes you confident that there could be no Trojan horses (or even security relevant bugs) in the code.

TTL (Time to Live)—a field in the IP header that is decremented by each router that forwards the packet, so that a packet can be deleted from the network if it is looping, due to temporary routing instability after a topology change.

Turing test—a test proposed by Alan Turing for testing whether a computer had achieved artificial intelligence. The test was that a person would communicate by keyboard to either the computer or to a human, and if the tester couldn't tell which was the human and which was the computer, then the computer had passed the Turing test.

UA (user agent)—the first layer of software insulating the user from the vagaries of the electronic mail infrastructure.

UDP (User Datagram Protocol)—the datagram transport layer protocol defined in the Internet suite of protocols.

uudecode—a UNIX utility for reversing the effects of uuencode.

uuencode—a UNIX utility for encoding arbitrary binary data as harmless printable characters by encoding six bits of binary data per character.

verify a signature—perform a cryptographic calculation using a message, a signature, and a public key to determine whether the signature was generated by someone knowing the corresponding private key signing the message.

virus—a piece of a computer program that replicates by embedding itself in other programs. When those programs are run, the virus is invoked again and can spread further.

VMS (Virtual Memory System)—a Digital Equipment Corporation proprietary operating system.

VPN (Virtual Private Network)—a network using encrypted tunnels across the Internet as if they were private links.

work factor—an estimate of the computational resources required to defeat a given cryptographic system.

workstation—a single-user computer such as a PC. Sometimes the term workstation implies the computer is running UNIX, but for the purpose of this book, the specific hardware and specific operating system of the user's computer is irrelevant.

worm—a self-contained program that replicates by running copies of itself—usually on different machines across a computer network.

X.400—a CCITT standard for electronic mail.

X.500—a CCITT standard for directory services.

X.509—a CCITT standard for security services within the X.500 directory services framework. The X.509 encoding of public key certificates has been widely adopted; the other protocol elements of X.509 have not.

YP—Yellow Pages, a directory service part of Sun Microsystems distributed environment.

zero knowledge proof—1. a scheme in which you can convince someone you know a secret without actually divulging the secret. You know a secret; they know something equivalent to a public key. You answer questions, and the answers convince the other that you know the secret without giving them any information that will help them find the secret. 2. what you write when you're faking an answer on a math test.

Z_n— the integers mod n.

Z_n*—the integers relatively prime to n, mod n.

INDEX

D

Q

R

S